TELLING TIMES

TELLING TIMES

Writing and Living, 1954–2008

NADINE GORDIMER

HAMISH HAMILTON
CANADA

HAMISH HAMILTON CANADA

Published by the Penguin Group

Penguin Group (Canada), 90 Eglinton Avenue East, Suite 700, Toronto, Ontario, Canada
M4P 2Y3 (a division of Pearson Canada Inc.)

Penguin Group (USA) Inc., 375 Hudson Street, New York, New York 10014, U.S.A.
Penguin Books Ltd, 80 Strand, London WC2R 0RL, England
Penguin Ireland, 25 St Stephen's Green, Dublin 2, Ireland (a division of Penguin Books Ltd)
Penguin Group (Australia), 250 Camberwell Road, Camberwell, Victoria 3124, Australia
(a division of Pearson Australia Group Pty Ltd)
Penguin Books India Pvt Ltd, 11 Community Centre, Panchsheel Park, New Delhi – 110 017, India
Penguin Group (NZ), 67 Apollo Drive, Rosedale, North Shore 0745, Auckland, New Zealand
(a division of Pearson New Zealand Ltd)
Penguin Books (South Africa) (Pty) Ltd, 24 Sturdee Avenue, Rosebank, Johannesburg 2196, South Africa

Penguin Books Ltd, Registered Offices: 80 Strand, London WC2R 0RL, England

Published in Canada by Penguin Group (Canada), a division of Pearson Canada Inc., 2010. Simultaneously
published in Great Britain by Bloomsbury Publishing Plc, 36 Soho Square, London W1D 3QY.

1 2 3 4 5 6 7 8 9 10 (WEB)

The publishers are grateful to Leo Carey for his meticulous work in preparing the
manuscript of this book for press.

Manufactured in the U.S.A.

LIBRARY AND ARCHIVES CANADA CATALOGUING IN PUBLICATION
Gordimer, Nadine
Telling times : writing and living, 1950-2008 / Nadine Gordimer.
ISBN 978-0-14-316794-5
I. Title.
PR9369.3.G6A6 2010   824   C2010-900580-5

British Library Cataloguing in Publication data available

Visit the Penguin Group (Canada) website at www.penguin.ca

Special and corporate bulk purchase rates available; please see
www.penguin.ca/corporatesales or call 1-800-810-3104, ext. 2477 or 2474

Reinhold Cassirer

12 March 1908–17 October 2001
1 March 1953–17 October 2001

Contents

The 1950s

The 1960s

The 1970s

The 1980s

The 1990s

The 2000s

The 1950s

A South African Childhood

Allusions in a Landscape

Growing up in one part of a vast young country can be very different from growing up in another, and in South Africa this difference is not only a matter of geography. The division of the people into two great races – black and white – and the subdivision of the white into Afrikaans- and English-speaking groups provides a diversity of cultural heritage that can make two South African children seem almost as strange to each other as if they had come from different countries. The fact that their parents, if they are English-speaking, frequently have come from different countries complicates their backgrounds still further. My father came to South Africa from a village in Russia; my mother was born and grew up in London. I remember, when I was about eight years old, going with my sister and mother and father to spend a long weekend with a cousin of my father's who lived in the Orange Free State. After miles and miles of sienna-red ploughed earth, after miles and miles of silk-fringed mealies standing as high as your eyes on either side of the road and ugly farmhouses where women in bunchy cotton dresses and sun-bonnets stared after the car as we passed (years later, when I saw *Oklahoma!* in a Johannesburg theatre, I recalled that scene), we reached the dorp where the cousin lived in a small white house with sides that were dust-stained in a wavering wash, like rust, for more than a foot above the ground. There we two little girls slept on beds of a smothering softness we had never felt before – feather beds brought from Eastern Europe – and drank tea drawn from a charming contraption, a samovar. There – to our and our mother's horror – we were given smoked duck, flavoured with garlic, at breakfast. The two children of the house spoke only Afrikaans,

like the Boer children who played in the yards of the mean little
houses on either side, and my sister and I, queasy from the strange
food and able to speak only English, watched their games with a
mixture of hostility and wistfulness.

How different it all was from our visit to our mother's sister, in
Natal! There, with the 'English' side of the family, in the green,
softly contoured hills and the gentle meadows of sweet grass near
Balgowan, we might almost have been in England itself. There
our cousins Roy and Humphrey rode like young lords about their
father's beautiful farm, and spoke the high, polite, 'pure' English
learned in expensive Natal private schools that were staffed with
masters imported from English universities. And how different
were both visits from our life in one of the gold-mining towns of
the Witwatersrand, near Johannesburg, in the Transvaal.

There are nine of these towns, spread over a distance of roughly a
hundred and forty miles east and west of Johannesburg. The one
in which we lived was on the east side – the East Rand, it is called
– and it had many distinctions, as distinctions are measured in
that part of the world. First of all, it was one of the oldest towns,
having got itself a gold strike, a general store, a few tents and a
name before 1890. In the pioneer days, my father had set himself
up in a small, one-man business as a watchmaker and jeweller,
and during the twenties and thirties, when the town became the
most rapidly expanding on the Witwatersrand, he continued to
live there with his family. In the richest gold-mining area in the
world, it became the richest square mile or so. All around us,
the shafts went down and the gold came up; our horizon was an
Egyptian-looking frieze of man-made hills of cyanide sand, called
'dumps', because that is what they are – great mounds of waste
matter dumped on the surface of the earth after the gold-bearing
ore has been blasted below, hauled up, and pounded and washed
into yielding its treasure. In the dusty month before spring – in
August, that is – the sand from the dumps blew under the tightly
shut doors of every house in the town and enveloped the heads of
the dumps themselves in a swirling haze, lending them some of

the dignity of cloud-capped mountains. It is characteristic of the Witwatersrand that any feature of the landscape that strikes the eye always does so because it is a reminder of something else; considered on its own merits, the landscape is utterly without interest – flat, dry, and barren.

In our part of the East Rand, the yellowish-white pattern of the cyanide dumps was broken here and there by the head of a black hill rising out of the veld. These hills were man-made, too, but they did not have the geometrical, pyramidal rigidity of the cyanide dumps, and they were so old that enough real earth had blown on to them to hold a growth of sparse grass and perhaps even a sinewy peppercorn or peach tree, sprung up, no doubt, out of garden refuse abandoned there by somebody from the nearby town. These hills were also dumps, but through their scanty natural covering a blackness clearly showed – even a little blueness, the way black hair shines – for they were coal dumps, made of coal dust.

The coal dumps assumed, both because of their appearance and because of the stories and warnings we heard about them, something of a diabolical nature. In our sedate little colonial tribe, with its ritual tea parties and tennis parties, the coal dump could be said to be our Evil Mountain; I use the singular here because when I think of these dumps, I think of one in particular – the biggest one, the one that stood fifty yards beyond the last row of houses in the town where we lived. I remember it especially well because on the other side of it, hidden by it, was the local nursing home, where, when my sister and I were young and the town was small, all the mothers went to have their babies and all the children went to have their tonsillectomies – where, in fact, almost everyone was born, endured an illness, or died. Our mother had several long stays in the place, over a period of two or three years, and during these stays our grandmother took us on a daily visit across the veld to see her. Immediately lunch was over, she would spend an hour dressing us, and then, brushed and beribboned and curled, we would set off. We took a path that skirted the coal dump, and there it was at our side most of the way – a dirty, scarred old mountain, collapsing into the fold of a small ravine here, supporting a twisted peach tree there, and showing bald and black through patchy grass. A fence consisting of two threads of barbed wire looped at intervals through low rusted-iron poles, which once had surrounded it completely, now remained only in places, conveying the idea of a taboo rather than providing an effectual means of isolation. The whole coal dump looked dead, forsaken, and harmless enough, but my sister and I walked softly and looked at it out of the corners of our eyes, half fascinated, half afraid, because we knew it was something else – inert. Not dead by any means, but inert. For we had *seen*. Coming back from the nursing home in the early-winter dusk, we had seen the strange glow in the bald patches the grass did not cover, and in the runnels made by the erosion of summer wind and rain we had seen the hot blue waver of flame. The coal dump was alive. Like a beast of prey, it woke to life in the dark.

The matter-of-fact truth was that these coal dumps, relics of the pre-gold-strike era when collieries operated in the district, were burning. Along with the abandoned mine workings underground, they had caught fire at some time or other in their years of disuse, and had continued to burn, night and day, ever since. Neither rain nor time could put the fires out, and in some places, even on the coldest winter days, we would be surprised to feel the veld warm beneath the soles of our shoes, and, if we cut out a clod, faintly steaming. That dump on the outskirts of the town where we lived is still burning today. I have asked people who have studied such things how long it may be expected to go on burning before it consumes itself. Nobody seems to know; it shares with the idea of Hades its heat and vague eternity.

But perhaps its fierce heart is being subdued gradually. Apparently, no one can even remember, these days, the nasty incidents connected with the dump, incidents that were fresh in memory during our childhood. Perhaps there is no need for anyone to remember, for the town now has more vicarious and less dangerous excitements to offer children than the thrill of running quickly across a pile of black dust that may at any moment cave in and plunge the adventurer into a bed of incandescent coals. In our time, we knew a girl to whom this had happened, and our mother remembered a small boy who had disappeared entirely under a sudden landslide of terrible glowing heat. Not even his bones had been recovered, but the girl we knew survived to become a kind of curiosity about the town. She had been playing on the dump with her friends, and all at once had found herself sunk thigh-deep in living coals and hot ashes. Her friends had managed to pull her out of this fiery quicksand, but she was horribly burned. When we saw her in the street, we used to be unable to keep our eyes from the tight-puckered skin of her calves, and the still tighter skin of her hands, which drew up her fingers like claws. Despite, or because of, these awful warnings, my sister and I longed to run quickly across the lower slopes of the dump for ourselves, and several times managed to elude surveillance long enough to do so. And once, in the unbearable terror and bliss of excitement, we clutched each other on the veld below while, legs pumping wildly, our cousin Roy, come from Natal to spend the holidays with us, rode a bicycle right to the top of the dump and down the other side, triumphant and unharmed.

In the part of South Africa where we lived, we had not only fire under our feet; we had, too, a complication of tunnels as intricate as one of those delicate chunks of worm cast you find on the seashore. All the towns along the Witwatersrand, and the older parts of Johannesburg itself, are undermined. Living there, you think about it as little as you think about the fact that, whatever your work and whatever your life, your reason for performing it where you do and living it where you do is the existence of the gold mines. Yet you are never allowed to forget entirely that the ground is not solid beneath you. In Johannesburg, sitting eight or ten storeys up, in the office of your stockbroker or in your dentist's waiting room, you feel the strong shudder of an earth tremor; the vase of flowers skids towards the magazines on the table, the gossip of the ticker-tape machine is drowned. These tremors, never strong enough to do any serious damage, are commonplace. By ascribing them to the fact that the Witwatersrand is extensively undermined, I am inadvertently taking sides in a long, discreet controversy between the seismologists and the Chamber of Mines. The seismologists say that the tremors are not, geologically speaking, earth tremors at all but are caused by rocks falling from the ceilings of either working or abandoned mines. The Chamber of Mines insists that they are natural and not man-caused phenomena. And jerry-builders take advantage of the dispute, greeting the evidence of cracked walls in houses with a shrug of the shoulders that lets the responsibility fall on God or the Chamber of Mines, take your choice.

Our life in the mining town, in one of the ugliest parts of a generally beautiful continent, was narrow and neighbourly – a way of life that, while it commonly produces a violent reaction of rebelliousness in adolescence, suits young children very well. The town had sprung into existence because of the mines, had grown up around the mines. The shopkeepers had come – first with their tents, then with their shanties, and, at last, with their corner sites and neon signs – to fill and profit from the miners' needs. At the start, the miners wanted only the necessities of life – stoves and workmen's clothing and meat. Soon they wanted everything – cinemas and shiny wooden cocktail cabinets and tinned asparagus. My father's little business was a good example of how trade grew into the full feather of provincial luxury from scrawny beginnings in utility. When he arrived in the town, just before the Boer War, he used to tramp from mine to mine carrying a cardboard suitcase full of pocket watches. The watches sold for less than a dollar each. They ticked as loudly as the crocodile who pursues Captain Hook in *Peter Pan*, and they were as strong as they sounded. They were a necessity for the mine-workers, who found that ordinary watches became rusted and ruined in no time by the damp and heat underground. So my father, a tiny, dapper, small-featured youth with feet no bigger than a woman's, made his living by selling watches to, and repairing watches for, the great, hefty Afrikaners and the tough Scots and Irishmen who produced gold. He had a little wood-and-iron cottage, where he lived with a black retriever named Springbok, two German roller canaries, and his watchmaker's worktable.

By the time my father married my mother, he was living in the newly built local hotel, owned a horse and trap, and had rented a glass-fronted shop, where he sold diamond engagement rings. By the time my sister and I were old enough to notice such things, his shop had showcases full of silver sports cups, walnut mantel clocks, stainless-steel cutlery, and costume jewellery from America and Czechoslovakia. A stone-deaf relative had been imported from Leningrad to do the watch repairing; he sat behind an engraved glass partition, out of sight of the customers, who were now towns-people – the families of other shopkeepers, municipal officials, civil servants – as well as white workers from the mines. The white miners wore the new Swiss water-and-shock-proof watches. The only potential customers for cheap pocket watches were now the tribal Africans – migrant labourers who were employed to do all the really hard work in the mines – and these bewildered men, still wearing earrings and dressed in ochre-dyed blankets, mostly made their purchases at government-concession stores on mine property and did not venture into a jeweller's shop in the town.

The mine people and the townspeople did not by any means constitute a homogeneous population; they remained two well-defined groups. Socially, the mine people undoubtedly had the edge on the people of the town. Their social hierarchy had been set up first, and was the more rigid and powerful. There was a general manager before there was a mayor. But even when the town did create civic dignitaries for itself, even when we did get a country club, there were those among us who neither knew nor cared about the social scaffolding that was going up around them, whereas at each mine the G.M. was not only the leader of society but also the boss, and if one did not revere him as the first, one had to respect him as the second. The dignitaries on both sides – the G.M.s and their officials from the mines, and the city fathers, the presidents of clubs in the town, and so on – invited each other to dinners and receptions, and the teams of the sports clubs of mine and town competed with each other, but there was little mixing on the more intimate levels of sociability. The mine officials and their wives and families lived on 'the property'; that is, the area of ground, some-times very large, that belonged to each mine and that included, in addition to the shaft heads and the mine offices and the hospital, a

sports ground, a swimming pool, a recreation club, and the houses
of the officials – all built by the mine. The G.M. lived in the largest
house, usually a spacious and very pleasant one, situated in a garden
so big that one might almost have called it a park. The garden
was kept in full bloom all year round, right through the sharp,
dry Transvaal winter, by African labour diverted from the mines,
and the liquor stock indoors was ample and lavishly dispensed.
The assistant manager's house was smaller, but decent enough;
then came the underground manager's, and then the compound
manager's (he was in charge of the four-sided barracks, with all
its windows opening on a courtyard and only one gateway, always
guarded, to the world without, in which the African labourers were
fed and housed in celibacy, having left their families in distant
kraals), and then the mine secretary's, and so on down the salary
and social scale, the houses getting smaller, the gardens getting
less elaborate. Most of the mine families lived only a few miles
out from the town, but their self-sufficiency surrounded them
like a moat. Their offspring could go from the cradle to the grave
without having anything to do with the town other than attending
its high school, placing weekly orders with the butcher and the
grocer, and paying three visits to church – one for christening, one
for marrying, one for burying.

We, of course, were town people. All my childhood, we lived
in the little house, in one of the town's earliest suburbs, that my
parents had bought before I was born. Other people moved to the
newer suburbs of flat-roofed villas, pseudo-Tudor houses, and, later,
houses inspired by American magazines, with picture windows
looking out on the bare veld. But we stayed. Ours was a bungalow-
type house with two bow windows and a corrugated-iron roof, like
almost all the other houses that were built in the Witwatersrand
gold-mining towns during the twenties and early thirties. It stood
in a small garden, one of several similar houses on a street along
whose sidewalk grew leathery-leaved trees, which in summer put
out bunches of creamy, bell-shaped flowers. When my sister and I
were little, we used to fit these flowers over our fingertips, like tiny
hats; when we were old enough to own bicycles, we would ride up

heavy bloom of pollen which makes hazy the inner convolutions of certain flowers. Streams oozed down from the hills and could be discovered by the ear only, since they were completely covered by low, umbrella-shaped trees (these are seen to better advantage on the hills around Durban, where their peculiarly Japanese beauty is unobstructed by undergrowth), latticed and knitted and strung together by a cat's cradle of lianas and creepers. My sister and I would push and slither our way into these dim, secret places, glimpsing, for the instant in which we leaned over, the greenish, startling image of our faces in water that endlessly reflected back to the ferns the Narcissus image of their own fronds.

More cheerfully, in the bush along the road we would sometimes hear that incredibly light-hearted, gossipy chatter which means that monkeys are about. The little Natal coast monkeys are charming creatures, in appearance exactly the sort of monkey toy manufacturers choose; in fact, they are just what one would wish a monkey to be. They bound about in the treetops, nonchalant and excitable at the same time, and unless they are half tame, as they have become around some of the road-houses on the outskirts of Durban, they move off almost too quickly to be clearly seen; you find yourself left standing and gazing at the branches as they swing back into place and listening to the gaiety as it passes out of hearing, and the whole thing has the feeling of a party to which you have not been invited. If the monkeys, like distant relatives who wish to make it clear that there is *no* connection, ignored us, there were creatures who, because their movements were attuned to some other age of slime or rock, could not escape us. On the trailing plants near the rocks, sleepy chameleons stalked shakily, or clung swaying, their eyes closed and their claws, so like minute, cold human hands, holding on for dear life. If they saw you coming for them, they would go off nervously, high-stepping across the sand, but with a kind of hopelessness, as if they knew that all you had to do was lean over and pick them up. And then, unable to bite, scratch, sting, or even to make any protest other than to hiss faintly and hoarsely, they wrapped their little cold hands around your finger like a tired child and went as pale as they could – a lightly spotted creamy beige that was apparently their idea of approximating the colour of human skin. My sister was particularly fond of these resigned and melancholy creatures. Twice we took one home to the Transvaal with us on the train, and twice we watched and wept in anguish when, after two or three happy months on the house plant in my mother's living room, the poor thing lost first his ability to change colour, fading instead to a more ghostly pallor each day, and then, literally, his grip, so that he kept falling to the floor. The Transvaal winter, even indoors, was too much for chameleons.

In the heavy green water of the lagoon at the South Coast village where we used to stay, there appeared to be no life at all, though some people said that under the rocks at the bottom there were giant crabs. When the weather was bad for a few days, and the combination of the sea's rising and the lagoon's flooding washed away the sandbanks between the lagoon and the sea, the dark river water in the lagoon poured in a deep channel down into the waves, and the waves mounted the river water, frothing over the swirl. Decaying palm leaves, the rotten ropes of broken lianas, and fallen vegetable-ivory fruit, as hard and round as cricket balls, were washed out of the stagnant bed of the lagoon and brushed you weirdly while you swam in the sea. Once, late one afternoon, my mother and I were lying on the sand watching a solitary swimmer who evidently did not mind the dirty sea. Suddenly we saw the rhythmic flaying of his arms against the water violently interrupted, and then he heaved clear up into the air, gripping or in the grip of a black shape as big as he was. My mother was convinced that he had been attacked by a shark, and went stumbling and flying over the sand to get help from the hotel. I went, with that instinct to seek human solidarity in the face of any sort of danger towards humankind, to stand with some excited children who had been playing with toy boats at the water's edge. I was four or five years older than the eldest of them, and I kept holding them back from the water with the barrier of my outspread arms, like a policeman at a parade. What danger I thought there could be in two or three inches of water I cannot imagine, but the idea that there was a monster in the vicinity seemed to make even the touch of the water's edge a touch of menace.

In minutes, the whole village was on the beach, and out there, but coming nearer with every wave, were the swimmer and the dark shape, now together, now apart, now lost, now discovered again. As the lifesaving rope was unreeled and the volunteer lifesavers plunged into the sea, supposition was shrill, but hastily silenced at the occasional cry of 'Look, there he is!' There was a feeling of special horror, oddly, because it was obvious that the creature was not a shark; with a shark, one knew exactly what it was one had to be afraid of. And then the cry went up: 'It's a crocodile! It's a crocodile!' Even the lifesavers heard it, and looked back towards the shore, confused. Before they could get to the swimmer, he was in water shallow enough for him to stand, and we could see him very clearly, his face grim and wild with water and effort, his hands locked around the long snout of a big reptile, which seemed to gather up the rest of its body in an attempt to kick him, rather than to thrash at him with its tail, as crocodiles are said to do. 'A crocodile!' the cry went up again. 'Enormous!' Men rushed into the shallow water with pocketknives and weapons of driftwood. Yet the man staggered up on to the beach with his monster alone. He was a short, stocky man, and it was true that the thing was as big as he was. It seemed stunned, and he kept hitting it across the snout with his fist, as if to say, 'That will show you!' Amid the screams and the squeals, and the confusion of lifesavers, rope, brandished driftwood, and Boy Scout knives, he beat it to death himself; it was plain that, exhausted though he was, he wanted the privilege of being the conqueror. Then he sat on the sand, sniffing deeply, his chest heaving, a flask of brandy trembling in his hand; I remember so well how he said, in an incredulous, rasping voice, 'Crocodile that size could've torn one of those kids in half.'

The man was a great hero for half an hour. Then an old retired major who had lived in the district for many years and was a botanist and naturalist came over the sand, leaning on his little cane, and prodded at the monster lying there disfigured by blows and sand. 'Leguan,' the major said. 'Old leguan – poor old lizard wouldn't harm a fly. Must've been trying to get back to the lagoon.' The major was quite right. The beast was not a crocodile but one of those giant lizards, the leguans, that are still fairly common all over South Africa but are careful to keep out of the way of man – as timid and, indeed, except for their frightening size and resemblance to the crocodile family, as defenceless as the chameleon. He would not have bitten the swimmer, and he was too stupid and clumsy even to use his weight to defend himself. The man had done battle with the most reluctant of dragons. So, with the wiliness of human beings, who hate to admit that they have been taken in and must turn their gullibility to advantage somehow, the people in the village and at the hotel were quick to make a kind of joke of the swimmer; where before his words 'Could've torn one of those kids in half' had made him seem the saviour of their children, now they saw something absurd in the dramatic way he had struggled to bring the creature in instead of making for the shore and his own safety. He went about the hotel for the rest of his holiday very much alone, and a little sullen perhaps.

By the time my sister and I were in our middle teens, we had lost our taste for solitude and the gentle wilderness. Our childhood love of Durban returned – for different reasons, of course – and I think that then we came to love the place for what it really is: in many ways a fascinating city, even if rather dull and smug intellectually. One of our chief delights at this time was our discovery of the Indian quarter of the town, and the Indian market. We enjoyed turning away from the pseudo-American and neo-Tudor architecture of the shopping centre and wandering down wide Grey Street, where the shops were small and crowded together and the balconies picked out in gaudy curlicues, and here and there a silver minaret or cupola shone. Among the more conventional stores, which sold men's outfitting in fierce competition, were shops full of gauzy, tinselled lengths for saris, and Indian jewellers whose crammed windows seemed almost to tinkle with rows and rows of long gold earrings, and pendants strung upon thread. Those shops that were especially designed to entice European visitors like ourselves burned incense. Their dry, sweet odour was pleasant after the hot street, where splashes of chewed betel nut looked like blood on the pavement. In the Indian market there were piles of sweetmeats coloured violent pink and putrescent yellow, which smelled as revolting as they looked. We would return from these small expeditions with a particular type of sandal, thonged over the big toe, or a pair of earrings that looked as if they had been stamped out of thin gold tinfoil and that hung from the lobe to the shoulder. The sandals were called, if I remember rightly, *chappals*, and I know they were imported from India, but I do not remember ever seeing an Indian woman in Durban wear them. The earrings, without the folds of a sari to back them up, looked cheap and foolish in Western ears.

Like most South Africans, once I had been to Cape Town I wondered how I had ever thought Durban beautiful. Before I was quite grown up, I went alone with my father to Cape Town and we took a cable car to the top of Table Mountain. We stood there, on a clear, calm, perfect day, and, truly, for a little girl, that was god's-eye look at the world. On such a day, you can see the whole Cape Peninsula, from Fishhoek on the one side, right around the ribs of mountain rising out of the sea, to Camps Bay on the other side. Some people even claim that you are looking at two oceans – the Atlantic on one side and the Indian on the other. But that is in dispute, for it is difficult to say where one ocean begins and the other ends. Anyway, the vast waters that lie before you are enough for two oceans. No peacock's tail ever showed such blues and greens as the seas do from that height; all the gradations of depth are miraculously revealed, and, looking far, far down, where the colour crinkles and breaks into white near the shore, you see pale translucent areas in which the rocks show as boldly as if you were looking through the glass bottom of a boat directly above them.

It is something splendid, an almost superhuman experience, to see the tip of a continent, alive, at your feet. I know that I stumbled back to the cable station that day smiling constantly at my father but with the feeling of tears behind my eyes, in a confused state of exaltation that made it impossible for me to speak, and because I was so young, I immediately lost my exaltation in anger

when I saw that many people who had come up with us on the
cable car had been spending their half hour before the cable took
us all down again writing postcards that would bear the postmark
'Table Mountain'. These absorbed visitors scarcely glanced out of
the windows at what they had come to see.

For some reason, our family did not visit the Kruger National Park
until I was sixteen and in my last year at high school. Just how
unusual this abstinence is, is difficult to explain to anyone who is
not South African. For whatever else the South African in general,
and the Transvaaler in particular, may or may not do for his family,
he will manage somehow to get them to Kruger Park, the great
wildlife preserve in the Transvaal. If he has no car, he will borrow
one, and if he cannot do this, he will persuade a friend that two
families can travel as uncomfortably as one, and beg a lift. The Park
opens at the beginning of winter, in late April or early May, and
by dawn on the opening day, cars and trucks loaded with camping
equipment and tinned food are lined up in mile-long queues outside
the various camps that serve as points of entry to the preserve.

I had heard so many tales and seen so many home movies about
the Kruger Park ('My dear, and then the lioness walked right up
to the car and sniffed the tyres!') that I almost dreaded going. I
regarded listlessly the prospect of overcrowded camps, *boerewors*
(a coarse, highly seasoned sausage held in sentimental regard by
both Afrikaans- and English-speaking South Africans) cooked
over an open fire, and long processions of cars crawling along the
dusty roads in the stern rivalry of who would sight the most lions
soonest. But when we went, it was very different from that. We
went in October, during the last few days before the park closes
for the summer rains and the calm that is granted the beasts for
their breeding season. We stayed at a camp with a beautiful name
– Shingwedsi – and we had the shade of its trees and the red blossoms of the cacti almost to ourselves. The peace of the bushveld was
scarcely disturbed by the few cars on the roads.

The rainy season was a month off, but the first night we were at
Shingwedsi the fantastic roar of a freak storm woke us at midnight

and flooded the camp, marooning us for nearly twenty-four hours. During the next day, while we were shut in by drumming rain, my Uncle Robert, our mother's younger brother, drank beer with and received the confidences of an engineer who lived and worked in the Park all the year round, watching over the boreholes that guarantee the animals' water supply. At that period, I had just begun to read Hemingway, and it seemed to me that for the first time in my life something in fact had measured up to fiction. The engineer was just such a man as poor Francis Macomber might have chosen as an escort on a hunting trip. (And, on reflection, just such a man as Mrs Macomber might have wished him to choose.) He had a taciturn, world-weary air, and, in the cosy confinement of the rain, over the beer, he made Robert (since he was only ten years older than I, we girls did not call Robert 'uncle') feel that he, Robert, was the first person in years to whom he had been able to talk as he was talking, the first man whose sporting sense and sensitivity matched the engineer's own, a man — at last! at last! — who instinctively would understand the boredom and tameness, for a man of spirit, of life in a sanctuary, with no one to talk to but gaping tourists. In fact, the engineer was one of those people who make others feel chosen. At five in the afternoon, when the rain had stopped, he stood up, flexed his tanned, muscular knees, and said, with a kind of stern, sardonic glee, 'This is the time for elephant, if you want elephant. This water'll keep the wardens out of my way for a day or so.'

Robert and I were agog, as we were meant to be. While Robert questioned him, unconsciously adopting the engineer's terse manner as he tried to show that he 'belonged', I kept close by his side, determined not to be left out of this. The way to see elephants, to get right up close to them and just about feel them breathe on you as you photographed them, said the engineer, was to take a light truck and go after them fast, ignoring the strict twenty-five-mile-an-hour speed limit in force in the preserve, and then, when you sighted them, to get out and stalk them on foot, ignoring the still stricter rule that no visitor may leave his car. Robert and I grinned with excitement. 'But you can only do it when those

bastards are sitting with their feet in mustard water,' said the engineer, referring to the wardens. Well, that was now.

Robert and I slipped away from the rest of the family – I was
extremely anxious to have this adventure exclusive of my sister
– and in half an hour the engineer had Robert, me, and Robert's
movie camera in his truck. While the wild passage of the truck
through water and mud shook loose every nerve in our bodies,
he told us that what we were going to do was perfectly safe, and
then, almost in the same breath, that what we were going to do
was terribly dangerous but that we need not worry, for he knew
exactly how to do it and get away with it. I wanted to close my
eyes with the speed and exhilaration, but the leaps of a herd of
impala deer that we had startled into a Nijinsky-like retreat of
alarmed grace brought me out of my tense passivity almost as
abruptly as the deer had been brought out of theirs. After about
twenty minutes, we reached a river bed, and there, with their
great columns of legs in the newly flowing water, stood three
magnificent elephants.

The shattering life of the truck came to an abrupt halt. The engineer said 'There you are!', and sent Robert and me stalking on
foot. It seemed as if our hush of intensity had brought home to the
engineer his boredom with this sort of adventure; he looked around
for a dry boulder where he could sit and smoke his pipe while
he waited. The truck was, I suppose, about two hundred yards
from the river. When Robert and I were very near indeed to the
elephants, and the beetle-wing whir of the camera was sounding,
one of the great beasts slowly swung his head erect and towards us.
Then he walked out of the shallow water, trailing his huge feet like
a clumsy child, and advanced to within thirty feet of the camera,
Robert, and me. And there the elephant stood, slowly flapping
those wide, palmetto-like ears that African elephants have. I don't
think he seemed real to us; we thought only of the camera, and saw
the elephant as he would loom on the screen rather than as he was,
a slack-skinned splendid hulk, standing there before us. Then, all
in the same instant, I smelled liquorice tobacco and felt myself
violently grasped by the arm. The same thing must have happened

to Robert, for at once we were jerked furiously around, met the impatient and alarmed face of the engineer, and were running, pushed roughly along by him, for the truck. I suppose it was the beating of my own heart that I thought was the pounding of the elephant coming up behind us.

Driving back to Shingwedsi camp, the engineer grinned fascinatingly – it was difficult to say who was more under the spell of that grin, Robert or me – and remarked, 'Those pictures will be quite good enough as it is. You don't want to scare your friends, do you?' And Robert and I laughed, to show that we, too, knew there hadn't really been any danger. It was only next day, when our party had moved on to Pretorius Kop camp to see lions, that I suddenly remembered that the engineer hadn't had to start the truck when we jumped in; he had left the engine running all the time. Some years later, I was told that there is reason to believe that when an elephant flaps his ears, he does it to fan the scent of his enemy more strongly towards his nostrils, in preparation for a charge.

In a country where people of a colour different from your own are neither in the majority nor the ruling class, you may avoid altogether certain complications that might otherwise arise in the formation of your sense of human values. If the Chinese, say, remain a small, exiled community in Chinatown, and the Red Indians are self-contained on their reservation, you can grow up to have a reasonable standard of personal ethics without taking consideration of their presence. The problem of how you would behave towards them if you met them can be almost purely academic; you need not meet them, if you don't wish to. In South Africa, this is not possible. There are people who try it, who arrange their lives for it, but they never succeed, for it cannot be done. Even if you are the most diehard reactionary, you cannot get away with it in a country where there are three million white people and nine million black and coloured.

For me, one of the confusing things about growing up in South Africa was the strange shift – every year or two when I was small, and then weekly, daily almost, when I was adolescent – in my consciousness of, and attitude towards, the Africans around me. I became aware of them incredibly slowly, it now seems, as if with some faculty that should naturally, the way the ability to focus and to recognise voices comes to a baby in a matter of weeks after birth, have been part of my human equipment from the beginning. The experience of the warm black bosom of the mammy (in South Africa she would be known as the nanny) has been so sentimentalised that I must say I am glad it is one I missed, though not for the reason that I missed it. The reason was simply that my mother, like many good South African mothers from England and Europe, would not have dreamed of allowing any child of hers to nestle in the bosom of a dirty native girl. (That was exactly the phrase – a phrase of scornful reflection on those mothers who did.) And if, at the age of five or six, it had been suggested to my sister or me that we should go up and give our native servant a hug, we would have shrunk away. We accepted the fact that natives were not as clean as we were in the same way we accepted the fact that our spaniel had fleas. It was not until years later that it occurred to me that if our servants were not so well and frequently bathed as ourselves, the circumstance that no bathroom or shower was provided for them might have had a great deal to do with it. And it was later even than that when the final breaking down of this preconceived notion came about. I was a long time learning, and each stage of enlightenment brought its own impulse of guilt for the ignorance that had gone before.

Our successive attitudes towards the Indians are another example of the disturbing shift in values that is likely to beset any child growing up in South Africa. The Indians are a minority group here, but even before their treatment became an issue at the United Nations, affecting the attitude of the rest of the world towards South Africa, they could not comfortably be ignored, because they belonged to the great mass of the Other Side – the coloureds. The Indians were imported into the country as indentured labour for the Natal sugar-cane fields in the mid-nineteenth century, and now, except for a considerable number of businessmen in Natal, a few traders in nearly every Transvaal town, and the considerable number who are employed in hotels and restaurants, they seem to be occupied chiefly as vendors of fruit, vegetables and flowers. In our East Rand mining town, the Indian traders were concentrated in a huddle of shops in one block, bought by them before the passage of what is known as the Ghetto Act of 1946, which, in effect, bars them from owning or leasing property in any but restricted, non-European areas. These were tailor shops, or they were 'bazaars' where cheap goods of all kinds were sold, and they were the object of dislike and enmity on the part of the white shop-keepers. In fact, a woman who was seen coming out of an Indian bazaar with a basket of groceries immediately earned herself a stigma: either she was low-class or, if her husband's position as an official of one of the gold mines put the level of her class beyond question, she must be stingy. 'She's so mean she even goes to the Indians' was the most convincing allegation of miserliness in our town. It was bad enough to be penny-pinching, but to stoop so low as to buy from an Indian trader in order to save!

For some reason I have never understood, it was quite respectable and conventional to buy your fruit and vegetables from the Indians who hawked from door to door with their big red or yellow lorries. Our household, like most others, had its own regular hawker, who called two or three times a week. Whatever a hawker's name (and it was always painted in large, elaborate lettering, a kind of fancy compromise between Indian and English script, on his lorry), he was invariably known as Sammy. He even called himself Sammy, rapping at kitchen doors and announcing himself by this generic. There was a verse, parodying the hawkers' broken English, that children used to chant around these lorries:

> Sammy, Sammy, what you got?
> Missus, Missus, apricot.

There were many more verses with the same rhyme scheme, becoming more and more daring in their inclusion of what struck the children as giggle-producing obscenities, such as 'chamber pot', and a few genuine old Anglo-Saxon shockers, which they pronounced quite calmly.

If you did not serenade the Indian with rude songs, and your mother was a good buyer and payer, he might hand you down a peach or a bunch of grapes from his lorry, but if you were an urchin without family backing, he would shout and shoo you away, lest your quick hand filch something while his back was turned. It is interesting to me now, too, to remember how yet again the bogy of uncleanliness came up immediately with the gift of the peach from Sammy; my mother, too polite to offend him by saying anything, pronounced such a warning with her eyes that I would not dare put my teeth to that peach until I had taken it inside to be washed. Sammy had 'handled' it. Sammy was an Indian. In fact, Sammy was Not White. Heaven knows, I don't suppose the man *was* clean. But why did no one ever explain that the colour had nothing to do with cleanliness?

So my sister and I began by thinking of the Indian as dirty, and a pest; the vendors whom I have described as annoying us on the beach at Durban were the prototype. Then we thought of him as romantic; our wanderings in the Indian market in Durban were, I suppose, part of a common youthful longing for the exotic. And finally, when we were old enough and clearheaded enough and had read enough to have an abstract, objective notion of man, as well as a lot of jumbled personal emotions about him, the Indian became a person like ourselves.

I suppose it is a pity that as children we did not know what people like to talk of as 'the real Africa' – the Africa of proud black warriors and great jungle rivers and enormous silent nights, that anachronism of a country belonging to its own birds and beasts and savages which rouses such nostalgia in the citified, neighbour-jostled heart, and out of which a mystique has been created by writers and film directors. The fact of the matter is that this noble paradise of 'the real Africa' is, as far as the Union of South Africa is concerned, an anachronism. Bits of it continue to exist; if you live in Johannesburg, you can still go to the bushveld for solitude or shooting in a few hours. And bits of it have been carefully preserved, with as little of the taint of civilisation as is commensurate with the longing of the civilised for comfort, as in the Kruger Park. But the *real* South Africa was then, and is now, to be found in Johannesburg and in the brash, thriving towns of the Witwatersrand. Everything that is happening on the whole emergent continent can be found in microcosm here. Here are the Africans, in all the stages of an industrial and social revolution – the half-naked man fresh from the kraal, clutching his blanket as he stares gazelle-eyed at the traffic; the detribalised worker, living in a limbo between his discarded tribal mores and the mores of the white man's world; the unhappy black intellectual with no outlet for his talents. And here, too, are the whites, in all the stages of understanding and misunderstanding of this inevitable historical process – some afraid and resentful, some pretending it is not happening, a few trying to help it along less painfully. A sad, confusing part of the world to grow up and live in. And yet exciting.

1954

Hassan in America

We have a friend in Cairo who is a prefabricator of mosques. I do not offer this as an item from Ripley, or as an insinuation that our friend belongs under any exhibitionist heading of Unusual Occupations, along with sword-swallowers and bearded ladies. On the contrary. He is a thin, wiry aesthete of great charm, member of a famous continental banking family by birth, Arab by inclination, and the beauty of his profession (for me, at any rate) is that there is nothing intrinsically outlandish or freakish about it; it is simply a combination of two perfectly ordinary occupations which happen to belong, in time and space, worlds apart. Mosques have been going up in the East since the seventh century,

at the shoddy white sugar-cube blocks going up where the palaces
were left to become rubble beneath the feet of men and the hooves
of goats; he catches his breath at the sight of a beautiful keyhole
doorway, still standing, a little house with a cool courtyard, that
might yet be saved. He wants to buy them all. Driving with him
through the lanes of the old town, I saw that his black eyes were not
on the yelling dawdling traffic – there was no hooter in his car, and,
dangling one hand out of the window, he beat on the bodywork to
give warning of his approach – but looked all the time at windows,
doors, balconies and gateways, mosques fallen away like cliffs, houses
like broken honeycomb. He wants to buy them all, to save what can
never be built again. He is not appalled by dirt, by poverty, by the
degeneration of the humans who shelter and breed in pace with this
decay. That is Allah's affair. He wants only to hold together a little
longer the beauty that has held out so long.

It was this passion of his that led him to quick fatalistic anger
when he heard that someone whom he knew was building an
'Arab style' house, with modern steel doors beneath a traditionally shaped portal. *He* knew where he could find a magnificent
carved door dating from the eighteenth century. He could buy
it for five – no, less – three pounds. It was there for the taking,
almost. All it needed was sandpapering, and a new piece of wood
where the bolt was fitted. And he knew someone who could do
that properly, too.

He was even more despairing when he saw a 'modern' mosque
going up with a *mimbar*, or pulpit, made of lacquered plywood
instead of the carved and inlaid panelling and *meshrebiya* work – a
delicate, hand-made wooden lattice – which is traditional. He told
the people who had perpetrated this offence that even if the microphone had replaced the *muezzin*, there was no need for the *mimbar*
to be a vulgar travesty. He could have got them a *mimbar* made of
centuries-old ivory and wood, and restored by the last man in Cairo
who truly understood the technique of the work . . .

They were not only chastened, but interested. Some short time
later he received a call from two gentlemen from out of town.

Would he contract to supply, ready-made, a traditional *mimbar* for a new mosque under construction in Alexandria?

He was in the prefabricated mosque business.

When we were in Egypt in March last year, the work for the mosque in Alexandria was completed. Wally had taken a little trip there, to see his contract honoured, his beautiful *mimbar* delivered and set up against the wall to the right of the niche – the *mihrab* – which indicates the direction of Mecca. 'But now I'm on something big, something much bigger,' he murmured, when we congratulated him on the success of this first venture. His black eyes, mournful and gay at the same time, invited questions. But he couldn't wait to be asked. He went on: 'A mosque, oh yes. But not here. Far away You'll laugh . . . A mosque in Washington.'

'Wally, we're going to Washington,' warned my husband.

'No, it's true. You can go and see it. I *want* you to go and see it for me.'

I was not so sceptical as my husband. I had never travelled before. If Cairo existed at one end of a continent on which Johannesburg, where I live, is at the other. I was ready to believe that I might find a mosque as well as a White House in Washington.

'I am making – at least my man Hassan is making – a *mimbar* for a mosque that's going up in Washington. Tomorrow I'll take you to see the work he's doing. It's beautiful.' English is a little-used fourth language for Wally, whose real fluency belongs to French, German and Arabic, and in his mouth the adjective is still an incomparable superlative.

We pestered him with questions, in which he wasn't really interested. Who was building a mosque in Washington! And what for? Who would worship there! His answers were vague. Diplomatic personnel, he supposed. What did it matter, anyway? The important thing was that this mosque, whether in Washington or Timbuctoo, would have a beautiful *mimbar*, made by Hassan in exactly the same way as it had been made for centuries. Old Hassan and his son were, so far as he knew, the last men in Cairo who still practised this ancient craft. We would see for ourselves tomorrow how perfect the *mimbar* was going to be.

Wally came to our hotel to fetch us after a late breakfast next morning. It was a week of riot and crisis in Egypt, when Nasser deposed Neguib and then Neguib deposed Nasser, and we got into the old Dodge under the eyes of a bored Egyptian soldier who crouched, half hidden by dusty shrubs, over one of the Bren guns that pointed at the steel from the Ezbekieh Gardens. We went, I suppose, the long way round to the workshop of Hassan the carpenter, because, as I quickly discovered, Wally never could resist making detours to take in places he loved, or another look at some old house with windows that he admired and hoped to buy or borrow. On this day he drove us via the site of the summer villa, on the Nile bank opposite the Nilometer, where my husband had lived while he worked for British Intelligence during the war. I had seen this little house on many photographs, knew exactly the disposition of its rooms, and its relation to the three great palm trees in the courtyard. Now only the three palm trees remained, on a piece of cleared sand overlooking the river. Wally had built that little house himself – without permission, on a piece of land belonging to someone else.

My husband paced out the familiar steps from one palm to another, looking lost. But Wally did not seem to mind the disappearance of the little house, its confiscation and demolition. 'It's a pity, isn't it?' he said cheerfully. 'I've got a place in mind,' his voice had dropped to its confidential low, 'further along the Nile, out of town entirely. I'll show you, soon. That façade I showed you on Sunday, you liked it? If I don't need it for one of my prefabrication jobs, I want to use it for myself.'

Before we reached Hassan's workshop we made another stop, this time at the Ibn Tulun mosque. Wally would not let us go into the famous mosque at the Citadel, nearby. 'Rubbish,' he said. 'Impure style. This,' ushering us into the Ibn Tulun, 'this is, I think, my favourite mosque. Twelfth century.' Inside the great mosque, in the sunlit square open to the sky, we did not talk at all. We crossed it and then walked slowly round all four sides beneath the repetitive vista of the colonnades, falling away behind us with the beautiful monotony of ripples in water. It was dark under the high roof, after the bright sun: the dark was repeated, out in the sun of the square, in the dark bodies of the kites which, when we looked out, passed between our eyes and the light like those proverbial clouds no bigger than a man's hand. The mosque was deserted except for two old men who slept peacefully on straw mats.

Once we had left the mosque, the old car plunged and bucked into streets scarcely wide enough for a loaded donkey. We reinforced Wally's thumping of the bodywork with yells and cries. Bare-bottomed brats pressed out of our way against filthy walls. At last we left the car and walked up a steep, humped and winding street, stale with age, strong with poverty. The children had their life in public, coming out the way rats emerge to play quietly next to their refuse heap. The girls especially did not look much like children; with their painted eyes, they were more like frail women, shrunken through long illness. One was beautiful, under the grotesquerie of kohl, an actress who had forgotten to take off her make-up – until you saw that only her head looked young and alive; the rest of her was shrivelled before it had grown, like an anemone plant I once transplanted when it was already in bud. This child was being nursemaid to the baby of the family, one of those appalling Egyptian babies which made me shudder, and then feel ashamed of my horror. When they are six or eight months old they are no bigger than a newborn, but their pocket-watch-sized heads, covered with straight black hair, are veteran with survival of the dirt in which they feebly lie, and which would have killed the fat, pink-cheeked kind within days of birth. Past the baby, the street ended at the entrance to a kind of courtyard. Once, I suppose, it had been a garden. Now grass or flowers or paving were replaced by a surface of rubble from the crumbling building to which the courtyard belonged. In the middle stood a well-used grey Peugeot car.

Wally was smiling. 'Come,' he said, and took my arm, 'This is Hassan's place. He is here.'

*　　*　　*

There was no door. We stepped, in the calm sunlight – the courtyard preserved still its old function of creating a space of quiet
between the dwelling and the street – over fallen stone and wood. A
stairway led nowhere; it seemed terribly light inside; a fat, pleasant-
faced, middle-aged Arab in shirt and trousers called out a greeting
to Wally and came over to us. We were introduced to Hassan, and I
saw one or two fine feathers of wood-shaving, curled on his clothes
and hair. Slightly awkwardly, with an air, if no words of apology
(he spoke little English) he drew Wally away to consult with him
in Arabic. They argued, considered, explained in the manner of
men who are in business together. My husband and I saw that we
were in a great, floorless room – perhaps two or three rooms from
which the intervening walls had been taken or had fallen down.
Planks of new wood rested crazily against the old walls, sawdust
was mixed with rubble underfoot, and, at the far end, there was a
workman's bench, a lathe and other carpenter's tools. The walls
were very high. Higher still, there was the sky. There was no roof.

Picking my way, I went through a beautiful arched doorway and
found myself in another room. Where the floor had been there were
piles of what at first glance appeared to be litter and rubbish, but
which, when I looked again, I guessed must be Wally's stores. Four
broken Greco-Roman columns were stacked next to a porcelain toilet
pan bearing the name of a firm of English plumbers. A huge carved
door, half-destroyed by dry rot, lay on its side. A neat pile of pinkish
stone blocks, numbered in chalk, stood near where I had entered.
While I looked, there was a stir behind the columns, and a white
duck came flatly towards me, blinking her quick eyes and shaking at
a piece of rotting vegetable peel that she held in her beak.

This shell was a place of elegant proportion; even now, with
the strange assortment of objects, and the duck, scavenger of the
mud, in possession, it was the sort of place in which you must
stand still a moment, as you enter, and feel how pleasingly you
are enclosed. Half the ceiling remained intact above the ruin; the
walls curved in to meet it, and this curved cornice and the ceiling
itself were painted in a close, delicate, formal design of red and
blue and gold. The colours were still perfectly clear but the ceiling

ended jaggedly, halfway across the span of the room. In the gaping
space of sky, kites wheeled slowly, as they did over the Ibn Tulun
mosque. It was splendid.

Wally came in behind me, saying 'shoo' to the duck, who knew
him and took no notice.

'What *was* this?' I said. My face must have shown my astonish-
ment, awe, almost, the strain of the impact of a world that had
flourished and rotted before I had come, alien and impudent as the
duck, to look upon it.

'Early eighteenth-century palace. Must have belonged to some
prince. This was the salon.' He stood with his hands on his skinny
hips, admiring the ceiling.

'But to whom does it belong?'

'Nobody.'

'How nobody?'

'These palaces were family seats. Passed from father to son. But
they lost power, money. Years ago, the descendants got too poor
to keep up such places. Three or four or five families lived in them
together. They fell to bits. Nobody ever restores anything, here.
Everything decays, is lost. In the end the inheritance is divided
among so many, nobody owns it. Nobody can live in it, nobody can
afford to keep it – what is the word – habitable. But come on, you
haven't seen what I brought you here for. Don't you want to see the
mimbar for Washington?'

The duck ran once or twice before us like someone hurrying
against the stream on a crowded sidewalk. 'Get,' said Wally, or
maybe it was some Arabic word that sounded the same. The duck
dived out of the way.

When Wally and I came back through the arched doorway, Hassan
and my husband were talking in French beside the carpenter's
bench. Hassan wiped some small object in his hand with the palm
of the other, and smiled at me with his head wrinkling his fat neck
to one side, like one of those pictures of foreign children one is
tempted to take on quaysides, recording an attitude at once shy
and yet amusedly tolerant. Wally called out something to him in

Arabic, and he disappeared for a moment behind a pile of planks
and carved timber. From the wood powder that covered the bench I
picked up the spool-shaped piece of wood, about an inch and a half
long, that he had dropped there. I turned it over and saw that there
was a slot cut across the back of it. My husband leaned over my
shoulder and put into my hand a thin slat of wood, a little longer
than the spool. It fitted smoothly into place.

Hassan came back with a handful of such slats and little carved
wooden shapes – some were spools, like the one I held, but most of
them looked like segments cut from a narrow picture frame. Some
were of black wood, some nut-coloured, some rosy mahogany.
There were two or three very small diamond-shaped pieces which
were made of yellowed ivory. Not quickly, but with the calm
rhythm of fingers that are doing work to which they have long
been accustomed, Hassan fitted together shapes, slats and ivory.
The picture frame segments formed diamonds, the ivory diamond
shapes fitted within the black wooden ones, and a spool united each
of the four angles of each wooden diamond to an angle of another.
Grooves in the pieces themselves, and the thin wooden slats that
slid in behind, held the whole pattern rigidly and sweetly in place
without a single nail. Later Wally was to show me huge screens
made this way, and the balconies which, in old Arab houses, cover
the windows and have a tiny peep-hole window out of which the
veiled women are allowed to observe the street, and, most beautiful
of all, a centuries-old *mimbar* in an ancient Cairo mosque, from
which not the smallest fragment of wood had worked loose. Hassan
went away again and brought back with him a cardboard box in
which his wooden confetti lay thick.

'So!' he said, assembling another pattern.

'That's partly very old stuff.' Wally interpreted for the carpenter,
'I brought him a screen – beautiful, very fine work,' he picked up
a tiny triangle, 'but in bad repair, half destroyed. Now he's making
new pieces to replace those which have been lost.'

The jagged square mosaic Hassan handed to me had a uniform
patina. 'How is it that you can't tell the old from the new?' I asked.

'He cleans and emery-papers the old pieces, and his replacements are identical with them,' said Wally.

'Patient work!' I said.

Wally shrugged. 'He is the last,' he said, 'it's a dying art. Even in Egypt, there is no time, any more.'

Hassan went off with his easy, shambling walk and came back carrying a large section of wooden mosaic. He laid it before us on the bench, clearing a space for it with his forearm. It was part of the *mimbar*, the pulpit for the mosque in Washington.

'There you are!' said Wally.

Hassan pulled a few segments free, fitted them on to the pattern again. He pressed two pieces into my hand, motioned me to try. It was harder than I thought, because the pieces were made to fit so snugly. Hassan watched me proudly, as if I were a pupil.

'He's making every piece for the Washington pulpit here, himself?' I asked Wally.

'His son helps,' said Wally.

I looked round at the ruined palace, open to the sky. 'And when it's finished,' I said. 'When it goes from here to – there. Will it be shipped complete? It'll be such a huge thing.'

'We'll probably take it all to pieces for shipping,' said Wally. 'Hassan may go along to Washington to assemble it again, piece by piece. That's prefabricating.'

'Hassan in America,' I said.

Hassan heard the two names, guessed of what we were speaking and smiled, his plump man's breasts lifting against his old shirt with a shrug. I noticed that the carpenter doodled, though leisurely, not nervously, with his little bits of wood: making and pulling apart patterns he did not even look at.

From here to there.

Hassan walked with us, respectfully, out into the courtyard. He and Wally joked together in Arabic, conspiratorially. Hassan giggled deep in his chest. 'Is that his car?' my husband asked Wally, looking at the grey Peugeot. Hassan put an arm on it, leaning upon it as on an old wife. 'How do you get it in here, for heaven's sake?'

my husband said to him in English. I do not know whether or not the carpenter understood; he raised his big curved brows, laughing, in a kind of pantomime of one of Wally's favourite answers: 'We have our methods.' As we left, waving to Hassan, I looked up round the courtyard once more, and noticed a shirt fluttering at a window. In what perhaps had once been the servants' quarters of the palace, on the street side of the courtyard, a room was still standing, a room with a roof. Whatever inner communication to it there had been was no longer there; it was reached by a wooden ladder. It was in that room that Hassan lived, perhaps with his whole family. But he had his Peugeot. He merely camped out in the eighteenth century.

I wonder if we ever really believed in the mosque in Washington.

We were in New York in April and decided to spend the Easter weekend in Washington. 'Ah, the cherry blossom,' friends said, knowingly. 'Well, the National Gallery, actually,' said my husband. 'And we must remember to ask about the mosque,' I murmured, but nobody heard me.

It was only late on our last afternoon in the capital that we remembered, or rather that we didn't think of something else we *must* see, instead. We had been to the White House and the Lincoln Memorial, and out along the smooth parkway to Mount Vernon. I had had my picture taken against the wisteria in front of the National Gallery, and again before an espaliered pear tree in Washington's delightful kitchen garden. (The cherry blossom had been out, it appeared, the week before, and was as bedraggled and stained as an old ball dress.) A gentle rain steamed the grass and trees of the public gardens and boulevards all day, and over all the lovely city there was the wan, soft atmosphere of a hothouse, the smell of warmth and water. We had to take a friend home to his house in a fairly distant suburb, and by the time we set out to find the mosque, it was near twilight.

'I think we should get on straight back to New York,' said my husband.

'No, I'm going to see that mosque.'

We found it, of course, on Massachusetts Avenue, along the wide way lined with foreign embassies. It is part of the new Islamic Centre, built by the countries belonging to the Arab League, and is contiguous with lecture and other public rooms. When we saw it, it was near completion, though the builder's and architect's boards were still up. We sat and looked at it, from the car on the other side of the road. Close to the sidewalk, five pillared archways lead to the courtyard of the mosque, flanked by arched keyhole windows repeating the pattern in the secular rooms to left and right. The building, of pale stone, is two storeys high and ends in a silhouetted balustrade of a delicate design, almost exactly like that of the Doge's Palace in Venice. Tiered above this, there is a broad square tower, with the same decoration, and from the front wall of the broad tower rises a slender square tower culminating in a kind of balcony from which the minaret points. Near its peak, the minaret has its own round balcony, above which it is nipped into a slender waist; from this the graceful onion-shaped peak curves out and then in again. The crescent of Islam balances on its tip. There in the misty twilight, with the street lights superimposing, like scratches on a picture, the trees and buds of spring on an American sidewalk, was Wally's mosque.

We scrambled out of the car and scuttled recklessly across the avenue over the shivering lanes of light from the great eyes of American cars. The earth between the sidewalk and the entrance to the Islamic Centre was uneven with rubble; new rubble, builder's rubble, this time, adulterating the spring smell of wet soil with the cold odour of cement. We went through one of the five pillared archways into the courtyard. But it was not yet paved, and we had to skirt wide pools of rainwater in order to cross it. It was in the process of being decorated in a bright, light blue. The way into the mosque was barred with builder's boards. We could not even see in.

We came out of the courtyard and walked all round the Islamic Centre. All doors were locked. 'Look,' said my husband. He had noticed that the elaborate keyhole windows were filled in with modern steel, glass-paned frames. The steel was painted blue. Inside, I could picture lecture rooms, planned for acoustic perfection, washrooms with clean tiles and a machine that dries your hands with a stream of hygienic, warmed and disinfected air. We came out on the other side of the building and found ourselves at the right-hand entrance to the courtyard. I stepped into it once more, for a last look. Here, the builders must have settled themselves for their lunch – empty beer cans lay at the foot of one of the arches. 'The beer that made Milwaukee famous,' I read, kicking over one of the cans.

As we drove away, I screwed my neck round to have a last look at the brand-new mosque to which Wally's prefabricated pulpit was coming. In a few moments all I could see of it was the Islamic crescent, caught in the treetops of Washington like the moon itself.

1955

Egypt Revisited

The friend who had come to meet me at the airport said with satisfaction, 'It's worse than ever here, it's lovely.' He was a foreigner, expressing in seven words a viewpoint doubly foreign: no citizen of the United Arab Republic would admit that graft is thriving in Egypt more rankly than ever, and no other member of the remnant of the foreign community whom I met would agree that life there is lovely. Yet the eccentric viewpoint given by my friend, who has spent the whole middle thirty years of his life in Egypt, is less than half a joke. Perhaps you have to come, as I do, from Africa and not from Europe, to pick the truth from the laugh. All over the Afro-Asian world there must be isolated Europeans who secretly rejoice in the bitterness of their own banishment, because they love the life and temperament of the country of their adoption so much and so tolerantly that they luxuriate even in the intensification of national failings that so often seems to follow on independence of foreign domination.

I was last in Cairo nearly five years ago, in March 1954, during the week when Nasser deposed Neguib. There were machine guns snouting at you through the dusty leaves of the shrubs in the Ezbekieh Gardens, then, and military trucks delivered their loads of soldiers at the street corners every morning, where they sipped coffee on the alert, all day. Now the impromptu, trigger-happy atmosphere has gone. Suez hangs in the air, a confidence that inflates even the meanest street-urchin chest. Nasser has had the good sense and the imagination to do one or two things that show: a beautiful corniche has swept away the jumble of little villas that used to obscure the town bank of the Nile, there are new bridges, and new wide roads, and white blocks of newly built workers' flats that, spaced on their cleared ground, look as much like institutions as all workers' flats seem to everywhere in the world. One of the new roads, which leads up to the Mokattam hills, cuts a wide tarred swathe through the Dead City, and in another part of the city the great dunes of rubble that are ancient Cairo, crumbled to dust, are being bitten into and smoothed to a new level for the dwelling places of the latest wave of civilisation. (Watching the cranes and bulldozers, you can see an archaeological discovery of the future in the actual making.) All this, along with the colossus that has been raised from the sands of Memphis and put up outside the main railway station, and the boyishly-grinning pictures of Nasser that cover the faded squares where once Farouk's picture hung on the walls of shops, is the maquillage on an old face that has known so many. But it's an impressive job, and one which encourages one to believe that there's been some bone-surgery too, some improvement of the structure beneath the paint.

I soon discovered that there are two almost completely different versions of the range and effect of this surgery, and that while I should have full opportunity to hear one, I should have to gather the other, and most important, one chiefly by sharpening my own eyes and ears and the shiver of receptivity on my skin. As a white visitor without any Arabic, I naturally found myself socially stranded

among the remnants of the European 'foreign' community; I could
not expect to cross the very few old and personal bridges between
European society and Egyptian society that have survived, successfully, the Palestine War, the Officers' Revolution and Suez, and
I could not expect, without a word of their language, to reach a
confession of the hopes, fears and prides of the people of the streets.
While I was in Cairo I did not let myself forget that the voice in my
ear – a measured, intelligent and mostly unembittered voice – was
not the voice of the people; that coarse and muffled note I should
have to pick up for myself.

Cairo as seen by the few members of the old community who
still manage to live there is a depressing place; an intimate whose
sight is going and from whose mind the mobility of memory is
fading. This is not entirely blimpish nostalgia for good old days.
The ancient city that only a few years ago was one of the elegant
centres of the modern world has forgotten its sophistication. Lack
of foreign currency has emptied the Kasr-el-Nil shops of nearly
everything imported; they are filled with decent cloth of unin-
spired design made in Egyptian textile mills, and unbeautiful
shoes fairly well made by Egyptian factories. Even Groppi's famous
delicatessen exposition has shrunk; there *are* one or two delicacies you cannot buy there, now. In those smart restaurants which
are still open, the head chef has gone (banished to that 'home' in
France from which he came perhaps two generations ago?) and
the second-in-command is following the recipes, but not the flair.
The great artists and musicians of the world no longer come to
Egypt, and there are few who come to hear them if they do. The
only evidence I saw of the cultural life of the year in Cairo was the
peeling remains of tremendous posters advertising a Soviet ballet
and theatre company (a third-rate one, I was told) that had come
and gone. The *luxe* of Europe has been banished, but what is left, of
course, is the pandemic inanity of Hollywood. The entertainment
life of Cairo has become that of a complex of villages, each with its
ten-foot-high paper face of Marilyn Monroe.

In the eloquent silence of a departed presence that Europe has
left behind in Cairo – a silence that you are aware of beneath the

unchanged racket and tinkle of the street – a sound forms. The hoarse scraping of the palms of deserted gardens in Maadi is the nervous clearing of the throat; the faint stir of air in the peacock's tail of fallen leaves before the door of the British Embassy is the taking of a preparatory breath – and there, it is out. 'Sequestrated'. Sibilant and fateful, this is the last word on the destiny of nearly every European you meet and every second shop or bank you pass. It is the excuse, the explanation and the apotheosis of city life.

With the immediate past of the city under sequestration, the present seems to be passing into the hands of the army officers and their wives. They are the new elite; the officers' wives are the women who spend hours and money at the beauty parlours, now, and (it is said with a touch of malice) picnic on the Gezirah Club golf course because they haven't yet got so far as learning the game itself. There is a splendid new officers' club, too, where the officers take the ease of top men. No doubt these are the people for whom the new suburb, dubbed Mokattam City, is intended. The development has the authentic, sad, *nouveau riche* stamp; bold, cocky, unsure in taste but sure of *right* – in this case the right to plan ugly villas on the moon-landscape of the Mokattam hills. This certainly is one of the most beautiful places in the world to live, if you feel you could stand the unearthliness of it. Withdrawn from the softening presence of the Nile, these austere heights have no geological memory of green or root or growth; as some mountains are above the tree belt, so these are, so to speak, above the life belt. They drop sheerly from level to level, the higher ones carved into deep escarpments of rock and sand, and the lower ones pitted and cragged by the quarrying that has built Cairo for years. From the foot you see a landslide of hardened Demerara sugar, sliced here, scooped out there, gouged and layered. From the top, with the strange, coarse crumbs of a substance that does not seem to be the surface of the earth underfoot, you look, far below, on the peace of the Dead City, a place from which at this height only the sound-track seems missing; and beyond it to the whole marvellous city, from the medieval minarets and domes to the cubist shapes of light and shade made by modern blocks; and, at last, to the desert itself.

I went into a Fatimid tomb that has stood alone, up there, through
the centuries; and I had lunch at the new casino, a vast grand piano
of a building whose 'free lines' have begun to peel before it is quite
completed.

On another day I drove past deserted Mena House – open, I
believe, but listless – and went to eat *tahina* and *kebab* at another
new restaurant, this time at the foot, or rather under the nose,
of the Sphinx. This one is called 'Sahara City' and it is run by a
Sudanese who looks like Uncle Tom and as a small boy was a page
at the court of Franz Joseph of Austria. Both the casino restaurant
and 'Sahara City' were empty; 'Nobody goes anywhere,' said my
friends. But that night, at a restaurant I had remembered from my
last visit, the tables were full and people stood ten deep around the
bar – avaricious-looking women, men who watched everyone who
came in.

'Then who are these?' I asked.

'The local representatives of international crooks,' said my
companion boredly.

The cosmopolitan city of Cairo is dead as the Dead City itself.
But does it matter? Does it really count? When I sat in the train,
waiting to leave for Upper Egypt, I had a sense of release from
involvement with a prevalent emotional atmosphere that had
little or nothing to do with me; my emphatic identification with
the dispossessed foreign community left me, and I very properly
took up my own role again, which was that of a stranger in a
strange land. The train took a long time to get started; a boy with
rings of sesame-studded bread braceleting his arms from armpit
to wrist ran up and down the platform; trolleys full of fowls in
cane cages were wheeled past; the crowd, predominantly male, as
usual, took an elaborate farewell of the passengers. I had plenty
of time to think, and look. The scene on the platform was just
as it would have been, five years ago. The streets of Cairo, too,
with the exception of the 'foreign' streets, were just as before.
At sunset that afternoon, I had stood on the balcony of the flat
where I was staying, and had watched the people below, never

ant-like as in big cities of the West, but leisured, in full cry, pushing carts, selling peanuts and roasted maize cobs, balancing coffee cups, zigzagging the hazard across hooting cars and the little red petrol tanks (from which householders buy the spirit for their stoves) drawn by jingling, brass-cluttered donkeys. As I had come out of the building to make for the station, I had passed the caretaker, sitting resting his back against the blast-wall that was put on during the War and has never been taken down; he was eating his bean soup supper preparatory to his night's work, which consists of climbing into the bed that is pushed into the foyer every evening, and falling asleep under his yellow coverlet.

Here, among the real population, the people themselves, not enough seemed to have changed. Nasser's infant industrial plans are not yet sufficiently under way to thin out the ranks of the thousands who exist on half-jobs, waiting for a share of a half-job, or simply waiting for the opportunity to turn some absurd and unwelcome service into a job — the urban manifestation of an over-populated country that is increasing its count of souls by the disastrous number of a million every two years. And while the military caste is raising its standard of living hand over fist along with its social position, the civil servants are struggling to keep up decent appearances on salary scales that would have been adequate before the last war. Many people told me that these totally unrealistic salaries were largely responsible for corruption; families could not hope to make ends meet without the 'little extra' brought in by bribes.

Yet though these facts were disappointing — they were at least negative — by and large, they had not been brought about by the new regime; the new regime had failed, as yet, to change them.

One of the things I had liked about Cairo, five years after the revolution, I decided, was what I cautiously call national confidence — something that I don't believe has anything to do with the braggart 'Voice of Cairo' or Pan-Arabism, or, indeed, anything more ambitious or aggressive than an inner assurance that each man is a man measured against his own people, and not a cipher found wanting against the standards of those who are born of other countries and to other opportunities. All of a piece with this was my satisfaction when I saw what good care the new government is taking to preserve many of those great hunks of the past which jut out here and there, all over Cairo – walls and city gates as well as more obvious and spectacular monuments. When I went to the Cairo Museum, that very morning of my last day in Cairo, I was not surprised to see that although the tourists were reduced to myself, two whispering Indian girls and an American couple sitting exhaustedly in a window embrasure, the museum was full of parties of Egyptian schoolboys and girls; it seemed to me natural that a young and poor nation should be eager to teach its children that it is not so young or so poor, after all.

But what *was* a horrifying surprise was the state of the museum. It was dusty and dingy as a second-hand dealer's; many exhibits had lost their labels, and those of others were almost indecipherable. Vaguely military-looking attendants lounged about, their sticky tea-glasses stowed away in dark corners. Even in the Tutankhamen rooms the jewellery is falling to pieces and the gold is flaking off the incomparable splendour of the shrine. Such neglect of the exquisite work of human hands that has survived time almost long enough to have achieved immortality gives you a feeling of real distress; I had hastened back into town to find someone who could explain to me why this was being allowed to happen. And then I heard about another side of national pride, a foolish, childish side, that will see its wonderful artistic heritage rot rather than let the foreigner – any foreigner – bring the expert help and knowledge that is needed to preserve it.

The train finally did go, and I woke up next morning in an Egypt that is not Cairo. For the next few days I followed the life of the Nile. Where in the world do you get a statement of the human condition as simple and complete as this? Look out of the train or car window and the entire context of the people's lives is there – the river, the mud, the green of crop and palm it nurtures, the desert. There is no existence outside the beneficence of the river, the scope of the mud, the discipline of the desert. This pure statement comes like peace, after the complexity and fragmentariness of life as we know it.

The land looks as it has always looked – 'always' is an impudent five years, for me, out of many thousands. Although the big estates have been broken up under a fairly vigorous and, most people agree, fairly successful agrarian reform, they are worked by the same people in the same way. I was struck again by the unfair picture of these people that soldiers who had been in Egypt during the War gave to their Western countries. I know that South Africans built up for me a caricature of a squinting, cringing, night-shirted Egypt – 'those old Gyppos'. The fact is that many of the peasants, who went on with their work in dogged dignity, as we walked past, are good-looking, while the youths, especially the Nubians round Aswan, are as beautiful as the lovely faces in tomb carvings. This is extraordinary when you remind yourself that these people have been underfed and debilitated by bilharzia and malaria for many generations, and that ever since year-round irrigation was achieved, they have been overworked as well.

Strung along the Nile, their villages appear as single units – no straggler houses, and a shelter of palms drawn in around them, fortressed against the sun. In the distance they seem to be those very oases that appear in the deserts of fairy tales. The beauty of this poverty has to be shaken off. Then you see that these people are breathtakingly poor, even by the standards of African poverty that I know in South Africa. How, you ask yourself, mentally groping down to confine comparisons only to those things which seem reasonably essential to life – how can they live, so possessionless, so stripped? Apart from a more equitable distribution of land – no one is allowed to own more than 300 feddans (315 acres) and fifty feddans for each of his first two children, and the vast absentee-owned estates have been distributed among the landless – the regime has brought one obvious enrichment to village life. Nearly every village now has a fine modern school, just outside its confines, and it was good, in the mornings, to see the children running out of the dark, close mud walls across to the spanking new white buildings with big windows. Oddly enough, contemporary architecture does not look out of place beside mud brick and tea-cup domes; I wondered about this until I remembered the model of an ancient Egyptian villa that I had seen in a dusty case in the Cairo Museum – it made use of the same juxtaposition of simple rectangles as one sees in contemporary buildings.

At last, I stood at Aswan on the barrage and felt the power of the Nile water thudding up through the concrete under my hands as it forced through the sluices. 'Aswan' has become a place-name of immense overtones to anyone who reads a newspaper; since 1956 its pronouncement as a colossal barrage of the Nile to be created there has stirred feelings – loyalties, resentments, fears, satisfactions, guilts – rather than conjured up the imaginative picture of a town. It was quite a surprise – it was as if I had forgotten – to find that Aswan was a place where people lived; a lively Arab town, a view of the Nile flowing in great hanks of calm water round islands of granite behind which the feluccas appeared and disappeared in scythes of white. A few miles from the town, standing on the barrage itself, it is difficult not to indulge in the dramatic feeling that you have all the life of Egypt piled up there behind you in the great dam, and in the still greater dam whose plan lies, bandied about in the abstractions of international politics and finance, but marked out clearly on the landscape, not many miles behind it. I walked along the barrage to the hydro-electric power station which is under construction, cutting into the west shore. The clumsy steel giants of Europe were busy there; great turbines and cables and cranes from Switzerland, Germany and Austria. A workman waved me back; and laughed like a boy with a firecracker when I jumped at the hollow boom of an explosion. We leaned together over the steel rail and watched the granite dust settle, far down in the immense rock basin that has been blasted out.

I am not a watcher at the peep-holes so considerately provided by builders when they are at work; the sight of men swarming about their jobs on some project that will swallow the work in their hands anonymously in its immensity is more likely to depress than thrill me. But I found myself watching the Egyptian workmen labouring below on their power station, and I felt I could go on watching for a long time. There was something hopeful and even exciting about the sight of these men with their energies caught up by the demands of a huge imaginative task – not the labour of the cotton and the bean field whose fruits are used up each day by the day's existence, and nothing more to show for it. When the power station is completed, it will be theirs to use; it does not merely feed them now, but will change their lives. Surely these people need so badly not merely to be fed better and to live better, but also, after so many centuries of humbleness, to achieve, as other people do? I hope that Nasser will not forget them in dreams of world power, as all their rulers in the past have forgotten them or sold them out, for one reason or another. People who 'know Egypt' and deplore the Nasser regime tell me that 'kings and governments come and go, but it makes no difference to the fellah'. How tragic is the smug comfort of this remark if, this time again, it should prove to be true.

1959

Chief Luthuli

There are three million white people and more than nine million black people in the Union of South Africa. Only a handful of the whites have ever met Albert John Luthuli. He has never been invited to speak over the radio, and his picture rarely appears in the white daily press in South Africa. Yet this government-deposed African chief – who, far from losing his honourable title since he was officially deprived of it, is generally known simply as 'Chief' – is the only man to whom the nine million Africans ('African' is becoming the accepted term for a South African black) give any sort of wide allegiance as a popular leader. He is a man in black politics in South Africa whose personality is a symbol of human dignity which Africans as a whole, no matter what their individual

or political affiliations are and no matter what state of enlightenment or ignorance they may be in, recognise as *their* dignity.

Luthuli is a sixty-year-old Zulu and an African aristocrat. His
mother was a Gumede – one of the most honoured of Zulu clans –
and his grandmother was given, as was the custom with the daughter
of a prominent tribal chief, to the court of the famous paramount
chief of unconquered Zululand in the 1870s, Cetshwayo. Luthuli
has a number of those physical characteristics which are regarded
as typical of the warrior Zulu and to which even the most ardent
supporter of apartheid would pay grudging admiration. His head is
large and set majestically back on a strong neck; he has a deep, soft
voice; and although he is not a tall man he seems always to look as
big as anyone else in the room.

Among his less obvious characteristics is a sense of repose; sometimes a monumental quiet. If more white South Africans could
meet him, or even hear him speak on a public platform, they would
be astonished (and perhaps even a little ashamed – he makes that
sort of impression) to measure the real man against the bloodthirsty
demagogue that is the African leader as they imagine him. Apart
from anything else, he speaks English with a distinct American
intonation, acquired along with his education at schools run by
American missionaries.

Luthuli's ancestral home is Groutville Mission, in the Umvoti
Mission Reserve on the coast of Natal, near Durban, and his
personality stands sturdily upon this little corner of Africa. He
has never, even as a child, lived in the collection of thatched mud
huts in which tribal Africans usually live because Reverend Grout,
an American missionary who came to South Africa in 1835, had
planned his mission village on the European pattern, with houses;
and if as a child the young Luthuli did his share of herding cattle,
he did it after school hours, because Grout had seen to it that there
was fenced common that would free the children to attend school.
As the Umvoti Reserve is a mission and not a tribal reserve, the
chiefs are elected, and there is no dynasty in the hereditary sense.
Yet ability has tended to create a dynasty of its own; a number of
the elected chiefs have been members of the Luthuli family. When

Luthuli was a child, his uncle was chief, but after 1921 the chief-tainship went out of the hands of the family until 1936, when Luthuli himself, then a teacher at Adams College (one of the most respected of mission educational establishments for Africans) was elected.

Luthuli was educated at various mission schools and at Adams College, and in 1921 he qualified as an instructor in the teachers' training course and joined the staff of Adams. He could look back on a gentle, almost sheltered childhood in the protective shadow of his uncle's house and the mission at Groutville. The one had given him the confidence that comes to children who belong to an honoured family; the other, which provided his first contact with the world of whites, did not impose the harsh impact of the colour bar too early on his young mind. Perhaps as a result of this, even today, when the white government of South Africa has deposed him as chief of his people, several times banned him from free movement about the country, and arrested him – as President-General of the African National Congress and a leader of the liberation movement of Africans in South Africa – on a charge of treason that kept him in court through almost a year of inquiry, he has no hate in him. He has never been anti-white and believes he never will be. He started off his life by seeing human beings, not colours. It is a very different matter today for the urban African child who is born and grows up in the slum areas of big cities in South Africa, cheek by jowl with the whites in the paradox of the colour bar; he is made aware, from the start, that his blackness is a shroud, cutting him off, preparing him to be – as the Africans often describe themselves as feeling – 'half a man'.

Luthuli seems to have come to politics through an ideal of service fostered by religion rather than by way of any strong ambition. As early as his primary school days, what he calls the 'Christian ideal' of service captured his faith and his imagination. Many politically minded Africans deplore the influence the missions – which brought education to Africa and which have continued, because of government neglect of its obligation, to dominate African educa-tion – have had among their people in the past. The cry is that the missions have used their influence to reconcile the people to white domination rather than to encourage them to demand their birthright as free human beings. But Luthuli's experience has been that mission teaching gave him a sense of the dignity of man, in the sight of God, that he wants to see made a reality for all colours and creeds.

The truth probably lies somewhere in the fact that for those, like Luthuli, who had eyes for it, there was a glimpse of freedom in the gospel of humble submission to a discipline greater than man-devised. Out of that glimpse, more than any reasoning of politics and experience, a man may come to say, as Luthuli did when he gave up his chieftainship under government pressure in 1952, 'Laws and conditions that tend to debase human personality – a God-given force – be they brought about by the State or any other individuals, must be relentlessly opposed in the spirit of defiance shown by Saint Peter when he said to the rulers of his day, "Shall we obey God or man?" '

Luthuli's consciousness of the disabilities of the African people awoke as soon as he began to teach. 'Before that,' he explains,

> when men like myself were children at school and college students, we didn't have much chance to compare our lot with that of white people. Living in a reserve and going to a mission school or college, far away from the big white cities, our only real contact with white people was with the school principal and the missionary, and so if we suffered in any way from discriminatory treatment by white men, we tended to confuse our resentment with the natural resentment of the schoolboy towards those in authority who abuse him.

But the moment he was adult and a teacher, the normal disabilities of being a black man in South Africa, plus the disabilities of being a black teacher, plus the special sensitivity to both that comes about through being an educated and enlightened person, hit home. Through church work and the activities of the teachers' association, he busied himself with trying to improve the world of his people within the existing framework that the white world imposed upon it; he was too young and, in a sense, too ignorant to understand then, as he came to later, that the desire and the context in which it existed were contradictory.

In 1936, after some deliberation and misgiving, for he loved to teach, Luthuli left Adams College and teaching for ever and went home to Groutville as chief. The duties and responsibilities of chieftainship were in his blood and his family tradition, so from one point of view the change was not a dramatic one. But from another aspect the change was to be total and drastic. His thirty-eight years as a non-political man were over; he found himself, as he puts it, 'plunged right into South African politics – and by the South African government itself'.

The year of the Hertzog Bills was 1936. They were two: the Representation of Natives Bill and the Native Trust and Land Bill. The Representation of Natives Bill took away from all non-whites in South Africa the hope of an eventual universal franchise that they had been told since 1853 they would someday attain. It offered Africans in the Cape Province representation through the election, on a separate voters' roll, of three white members of Parliament. It offered Africans in the rest of the Union the opportunity to elect – not by individual vote but by means of chiefs, local councils and advisory boards, all acting as electoral colleges – four white senators. Finally, a Natives' Representative Council was to be instituted, to consist of twelve elected African representatives, four government-nominated African representatives, and five white officials, with the Secretary for Native Affairs as chairman. Its function was to be purely advisory, to keep the government acquainted with the wants and views of the African people.

The Native Trust and Land Bill tightened once and for all the Natives' Land Act of 1913, whereby Africans were prohibited from owning land except in reserves. The new bill provided 7.25 million morgen of land to be made available for African occupation and a trust fund to finance land purchase. (Twenty-two years later, this provision has not yet been completely fulfilled.)

Once the bills were law, Luthuli had vested in his authority as chief of the Umvoti Mission Reserve the collective vote of his five thousand people. White men and black canvassed him eagerly. He, who had scarcely talked politics at all, found himself talking scarcely anything else. For him, the reserve and its troubles had come into focus with the whole South African political scene. At the same time, he took up his traditional duties as chief – that combination of administrator, lawgiver, father-confessor, and figurehead. He found his chief's court or *ibandla*, held under a shady tree, 'a fine exercise in logical thinking', and the cases on which he gave judgement, according to a nice balance of tribal lore and the official Code of Native Law, varied from boundary disputes to wrangles over the payment of *lobolo* (bride price). He could not make the land go around among his people – not even the uneconomic five-acre units without freehold which were all that Groutville, a better reserve than most, had to offer – but he tried to help them make the best of what they had: he even formed a black cane growers' association to protect those among his tribesmen who were small growers of sugar. 'The real meaning of our poverty was brought home to me,' he says. 'I could see that the African people had no means of making a living according to civilised standards, even if they belonged, as we did in Groutville, to a civilised Christian community, so far as African communities go.'

From 1945 until 1948, Luthuli himself sat on the Natives' Representative Council. The Council proved to be a 'toy telephone' (in the phrase most tellingly used at the time) and no one regretted its passing when the Nationalist government of Dr Malan abolished it when it came into power in 1948. No one was much surprised, either, when it was not replaced by something more effective, for this was the first government actually dedicated to apartheid instead of merely committed to the bogus paternalism of Smuts. What the Africans got in place of the Council was yet another act – the Bantu Authorities Act, which, like many others affecting his people, Luthuli knows almost by heart and can reel off clause by clause. 'It was a velvet-glove act,' he says, 'designed to give Africans in the reserves some feeling of autonomy, of a direct hand in their own affairs, while in fact using the decoy of their own chiefs to attract them to accept whatever the apartheid government decided was good for them. Under the Act, the chief becomes a sort of civil servant and must cooperate with the government in selling the government's wishes to the people.'

In the late forties, Luthuli went to the United States at the invitation of the American Missionary Board to lecture on Christian missions in Africa. (The church had provided him with a chance to get to know other countries and peoples once before, when in 1938 he had gone to Madras as the Christian Council delegate to an International Missionary Council meeting.) He spent nine months in the United States, and he enjoyed his visit tremendously despite one or two incidents, those moments – a door closed in one's face, a restaurant where a cup of coffee has been refused – that jolt the black man back to the realisation that, almost everywhere he travels, race prejudice will not let him be at home in the world.

The same year in which Luthuli took up his seat on the Natives' Representative Council, he had joined an organisation to which, in time, no government was to be able to turn a deaf ear. This was the African National Congress. The Congress Movement began in 1912, just after the Act of Union that made the four provinces of South Africa into one country, when the Africans realised that the union's motto, 'Unity is Strength', was to refer strictly to the whites. 'When the ANC started,' Luthuli says, 'it had no idea of fighting for a change in fundamentals. It was concerned with the African's immediate disabilities – passes, not issues. The question of the fight for political rights may have been implied, but was not on the platform at all.'

Other Africans would not agree with him about this. Be that as it may – the history of Congress, a movement shrinking and spawning, according to the times, over the years, is not very well documented except perhaps in the secret files of the Special Branch of the South African Police – the first meeting of Congress laid down at least one principle that has characterised the movement to this day: it was to be 'a greater political and national body, uniting all small bodies and the different tribes in South Africa'. It has since pledged itself to the goal of a multi-racial society in South

Africa with equal rights for all colours. 'But it was only after 1936,' says Luthuli, 'when the Hertzog Bills acted as a terrific spur, that Congress began to show signs of becoming a movement that aimed at getting the government to bring about changes in policy that would give equal rights to non-whites in all fields.' At the same time, Luthuli's new responsibility as chief was proving to him the futility of any attempt to secure human rights without political rights; experience was shaping him for Congress, as it was shaping Congress for its historic role to come.

When he joined Congress in 1945, he was elected to the executive of the Natal Branch at once, and he remained on it continuously for the six years during which the movement felt its way to effectiveness, leaving behind the old methods – deputations, petitions, conferences that enabled the government to 'keep in touch with the people' without having to take their views into account – that had failed to achieve anything for the Africans. Finally, in 1949 Congress drafted a Programme of Action that was based on the premise that in South Africa freedom can come to the non-white only through extra-parliamentary methods. A year later, when Luthuli had just been elected Provincial President of Natal, Congress decided to launch a full-scale passive resistance campaign in defiance of unjust colour-bar laws. 'This decision,' he comments, 'had my full approval.'

The official-sounding, platitudinous remark covers what was the result of considerable heart-searching on Luthuli's part. Luthuli sees it and, for himself, used it as Gandhi conceived it – not only as a technique but as a soul force, *Satyagraha*.

In 1952 the African National Congress, the South African Indian Congress, and other related associations organised defiance groups all over the country. Thousands of Africans and, in lesser numbers, Indians, and even some whites, defied the colour-bar laws and invited arrest. Africans and Indians entered libraries reserved for white people, sat on railway benches reserved for white people, used post office counters reserved for white people, and camped out in open ground in the middle of the white city of Durban. Black and white, they went to prison. Luthuli was everywhere in

Natal, addressing meetings, encouraging individuals, carrying with him in the most delicate situations, under the nose of government ire and police hostility, an extraordinary core of confidence and warmth. All his natural abilities of leadership came up simply and strongly.

The Defiance Campaign went on successfully for some months before it was crushed by the heavy sentences imposed upon defiers under new legislation specially devised by the government, which fixed the high penalties (up to three years' imprisonment or a fine of £300) that may be applied to anyone protesting against any of the racial laws or inciting others to do so.

Luthuli had gone into the Campaign a country chief; he came out a public figure. In September 1952, while Defiance was still on, he was given an ultimatum by the Native Affairs Department: he must resign from Congress and the Defiance Campaign or give up his chieftainship. 'I don't see the contradiction between my office as chief and my work in Congress,' he answered, courteously but bluntly. 'In the one I work in the interests of my people within tribal limits, and in the other I work for them on a national level, that's all. I will not resign from either.'

On Wednesday 12 November 1952, the Native Commissioner announced that Chief A. J. Luthuli was dismissed by the government from his position as chief of the Umvoti Mission Reserve. In reply to this, the African National Congress issued a statement by Luthuli under the title 'Our Chief Speaks'. It is a statement that has been much quoted, in and out of South Africa, both in support of those who believe that right is on the side of the Africans in their struggle against racial discrimination and in support of those who regard the black man's claim to equality of opportunity with the white man as a fearful black nationalism that aims – to quote, in turn, one of the favourite bogies of white South Africa – 'to drive the white man into the sea'.

The lengthy statement is written in the formal, rather Victorian English, laced with biblical cadence and officialese, that Luthuli uses – the English of a man to whom it is a foreign or at best a second language, but impressive, for all that. 'In these past thirty years or so,' he said,

> I have striven with tremendous zeal and patience to work for the progress and welfare of my people and for their harmonious relations with other sections of our multi-racial society in the Union of South Africa. In this effort I have always pursued what liberal-minded people rightly regarded as the path of moderation . . .
>
> In so far as gaining citizenship rights and opportunities for the unfettered development of the African people, who will deny that thirty years of my life have been spent knocking in vain, patiently, moderately, and modestly at a closed and barred door?
>
> . . . Has there been any reciprocal tolerance or moderation from the Government, be it Nationalist or United Party? No! On the contrary, the past thirty years have seen the greatest number of Laws restricting our rights and progress until today we have reached a stage where we have almost no rights at all: no adequate land for our occupation, our only asset – cattle – dwindling, no security of homes, no decent and remunerative employment, more restrictions to freedom of movement through passes, curfew regulations, influx control measures; in short we have witnessed in these years an intensification of our subjection to ensure and protect white supremacy.
>
> It is with this background and with a full sense of responsibility that . . . I have joined my people in . . . the spirit that revolts openly and boldly against injustice and expresses itself in a determined and non-violent manner . . . Viewing Non-Violent Passive Resistance as a non-revolutionary and, therefore, a most legitimate and humane political pressure technique for a people denied all effective forms of constitutional striving, I saw no real conflict in my dual leadership of my people.

A month after his deposition as chief, Luthuli was elected President-General of the African National Congress and became leader of the entire Congress movement in South Africa. Wherever he went, he was greeted by cheering crowds of Africans; at last they had a leader who had shown himself a leader in places less comfortable and closer to their lives than conferences and conventions.

The government found that ex-Chief Luthuli seemed to be more of a chief than ever. A ban was served on him under one of those new powers that had been legislated to deal with the Defiance Campaign, a ban which debarred him for a year from all the important cities and towns in South Africa. The day it expired, Luthuli opened the South African Indian Congress in Durban and, guessing that his time was short, left at once by air for Johannesburg to attend a protest meeting about Sophiatown removals. It was his first visit to Johannesburg since he had become President-General, and the people of Sophiatown, under arbitrary orders to quit their homes and move to a settlement farther away from the white city, were heartened at the idea of having him among them as champion of their protest.

As he stepped off the plane at Johannesburg, the Special Branch police served him with a second ban. And what a ban! This time he was to be confined for two years to a radius of about twenty miles around his home in Groutville village. During the long period of confinement he suffered a slight stroke, and while he lay ill in his house in Groutville, his wife had to beg permission from the police to let him be taken to a hospital in Durban, sixty miles away. Permission was granted, and he was rushed to Durban. There he spent two months in the hospital, and from the second day Special Branch men hung about his ward in constant attendance. Despite these unwelcome presences, who, he says, day after day used to inquire sheepishly after his health, Chief made a complete recovery except for a barely perceptible droop that shows itself in his left eyelid when he is tired.

His ban expired in July 1956. He was free to move about the country again; but not for long. About four in the morning of 5 December, there was a loud knocking at the door of the Luthulis' house in Groutville. The Luthulis struggled out of sleep. Four white Special Branch men were at the door; they had come to arrest Chief on a charge of treason. He was flown to Johannesburg and taken straight to prison at the Johannesburg Fort. And there he found himself accused of treason with 155 others. Some were his respected colleagues over many years; some represented ideologies that were largely or partly distasteful to him; some he had never heard of before.

The preliminary hearing of the Treason Trial (the first in the history of peacetime South Africa) began in January 1957, and the trial has been in progress, in one form and another – nine months of preliminary hearing, several sessions of the trial itself, with a number of adjournments – for two years. 'Treason' is a word with ugly associations. They have become uglier still during the years since the war, now that the word has become part of the vocabulary of the witch hunters of the world. Like 'Communist', 'treason' may be used, in certain countries and circumstances, to blot out the name of anyone who puts up any sort of opposition to race discrimination and the denial of freedom of movement, opportunity and education.

Among the 156 of the original accused, there was a sprinkling of ex-Communists and fellow travellers – almost exclusively among the twenty-three whites – but the great majority were simply people who abhor the injustice and misery of apartheid and want all races in South Africa to share freely in the life of the country. At various stages in the trial, the number of accused has been reduced, and the government has not yet succeeded in formulating a satisfactory statement of the charge against them; but the trial drags on and, at the time of writing, the Attorney General has just made a statement that he intends to draw up a fresh indictment against the remaining accused.

The first list of those against whom charges had been withdrawn was announced in December 1957, when the preliminary inquiry was in recess. Among the names was that of Chief A. J. Luthuli, President-General of the African National Congress. Chief was at home in Groutville after the nine-month ordeal in court, preparing for the wedding of his medical-student daughter, when the news came, followed by a paper storm of congratulatory telegrams. His feelings were mixed: he could not see why he should be freed while his colleagues in the liberation movement were held; on the other hand, he was glad to be able to get on with Congress work outside the Drill Hall. A few weeks later, charges were withdrawn against some more accused, bringing down to ninety-one the number of those who were committed for trial for high treason in January 1958.

The particulars of the 'hostile acts' which were read under the charge of high treason included 'the hampering or hindering of the said Government [of the Union of South Africa] in its lawful administration by organising or taking part in campaigns against existing laws'. The laws named included the Natives Resettlement Act and the Group Areas Act, which involve the uprooting of African, Indian and coloured communities in order to move them out of white areas; the Bantu Education Act, which has lowered the standard of education available to African children; and the Bantu Authorities Act.

The defence applied for the discharge of the ninety-one, saying that the Crown, by the way it had formulated the charges, had established 'nothing other than a desire to put an end to any form of effective opposition to the Government of this country – a desire to outlaw free expression of thought and ideas which people in all democratic countries of the West assert the right to hold and utter'. The application for discharge was refused. In the public gallery of the Drill Hall (divided down the middle by a token barrier of low chains and posts to ensure that whites sat on one side and blacks on the other) Luthuli heard the magistrate's decision. Why he was not still among the accused in the dock was as much of a mystery to him as to anyone else. Whatever the reason, Chief sat in the Drill Hall as a spectator and a free man that day, and many heads, black and white, turned to look at him. When the court adjourned, he walked out among the free men, too; free to travel about the country and address meetings and attend gatherings where he pleased. For how long, of course, he could not guess.

So far – a year later – he has not been served with a ban again, though he has not minced words, whether addressing the small white Liberal Party or Congress. At a meeting before a white audience he was beaten up by white hooligans. At angry meetings

of the Transvaal Branch of Congress in Johannesburg Africanists
attempted to oust Chief and his kind from leadership and commit
the African National Congress to what he calls 'a dangerously
narrow African nationalism'. In April 1959 this group broke away
to form the Pan-Africanist Congress.

But that day at the beginning of 1958, when he walked out of
the Drill Hall, the sudden release of his freedom was fresh upon
him, lightheaded, like a weakness, though the weight of the ordeal
of trial to which his colleagues were committed oppressed him,
and he even looked a little lonely. And such are the paradoxes of
human behaviour that, as Luthuli crossed the street, two of the
white police officers who had become familiar figures on duty
in the Drill Hall all through the preparatory examination came
around the corner and called out, forgetful, across the barrier of
apartheid that seeks to legislate against all human contact between
black and white and across the barrier of hate that the pass and the
baton have built between the police and the black man in South
Africa, 'Well, hullo! You look fine! What are you doing around
here? Can't you keep away from the old Drill Hall, after all?' And
rather gingerly, Chief was amiable in reply.

1959

Postscript: Chief Albert Luthuli received the Nobel Peace Prize in
1960. He died in 1967.

Apartheid

Men are not born brothers; they have to discover each other,
and it is this discovery that apartheid seeks to prevent . . .
What is apartheid?

It depends who's answering. If you ask a member of the South
African government, he will tell you that it is separate and parallel

development of white and black – that is the official, legal definition. If you ask an ordinary white man who supports the policy, he
will tell you that it is the means of keeping South Africa white. If
you ask a black man, he may give you any one of a dozen answers,
arising out of whatever aspect of apartheid he has been brought
up short against that day, for to him it is neither an ideological
concept nor a policy, but a context in which his whole life, learning,
working, loving, is rigidly enclosed.

He could give you a list of the laws that restrict him from
aspiring to most of the aims of any civilised person, or enjoying
the pleasures that every white person takes for granted. But it is
unlikely that he will. What may be on his mind at the moment
is the problem of how to save his child from the watered-down
'Bantu Education' which is now standard in schools for black children – inferior schooling based on a reduced syllabus that insists
the black child cannot attain the same standard of education as the
white child, and places emphasis on practical and menial skills.
Or perhaps you've merely caught him on the morning after he's
spent a night in the police cells because he was out after curfew
hours without a piece of paper bearing a white man's signature
permitting him to be so. Perhaps (if he's a man who cares for such
things) he's feeling resentful because there's a concert in town he
would not be permitted to attend, or (if he's that kind of man, and
who isn't?) he's irked at having to pay a black-market price for the
bottle of brandy he is debarred from buying legitimately. That's
apartheid, to him. All these things, big and little, and many more.

If you want to know how Africans – black men – live in South
Africa, you will get in return for your curiosity an exposition of
apartheid in action, for in all of a black man's life – all his life –
rejection by the white man has the last word. With this word of
rejection apartheid began, long before it hardened into laws and
legislation, long before it became a theory of racial selectiveness
and the policy of a government. The Afrikaner Nationalists (an
Afrikaner is a white person of Dutch descent whose mother tongue
is Afrikaans; a Nationalist is a member or supporter of the National
Party, at present in power) did not invent it, they merely developed

it, and the impulse of Cain from which they worked lives in many white South Africans today, English-speaking as well as Afrikaner.

Shall I forget that when I was a child I was taught that I must never use a cup from which our black servant had drunk?

I live in the white city of Johannesburg, the largest city in South Africa. Around the white city, particularly to the west and north, is another city, black Johannesburg. This clear picture of black and white is blurred only a little at the edges by the presence of small coloured – mixed blood – and Indian communities, also segregated, both from each other and from the rest. You will see Africans in every house in the white city, of course, for servants live in, and every house has its servants' quarters, in a building separate from the white house. Sophisticated Africans call this back-yard life 'living dogs-meat' – closer to the kennel and the outhouses than to the humans in the house.

But no black man has his *home* in the white city; neither wealth nor honour nor distinction of any kind could entitle him to move into a house in the street where I or any other white person lives. So it easily happens that thousands of white people live their whole lives without ever exchanging a word with a black man who is on their own social and cultural level; and for them, the whole African people is composed of servants and the great army of 'boys' who cart away or deliver things – the butcher's boy, the grocer's boy, the milk boy, the dust boy. On the basis of this experience, you will see that it is simple for white men and women to deduce that black men and women are an inferior race. Out of this experience all the platitudes of apartheid sound endlessly, like the bogus sea from the convolutions of a big shell: *they're like children . . . they don't think the way we do . . . they're not ready.*

Black men do all the physical labour in our country, because no white man wants to dig a road or load a truck. But in every kind of work a white man *wants* to do, there are sanctions and job reservations to shut the black man out. In the building trade, and in industry, the Africans are the unskilled and semi-skilled workers, and they cannot, by law, become anything else. They cannot serve behind the counters in the shops, and cannot be employed alongside white clerks. Wherever they work, they cannot share the wash-rooms or the canteens of the white workers. But they may buy in the shops. Oh yes, once the counter is between the black customer and the white shopkeeper, the hollow murmur of the apartheid shell is silenced – they *are*, ready, indeed, to provide a splendid market, they *do* think enough like white people to want most of the things that white people want, from LP recordings to no-iron shirts.

The real life of any community – restaurants, bars, hotels, clubs and coffee bars – has no place for the African man or woman. They serve in all these, but they cannot come in and sit down. Art galleries, cinemas, theatres, golf courses and sports clubs, even the libraries are closed to them. In the post offices and all other govern-ment offices, they are served at segregated counters. They have no vote.

What it means to live like this, from the day you are born until the day you die, I cannot tell you. No white person can. I think I know the lives of my African friends, but time and again I find that I have assumed – since it was so ordinary a part of the average white person's life – that they had knowledge of some commonplace experience that, in fact, they could never have had. How am I to remember that Danny, who is writing his PhD thesis on industrial psychology, has never seen the inside of a museum? How am I to remember that John, who is a journalist on a lively newspaper, can never hope to see the film I am urging him not to miss, since the township cinemas are censored and do not show what one might call adult films? How am I to remember that Alice's charming children, playing with my child's toy elephant, will never be able to ride on the elephant in the Johannesburg Zoo?

The humblest labourer will find his life the meaner for being black. If he were a white man, at least there would be no ceiling to his children's ambitions. But it is in the educated man that want and need stand highest on the wrong side of the colour bar. Whatever he achieves as a man of learning, *as a man* he still has as little say in the community as a child or a lunatic. Outside the gates of the university (soon he may not be able to enter them at all; the two 'open' universities are threatened by legislation that will close them to all who are not white), white men will hail him as 'boy'. When the first African advocate was called to the Johannesburg bar, back in 1956, government officials raised objections to his robing and disrobing in the same chamber as the white advocates. His colleagues accepted him as a man of the law; but the laws of apartheid saw him only as a black man. Neither by genius nor cunning, by sainthood or thuggery, is there a way in which a black man can earn the right to be regarded as any other man.

Of course, the Africans have made some sort of life of their own. It's a slum life, a make-do life, because, although I speak of black cities outside white cities, these black cities – known as 'the townships' – are no Harlems. They are bleak rectangular patterns of glum municipal housing, or great smoky proliferations of crazy, chipped brick and tin huts, with few street lights, few shops. The life there is robust, ribald and candid. All human exchange of the extrovert sort flourishes; standing in a wretched alley, you feel the exciting blast of a great vitality. Here and there, in small rooms where a candle makes big shadows, there is good talk. It is attractive, especially if you are white; but it is also sad, bleak and terrible. It may not be a bad thing to be a township Villon; but it is tragic if you can never be anything else. The penny whistle is a charming piece of musical ingenuity; but it should not always be necessary for a man to make his music out of nothing.

Some Africans are born, into their segregated townships, light enough to pass as coloured. They play coloured for the few privi-leges – better jobs, better housing, more freedom of movement – that this brings, for the nearer you can get to being white, the less restricted your life is. Some coloureds are born, into their segregated townships, light enough to pass as white. A fair skin is the equivalent of a golden spoon in the child's mouth; in other countries coloured people may be tempted to play white for social reasons, but in South Africa a pale face and straight hair can gain the basic things – a good school, acceptance instead of rejection all the way along the line.

It is the ambition of many coloured parents to have a child light enough to cross the colour bar and live the precarious lie of pretending to be white; their only fear is that the imposture will be discovered. But the other night I was made aware of a different sort of fear and a new twist to the old game of play-white. An Indian acquaintance confessed to me that he was uneasy because his thirteen-year-old son has turned out to have the sort of face and complexion that could pass for white. 'He's only got to slip into a white cinema or somewhere, just once, for the fun of it. The next thing my wife and I know, he'll be starting to play white. Once they've tried what it's like to be a white man, how are you to stop them? Then it's lies, and not wanting to know their own families, and misery all round. That's one of the reasons why I want to leave South Africa, so my kids won't want to grow up to be something they're not.'

I've talked about the wrong side of the colour bar, but the truth is that both are wrong sides. Do not think that we, on the white side of privilege, are the people we might be in a society that has no sides at all. We do not suffer, but we are coarsened. Even to continue to live here is to acquiesce in some measure to apartheid – to a sealing off of responses, the cauterisation of the human heart. Our children grow up accepting as natural the fact that they are well clothed and well fed, while black children are ragged and skinny. It cannot occur to the white child that the black one has any rights outside of charity; you must explain to your child, if you have the mind to, that men have decided this, that the white shall have and the black shall have not, and it is not an immutable law, like the rising of the sun in the morning. Even then it is not possible entirely to counter with facts an emotional climate of privilege. We have the better part of everything, and it is difficult for us not to feel, somewhere secretly, that we *are* better.

Hundreds of thousands of white South Africans are concerned only with holding on to white privilege. They believe that they would rather die holding on to it than give up the smallest part of it; and I believe they would. They cannot imagine a life that would

be neither their life nor the black man's life, but another life altogether. How can they imagine freedom, who for years have been so
vigilant to keep it only to themselves?

No one of us, black or white, can promise them that black domination will not be the alternative to white domination, and black
revenge the long if not the last answer to all that the whites have
done to the blacks. For – such is the impact of apartheid – there
are many blacks, as well as many whites, who cannot imagine a life
that would be neither a black man's life nor a white man's life.

Those white South Africans who want to let go – leave hold –
are either afraid of having held on too long, or are disgusted and
ashamed to go on living as we do. These last have become colour-
blind, perhaps by one of those freaks by which desperate nature hits
upon a new species. They want another life altogether in South Africa.
They want people of all colours to use the same doors, share the same
learning, and give and take the same respect from each other. They
don't care if the government that guarantees these things is white or
black. A very few of these people go so far as to go to prison, in the
name of one political cause or another, in attempts that they believe
will help to bring about this new sort of life. The rest make, in one
degree or another, an effort to live, within an apartheid community,
the decent life that apartheid prohibits.

Of course, I know that no African attaches much importance to
what apartheid does to the white man, and no one could blame him for
this. What does it signify to him that your sense of justice is outraged,
your conscience is troubled, and your friendships are restricted by the
colour bar? All this lies heavily, mostly unspoken, between black and
white friends. My own friends among Africans are people I happen to
like, my kind of people, whose friendship I am not prepared to forgo
because of some racial theory I find meaningless and absurd. Like that
of many others, my opposition to apartheid is compounded not only
out of a sense of justice but also out of a personal, selfish and extreme
distaste for having the choice of my friends dictated to me, and the
range of human intercourse proscribed for me.

I am aware that, because of this, I sometimes expect African
friends to take lightly, in the ordinary course of friendship, risks

that simply are not worth it, to them, who have so many more basic things to risk themselves for.

I remember a day last year when some African friends and I went to the airport to see off a close friend of ours. I had brought a picnic lunch with me, and so had Alice, my friend, for we knew that we shouldn't be able to lunch together in the airport restaurant. What we hadn't realised was that there was no place where we could eat together. I wanted to brazen it out, sit somewhere until we were ordered off into segregation; it was easy for me, I am white and not sensitised by daily humiliation. But Alice, who has to find words to explain to her children why they cannot ride the elephant at the zoo, did not want to seek the sort of rebuff that comes to her all the time, unsought.

Black and white get to know each other in spite of and under the strain of a dozen illegalities. We can never meet in town, for there is nowhere we can sit and talk. The legal position about receiving African guests in a white house is unclear; we do have our friends in our houses, of course, but there is always the risk that a neighbour may trump up a complaint, to which the police would always be sympathetic. When you offer an African guest a drink, you break the law unequivocally; the exchange of a beer between your hand and his could land you both in the police court on a serious charge.

Officially, you are not supposed to enter an African 'location' without a permit, and when we go to visit friends in a black township we take the chance of being stopped by the police, who are looking for gangsters or caches of liquor but will do their duty to apartheid on the side.

Towards the end of last year I was one of a small group of white guests who had to get up and leave the table at the wedding reception of an African medical student; a white official of the gold-mining company for whom the bride's father worked, and on whose property his house was, drove up to inform us that our invitations to the wedding were not sufficient to authorise our presence in African living quarters.

No friendship between black and white is free of these things. It is hard to keep any relationship both clandestine and natural. No matter how warm the pleasure in each other's company, how deep and comfortable the understanding, there are moments of failure created by resentment of white privilege, on the one side, and guilt about white privilege, on the other.

Another life altogether.

Put the shell to your ear and hear the old warning: do you want to be overrun by blacks?

I bump an African's scooter while parking, and before he and I have a chance to apologise or accuse, there's a white man at my side ready to swear that I'm in the right, and there are three black men at his side ready to swear that he is in the right.

Another life altogether.

Put the shell to your ear and hear the old warning: are you prepared to see white standards destroyed?

A friend of mine, a dignified and responsible African politician and an old man, is beaten up by white intruders while addressing a meeting of white people.

Living apart, black and white are destroying themselves morally in the effort. Living together, it is just possible that we might survive white domination, black domination, and all the other guises that hide us from each other, and discover ourselves to be identically human.

1959

The 1960s

The Congo

. . . a place of darkness. But there was in it one river especially, a mighty big river, that you could see on the map, resembling an immense snake uncoiled, with its head in the sea, its body at rest curving afar over a vast country, and its tail lost in the depths of the land.

Joseph Conrad, *Heart of Darkness*

Begin with a stain in the ocean. Three hundred miles out to sea, off the west coast of Africa, the mark of a presence the immensity of seas has not been able to swallow. Mariners saw it in the age of exploration, when each voyage held the fear that a ship might sail off the edge of the world. They knew it was the stain of land; mountains had coloured it, the rotting verdure of forests, perhaps, the grass of plains. A massive land, a continent, giving rise to and feeding a river great enough to make a dent in the sea.

The continent parts; the river opens a way in. Many journeys have beginnings flat and unworthy, but not this one.

I stayed a day or two at a beach on the west coast of Africa at the river's mouth. Though the water was salt to my tongue and the tides rose and withdrew, it was not the sea that lay below the ochre cliff. It was the Congo River. All the Atlantic Ocean, as far as I could see, was the Congo River. In the bright sun, the water glittered like a seal's coat; under the heavy skies of the rainy season, it was quite black. When I swam in it, even in the evening, it was warmer than the warm air. I had read that the Congo, measured by its year-by-year flow, is the second greatest river in the world; now the conception of the dry fact flowed around me, a vast environment.

Strange creatures live in the Congo River. From a small boat following the water maze of mangroves, with their cages of whitish roots set over a footing of black ooze, I saw the climbing fish *periophthalmus*. Pop-eyed, startled little creatures, they ran nimbly up the roots, but hobbled and flopped on the ooze. They are the colour of mud, they live in mud that is neither land nor water, and their lives span quietly the gasping transition that evolution made millennia ago, bringing life out of the sea. The manatee, a sea mammal with white breasts (the creature on which the fiction of the mermaid is based), is sometimes caught here.

A slender spatula of land runs out from the mangroves at the shining gape of the river's open mouth. On it is a strip of a town, so narrow that you can see through the gaps between the rows of coconut palms and the smart little villas to the water on the other side. There are no blocks of buildings; the only objects of height and bulk are the ocean-going ships moored off the jetty. This town is Banana, an old slave port and the oldest white settlement on the Congo. It looks like a bright prefab; no memory, here, of the ships that passed, heavy with human cargo, taking Africa to the rest of the world – a world that lived to see a new nation in Brazil, a Negro 'problem' in the United States, riots in London's Notting Hill. I could not believe that those extraordinary beginnings could have been wiped out entirely, but all I could find was a neglected graveyard by the sea. Dutch, French, Portuguese, English and German names were on the headstones, and the earliest was dated 1861. Nobody stayed in Banana unless he died there; nobody built a house meant to last; there were no solid monuments to community pride among slave traders.

Perhaps, while I am writing, the new past, so recent that it is almost the present, is disappearing without trace as the older one did. The white personnel from the Belgian naval base, and the comfortable hotel where Belgians from the stifling interior used to come to swim and lounge in the harlequin garb of resorts the world over – will there remain, soon, much sign of their passing?

A few miles up the same – and only – coast road that led past the graveyard, there was a fishing village that was unaware not only of the past but even of the passing present. On swept sand under coconut and Elaeis palms the bamboo houses of the village had the special, satisfying neatness of fine basketwork; big nets checkered the shore and a flotilla of pirogues lay beached. Squat monsters of baobab trees, fat-limbed and baggy, sounded tuba notes here and there among the string ensemble of the palms. In the hollow trunk of one of the baobabs was a chicken house, reached by a little ladder. Two old men sat making nets in the sunlight sliced by the poles of palms. One was rolling the thread, using the reddish bark fibre taken from a baobab not ten feet away. A woman came out of a house and took in a basket of flame-coloured palm nuts, ready to be pounded for oil. Under the eaves of her house hung the family storage vessels, bunches of calabashes engraved with abstract designs. These people had none of the aesthetic deprivations I associate with poverty. They walked between classic pillars of palm, and no yesterday's newspapers blew about their feet. They were living in a place so guileless and clean that it was like a state of grace.

A fast motor launch took me in five hours from the West African Coast to the cataracts that kept the white man out of Central Africa for 300 years. The mangroves were left behind at once, the river continued so wide that the distant banks seemed to be slipping over the horizon, and islands appeared faintly as mirages and then came close, shapes extinguished beneath a dark cloth of creepers. The undersides of the clouds were lit by sunlight shaken glitteringly off the purplish-brown storm-coloured water that heaved past us. As we took the highway against the main current, far off, Africans moved quietly on the verges of the river, their slender pirogues threading the darkness of overhanging trees.

Ocean liners come this way up the Congo to Matadi, the town at the foot of the cataracts, and it has the air of a nineteenth-century seaport. The steep, twisting streets that lead down to the docks are sailors' streets; there is even a notice in the hotel: No parrots allowed. The Congo here looks as I was never to see it anywhere else. It has just emerged from the skelter and plunge 200 miles down a stairway of thirty-two cataracts in a total drop five times the height of Niagara Falls. It is all muscle, running deep between the high confines of granite hills, and straightening out in swaths from the terrible circular pull of whirlpools.

I saw the rock of Diego Cão, naval officer and Gentleman of

the Household to Dom João II, King of Portugal, who reached the mouth of the Congo in 1482. He set up a stone pillar on the southern point of the six-mile-wide mouth of the estuary, and so the river got its first European name, Rio de Padrão, the Pillar River. Diego Cão came back twice. On his third trip he sailed ninety-two miles up the river until he was turned back by impassable cataracts. He left an inscription carved on rock to show how far he had got; for more than three centuries this was the limit of the outside world's knowledge of the river.

On the face of volcanic rock above the powerfully disturbed waters of the first cataracts, a mile or two above Matadi, was the cross, the coat of arms of Dom João II of Portugal, and the names of Cão and his companions, cut in the beautiful lettering of an illuminated manuscript. The inscription had the sharp clarity of something freshly finished instead of nearly five centuries old.

The place of the rock, where Diego Cão turned back, is a dark place. No earth is to be seen there; only great humps of grey-black rock, and, like rock come to life, tremendous baobabs (those anthropomorphic, zoomorphic, geomorphic living forms, always less tree than man or beast or stone) with their wrinkled flesh that looks as if it would cringe at a touch, their token disguise of brilliant leaves, and their mammalian fruit pendent from long cords. I took one in my hands; it was fully a foot and a half long and must have weighed five pounds. The light-green velour skin was fuzzy as a peach. There came to me, through my hand, all the queerness of the continent, in the strange feel of that heavy-hanging fruit.

There is a road bypassing the cataracts that once barred the way into equatorial Africa, and a railway. Without that railway, Stanley said, all the wealth of Africa behind the cataracts was not worth 'a two-shilling piece'. Stanley himself hacked and dragged his way on foot, sometimes following hippopotamus trails, over the hills and through gallery forests – the dense tunnels of green that cover water courses. The black men dubbed him – with grim admiration, since many of their number died portering for him – Bula Matari, 'Breaker of Rocks'. But it is easy, now, to come upon the splendid sight of Stanley Pool (Pool Malebo), the 360-square-mile river-lake above the cataracts, and the beginning of a million square miles of accessible river basin.

On the south bank of the Pool is Léopoldville (Kinshasa), one of the few real cities in Africa, if one of the most troubled, where last year the splendid celebrations of Congolese Independence Day gave way at once to riots and political chaos. Ever since the first agitation for independence, in 1959, there have been riots from time to time, and worse, the fear of riots all the time. When trouble does come, city people white and black flee in their thousands across Stanley Pool to Brazzaville until things cool down again. Brazzaville stands on the north bank, the capital of another Congo Republic, a slightly senior and entirely peaceful independent black state that was formerly part of French Equatorial Africa.

Many big airlines alight here, beside Stanley Pool, at Léo or Brazza, migrant birds always on their way to somewhere else; they bring the world thus far, with their thin filaments of communication they touch thus lightly upon the vast and lazy confidence of the great river that opens an eye of dazzling light beneath them as they take off and go away; the river that carries with ease the entire commerce of the deep Africa through which it is the only highway.

The Pool has always been the point where all the trade of the river, and that of the interior that comes down the river, logically converges, and life there since ancient times must have been a little different from that of the rest of the river. Life on either side of the Pool today is dominated by the presence of the new African – the young men with Belafonte cuts and narrow trousers. One sits behind a teller's chromium bars in an air-conditioned bank, another may only sell lottery tickets in the streets, but they are all *évolué* – for good – from the old African, who sold his land and, as it turned out, his way of life to the white man for a few bottles of gin and some bolts of cloth.

On the south bank, Léopoldville's Congolese cities of 360,000 people shuttle with vitality night and day, while the 'white' city – no longer segregated by anything except old usage, new fears and the black man's poverty – is dead after the shops shut. On the eve

of independence, 21,000 white people were living there; it is difficult to get a figure for those who live there now, for of the numbers
who fled last year, some have quietly come back, and of course
there is the shifting population of United Nations personnel.

The bloody foundering of the new state naturally has focused
attention on what the Congolese have *not* got: not a single doctor or
lawyer among them and not so much understanding of democracy
as you might hope to find in an election of officers of a sports club.
These are not sneers but facts. When you go about Léopoldville
among the Congolese, you are reminded that if there are no
Congolese doctors or lawyers, it is nevertheless also a fact before
your eyes that the fishermen and warriors that Stanley encountered
eighty-one years ago have become clerks, laboratory technicians,
ships' captains and skilled workers. They also reveal an aptitude
for spending hours talking politics, reading party newspapers and
drinking beer – a way of passing time that is characteristic of some
of the most civilised cities in the world, and that has been the
beginning of many a man's political education. They stood small
chance of making a success of governing themselves when independence fell into their clamouring hands; now they may have to
pick their way through years of near-anarchy before they defeat
tribalism, evade or survive foreign domination, and learn, a tragically hard way, how to run a modern state.

The city Congolese have the roaring capacity for enjoyment that
looks as if it is going to be one of the pleasanter characteristics of
the new African states. Dancing begins in the open-air cafés at two
o'clock in the heat of a Sunday afternoon, only a few hours after
the last cha-cha-cha of Saturday night has ended, and the influence
of the weekend hangs over well into Monday, even in these lean
times.

On a Monday morning I visited the Léopoldville market, that
colossal exchange of goods, gossip and sometimes hard words.
Two or three thousand vendors, mostly women, were selling fruit,
vegetables, miles of mammy cloth as dazzling as the patterns you
see in your own eyelids; patent medicines and nail varnish, and
also several things you would never think of, such as chunks of

smoked hippo meat and piles of dried caterpillars sold by the newspaper poke. At least five thousand people were buying there. Lost among them, I understood for the first time the concept of the values of the market-place. For it was clear that these people were not just doing their shopping; they were expressing the metropolitan need to be seen at the theatre, the city instinct of participation that fills the galleries of houses of parliament and the foyers of fashionable hotels. They had come to hear what was going on in their world, and what a man's reputation was worth at current prices.

When I emerged from this vociferous and confident press, the Congolese taxi driver who drove me away remarked, 'Ah, it's a pity that you saw it on such a quiet day. No one comes to market on a Monday – all too tired after the weekend. You should have come on a Friday, when it's full of people.'

The Congo crosses the Equator twice in its 2,900-mile length, and it is the only river system in the world whose main stream flows through both northern and southern hemispheres. Some of its tributaries are on one, some on the other side of the Equator. This means that the river benefits from both rainy seasons – April to October from the north, and October to April from the south – and instead of rising and falling annually, it has two moderate highs and two lows each year. It does not flood, and though navigation in times of low water is sometimes tricky, it is always possible.

The Congo is shorter than the Nile, the Ob, the Yangtze and the Mississippi–Missouri system, but only the Amazon exceeds it in volume of water discharged into the sea. Its hydraulic energy is estimated at a sixth of the world's potential, and there are a thousand known species of fish in its waters.

From Stanley Pool the Congo opens a way more than a thousand miles, without a man-made lock or a natural obstacle, through the centre of Africa. It leads to what Joseph Conrad called the heart of darkness; the least-known, most subjectively described depths of the continent where men have always feared to meet the dark places of their own souls.

No bridge crosses the river in all this distance. No road offers an alternate way for more than short stretches, and these always lead back to the river. The river alone cleaves the forests and reveals, in its shining light, the life there. Sometimes, for hours, there is no break in the wall of forest. Sometimes, beyond an open stretch of papyrus, a group of palms stands like animals arrested in attitudes of attention. One morning crowds of pale-green butterflies with black lacy frames and veinings to their wings came to settle on the burning metal of the jeeps that were tethered to the barge in front of our boat.

This boat – the *Gouverneur Moulaert* – pushed a whole caravan: two barges and another boat, the *Ngwaka*, for third-class passengers – mostly black. The pace, night and day, was six miles an hour; a little more than the pace of a man. We were never out of touch with the life of the shore. All day long, pirogues paddled out to hitch up alongside our bulky complex, and the people came aboard to sell dried fish and palm or banana wine to the passengers of the *Ngwaka*. Two huge catfish, each with a mouth big enough to take a man's head, were lugged aboard for sale to the crew, and once a basket of smoked crocodile feet was casually handed up. For the wilderness was inhabited everywhere, though it often seemed empty to our eyes, accustomed to landscapes where, even if few people are to be seen, there are evidences of men having made their mark in the way the country looks. These people, slipping out of the forest into the sight of the river, didn't obtrude; their flimsy huts, roofed with the fronds that the forest can abundantly spare, lay far down among the humus litter at the forest's feet; their manioc and bananas were merely patches of vegetation a little differently organised from the rest of the wilderness.

There were many peoples, of course. Every day we saw different faces turned to us from the visiting pirogues. North of the Equator, tattooing was no longer a matter of misplaced vaccination scratches. There were patterns of serrated nicks that sometimes made a bold second pair of eyebrows; there were round engravings like beauty patches on women's cheeks. On some faces the distortion was beautiful; they were formalised into sculpture in flesh. On the faces of the old, artifice had given way to nature, and the imposed face was broken up by the patient triumph of wrinkles.

Our water caravan did not halt for the first night and day, but in the small hours of the second night I was awakened by the sudden stillness of the engines. There were muffled cries in the air; I got up and went on deck. Out of the darkness and dark warmth the two great spotlights of our boat hastily framed a stage setting. A few palm trees were the only props. Before them, on the twenty feet or so of water between our caravan and the shore, black pirogues moved, silent and busy. The third-class ship ahead of ours glowed with light as if it were afire; everyone aboard was up, and life was going on purposefully. I saw the whole scene as if I had carried a lantern into a cave. Once, twice, the non-existent land showed the incredible sight of the lights of a car, carving through it and away. The calls of men and women traders graceful as shades in some watery level of a Dantesque Lethe, came to me as the caravan began to move away. The pirogues showed tiny candle halos of orange light; there was silence. Then a long cry: '*Ivoire!*'

By daylight, these ports of call were signalled by a mile or two of bank tamed by occupation; the red-brick buildings of a mission set back on a grassy slope, a palm-oil refinery or coffee-plantation headquarters. As well as the river people, and the workers from the refinery village, whatever white people there were always came down to the shore to survey us across the water: an old priest with a freshly combed, yellow-stained beard hanging to his waist, a couple of jolly-looking missionaries in cotton frocks, a Portuguese trader's wife, with sad, splendid eyes and a moustache, who never waved back.

At Coquilhatville (Mbandaka), exactly on the Equator, I went ashore for the first time. It was a small modern town with its main street set along the river, and an air of great isolation. There is a magnificent botanical garden there, with trees and plants from the jungles of the Amazon as well as nearly all known varieties native to tropical Africa. The Belgian director was still there, then, a happy misogynist living alone with a cat. He opened his penknife and cut me a spray of three cattleya orchids from the baskets blooming on his open verandah. When I got back to the boat, I found that cargo was still being loaded, so I put the orchids into a mug and crossed the road from the dock to the main street again, where I had noticed the *Musée de l'Équateur* housed in a little old building. Striped wasps droned inside, tokening the peculiar resistance of the Equatorial forest to the preservation of material things; but if heat and damp threatened to invade the fetish figures and the carved utensils behind glass, it did not matter, because they were all in everyday use in the region, with the exception, perhaps, of a coffin, about twelve feet long, in the form of a man. It was an expression of rigor mortis in wood – angular, stern and dyed red. The face was tattooed, and in the crook of the left arm there was a small figure representing the dead man's wife. But I was told that people in that part of the country usually bury their dead in ant heaps, and certainly I never saw a cemetery near any village along the river.

Conrad romanticised the Congo; Stanley, for all his genius of adventurousness, had a vulgar mind. Conrad projected his horror of the savage greed with which the agents of Léopold II brought 'civilisation' to the river in the 1880s, into the look of the river itself. The inviolate privacy of the primeval forest became a brooding symbol of the ugly deeds that were done there, the tattooed faces became the subjective image of life without the organised legal and moral strictures with which the white man keeps the beast in himself at bay. Stanley sometimes saw the river as a potential old-clothes mart; the tattooed and naked people irresistibly suggested to him a 'ready market' for the 'garments shed by the military heroes of Europe, of the club lackeys, of the liveried servants'.

Neither vision fitted what I saw on the Congo, though some of the anti-white and inter-tribal atrocities that have been committed since independence have matched in horror what white men did in the name of civilisation less than a century ago, and Conrad's vision of this part of Africa as the heart of man's darkness has taken on the look of prophecy. For myself, I had not been many days on the river when I stopped thinking of the people around me as primitive, in terms of skills and aesthetics. Their pirogues and all the weapons and tools of their livelihood were efficient and had the beauty that is the unsought result of perfect function. The pirogues were masters of the water, and like their gear, many of them were chased with carving of great restraint and discipline. The armoury of fishing spears, with their variety of tips and barbs, represented hand-forging and metalwork of a long skilled tradition, and a jeweller's eye for the beauty inherent in the strength of metals. Any paddle or bailing scoop – common articles of everyday use among riparian people – could have gone straight into an art collection; which is as if to say one could pick up a plastic spoon in a white man's kitchen, a spade in a suburban garden, and confidently put them on exhibition.

After Coquilhatville the river mustered such a day-and-night assault on the senses that you could not read. In the slowly passing forest were the halls and mansions of prehistory: great mahogany trees, ficus, and, out-topping the tallest palm, the giant kapok with its trunk like pale stone. There were times when the pull and contrast between the elements of land and water seemed to disappear altogether. On golden water, garlands of green islands floated. As the light changed, the water became smooth as ice; our length, our bulk skimmed it like a waterbug. Then the floating islands, with their hazy, lengthening reflections, coloured a surface like that of a mirror on which the quicksilver is worn; and perfume came to us from the forest. There were many flowering creepers – an orchid-pink one that spread itself out to the sun over a tree, an occasional red or orange one – but the perfume was the cold, sweet, unmistakable one of white flowers, and came from a waxy trail of blossoms, deadly poisonous, very beautiful.

A storm in the night brought tremendous rain hosing down on us. The sky swelled and thinned with lightning like the overblown skin of a dark balloon. In the morning, the jungle was dripping and brilliant, and an hour-long forest of trees suddenly appeared, covered with ethereal orchilla moss, their beards matted with water. Other trees had ant-heaps looking like spools of thread wound high up on their branches. When the boat drew near an island – there are four thousand of them in this stretch of the Congo – or passed close to one of the banks, the raucous gossip of grey-and-red African parrots was overheard. The Africans catch young parrots by letting a ball of latex, from the wild rubber lianas, down the hollow trees where the parrots nest; the claws of the young become entangled in the tacky ball, and when it is drawn up they come with it. They are caught to sell as white people's pets, unlike the monkeys, which are favoured as food. In a lonely stretch of forest, two men wearing nothing but loincloths of bark startled me by holding up a monkey they had just found and killed in one of the traps they set up along the river.

Not long after the caravan had left Bumba, its most northerly stop in the curving course of the river and the point at which the Congo–Nile road down Africa meets the Congo, we approached a village where a whole armada of pirogues came out to meet us. From our galley came a shower of jam tins; men, women and children leaped for them from the pirogues into the water. The men were naked; the women were wrapped in mammy cloth but they too seemed unencumbered. Some who boarded our boat did not leave it for several miles, when the pirogues had left them behind long ago; they simply stepped off into our swirling wake and swam back home. They are the only people I have ever seen who swim as others walk or run.

We passed, and sometimes made a stop at, places that were once the Arab fortresses of Tippu Tip, a powerful Arab slave trader whose help Stanley was ironically forced to seek in his journeys, although one of the professed objects of the association for which Stanley worked was to wipe out the slave trade. One of these places was Yangambi, which Stanley came upon in 1883 as a populous village in ruins, with its male population murdered and its women and children fettered by the neck or leg in an Arab slave camp built of the remains of their home.

The Belgians built a fine agricultural research station at Yangambi, the biggest in Africa, a garden town with its own shops, school, hospital, club and pleasant houses as well as laboratories and experimental plantations. It belonged, like everything else, to the new Congolese state, and it still had its complement of

Belgian scientists when I was there, but the disorder that has since descended on nearby Stanleyville (Kisangani) may have brought its usefulness to a standstill.

Across the river, from a great village that stretched for several miles along the bank, Topoke people brought huge forest pine-apples to sell us. The tribesmen were intricately tattooed, with the attentive eyes of merchants, though they grow bananas and catch fish. Many of them are followers of what is known as the Kitiwala – an African corruption of the name as well as the character of the Watch Tower Society, which (like a number of other harmless religious sects in a country where Christianity, traditional animism and black nationalism provide a heady inspirational mixture) has become a subversive secret society. So much so that the Belgian colonial administration outlawed the distribution of those apocalyptic pamphlets familiar on street corners all over the world.

At Stanleyville the river's great right of way through twelve hundred miles ends; the Stanley Falls (Boyoma Falls) break it – they are rapids, really – and the Equator is crossed again. On the other side, in the southern hemisphere, is the stretch of the Congo that leads to its source near the copper belt of the south; it has another name, Lualaba. Livingstone 'discovered' it (for Europe) but did not dream that it could be the distant Congo, known far away in West Africa.

Stanleyville lies just below Stanley Falls, as Léopoldville lies just above the lower Congo rapids. But the river at Stanleyville is of a size the eye can encompass, and in fact the town is on both sides of it. Here is a place deeply of Africa, sunk in Africa. In Léopoldville the tropical vegetation is not dwarfed by, but a match for, the giant modern buildings; the modest colonial buildings of Stanleyville make no challenge to the towering fecundity of the tropics. There is a lofty feeling that comes from living things, not buildings; palms, whose trunks are covered with a cool compress of moss, bright as seaweed and feathered with ferns, hang above the avenues, and the Traveller's Tree – an exalted relation of the banana palm that stores cool water for the passer-by at the base of fringed fronds arranged like the spread of a peacock's tail – is common.

Stanleyville is – or was – the late Patrice Lumumba's town, and it has become a place of terror for white people. From time to time, now, it is cut off from communication with the rest of the country, and the world; planes cannot land there, and the river convoy service from Léopoldville, carrying food and other supplies, is disrupted by unrest. But the *Gouverneur Moulaert* and its water caravan reached the end of their journey at Stanleyville during an interval of calm. There, I was even able to have one last experience of the river before I left it to continue my journey by land.

I went with the Wagenia fishermen to visit their fishing grounds in the rapids of Stanley Falls. I found them at home in an ugly 'Arabised' village a mile or two from the town. It was a poor collection of low mud houses like a heap of sandcastles that a tide had lapped over; the extent of its Arabisation seemed to consist of the one mud hut, daubed with white and a line of shaky Arabic script, that served as a mosque. African villages such as this one on the riverbank are relics of the proselytising for Islam that was a sideline of Arab slavers from the East Coast.

It was just five in the afternoon when I got to the Wagenia village, and I had to wait while the crew mustered, struggling out of the patchy decency of the white man's cast-offs that they wore to work in Stanleyville, and emerging from their dark mudholes in shorts and loincloths. There were twenty-five paddlers and three musicians, and we took to the water in a big pirogue that held us all comfortably. A coxswain stood in front of me where I sat in the middle, and another, a lean and handsome old man, stood up aft. He was the leader of the chanting; sometimes this accompanied the drumming, sometimes followed on the beat of the drums, and sometimes was beaten into silence by the master voice of the drums. The pirogue skidded and shot across the rapids, the bodies of the paddlers jabbing and rising, and as the water became wilder the drums hammered up the energy of the men, deafening and dramatic.

We crossed the river and landed among reeds where rocks jutted

out half-hidden by very fast and evil-looking rapids. Giant cornu-
copias of fish traps hung from an incredible catwalk of huge logs
and lianas strung over the dreadful waters. Three of the fishermen
shinned over the lianas and logs and, balancing like high-wire
artists, pulled up the traps full of slapping fish. I found myself in a
scene I recognised as identical in every detail with the sketch reproduced in Stanley's account of the Wagenias when he founded his
first river station at the Falls in 1885; they fish the wild, twisted
water exactly as they did then.

Returning downstream towards Stanleyville, the going was
smoother and the paddlers made a great show of speed, rhythm
and drumming. We cut across the path of the ferryboat that plies
between the 'black' town on one bank and the 'white' town on the
other; the cranes on the dock were at work on their slow devouring
and disgorging. It was an odd feeling to be the centre of a kind of
floating war dance in the middle of a modern port preoccupied with
political fervour; while I enjoyed the show-off of the Wagenias, I
felt something was fraudulent, and could not make up my mind
whether it was the modern port or the old pirogue. Yet the Congo
River was not demeaned either way. The Congo, like that other
stream, of time, is neither past nor present, and carries both in an
immense indifference that takes them to be one. There is no old
and no new Africa to the great river; it simply bears a majestic
burden of life, as it has always done.

While I was travelling on the Congo River I might have forgotten for
days at a time that I was in a land suffering the great political crisis of
its existence. Yet all through the thousand-mile river journey from
Léopoldville to Stanleyville, while the banks of the Congo showed
a life regulated by other mores and even other gods than those of
the contemporary world of history, a scribble, chalked by an idler
in Léopoldville on one of the barges in the water caravan in which
I travelled, remained: 'Vive le Roi M. Kasavubu et l'Indépendance'. In
all the traffic of the caravan's progress, the scribble was not rubbed
off. And whenever it caught my eye there was brought home to me
the realisation that Africa, however troubled it may be, has never

been more interesting than it is in this decade; it may never be so interesting again. The Africa the nineteenth-century explorers found – the jungle and the scarified faces that I myself was seeing on the river – and the Africa I had seen emergent in the city life of Stanley Pool are in living coexistence though centuries apart. These are the two great periods of the continent; the colonial Africa that came between them was the dullest, despite its achievements and historical necessity.

When Stanley was busy opening up the Congo River to trade in the name of Léopold II of Belgium, he met in the wilderness Pierre Savorgnan de Brazza, who was equally busy staking out rival claims for the French. Opposite Léopoldville, which Stanley founded, across the great width of Stanley Pool is Brazzaville, which de Brazza founded. Four years ago the Pool was French on one bank and Belgian on the other; now Brazzaville is the capital of one Congo Republic, and Léopoldville is the capital of another. The new definitions are only a little less artificial than the old colonial ones; for the people on both banks of Stanley Pool are the same people – the Bakongo – who had a kingdom of their own in the fifteenth century. The definitions are less artificial only because the people of the right bank and the people of the left bank have entered into community with the modern world under two different influences – the one French, the other Belgian – and certain approaches to life characteristic of the French, and others characteristic of the Belgians, will probably distinguish the two African peoples for ever, despite the fact that the Congolese of the former Belgian Congo have shown a fanatic revulsion against the Belgians.

On a Saturday night I took the ferry across Stanley Pool to what used to be the French side, and went to an open-air café in the Poto Poto district of Brazzaville, a vast black slum that is the real city, although its swarming existence in shacks and unlit streets goes on completely buried under an extravagant growth of creepers and palms, while the pleasant colonial town built by the French shows up more prominently through the tropical green.

Chez Faignon lay behind a dirty alley full of amiable hangers-

about, a barber's stall doing good business, and an old, blind house.
Yet it turned a face to the sky as a moon-flower; there was a raised
dance floor, a marvellous band panting out to the night the triumph
of its return from a Left Bank engagement in Paris, a pungent atmosphere of cats and spilled beer, and a collection of women whose
blatant gorgeousness is the only grand style of beauty I know of in
the world today.

These ladies of joy – as many of them were – suggested all the
wickedness of courtesans of the great age; they also giggled and
whispered in each other's ears like schoolgirls. They were wearing –
carried to the nth degree – the form of dress that the modern women
of the Congo basin have evolved for themselves, and that, though
it goes by the humble French word *pagne* – loincloth – combines
the grace of the sari with the revelations of the bikini. It consists
of a décolleté, almost backless tight bodice, a bandage-narrow skirt
from pelvis to ankle, and some yards of material draped to cover
the gap between bodice and skirt. The ladies dance the paso doble
in this outfit, and the gesture with which they unhitched and rearranged the drape recalled the business of the cape before the bull
and also revealed, for quick glimpses, smooth, bare belly.

I sat at a table with French friends and pointed to various people
around us: 'Who would they be?' There were a few white couples
among the gay ladies and town bachelors.

'Just people who like a good band to dance to on a Saturday
night.'

'And that man over there?' He was a white-haired white man
with a smooth, pink jaw, impeccably dressed in quite a different
way from that of the Congolese bachelors, who were elegant in the
manner of young Americans trying to look like young Italians. I
was told he was Monsieur Christian Gayle, Minister of Information
at the time – the only white man in Africa holding a cabinet post
in an independent black government. A little later the Minister of
Information left his party of African friends – which included the
Minister of Finance and also a spectacular six-foot Senegalese lady
in turquoise chiffon *pagne* and diamonds – and joined us. He was a
calm, charming man who wore the ribbon of the Légion d'Honneur

and was once a member of the French Chamber of Deputies. The finish of Europe lay upon him invisibly but effectively; he was serenely unaware of any temptation to Africanise himself. He told me that he had come to Brazzaville seven years ago on a stopover between planes, and had lived there ever since.

'The only way a white man in Africa keeps his self-respect now is when he is working with independent Africans. Last year, when I was Speaker, the leader of the opposition knocked me over the head with a portable radio. I remained calm. That is one of the important things left to do in Africa – to keep the peace between Africans, who don't really understand the principle of loyal opposition – of putting the country first.'

A few weeks later Léopoldville, on the other side of the river, was a place of brutality again, with the Congolese battering a bewildered assertion of their freedom on the heads of one another, as well as on white heads, and the size of the task M. Gayle had foreseen became clear. Since then, even the United Nations has seemed less than equal to this important thing left to do in Africa.

When the river had taken me halfway across the continent to Stanleyville, I continued by road north and east through other parts of the centre of Africa, a spread of more than 900,000 square miles that was colonised by the Belgians. It is eighty times the size of Belgium itself – indeed, the whole of Western Europe could be contained within its borders. Almost the whole of the Congo River basin belongs in it, the Mountains of the Moon, many thousands of miles of tropical rain forest, and beyond the forest, rich copper, diamond and other mineral deposits. Men and animals extinct or unheard-of anywhere else still live in the Equatorial jungle, and the uranium for the bombs of Hiroshima and Nagasake came from the mine at a tiny place called Shinkolobwe in the savannah.

Vive l'indépendance. There was no mud hut so isolated, no road so lost in this wilderness that the message of that scribble on the river barge had not reached it. On the way north, in a country hotel on a lonely road where men carry bows and arrows just as we carry umbrellas and newspapers, and pygmy women run like shy deer twenty yards into the forest before they turn to pause and look at you looking at them, a huge yellow American car brought a couple of party politicians to put up for the night in the room next to mine. They were urbane young black men, and after drinking French wine with their dinner, they set off to address a meeting in the village. The people round about were the Mangbetu, whose artistic sense has led them to the elegant distortion of their own skulls; they have artificially elongated heads as a result of the custom of binding them in babyhood, and the taut skins of their brows give both men and women the look of women who have had a face-lift.

I had seen one of their beautifully decorated courthouses that day. Its mud walls were covered, inside and out, with abstract designs incorporating the figures of animals and weapons in terra-cotta, black and white. The court was in session and a group of women were listening to the drone of somebody's grievances and passing silently among themselves a bamboo water pipe, also decorated. They were unsmiling women who wore the *negbwe*, a concave bark shield, on their behinds, and little else. But their near-nakedness wore the forbidding expression that my limited experience is familiar with only on faces. Among them, I had the curious impression that I was not there.

Early next morning I passed the open door of my neighbours' room and saw the two politicians, in shirtsleeves and bow ties, sitting on their beds counting a great pile of currency contributed to party funds by the Mangbetu, who had attended in full force at the meeting the night before.

And there was no part of the country, however remote, where you might not be startled by the sudden appearance of a group of ragged children, yelling at the car as it passed. Speed whipped the cry away; but it was always recognisable as the same one: ' '*dépendance!*' Perhaps, deep in the forest they had never left, they did not realise that they had got it; perhaps only when the cotton crop was gathered, and there was no one to buy it, and they were hungry, would they realise the change had come.

Once my companions and I met with an older form of African confidence, and one that belonged to a different kind of independence

– a kind safe from disillusion. We had stopped to quench our thirst on warm soda water on a road that led through a neglected palm grove, old and taken over by the jungle. A Congolese with a demijohn of palm wine came over the rise towards us, his wavering progress given a push by gravity. A lot of the wine was inside him instead of the demijohn, and when he drew level with the car, he stopped, greeted us and then stood a minute, watching us with a fuddled amiability that presently turned to amused patronage. He pointed to the soda water. 'That's your drink,' he said. Then he lifted the demijohn. 'This's ours.'

For years travel maps have shown the continent of Africa populated apparently exclusively by lions and elephants, but these maps are out of date now, and will have to be replaced with something ethnographic as well as zoogeographic. For the people have come back; they are no longer discounted by the world as they were for so long. The people have come back into their own, no matter how strife-torn they may be; and the animals have not gone yet. This, if he can dodge between riots and avoid the crash of toppling governments, is a fascinating combination of circumstances for a traveller.

Gangala-na-Bodio – the hill of Chief Bodio – is high up in the Uele district, the north-east corner of the Congo, out of the Equatorial forest and lost in the bush near the Sudan border. On the hill, in the middle of the home of the last great herds of African elephants, was the only African elephant-training station in the world. I write 'was' because I must have been one of the last visitors to go there, and in a matter of weeks after that, all news from this remote corner of the Congo ceased. The few white people in the district fled to the Sudan, and I imagine that the Belgian commander of the station – the only white man there – must have been among them. It is doubtful if the Congolese – even those who treated their elephant charges with such loving care – will be able to look upon elephants as anything but potential food, now, with the country's economy in a state of collapse, and hunger general.

I arrived at Gangala-na-Bodio two weeks after the capture of two wild young elephants. Each was attended by a pair of monitor elephants, old, wise and immensely patient, who hustled them gently but firmly through the routine of the day; but there was a nightly crisis when they were led off to be bedded down in their stockades. On my first afternoon at the station I was charged by Sophie, the wilder of the two. I was standing with a couple of other visitors, watching her being eased into her stockade by the trunks and tusks of her monitors and the shouts and prods of cornacs – trainers – armed with pronged forks. Suddenly she broke through the legs of one of her monitors and hurtled straight for me, her eyes mean with infant rage, her trunk raised for battle and her ears flaring. I lost my head and ran – the wrong way, right among the immense columns of the monitors' legs. They trumpeted, but though the sound was alarming, it was, in a manner of speaking, a mere tut-tutting – a mature deprecation of Sophie's behaviour and mine. I scrambled up into a fodder cart, quite safe.

The majestic charm of elephants creates a wonderful atmosphere to live in. In the morning, their great shapes constantly detached themselves from and merged with the heat-hazy shapes of the bush, where they were out to pasture, or they would appear, with the pausing momentum of their gait, suddenly blocking the bright end of a leafy path at the station. Harnessed to clumsy carts, they did all the hard work of the camp. At four in the afternoon all thirty-one of them were led to the river for their daily bath. Each day I watched them career slowly past me down the riverbank and into the brown water. Some had cornacs on their backs, and they were careful not to dunk them; the men scrubbed luxuriously behind the beasts' ears with handfuls of grass. Some linked trunks and played well out in the river, and rolled each other over with a whoosh that sent four great stubby feet waving in the air. As they came out, in strolling twos and threes, they plastered their foreheads with sand from a pile dumped there specially for them. The cornacs shouted, the laggards broke into a heavy trot to catch up, and the whole procession (wild Sophie with her tail a stiffly held aerial of alarm) trailed home through the trees while the cornacs broke raggedly, then more surely, into 'Alalise' or 'Dina Dina,' two Hindi elephant songs the Indian mahouts left behind them long ago.

From Gangala-na-Bodio I went out into the bush on one of the station elephants. A cornac in a smart trooper's hat was up in front, and I sat behind on a hard little seat strapped to the elephant's back. We were accompanied by another elephant and his cornac. The cornacs and I had no common language (they belonged to one of the Sudanese tribes of the north-east Congo) but they seemed to have one in common with the elephants, and as we swayed regularly through the early-morning air, first wading across the river (our elephant filled his mouth as he went, like a car taking petrol), my cornac kept up a nagging, reproachful, urging monologue in the elephant's enormous ear. A family of giraffe crossed our path, and though I admire them, from the vantage point of an elephant's back I felt less impressed than usual by their loftiness. Then we stopped within a few yards of a herd of bushpigs, who showed no sign of wanting to run, and passed before the serene eyes of a Thomas's Cob – a lovely antelope – without startling him.

We saw a herd of elephant in the distance to the east, and slowly swung off towards them through the trees. I held my breath as our two elephants moved right up to mingle on the fringe of the herd of five cows, three calves and a monumental bull. But the wild elephants seemed unaware of the two who bore men on their backs, and the tame elephants showed no remembrance of the freedom from which they once came. I have often seen the wild animals of Africa from a car, or even on foot, in game reserves, but I have never expected or felt myself to be anything but an intruder among them. On elephant-back, they accepted me as one of themselves; it was a kind of release from the natural pariahdom of man in the world of the beasts – an hour, for me, that early morning, which was the reverse of that hour at midnight on Christmas Eve when it is said that beasts can speak like men.

From Stanleyville, at the end of the thousand-mile main navigable stretch of the Congo River, a road follows the old slave and ivory caravan trail through the Ituri Forest, the primeval jungle through which Stanley walked for 160 days, almost without seeing the light.

The life of the forest is an internecine existence; completely enclosed, each step, each minute sealed off from the next by a conspiracy of leaves, lianas and deadening mosses. The trees are host to all sorts of other living forms. Some are held by lianas in a deadly embrace that eventually hugs them out of existence, so that only the lianas remain, locked soaring upright; through them you can see the space where the tree used to be. Shell-shaped wasp nests stand like platforms on the tree trunks. Bunches of swordfern and fungus are stuffed in every crevice. On the floor of the forest, stiff waxy lilies are hatched out by the ancient humus.

The forest creaks like an enormous house. In the silence of the day, showers of small leaves fall from so high up you cannot see where. But most of the things that lie fallen are tremendous; pods from the beanstalk Jack might have climbed, huge silky seed cases, green on one side, silvery fur on the other.

At night the forest is as noisy as a city. Among the barks, grunts and cries there was one Greek and immortal in its desperate passion, gathering up echoes from all the private wailing walls of the human soul. It turned out that it came from an outsize guinea pig of a creature called a tree hyrax; I saw one in captivity in one of the villages where, like parrots, monkeys and pythons, they are popular pets of the few white inhabitants.

Most of the animals of the forest do not show themselves, but on the Epulu River, deep in the jungle, I visited a trapping and breeding station where I had a chance to see the rarest and most timid, the okapi, the forest giraffe. The station was simply a part of the forest enclosed, and I came upon the okapi in the cathedral light for which their being has evolved. They were the most luxurious-looking animals imaginable, as big as horses, with legs striped waveringly in clear black and white as if they were standing in rippling water, and a rich sable sheen on the rump shading into glowing auburn that changed in movement, like a woman's hair tinted different colours at different levels.

The pygmies, who belong to the forest just as the okapis do, venture out of it hardly more. They are the only autochthonous people of the forest, and in parts they live a nomadic life, hunting,

and are at home wherever they twist together the few branches
and leaves that provide shelter for a short time. (These huts are
not much more elaborate than the gorilla nest I saw later on an
extinct volcano.) But many pygmy groups have attached themselves to other African communities, who live where the forest has
been cleared for cultivation, and these have adopted a more permanent way of life and live in the villages. Pygmies have interbred,
too, with full-size people, and in many villages there is a confusing
variety of sizes that don't necessarily correspond with ages. A boy
of seven can be as big as his grandfather, and what looks like a
man's small daughter turns out to be one of his wives.

Driving along a road one morning where the forest had been
pulled down to make way for coffee and banana plantations, we
heard drums in one of these villages. A child had just been born; a
small tam-tam and biggish beer-drink were in progress as a celebration. Two fine young men stood at long drums suspended over
smouldering logs to keep the skins taut. Around them a company
of men, women and children shuffled and sang. There were several
gnomes of men with the huge eyes that pygmies have, like the eyes
of some harmless night-prowling creature.

There was a tall man, small-featured and handsome, who wore at
an angle, in drunken parody of his own natural dignity, a straw and
parrot-feather toque exactly like the one in a sketch that Stanley
reproduced, as an example of dress in the region, in one of his Congo
exploration books. There were people with filed teeth and others
with tattooed navels. Young girls and old crones who wore only
small aprons of beaten bark were the most enthusiastic dancers, the
crones inspired by drink, the girls perhaps by the wonderful intri-
cacy of their coiffures – corrugated, helmeted, deeply furrowed as
if the very cranium had been cleaved in two.

Pygmies and other forest Congolese use the road to walk on,
but there is no feeling that it connects them to anything. They are
complete, in and of the forest. The women peer from under the
forehead band that supports a huge, papoose-shaped basket filled
with bananas, wood or palm nuts; often a baby sits on top of it. The
men carry their bows and arrows, pangas and hunting spears, and

the great bark-fibre nets with which they trap animals. Sometimes they have with them the little Basenji dogs that look like mongrel fox terriers with wide pointed ears, and cannot bark. Often there are people playing musical instruments as they walk; harps with resonators of stiff buckskin, and the *likembe*, a small box with metal tongues that is heard, plaintively plangent, all over Africa.

The landmarks here are giant red sandcastles of ant heaps, carefully covered with palm leaves over a stick frame; the cover prevents the winged grubs inside from flying off, by suggesting a night which ends only when the Africans open the heap to eat them. Cars that falter on the way provide, for a while, other landmarks; the hulks of recent American and Continental models lie abandoned here and there, the creeping plants beginning to cover them within a year or two of their announcement as an innovation in motoring. Soon they disappear under the green.

Stanley almost gave up hope of emerging from the forest into the light, but after five months the day came. 'Instead of crawling like mighty bipeds in the twilight, thirty fathoms below the level of the white light of the day, compelled to recognise our littleness, by comparison with the giant columns and tall pillar-like shafts that rose by millions around us, we now stood on the crest of a cleared mount.' The end of the forest is just as dramatic today, from the road that leads east. Perhaps more dramatic, for you can drive in one day from the Equatorial forest to the sight of snow.

At four in the afternoon, the trees fell away before us, the green land fell away beyond that, and a great blue ghost of a mountain hung across the horizon. It was an infinity; a palm or two stood up clear in the foreground against swimming blue. Then the cloud at the top of the blue shape shifted a little, the outline neared and hardened; we saw the white glitter, the soft contour of snow on the jagged peaks of a whole range. It was the Ruwenzori – Ptolemy's Mountains of the Moon. And we came upon them, remote as the moon, from out of the close warm forest and the pygmies burrowing there.

Across the Semliki Plain we drove towards the mountains through elephant grass, spiked acacias and companies of royal palms. There were banana and paw-paw plantations, too, down where we were; and, up there, the alps. At the foot of the mountains there was a hotel that seemed to float in the radiance that came up from the plain. A water garden of three swimming lakes held, upside down, the snow flash of the mountains' highest peak, 16,795-foot Margherita; and between hotel and peak there was a five-day climb, for the hardy, through every type of vegetation from Equatorial to alpine.

This part of the Congo – the Kivu province – and the neighbouring territory of Ruanda-Urundi (still under Belgian trusteeship), is unlike any other part, not only of the Congo but of all Africa. From the Mountains of the Moon driving three days to Lake Tanganyika, the car seemed to be pulled from side to side by mountains and lakes that reduced most famous drives to the stature and duration of a scenic railway in the painted canvas of a fairground.

Tourist pamphlets, with their passion for making everywhere sound like somewhere else, used to call this the Switzerland of Africa, and no doubt will again when the country is once more open to pleasure travel, but it is not much like Switzerland, and if it were, who would bother to seek in Africa what is so handy in Europe? It is unlike the rest of Africa because it is the high reservoir – watershed of both the Congo River and the Nile – of a continent, seared through by the Equator, which is largely baked dry where there is any altitude to speak of, and steaming wet where there is none. It is unlike Switzerland because many of its green mountains are volcanoes (two are still active); its strange pale lakes have floors of lava; its cattle (my first sight of a cow in all the Congo) are long-horned beasts like the cow-god Hathor in Egyptian tomb paintings; and on the roads behind the villas that the Belgians built on Lake Kivu you see brown giants and pygmies. The giants are the Hamitic Watusi of Ruanda-Urundi, and the pygmies, not the pure forest breed, are the Batwa.

In the middle of this mountain and lake-land, enclosing three-quarters of the shores of Lake Edward (Lake Rutanzige) and reaching to Lake Kivu, is Albert Park, a wonderful game preserve on the floor of the Great Rift Valley. I drove straight through it, for I was on my way over the border of the Congo into Uganda – the frontier runs over the Mountains of the Moon, through Lake Edward and over three volcanoes – because of an animal that can only be seen outside a game preserve – the mountain gorilla. There are many on the Congo side of the volcanoes that cross the Great Rift Valley from West to East, but, under Belgian administration at least, no one was allowed to go up after them. At the Uganda frontier post of Kisoro, there is a tiny country hotel whose proprietor had permission, and himself provided the guide, to take people up the side of the extinct volcano, Muhavura, where gorillas live.

I set off up Muhavura early in the morning and climbed to 10,000 feet, well into the bamboo belt. The gorillas do venture up the full 14,000 feet of the volcano, but bamboos provide their beds – a fresh one each night – and a favoured food, and the guide felt that if we were to come upon them at all, it would be there among the bamboos that enclosed us like the bars of a vegetable prison. Progress was a matter of squeezing between them, usually on hands and knees because the glassy-wet earth gave no foothold. We were within a degree of the Equator – but it was dripping cold, up there; where there was no bamboo, there were leafless, lichen-scaly trees spun all over with a floss of moss that came against your face like a wet sponge.

A broken stalk of wild celery, a huge, knobbly-surfaced mushroom, nibbled and discarded, made a trail read by the guide. Soon he showed me five fresh gorilla beds, that had been slept in the night before. They looked more like giant nests than beds; the stout bamboo poles were bent together five or six feet above ground, and then roughly thatched with leaves. There was fresh dung, and in the wet earth, huge knuckle-marks – like us, the gorillas use hands as well as feet to get along on the mountain. This deserted bedroom had an odour that curiously matched the gorilla's own place in creation; not quite man, not entirely beast, a compound of lodging-house back room and zoo enclosure.

I did not see the gorillas although we trailed them for four hours. Apparently people who do come upon them do so quite suddenly; the male, who may be a 600-pound six-footer, then stands his

ground, beating his breast and arms and giving a blood-freezing
battle cry, while the females and young make off. How the exhilarating mixture of curiosity and pure funk with which I sought this
experience would have stood up to it, I shall not know until I go
back one day and try again; for this time, my sense of let-down was
forgotten by the surprise when I turned my back on Muhavura for
the climb down, and saw before me a marvel of a plain far below,
with little volcanoes set in it like cupcakes fallen in in the middle,
and the grain and counter-grain of the scratchings of agriculture,
and more volcanoes, ringed from base to summit with contoured
planting in a pattern as ordered as the plaiting on the Africans'
heads, and the pale moonstone gleam of yet another volcano that
held, instead of fire and brimstone, a lake.

Climbing down, we sank slowly, like birds coming to rest, to the
level of this plain.

The white man, as a power, is fast becoming extinct in Africa; it
may be that the wild animals will follow him. Africans and animals
have lived together so long that one is inclined to think of them
as belonging together in a natural order, but the truth is that the
domain of the beasts has long been a puppet kingdom, upheld by
white governments not only by means of game preserves and sanc-
tuaries, but, more important, by stringent hunting laws outside
them. Once the greater part of the continent is ruled independently by the Africans themselves, it is unlikely that they will be
able to regard the beasts as anything but a supply of meat and an
obstacle to the expansion of farmland. By the time the Africans
have secured confidence in their place in the twentieth century,
it may be too late to remedy the sacrifice of the beasts. It is just
possible that this sacrifice might be avoided if the African states
would agree to let the game preserves be the responsibility of an
international authority, such as the United Nations.

Whatever happens, the hour of man has struck in Africa. We
have swarmed over the whole of creation; it would be humbug to
pretend not to hear, simply because elephants often seem so much
nobler than men, buck more beautiful and even lion less menacing.

I left the Congo with men's voices in my ears. It was in Katanga
(Shaba), the rich province that was the first to secede from the central
government. Katanga, with its copper, uranium, diamonds, gold,
cobalt and tin, is richer in minerals than any other part of Africa
(with perhaps the exception of the Union of South Africa) and once
supplied more than half the national income of the old Belgian
Congo. The Belgians in particular, and international mining interests in general, have managed to retain powerful influence in this
prize territory, and its Congolese president, Moise Tshombe, is
regarded in most other independent African states as a white man's
stooge – a puppet animated by the old colonial strings.

For the first few months after independence, in June 1960, the
breakaway state of Katanga was the one part of the former Belgian
Congo that remained peaceful. But later tribal fighting began
there, and in certain mining and industrial centres the whites were
subjected to a reign of terror just as bad as those that hit the late
Lumumba's Stanleyville, or Kasavubu's Léopoldville.

On a Sunday morning the town square of the prosperous copper
town and capital of Katanga, Elisabethville (Lubumbashi), was
ready to receive President Tshombe on his return from the Brussels
Conference at which the Congo had been granted independence.
The day before, I had seen chiefs in leopard-skin regalia lunching
at the Léopold Deux, the most elegant hotel; they had arrived from
the country to welcome him. And early on Sunday morning I had
been wakened by the sound of ululating cries in the streets, as less
exalted supporters came into town by lorry and on foot.

The scene in the square was one of dazzling, jazzing holiday joy.
Twenty thousand faces looked from the branches of the flowering
trees, from the top of buildings, from a solid phalanx in the streets
– all black. There were Boy Scouts and religious sects in white and
blue robes and chiefs in fur, feather and beads, and young men in
forage caps and party uniform. There were several hundred women
whose faces and arms were painted white and whose hair stuck out
like pipe cleaners in tiny plaits all over their heads. There were
drummers and dancers with tribal masks on their faces, and on
their feet the issue boots they wear in the copper mines. While

they stamped and sang, a white man in shorts held a microphone impassively before them.

After a two-hour wait, a party official leaped on to the red and white striped official stand, stilled the drums and the din, and held up a gentleman's overcoat, of discreet colour and the best tailoring. Like a thump on a gong, a tremendous cry rang out from the crowd and hung on the air: the coat was a sign, brought by dispatch rider from the airport, that their leader had truly arrived.

Soon Tshombe came in person, a beamish, very young-looking man, as many African statesmen tend to be, standing up in an open car, a very large pink one, as many African statesmen's cars tend to be. It had been announced that photographing of his person was forbidden: the reason – not announced – was that no one is yet quite sure that there may not be something in the old African belief that, by sticking pins into or casting a spell over an image, you may be able to bring harm to the person it represents.

He looked afraid of nothing, nothing at all, this young man in the blue lounge suit. Yet as I watched him up there on his platform of welcome I could see that he was surrounded by everything that Africa has to fear. The faces of white men – men of prey or good will, who could tell? – were there, few and ominous, close beside him before the black crowd. And, just behind him, there was a mountainously fat chief, holding a fly whisk with the authority of a sceptre.

1961

Party of One

Americans invented the word 'image' in the sense in which it is now associated with consumer goods everywhere. Oddly enough, it was American writers who began the image-making. In the early days of independence, the fact that English remained the language of the Americans, even though they had won the war, was a tender place on the hide of the new nation. The mandarin prose of New England was too closely associated with England; yet the slangy vitality of Artemus Ward and Mark Twain seemed too rough-and-ready to provide an American idiom. For some generations, American writers felt about uneasily for words of their own; long after they had found them, the idea of an American idiom was taken over and blurred, changed; confused with the idea of the American image. The one was a search; the other is a gimmick. I believe the American writer's share in it was innocent; certainly – to borrow his own idiom – he wants no part of it today.

The difference between the America of films, magazines and packaged goods, and the America of Faulkner, Hawthorne, Saul Bellow, Carson McCullers, James Baldwin, Melville – I stab the names with a pin, hitting on past as well as present, because the *then* in every country is contained in its *now* – is extraordinary. (It is interesting that that marvellous American invention, sick humour, is based on this very difference: life as you've been told to want it, and life as it is.) One can't explain away the gap in terms of the difference between art and commercialism. For though shamelessly used by commerce, the American image is also held up by Americans in high and serious places, political ones, for example. The image exalts youth, success, unquestioning patriotism, the love of a good man/woman, the confidence of freedom and of being right. The best of American writers are concerned with the difficulty of fulfilment; the corruption of integrity; the struggle for moral standards in public as well as private life; the truth of love, whatever its form, hetero- or homosexual; the battle of the individual against the might of society; and the doubt that one is right.

I don't mean by this that what foreigners get from American writers is an exposé of America. It is a world of real human beings grappling with real life, asking the questions instead of accepting that they know all the answers. Why do we accept the verity of this world while rejecting that of America on the back of the cereal package? For the simple reason that, being alive, we ourselves know that life is not a Happy Families game of matching sorrow with death, joy with love, freedom with a declaration of independence.

It is a matter of questioning these things afresh every time they come up in individual lives; in fact, when it comes to freedom, it is a matter of measuring it by one's right and impulse to question it constantly.

Melville wrote: 'I love all men that *dive* . . . the whole corps of intellectual thought-divers that have been diving and coming up again with bloodshot eyes since the world began.'

Of course, I am speaking of the divers with bloodshot eyes – the real American writers. In the context of literature, the hacks don't concern us except as an aside: why is it that the competent, decently written library novel, a good yarn or a nice love story, is on a much higher standard in England than in America? In fact, to most non-Americans, the run-of-the-mill American novel is unreadable. (From *Gone With the Wind* to *Advise and Consent* it's come in thousand-page hunks, too.) We see the film, but we can't read the book.

I think it is because although this sort of book may be expected to fill loosely the gap between the comfortable conventions and reality, advancing timidly towards one while returning, on the final page, to the other, in America the nature of the conventions – the America of the cereal package – is so remote from reality that even this is not possible. If a writer is not good enough to be able to go the whole way, he has to dream on between the genuine percale sheets. If the gap is filled in at all, it is in a different way, and by people who are not hacks but sociologists with a knack of making themselves readable to the layman. I don't suppose the foreigner's interest in books such as *The Lonely Crowd* and *The Affluent Society* has anything of the intensity with which Americans seize upon them for self-revelation; but, by analysing the gap, these books do fill it to the extent by which knowledge of the exact measurements of the height, depth and cubic capacity of a hole can be said to stop it up.

Apart from bringing information about the kinds and character of life in America, what does American writing mean to the outsider? There have been no American novelist-philosophers, no Camus, for example, showing man dealing with the absurdity of his position as a finite being possessed of infinite possibilities. No novelist-humanists, either: no E. M. Forster showing that the connection between individuals, though full of the sudden infuriating silences of a bad telephone line, is sometimes made. What American writers do give is the quality of life. The sight, smell, taste, feel, sound of it; from Thoreau to Hemingway and Fitzgerald, from Katherine Anne Porter to Henry Miller and Kerouac, Americans are writers of the five senses. Many of them have been journalists as well as writers, and they have brought to creative writing the feel for the immediacy of experience that journalism demands – get it down and get it straight. If you manage to do that, you won't need any rigmarole to explain it; it'll explain itself. This journalist's *method*, used with the creative intelligence, the precision, and the time a journalist hasn't got, has become one of the strong influences of American writing on the literature of other countries. Not only is Hemingway – its greatest exponent if not its inventor – the most famous American writer in world literature, but there is scarcely a contemporary writer in France, Italy or Germany, let alone in the English-speaking world, who does not show traces of this influence even if he supports the current sober and sour reassessment of the tough guy who ended up as Papa.

If Hemingway is the most famous American writer, then, to the non-American, Henry James is surely the greatest. James is the nearest to an American novelist-philospher, but we read him not so much for his marvellously complex moral structure in general as for the profundity of his understanding of America's relation to Europe. Why is it that his Millys and Daisys are more American than Uncle Sam; speak to us more deeply of America than anyone we've met with right up until that unexpected encounter with Captain Yossarian, in *Catch*-22, last year?

As a matter of fact, James, who seems at first thought to have nothing in common with his fellow American writers, actually shares several literary, familial traits. One of them is the curiously *maddening* quality of some of the American writers who turn out to be most rewarding, even wonderful. I don't mean just the turgidity that Faulkner, in his different way, shares with James, and ultimately

with Saul Bellow, Ralph Ellison and others; I don't mean the sheer
fighting with briars and lianas of words which one now and then
gives up in heavy-breathing despair. I mean the obstinate attraction exuded by this writing which gets one dazedly on to one's
mental feet again, set on getting into the dense, closed world that
the writer has made, where landmarks can only be followed once
you know your way about within it blindfolded and no longer need
them. Faulkner's Yoknapatawpha County is the obvious example;
but what about the New York apartment where J. D. Salinger's
Glass family lives? Salinger's prose is like a very clean window-
pane, yet to get into the room beyond needs quite a sustained effort
to suspend one's consciousness of all terms of reference other than
those that direct the life of the Glasses.

Certain kinds, and at least one period, of the literature of the
English-speaking world seem to belong to America. When an
Englishman thinks of the twenties, he'll think of Fitzgerald. If (I'm
told) you ask a Russian to name a 'collectivist' novelist in the West,
he'll name Dos Passos. And ask anyone to list the best humorous
writers in the English language, and he'll start with Mark Twain
and go on to Thurber and Perelman – an all-American roster, unless
he suddenly remembers Max Beerbohm. American wits – the
Woolcotts and Menckens – are not much known outside. Neither
are the home-spun philosophers – who is that Harry Golden man,
by the way? But at least two essayists are read, beginning with
Thoreau and making the logical descent in time, not quality, to E.
B. White.

Philip Toynbee has recently called Edmund Wilson the most
distinguished man of letters in the English-speaking world; and
many people, like myself, are more than satisfied to find the term
defined thus. Edmund Wilson sent the dusty blinds shuddering
up and flung the door wide on the scholarly preserves of English
criticism. He has made himself indispensable to English literature not by popularisation, but by bringing to criticism along
with scholarship a unique range of awareness of the contemporary world, psychological, political, linguistic, philosophical and
social. Under his scrutiny, a work of art does not fall apart; it

flies together in a new unity one would never have discovered for oneself. Kipling becomes as interesting as Dostoevsky; and the minor writings about the American Civil War become the best insight into that event one has ever read. Other American critics – Harry Levin, Lionel Trilling, Alfred Kazin, Leslie Fiedler and Harold Rosenberg – are almost indispensable too, along with the little magazines in which we first read them. And the only English-writing woman who has an international reputation in literary criticism is, of course, Mary McCarthy; her bitchy brilliance is enjoyed far beyond the confines of the literati and their appreciation of her integrity and erudition.

To us it certainly seems due to the existence of little magazines and the good commercial magazines that America has produced such outstanding short-story writers. I suppose Poe began it, followed by Sherwood Anderson, but the new life given to the short story in the New World started, so far as we are concerned, with the early stories of Hemingway. Whatever we think about his later novels, these stories put him up there with de Maupassant and Chekhov. O. Henry is half-forgotten, but still they come: very different, very brilliant – from Eudora Welty and Katherine Anne Porter to Bernard Malamud, Flannery O'Connor, John Updike and James Purdy.

The giants T. S. Eliot and Ezra Pound have long been appropriated by English-language poetry in general, and one almost forgets that they belong to America.

One is inclined to forget, too, that America and not England shares with France the break with poetic tradition that came about with Baudelaire and Poe just over a hundred years ago, and resulted in what has been known since, in all its various experiments and movements, as modern poetry. America has produced some important poets in this 'tradition of the new' (the phrase of critic Harold Rosenberg) that is partly an American achievement, but often it is its curiously original offshoots, like Marianne Moore, that seem particularly interesting to us. Poetry means something to the few, everywhere in the world; and even among those few, there are more individual blind spots than in the appreciation of any other form of writing – I know that to me Whitman is a garrulous bore; there are some who think of American poetry as Ogden Nash, or at most, e. e. cummings. But out of a catholic admiration for the various voices of Hart Crane, Robert Frost, William Carlos Williams, Wallace Stevens, Louise Bogan, Theodore Roethke, Archibald MacLeish, John Crowe Ransom, Elizabeth Bishop, Allen Ginsberg and Kenneth Rexroth – to name some of the poets most of us know – we have come increasingly to regard Robert Lowell as the most splendidly gifted poet writing in America now, and for a long time.

Poised against the Mayflower is the slave ship.

William Carlos Williams's image (I use the word in the legitimate, poetic sense, this time) posits a balance between two forces – a balance that American writers accepted long before Congress, and, indeed, beyond the way that the law and legislation ever can. The question of this balance, implying as it does the *necessity of the one force for the other*, is one of the themes in American writing that mean most to non-Americans. Not 'taken up', but integral to the being of some of the best American writers; through their writings it has been clear to us rather sooner than to Americans that this theme was not just Southern writing, dealing with a geographically and politically defined region, but with a region of the human condition. All the white world, through the ramifications of history, shares the white man's guilt before, and fear of, the black man. All the black world shares the black man's humiliation by, and resentment towards, the white man. That is why the cult of *négritude* in literature (invented by the Martiniquais poet Aimé Césaire and developed by Negroes in French-speaking Africa) reached English culture through the writings of American blacks, far from their origins in Africa; and that is also why the most profound attempt to draw up the account and present the balance between white man and black still comes from America, although most of Africa has found its freedom and its voice. William Faulkner, Richard Wright, Carson McCullers, Harper Lee, Langston Hughes, Ralph

Ellison – in them we find the equivocalities, the contradictions, the whole emotional and moral muddle of colour; in James Baldwin we have terrifying sense made of it all. His is not 'Negro writing'. It is perhaps the end of 'Negro writing' for good. It takes it to the point where a man is stripped of all kicks, kindness, rejection, patronage, and takes his identity as a man – or nothing.

Among American themes we are naturally drawn to those that touch chillingly or illuminatingly on the conditions of life that we have in common with Americans. Materialism, that big, glittering fake that we've all had come apart in our hands, may have reached its apotheosis in America, but American writers have matched this by ferociously picking up the jagged pieces as other writers have not done. This, for grown-ups if not for the university students all over the world who have *Tender is the Night* stuffed in their pockets, is surely the source of our admiration for Scott Fitzgerald, who, if he thought the rich had special voices, showed that they end up calling in a void. No writer has handled the loneliness and aliena-tion concomitant with a materialist society as Nathanael West did in *Miss Lonelyhearts* and *The Day of the Locust*. The truculent and unsqueamish honesty of Saul Bellow's *Henderson, the Rain King*, Nabokov's *Lolita*, and Joseph Heller's magnificent *Catch-22* last year, find no comparison in contemporary English writing, and this last book can only be matched by that extraordinary novel out of Germany, Günter Grass's *The Tin Drum*.

Like Grass's Oscar, Heller's Captain Yossarian is a kind of Last Man – a sum total of humanness ('humanity' is the wrong word; 'humanity' is one of the big abstractions they're up against) in a world where men have imprisoned themselves. The law of supply and demand grills and drills them, God is a searchlight turned on now and then by the jailers in the observation tower, and the only cry that goes up is not '*Ecce homo!*' but 'Why me?'

Captain Yossarian, a bombardier, opposes this world by making the extraordinary decision 'to live forever, or die in the attempt'. It is a splendid battle cry on the side of life; it recognises the ultimate enemy, come peace or war, in *Catch-22* – the clause that 'fixes' you so that you can't win.

There was only one catch, and that was Catch-22, which specified that a concern for one's own safety in the face of dangers that were real and immediate was the process of a rational mind. Orr was crazy and could be grounded. All he had to do was ask; and as soon as he did, he would no longer be crazy and would have to fly more missions. Orr would be crazy to fly more missions and sane if he didn't, but if he was sane he had to fly them. If he flew them he was crazy and didn't have to: but if he didn't want to he was sane and had to. Yossarian was moved very deeply by the absolute simplicity of this clause of Catch-22 and let out a respectful whistle.

This is Yossarian's first encounter with the Catch, but he continues to run head-on against it, not only in his struggle with authority in the person of Colonel Cathcart, who keeps putting up the number of missions in a tour of duty, in order to win promotion for himself on the ground, but also in his experience of big business, in the person of the pilot turned entrepreneur, Milo Minderbinder. Milo starts a 'syndicate' to supply the squadron with delicacies bought in job lots all over the world and flown to Pianosa, off the Italian coast, in the squadron's planes and those of other outfits pressed into the syndicate. Milo gets so rich and deal-drunk that he ends up accepting a reasonable offer from the Germans – cost plus 6 per cent for undertaking on their behalf to bomb his own squadron's airfield with its own planes.

Yossarian survives Cathcart, Minderbinder and many more, and on the last page is about to attempt a getaway to Sweden. A friend asks:

> 'How do you feel, Yossarian?'
>
> 'Fine. No, I'm very frightened.'
>
> 'That's good,' said Major Danby. 'It proves you're still alive. It won't be fun.'
>
> Yossarian started out. 'Yes it will . . .'
>
> 'You'll have to jump.'
>
> 'I'll jump.'

Yossarian jumps. The fear; the aliveness; the jump – the first two are the situation, the last the necessity that we all recognise and that few writers anywhere have tackled, none with the wit and vitality of Heller.

Beat writing is the American writer's other answer to a life that harries and cheats all of us, Americans and non-Americans alike. But beat writing itself, in spite of the physical free-ranging of the characters it deals with, is curiously lacking in the vigour and demand that really make the rest of us sit up. Beat books remain a kind of spirito-literary Esperanto, in which no real spiritual revolution could find expression.

Ever since Baudelaire adopted Poe for the French, non-Americans have differed from Americans in their enthusiasm for certain writers, and I think that it is most usually the theme rather than the individual quality of the writer that decides this. The name of Thomas Wolfe, for instance, is likely to bring to the eyes of a non-American the polite gaze that is produced by mention of a book that one ought to have read; or worse, that one was unable to finish. Though *A Death in the Family* has its following, many people produce the gaze for Agee, too. The preoccupation of these writers with childhood origins, the womb and nest of their personalities, is something that we find wearisome, however (for me, in the case of Agee) exquisitely accurate the findings may be. This obsessively personal quality of some American writing is suspect – whether it has broad, Whitmanesque overtones, or tends to the domestic cosiness that, alas, is creeping into the writing of John Updike, or the shrine-cosiness that now encloses J. D. Salinger.

Who but an American could have written *Advertisements for Myself*? Or, having written it, would have given it that title? Even Norman Mailer begins to show that the fatal flaw in his strong but flawed talent may be this obsessive turning in on himself, a rending apart if not a contemplation of the navel. If he is in fact attempting to be America's first existentialist writer, this tendency points to the unlikelihood that he will succeed. Self-obsession rules out the explicit moral clarity demanded by an existentialist approach; it even rules out the dispassion needed for that existentialist offshoot, a sense of the 'absurd'.

We turn away from inspired self-celebration not in the same way as from beat Esperanto, but nevertheless restlessly. This inner restlessness, born of our times rather than ourselves, looks back to the moral isolation of Melville's Billy Budd and Captain Ahab, and finds its expression in its own events and time, in the bizarre, awful, funny, cruel, crazy lives of Joseph Heller's Captain Yossarian and Günter Grass's dwarf with the tin drum. These are the means by which the *geist* of contemporary life seems to be brutally best invoked. This is why, as a writer as well as a reader, I must admit that in a year that brought from America both the hollow-eyed beauty of Katherine Anne Porter's *Ship of Fools*, as uncompromising, in its classic, profoundly disillusioned way, as Heller's book, I would rather have written *Catch-22*.

1963

A Bolter and the Invincible Summer

My writing life began long before I left school, and I began to leave school (frequently) long before the recognised time came, so there is no real demarcation, for me, between school and 'professional' life. The quotes are there because I think of professional life as something one enters by way of an examination, not as an obsessional occupation like writing for which you provide your own, often extraordinary or eccentric, qualifications as you go along. And I'm not flattered by the idea of being presented with a 'profession', *honoris causa*; every honest writer or painter wants to achieve the impossible and needs no minimum standard laid down by an establishment such as a profession.

This doesn't mean that I think a writer doesn't need a good education in general, and that I don't wish I had had a better one. But maybe my own regrets arise out of the common impulse to find a justification, outside the limits of one's own talent, for the limits of one's achievement.

I was a bolter, from kindergarten age, but unlike most small children rapidly accustoming their soft, round selves to the sharp angles of desks and discipline, I went on running away from school, year after year. I was a day scholar at a convent in Springs, the Transvaal gold-mining town where we lived, and when I was little I used to hide until I heard the hive of voices start up 'Our Father' at prayers, and then I would walk out of the ugly iron gates and spend the morning on the strip of open veld that lay between the township where the school was and the township where my home was. I remember catching white butterflies there, all one summer morning, until, in the quiet when I had no shadow, I heard the school bell, far away, clearly, and I knew I could safely appear at home for lunch. When I was older I used to take refuge for hours in the lavatory block, waiting in the atmosphere of Jeyes' Fluid for my opportunity to escape. By then I no longer lived from moment to moment, and could not enjoy the butterflies; the past, with the act of running away contained in it, and the future, containing discovery and punishment, made freedom impossible; the act of seizing it was merely a desperate gesture.

What the gesture meant, I don't know. I managed my school work easily, and among the girls of the class I had the sort of bossy vitality that makes for popularity; yet I was overcome, from time to time, by what I now can at least label as anxiety states. Speculation about their cause hasn't much place here, which is lucky, for the people who were around me then are still alive. Autobiography can't be written until one is old, can't hurt anyone's feelings, can't be sued for libel, or, worse, contradicted.

There is just one curious aspect of my bolting that seems worth mentioning because it reveals a device of the personality that, beginning at that very time, perhaps, as a dream-defence, an escape, later became the practical subconscious cunning that enabled me to survive and grow in secret while projecting a totally different, camouflage image of myself. I ran away from school; yet there was another school, the jolly, competitive, thrillingly loyal, close-knit world of schoolgirl books, to which I felt that I longed to belong. (At one time I begged to go to boarding school, believing, no doubt, that I should find it there.) Of course, even had it existed, that *School Friend* world would have been the last place on earth for me. I should have found there, far more insistently, the walls, the smell of serge and floor polish, the pressure of uniformity and the tyranny of bell-regulated time that set off revolt and revulsion in me. What I did not know – and what a child never knows – is that there is more to the world than what is offered to him; more choices than those presented to him; more kinds of people than those (the only ones he knows) to which he feels but dares not admit he does not belong. I thought I *had* to accept school and all the attitudes there that reflected the attitudes of home; therefore, in order to be a person I had to have *some* sort of picture of a school that would be acceptable to me; it didn't seem possible to live without it. Stevie Smith once wrote that all children should be told of the possibility of committing suicide, to console them in case they believed there was no way out of the unbearable; it would be less dramatic but far more consoling if a child could be told that there is an aspect of himself he *does not know is permissible.*

The conclusion my bolting school drew from the grown-ups around me was that I was not the studious type and simply should be persuaded to reconcile myself to the minimum of learning. In our small town many girls left school at fifteen or even before. Then, after a six-week course at the local commercial college, a girl was ready for a job as a clerk in a shop or in the offices of one of the gold mines which had brought the town into being. And the typewriter itself merely tapped a mark-time for the brief season of glory, self-assertion and importance that came with the engagement party, the pre-nuptial linen 'shower', and culminated not so much in the wedding itself as in the birth, not a day sooner than nine months and three weeks later, of the baby. There wasn't much point in a girl keeping her head stuck in books anyway; even if she chose to fill the interim with one of the occupations that carried a slightly higher prestige, and were vaguely thought of as artistic – teaching tap-dancing, the piano, or 'elocution'.

I suppose I must have been marked out for one of these, because, although I had neither talent nor serious interest in drumming my toes, playing Czerny, or rounding my vowels, I enjoyed using them all as material in my talent for showing off. As I grew towards adolescence I stopped the home concerts and contented myself with mimicking, for the entertainment of one group of my parents' friends, other friends who were not present. It did not seem to strike those who were that, in their absence, they would change places with the people they were laughing at; or perhaps it did, I do them an injustice, and they didn't mind.

All the time it was accepted that I was a candidate for home-dressmaking or elocution whom there was no point in keeping at school too long, I was reading and writing not in secret, but as one does, openly, something that is not taken into account. It didn't occur to anyone else that these activities were connected with learning, so why should it have occurred to me? And although I fed on the attention my efforts at impersonation brought me, I felt quite differently about any praise or comment that came when my stories were published in the children's section of a Sunday paper. While I was terribly proud to see my story in print – for only in print did it become 'real', did I have proof of the miracle whereby the thing created has an existence of its own – I had a jealous instinct to keep this activity of mine from the handling that would pronounce it 'clever' along with the mimicry and the home concerts. It was the beginning of the humble arrogance that writers and painters have, knowing that it is hardly likely that they will ever do anything really good, and not wanting to be judged by standards that will accept anything less. Is this too high-falutin' a motive to attribute to a twelve-year-old child? I don't think so. One can have a generalised instinct towards the unattainable long before one has actually met with it. When, not many years later, I read *Un Cœur simple* or *War and Peace* – Oh, I knew this was it, without any guidance from the list of the World's Hundred Best Books that I once tried to read through!

I started writing at nine, because I was surprised by a poem I produced as a school exercise. The subject prescribed was 'Paul

Kruger', and although an item of earliest juvenilia, in view of what has happened between people like myself and our country since then, I can't resist quoting, just for the long-untasted patriotic flavour:

> Noble in heart,
> Noble in mind,
> Never deceitful,
> Never unkind . . .

It was the dum-de-de-dum that delighted me rather than the sentiments or the subject. But soon I found that what I really enjoyed was making up a story, and that this was more easily done without the restrictions of dum-de-de-dum. After that I was always writing something, and from the age of twelve or thirteen, often publishing. My children's stories were anthropomorphic, with a dash of the Edwardian writers' Pan-cult paganism as it had been shipped out to South Africa in Kenneth Grahame's books, though already I used the background of mine dumps and veld animals that was familiar to me, and not the European one that provided my literary background, since there were no books about the world I knew. I wrote my elder sister's essays when she was a student at the Witwatersrand University, and kept up a fair average for her. I entered an essay in the literary section of the Eisteddfod run by the Welsh community in Johannesburg and bought with the prize chit *War and Peace*, *Gone with the Wind*, and an Arthur Ransome.

I was about fourteen then, and a happy unawareness of the strange combination of this choice is an indication of my reading. It was appetite rather than taste, that I had; yet while it took in indiscriminately things that were too much for me, the trash tended to be crowded out and fall away. Some of the books I read in my early teens puzzle me, though. Why Pepys's *Diary*? And what made me plod through *The Anatomy of Melancholy*? Where did I hear of the existence of these books? (That list of the World's One Hundred Best, maybe.) And once I'd got hold of something like Burton, what made me go on from page to page? I think it must have been because although I didn't understand all that I was reading, and what I did understand was remote from my experience in the way that easily assimilable romance was not, the half-grasped words dealt with the world of ideas, and so confirmed the recognition, somewhere, of that part of myself that I did not know was permissible.

All the circumstances and ingredients were there for a small-town prodigy, but, thank God, by missing the encouragement and practical help usually offered to 'talented' children, I also escaped the dwarf status that is clapped upon the poor little devils before their time (if it ever comes). It did not occur to anyone that if I wanted to try to write I ought to be given a wide education in order to develop my powers and to give me some cultural background. But this neglect at least meant that I was left alone. Nobody came gawping into the private domain that was no dream-world, but, as I grew up, the scene of my greatest activity and my only discipline. When schooldays finally petered out (I had stopped running away, but various other factors had continued to make attendance sketchy) I did have some sort of show of activity that passed for my life in the small town. It was so trivial that I wonder how it can have passed, how family or friends can have accepted that any young person could expend vitality at such a low hum. It was never decided what I should 'take up' and so I didn't have a job. Until, at twenty-two, I went to the University, I led an outward life of sybaritic meagreness that I am ashamed of. In it I did not one thing that I wanted wholeheartedly to do; in it I attempted or gratified nothing (outside sex) to try out my reach, the measure of aliveness in me. My existential self was breathing but inert, like one of those unfortunate people who has had a brain injury in a motor accident and lies unhearing and unseeing, though he will eat when food comes and open his eyes to a light. I played golf, learned to drink gin with the RAF pupil pilots from the nearby air station, and took part in amateur theatricals to show recognisable signs of life to the people around me. I even went to first aid and nursing classes because this was suggested as an 'interest' for me; it did not matter to me what I did, since I could not admit that there was nothing, in the occupations and diversions offered to me, that really did interest me, and I was not sure – the only evidence was in books – that anything else was possible.

I am ashamed of this torpor nevertheless, setting aside what I can now see as probable reasons for it, the careful preparation for it that my childhood constituted. I cannot understand why I did not free myself in the most obvious way, leave home and small town and get myself a job somewhere. No conditioning can excuse the absence of the simple act of courage that would resist it. My only overt rejection of my matchbox life was the fact that, without the slightest embarrassment or conscience, I let my father keep me. Though the needs provided for were modest, he was not a rich man. One thing at least I would not do, apparently – I would not work for the things I did not want. And the camouflage image of myself as a dilettantish girl, content with playing grown-up games at the end of my mother's apron strings – at most a Bovary in the making – made this possible for me.

When I was fifteen I had written my first story about adults and had sent it off to a liberal weekly that was flourishing in South Africa at the time. They published it. It was about an old man who is out of touch with the smart, prosperous life he has secured for his sons, and who experiences a moment of human recognition where he least expects it – with one of their brisk young wives who is so unlike the wife he remembers. Not a bad theme, but expressed with the respectable bourgeois sentiment which one would expect. That was in 1939, two months after the war had broken out, but in the years that followed the stories that I was writing were not much influenced by the war. It occupied the news bulletins on the radio, taking place a long way off, in countries I had never seen; later, when I was seventeen or eighteen, there were various boyfriends who went away to Egypt and Italy and sent back coral jewellery and leather bags stamped with a sphinx.

Oddly enough, as I became engaged with the real business of learning how to write, I became less prompt about sending my efforts off to papers and magazines. I was reading Maupassant, Chekhov, Maugham and Lawrence, now, also discovering O. Henry,

Katherine Anne Porter and Eudora Welty, and the stories in *Partisan Review*, *New Writing* and *Horizon*. Katherine Mansfield and Pauline Smith, although one was a New Zealander, confirmed for me that my own 'colonial' background provided an experience that had scarcely been looked at, let alone thought about, except as a source of adventure stories. I had read 'The Death of Ivan Ilyich' and 'The Child of Queen Victoria'; the whole idea of what a story could do, be, swept aside the satisfaction of producing something that found its small validity in print. From time to time I sent off an attempt to one of the short-lived local politico-literary magazines – meant chiefly as platforms for liberal politics, they were the only publications that published poetry and stories outside the true romance category – but these published stories were the easy ones. For the other I had no facility whatever, and they took months, even years, to cease changing shape before I found a way of getting hold of them in my mind, let alone nailing the words down around them. And then most of them were too long, or too outspoken (not always in the sexual sense) for these magazines. In a fumbling way that sometimes slid home in an unexpected strike, I was looking for what people meant but didn't say, not only about sex, but also about politics and their relationship with the black people among whom we lived as people live in a forest among trees. So it was that I didn't wake up to Africans and the shameful enormity of the colour bar through a youthful spell in the Communist Party, as did some of my contemporaries with whom I share the rejection of white supremacy, but through the apparently esoteric speleology of doubt, led by Kafka rather than Marx. And the 'problems' of my country did not set me writing; on the contrary, it was learning to write that sent me falling, falling through the surface of 'the South African way of life'.

It was about this time, during a rare foray into the nursery bohemia of university students in Johannesburg, that I met a boy who believed I was a writer. Just that; I don't mean he saw me as Chosen for the Holy Temple of Art, or any presumptuous mumbo-jumbo of that kind. The cosmetic-counter sophistication that I hopefully wore to disguise my stasis in the world I knew and my uncertainty of the possibility of any other, he ignored as so much rubbish. This aspect of myself, that everyone else knew, he did not; what he recognised was my ignorance, my clumsy battle to chip my way out of shell after shell of ready-made concepts and make my own sense of life. He was often full of scorn, and jeered at the way I was going about it; but he *recognised the necessity*. It was through him, too, that I roused myself sufficiently to insist on going to the University; not surprisingly, there was opposition to this at home, since it had been accepted so long that I was not the studious type, as the phrase went. It seemed a waste, spending money on a university at twenty-two (surely I should be married soon?); it was suggested that (as distinct from the honourable quest for a husband) the real reason why I wanted to go was to look for men. It seems to me now that this would have been as good a reason as any. My one preoccupation outside the world of ideas was men, and I should have been prepared to claim my right to the one as valid as the other.

But my freedom did not come from my new life at university; I was too old, in many ways, had already gone too far, on my own scratched tracks, for what I might once have gained along the tarmac. One day a poet asked me to lunch. He was co-editor of yet another little magazine that was then halfway through the dozen issues that would measure its life. He had just published a story of mine and, like many editors when the contributor is known to be a young girl, was curious to meet its author. He was the Afrikaans poet and playwright Uys Krige, who wrote in English as well, had lived in France and Spain, spoke five languages, was familiar with their literature, and translated from three. He had been a swimming instructor on the Riviera, a football coach somewhere else, and a war correspondent with the International Brigade in Spain.

When the boy (that same boy) heard that I was taking the train into Johannesburg for this invitation – I still lived in Springs – he said: 'I wouldn't go, if I were you, Nadine.'

'For Pete's sake, why not?'

'Not unless you're prepared to change a lot of things. You may not feel the same, afterwards. You may never be able to go back.'

'What on *earth* are you talking about?' I made fun of him: 'I'll take the train back.'

'No, once you see what a person like that is like, you won't be able to stand your ordinary life. You'll be miserable. So don't go unless you're prepared for this.'

The poet was a small, sun-burned, blond man. While he joked, enjoyed his food, had an animated discussion with the African waiter about the origin of the name of a fruit, and said for me some translations of Lorca and Eluard, first in Afrikaans and then, because I couldn't follow too well, in English, he had the physical brightness of a fisherman. It was true; I had never met anyone like this being before. I have met many poets and writers since, sick, tortured, pompous, mousy; I know the morning-after face of Apollo. But that day I had a glimpse of – not some spurious 'artist's life', but, through the poet's person, the glint of his purpose – what we are all getting at, Camus's 'invincible summer' that is there to be dug for in man beneath the grey of suburban life, the numbness of repetitive labour, and the sucking mud of politics.

Oh yes – not long after, a story of mine was published in an anthology, and a second publisher approached me with the offer to publish a collection. The following year I at last sent my stories where I had never been – across the seas to England and America. They came back to me in due course, in hard covers with my name printed on the coloured jacket. There were reviews, and, even more astonishing, there was money. I was living alone in Johannesburg by then, and was able to pay the rent and feed both myself and the baby daughter I had acquired. These things are a convenient marker for the beginning of a working life. But mine really began that day at lunch. I see the poet occasionally. He's older now, of course; a bit seamed with disappointments, something of a political victim, since he doesn't celebrate his people's politics or the white man's colour bar in general. The truth isn't always beauty, but the hunger for it is.

1963

Censored, Banned, Gagged

Peter Abrahams, Harry Bloom, Hans Hofmeyer, Daphne Rooke, Ezekiel Mphahlele, and I myself are some of the South African writers who share the experience of having had books banned in our own country. Why were our books banned? If one were to judge by the monotonous insistence with which the necessity to protect pure young minds from 'cheap filth', etc., was invoked as justification for the new censorship bill in recent parliamentary debates in South Africa, one would conclude that these books must be pornographic. In fact, of the six writers I have mentioned, none deals sensationally or with more than passing frankness with sex, and two (in those books of theirs which were banned) do not, by reason of their subjects, touch upon sexual relations at all. Although the Minister of the Interior and the Nationalist Members of Parliament never mention political reasons for censorship, these books, and almost without exception *all* those books by South African writers which have been banned, have been banned for a political reason: non-conformity with the picture of South African life as prescribed and proscribed by apartheid.

I think I am the only one who has ever been favoured with an explanation for a book banning. I was informed that the official attitude to my second novel – banned in the Penguin edition in which it would have reached its widest public in my country – was that the book 'undermines the traditional race policy of the Republic'.[1]

That was the truth, for once, the truth behind pious concern

---

1 My latest novel, *Occasion for Loving* (London: Gollancz; New York: Viking, 1963), was held under embargo for a while, but has now been released; its fate, once it is published in a cheaper edition, probably will be the same as that of the earlier novel. [In fact *Occasion for Loving* was not ultimately banned; possibly because, amongst other things, it dealt with the failure of an inter-racial love affair.]

for young minds: it's not four-letter words that menace them, but the danger that they may begin to think, and, under the stimulus of certain books, come up with some doubts about the way their lives are ordered. The minds of people who can afford five shillings for a paper-cover edition of a book are apparently considered more tender (or more susceptible?) than those of people who pay eighteen-and-six for a hard-cover edition, since some books are banned in the paper-cover edition only. This is not as illogical as it seems; it assumes that more affluent people (affluent = white) are likely to be living too easy to want to see any change in the 'traditional race policy of the Republic' whereas poorer people (poorer = black) are likely to be encouraged by any suggestion that it is possible to 'undermine' it.

The machinery of censorship which has served to ban all these books has now been superseded by a more stringent, sin-mongering, and all-devouring system under the new censorship laws, promulgated in the Publications and Entertainments Act of 1963. Among the defects of the old machinery – from the point of view of a state evidently bent on introducing thought-control – was that it did not provide for internal censorship (that is, of publications produced within the Republic itself) other than in respect of pornography. This is not quite such a gap as it sounds; English-language publishers in South Africa are few, and they stick mainly to graceful, gift-book Africana and adventure yarns; the thriving Afrikaans publishing houses draw both authors and readers from that section of the community which loyally supports the government and, so far,[2] has been unlikely to produce anything that undermines any government policy. At any rate, whatever is published within the country will now be subject to censorship along with whatever is imported, and the decisions as to what should be banned and what may be read will

2 Some of the younger Afrikaans writers are beginning to feel stifled by a literary tradition that ignores the glaring realities of our country's life. If they are moved to write books that do not conform to the tradition of Afrikaans writing, who is to publish them? Afrikaans is not spoken outside South Africa, the European Protectorates, and the Rhodesias.

be made by a Publications Control Board, presently to be set up
by the Minister of the Interior.

The Board will consist of nine members, all appointed by the
Minister, of whom not fewer than six shall be 'persons having special
knowledge of arts, language, and literature, *or* [my italics] the administration of justice.' The chairman (Minister-designated, again) must
be one of the 'special knowledge' members, but a quorum is constituted by only four members and, in the absence of the chairman and
vice-chairman, an ordinary member may preside. Special committees can be set up to deal with the work of the Board – which will
be prodigious, to say the least, since it covers films, plays, 'objects',
magazines, etc., as well as books. A committee is to consist of one
member of the Board (not specified that this should be one with
'special knowledge') and at least two other persons appointed as
members from a panel designated by the Minister. So that, in fact,
whether South Africans will be permitted or not to read any particular piece of literature can and frequently will be decided by three
persons, all appointed by the Minister, not one of whom need have
even the dubious qualification, where literary judgement is required,
of 'special knowledge' of the 'administration of justice'.

There will be no representation whatsoever on the Board or
committees outside the Minister's personal choice; but any person
may, at any time, upon payment of a nominal fee, submit for the
consideration of the Board a publication which *he* personally thinks
ought to be banned. Under the old system there was a board of
censors which examined books referred to it by Customs, Post
Office, or other officials under various relevant Acts, including
the Suppression of Communism Act; but the old Board was not
a Grundy ombudsman to whom, as well, cranks, crackpots, and
political informers could take their grudges, confident, on the
incredibly wide grounds on which there is provision for them to
claim offence, of a hearing.

A publication is deemed 'undesirable' if it, or any part of it, is

indecent or obscene or is offensive or harmful to public morals; is
blasphemous or offensive to the religious convictions or feelings of

any section of the inhabitants of the Republic; *brings any section of the inhabitants into ridicule or contempt; is harmful to the relations between any sections of the inhabitants*; is prejudicial to the safety of the State, the general welfare, or the peace and good order.

The definition of what may be considered indecent, obscene, offensive or harmful to public morals includes the portrayal of:

murder, suicide, death, horror, cruelty, fighting, brawling, ill-treatment, lawlessness, gangsterism, robbery, crime, the technique of crimes and criminals, tippling, drunkenness, trafficking in or addiction to drugs, smuggling, sexual intercourse, prostitution, promiscuity, white-slaving, licentiousness, lust, passionate love scenes, sexual assault, rape, sodomy, masochism, sadism, sexual bestiality, abortion, change of sex, night life, physical poses, nudity, scant or inadequate dress, divorce, marital infidelity, adultery, illegitimacy, *human or social deviation or degeneracy*, or any other similar or related phenomenon.

My italics are there as a reminder that the racial laws of the country, and its traditional race policies, are such that social as well as sexual intercourse between white and coloured people could be interpreted as 'human or social deviation or degeneracy'; and that, in the practical and ideological pursuit of apartheid, *any* mixing between the races is considered 'harmful', and criticism of or satire on this curious belief could easily be construed, by those who uphold it, as 'ridicule and contempt'.

In determining whether a book should be censored or not, 'no regard shall be had to the purpose' of the author; which means that no distinction can be drawn between *Ulysses* and *What the Butler Saw in the Boudoir*, or between a revolutionary pamphlet advocating the bloody overthrow of the white man and a serious study of such aspirations. There is a provision that the Board may exempt, at its pleasure to recall the exemption at any time, a publication of a 'technical, scientific, or professional nature *bona fide* intended for the advancement of or for use in any particular profession or branch of arts, literature, or science'. But how the Board will go about deciding what is *bona fide* and what is not, is not stated.

Much has been made of the concession of the right of appeal to the courts, not included in the Act in its earlier forms (there have been three), but now granted. An author now has the right of appeal to the Supreme Court after his book has been banned by the Board, but he must lodge notice of the appeal within thirty days of the Board's decision. As a book may be banned, at the instigation of anyone, at any time (maybe months or years after publication) and the notice of its banning is not communicated to the author but merely published in the *Government Gazette*, it could easily happen that the thirty days might elapse before the author became aware of the ban. And a Supreme Court action is an extremely costly privilege by means of which one is allowed, at last, to defend a work which has already been condemned without trial.

The censorship system applies to magazines and periodicals as well as books, of course, and also to exhibitions, films, plays and entertainment of any kind. (The long list of special restrictions on films includes any scene that 'depicts in an offensive manner intermingling of white and non-white persons'.) The daily and weekly press, both opposition and government, is exempt because the Newspaper Press (Proprietors) Union of South Africa accepted a 'code' – self-censorship responsible to their own organisation – as the lesser evil, when confronted with the alternative of government censorship. The radical left-wing and liberal publications – weeklies, fortnightlies, and monthlies – have been successfully decimated (the last may have disappeared by the time this is in print) without the help of the new Act, by the simple means of making them staffless – first under the Suppression of Communism Act, by prohibiting all people banned under the Act, or who were even only members of an organisation suppressed by it, from association with any organisation which 'in any manner prepares, compiles, prints, publishes, or disseminates' a newspaper, magazine, pamphlet, handbill or poster; second, under the General Law Amendment Act, 1962 (commonly called the Sabotage Act), by prohibiting five journalists from in any way carrying on their profession.

The special provisions governing paperbacks are making booksellers wish they had become bakers instead. For example, the importation of paperbacks that cost the bookseller less than 2s. 6d. each is forbidden. This piece of legislation was no doubt genuinely intended to keep out trash; but it failed to take into account that thousands of reputable books, including classics, reference, and handbooks prescribed for schools and universities, are imported in paperback editions. If the bookseller wants to import any particular book or series, he may apply, on payment of a fee, to have the Board examine it, decide whether it is 'undesirable' and, if not, grant him permission to import it. Similarly, exemptions may be granted in the case of books published by a specified publisher; or a specified class of publication from such a publisher; or if they deal with any specified subject. Of course, these blanket releases work t'other way about, too: blanket bans may be invoked for specified books, series, editions and publishers. As for magazines, presumably if one number were to be pronounced undesirable, either that particular number could be banned, or a blanket ban could descend on the magazine.

All the dreary legalese through which I have followed the writer's situation thus far belongs to the hot war of censorship. But there is also a cold war going on all the time, outside the statute books, and as it is likely to get colder and colder with the new Act, I should like to explain it. One hears a lot (quite rightly) about the effect the new internal censorship will have on South African (virtually, Afrikaans) publishers: how they will hesitate to publish if they feel there is any risk of banning, so prejudicing the chances of existing or aspirant writers who publish in the Republic. But this censorship cold war began long ago for writers with a wider public, that is abroad as well as in their own country, whose books are published in England and imported to South Africa as part of the literature of the English-speaking world.

South African booksellers are wary of books by serious South African writers who deal with the contemporary scene. Whatever the interest of the book, whatever the selling power of the author's name, the booksellers risk only very small orders, perhaps a third of what they know they could sell, because they fear to find themselves burdened with hundreds of copies of a book that may be banned either on arrival in the country, or later. (Some publishers ship copies on the understanding of return in the case of banning; others do not.) Publishers are afraid to risk advance publicity for the book in the Republic; the general idea is that it is better to have the book slip in quietly and sell modestly than to be unable to sell it at all. If the book is subsequently banned, the author has the satisfaction of knowing that at least it has had some chance to be read, if not widely. If it is not banned, its potential distribution and readership have been limited by the intimidation of censorship to an extent that, especially in the case of lesser-known writers, cannot easily be made up by subsequent sales. By the time the bookseller feels 'safe' to re-order (remember, anyone can submit the book to the Board at any time), interest in the book may well have died down.

Back to the hot war, now. As I have already indicated, not only censorship afflicts writing and writers in my country. So far as I know, only one author has been affected as yet by what one might call the Mutilation Act, one of the gagging provisions of the Sabotage Act. Tom Hopkinson – South African by adoption for a number of years – was obliged to remove from his autobiographical record of experience in Africa a statement by Chief Luthuli, who, like all banned persons, may not be quoted. Not a matter of much importance in this particular book, maybe; not enough to distort it seriously: but quite enough to establish the principle of mutilation of books through censorship. Enough to show the authors of non-fiction – the sociological, historical, and political studies, the analyses, reminiscences, and biographies – that they are no longer free to present as full a picture of South African life and thought as their subjects and talents can command. The balance has gone from the picture; and the truth, in direct proportion to what must be left out.

The links between this and the Sabotage Act are clear. Under the

Sabotage Act it may be considered a crime 'to further or encourage the achievement of any political aim, *including the bringing about of any social or economic change in the Republic*'. (As usual, my italics.) The gagging clauses of the Act make the incredible provisions whereby more than 102 people have been forbidden to make any communication whatsoever with the public, either in speech or in the written or quoted word. Among these people are twelve journalists and two or three creative writers – the number does not matter; so long as there were to be even one, this Act would provide an example of suppression of writers that far exceeds any restrictions suffered by any other profession. The gagged journalist and writers are prohibited from publishing *any writing whatever*, however remote from politics it might be. This means that Dennis Brutus, writing poetry, Alex La Guma, writing a novel while under twenty-four-hour house-arrest, cannot publish either.

Censored, banned, gagged – the writers of my country may be said to be well on the way to becoming a victimised group. They have resisted variously. So far as censorship is concerned, English-speaking writers began to oppose its growth several years ago, with vigour in the case of individuals, rather ponderously and timidly in the case of our only English-speaking writers' organisation, PEN. Nevertheless, PEN did submit to the Select Committee on the Publications and Entertainments Bill an excellent memorandum that probably had a mitigating effect on the form in which the Bill finally became an Act. With the exception of a few splendidly outspoken people, such as the poet Uys Krige, the Afrikaans writers seemed to feel that censorship was none of their business until the new Publications and Entertainments Act, with its provision for internal censorship, right here at home where their books are published, changed their minds for them. Once this happened, they began the familiar round of collecting signatures for protest, etc., with which the English-speaking writers were already so familiar, and which, alas, while in the combined effort may have softened the Act a little between its first draft and final form, did not, could not hope to succeed in getting it scrapped.

The attitude towards gagged writers and journalists is more complicated, because organisations and individuals in general are inclined to be frightened off by the fact that these are leftist[3] writers and journalists, some of them named Communists. The sad old paradox arises of those who will fight for the freedom to write what *they* want to write, but are not sure it really ought to be extended to other people who may want to write something different. Perhaps, like the Afrikaans writers, who thought censorship wouldn't touch them, people who keep silent on the subject of gagged writers will wake up, too late, to find that freedom is indivisible and that when professional freedom was withheld from one or two little-known leftist writers, it was lost to them, too. Individual writers and PEN have issued protests on behalf of gagged persons. The South African Society of Journalists is putting up a strong fight on behalf of the gagged journalists.

Within the small group of intellectuals in South Africa, writers represent an even smaller group; and for that reason perhaps the people of the country might be content to ignore what is happening to them.

But what of the readers? What of the millions, from university professors to children spelling out their first primers, for whom the free choice of books means the right to participate in the heritage of human thought, knowledge and imagination?

Yes, they still have a great many uncensored books to read, Shakespeare, Plato, Tolstoy, and many modern writers in world literature – though even the classics have been shown not to be immune from South African censorship (much of Zola; *Moll Flanders*; some of Maupassant as well as Marx); serious writers of all times and origins have been axed. But surely the people realise that no one can be well-read or well-informed or fitted to contribute fully to the culture and development of his own

---

3   An imprecise definition in South Africa, at the best of times. Randolph Vigne and Peter Hjul are members of the Liberal Party who were running a liberal fortnightly, as was its founder, Patrick Duncan, at the time he was put under ban – subsequently he went into exile in Basutoland, left the Liberal Party and aligned himself with the anti-Communist, militantly black nationalist Pan-Africanist Congress.

society in the democratic sense while he does not have absolutely free access to the ideas of his time as well as to the accumulated thought of the past, nor while, in particular, there are areas of experience in the life of his own society and country which, through censorship, are left out of his reading? It is interesting to note, in this context, that while the South African government is anxious to convince the world of its eagerness to raise to 'civilisation' the African people, it has at the same time largely suppressed the first proofs that some Africans have indeed already achieved complete emergence into the intellectual standards of the democratic world. Most of the writings of black South Africans who have recorded the contemporary experience of their people – including Peter Abrahams's autobiography, the literary essays of Ezekiel Mphahlele, the autobiographies of Alfred Hutchinson and Todd Matshikiza, and an anthology of African writing which included stories and poems of a number of black writers from South Africa – are banned. These books were written in English and they provide the major part of the only record, set down by talented and self-analytical people, of what black South Africans, who have no voice in parliament nor any say in the ordering of their life, think and feel about their lives and those of their fellow white South Africans. Can South Africa afford to do without these books?

And can South Africans in general boast of a 'literature' while, by decree, in their own country, it consists of *some* of the books written by its black and white, Afrikaans- and English-speaking writers?

1963

Great Problems in the Street

People who don't live in South Africa find it difficult to hold in their minds at once an image of the life lived by the banished, banned, harried and spied-upon active opponents of apartheid, and the juxtaposed image of life in the sun lived by a prosperous white population that does not care what happens so long as it goes on living pleasantly. Even those of us who do live here – once out of the country, the situation we have just left and to which we are about to return seems improbable. For the gap between the committed and the indifferent is a Sahara whose faint trails, followed by the mind's eye only, fade out in sand. The place is not on the map of human relations; but, like most unmapped areas, there is a coming and going that goes unrecorded; there is a meeting of eyes at points without a name; there is an exchange of silences between strangers crossing one another far from the witness of their own kind – once you are down there on your own two feet you find the ancient caravan trails connecting human destiny no matter how much distance a man tries to put between himself and the next man.

Of course, the committed know this – it is at the base of liberal and leftist politics, and most philosophies – but the indifferent don't, or won't. To them the desert seems absolutely foolproof, reassuringly impassable. Nothing can get to me through *that*, they are saying, when they turn to the sports page after a glance at the latest list of house arrests or banning orders. Those sort of people are black, or communist or something – they have nothing whatever to do with *me*, though I may be jostled among them in the street every day. If it happens to be a white person who has been arrested, the indifference may be enlivened by a spark of resentment – 'people like that, ratting on their own kind, they deserve all that's coming to them'.

Kindly and decent, within the strict limits of their 'own kind' (white, good Christians, good Jews, members of the country clubs – all upholders of the colour bar though not necessarily supporters of the Nationalist government), the indifferent do not want to extend that limit by so much as one human pulse reaching out beyond it. Where the pretty suburban garden ends, the desert begins. This 'security' measure brings about some queer situations when the indifferent stray into the company of a committed person, as it were by mistake. During the State of Emergency after Sharpeville, a friend who is a frequent visitor to my house was among those imprisoned without trial. A couple who had met him when dining with us, and had found him amusing and charming, heard about his arrest. (Newspapers were forbidden to publish the names of people taken into custody in this way.)

'Is it true that D— B— is in prison?'

'Yes, he was picked up last Thursday night.'

'But *why*? He seems such a fine person. I mean I couldn't imagine him doing anything wrong—'

'Do you think it's wrong for Africans to demonstrate against the pass laws?'

'Well, I mean, that's got to be put down, that's political agitation—'

'Yes, exactly. Well, D— B— thinks the pass laws are wrong and so, quite logically, since he is a fine person, he's prepared to do what he can to help Africans protest against them.'

How could the indifferent keep at a safe distance this man whom they had accepted and who was at once the same man who sat in prison, *nothing whatever to do with them*? The subject was dropped into the dark cupboard of questions that are not dealt with.

But it is not in private, drawing-room encounters that indifference meets commitment most openly. Nietzsche said, 'Great problems are in the street.' South Africa's problems are there, in the streets, in the tens of thousands of Africans going about their city work but not recognised as citizens, in the theatres and libraries and hotels into which the white people may turn, but the black people must pass by; in the countless laws, prejudices, 'traditions', fallacies, fears that regulate every move and glance where white and black move together through the city. The great problems are alive in the street, and it is in the street, too, that (until now) they have always been debated. The street has held both the flesh and the word. For the meeting-halls of African political movements have been the open spaces in the streets, in the townships and on the city's fringe, and progressive movements in general have used the City Hall steps in Johannesburg as a platform, and also as a final rallying-point in protest marches. In the townships or down in Fordsburg the supporters gathered close to hear Mandela or Tambo or Naicker speak, while the Special Branch took notes, and idlers and children hung about; in times of a campaign the crowd of supporters swelled enormously. At the City Hall steps at lunch-time speakers from the Congress of Democrats, the Liberal Party, or some other liberatory or progressive movement would stand among their placards with a small band of supporters. Slowly their numbers would grow; the pavements thicken with silent faces, black and white, office cleaners and executives, young students from the University and old bums from the Library Gardens. The antenna of an attendant police car would poke a shining whisker out of the traffic.

Probably the meetings in the townships will prove to have been the decisive ones in the future of this country, in the long run. But the meetings on the City Hall steps made the flesh and word of great problems curiously manifest because these meetings took place in the one place where black and white participated in them together. And they happened right in the middle of the daily life of the city, under the eyes of all those people who were going about their own business – which excluded, of course, things like the Extension of University Education Act (it provided the exact opposite; not extension but restriction of the universities, formerly part 'open', to whites only) or the Group Areas Act (it has enabled the government to move Africans, coloureds and Indians living or trading in areas declared white). Their children were white and would have no difficulty in getting into a university; they did not fall into any racial category affected by removals; these things had nothing to do with them. Yet they were confronted with them in the street, they read the posters on the way to pick up the latest kitchen gadget at the bargain basement, they paused a moment (another face showing among the dark and light faces in the crowd) or walked quickly past to the business lunch, carrying with them a snatch of the speaker's words like a torn streamer.

The atmosphere of these meetings hung about the city, an unease, after two o'clock. Like the more formal mass meetings called from time to time in the City Hall itself, at night, they sometimes ended in an ill-defined scuffle on the edge of the melting crowd: hooligans, in their blind and violent way giving vent to the resentment the city feels at being forced to admit the guilt and fear that lie under indifference.

The march through Johannesburg last year when the Sabotage Bill was introduced was the last for no one can say how long, since one of the restrictions imposed by the Bill itself was an end of gatherings on the City Hall steps and to protest demonstrations generally. The march was also one of the biggest there has ever been, and it drew a tension between marchers and onlookers that was an extraordinary experience. Assembling for a demonstration of this kind is always a rather foolish-making business: the individuals coming up awkwardly, craning about for the sight of friends; the shuffling and coming and going; the detachment of a figure from the watching crowd, and his sudden appearance beside you in the ranks – has a longing for freedom burst in him like a blood vessel? Is he a paid rowdy muscling in to break up the ranks? Is he merely one of those nameless, placeless pieces of city driftwood that are attracted to any stream of humanity going anywhere? Behind these nervous speculations is a fierce longing to seize the tendrils of impulse which are running, in spite of themselves, from the watchers; the desire of those within the ranks to pull on those feelers of awareness – insults, laughter, embarrassment – *anything* that offers a hold, a sign of life by which the onlookers might be drawn in to speak up for it.

On the day of that last march, as on other occasions, the onlookers let the hooligans speak for them. And this time, the last time before their mouths were stopped up once and for all by the accumulation of public safety bills, press bills, censorship bills, they let the hooligans speak in word and deed more uninhibitedly and wildly than ever. All the white man's battened-down fear of the consequences of the 'South African way of life' he has chosen poured out in a mess of infantile regression – senseless blows, rotten eggs, foul words. As the marchers went through the city – filling the width of the street, several thousand strong – these fell upon them at intervals. In between, there was the gaze of flat-dwellers and office workers looking down silently on the passing backs. When the procession passed an elegant first-floor restaurant, five well-dressed men came out on to the balcony, whiskies in hand, to watch. An equally well-dressed man walking near me broke the ranks. The five waved to him, but he stood there in the street, legs apart, palms up, and called: 'Why don't you come down here with us?'

They laughed, and one of them called back, 'You always were crazy, Reg.'

For a moment the eyes of the procession were on that balcony where the five men stood glass in hand; then the five turned and went in.

And so the last march came to its end. The meetings on Freedom Square ended long ago, with the banning of the African National Congress and subsequently the Pan-Africanist Congress, in 1960. The South African Communist Party has been banned since 1950. The Congress of Democrats is banned, too, and the Federation of South African Women, the Liberal Party and others are refused the special permission necessary, now, to hold meetings at the City Hall steps or at any other rallying point in the streets. The speakers who defended human rights against the attrition of one repressive apartheid measure after another, all committed to this over and above their varying political standpoints in the opposition – all are banned, in exile, or under house arrest. Even the posters of the newspapers will soon no longer provide any unwelcome reminders; those that are not closed down by the censorship bill will be guided by it. There is silence in the streets. The indifferent are left in peace. There is nothing to disturb them, now, but the detonations of saboteurs, and the hideous outbursts of secret society savagery.

1963

Notes of an Expropriator

I've never before thought of English (Scottish, Irish, Welsh) literature as something that didn't belong to me as much as to any Briton. It's quite a shock to be confronted with the old familiars – Hugh Lofting and Chaucer and Burton, Donne, the two Eliots, Lawrence, Greene, Braine and Wain – and be asked politely how they strike me, as if I were a foreigner being shown the crown jewels. I make no claim on your crown jewels; but growing up in South Africa with English as my mother tongue there was no other literature but yours for me to appropriate.

What has it meant to me? What less can I say than everything? From the day I learned to read, British writers provided my vision of the world; for it seemed, reading what living in that world was like, that I lived outside it – until later, when British literature introduced me to the world of ideas, and made me realise that to *this* our life belonged just as much as the life of Europe: the only difference was that so little had been thought about or written of our life in Africa.

Since I know no other language well enough to read what I want in the original, it was through British literature, as well, that I came to know other literatures. I got my Greek drama from Gilbert Murray. Constance Garnett brought me Dostoevsky and Tolstoy, Spender introduced me to Lorca, and even Petrarch was first discovered strangely Irished by Synge. It seems incongruous, now, to see myself lying in our dusty garden among the mine dumps, reading aloud:

> If my dark heart has any sweet thing it is turned away from me,
> and then farther off I see the great winds where I must be sailing.
> I see my good luck far away in the harbour, but my steersman is
> tired out, and the masts and the ropes on them are broken, and the
> beautiful lights where I would be always looking are quenched.

Why Synge? Well, why not? One of the freedoms of expropri-
ating a literature from 6,000 miles away is that you do not take
along with it any of the deadweight of a traditional approach – I
was not coerced in my tastes by the kind of education, libraries,
journals, conversation, class distinction and even ancient buildings
which surround a literature in the country and among the people of
its origin. Once you had got through Pooh and Dr Dolittle, Alice
and the Water Babies, you were a bibliophagist on the loose. The
local library had a steady traffic in novels whose uniform scuffed
municipal binding was an honest indication of their unvarying
content. But there were some books on the shelves that did not
go out from one year to the next; one day, if all the Cronins were
bespoken, you might find yourself obliged to try Samuel Butler. By
such haphazard means great cracks appear in the washable plastic
of daily life. To be literate is to be someone whose crucially formative experience may come just as well from certain books as from
events. I know that until I was at least twenty nothing and no one
influenced me as much as certain poets and writers. Most of them
were British.

These writers who first set your puny ego roughly on its own feet
are usually the ones you don't remember. One 'forgets' them in the
self-preservation of letting old ties fall away, and one doesn't have
to feel guilty about it, the way one does over old friends. What the
writers did for you has long since become your own, exists perhaps,
unrecognisable, somewhere in that rock-bottom on which the coal-
flower of self proliferates. Lawrence was the one I can't pretend to
forget: *Sons and Lovers*, and the stories, and the beast and flower
poems. All that was mealy-mouthed, genteelly hypocritical and
petty respectable – the whole smug suet of white provincialism
that covered my seventeen years, swaddling and shroud in one –
became something to kick flying. What other writer anywhere
could instil the confidence of a minority of one as Lawrence could?
And it was not only rebellion, it was also assertion of the splendour of everything that I was already intoxicatingly drawn to – the
claims of friendship rather than the local country club, the strength
of the sun, the joyfulness of the natural world and the place in it of

human sex. Lawrence's peevishness and bile went unnoticed; oddly, it is only now, when I have learned for myself that you don't get splendid anger without side-effects, that I find some of his later writings unreadable.

I was amused to discover, post-Leavis and years after my Lawrence phase was over, that the time when I was deeply under his influence was in fact the time when he was 'forgotten'. This, again, was one of the freedoms of an expropriated literature. I had been too far away to know, and too obscure to care, whether certain authors were fashionable or not. It was quite possible for me to be, while ten years behind current taste in the literary world, at the same time ten years ahead of it . . .

The serendipity of the library had provided me with Pepys's diaries at the age of fifteen or thereabouts, but soon after, Everyman's made my acquaintance with English literature less fortuitous. I had enjoyed Pepys more than I enjoyed Dickens (regarded then, in my canon, as school-prize calibre; I grew up to know better) and I formed a great liking for egocentric and eccentric writers. Burton's *Anatomy of Melancholy* fed my hunger for introspection, and the close-printed list of 'other titles' offered similar dark satisfactions. I got from English eccentrics and egocentrics not just encouragement for my own brooding, but also a sense of the hoary variety of British life, and the extraordinary contradiction of a tolerance of so many odd people with astonishing ideas, along with what British writers never tire of exposing as an awesome system of class distinction.

Perhaps because of the sort of reading I had been doing, Joyce and *Ulysses* did not surprise me as much as one might have expected. That great sunburst of night-flowering prose carried the inference of multiform to the ultimate. Life was tremendous *anywhere*, once you admitted it all. Every man his own Dublin. What you experienced in the lavatory was as relevant to the state of being as what you experienced in the pub or in church. The thin hum of your consciousness as you went about the streets was orchestrated richly with the conversation, sensations and unspoken thoughts of others. What other writer can make one as aware of the sheer range of the state of being? Virginia Woolf did as much for the texture of life, of course. Yet, fearless as she was in style and spirit, making her own prose for her own purpose, not shrinking from her own madness, even, there is a point at which all her writings seem fixed to that mark on the wall. It is the point at which the desire to grasp reality becomes the compulsion to fix one's attention on an object in order, by assuring oneself of the details of its existence, to confirm one's own. It is the compulsion one feels, when distrait, to stare at a chair or a light bulb on its string. By the way, why (to my knowledge) has no one pointed out to the *nouvelle vague* that this sort of attempt to prove existence was done so much better by her?

Most writers make their impact on one once and for all or not at all, but E. M. Forster's novels seem to contain a series of time-fuses, for me. I am convinced I could go on re-reading them at ten-year intervals all my life, and each time find something apparently revealed specifically for the time – both the historic and personal variety. After all, when I first read him his Edwardian delicacy and his fastidious faith in the sanctity of human relationships were already dated – the war was making nonsense of both: I was also reading *The Way We Live Now* in Penguin New Writing. Yet after the war, after the gas-chambers and the appearance of the first mushroom cloud, where was there to turn, in the ruins of institutions and political beliefs, but back to individual personal relationships, to learn again the human A B C? And when the recovery was materially triumphant but strangely hollow, *Howard's End* and *A Room With a View*, with their peculiar understanding of the hollowness of the Haves and the strength-without-power of the Have-nots, became newly illuminating. *A Passage to India*, written while colonialism was in its heyday, remained until the publication last year of James Baldwin's *The Fire Next Time* the most truthful and far-sighted piece of writing ever done about the relationship between coloured people and whites. It is still the best novel on the theme.

What about George Eliot (Dorothea Casaubon, that priggish lioness, is my favourite female character in any fiction), Chaucer, Thomas Wyatt, Gerard Manley Hopkins, Sterne, Angus Wilson,

Ivy Compton-Burnett, and many other British writers I couldn't do without? There is not space to do more than salute them, like beacons, in passing. Shakespeare presents a problem, too; does he go without saying in any context such as this? Alternatively, by halfway through this year, will anyone be able to bear to read another word about him? I should like, however, to slip in a quick word against Lamb's Tales – like all abridgements, stories of the film. etc., they ought to be abolished. I blame Lamb for the fact that I have never been able to read the comedies with any pleasure (the 'tale' without the poetry killed them for me, once and for all); the historical plays and the tragedies, as legendary allegory of the human spirit, have taken for me what might be thought of as the place of the Greeks.

Shakespeare's sonnets have never meant as much to me as Donne's; Eliot has been my poet rather than Auden: in general, it's the metaphysical that I respond to in British poetry. The romantics never gained much hold on my imagination. The poetry of Shelley, Byron and Keats always seemed to be as much in their lives as in their work. Yet Yeats is the British (Irish) poet who has influenced me most. More than any other poet I have read, he has been able to use, in the intensely private and personal terms of his poetic vision, the (from a poet's point of view) curiously abstract historical events of which he was part, and even the personalities involved – the stuff of newspapers and political platforms taken into poetry. Can you imagine anyone writing something like 'Easter 1916' about the nuclear disarmament protest marchers, or men and women who are in the struggle against apartheid in South Africa today?

Like all former colonial subjects, I am finally ready to turn the advantages gained while under subjection to the purpose of pointing out what these have failed to provide. 'Everything' becomes 'Everything but—'. In the 1960s, if one read nothing but British literature, where would one look for novels in the great nineteenth-century British tradition? Since Angus Wilson, there is no writer who has used this tradition, expanding it seriously: recently, the best novel I have read for a long time did so splendidly – but it was written by an Indian from Trinidad (A House *for Mr Biswas*, by V. S. Naipaul). The picaresque fantasy-novel – didn't it originate in England? – has lately made a come-back: but in German, with *The Tin Drum*. The splenetic vein of Wyndham Lewis has dried up; the inheritance of Wells and Huxley is frittered away in the small change of science fiction.

These are grouses in the she-ain't-what-she-used-to-be strain. The real gap that I am conscious of in my expropriated literature is the lack of novelist-philosophers. Among my contemporaries in British writing there is a lot of lively blind dissatisfaction – hitting out for the hell of it at telly civilisation or shying (again) at that apparently Welfare State-proof old coconut, the class barrier. From outside, however admirably well done, and sometimes witty, it all seems rather parochial. Then there are the Catholic novelists, from Graham Greene – whose marvellous laconic style, reflecting the profound pessimism that sometimes affects one who knows men to the last cell, makes him appear too unheroic, even in his despair, for greatness – to Muriel Spark, whose dialogue is the first ever to match the telegraphic brilliance of early Waugh, and whose two most recent books seem to indicate that she has chosen for good, the confines of some girls' institution as her private vision of the world; there are stockings dangling to dry above every page. The only British novelist who is close to being a novelist-philosopher outside the limits of a religious dogma is William Golding. To me he is the most exciting and interesting of contemporary British writers.

But where is the British equivalent of a Camus – not just the individual genius, but the writer with the sense of the past (unwistfully) and the future (unprophetically) present in himself, and a cool purpose, born of real passion for life, to explore its possibilities at this stage of half-understood, totally threatened human existence?

1964

Taking into Account

Simone de Beauvoir's *Force of Circumstance*

You can seize hold of this final(?) instalment of the autobiography of Simone de Beauvoir and worry away at it from
a number of points of view. But which is the one that will yield,
wriggling, the individual herself? In the end, what does one make
of her? What does she make of herself? To write an autobiography
is to sum up: and to read it is to examine the process and arrive at a
total of one's own – never objective, of course, but subject to a set of
opinions, prejudices and emotions that differ in kind and/or degree
from those of the author. Entertained, appalled (once or twice), irri-
tated (occasionally), enthralled (often), amused (in places where this
was not the author's intention), moved and, above all, compelled to
stay with her to the last page. I stand back from volume three and,
for me, this life gives purchase most clearly in three aspects and in
this order: the experience of being French during the Algerian war;
the position of the Leftist outside the Communist Party; woman as
intellectual. Here is Simone de Beauvoir.

Being female was a precondition, yet, in order of importance, I
put it third in the forces that have shaped her life because she has
dealt with it, in the particular context of that life, successfully –
even triumphantly – and in this last volume it crops up more in
the light of reflection on these triumphs than in the glare of battle
enjoined. I am referring here to the intellectual woman's problem
of being regarded as what Simone de Beauvoir calls a 'secondary
being' rather than that of being, in the narrowest sense – sexually –
a female, and so we can turn a deaf ear to that mournful cry of the
ageing woman towards the end of the book: 'Never again a man!'
Anyway, might it not just as easily come from a man – the cry:
'Never again a woman!'?

Intellectual women have, a generation ago at least, disowned the old feminist stand that women are, so to speak, men with frills on. A woman no longer has to see herself emancipated in the image of a man; just as the black man (rather later) no longer sees himself in the image of the white man. *Equal but different*; that's not only acceptable, it's what women want and what we have had ratified (even if the law, opportunity and custom lag behind here and there) by a man's world. It is a man's world still, largely because men kept it to themselves so long, and because many women share in common with other oppressed peoples the development of a slave mentality and are the first to turn their red fingernails on their sisters who not only walk out on the seraglio but, worse, refuse the status of 'honorary males'. (De Beauvoir's phrase again.) Feminism as such – whether in this negative or in its positive aspects – has become a bore. The attacks on Simone de Beauvoir *as a woman* after she had published *The Second Sex* glanced off because she was confident of having no special inadequacies to defend. 'No; far from suffering from my femininity, I have, on the contrary, from the age of twenty on, accumulated the advantages of both sexes; after *She Came to Stay*, those around me treated me both as a writer, their peer in the masculine world, and as a woman' and she adds, 'Oh how insufferable to the suffragette and the sultan! . . . at parties I went to the wives all got together and talked to each other while I talked to the men, who nevertheless behaved towards me with greater courtesy than they did towards the members of their own sex'. For a woman as little given to feminine glee as this one, it must take tremendous self-confidence to come out with *that* – the heady first success of every little small-town intellectual Bovary as well as the experience of the Simone de Beauvoirs and Mary McCarthys.

In her sexual and emotional relationships Simone de Beauvoir seems again to have managed to achieve the best of both worlds. A lifelong bond with 'the man whom I placed above all others', plus two deep and passionate love affairs which left the bond untouched; this compact of 'contingent love' has proved the best of marriages. Like any Joan sitting with her Darby (Simone de Beauvoir, in her late fifties, sees herself in old age) she wonders, now, which one of them will 'go' first, and how shall the survivor bear it? Apart from their lifelong dialogue, they have had a silent understanding that persisted without a break in communication even when travelling abroad in a foursome composed of themselves, her lover and his mistress. Only once does she admit to suffering fear and feeling threatened by Sartre's relationship with a woman and soon the solemnity of the unsolemnised marriage won out for her. As for her own grand passions, both seem to have ended in special friendships and the secret consolation that although *he* wished it, she wouldn't marry Nelson Algren, and Lanzmann was born a generation too late to provide more for her than, in her middle forties, a highly gratifying second spring. She is a woman who has been loved by three men; and in freedom; without yielding an inch or hour of 'the autonomy that has been bestowed on me by a profession which means so much to me'. She has not allowed herself to be forced to assume, on the side, the domestic obligations in one form or another that follow hot on the love-talk for most intellectual women as for all others, except perhaps the wealthy bourgeoise whom she despises. That's no mean achievement. Even the man who is the peer of an intellectual woman fails to see why he, just as well as she, should wash his shirt. Sartre must be the exception. Of course, he *has* lived at home with his mother quite a lot of the time.

De Beauvoir may have avoided washing his shirts, but she has constantly been accused of wearing his opinions. She gives quite a lot of space to refuting this. If, as she seems to think, the allegation comes from the old anti-feminist guard, why grant it so much attention? They have long since lost the power to 'draw' her when they touch upon other aspects of her life. If, on the other hand, she is accused without prejudice, as an intellectual, of being unduly under the influence of the thought of another, and one takes her refutation in this context, fair enough. We can accept that we cannot know the extent to which these two very different − we can tell that, from their books, without any explanation from her − minds have interacted; the trouble is that her autobiography provides circumstantial evidence that *Words*, confined to that 'poodle of the future', the infant Sartre, cannot. And there's not much reason to believe, on the evidence of *Words*, populated entirely by Sartre himself in the many avatars of childhood fantasy (grandfather, mother, schoolmaster: chair, table, lamp, on an empty stage set for his performances), that later volumes of his autobiography will find it necessary to admit other people. (This is not a criticism, but the description of a method. With her, you are under the clock on the street corner, always at the point at which she meets the world; with him, you are in that interior being to which he has carried away the world's phenomena.) Throughout her book, Simone de Beauvoir has an irritating habit of writing 'we thought', when surely, since this is her own story she is telling, her own development, however closely entwined with another's, that she is describing, she ought to be writing 'I thought'. For the purposes of this particular narrative. Sartre simply happens to hold the same opinion.

'It was not of my own free will . . . that I allowed the war in Algeria to invade my thoughts, my sleep, my every mood.'

Almost exactly halfway through *Force of Circumstance* this invasion begins. By the time the last page is reached, it has established itself as the definitive experience of the writer's life. It is a destruction, not a culmination; and that is the real reason why this woman, who can say 'when I look back over the past, there is no-one I envy', at the same time ends her book in despair.

For as it turned out, it has been the Algerian war and not the Resistance that has proved to be the testing-ground for de Beauvoir's beliefs and convictions, and most of her loyalties. Looked back upon, the Resistance (with which one can't deny she identified herself absolutely, even if, as her detractors point out, she was not herself active in the movement) was a period of blessed moral certitude; the enemy might have been in Occupation, but came from Without. There were collaborators, of course, but they were not drawn from the ranks of her friends. It still meant something to be a Frenchwoman; one did not have to repudiate one's heritage of the nation's whole past – from its intellectual tradition to its gastronomy – because of the present this resulted in. The touchstone of socialist principles was lodged in what a man said and did and thought *then*, in relation to the Germans, and not in relation to how he would think or write or act in other forms of social conflict. It was possible to belong to the Left and not be a Communist, without being reviled by the Right or scorned by the Communist, because if the Underground was a battle-field it was also an area of agreement. For those years the forces of human regression wore the same face for all: the face of the German soldier. And after the war there was a brief honeymoon of the Peace when Simone de Beauvoir and Sartre, in common with others, felt that the moral force that had been put up against that face would now be hurled against all the other horrors bobbing in the human coconut-shy; there would be a new France, if not a new world.

They considered themselves socialists and the future was, by defi-nition, socialism. Yet neither would join the Communist Party; she was 'close to the Communists certainly, because of my horror of all that they were fighting against; but I loved truth too much not to demand the freedom to seek it as I wished'. As for Sartre, she insists that 'a dialogue (with the Communists) was possible'; nevertheless, soon after the war he was already experiencing an ironic situation that was to continue for most of his life: the Communists used, as a stick to beat him with, the interpretation of his thought taken up by the Right – 'the bourgeois public interpreted Existentialism as a spare, emergency ideology. The Communists took the same view.' This classic form of punishment reserved for the fellow trav-eller has been the lot of both de Beauvoir and Sartre for a good distance on the long road that has led 'the jackal with a fountain pen' (Sartre, as once described by a Communist) finally to the acco-lade from Castro and (surely not so pleasant) the arms of Surkov. There have been some casualties on the way, particularly in the fields of literary judgement and private friendship. The latter are inevitable; you have to lose some friends if you want to keep your convictions. But the former make one shake one's head: is Simone de Beauvoir really content with the political priggery of her appraisal of *The Rebel* as 'a statement of his [Camus's] solidarity with bourgeois values'?

If de Beauvoir and her man have at last won from the Communists the recognition of their position 'close to' but not within the Party, it hasn't come about through that 'dialogue' she was convinced was possible, but as a result of their stand throughout the Algerian war. For her, at least, although she does not say so, it must be like receiving a citation whose words can hold little of what really happened. '. . . the horror my [the middle] class inspires in me has been brought to white heat by the Algerian war': it was not that her experience of that war went deeper than her politics, but that her political convictions found their depth in her experience of that war.

Other things central to her being were put to the test by the same event – love of country, even love of life. The first did not survive; the second seems damaged beyond healing. All through the last half of this volume the record of destruction grows.

> What did appal me was to see the vast majority of the French people turn chauvinist and to realize the depths of their racist attitude. Whole battalions were looting, burning, raping, massacring. Torture was being used as the normal and indispensable method of obtaining information . . . My compatriots did not want to know anything about all this . . . no-one turned a hair.

And yet

> Every evening a sentimental audience wept over the past misfortunes of little Anne Frank; but all the children in agony . . . at that moment in a supposedly French country were something they preferred to ignore. If you had attempted to stir up pity for them [Algerian children] you would have been accused of lowering the nation's morale. This hypocrisy, this indifference, this country, my own self, were no longer bearable to me. All those people in the streets, in open agreement [with the war] or battered into a stupid submission – they were all murderers, all guilty. Myself as well. 'I'm French.' The words scalded my throat like an admission of a hideous deformity. For millions of men and women . . . I was just one of the people who were torturing them . . . I deserved their hatred because I could still sleep, write, enjoy a walk or a book.

... I had been labelled, along with several others, anti-French. I became so. I could no longer bear my fellow citizens ... At the cinema we had to swallow newsreels showing the fine work the French were doing in Algeria ... Just having coffee at a counter or going into a bakery became an ordeal ... I had liked crowds once; now even the streets were hostile to me. I felt dispossessed as I had when the Occupation began. It was even worse, because, whether I wanted to be or not, I was an accomplice of these people I couldn't bear to be in the same street with. That was what I could least forgive. Or else they should have trained me from childhood to be an SS, a para, instead of giving me a Christian, democratic, humanist conscience: a conscience ... I was seeing myself through the eyes of women who had been raped twenty times, of men with broken bones, of crazed children: a Frenchwoman.

If hell is seeing horrors done in one's name, then many of us have been down there with her. 'I'm French.' 'I'm German.' For me, a South African, 'I'm white.' As a testament of the shaking of the foundations of individual existence in this situation, this autobiography has no rival I have read. Simone de Beauvoir's sorrowful sense of disgust with life is surely not so much the inability to accept an ageing body, as the other kind of self-loathing that comes from having to accept that for years one has no longer been able to bear one's fellow citizens. Let this stand against the judgement of some French critics that the sorrow is the confession of the failure of a philosophy, and against the world's jealous insistence that a woman so brilliant, celebrated, and (by now) even rich, *ought* to arrive at a different reckoning.

1966

One Man Living Through It

My memory for the sequence of events in getting to know people is bad – the preliminaries tend to run together into the colour and quality of the relationship that develops. But I do remember clearly the first time I met Nat Nakasa. It was perhaps seven years ago and I was expecting Lewis Nkosi. He brought with him that day a round-faced boy who, faced with the prospect of being left alone to amuse himself while Lewis and I went off for a private talk, said, just as if there were not plenty of books and papers in the room – 'Haven't you got any records I can play?' He was not ill at ease, but carried the youthful confidence in his own interests that marks the city-bred. Here was someone who would skid through the conventions of white houses as nippily as, a few years earlier, he would weave a bicycle in and out of the stream of Durban's big cars.

I knew he must mean jazz records, and felt he would find mine meagre and 'commercial', but I gave them to him. And when Lewis and I came back to the room he was stretched full-length in a chair, attentive to the music and inoffensively indifferent to both our absence and return.

That was Nat, newly arrived in Johannesburg. That was Nat at the beginning of the period he describes in an essay 'Johannesburg, Johannesburg'. That was the period of no fixed abode. And yet he was going somewhere; by the very nature of the way he was living, he was set upon the only course that was valid for him: the course of independent self-realisation. Although I barely recognise that boy sitting in the chair stirring his toes inside his shoes to the beat, just as I barely recognise the man who ended his own life early one summer morning in New York, both were part of the young man who became my close friend. So do the limits of human relation-ships constantly fling us back; so do one's hands fall, helpless, before the quintessential loneliness of each human being. It is keeping this in mind that I write of him, respecting the ultimate despair that took him beyond the understanding of friends, aware that what each of us knows of him was only part of what he was, and lived, and suffered, and that even when we have put it all together there will always be something – perhaps the unbearable sum of the total in itself? – that he kept to himself and died of.

I saw quite a lot of Nat at parties or when friends simply gravitated together to talk, but it was when he launched out into the founding of the *Classic*, a defiant literary journal, and I became a member of the small committee formed to help him run it, that he was drawn into the working life of our house. He heard squabbles and learned private jokes. He lost his fear of the bulldog and endured its smelly presence at his feet; he was asked to pick up a schoolboy from the bus stop or to buy a pint of milk while on the way from town. The process is known as becoming one of the family and it implies chores as well as privileges. He and I found that one of the times that suited both of us best, if we had *Classic* matters to work on, was about two o'clock in the afternoon. Very often he would rush in then, carrying his bulging attaché case, and we would eat bread and cheese on the verandah in the sun, laughing a lot (he was a brilliant mimic) and getting on with the work at the same time. His social instincts were sure, and even in easy friendship he never lost his precise judgement of exactly the time to get up and go. He always seemed to sense when you had work or some other preoccupation that you must get back to. This leads me, only now, while writing, to realise that I never ever remember him being a bore. He didn't even have those moments of recurring tediousness on pet subjects that most of us have. Sensitivity is a term whose mention may itself cause a suppressed yawn, but the fact is that he was too sensitive to be a bore. Too conscious, in the best and most open way, of the feelings of other people. And this reminds one how, on the last evening of his life, when in all his final anguish of mind he talked until late with his friend Jack Thomson and his wife, he had still some instinct that made him shrink from burdening them with the mention of his impulse to suicide.

Nat's approach to the *Classic* was serious and yet light-hearted, candid and unflustered. He was a clever young newspaperman but had no literary background or experience – yes. There was not enough money for the venture and there were endless practical difficulties – yes. But he felt that day-to-day journalism floated, like oil indicating the presence of a submarine, on the surface of African life, and he wanted to make soundings of his own. He asked for help, and what's more, he did so aware that help more often than not must take the form of criticism, and in the self-knowledge that he could take *that*, too. As for money, he managed as best he could with what there was; and as for the other difficulties, he dealt with them with what I am prepared to say is a particularly African resilience, vigorously born of harsh necessity, early on.

One of the practical difficulties was that it was hard to get white printers (our first one, certainly) to accept that this black man was the editor and not a white editor's office boy. Nat's manner with the man was amusing and highly successful – he treated him kindly but firmly as someone who has had a nasty shock, but really not *so* bad, after all, and wasn't he getting used to it, wasn't he feeling better already? Nat did not do as well with the wife, an ink-haired, flour-faced lady sitting up among her invoices on a high stool, like a grim *madame* in a late-nineteenth-century French painting, but he had the husband confiding his business troubles to him, and *almost* calling him 'Mr Nakasa' . . .

He would bring to me a manuscript that he liked particularly, to share the pleasure of it, and he brought me those whose interest or quality he felt uncertain about. If he was strongly in favour of something, he would publish it anyway, no matter what anyone thought of it. He had read no poetry outside a school primer and I often told him that some poems he considered publishing in the magazine were rubbish.

He would say, 'Oh. Well, why?' And would force me to state the grounds of my attack, line by line. Sometimes he would come back days later – scratching down through the nest of dog-eared manuscripts in the attaché case – and dig out one of the same poems over again.

'What about this line here? – you said it was meaningless but I think what he's getting at here –' And so he sometimes caught me out.

Once he plonked down a poem – 'Now that's really got something!'

I read it over; 'Yes, but what it's got is not its own,' and I fetched down the Lorca and showed him the poem from which the other had borrowed the form and imagery that distinguished it.

He was not at all touchy about gaps in his knowledge and experience; he had none of the limitations of false pride. He sat down to Lorca with the pleasure of discovery. One of the reasons why he hoped to go to Harvard was because he wanted time to read the great poets and imaginative writers; he felt strongly that he needed a wider intellectual context than the day-to-day, politically orientated, African-centred one in which he had become a thinking person, and on which, so far, even his artistic judgements must be empirically based. I wonder if he ever found that time to read; somehow, I don't think he did. Too many well-meant invitations to speak here and there about Africa, too many well-meant requests to appear on television programmes about Africa, too many requests to write articles about how an African looks at American this and that. Nat remained trapped in the preoccupations of his time – the time measured by those multiple clocks in airports, showing simultaneously what hour it is at Karachi, Vladivostok, Nairobi and New York, and not the dimension in which one can sit down and read. There seems to be no fellowship that provides for that.

Nat was a good talker and had the unusual ability to tell an anecdote in such a way that he himself was presented as the 'feed', and the bright lights illuminated the character of someone else. The oblique picture that emerged of him was one of wit and calm, sometimes in bizarre situations. He was given to analysis – of himself and others – rather than accusations and self-pity, and so did not react with self-dramatisation to the daily encounters with white laws and prejudices. White people used to say of him that he, unlike others, was not 'bitter'; I don't know quite what they meant by this – because he was as bitterly hurt by the colour bar as the next man – unless they mistook for resignation the fact that he managed to keep his self-respect intact.

In the years I knew him fragments and segments of his life came out in talk, without chronology, as these things do between friends; he was telling me, one Sunday, how as a small boy he used to be up at four in the morning to be first on the streets with the newspapers. He was not telling me about his hardships as a poor black child, but of how mysterious and exciting Durban was at that hour, for a little boy – the deserted city coming up with the sun out of the mist from the sea. Then, last year while I was in London, I met his younger brother, who was about to go up to Oxford. When I told Nat – who had helped to pay for the boy's schooling – how impressed I had been by his brother's keen mind, he told me how he had been in the room when the boy was born, and how, since the mother became ill soon after and was never again able to look after her children, he had simply 'taken the baby around with me until he could walk'. Again, it was the quality of the experience he was conveying, not a hard-luck story presenting himself as a victim. Of course, he *was* a victim of this country; but never accepted the character of the victimised in himself.

I always hoped that one day he would write about these things – the child in Durban, the life he and Lewis Nkosi shared, homeless and yet, curiously, more at home in Johannesburg than those behind their suburban front doors. I think that the writing in his weekly column in the Johannesburg *Rand Daily Mail* was a beginning, and is the best writing he did. It was journalism, yes, but journalism of a highly personal kind; all the news came from inside Nat. He dredged into his mind and feelings as he had never done before, he wrote only of what was real to him, throwing away all the labels conveniently provided by both protest writing and government handouts, accepting without embarrassment all the apparent contradictions in the complexity of his reactions to his situation – and ours, black and white. (He didn't even balk at coming out with the pronouncement that he felt sorry for young Afrikaners!) 'Bitterness'; 'resentment'; 'prejudice'; these terms are as easy to use as the airmail stickers free for the taking in post offices. Nat presented the reality, in daily life and thought, from which these abstractions are run off. He showed us what it was all about, for one man living through it.

This writing – reflecting the gaiety of a serious person – came from his central personality and, in giving himself the fullest expression he had yet known, during the year that he was writing his column and concurrently running *Classic* he developed amazingly. It was a strange time, that last year in South Africa. On the one hand, he was making a name for himself in a small but special way that no African had done before; his opinions and ideas were being considered seriously by white newspaper-readers whose dialogue across the colour line had never exceeded the command, do-this-or-that, and the response, yes-*baas*. On the other hand, he had been awarded a fellowship to Harvard and was involved in the process of trying to get a passport – for an African, a year-long game in which the sporting element seems to be that the applicant is never told what you have to do to win, or what it was he did that made him lose. Knowing the nature of the game, Nat had to consider from the start how the refusal of a passport would affect his life. He had to decide whether the place he had made for himself, astride the colour bar, merited electing to stay, should the passport be refused; or whether he should, like others, accept exile as the price of a breath of the open world. It was not a decision to be dictated only by personal ambition; part of his development was that he had come to the stage, now, when he had to weigh up the possible usefulness to his people of the position he had gained. It was not, of course, a political position, and its value was not something that could easily be measured; there is no scale for the intangibles of the human spirit.

Quite suddenly, he made the decision to go, although he had been refused a passport. He took what every other young man of outstanding ability – but of a different colour – takes for granted, and gets without the necessity of an agonising decision to exile himself from home, country, friends and family – a chance to travel and seek education. I saw him off at the airport – twice. The first time he missed the plane (no, it was not what white people call

African time; it was a hitch over the issue of traveller's cheques) and the crowd of friends who had come to say goodbye dispersed rather flatly. Not all could come back again next day; but this time it went without a hitch, weigh-in, customs, finally passport control and the exit permit open on the counter. I looked at it; it was valid for one exit only, and the undersigned, Nathaniel Nakasa, was debarred from 'entering the Republic of South Africa or South West Africa' again. There was the printed admonition: 'This is a valuable document. Keep it in a safe place.'

Nat was gone. He never came back. But he was the beginning, not the end of something. In so many ways he was starting where others left off. I have heard that shortly before his death he made an impassioned anti-white speech before a Washington audience; but the report comes third-hand and I do not know whether this interpretation of his address is a true one. Similarly, if in direct contradiction, I have heard it said that through his association with white friends he had become a 'white' black man. The truth is that he was a new kind of man in South Africa – he accepted without question and with easy dignity and natural pride his Africanness, and he took equally for granted that his identity as a man among men, a human among fellow humans, could not be legislated out of existence even by all the apartheid laws in the statute book, or all the racial prejudice in this country. He did not calculate the population as thirteen million or three million, but as sixteen. He belonged not between two worlds, but to both. And in him one could see the hope of one world. He has left that hope behind; there will be others to take it up.

1966

Why Did Bram Fischer Choose Jail?

In South Africa on May 9 1966, Abram Fischer, Queen's Counsel, a proud Afrikaner and self-affirmed Communist, was sentenced to imprisonment for life. The main counts against him (conspiring to commit sabotage and being a member of, and furthering the aims of, the Communist Party) were framed under the Suppression of Communism Act, but anti-Communists could take no comfort from that: this Act is the much-extended one under which all extra-parliamentary opposition to apartheid, whether inspired by socialism, capitalism, religious principles, a sense of justice or just plain human feeling, is at least under suspicion in South Africa.

In his address to the court a few days before, Fischer himself had pointed out, 'The laws under which I am being prosecuted were enacted by a wholly unrepresentative body ... in which three-quarters of the people of this country have no voice whatever.' He went on to say, 'These laws were enacted not to prevent the spread of Communism, but for the purpose of silencing the opposition of a large majority of our citizens to a Government intent upon depriving them, solely on account of their colour, of the most elementary human rights.'

All through his trial, Fischer listened and took notes – even when some erstwhile friends turned state witnesses stood a few feet away, testifying against him – with the same composed alertness that had been his demeanour when appearing as counsel in this same Palace of Justice at Pretoria. The smile, beginning in the brilliant, flecked blue eyes, was his familiar one, as he turned from the dock to face the public gallery, and sought the faces of family or friends. The panoply of the court, the shouts drifting up from the cells below, the press tiptoeing restlessly in and out, his colleagues in their robes, Mr Justice Wessel Boshoff on the bench – all this was the everyday scene of his professional working life as an advocate. But he stood in the prisoner's dock. Hemmed in by the intimidating presence of plain-clothes security men and scrutinised by uniformed policemen, the spectators in the gallery stared into the well of the court as into Fischer's private nightmare, where all appeared normal except for this one glaring displacement.

Yet it was clear that Abram Fischer recognised the reality of his position, and knew it to be the climax of the collision course upon which he and his countrymen were set, nearly thirty years ago, the day he rejected his student belief in segregation. He told the court:

> All the conduct with which I have been charged has been directed towards maintaining contact and understanding between the races of this country. If one day it may help to establish a bridge across which white leaders and the real leaders of the non-whites can meet to settle the destinies of all of us by negotiation and not by force of arms, I shall be able to bear with fortitude any sentence which this court may impose on me. It will be a fortitude strengthened by this knowledge at least, that for twenty-five years I have taken no part, not even by passive acceptance, in that hideous system of discrimination which we have erected in this country and which has become a byword in the civilised world today.

Not even those Afrikaners who regard Abram Fischer as the arch-traitor to Afrikanerdom would deny that if he had been able to stomach white overlordship and the colour bar there would have been no limit to the honours and high office he might today have attained in the republic his forebears won from British imperialism. He comes from the right stock, with not only the brains but also the intellectual savoir-faire coveted by a people who sometimes feel, even at the peak of their political power, some veld-bred disadvantage in their dealings with the sophistications of the outside world.

He was born in 1908 in the Orange River Colony – formerly the old Boer republic of the Orange Free State – grandson of its only Prime Minister before Union in 1910. His father became Judge-President of the Orange Free State – after Union a province of South Africa. The Boer War defeat at the hands of the British remained a bitter taste in the mouth of the grandfather; as a school cadet, it is said that the grandson refused to be seen in the British conqueror's military uniform.

He was a brilliant scholar, and when he had taken his law degree at Bloemfontein, won a Rhodes scholarship to New College, Oxford. At twenty-nine he married the daughter of another distinguished Afrikaner family, Susannah (Molly) Krige, and began a thirty-year career at the bar in Johannesburg. He reached the top of his profession and was regarded as an expert on mining law. His services were engaged by the insurance companies, the newspaper consortiums and the big mining houses.

His success coincided with the growth of Afrikaner political power, but his recognition of the subjection of the black man on which this power was built precluded him from taking any part in it. While he saw his people as the first in Africa to win liberation from colonial domination and therefore well able to understand and fitted to encourage African aspirations, they were busy codifying the traditional race prejudice of white South Africans, whether of Boer, British or any other descent, as an ideology and the 'South African way of life'.

It was within this situation that Fischer, as a young man, had become a Communist. The rise of Fascism in the world at that time was turning many of his contemporaries in other countries to the left. In England, for example, his counterpart would have gone off to fight with the International Brigade in the Spanish Civil War. But Fischer's battle was to be fought at home. His instigation was not youthful idealism, but the injustice and indifference to injustice that he saw around him every day, and that, indeed, as the first Nationalist prime minister of a student parliament, and a segregationist, he had been party to. It was Hitler's sinister theory of race superiority, combined with a 'strange revulsion' that Fischer experienced when, as a formality at a philanthropic meeting he had to take a black man's hand, that had opened his eyes. Since the days when, as a child, he had made clay oxen with black children on his family's farm, he had been conditioned to develop an antagonism for which he could find no reason. He came to understand colour prejudice as a wholly irrational phenomenon.

At his trial in Pretoria, he told the court why he had been attracted to the Communist Party. There was this

> glaring injustice which exists and has existed for a long time in South African society . . . This is not even a question of the degree of humiliation or poverty or misery imposed by discrimination . . . It is simply and plainly that discrimination should be imposed as a matter of deliberate policy, solely because of the colour which a man's skin happens to be, irrespective of his merits as a man.

Three decades ago there was certainly not much choice for a young man looking for participation in political activity unequivocally aimed to change all this. The Communist Party was then, and for many years, the only political party that observed no colour bar and advocated universal franchise. (Today, more than thirty years later, there is only one other white political party advocating universal franchise – the Liberal Party, founded in 1953.) At his trial Fischer explained:

> My attraction to the Communist Party was a matter of personal observation. By that time the Communist Party had already for two decades stood avowedly and unconditionally for political rights for non-whites, and its white members were, save for a handful of courageous individuals, the only whites who showed complete disregard for the hatred which this attitude attracted from their fellow white South Africans. These members . . . were whites who could have taken full advantage of all the privileges open to them because of their colour . . . They were not prepared to flourish on the deprivations suffered by others.
>
> But apart from the example of white members, it was always the Communists of all races who were prepared to give of their time and their energy and such means as they had, to help . . . with night schools and feeding schemes, who assisted trade unions fighting desperately to preserve standards of living . . . It was African Communists who constantly risked arrest . . . in order to gain or retain some rights . . . This fearless adherence to principle

must always exercise a strong appeal to those who wish to take part in politics, not for personal advantage, but in the hope of making some positive contribution.

Fischer's contemporaries among the angry young men in the Western world of the thirties have lived to see a peaceful social revolution in England and the vigorous pursuit of civil-rights legislation against segregation in the United States. Within the same span, in South Africa, Fischer has seen the deeply felt grievances of the non-white population of his country increasingly ignored, their non-violent campaigns against discriminatory laws in the fifties ruthlessly put down, in the sixties their Congresses banned, responsible leaders jailed and house-arrested, along with white people of many political beliefs who have supported them, and a year-by-year piling up of legislation – Bantustans, job reservation, ghetto acts – increasing restriction by colour in every aspect of human activity.

Those contemporaries who shared what now seems to them a hot-headed youth may sit back in good conscience and ask why Fischer did not leave behind leftist beliefs, as they did, in the disillusion of the Stalinist era. One can only state the facts. Though Fischer never proselytised, he was and remains a doctrinaire Marxist; South Africa, in her political development in relation to the colour problem, has never offered him an acceptable alternative to his socialist beliefs.

At his trial he affirmed in orthodox Marxist terms the theory that political change occurs inevitably when a political form ceases to serve the needs of people who are living under new circumstances created by the development of new economic forces and relations. He obviously sees the colour problem in South Africa as basically an economic one: the white man's fear of losing his job to the overwhelming numbers of Africans, the black man so insecure economically that the numbers of unemployed Africans are never even recorded accurately. Fischer said, 'South Africa today is a clear example of a society in which the political forms do not serve the needs of most of the people', and pointed out that ownership of

factories, mines and land used for productive purposes is becoming
more and more concentrated – in the hands of whites, of course.

Outside the banned Communist Party, there is no group or party
open to whites that, however it proposes to go about removing
colour discrimination, also visualises radical change in the ownership of the means of production which underpins the present
system of white supremacy. Fischer openly told the court: 'I believe
that socialism in the long term has an answer to the problem of
race relations. But by negotiation, other immediate solutions can
be found . . . Immediate dangers [a civil war which he visualised
as dwarfing the horrors of Algeria] can be avoided by bringing our
state at this stage into line with the needs of today by abolishing
discrimination, extending political rights, and then allowing our
people to settle their own future.'

In prison or out, Abram Fischer maintains a dramatic position
in South African life. For some years, circumstances surrounding
him have been extraordinary. If Afrikaner Nationalist propagan-
dists present him as the anti-Christ, then, curiously moved to lay
aside his socialist rationalism, he has taken upon himself some of
their sins in an almost Christlike way. In addressing the court he
returned again and again to statements like

> What is not appreciated by my fellow Afrikaner, because he has
> cut himself off from all contact with non-whites, is that . . . he
> is now blamed as an Afrikaner for all the evils and humiliations
> of apartheid. Hence today the policeman is known as a 'Dutch'
> . . . When I give an African a lift during a bus boycott, he refuses
> to believe that I am an Afrikaner . . . All this has bred a deep-
> rooted hatred for Afrikaners among non-whites . . . It demands that
> Afrikaners themselves should protest openly and clearly against
> discrimination. Surely there was an additional duty cast on me, that
> at least one Afrikaner should make this protest actively . . .

Those people, including Afrikaner Nationalists, who know
Fischer personally have a special affection and respect for him, no

matter how anti-Communist they may be. He himself has always shown respect for the right of anyone to work for social reform in his own way, just so long as the obligation is not smugly ignored. No other figure is at once so controversial and so well-liked. Even people who have never been able to understand his adherence to, let alone accept, his socialist views will add: 'But he is a wonderful *person*.' This is due to nothing so superficial as charm – though Fischer has plenty of that; there has been, about Abram Fischer and his wife and children, the particular magnetism of deeply honest lives. Paradoxically, the pull is strong in a country where so many compromises with conscience are made by so many decent citizens.

In his profession, as well, Fischer has borne something of a charmed life. From the fifties, when political trials got under way in South Africa, he would refuse conventionally important briefs in order to take time to defend rank-and-file Africans, Indians and whites on political charges. Such was his professional prestige that the financial Establishment continued to seek his services as before. From 1958 to 1961 he devoted himself to the defence of Nelson Mandela, the African National Congress leader, and twenty-nine other accused in the first mass political trial that, because it repre- sented so many shades – both skin and ideological – of political thought, became known as 'the Opposition on trial'. In 1964 Fischer was leading defence counsel at the trial of the 'High Command' of combined liberation movements, which had been based at Rivonia, north of Johannesburg. Later that year, his invisible armour was pierced for the first time; he was imprisoned, briefly, under the ninety-day-detention law. And then, in September of 1964 he was arrested, with thirteen others, on five charges including those of being a member and furthering the objects of the Communist Party.

Because of the esteem in which Fischer was held, his request for bail was supported by many of his legal colleagues and granted by the court, although he had been named chief accused. During the course of the trial, he was even given a temporary passport to enable him to go to London to represent an internationally known pharmaceutical company at the Privy Council. He could expect

as much as a five-year sentence at his own trial: would he come
back? He had given his word, and he did. Having won the case,
he returned discussing the new plays he had seen in the West End,
just as if he had come home to face nothing more than the letdown
after a holiday.

He had been in South Africa a month or so when, on 25 January
1965, he disappeared overnight, leaving a letter to the court saying
that he was aware that his eventual punishment would be increased
by his action, but that he believed it was his duty both to remain
in South Africa and to continue to oppose apartheid by carrying
on with his political work as long as he was physically able. He
referred to his career at the Bar, in relation to the injustice of apartheid upheld by the law: 'I can no longer serve justice in the way I
have attempted to do during the past 30 years. I can do it only in
the way I have now chosen.'

For ten months he eluded a police hunt that poked into every
backyard and farmhouse in the country, and brought into detention
anyone suspected of being able to blurt out, under persuasion of
solitary confinement, Fischer's whereabouts. On 11 November last
year, he was arrested in Johannesburg, thin, bearded, his hair dyed.
Except for the eyes, he was unrecognisable as the short but well-set,
handsome man with curly white hair that he had been – and was
to be again, by the time he appeared in court on 26 January of this
year to face fifteen instead of the original five charges against him.

Why did Abram Fischer abscond? What did he achieve by it? So
far as is known, he does not seem to have managed to initiate any
significant new political activity while in hiding.

His fellow white South Africans, the majority of whom are indifferent to the quality of life on the other side of the colour bar, living
their comfortable lives in the segregated suburbs where, once, he
too had a house with a swimming pool, and among whom, last
year, he lived as a fugitive, express strong opinions about what he
had done with his life. His colleagues at the Bar, taking the position that absconding from his original trial was conduct unseemly
to the dignity of the profession, hurriedly applied within days of

his disappearance to have him disbarred. Some people assure themselves that he acted in blind obedience to 'orders from Moscow' – the purpose of which they cannot suggest. Well-meaning people who cannot conceive that anyone would sacrifice profession, home, family and ultimately personal liberty for a gesture affirming what he believed to be right, say that the tragic death of his wife, Molly, in a motor accident in 1964, must have disorientated him. Others, who have themselves suffered bans and lost passports as a result of courageous opposition to apartheid, feel that Fischer's final defiance of the law was a gratuitous act, ending in senseless tragedy: 'Why has Bram thrown himself away?'

While Fischer was 'at large' for those ten months, some people were saying, 'Now he is our Mandela.' (The reference was to the period when Nelson Mandela escaped a police net for more than a year, travelled abroad, and worked among his people from 'underground'.) In the jails last year (where there were more than three thousand political prisoners), when African politicals were allowed to see anybody, their first question was commonly not about their families but whether 'Bram' was still 'all right'. And a few days before sentence was to be passed on him, an African couple begged his daughter to let them borrow one of his suits, so that a witch doctor might use it in a spell to influence the judge to give a deferred sentence.

For the Fischer family, 1964–5 was a year to turn distraught any but the most tough and selfless minds. It has since become clear that, as defence counsel at the Rivonia Trial, Fischer had to muster the nerve and daring to handle evidence that might at any moment involve himself. Directly after the trial, he and his wife were driving to Cape Town to celebrate the twenty-first birthday of their daughter Ilse, a student at the University of Cape Town, and to enable Fischer to visit Mandela and the other convicted trial defendants imprisoned off the coast on Robben Island, when his car plunged into a deep pool by the side of the road and Molly Fischer was drowned.

The Fischers have always been an exceptionally devoted family, sharing as well as family love a working conviction that daily life

must realise in warm, human action any theoretical condemnation of race discrimination. In Molly Fischer the very real tradition
of Afrikaner hospitality triumphantly burst the barriers it has
imposed on itself; her big house was open to people of all races,
and, unmindful of what the neighbours would say, she and her
husband brought up along with their own daughters and son an
orphaned African child.

Molly Fischer taught Indian children, worked with women's
non-racial movements and spent five months in prison, detained
without trial, during the 1960 State of Emergency. At her huge
funeral people of all races mourned together, as if apartheid did
not exist. No one who saw him at that time can forget the terrible
courage with which Fischer turned loss into concern for the living;
neither could they confuse this with the workings of an unhinged
mind. Almost at once, he set out again for Cape Town to visit the
men on Robben Island.

If one wants to speculate why he disappeared in the middle of
his trial and yet stayed in South Africa, fully aware that when,
inevitably, he was caught he would incur greatly increased punishment, one must surely also ask oneself why, when, he was allowed
to go abroad while on bail, he ever came back. Some friends half
hoped he wouldn't; a government supporter nervously remarked
that there was nothing to stop Fischer turning up at The Hague,
where, at the time, the World Court was hearing the question of
South Africa's right to impose apartheid on the mandated territory
of South West Africa (Namibia). There would have been no extra-
dition, but a hero's role for him there.

People of different backgrounds who know Fischer best seem to
agree that what brought him back from Europe and what made him
turn fugitive were one and the same thing, the touchstone of his
personality: absolute faith in human integrity. It seems reasonable to
conclude that he came back because he believed that this integrity
was mutual and indivisible – he believed he would never be betrayed
by the people with whom he was working in opposition to apartheid,
and, in turn, he owed them the guarantee of his presence.

As for the 'gesture' of the ten months he spent in hiding, he has given, in court, his own answer to those fellow citizens – legal colleagues, firms, enemies, the white people of South Africa – who seek to judge him:

It was to keep faith with all those dispossessed by apartheid that I broke my undertaking to the court, separated myself from my family, pretended I was someone else, and accepted the life of a fugitive. I owed it to the political prisoners, to the banished, to the silenced and to those under house arrest not to remain a spectator, but to act. I knew what they expected of me, and I did it. I felt responsible, not to those who are indifferent to the sufferings of others, but to those who are concerned. I knew that by valuing, above all, their judgment, I would be condemned by people who are content to see themselves as respectable and loyal citizens. I cannot regret any such condemnation that may follow me.

The judge sentenced him to prison 'for life' and, while others wept, Fischer himself received the pronouncement with fortitude. No one can guess what goes on in a man's mind when he hears such words; but perhaps Abram Fischer, sitting it out in prison, now, may ask himself, taking courage, 'Whose life? Theirs – the government's – or mine?'

1966

Postscript: In prison Fischer suffered terminal cancer and when the news became public there was a campaign for his release. He left prison in 1975 under house arrest at the home of a relative as permission was refused for him to abide by this restriction at his daughters' home. He died on 8 May that year and his ashes were forbidden to be given into the daughters' possession lest they would become an object of political pilgrimage.

The Short Story in South Africa

Why is it that while the death of the novel is good for post-mortem at least once a year, the short story lives on unmolested? It cannot be because – to borrow their own jargon – literary critics regard it as merely a minor art form. Most of them, if pressed, would express the view that it is a highly specialised and skilful form, closer to poetry, etc. But they would have to be pressed; otherwise they wouldn't bother to discuss it at all. When Chekhov crops up, it is as a playwright, and Katherine Mansfield is a period personality from the Lady Chatterley set. Yet no one suggests that we are practising a dead art form. And, like a child suffering from healthy neglect, the short story survives.

'To say that no one now much likes novels is to exaggerate very little. The large public which used to find pleasure in prose fictions prefer movies, television, journalism, and books of "fact",' Gore Vidal wrote recently (*Encounter*, December 1967). If the cinema and television have taken over so much of the novel's territory, just as photography forced painting into wastelands which may or may not be made to bloom, hasn't the short story been overrun, too? This symposium is shop talk and it would seem unnecessary for us to go over the old definitions of where and how the short story differs from the novel, but the answer to the question must lie somewhere here. Both novel and story use the same material: human experience. Both have the same aim: to communicate it. Both use the same medium: the written word. There is a general and recurrent dissatisfaction with the novel as a means of netting ultimate reality – another term for the quality of human life – and inevitably there is even a tendency to blame the tools: words have become hopelessly blunted by overuse, dinned to death by admen, and, above all, debased by political creeds that have twisted and changed their meaning. Various ways out have been sought.

In England, a return to classicism in technique and a turning to the exoticism of sexual aberration and physical and mental abnormality as an extension of human experience and therefore of subject matter; in Germany and America, a splendid abandon in making a virtue of the vice of the novel's inherent clumsiness by stuffing it not with nineteenth-century horsehair narrative but twentieth-century anecdotal-analytical plastic foam; in France, the 'laboratory novel' struggling to get away from the anthropocentric curse of the form and the illusion of depth of the psychological novel, and landing up very much where Virginia Woolf was, years ago, staring at the mark on the wall. Burroughs has invented the reader-participation novel. For the diseased word, George Steiner has even suggested silence.

If the short story is alive while the novel is dead, the reason must lie in approach and method. The short story as a form and as *a kind of creative vision* must be better equipped to attempt the capture of ultimate reality at a time when (whichever way you choose to see it) we are drawing nearer to the mystery of life or are losing ourselves in a bellowing wilderness of mirrors, as the nature of that reality becomes more fully understood or more bewilderingly concealed by the discoveries of science and the proliferation of communication media outside the printed word.

Certainly the short story always has been more flexible and open to experiment than the novel. Short-story writers always have been subject at the same time to both a stricter technical discipline and a wider freedom than the novelist. Short-story writers have known – and solved by nature of their choice of form – what novelists seem to have discovered in despair only now: the strongest convention of the novel, prolonged coherence of tone, to which even the most experimental of novels must conform unless it is to fall apart, is false to the nature of whatever can be grasped of human reality. How shall I put it? Each of us has a thousand lives and a novel gives a character only one. *For the sake of the form.* The novelist may juggle about with chronology and throw narrative overboard; all the time his characters have the reader by the hand, there is a consistency of relationship throughout the experience that cannot and does not convey the quality of human life, where contact is more like the flash of fireflies, in and out, now here, now there, in darkness. Short-story writers see by the light of the flash; theirs is the art of the only thing one can be sure of – the present moment. Ideally, they have learned to do without explanation of what went before, and what happens beyond this point. How the characters will appear, think, behave, comprehend, tomorrow or at any other time in their lives, is irrelevant. A discrete moment of truth is aimed at – not *the* moment of truth, because the short story doesn't deal in cumulatives.

The problem of how best to take hold of ultimate reality, from the technical and stylistic point of view, is one that the short-story writer is accustomed to solving specifically in relation to an area – event, mental state, mood, appearance – which is heightenedly manifest in a single situation. Take fantasy for an example. Writers are becoming more and more aware of the waviness of the line that separates fantasy from the so-called rational in human perception. It is recognised that fantasy is no more than a shift in angle; to put it another way, the rational is simply another, the most obvious, kind of fantasy. Writers turn to the less obvious fantasy as a wider lens on ultimate reality. But this fantasy is something that changes, merges, emerges, disappears as a pattern does viewed through the bottom of a glass. It is true for the moment when one looks down through the glass; but the same vision does not transform everything one sees, consistently throughout one's whole consciousness. Fantasy in the hands of short-story writers is so much more successful than when in the hands of novelists because it is necessary for it to hold good only for the brief illumination of the situation it dominates. In the series of developing situations of the novel the sustainment of the tone of fantasy becomes a high-pitched ringing in the reader's ears. How many fantasy novels achieve what they set out to do: convey the shift and change, to and fro, beneath, above and around the world of appearances? The short story recognises that full comprehension of a particular kind in the reader, like full apprehension of a particular kind in the writer, is something of limited duration. The short story is a fragmented and restless form, a matter of hit or miss, and it is perhaps for this reason that it suits modern consciousness – which seems best expressed as flashes of fearful insight alternating with near-hypnotic states of indifference.

These are technical and stylistic considerations. Marxist criticism sees the survival of an art form in relation to social change. What about the socio-political implications of the short story's survival? George Lukács has said that the novel is a bourgeois art form whose enjoyment presupposes leisure and privacy. It implies the living room, the armchair, the table lamp; just as epic implies the illiterates round the tribal story-teller, and Shakespeare implies the two audiences – that of the people and that of the court – of a feudal age. From this point of view the novel marks the apogee of an exclusive, individualist culture; the nearest it ever got to a popular art form (in the sense of bringing people together in direct participation in an intellectually stimulating experience) was the nineteenth-century custom of reading novels aloud to the family. Here again it would seem that the short story shares the same disadvantages as the novel. It is an art form solitary in communication; yet another sign of the increasing loneliness and isolation of the individual in a competitive society. You cannot enjoy the experience of a short story unless you have certain minimum conditions of privacy in which to read it; and these conditions are those of middle-class life. But of course a short story, by reason of its length and its *completeness*, totally contained in the brief time you give to it, depends less than the novel upon the classic conditions of middle-class life, and perhaps corresponds to the break-up of that life which is taking place. In that case, although the story may outlive the novel, it may become obsolete when the period of disintegration is replaced by new social forms and the art forms that express them. One doesn't have to embrace the dreariness of conventional 'social realism' in literature to grant this. That our age is thrashing about desperately for a way out of individual human isolation, and that our present art forms are not adequate to it, is obvious to see in all the tatty dressing-up games, from McLuhan's theories to pop art, in which we seek a substitute for them.

This symposium is also concerned with the short story as a means of earning a living. I'd like to say here that I have never understood why writers are always asked bluntly what they earn (as if we were children, whose pocket money must be flatteringly exclaimed over) while businessmen would never be expected to reveal the intimacies of tax return and bank balance. I'd like to think that this is because they know we're after something more than money; and it's *that* they're not old enough to know about . . . Snobberies aside, writing stories is generally regarded as the most unlikely way of earning money, only just less hopeless than writing poetry. It goes without saying that publishers nurture their short-story writers mainly in the hope that they will write novels sooner or later. And yet I believe that writers of short stories (I'm not talking about popular hacks, of course) have more chance of working without compromise than novelists have. The novel that doesn't sell represents anything from one to five years' work – years that, economically speaking, then, the locusts have eaten. If a short story doesn't find a home (and sometimes one's more interesting stories must wait until the particular review or anthology, in which their quality is recognised, comes along), it does not represent the same loss in terms of working time. Other stories have been written within the same few months or the same year that enable the writer to go on eating. The novelist whose book sells poorly may have to turn to some other means of earning, during the next few years while he is writing (or would like to write) another novel – the journalism, teaching, etc., that takes him away from the only work he really cares to do. The short-story writer, with less capital tied up over a long period of time, as it were, has a better chance of keeping the integrity of assiduity to his own work. Also, once out of the best-seller class (and this would include a majority of serious novels, and virtually all experimental ones) a novel is dead, so far as sales are concerned, after a year. A short-story collection often represents stories that before book publication have earned money through individual publication in magazines, and which will continue to earn, long after publication and sale of the book, through individual publication in anthologies. I know that certain stories of mine are still earning money for me, fifteen years after they were written.

Although my novels have always sold better, initially, than my story collections, and now and then I have had unexpected wind-falls from novels (mainly through translations), I think I can say that my short stories have provided my bread-and-butter earnings. (And this despite the fact that there are two of the highest-paying American magazines to whom my work is not offered, because I should not like to see it published in them.) Of course, part of the reason is that quite a large number of my stories have been published in *The New Yorker*. My living as a short-story writer has been earned almost entirely in America. In England, only *Encounter* and *London Magazine* regularly publish stories of quality, for which the payment is meagre. Sporadically – apparently for prestige – one of the Sunday newspaper colour magazines buys a story for a more realistic sum – say £80 or £90: about the level of an American literary review. No story-writer could write only what he pleased and continue to eat, in England. In my own country, South Africa, both the limited size of the publishing industry and the limited size and tastes of the reading public would make it impossible for any serious writer to live off local earnings. And yet – such is the resilience and obstinacy of short-story writers – almost all the interesting fiction written by local Africans (not *white* South Africans) has taken the form of short stories.

In literature, the short story has always been a small principality. If threatened, it seems to me still remarkably independent, glori-ously eccentric, adventurous and free. After all, in the last few years, Ingeborg Bachman wrote 'Among Murderers and Madmen', Borges wrote 'The Handwriting of God', and LeClézio wrote his 'little madnesses', including 'It Seems to Me the Boat Is Heading for the Island'.

1968

Madagascar

A four-letter word brought me to Madagascar. Not the usual sort. A single word in the local tongue. I read that in the Malagasy language the world 'lolo' means both 'soul' and 'butterfly', identifying the chrysalis with the shrouded corpse, and the butterfly that emerges from it with the soul from the body of the dead. A people who could express the concepts of resurrection and the eternal renewal of life in a single image conjured up by one short word – they took a hold on my mind. That was why I went to their island in the Indian Ocean, which otherwise had attracted me neither more nor less than the dozens of others floating about the warm seas of the world under the general heading of Island Paradise: a time-spotted Gauguinesque romanticism that seems to survive for all except the inhabitants themselves, now flying the flags of their doll-sized independent nations and hoping for the discovery of off-shore oil or on-shore uranium.

Island Paradise sources of information labelled Madagascar the Great Red Island; home of the gryphon; fourth biggest island in the world. Flying over it at last, I was not surprised to find that it was, of course, not red at all: a deep, contused glow in the skin of mountains and hills cosmically wrinkled below, a flush the colour of purplish jasper that came up under the thinning grass of the dry season. Amber rivers opaque with mud moving strongly in U-curves along the valleys, roads (where there are any at all) following the same line of looping low resistance, the colour of powdered rust. As for size – while I zigzagged about the island either on land or by air (a thousand miles from end to end, three hundred and sixty across at the broadest point) with climate and landscape constantly changing, what became a reality for me was a pocket continent. And as for the poor giant gryphon bird whose last known egg, holding more than two gallons of omelette ingredient, was taken to Paris for exhibit in 1850 – the present wild-life population of lemurs proved so elusive that they might just as well have been extinct along with her. But the people were there. The Malagasy, of whose language I went knowing just one word, were not at all elusive and very much alive in the tenth year of their independence both as one of the former French colonies still under the skirts of the French Community, and as a member state of the Organisation of African Unity.

Wherever you fly in from, you alight on Madagascar at the capital, Antananarivo, four thousand feet up on the high plateau among the ribbed shapes of shining rice paddies. The island lies 250 miles across the Mozambique Channel from the south-east coast of Africa and was once probably joined to it; no one really knows. No one knows either where exactly the inhabitants came from and when, although ethnologists presume it was from the south-west Pacific in the succession of migrations from some centuries before the birth of Christ until the fifteenth century. The first thing you notice in Antananarivo is how strikingly Polynesian as opposed to African their descendants, the people in the streets, the Merina, look, and the Merina's language, which over the centuries and through their long political dominance has become the language even of the coastal tribes who have an admixture of negroid and Arab blood, is a Malayo-Polynesian dialect full of repeated syllables and long names beautiful to look at but hellish to remember. The first Merina king recorded by colonial history has a prize one: Andrianampoinimerinandriantsimitoviaminandriampanjaka. Known now as Andrianampoinimerina, it was under his rule in the eighteenth century that the Imerina kingdom began to extend its sovereignty over lesser tribal kingdoms of the island. Among the portraits of the Merina dynasty I saw hanging in the palace complex that is still perched above Antananarivo city, his picture is the only one that shows a 'native' king – naked except for a loin-kilt, feather in hair, spear in hand. When he died in 1810 his son Radama I welcomed the English and French, primarily in the hope of using the white man to help him complete the Merina conquest of the island. The portraits of all succeeding monarchs show dark-skinned queens and princes in Napoleonic satin and Victorian hour-glass velvet: the white man, in the form of the rival influences of France and England, had begun to use *them*.

Of course the riff-raff of the white world – pirates such as John Avery and William Kidd – had found the Madagascar coast a useful base, the Portuguese had discovered it in 1500 and abandoned their trading posts there two hundred years later, the Arabs had made foot-hold settlements as early as the seventh century and the French chartered companies of Louis XIV's reign had unsuccessfully attempted to colonise the south-east coast. But on Madagascar just as on the continent of Africa itself, it was in the nineteenth century that Europe's acquisitive scramble for colonies really began. France and Britain bristled at each other half-heartedly for years over 'influence' with the Merina; neither seems seriously to have wanted to take on the place. Their fortunes at the Merina court rose and fell, often promoted unofficially by eccentric individuals like the extraordinary Jean Laborde, a shipwrecked blacksmith who became Queen Ranavalona I's favourite and taught the Merina to make cannon, textiles, paper and sugar, and Cameron, a Scot, who is responsible for having fossilised the charming wooden palace in its present stone carapace. The French and English were alternately welcomed and rebuffed. Which power would take over the island finally was decided in the casual way European powers handed out other people's countries among themselves in those days of piously professed concern for the poor heathen: England swopped her chances in Madagascar in exchange for a hands-off Egypt on the part of France.

Nobody asked the Malagasy how they felt about being disposed of by this gentlemen's agreement; there were several Franco–Malagasy wars before France annexed Madagascar in 1896.

Tsihy be lambanana ny ambanilanitra – Men form one great mat

For nearly a century before the French conquest, the Merina had ruled the greater part of the island from Antananarivo. Now that the French have gone, unlike so many capitals on the African mainland it is not a white man's town from which the inhabitants have decamped; it's what it always was, long before the white man came – the island's own metropolis. It has grown more in the last ten years than in the preceding fifty, and in the new quarters of Ampefiloha there are the big apartment blocks of international middle-class living, but the lifestyle of the city radiates from the daily market – the *zoma* – of the Analakely quarter to which the splendid boulevard of the Avenue de l'Indépendance leads theatrically, overlooked by the *haute ville*, the hill faced with tall houses in smudgy pastels all the way up to the queen's palace. A wide flight of steps debouches into the blue and white umbrellas of the market from either side of the city; walking down the Escalier de Lastelle from my hotel on my first morning, I felt I was making an entrance of some sort. Indeed, it was Friday and the show was on. Every Friday the *zoma* bursts out and spreads down the entire length of the Avenue de l'Indépendance for the full width of the sidewalks and the arcades of the conventional shops.

No wonder the Merina – those makers of enviable imagery – visualise human interdependence in terms of weaving. Although the *zoma* stalls sell everything from furniture to horoscopes and rose quartz, from delicious oysters to dried octopus like stiff old gloves, and medicinal ingredients that looked as if they might quite possibly be the tongues of newts, what most people were selling was made of straw. Impossible to catalogue so many different objects woven in so many ways out of different kinds of straw – rice, maize, palm, banana-leaf, raffia. There's nothing more satisfying to buy than something made of straw; it's beautiful, cheap, and cannot last – thus gratifying the eye, the desire to get something for nothing, and leaving one free of the guilt of laying up treasures less ephemeral than the flesh.

And picking a way through the weavers' stalls was also to become threaded into the great mat of people who were trading or buying. A quarter of a million live in Antananarivo; most of them seemed to be in the streets, but it was not noisy and nobody jostled – if anyone did, nobody lost his temper. The Merina, whether or not

they have adopted Western dress (all the women have), still wear
the *lamba*, a long cloth, usually white but sometimes a surprising
saffron, draped Mexican-style across the shoulders. It looked
very fine with ordinary trousers and jacket, and on women with
babies enveloped the baby head and all against the mother's body.
Malagasy babies must feel extremely secure in this intermediary
stage between the womb and the world.

Every man was wearing a hat, and everyone who wanted to look
a man – that is, every little barefoot urchin. A straw hat of course,
and usually sombrero-shaped. The sombrero and the poncho are
a dashing combination: but the Merina are not dashing at all, on
them this outfit confers a sombre dignity. If there is anything
definitively un-African about them apart from their looks, it is this
quiet demeanour. In place of black ebullience, brown calm.

I was in a taxi one day when it was almost run down by another.
The two drivers, eye to eye through glass, paused for a long moment.
No word, no gesture from either. We drove on. Are there no curses
in Malagasy? Even if there are not, neither driver resorted to the
riches of French invective. In place of temperament, withdrawal.

Zanahary ambonin'ny tany – Gods on earth

It turned out that the one word *I* knew was a key one. For the
Malagasy, both the Merina of the high plateau and the *côtiers* – the
coastal tribes – the dead are part of life. *Lolo* is dead soul ghosting
the earth, and living butterfly. The *lamba* is precisely the same
garment as the shroud. In ancient times there was a civilisation
stretching from the Indian Ocean to Melanesia, based on the cult
of the dead and the cultivation of rice. The ancestors of the Merina
brought from the Pacific the art of cultivating rice in irrigated
paddies, and possibly the cult of the dead along with it. Both have
survived into the present day. The dead are believed to be the sole
source of happiness, peace, and above all, fertility. The greatest
virtue for a Malagasy lies in actual physical contact with the corpse;
during the dry season from May to September, as often over the
years as they can afford it, the family gathers, sometimes from

great distances, at the family tomb to exhume the bodies, give them fresh shrouds and a breath of air, and celebrate their presence with drinking and feasting. Christian conversion (about 40 per cent of the population practise Christianity) and conversion to Islam (about 5 per cent are Moslem) have been accommodated to the custom by the Malagasy instead of resulting in its abolition. President Philibert Tsiranana's democratic government, which would prefer people's energies to be directed to raising production as a means of attaining peace, happiness, fertility, etc., has to tread delicately in its efforts to discourage it.

I wasn't sure whether I wanted to join the party at an exhumation. But I did want to see the tombs, whether the occupants were taking the air or not, because the cult has given rise to an extraordinary religious art – grave sculptures in wood. I knew that the best examples were to be seen far from Antananarivo, in the south, near the west coast ports of Tuléar and Morondava. The charming and helpful Malagasy in Antananarivo were unexpectedly discouraging when I said I would go by car – why not fly? I would settle for Morondava, then, if Tuléar was too far to drive. I was a bit puzzled when it was calculated that Morondava – only 250 miles – would take as long to reach, but didn't want to listen to any more objections, and set off in a new hired French car with a skilful Malagasy driver on a route marked as a national highway. We did get there – after two days, the second a knuckle-whitening climb over the spine of the island and down through the mountains by way of stony gullies, carrying our own petrol and always hoping the next bridge wouldn't be down. My apprehension was put to shame by the fairly frequent appearance of small shoe-box-shaped buses, marked *taxi brousse* (bush taxi) that rocked by, crowded with serene faces. Anyway I had jolted into me unforgettably that the greatest need of the island is roads. It has one of the best networks of internal air services in the world – used by foreign businessmen, government officials and visitors. Air tickets are far beyond the pocket of the average Malagasy, and apart from the line connecting Antananarivo with the principal port, Tamatave, there are only a few strips of railroad. If half the country's 1963–73 development plan funds have been earmarked for the improvement of transport, there's not much to show for the money so far on Highway 24.

Down on the other side of the mountains was flat country with the peculiar hot silence of the bush invested, like power, in the monolithic growth of baobab trees; forms from the sophisticated imagination of a Miró, planked down in the nowhere. Morondava was a one-street town of Indian and Chinese shops, an old colonial hotel enclosed by jalousies, and a lovely beach with the Indian Ocean rolling in. I set off for the grave sites. First a visit to the chief's village at Maravoay; this part of the island was once the kingdom of Sakalava and is still inhabited by Sakalava tribes, who are negroid, so the old man in a loincloth was unmistakably African. He refused permission to view the graves: recently somebody had sawn off grave figures and taken them away. While the driver protested my honest intentions, I was watching a woman making-up in a cheap store mirror, drawing a dotted pattern in white clay across her cheekbones and down her nose. Better housewives were occupied threshing rice. We had to return to Morondava to buy a bottle of rum; then the chief stiffly relented. We drove through dry winter bush from the village of the living to the village of the dead. In a clearing among paper-bark trees with livid trunks sloughing tattered parchment, were the small fenced allotments the dead occupy. These were all about six by eight feet, and the shoulder-high palings were decorated with finial carvings of birds and humans, and tall, totemic geometrical cut-outs, so that the place seemed peopled above ground as well as below. It was very quiet; I saw that butterflies were hovering everywhere. . . .

The tombs I had seen in other areas were blind cement or stone structures, some with a kind of doll's house on top, and the form that grave sculptures take also varies according to region. The Mahafaly sculptures farther south are totems, sometimes surmounted by miniature tableaux from the dead man's life – his cattle, his house, his family; the horns of sacrificed Zebu cattle are part of the monument. The Vezo (a Sakalava tribe) sculptures around Morondava are unique in their eroticism. At Maravoay, among the representations of colonial messengers in de Gaulle caps, ladies in European blouse and skirt complete with high-heeled pumps and dangling handbag, there was a single couple shown in The Act, he, still wearing his messenger's cap, peering rather nervously from behind her intimidatingly female body as if caught in an irresistible indiscretion while on duty.

But at Ambato, a site a few miles up the coast among deserted sand dunes within view but not sound of the sea, the first sight of the village of the dead was of a village petrified in orgy. On the fifty-odd graves, couples – and an occasional threesome – are represented in almost all the common and uncommon variations of sexual intercourse. In this desolate place the sight comes as a *statement* rather than a spectacle: through the moment of man's most intense experience of his own body, the assertion of his fecundity against nothingness. It has the audacity of a flag stuck on the moon.

Of course, for a non-believer (in the context of ancestor-worship) it's tempting to see the fierce joy of coupling as defiance of the loneliness of the grave, Andrew Marvell's fine and private place where none embrace. But this is as subjective as my driver's explanation that these dead had been 'very fond of women'. Apparently the truth has little to do with either the grave occupants' sexual capacity or resentment against death; the skilful lovers symbolise the fertility that, like all good things, comes to the living from the dead.

While the clothed and painted figures are naive in conception and execution, and the partly-clothed couples lean towards caricature, many of the naked couples are works of extraordinary beauty and technical achievement. Since they are embellishment first and faithful representation only second, artistic licence is dictated by the necessity to show all positions as vertical. The way in which the sculptor has solved problems of form and volume in dealing with the interplay of limbs and bodies is often masterly. Some of the sculptures have a classical tenderness rather than the expressionism or symbolism associated with other 'primitive' sculpture. And there was one grave in particular where the total conception showed a complex creative vision: human couples were alternated with pairs of mating birds, the sacred ibis with their slender beaks affectionately intertwined, one pair linked by a small fish, its tail in the one beak, its head gripped by the other.

Malagasy sculptors often hand down their art, not only from father to son but also from mother to daughter. A family tree of the sculptors of Iakoro hangs in the ethnological museum in Antananarivo. But the artistic tradition is dying out, the grave sites are not protected, and not one of the magnificent grave sculptures from Morondava is preserved in a museum in Madagascar. I righted a grave-post topped by a lovely bird that was being ground to dust by the jaws of ants; there were so many others, powdering into the sand. I suppose soon the only ones left will be those that appear, mysteriously (export is forbidden) in the rich art collections of Europe and America. There was that story of the old chief at Maravoay: 'some people had sawn off figures and gone away . . .'

Out of the cult of the dead, the oligarchy of the Merina, the oligarchy of the French that followed – the *lolo* of the Malagasy Republic that emerged in 1960 has had time to dry its wings in peace. President Tsiranana and his PSD (Social Democratic Party) – extremely conservative, despite the name – stay comfortably in power while on the mainland of Africa coups and counter-coups come and go. Tsiranana (of the Tsimihety tribe) and many of his top men are *côtiers*, and although they are anxious to prove that they stand for a democratic, non-tribal government and have largely succeeded, they represent the final defeat of the aristocratic Merina as well as independence of white rule. Yet the Merina with their monopoly of the capital province, their lingering caste system, their educational superiority and natural aloofness remain an overwhelming presence when you are on the island – their palace may be empty, but they *are* Madagascar as no other single element is. The French presence also remains in evidence, particularly in Antananarivo; the governor's rose-coloured, tin-roofed palace becomes the French Embassy, the work of Boris Vian and Malraux being presented at the *Centre Culturel Albert Camus*, French food and wine in every restaurant (if you have to be colonised at all, how lucky to be colonised by the French). French culture 'takes', and survives political bitterness in her former colonies. Jacques Rabemananjara, Minister of Foreign Affairs, once one of the famous rebels exiled from Madagascar after the bloody 1947 uprising against France, is a Malagasy poet who writes in French, just as Senghor, poet and President of Senegal, belongs also to French literature. Whether due to French influence or the traditional oral culture of the Malagasy with its *ankamantatra* (riddles), *ohabolana* (proverbs), and *anatra* (good advice), often combined in short, sometimes erotic poems called *hain-teny*, Antananarivo publishes more newspapers than any place I've ever been. On the Escalier de Lastelle, among the booths selling cheap sunglasses and the island's semi-precious stones, I counted fourteen Malagasy newspapers pegged up for sale round a cigarette stall; but there are, in fact, about 155, some in French, for a total population of six million people. Writing poetry seems to be a prestigious pastime; among the papers were privately printed booklets of amateur verse with the dim picture of a bespectacled teacher or civil-servant author on the cover.

President Tsiranana, who needs only a lei round his neck to look like a welcoming Polynesian host in a travelogue, was a particularly close friend of General de Gaulle and no doubt will now embrace Pompidou as warmly. France remains the island's main source of economic aid and biggest customer for its products, mainly stimulating, nourishing, sweet or fragrant – coffee, tobacco, rice, manioc, sugar, cloves and vanilla. The United States is next best customer; the trade began in pirate days when an American buccaneer vessel introduced Malagasy rice to North Carolina. The Malagasy I talked to were disappointed at the smallness of American investment and aid, though. In five years after independence the US gave only $13 million.

The island can feed itself abundantly, but apart from nickel on the eastern side – and of course there is the inevitable oil-prospection going on – has none of the important mineral discoveries that bring the white world flying in to promote development. For this reason it is making a late and hasty entry in the Island Paradise lists, and has begun a jet service that links it with the regular tourist run down Africa. Nossi-bé, a tiny island off the north-west coast

of the main one, has been decided on as the main draw outside
Antananarivo itself. And no wonder – you don't have to drive
to get there, and a short flight lands you in a place that really
does seem to have escaped debased Gauguinism. Brilliant sugar
cane lying stroked back, silky, in the breeze, sudden dark walls
of tropical forest, coffee bushes flowering white rosettes, ylang-
ylang perfume trees weirdly espaliered, great glossy-leaved mango
trees ivied with pepper vines – the whole island rustles softly and
breathes sweet. The government-owned hotel in a coconut grove
on one of the beaches has a tiny casino under a banana-leaf roof
where you can play baccarat (why is it presumed that at the end of
getting away from it all, as at the end of the rainbow, there's got to
be a pot of gold?) but the real action was down the beach on Sunday
morning, when two busloads of Sakalava arrived for some occasion
I'm sure was more important than a mere picnic. On this shore of
Madagascar, nearest to the East Coast of Africa and African and
Arab influences along the ancient trade routes of the Indian Ocean,
the *lamba* becomes a brilliant cotton robe worn by women – I could
see the restless pollen-yellow, purple, red, orange, from afar. They
wore elaborately filamented Arab-style jewellery on ears and necks,
turbans, flowers picked from the forest that shaded the edge of the
sand, and some used lipstick as well as sophisticated variations of
the clay-patterned maquillage I had seen down south, at Maravoay.
Drums, flutes and clappers entertained the company. They drank
and ate from enormous black boarding-house pots that were then
scrubbed clean in the sea by the painted ladies with their robes
hitched up. The men put on smart nylon trunks from France and
went in for a swim. Then the whole party was drummed, piped and
clappered back into their *taxis brousse*.

At the inauguration of the Organisation of African Unity in Addis
Ababa in 1963, President Tsiranana hopefully suggested that the
Organisation's title should include the words 'and Malagasy' after
'African'; he was curtly told that if the Malagasy didn't consider
their state African, they had no place in the Organisation at all. But
Merinas and *côtiers* alike, the islanders privately don't really regard

themselves as Africans even now, when for political and economic reasons as well as ancient geographical ones, their destiny is lumped in along with that of the Third World. Tsiranana, in addition to his natural conservatism, fears the proximity of the Chinese-Communist-controlled island of Zanzibar, and places Madagascar 'without any bad conscience' among the moderate African states in the OAU and not the revolutionary ones; but he also allows himself to have no bad conscience over the fact that the new jet service is run in collaboration with South Africa, and Madagascar is receiving trade missions from there, while the OAU condemns any contact with the country of white minority rule and colour bar. Of course, the agricultural machinery Madagascar buys from France would be so much cheaper, imported from nearby South Africa . . .

It was only in my last two hours on the island that I went up to the queen's palace that I had seen from my bathroom window in Antananarivo every morning. One of those neck-dislocating rides to see the sights: here the Presidential Palace (once the Royal Prime Minister's) with its onion turrets and central glass dome of a steam-age exhibition building, there the old Royal tribunal, a Greek temple of pillars and pink stone – and then the group of strange mansions, large and small, that crowns the town and is known collectively as the *rova*. Beside the Manjakamiadana, the palace that Cameron turned to stone, is the Tranovola, the Treasury Palace, an enormous Victorian wooden doll's house, its white verandah arches of cathedral proportion, and inside, delightful naive murals in which fruit, flowers and people's eyes have the same open gaze. Beside the Tranovola, two tiny yellow-and-green pagodas on a stone platform – the royal tombs, to which the last Queen, Ranavalona III, was brought back from her exile's grave in Algeria in 1938. *Her* palace is like a country house built by one of those decadently Europeanised Russians in Turgenev: partly English, partly Swiss cuckoo-clock, with an Italianate touch.

Hidden among the decorative and architectural mannerisms of nineteenth-century England and Europe is Andrianampoinimerina's original royal Great Place; I use the African term for a king's quarters because 'palace' is too cheaply grandiloquent for this lofty shelter with tall crossed lances at either end of its steep roof. A dwelling like a tent made of thick black wood, divided internally only by the differentiation of the hearth from the rest of the tamped-earth floor. Round the walls are his carved wooden shields, his spears and muskets, and his drinking vessels made of clay given a pewter patina with graphite.

The museum curator (we showed off to one another, agreeing that some of the palace murals were pure Douanier Rousseau) apologised for rushing me, but there was a Japanese trade delegation in town, and she was due to escort them through the palaces any moment; they arrived just as I left, very small and neat and alert with the magpie curiosity they carry everywhere. What had they come to Madagascar to sell? What had they come to buy?

An hour later, waiting for the plane to take me away, I bought a newspaper and read an announcement that work had started in Antananarivo on the Madagascar Hilton. I remembered reading how President Tsiranana had once said, expressing the detachment of the Malagasy as well as a sly dig at Africa's troubles, 'If the *Bon Dieu* proposed to me that Madagascar should be rejoined to the African continent, I would ask him to let it remain an island.'

Well, we all know that no man is an island; but no island is an island, either – not now. Can't afford to be. From among the corpses and butterflies, the crook'd finger is beckoning, and sooner or later, for one reason or another the continents will close in.

1969

The 1970s

Merci Dieu, It Changes

Accra and Abidjan

Ghana five years after Nkrumah. I didn't ever see it in his time, but his presence has been so omnipresent in the consciousness of contemporary Africa that one approaches – at last – the physical reality of Accra in terms of a place where he once was. Black Star Square. The first of those vast independence celebration stadia that were built in country after country, and now stand, grandiose and deserted, eternally gouged of an occasion whose historical immensity, of course, can never come again. This one is backed by the huge rough seas that ride up the coast of West Africa. The empty arena looks lonely as power is supposed to be. The famous statue of Osagyefo isn't there; some harmless Unknown Soldier enthroned in its place. What about the victims, said to be Nkrumah's sacrifices to witchcraft, supposed to be buried there? Did they dig them up for decent burial, after the coup? Did they dig anyway, and find nothing? Is that what such legends are: the same nothingness, whether filled by the malice of white foreigners branding Africa eternally savage, or by the projected fears of bewildered Africans themselves?

Going about the town, every day I pass Flagstaff House (army headquarters), the broadcasting station, and police headquarters. Colonial-looking entrances with white walls, flags, sentry boxes, and that ivy of Africa, splurgy bougainvillea, lounging over all. But it was here the coup took place, the young Major Afrifa and his soldiers marched in, those in power fired back or escaped out of windows, there was a few days' confusion, a little blood, and it was done.

The airport is renamed after Colonel Emmanuel Kotoka, a

maker of the coup and victim of an abortive counter-coup a year later – he was taken there and shot. Accra is a lusty warren where the pressure of humanity overruns mere bricks and mortar and one hardly notices the buildings whose batteredness certainly predates the coup, but here and there are nameless edifices in Independence baroque whose expanse has no life behind it. In one, a window open, a piece of clothing hung out to dry; someone is perhaps camping within the shell. This was once the headquarters of the powerful United Ghana Farmers' Council, which, along with the women's movement, became the only expression of the people's will – and it seems he made sure their will was his – Nkrumah consulted once he had become both the Head of State and chief executive, Life Chairman and General Secretary of the governing Convention People's Party, and no longer even held party congresses. Other landmarks interest me in a detached way; this one stops me short, with a private melancholy. There are so few African countries where the people who live off the land become a power and have a real say in the direction of government policy: it was a noble beginning, even if it went badly wrong, this time. I want to accost someone, anyone, in the street and tell him: as a Ghanaian, as an African, it must be tried again. And again and again.

But to be white in the streets of Accra is to feel oneself curiously anonymous and almost invisible; one is aware of one's unimportance, in terms of what a white face has meant and now means to people. To be white is to have been rendered harmless: a rather pathetic centuries-old monster the source of whose power-myth has been revealed to be mumbo-jumbo.

Tema is a Sunday drive up the coast from Accra. It's Nkrumah's city in the way that a city is the possession of the man who has a beautiful scale model, tall buildings, perfect clover-leaf flyovers, miniature trees and gardens, cars and people – just as if it were real. Nkrumah must have had such a model somewhere in Christiansborg Castle. The half-realisation of Tema – the city has never been completed – shows that it would have been like all those Brasilias that have to go through a process of attrition by humans, in accordance with obstinate local styles of life that keep making nonsense of 'international' architecture. Meccano giants step up at every change of the car's perspective. They climb down to the port, carrying power from the Akosombo Dam – in terms of surface, the biggest man-made lake in the world – to the Kaiser aluminium smelter. From a long green plain away, industrial towers proclaim a new faith in place of the single steeple among the huts that used to proclaim that other white man's religion in African towns. The splendid roads loop and bend according to plan, but often debouch into a bank of weeds. There is a slope covered with good neat houses; against the walls of the refinery a shanty town made with packing cases has cooking fires smoking away – that's underdevelopment, it's a way of life dictated by necessity and as difficult to put an end to as to put out the grass fires that burn up Africa.

The famous deep-water harbour is very fine, with every bolt on its straddling cranes carefully vaselined against rust, but there are few ships and no one about, the quays so neat that I notice some spilt peanuts as the only evidence of cargo. Perhaps it's because it's Sunday; the figures show that Tema handles more traffic than the old harbour of Takoradi. As for the aluminium smelter, the government would like the American consortium to finance the exploitation of local, if low-grade, bauxite deposits at Kibi, instead of using raw material brought in by Kaiser from Jamaica and Australia. That's the present situation – a variation of but hardly emancipation from the colonial role in which Africa produced the raw materials and the processing into profitable finished products was the preserve of others.

On the way back to Accra, I drive down to the promontory where Christiansborg Castle has stood for three centuries. Blinding white, looking through palm trees at the sea, it appears Arab rather than Danish. If what one can see *is* the castle at all; it has been much built around and to various purposes through various occupancies. Now it is nobody's castle, an administrative block. You cannot enter, but you can walk round part of the thick white walls with stopped-up cannon in their embrasures. Nkrumah, whose palace this became, passed through this gateway in state one day and did not dream he would not come back. Following the walls towards the sea, I suddenly find a grave. Dr W.E.B. DuBois, American Negro, father of Pan-Africanism, came home from his race's long exile from Africa to die, and he lies here for ever.

Peace to the huts; war on the palaces.

The pennant that is hoisted over every revolution and every coup. Nkrumah spent £8 million to build State House for an eight-day OAU conference. When he left for Peking and Hanoi on his last journey as President of Ghana, he took £45,000 of the £51,000 left in the state treasury. The present regime, avowed as well as forced to economy by Ghana's national debt – estimated at $850 million – has been able to build no road or bridge since 1967. While I was in Accra there was a strike of sanitary workers because they had not been issued with gloves and protective clothing, and when some formality took me to a local police station, I saw that the policemen did not have complete uniforms, either. One of the issues taken up by a fiery little Accra newssheet, the *Spokesman*, was the elaborate house being built by President Kofi Busia in his home village. While lack of foreign exchange means that all sorts of essential imports must be forgone, thousands of cedis worth of luxury fittings and material for Dr Busia's house are being imported. It is no State House or Christiansborg, yet certainly it will be a palace in comparison with the yards of Accra, where children, chickens and rubble seem awash on open drains, and people are paying 20 pesewas (100 pesewas to the cedi; the cedi worth roughly a dollar) for two plantain bananas.

Although the government has just published a pamphlet on the subject of President Busia's willingness to open a dialogue with South Africa, stressing that the Ghanaian stand differed from that of the other main supporter of dialogue, the Ivory Coast, in that Ghana intended to continue to support the Liberation Movements at the same time, most people seemed more embarrassed than anything else by the idea of the first of the independent black states talking to one of the last strongholds of white power. The issue that was preoccupying the press in general and the members of the Opposition party was the government's proposal to change the chairmanship of the Regional Councils from an elected to a government-appointed position. Nkrumah abolished the Regional Councils; they have been reinstated and are the most important move, outside free elections, away from wholly centralised power and back to genuine contact with the needs and wishes of ordinary people.

Of course, the very fact that there is an Opposition to walk out of the House in protest over such matters, and a *Spokesman* exists to attack the nature of the asceticism of Dr Busia's regime, says something for that regime. As another visiting foreigner remarked to me – 'At least no one's in jail.' There are no political prisoners.

The faces in public office, like the façades of the buildings stripped of their original designation, carry still the Nkrumah image, in reverse. They are almost all men whom he denounced and discarded; the pedigree for high position is exile or imprisonment under Nkrumah. But the faces of the junta which ruled the country from 1966 to the first post-coup elections in 1969 are strikingly absent. Members of both the government and Opposition are vague about the present activities of these army (and police-) men, and meet stiffly the reasonable question: why has none of them come forward to serve, in politics, as a civilian?

So far as I could gather, all have relinquished their army careers. Ex-Colonel Afrifa is running that old West African money-maker, a transport business; nobody seemed to know what General Ankrah himself was doing these days, and at least one dignitary said with asperity that he didn't care, either. 'They promised to hand over to civilian government after a specified time, and they had to keep that promise.' Only Afrifa, under forty, had gone so far as to remark that the provision that the new president of Ghana must be over forty was an insult to the youth of the country; interpret that as frustrated political ambition of the highest order, if you like.

Everyone has heard of the mammy wagons of Ghana, a chaotic unscheduled bus service that gets people dangerously where they want to go without the dreary queueing and frustration insepa-rable from ordinary bus services. Everyone knows that these trucks bear sayings or slogans. There is something evangelistic about even the most hedonistic of them, something exhortatory and moral, that suggests their original inspiration must have been missionary: those texts on love or sin chalked on boards outside churches. What I didn't know before I went there was that Ghana taxis have their statements, too, in the form of stickers on the dashboards. One gets into the habit of looking for omens – a private text-for-the-day, a warning? – as one moves around in Accra. Perhaps there will be a message to be interpreted only by oneself (like letting a hotel Gideon Bible fall open where it will), in the next taxi one climbs into. One afternoon there was. Just two words that were the last word on everything I had seen and heard and done. 'It changes.'

Ivory Coast from the Accra–Abidjan plane had a brocade texture, the crowns of thousands of palms in plantation pattern.

Abidjan: like all cities built on water it has the extraordinary quality of perpetually looking at itself. Even the stream of evening traffic, seen twice over from across one of the lagoons – once on the road, once reflected in the water – is hypnotic, narcissistic, silenced and calmed into a flow of liquid darkness and floating flares. Why haven't I read it was like this? I decide it is one of those places you have to go to, that perhaps really don't exist at all unless you are in them. It certainly doesn't exist in any comparison I might try.

Abidjan is full of flowers you cannot and have no wish to identify – not merely that apoplectic bougainvillea and coarse hibiscus trumpeting 'tropical paradise', but huge trees pollened with yellow and pink, and verges knee-deep in delicate lilies like just-struck match flames. There are unexpected scents; not only the whiff of 'Femme' or 'Je Reviens' from one of the passing white French ladies, but the delicious sweat of warm flowers. The high-rise architecture is outstandingly imaginative, anyway, slender buildings standing on stork legs that emphasise the relation of the city to water, but the real reason why these blocks are so much more successfully rooted in their environment than is usual, is because for once the *scale* of natural growth within it matches them. There are trees, here, that are not dwarfed by a skyscraper. They look as if they had been waiting through centuries for men to learn how to build in the proportions of the tropical forest.

The hotel I live in, across the water from the city in the 'diplomatic' suburb of Cocody, has a swimming pool where wives of French businessmen spend the day watching their children; occasionally, in the outdoor bar overlooking the lagoon, a white couple entertain a rich or distinguished black man and his lady, in the way of business or diplomacy, with an air of exaggerated ease. Opposite the craftsmen's market in town, a coffee-shop-cum-bar-restaurant is filled with Frenchmen eating a businessman's lunch and reading the Paris papers, while pestering Senegalese traders, quick to recognise a tourist face among them, parade snakeskin sandals and indigo-dyed caftans along the terrace. In arcades and side-streets, Lebanese sit entombed by the rolls of wax-print cloth whose market they traditionally corner. Outside boutiques showing the current *fantaisie* of the Boulevard St Germain, black boys have their home-made stalls selling cigarettes and gum. Down in their big market Africans congregate endlessly round small purchases from the numerous petty traders, seated before a pyramid of a few tomatoes or eggs, dried fish or cola nuts, who all seem to make a living, in Africa.

In a bar where I go to escape the midday heat, the blonde *patronne* in hot pants and boots is making up her eyes before a mirror and the indifference of a very tall Latin wearing a handbag, while a black barman plays a worn Georges Moustaki record over and over. The tall man shoulders his handbag and leaves, and the *patronne* at once turns prettily: 'What can you do, Madame? – I love him. He's Italian, he has to go back to Rome. But when you fall in love – eh?'

Yes, Abidjan is a beautiful city. A beautiful colonial city, despite its ten-year independence. With all the colonial preoccupations, comforts and diversions. There are twice as many French here as there were before independence. In Accra *you* – the visitor – can't get a decent bottle of wine or find a taxi whose window handles aren't missing so that you can close up against the rain. But dirty Accra on a Saturday – the dinner-bells of traders ringing, the vast chatter and surge of the streets, the sense not of people on their

way through the streets but of life being lived there; the bars and
hotels of Accra, the female tycoons of trade and transport with flesh
and finery piled up splendidly, ringed hands round glasses, voices
holding forth to men puny by contrast, the dancers sauntering to
the lazy pluck and thump of highlife music, the little velvety-faced
tarts with narrow hands, assuming bored solitude on a bar stool or
taking over the ladies' room to adjust already exquisitely arranged
turbans or hitch the angle of a breast under cloth – the Ghanaians
are living their own life and all quarters of their shabby capital are
theirs. Accra belongs to them in a way that Abidjan doesn't seem
to belong to the Ivoiriens.

This remains valid although in the days that follow I go to
Treichville and Adjamé, the African quarters, and see for myself that
the Ivoiriens are materially better off than Ghanaians. Everywhere new
housing schemes have been realised, and the houses, though basic as
sub-economic habitations must be, are decent and imaginative. There
are schools with lacy brick walls to let in the air; and market-places
covered against the sun and provided with facilities to keep them
clean. These are the things that the people need; it is something of a
surprise to find them here, instead of the black slums which, in Africa,
usually lie behind the white men's air-conditioned shops and bars.

Ghana and the Ivory Coast started off similarly endowed with
natural resources – Ghana is the biggest cocoa producer in the world,
Ivory Coast the third biggest producer of coffee – and geared economically to the provision of raw materials for the industrial powers of
the developed world. For the rest, the neighbours could hardly have
been more different: Ghana under Nkrumah one of the most radical,
the Ivory Coast under Félix Houphouët-Boigny the most conservative of new African states. While Nkrumah has had his stool kicked
from under him, Houphouët-Boigny, who has put down whatever
discontents may have shivered from time to time across the lagoons
of Abidjan, still lives in the tall pagoda-shaped residence among
the palms and flowers of Cocody whose lack of any suggestion of
a fortress surely reflects confidence. Ghana, the richer country to
begin with, is hobbled by debt; Ivory Coast had a trade balance of
32 million Central African francs in 1969. She is the *enfant chéri* of

France, showered with loans and French capital that have helped her diversify her economy, in return for President Houphouët-Boigny's loyal promotion of French influence and interests within such important groups as his Conseil d'Entente (Ivory Coast, Dahomey, Niger, Upper Volta) and OCAM (Afro-Malagasy Common Organisation) all the way up to the OAU, where he leads the call for dialogue with apartheid Pretoria, while French arms sales to South Africa are difficult to explain away to African states.

Those African states dedicated to radical change in the life of the masses rather than broadening the base of a black elite have so far achieved less for the masses than conservative states who have been content to foster a black elite, perpetuate foreign private enterprise and foreign investment, and finance social uplift out of the fringe benefits of capitalism, so to speak. It seems ironic. But it is not conclusive. It's a blessing to be given decent sub-economic housing, schools, hospitals and markets. But will the people, particularly the people in the interior – always so different from the capital, in African countries – get any further than that, under Africanised but colonial-style capitalism? In West Africa more than 80 per cent of the people still live on the land. Will they ever be more than the beneficiaries of the charity of the elite?

There is no impudent *Spokesman* published in Abidjan; in fact, French journalists must take care, when reporting local issues to Paris, not to annoy the French government by criticising the Houphouët-Boigny regime. Apart from Houphouët-Boigny's there is a palace there, though of a curious kind – indeed, a whole 100,000-acre Versailles is under construction. The part-state, part-American-owned Hotel Ivoire, with its thousand rooms, casino, theatre and ice-skating rink, was just along the lagoon shore from my modest hotel. I wandered there one day by way of a path made by servants' and fishermen's feet, following the shore. Someone's little patch of maize was being cultivated; high grass touched my cheeks on either side. Once inside the movie-labyrinth of the hotel, I was still wandering – along soaring, carpet-muffled corridors, glass galleries, through lounges that reduce the human figure to a small stroke, past bars buried like Chinese boxes. There was a model of the total plan of which this place is only part: an 'international tourist area', 'garden city environment' for 120,000 people, that will encompass whole existing African villages for the diversion of those tourists for whom the attraction of golf clubs, convention halls and an Olympic sports centre palls. To 'see' Africa, natives and all, it will not be necessary to stir from this environment of grotesque home comforts created by the Californian architect and urban planner William Pereira and Mr Moshe Mayer, an Israeli millionaire whose family-portrait face is displayed along with a letter from President Houphouët-Boigny, welcoming the project and referring to Mr Mayer as 'my dear friend'. This part of Africa was once known as the White Man's Grave; now he sees it as his pleasure-ground. A shift in the angle of a timeless subjectivity? Hardly more, and little enough.

There are not many mammy wagons in Abidjan. Those that exist generally have no identification except their registration plates. But when I went to the bus station in Adjamé with a professor of philosophy who had sat marking *baccalauréat* papers in the open-air bar of our hotel, there was a message for me. While we talked, a mammy wagon was being loaded with passengers and bundles. It had a worn text, decorated with painted flowers, half-legible; I could just make out the words, *'Merci Dieu'*. Since I am a white South African and the professor was a black Ivoirien, it was natural that we should be discussing the idea of dialogue between our two countries. What was perhaps a little less predictable was that I was arguing against dialogue, because – as I was quick to illustrate my point – the kind of contact between two enfranchised individuals he and I were having was what was needed within my country, rather than talk between the white establishment of that country and black statesmen from other countries – and he, on the basis of how well *we* got on, if nothing else, was prepared to give dialogue a trial. Well, yes – thank heaven for small mercies, not everything is predictable in Africa these days – whatever else has happened, the old equations, the defined roles, national and personal, good and bad, are all in question.

1971

Pack Up, Black Man

Americans who are repelled by a colour bar, but are at least prepared to consider that the South African 'separate development' political philosophy of apartheid may be something other than Jim Crow legislation under another name, have told me that they did not know what to think of the South African government's resettlement schemes for blacks. Living so far away, ignorant of local conditions, is one qualified to judge?

There are many white South Africans, living right in the country but at a distance from the conditions of the blacks no less palpable than the many thousand miles that separate New York and Johannesburg, who express similar reservations. Isn't decentralisation vital, anyway, for industrialised countries? Isn't it a good idea to clear rural slums? Politics aside – and in South Africa, separate development purports to aim at the eventual partition of the country, along lines laid down exclusively by the whites, between black and white – don't the industrial planners and community development experts know best?

I would say to Americans what I have said to my fellow white South Africans. You know well enough to eat when hungry, don't you? To turn on the heat when you're cold? To choose a place to live at the rent you can afford, on a transport route convenient to your work, your children's schools, and the pursuit of your interests?

That is all the expertise needed to judge the reasonable needs of any fellow human being. Forget about his colour or 'what he was used to'; he hungers, thirsts, and must work for a living just as you do. It is too easy for us to shelter behind the analyses of the behavioural sciences, that serve to rationalise the American 'hamlet' system in Vietnam as the 'restructuring' of society rather than the waging of war, and the crypto-behavioural theory of apartheid that rationalises arbitrary resettlement in South Africa on the premise that affinity of skin colour and race overrides all other human needs.

In South Africa, in ten years, 900,000 black people have been moved from their homes because the lands on which they were living – and some had been settled up to a hundred years – have been declared 'black spots' in a white area. The blacks have had no choice. The moves are decreed under laws they had no voice in making, since they have no vote. They are poor people, who lived humbly where they were; do not imagine that they are set down in some sort of model village, the shell of a bright new community waiting to be inhabited.

They are usually eventually granted some sort of compensation for the houses they leave behind to be bulldozed, but where they are sent, there are no new ones: at best, some basic building materials may be supplied, and they are expected to build new homes themselves, living meanwhile in tents that may or may not be supplied. There may be water nearby, and fuel; often they must walk miles for these necessities. If they are rural people and are moved to a bit of ground classified non-rural, they must sell their cattle before they go.

The bit of ground may be near a white town where work is available, or may not – it has not proved to be part of the 'planning' to ensure in advance that those who lose employment by the move shall be provided with alternative employment where they are ordered to live. Some settlements consist entirely of unemployables – officially termed 'surplus people', 'redundant people', 'non-productive people' – swept out of the towns since they cannot serve as units of labour.

The physical conditions of resettlement are practically without exception of such desolation that confronted with them, one is almost unable to think beyond bread and latrines. The sense of urgency aroused on behalf of people whose struggle for existence has been reduced to a search for wood to make a fire, a bucket of clean water to drink, 20 cents to pay a bus fare to a clinic, is inclined to set the mind safely on ameliorating such unthinkable concrete hardships. Newspaper accounts of these conditions have led the public of Johannesburg, for example, to do what is known locally as 'opening its heart' to pour forth from the cornucopia of white plenty, blankets, food and medicine to warm, feed and tend the tent-and-hovel black 'towns'.

This is done in the name of common humanity. But in the name of common humanity, how do white people manage to close their minds to the implications of the resettlement *policy* while at the same time 'opening their hearts' to its callous and inevitable results?

In the second richest country in Africa, in the new decade of the twentieth century, choosing to manipulate the lives of a voteless and powerless indigenous majority in accordance with a theory of colour preference, we in South Africa are reproducing the living conditions of nineteenth-century European famine victims allowed to labour under sufferance in another country. In a world with a vast refugee problem still unsolved from the last World War and the lesser ones that have succeeded it, we who have never suffered the destruction of our own soil and cities have created encampments of people living like the homeless refugees of Palestine, Biafra and Vietnam.

Every human life, however humble it has been, has a context meshed of familiar experience – social relationships, patterns of activity in relation to environment. Call it 'home', if you like. To be transported out of this on a government truck one morning and put down in an uninhabited place is to be asked to build not only your shelter but your whole life over again, from scratch. For the hundreds of thousands of blacks who are having this experience forced upon them in South Africa there is no appeal.

As for the whites – if our hearts were ever really to be opened perhaps all we should find would be, graven there, this comment from one of the inhabitants of a resettlement: *You can't say no to a white man.*

1971

Unchaining Poets

A few weeks ago South African censors banned a T-shirt bearing the legend, 'Help Cure Virginity'.

At the same time, long-standing bans on William Faulkner's *Sanctuary*, Ralph Ellison's *Invisible Man*, Nathaniel West's *Miss Lonelyhearts*, Philip Roth's *Goodbye Columbus* and Françoise Sagan's *A Certain Smile* were lifted.

Who was it who submitted a T-shirt for the censors' weighty consideration? Who or what made them read Ellison, Faulkner, etc., banned by their predecessors operating under South Africa's Customs and Post Office acts before the present Publications Control Board came into existence with the Publications and Entertainments Act in 1963?

The logic behind these decisions of the board is known only to its members, government appointees all.

T-shirts aside, my concern is literature. Unfortunately, the lifting of bans on a few books is not a general indication that censorship is about to be relaxed in South Africa. On the contrary. A committee representing seven government departments has been investigating 'new ways' of applying the Publications and Entertainments Act, since during the last few years there have been repeated criticisms of the board, whose rulings have been upset by court decisions.

For the right of appeal to the courts against bannings by the board exists, although since the writer is first pronounced guilty of producing something obscene or objectionable, and only then gets the chance to defend the work in question, the usual processes of law are reversed. Threats of abolition of the right have been brandished frequently; the Dutch Reformed Church has been zealous with this particular sword. Now the Minister of the Interior, Dr Connie Mulder, who has received the findings of the investigating committee, has announced that the right of appeal will not be abolished but there will be 'changes in the system of appeal' against the board's decisions.

Statements by the Minister himself and others in official positions do not inspire writers' confidence in the possible nature of these 'changes'. Dr Mulder commented that the present checkmate between judges and censors was unsatisfactory. Marais Viljoen, Minister of Labour, said that individual judges were being placed in an invidious position because 'having to give decisions on the country's morals was a difficult task'. And Andries van Wyk, retiring vice-chairman of the board, has predicted that censors will not relax their hardline attitude on matters involving race, sex and politics while the present government is in power.

At the same time as T-shirts are being banned, Faulkner is no longer illicit reading, and writers darkly await the censors' new ways of dealing with their work, the quiet phenomenon of new black poets – and publishers ready to risk publishing them – continues in Johannesburg.

It began last year with the publication of Oswald Mtshali's *Sounds of A Cowhide Drum*, also published in New York. Fourteen thousand copies were sold in South Africa; a wide readership for any poet, anywhere. This year *Yakhal'inkomo* (the cry of cattle at the slaughterhouse), the remarkable poems of another young black man, Mongane Wally Serote, have appeared under the same imprint. The publishers are three young white poets, Lionel Abrahams, Robert Royston and Eva Bezwoda. Another publisher has in preparation an anthology of the work of eleven black South African poets.

Why this upsurge of poetry under censorship?

Nearly all the seminal black writers in South Africa went into exile in the 1960s, and their works are banned. This has had a stunting effect on prose writing among young blacks; it seems it has produced, perhaps subconsciously, a search for a less vulnerable form of expression. Some of the people writing poetry are very talented; some are not. For all, poetry is a dragonfly released whose shimmer censors must find difficult to pin down to any of the Publications and Entertainments Act's ninety-seven definitions of what is undesirable. What poetry expresses is implicit rather than explicit.

1972

The New Black Poets

'Poetry does indeed have a very special place in this country. It arouses people and shapes their minds. No wonder the birth of our new intelligentsia is accompanied by a craving for poetry never seen before . . . It brings people back to life.'

This was written of the contemporary Soviet Union by Nadezhda Mandelstam, widow of the poet Osip Mandelstam, in her auto-biography, *Hope Against Hope*. But perhaps the same might be said of the new poetry being written in South Africa by black South Africans. Three individual collections have been published within eighteen months. I know of at least two more that are to come, this year. An anthology representative of the work of eleven poets is in the press at the time of writing. Poems signed with as yet unknown names crop up in the little magazines; there are readings at universities and in private houses, since the law doesn't allow blacks to read to whites or mixed audiences in public places. For the first time, black writers' works are beginning to be bought by ordinary black people in the segregated townships, instead of only by liberal or literary whites and the educated black elite.

Aspirant writers are intimidated not only by censorship as such but also by the fear that anything at all controversial, set out by a black in the generally explicit medium of prose, makes the writer suspect, since the correlation of articulacy and political insurrection, so far as blacks are concerned, is firmly lodged in the minds of the Ministers of the Interior, Justice and Police. Polymorphous fear cramps the hand.

Out of this paralytic silence, suspended between fear of expression and the need to give expression to an ever greater pressure of grim experience, has come the black writer's subconscious search for a form less vulnerable than those that led a previous generation into bannings and exile. In other countries, writers similarly placed have found a way to survive and speak through the use of different kinds of prose forms. Perhaps, if black writing had not been so thoroughly beheaded and truncated in the sixties, there would have been creative minds nimble enough to keep it alive through something like the *skaz* – a Russian genre, dating from Czarist times, which concentrates a narrative of wide-ranging significance in a compressed work that derives from an oral tradition of story-telling, and takes full advantage of the private and double meanings contained in colloquial idiom. Both the oral tradition and the politically charged idiom exist in black South Africa.

Or the solution might have been found in the adoption of the Aesopean genre – as in a fable, you write within one set of categories, knowing your readers will realise that you are referring to another, an area where explicit comment is taboo. Camus used this device in *La Peste*, and again, Stalin's generation of writers learned to be dab hands at it.

The cryptic mode is a long-established one; it has been resorted to in times and countries where religious persecution or political oppression drives creativity back into itself, and forces it to become its own hiding-place, from which, ingenious as an oracle, a voice that cannot be identified speaks the truth in riddles and parables not easily defined as subversive. In South Africa there are ninety-seven definitions of what is officially 'undesirable' in literature: subversive, obscene or otherwise 'offensive'. They are not always invoked, but are there when needed to suppress a particular book or silence an individual writer. Seeking to escape them, among other even more sinister marks of official attention, black writers have had to look for survival away from the explicit if not to the cryptic then to the implicit; and in their case, they have turned instinctively to poetry. Professor Harry Levin defines a poem as 'a verbal artefact' whose 'arrangement of signs and sounds is likewise a network of associations and responses, communicating implicit information'. In demotic, non-literary terms, a poem can be both hiding-place and loud-hailer. That was what black writers within South Africa were seeking.

There will be many people whose toes will curl at this crude pragmatic conception of how poetry comes to be written. One cannot simply 'turn' to poetry. It is not simply there, available to anybody with a few hours of home study to spare, like a correspondence course in accountancy or learning to play the recorder. As a prose writer, I don't need reminding of the levels of literature, where poets sit on Kilimanjaro. That snowy crown is not within reach of everyone who wants to write; even those who can start a grass fire across the prose plain will find themselves short of oxygen up at that height.

Poetry *as a last resort* is indeed a strange concept; and a kind of inversion of the enormous problems of skill and gifts implied in electing to write poetry at all. Many who are doing so in South Africa today are not poets at all, merely people of some talent attempting to use certain conventions and unconventions associated with poetry in order to express their feelings in a way that may hope to get a hearing. One of them has said:

> To label my utterings poetry
> and myself a poet
> would be as self-deluding
> as the planners of parallel development.
> I record the anguish of the persecuted
> whose words are whimpers of woe
> wrung from them by bestial laws.
> They stand one chained band
> silently asking one of the other
> will it never be the fire next time?

('To label my utterings poetry' by James Matthews)

From the Icelandic saga to Symbolism, from a Chaucer creating English as a democratic literary medium to a Günter Grass recreating areas of the German language debased by Nazi usage, writers in their place at the centre of their particular historical situation have been forced by this kind of empiricism and pragmatism to 'turn to' one form of expression rather than another.

There are two questions to ask of the black writers who have 'turned to' poetry in South Africa. In the five years since this spate of poetry began, these questions have been shown to be so bound together that I don't know which to put first. So, without prejudice at this point: Question – through the implicit medium of poetry, are black writers succeeding in establishing or re-establishing a black protest literature within South Africa? Question – are they writing good poetry?

These questions, as I have said, seem to have demonstrated an indivisibility that I hesitate to claim as a universal axiom. Where protest speaks from a good poem, even one good line, both questions are answered in a single affirmative. When Mandlenkosi Langa, in his 'Mother's Ode to a Still-born Child', writes:

> It is not my fault
> that you did not live
> to be a brother sister
> or lover of some black child
> that you did not experience pain
> pleasure voluptuousness and salt in the wound
> that your head did not stop a police truncheon
> that you are not a permanent resident of a prison island

his irony says more than any tract describing in spent emotives the life-expectations of the black ghetto under white oppression in the police state, etc. When, writing again of a newborn child already dead – symbol of the constant death-in-life that runs through this black poetry – Oswald Mbuyiseni Mtshali in 'An Abandoned Bundle' makes the image of dogs 'draped in red bandanas of blood' scavenging the body of a baby dumped on a location rubbish heap, he says more about black infant mortality than any newspaper exposé, and by the extension that the total vision of his poem provides, more about the cheapness of life where race is the measure of worth.

The themes chosen by the new black poets are committed in the main to the individual struggle for physical and spiritual survival under oppression. 'I' is the pronoun that prevails, rather than 'we', but the 'I' is the Whitmanesque unit of multi-millions rather than the exclusive first person singular. There is little evidence of group feeling, except perhaps in one or two of the young writers who are within SASO (South African Students' Organisation), the black student organisation whose politico-cultural manifesto is a combination of negritude with Black Power on the American pattern.

The themes, like those of the poets who preceded the present generation (they were few in number and were forced into exile), are urban — although it is doubtful whether one can speak of the tradition or influence of a Kunene or a Brutus, here. Few of the young aspirants writing today have read even the early work of exiled writers: it was banned while they were still at school. The striking development of Dennis Brutus's later and recent work, for example, is unknown except by a handful of people who may have spotted a copy of Cosmo Pieterse's *Seven South African Poets* or *Thoughts Abroad* that has somehow slipped into a bookshop, although the statutory ban on Dennis Brutus would mean that the book itself is automatically banned.

It is axiomatic that the urban theme contains the classic crises: tribal and traditional values against Western values, peasant modes of life against the modes of an industrial proletariat, above all, the quotidian humiliations of a black's world made to a white's specifications. But in the work we are considering I believe there also can be traced distinct stages or stations of development in creating a black ethos strong enough to be the challenger rather than the challenged in these crises.

The starting point is essentially post-Sharpeville — post-defeat of mass black political movements: the position that of young people cut off from political education and any objective formulation of their resentments against apartheid. The stations are three:

distortion of values by submission of whites; rejection of distortion; black/white polarity – opposition on new ground.

In terms of the personal, immediate and implicit within which the poems move, the first station – distortion by submission – is often demonstrated by apartheid through the eyes of a child. Mike Dues writes in his poem 'This Side of Town':

> Rested near swinging
> sliding playground
> with eager-eyed-black faces
> 'can we play on the swing'
> a cowing no
> in town the voice pleads
> 'I want to pee'
> a hackneyed no
> leads to the edge of town.

And James Matthews in 'Two Little Black Boys':

> Two little black boys
> standing in front of a public lavatory
> one not bigger than a grasshopper
> the other a head of hair taller
> you can't go in there
> the tall one said, pointing to the board
> it's white people only.

It is not insignificant that incidents such as this are written about again and again. Through the recurrence of apparent trivialities in a child's life, certain objects – a swing, a public lavatory – can be seen becoming reified with the value of a sacred totem of white supremacy from whose ground the black child learns he is excluded without knowing why. But the question will come. James Matthews's poem ends:

> Puzzled, the grasshopper replied
> don't white people shit like me?

And Mike Dues, more ominously:

> Later the face stronger
> and voice bigger
> will ask why.

A child's three questions in one of Oswald Mtshali's poems 'Boy on a Swing' – 'Mother!/Where did I come from?/When will I wear long trousers?/Why was my father jailed?' – illustrate by their unconscious grouping how victimisation undergoes transformation into one of the immutable mysteries of a natural order. The experience of these black children takes on a dreadful logic as preparation for their sort of future in Stanley Mogoba's poem 'Two Buckets' in which two buckets side by side, one a lavatory, the other filled with drinking water, define prison *as a destination*. Thrown into a cell at night, a man stumbles over the buckets:

> In this startled manner
> I made my entry
> into a dark world
> Where thousands of men
> Pine and are forgotten.

It is the world of the pass laws, and the pass document is not a booklet of simple identification but a hateful possession that must be cherished because one cannot live without it – another inversion of values demanded by the white man. In 'City Johannesburg', Mongane Wally Serote addresses the white city:

> This way I salute you;
> My hand pulses to my back trouser pocket
> Or into my inner jacket pocket
> For my pass, my life

. . . My hand like a starved snake rears my pockets

. . . Jo'burg City, I salute you;

When I run out, or roar in a bus to you,

I leave behind me my love – my comic houses and people, my
    donga and my ever-whirling dust

My death

That's so related to me as a wink to the eye

The city as an environment of distortion as well as dispossession creates the image in Njabulo Ndebele's poem:

I hid my love in the sewerage
Of a city; and when it was decayed,
I returned: I returned to the old lands.

Oswald Mtshali's country bird is shedding his identity along with his feathers when he takes a job as a city cleaner and says in 'The Moulting Country Bird':

I wish
I was not a bird
red and tender of body
with the mark of the tribe
branded on me as fledgling
hatched in the Zulu grass hut.

Pierced in the lobe of the ear
by the burning spike of the elderman;
he drew my blood like a butcher bird
that impales the grasshopper on the thorn.

As a full fledged starling
hopping in the city street,
scratching the building corridor,
I want to moult
from the dung-smeared down

tattered like a fieldworker's shirt,
tighter than the skin of a snake
that sleeps as the plough turns the sod.

Boots caked with mud,
wooden stoppers flapping from earlobes
and a beaded little gourd dangling on a hirsute chest,
all to stoke the incinerator.

I want to be adorned
by a silken suit so scintillating in sheen,
it pales even the peacock's plumage,
and catches the enchanted eye
of a harlot hiding in an alley:
'Come! my moulten bird,
I will not charge you a price!'

Njabulo Ndebele, one of the youngest of the new writers, is surely
speaking of the same man when he writes, in 'I hid my love in the
sewerage':

O who am I?
Who am I?
I am the hoof that once
Grazed in silence upon the grass
But now rings like a bell on tarred streets.

Ultimate submission is the acceptance of white materialist
values as a goal while at the same time they are by definition unattainable. Again Mtshali has understood this incomparably. In
much-imitated poems his city black wears shoes made in America,
has a wife who uses lightening cream, a mistress, a car, but:

He knows
he must carry a pass.
He don't care for politics

He don't go to church
He knows Sobukwe
He knows Mandela
They're in Robben Island,
'So what? That's not my business!'

('The Detribalised')

This city black does the 'Chauffeur Shuffle', 'a carving of black-wood/ in a peaked cap/clutching the wheel of the white man's car in white-gloved hands'; he is 'Always a Suspect', dressed like a gentleman in white shirt and suit but trudging 'the city pavements/side by side with "madam"/who shifts her handbag from my side to the other/ and looks at me with eyes that say/"Ha! Ha! I know who you are;/ beneath those fine clothes ticks the heart of a thief." '

The Sartrian and Fanonist theory of realising oneself in terms of the Other, of becoming someone else's projection rather than oneself (the orphan Genet a thief because that is the image in which society recognises his existence) reaches its apogee in the term 'non-white'. That is the official identity of any South African who is black, brown, coffee-coloured or yellow. Mtshali's non-white describes himself:

If I tell the truth
I'm detestable.
If I tell lies
I'm abominable.
If I tell nothing
I'm unpredictable.
If I smile to please
I'm nothing but an obsequious sambo.

('Always a Suspect')

And he accepts his non-white non-value by seeing, in turn, fulfilment as the vantage point from which the white man makes this valuation:

I want my heaven now,
Here on earth in Houghton and Parktown;
a mansion
two cars or more
and smiling servants
Isn't that heaven?

('This Kid Is No Goat')

The ironic note of the last phrase — no trumpet call, but ringing in the ears just the same — serves to mark the transition to the second station in the development of the black ethos as reflected in these poets. Mike Dues uses irony both as approach and technique in a terse poem, 'You Never Know', that is at once also an anecdote and a wry joke. We are eavesdropping on a telephone call to a sports event booking service:

'Hello. Duncan Taylor here.'
'I want nine tickets for Saturday.'
'Nine you said. Hold on I'll check the booking.
I can give you eight in one row. One in front or back.'
'Thank you. I'll collect at the gate. How much?'
'Well nine at R1.25. That is R11.25 Sir.'
'Why the difference? A friend paid seventy-five cents last night.'
'Oh! But that's non-white.'
'That's what we want.'
'I'm sorry, you sounded white.'

Soon the ironic note grows louder. Mandlenkosi Langa sets the scene in a 'non-whites' pension office with a white official behind the counter:

I lead her in
A sepia figure 100 years old.
Blue ice chips gaze
And a red slash gapes:

'What does she want?'
I translate: 'Pension, sir.'
'Useless kaffir crone,
Lazy as the black devil.
She'll get fuck-all.'
I translate.
'My man toiled
And rendered himself impotent
With hard labour.
He paid tax like you.
I am old enough to get pension.
I was born before the great wars
And I saw my father slit your likes' throats!'
I don't translate, but
She loses her pension anyhow.

('The Pension Jiveass')

The rejection of distortion of self, the rejection of reification, take many attitudes and forms. What has to be dismantled is three hundred years of spiritual enslavement; the poet is supremely aware that though the bricks and mortar of pass offices and prisons can be battered down, the Bastille of Otherness must have its combination locks picked from within. And this is not easy. In creative terms, there is a casting about for the right means. The reference of the metaphors of sexual love is extended to become a celebration of blackness as a kind of personal salvation, as in Njabulo Ndebele's love poems:

I am sweeping the firmament with the mop
of your kinky hair;
. . . I shall gather you
into my arms, my love
and oil myself,
Yea, anoint myself with the
Night of your skin,

That the dust of the soil may stick on me;
That the birds of the sky may stick on me;
. . . let me play hide-and-seek
With an image of you in the
Dark, plum-dark forests of
your kinky hair,
And I shall not want.

('Five Letters to M.M.M.')

(Echoes here of Leon Damas's *Rendez-moi mes poupées noires*.) Another means has been a use of the blues idiom of the Langston Hughes–Bessie Smith era, resuscitated in 'cat' vocabulary by Black Power writers in America. Pascal Gwala uses it, writing from Durban:

Been watching this jive
For too long.
That's struggle.
West Street ain't the place
To hang around any more
. . . At night you see another dream
White and Monstrous
Dropping from earth's heaven,
Whitewashing your own Black Dream.
That's struggle.
Struggle is when
You have to lower your eyes
And steer time
With your bent voice.
When you drag along –
Mechanically.
Your shoulder refusing;
Refusing like a young bull
Not wanting to drive
Into the dipping tank
Struggle is keying your tune

To harmonize with your inside.
. . . Heard a child giggle at obscene jokes
Heard a mother weep over a dead son;
Heard a foreman say 'boy' to a labouring oupa
Heard a bellowing, drunken voice in an alley.
. . . You heard struggle.
Knowing words don't kill
But a gun does.
That's struggle.
For no more jive
Evening's eight
Ain't never late.
Black is struggle.

('Gumba Gumba Gumba')

Mongane Wally Serote uses the jazz beat but with vocabulary and imagery less derivative or obviously localised – generalised definitions of blackness, or anything else, are not for him. He puts a craftsmanlike agony to making-by-naming (Gerald Moore's and Ulli Beier's definition of the particular quality of African poetry) in a vocabulary and grammar genuinely shaped by black urban life in South Africa. There is a piercing subjectivity in his work, in which 'black as struggle' becomes at times an actual struggle with the limits of language itself. He can discipline himself to the device of plain statement:

White people are white people
They are burning the world.
Black people are black people
They are the fuel.
White people are white people
They must learn to listen.
Black people are black people
They must learn to talk.

('Ofay-Watcher, Throbs-Phase')

He can see the elements of an almost untainted black identity in the old people and children who are recurring lyrical motifs in his work. But when he seeks to recreate that identity by learning how it was destroyed, deeply wounded and marked himself, he wanders among the signs of signs, the abstractions of abstraction. The persona of his poems is often named 'Ofay-Watcher' — one who watches Whitey, a definition that has overtones of the negative non-white clinging to it like grave-clothes around the resurrected. Ofay-Watcher says:

I want to look at what happened;
That done,
As silent as the roots of plants pierce the soil
I look at what happened,
Whether above the houses there is always either smoke or dust,
As there are always flies above a dead dog.
I want to look at what happened.
That done,
As silent as plants show colour: green,
I look at what happened,
When houses make me ask: do people live there?
As there is something wrong when I ask — is that man alive?
I want to look at what happened,
That done
As silent as the life of a plant that makes you see it
I look at what happened
When knives creep in and out of people
As day and night into time.
I want to look at what happened,
That done,
As silent as plants bloom and the eye tells you: something has happened.
I look at what happened
When jails are becoming necessary homes for people
Like death comes out of disease,
I want to look at what happened.

                                        ('Ofay-Watcher Looks Back')

Not only to look, but to express his findings in the long expletive of 'What's In This Black "Shit" ', gagging on its own bile of force-fed humiliation:

> It is not the steaming rot
> In the toilet bucket,
> It is the upheaval of the bowels
> Bleeding and coming out through the mouth
> And swallowed back,
> Rolling in the mouth
> Feeling its taste and wondering what's next like it.

Finally he turns the term 'black shit' on those who coined it:

> I'm learning to pronounce this 'shit' well,
> Since the other day
> at the pass office
> when I went to get employment,
> The officer there endorsed me to Middleburg
> So I said, hard and with all my might, 'Shit!'
> I felt a little better;
> But what's good is, I said it in his face,
> A thing my father wouldn't dare do.
> That's what's in this black 'Shit'.

The Word becomes Weapon. At times, for this writer, there is no calligraphy capable of containing the force of resentment and he destroys his very medium by exploding the bounds of coherence:

> WORDS.
> Trying to get out.
> Words. Words. Words.
> By Whitey
> I know I'm trapped.
> Helpless

Hopeless
You've trapped me Whitey! Meem wann ge aot Fuc
Pschwee ep booboodubooboodu blllll
Black books
Flesh blood words shitrrr Haai,
Amen.

('Black Bells')

You taught me language; and my profit on't/Is I know how to curse. Not
from the political platform or the prisoner's dock, but howling
from the subconscious, hate is conjured up in Serote's work. Yet he
himself is not free to hate; he is tormented by its necessity for the
black in South Africa:

To talk for myself
I hate to hate
But how often has it been
I could not hate enough.

('That's Not My Wish')

Preoccupation with the metaphysics of hate belongs to the station
of rejection of the distorted black self-image: James Matthews refers
to the book he has published with Gladys Thomas as a collection of
'declarations' and the unspoken overall declaration is that of those
who have learned how to hate enough, and to survive. His is the
manifesto of the black ethos as challenger, confronting the white
ethos on black ground. In a kind of black nursery jingle by Gladys
Thomas, entitled 'Fall To-morrow', it speaks to blacks:

Don't sow a seed
Don't paint a wall
To-morrow it will have to fall

and to whites:

Be at home in our desert for all
You that remade us
Your mould will break
And to-morrow you are going to fall.

The book is called 'Cry Rage!' and the theme is often expressed
in terms of actual and specific events. James Matthews is not
diffident about taking a hold wherever he can on those enormous
experiences of the long night of the black body-and-soul that prose
writers have ignored. His obsession with the subject of resettlement is no more than an accurate reflection of the realities of daily
life for the tens of thousands of blacks who have been moved by
government decree to find shelter and livelihood in the bare veld
of places dubbed Limehill, Dimbaza, Sada, Ilinge – often poetic
names whose meanings seem to show malicious contempt for the
people dumped there:

> Valley of plenty is what it is called;
> where little children display their nakedness
> and stumble around on listless limbs
> . . . where mothers plough their dead fruit into the soil
> their crone breasts dry of milk
> . . . where menfolk castrated by degradation
> seek their manhood in a jug
> of wine as brackish as their bile.

> ('Valley of plenty')

Njabulo Ndebele invokes the intimate sorrows of forced removal
less obviously and perhaps more tellingly. Limehills, Dimbazas –
these valleys of plenty seldom have adequate water supplies and
the new 'inhabitants' often have to walk a long way to fetch water:

> There is my wife. There she is
> She is old under those four gallons of water,
> It was said taps in the streets

Would be our new rivers.
But my wife fetches the water
We drink and we eat.
I watch my wife: she is old.

('Portrait of Love')

And Oswald Mtshali also takes as subjects some dark current events. He uses the Aesopean mode to write devastatingly of a ghastly recent disaster anyone living in South Africa would be able to identify instantly, although its horrors are transliterated, so to speak, into Roman times. A year or two ago a prison van broke down on the road between Johannesburg and Pretoria; the policemen in charge went off to seek help, leaving the prisoners locked inside. It was a hot day; the van was packed; they died of suffocation while the traffic passed unconcerned and unaware:

They rode upon
the death chariot
to their Golgotha—
three vagrants
whose papers to be in Caesar's empire
were not in order.

The sun
shrivelled their bodies
in the mobile tomb
as airtight as canned fish.

We're hot!
We're thirsty!
We're hungry!

The centurion
touched their tongues
with the tip

of a lance
dipped in apathy:

'Don't cry to me
but to Caesar who
crucifies you.'

A woman came
to wipe their faces.
She carried a dishcloth
full of bread and tea.

We're dying!

The centurion
washed his hands.

('Ride Upon The Death Chariot')

James Matthews writes of the Imam Abdullah Haron, one of the number of people who have died while in detention without trial. He writes of 'dialogue' as 'the cold fire where the oppressed will find no warmth'. Perhaps most significantly, he reflects the current black rejection of any claim whatever by whites, from radicals to liberals, to identify with the black struggle:

They speak so sorrowfully about the
children dying of hunger in Biafra
but sleep unconcerned about the rib-thin
children of Dimbaza.

('They Speak So Sorrowfully')

And again, in a poem called 'Liberal Student Crap!':

The basis of democracy rests upon
Fraternity, Equality and not LSD
I should know fellows
Progressive policy the salvation of us all
You just don't understand
There's no-one as liberal as me
Some of my best friends are
Kaffirs, Coolies and Coons
Forgive me, I mean other ethnic groups
How could it be otherwise?
I'm Jewish; I know discrimination
from the ghetto to Belsen
So, don't get me all wrong
Cause I know just how you feel
Come up and see me sometime
My folks are out of town.

Whatever the justice of this view of young white people militant against apartheid – and increasing numbers of them are banned and restricted along with blacks – on the question of white proxy for black protest he has a final unanswerable word:

can the white man speak for me?
can he feel my pain when his laws
tear wife and child from my side
and I am forced to work a thousand miles away?

does he know my anguish
as I walk his streets at night
my hand fearfully clasping my pass?

is he with me in the loneliness
of my bed in the bachelor barracks
with my longing driving me to mount my brother?

will he soothe my despair
as I am driven insane
by scraps of paper permitting me to live?

('Can The White Man Speak For Me?')

He does not spare certain blacks, either, nor fear to measure the fashionable against the actual lineaments of the black situation. He addresses one of the black American singers who from time to time come to South Africa and perform for segregated audiences:

Say, Percy dad
you ran out of bread that you got to
come to sunny South Africa to sing soul
or did you hope to find your soul
in the land of your forefathers?
. . . Say, Percy dad
will you tell nina simone back home
that you, a soul singer, did a segregated act
or will you sit back flashing silver dollar smiles
as they cart the loot from your Judas role to the bank.

('Say Percy Dad')

And he accuses:

my sister has become a schemer and
a scene-stealer
. . . songs of the village
traded in for tin pan alley
black is beautiful has become as artificial as the wig she wears.

('My sister has become a schemer')

Matthews uses indiscriminately the clichés of politics, tracts and popular journalism and these deaden and debase his work. But

occasionally the contrast between political catchwords and brutal
sexual imagery carries a crude immediacy:

> democracy
> has been turned
> into a whore
> her body ravished
> by those who pervert her
> in the bordello
> bandied from crotch to hand
> her breasts smeared
> with their seed . . .

('Democracy has been turned into a whore')

And in the context of fanatical laws framed in the language
of reason, within which he is writing, even clichés take on new
meaning: they mock the hollowness of high-sounding terms such
as 'separate development' or clinical ones such as 'surplus people'
– the behaviouristic vocabulary that gives a scientific gloss to mass
removals of human beings.

James Matthews is a paradigm of the black writer in search of
a form of expression that will meet the needs of his situation by
escaping strictures imposed on free expression by that situation.
He is older than other writers I have discussed; more than a decade
ago he was writing short stories of exceptional quality. There were
signs that he would become a fine prose writer. Whatever the
immediate reasons were for the long silence that followed, the fact
remains that there was little or no chance that the themes from
the cataclysmic life around him he would have wished to explore
would not have ended up as banned prose fiction. He stopped
writing. He seems to have accepted that for him to have dealt
honestly in prose with what he saw and experienced, as a coloured
man slowly accepting the black heritage of his mixed blood as
his real identity, might be written but could not be read. He is
the man who wrote the words I quoted at the beginning of this

survey: 'To label my utterings poetry/and myself a poet/would be self-deluding . . .'

He is indeed not a poet, although his old creative gifts, uneasy in a medium to which they are not suited, now and then transform his 'declarations' into something more than that. And so he is also an example of yet another distortion, this time within a black literature that expresses rejection of distortion and the assertion of new values for blacks: the black writer's gifts can be, and often are, squeezed into interstitial convolutions that do not allow him to develop in the direction in which development is possible for him as an artist.

At its best, 'turning to poetry' has released the fine talents of an Mtshali and a Serote, a Dues and a young Ndebele. At its least, it has provided a public-address system for the declarations of muzzled prose writers like Matthews. But if he stands where I have put him, as the symbolic figure of the situation of black writing, the sudden ban on his book 'Cry Rage!' (during the very time when I was preparing these notes) suggests that black writing in South Africa may once again find itself come full circle, back again at a blank, spiked wall. This is the first book of poems ever to be banned within South Africa. If there were to be a lesson to be learned in a game where it seems you can't win for long, it would seem to be that only good writing with implicit commitment is equal both to the inner demands of the situation and a chance of surviving publication, whatever the chosen literary form.

In terms of a literary judgement, yes, it is never enough to be angry. But unfortunately this does not hold good as an assurance that black poetry of real achievement can continue to be published and read in South Africa. Some of the best writing ever done by South Africans of all colours has not escaped, on grounds of quality, banning in the past. Black Orpheus, where now? How? What next?

1973

A Writer's Freedom

What is a writer's freedom?
To me it is his right to maintain and publish to the world
a deep, intense, private view of the situation in which he finds his
society. If he is to work as well as he can, he must take, and be granted,
freedom from the public conformity of political interpretation,
morals and tastes.

Living when we do, where we do, as we do, 'freedom' leaps to mind
as a political concept exclusively – and when people think of freedom
for writers they visualise at once the great mound of burned, banned
and proscribed books our civilisation has piled up; a pyre to which our
own country has added and is adding its contribution. The right to be
left alone to write what one pleases is not an academic issue to those
of us who live and work in South Africa. The private view always has
been and always will be a source of fear and anger to proponents of a
way of life, such as the white man's in South Africa, that does not bear
looking at except in the light of a special self-justificatory doctrine.

All that the writer can do, as a writer, is to go on writing the
truth as he sees it. That is what I mean by his 'private view' of events,
whether they be the great public ones of wars and revolutions, or
the individual and intimate ones of daily, personal life.

As to the fate of his books – there comes a time in the history
of certain countries when the feelings of their writers are best
expressed in this poem, written within the lifetime of many of us,
by Bertholt Brecht:

> When the Regime ordered that books with dangerous teachings
> Should be publicly burned and everywhere
> Oxen were forced to draw carts full of books
> To the funeral pyre,
> An exiled poet,

One of the best,
Discovered with fury when he studied the list
Of the burned, that his books
Had been forgotten. He rushed to his writing table
On wings of anger and wrote a letter to those in power.
Burn me, he wrote with hurrying pen, burn me!
Do not treat me in this fashion. Don't leave me out.
Have I not
Always spoken the truth in my books? And now
You treat me like a liar! I order you:
Burn me!

Not a very good poem, even if one makes allowance for the loss in translation from the German original; nevertheless, so far as South African writers are concerned, we can understand the desperate sentiments expressed while still putting up the fight to have our books read rather than burned.

Bannings and banishments are terrible known hazards a writer must face, and many have faced, if the writer belongs where freedom of expression, among other freedoms, is withheld, but sometimes creativity is frozen rather than destroyed. A Thomas Mann survives exile to write a *Dr Faustus*; a Pasternak smuggles *Dr Zhivago* out of a ten-year silence; a Solzhenitsyn emerges with his terrible world intact in the map of *The Gulag Archipelago*; nearer our home continent: a Chinua Achebe, writing from America, does not trim his prose to please a Nigerian regime under which he cannot live; a Dennis Brutus grows in reputation abroad while his poetry remains forbidden at home; and a Breyten Breytenbach, after accepting the special dispensation from racialist law which allowed him to visit his home country with a wife who is not white, no doubt has to accept the equally curious circumstance that his publisher would not publish the book he was to write about the visit, since it was sure to be banned.[1]

---

1   The Afrikaans poet Breyten Breytenbach returned to South Africa under a false name in August 1975 after years of self-imposed exile in Paris. Arrested shortly after his arrival he was sentenced on 26 November to nine years' imprisonment, having pleaded guilty to twenty-two

Through all these vicissitudes, real writers go on writing the truth as they see it. And they do not agree to censor themselves . . . You can burn the books, but the integrity of creative artists is not incarnate on paper any more than on canvas – it survives so long as the artist himself cannot be persuaded, cajoled or frightened into betraying it.

All this, hard though it is to live, is the part of the writer's fight for freedom the *world* finds easiest to understand.

There is another threat to that freedom, in any country where political freedom is withheld. It is a more insidious one, and one of which fewer people will be aware. It's a threat which comes from the very strength of the writer's opposition to repression of political freedom. That other, paradoxically wider, composite freedom – the freedom of his private view of life – may be threatened by the very awareness of *what is expected of him*. And often what is expected of him is conformity to an orthodoxy of opposition.

There will be those who regard him as their mouthpiece; people whose ideals, as a human being, he shares, and whose cause, as a human being, is his own. They may be those whose suffering is his own. His identification with, admiration for, and loyalty to these set up a state of conflict within him. His integrity as a human being demands the sacrifice of everything to the struggle put up on the side of free men. His integrity as a writer goes the moment he begins to write what he ought to write.

This is – whether all admit it or not – and will continue to be a particular problem for black writers in South Africa. For them, it extends even to an orthodoxy of vocabulary: the jargon of struggle, derived internationally, is right and adequate for the public platform, the newsletter, the statement from the dock; it is not adequate, it is not deep enough, wide enough, flexible enough, cutting enough, fresh enough for the vocabulary of the poet, the short-story writer or the novelist.

Neither is it, as the claim will be made, 'a language of the people' in a situation where certainly it is very important that imaginative

---

charges under the Terrorism and Suppression of Communism Acts.

writing must not reach the elite only. The jargon of struggle lacks both the inventive pragmatism and the poetry of common speech – those qualities the writer faces the challenge to capture and explore imaginatively, expressing as they do the soul and identity of a people as no thousandth-hand 'noble evocation' of clichés ever could.

The black writer needs his freedom to assert that the idiom of Chatsworth, Dimbaza, Soweto[2] is no less a vehicle for the expression of pride, self-respect, suffering, anger – or anything else in the spectrum of thought and emotion – than the language of Watts or Harlem.

The fact is, even on the side of the angels, a writer has to reserve the right to tell the truth as he sees it, in his own words, without being accused of letting the side down. For as Philip Toynbee has written, 'the writer's gift to the reader is not social zest or moral improvement or love of country, but an enlargement of the reader's apprehension'.

This is the writer's unique contribution to social change. He needs to be left alone, by brothers as well as enemies, to make this gift. And he must make it even against his own inclination.

I need hardly add this does not mean he retreats to an ivory tower. The gift cannot be made from any such place. The other day, Jean Paul Sartre gave the following definition of the writer's responsibility to his society as an intellectual, after himself having occupied such a position in France for the best part of seventy years: 'He is someone who is faithful to a political and social body but never stops contesting it. Of course; a contradiction may arise between his fidelity and his *contestation*, but that's a fruitful contradiction. If there's fidelity without *contestation*, that's no good: one is no longer a free man.'

When a writer claims these kinds of freedom for himself, he begins to understand the real magnitude of his struggle. It is not a new problem and of all the writers who have had to face it, I don't think anyone has seen it more clearly or dealt with it with such uncompromising honesty as the great nineteenth-century Russian, Ivan Turgenev. Turgenev had an immense reputation as a progressive writer. He was closely connected with the progressive movement in Tsarist

---

2   Chatsworth and Soweto are respectively Indian and African ghettos. Dimbaza is the notorious 'resettlement area' for Africans which is the subject of the film *Last Grave at Dimbaza*.

Russia and particularly with its more revolutionary wing headed by the critic Belinsky and afterwards by the poet Nekrasov. With his sketches and stories, people said that Turgenev was continuing the work Gogol had begun of awakening the conscience of the educated classes in Russia to the evils of a political regime based on serfdom.

But his friends, admirers and fellow progressives stopped short, in their understanding of his genius, of the very thing that made him one – his scrupulous reserve of the writer's freedom to reproduce truth and the reality of life, even if this truth does not coincide with his own sympathies.

When his greatest novel, *Fathers and Sons*, was published in 1862, he was attacked not only by the right for pandering to the revolutionary nihilists, but far more bitterly by the left, the younger generation themselves, of whom his chief character in the novel, Bazarov, was both prototype and apotheosis. The radicals and liberals, among whom Turgenev himself belonged, lambasted him as a traitor because Bazarov was presented with all the faults and contradictions that Turgenev saw in his own type, in himself, so to speak, and whom he created as he did because – in his own words – 'in the given case, life happened to be like that'.

The attacks were renewed after the publication of another novel, *Smoke*, and Turgenev decided to write a series of autobiographical reminiscences which would allow him to reply to his critics by explaining his views on the art of writing, the place of the writer in society, and what the writer's attitude to the controversial problems of his day should be. The result was a series of unpretentious essays that make up a remarkable testament to a writer's creed. Dealing particularly with Bazarov and *Fathers and Sons*, he writes of his critics:

> . . . generally speaking they have not got quite the right idea of what is taking place in the mind of a writer or what exactly his joys and sorrows, his aims, successes and failures are. They do not, for instance, even suspect the pleasure which Gogol mentions and which consists of castigating oneself and one's faults in the imaginary characters one depicts; they are quite sure that all a writer does is to 'develop his ideas' . . . Let me illustrate my meaning by a small example. I am an

inveterate and incorrigible Westerner. I have never concealed it and I am not concealing it now. And yet in spite of that it has given me great pleasure to show up in the person of Panshin [a character in *A House of Gentlefolk*] all the common and vulgar sides of the Westerners: I made the Slavophil Lavretsky 'crush him utterly'. Why did I do it, I who consider the Slavophil doctrine false and futile? Because, in the given case, *life*, according to my ideas, *happened to be like that*, and what I wanted above all was to be sincere and truthful.

In depicting Bazarov's personality, I excluded everything artistic from the range of his sympathies, I made him express himself in harsh and unceremonious tones, not out of an absurd desire to insult the younger generation, but simply as a result of my observations of people like him . . . My personal predilections had nothing to do with it. But I expect many of my readers will be surprised if I tell them that with the exception of Bazarov's views on art, I share almost all his convictions.

And in another essay, Turgenev sums up: 'The life that surrounds him [the writer] provides him with the content of his works; he is its *concentrated reflection*; but he is as incapable of writing a panegyric as a lampoon . . . When all is said and done – that is beneath him. Only those who can do no better submit to a given theme or carry out a programme.'

These conditions about which I have been talking are the special, though common ones of writers beleaguered in the time of the bomb and the colour bar, as they were in the time of the jackboot and rubber truncheon, and, no doubt, back through the ages whose shameful symbols keep tally of oppression in the skeleton cupboard of our civilisations.

Other conditions, more transient, less violent, affect the freedom of a writer's mind.

What about literary fashion, for example? What about the cycle of the innovator, the imitators, the debasers, and then the bringing forth of an innovator again? A writer must not be made too conscious of literary fashion, any more than he must allow himself to be inhibited by the mandarins, if he is to get on with work that is his own. I say 'made conscious' because literary fashion is a part of his working conditions; he can make the choice of rejecting it, but he cannot choose whether it is urged upon him or not by publishers and readers, who do not let him forget he has to eat.

That rare marvel, an innovator, should be received with shock and excitement. And his impact may set off people in new directions of their own. But the next innovator rarely, I would almost say never, comes from his imitators, those who create a fashion in his image. Not all worthwhile writing is an innovation, but I believe it always comes from an individual vision, privately pursued. The pursuit may stem from a tradition, but a tradition implies a choice of influence, whereas a fashion makes the influence of the moment the only one for all who are contemporary to it.

A writer needs all these kinds of freedom, built on the basic one of freedom from censorship. He does not ask for shelter from living, but for exposure to it without possibility of evasion. He is fiercely engaged with life on his own terms, and ought to be left to it, if anything is to come of the struggle. Any government, any society – any vision of a future society – that has respect for its writers must set them as free as possible to write in their own various ways, in their own choices of form and language, and according to their own discovery of truth.

Again, Turgenev expresses this best: 'Without freedom in the widest sense of the word – in relation to oneself . . . indeed, to one's people and one's history, a true artist is unthinkable; without that air, it is impossible to breathe.'

And I add my last word: In that air alone, commitment and creative freedom become one.

1976

English-Language Literature and Politics in South Africa

Speaking of South Africa, the association of politics with literature produces a snap equation: censorship. But is that the beginning and end of my subject? Indeed, it may be the end, in a literal sense, of a book or a writer: the book unread, the writer silenced. But censorship is the most extreme, final, and above all, most obvious effect of politics upon a literature, rather than the sum of the subject. Where and when, in a country such as South Africa, can the influence of politics on literature be said to begin? Politics, in the form of an agent of European imperialism – the Dutch East India Company – brought the written word to this part of Africa; politics, in the form of European missionaries who spread along with their Protestantism or Catholicism the political influence of their countries of origin, led to the very first transposition of the indigenous oral literature to the written word. When the first tribal praise-poem was put down on paper, what a political act that was! What could be communicated only by the mouth of the praise-singer to the ears of those present, was transmogrified into a series of squiggles on paper that could reach far beyond his living physical presence, beyond even the chain of memory of those who came after him. With that act a culture took hold upon and was taken hold upon by another.

Does not the subject begin quite simply, right there? And does not it extend, not simply at all, through the cultural isolation of whites who left their Europe over three centuries ago as the result of political events such as the revocation of the Edict of Nantes, the Napoleonic wars, the pogroms of Eastern Europe; does it not extend through the cultural upheaval of blacks under conquest; and the cultural ambiguity of the children one race fathered upon the other? The relationship of politics to literature in South Africa implies all of this, just as it does the overtly political example of writers forced into exile, and the subsequent development of their writings within the changed consciousness of exile. For some books are banned, and so South Africans never read them. But all that is and has been written by South Africans is profoundly influenced, at the deepest and least controllable level of consciousness, by the politics of race. All writers everywhere, even those like Joyce who cannot bear to live in their own countries, or those like Genet who live outside the pale of their country's laws, are shaped by their own particular society reflecting a particular political situation. Yet there is no country in the Western world where the daily enactment of the law reflects politics as intimately and blatantly as in South Africa. There is no country in the Western world where the creative imagination, whatever it seizes upon, finds the focus of even the most private event set in the overall social determination of racial laws.

I am not going to devote any time, here, to outlining or discussing how the Publications Control Board, the censorship system, works in South Africa. I take it that anyone interested in South African literature is familiar with the facts. But lest it be thought that I pass over that matter of censorship lightly, let me remark aside that personally, although I myself have continued and shall continue to bang my head in protesting concert against that particular brick in the granite wall, my fundamental attitude is that South Africans cannot expect to rid themselves of the Publications Control Board until they get rid of apartheid. Censorship is an indispensable part of an interlocking system of repressive laws.

There are other forms of censorship in South Africa. Anyone under a political ban may not be published or quoted; which means that the books of a number of white writers in exile, and those of a number of black writers in exile and at home, are automatically banned, no matter what their subject or form. Through this kind of censorship, the lively and important group of black writers who burst into South African literature in the 1950s and early 1960s disappeared from it as if through a trap door. A young black writer, Don Mattera, went the same way in 1973. Only those of us who care particularly for literature and writers remember; by the time the newspaper has been left behind on the breakfast table, most people have forgotten the banned authors and books listed there – the ultimate triumph of censorship.

I have said that South African literature was founded in an unrecorded political act: the writing down in Roman characters of some tribal praise-song. But the potted histories in DLitt theses always set its beginning with the writings of a white settler, an Englishman, Thomas Pringle. He was born the year the French Revolution started and came to South Africa in 1820, under the British government scheme of assisted immigration resorted to because of the agricultural depression in England that followed

Waterloo. For we white South Africans may somewhat unkindly be called, as Norman Mailer did his fellow Americans, 'a nation of rejects transplanted by the measure of every immigration of the last three hundred and fifty years'. Pringle led a Scottish party to settle on the border of the so-called Neutral Territory of the Cape from which the Xhosa people had been driven. Thus far, he is a classic white frontiersman; but this Scottish scribbler of album verse at once felt the awkward necessity to adapt his late Augustan diction and pastoral sentimentality to the crude events of Africa.

> First the brown Herder with his flock
> Comes winding round my hermit-rock
> His mien and gait and vesture tell,
> No shepherd he from Scottish fell;
> For crook the guardian gun he bears,
> . . . Nor Flute has he, nor merry song . . .
> But, born the White man's servile thrall,
> Knows that he cannot lower fall.

Pringle was never quite to find the adequate vocabulary for what moved him to write in Africa (Coleridge deplored his archaisms), but he astonishingly anticipated themes that were not to be taken up again by any writer in South Africa for a hundred years, and longer. Unlike the majority of his fellow frontiersmen, he refused to regard the cattle raids carried out by the Xhosa as proof that they were irredeemable savages. In a poem entitled 'The Caffer' he asks awkward questions of the whites.

> He is a robber?—True; it is a strife
> Between the black-skinned bandit and the white,
> (A Savage?—Yes, though loth to aim at life,
> Evil for evil fierce he doth requite.
> A heathen?—Teach him, then, thy better creed,
> Christian! If thou deserv'st that name indeed.)

He foreshadowed the contemporary South African liberal view, obliquely comforting to the white conscience, but none the less true, that any form of slavery degrades oppressor as well as oppressed:

> The Master, though in luxury's lap he loll . . . quakes
> with secret dread, and shares the hell he makes.

Pringle was one of the first and is one of the few whites ever to grant that blacks also have their heroes. He wrote a poem about the Xhosa prophet Makana who led an army of 10,000 tribesmen on the British Settlement at Grahamstown in 1819:

> Wake! Amakosa, wake!
> And arm yourselves for war.
> As coming winds the forest shake,
> I hear a sound from far:
> It is not thunder in the sky,
> Nor lion's roar upon the hill
> But the voice of HIM who sits on high
> And bids me speak his will
> . . . To sweep the White Men from the earth
> And drive them to the sea.

Pringle even wrote of love across the colour line, long before miscegenation laws made it a statutory crime and the so-called Immorality Act provided the theme of so many South African novels and stories:

> A young Boer speaks:
> '. . . Our Father bade each of us choose a mate
> Of Fatherland blood, from the *black* taint free
> As became a Dutch Burgher's proud degree.
> My brothers they rode to the Bovenland,
> And each came with a fair bride back in his hand;
> But *I* brought the handsomest bride of them all—
> Brown Dinah, the bondmaid who sat in our hall.

My Father's displeasure was stern and still;
My Brothers' flamed forth like a fire on the hill;
And they said that my spirit was mean and base,
To lower myself to the servile race.'

And the young Boer asks,

'. . . dear Stranger, from England the free,
What good tidings bring'st thou for Arend Plessie?
Shall the Edict of Mercy be sent forth at last,
To break the harsh fetters of Colour and Caste?'

Pringle himself was back in England the free after only six years in South Africa, hounded out of the Cape Colony by the English Governor, Lord Charles Somerset, for his fight against press censorship introduced to protect the British colonial regime against any mention of those controversial issues of the time, slavery, the condition of the blacks, and the anti-British feelings of the Boers . . .

After Pringle is packed off 'home' in 1826, a long colonial silence falls. Diaries are kept, chronicles are written by white missionaries and settlers, but no soundings are put down to the depths reached only by imaginative writing until Olive Schreiner writes *The Story of an African Farm* in the 1880s. It is a very famous book and one that, as a South African remembering it as a mind-opening discovery of adolescence, one tends to think of as all-encompassing: that is to say, that final accomplishment, the central themes of South African life given unafraid and yet non-exhibitionist expression by a writer whose skill is equal to them. But reading it again, and it is a book that stands up to re-reading, one finds that of course it is not that at all. It is one of those open-ended works whose strength lies at the level where human lives, our own and the book's characters, plunge out of grasp. The freedom that Lyndall, one of the two extraordinary main characters, burns for, is not the black man's freedom but essentially spiritual freedom in the context of the oppression of women through their sexual role; yet the passion of revolt is so deeply understood that it seems to hold good for all sufferings of oppression. The society Lyndall rejects is the shallow white frontier society; yet the rejection questions societal values that gave rise to it and will endure beyond it. It is a book whites in South Africa like to think of also as transcending politics; I have never met a black who has read it, with, ironically, the important exception of Richard Rive, who has just completed a book about Olive Schreiner's life and work. Certainly no black could ever have written *African Farm*. The alienation of Lyndall's longing to 'realise forms of life utterly unlike mine' is attempted transcendance of the isolation and lack of identity in a white frontier society; in the final analysis, this is a book that expresses the wonder and horror of the wilderness, and for the indigenous inhabitant that wilderness is home. The novel exists squarely within the political context of colonialism. Olive Schreiner's conscience was to reject colonialism, and her creative imagination to disappear in the sands of liberal pamphleteering, many years later. Perhaps she would have written no more imaginative work, anyway. But perhaps she took the conscious decision that Jean Paul Sartre, in the context of the Pan-African struggle, has said any writer should make, to stop writing if he is needed to do any other task that, as he sees it, his country requires of him. It is certain that political pressures, in the form of a deep sense of injustice and inhumanity existing within their society, can cause certain writers to question the luxury value of writing at all, within a country like South Africa.

The establishment of South African literature in English and (so far as it existed) in African languages as a literature of dissent came in the 1920s and early 1930s. The white man's military conquest of the blacks was over. The war between the whites, Boer and Briton, was over; the white man's other war, in which Boer and black had fought under the British flag along with the Briton, was over. In the State of Union of the four South African countries, the British Cape Colony and Natal, the Boer republics of the Orange Free State and Transvaal, blacks had been deprived of such rights as they had held at the pleasure of the more liberal of the separate governments. The black man's trusting willingness to identify his destiny with the white man's expressed in the victory praise-song-cum-poem of Samuel Mqhayi, a Khosa poet of the time, assumed a common black–white patriotism after the 1914–18 war:

Go catch the Kaiser, Let the Kaiser come and talk with us
We'll tell him how the Zulus won at Sandlwana
Of Thaba Ntsu where the Boers were baffled . . .

The assumption was met with rebuff and betrayal; only white men could be heroes, at home or in Valhalla.

Then William Plomer, aged nineteen, published in 1925 a work of genius, a forced flower fertilised upon an immature talent by reaction against racialism now entrenched under the name of a union of the best interests of all people in South Africa. *Turbott Wolfe* (Plomer's hero as well as the title of the novel) trails the torn umbilical cord of colonialism; Wolfe is not a born South African but an Englishman who plunges into Africa from without. But he understands at once: 'There would be the unavoidable question of colour. It is a question to which every man in Africa, black, white or yellow, must provide his answer.' The colonial cord is ruptured, early on and for ever, for South African literature because Plomer's novel does not measure Africa against the white man, but the white man against Africa. With it, a new literary consciousness was born: that no writer could go deeply into the life around him and avoid some sort of answer. Laurens van der Post's *In a Province* is awake to it, concerned with modern Africans in conflict with white-imposed values rather than Africans as exotic scenic props in the white man's story. So, fighting against it all the way, is Sarah Gertrude Millin's *God's Stepchildren*. This extraordinarily talented novel begs the question, as a kind of answer, by revealing the morality South Africa has built on colour and the suffering this brings to people of mixed blood, but nowhere suggesting that the sense of sin suffered by Barry Lindsell, play-white grandson of a white missionary and a Hottentot woman, is tragically, ludicrously and wastefully misplaced, until Barry Lindsell confesses to his young English wife that he has black blood and she says in surprised relief: 'Is that all?' Meanwhile, the novel has shown that it is, indeed, everything, in the life around her from which the author drew her substance.

Roy Campbell was the third of the famous triumvirate Plomer, van der Post, Campbell, who began in the 1920s the tradition of

exile, often self-imposed, that has afflicted South African literature with terrible blood-lettings ever since. Although accepted
and anthologised as one of those who, in his words about William
Plomer, 'dared alone to thrash a craven race/And hold a mirror
to its dirty face', Campbell provides a fascinating example of the
strange and complex mutations brought about by the effect of
politics upon writers and literature in South Africa.

Campbell was a writer whose work may be lifted like a transparency to show against the light certain dark and tangled
motivations where politics and the psyche struggle to accommodate
one another in the South African personality. It is there that South
African defence mechanisms are made. We shall see them reflected
in the work of other writers, too, subconsciously producing work
in answer to the need for various justificatory myths of political
origin. It is believed – certainly Campbell believed – that he left
South Africa because the colour bar was abhorrent to him. In his
poetry, he made biting and elegant attacks on white complacency. He wrote sensuously incomparable poems about blacks. But
he dismissed political and social aspirations with indiscriminate
contempt as 'the spoor and droppings of . . . the crowd emotions'.
The attributes of the brave black hunter with which he identified
were elitist rather than humanitarian, let alone egalitarian; in the
context of a white man's life, employed only for play, in blood
sports, not dictated by hunger, as for tribal Africans themselves.

I would say that Campbell left South Africa out of vanity; he did
not think the whites capable of appreciating his genius. It was true;
they were not. But his work did not ally itself in any way with the
destiny of the blacks either, in whose hands the culture of South
Africa must ultimately become definitive. The brilliant satirical
poet South Africa has never replaced ended as the last colonial,
romanticising himself as 'African' abroad, and irrevocably cut off
from all but the white majority he rejected at home.

Campbell's justificatory myth was tailored to an individual
need. But Pauline Smith, living in the 1920s in the isolation of
the Karroo as Schreiner did before her, created a justificatory myth
of the Afrikaner people that continues to answer, in literature, to

certain political pressures to this day. I must interrupt myself here to explain that I use the word 'myth' not in its primary dictionary sense of a purely fictitious narrative, but in the sense the anthropologist Claude Lévi-Strauss does, as a psychologically defensive and protective device. A myth is an extra-logical explanation of events according to the way a people wishes to interpret them.

Pauline Smith, a writer of Chekovian delicacy, was not an Afrikaner and she wrote in English. She wrote of rural Afrikaners, in whom her stories see poverty as a kind of grace rather than a limiting circumstance. Why? I believe that she was faithfully reflecting not a fundamental Christian view, but the guilt of the victor (British) over the vanquished (Boer), and also the curious shame that sophistication feels confronted by naivety, thus interpreting it as 'goodness'. One of the characters' main virtues is their total unfitness to deal with the industrial society that is going to come upon them with their defeat by the British. Her famous story 'The Pain' shows an old man and his dying wife terrified even by the workings of a hospital; the husband's humbleness is emphasised almost to the point of imbecility. This virtue in helplessness, in the situation of being overwhelmed by poverty, drought, economic depression, was to become a justificatory myth, in literature, of the Afrikaner in relation to the development of his part in the politics of domination. Based on it, at least in part, is the claim of Afrikaners to be a white African tribe; from Pauline Smith's *The Little Karroo* stories, through the long series of stoic novels in Afrikaans that André Brink has called 'a literature of drought and poor whites', to the tender and witty stories of an Afrikaner writing in English, Herman Charles Bosman, are Afrikaners not shown living close to the earth and natural disasters as any black man? The measure of poverty as a *positive value*, and the romanticising of pre-industrialism into a moral virtue are important aspects of Athol Fugard's plays, when these are about whites: his white characters are the children of Pauline Smith's rural Afrikaners, forced to the towns by drought and economic depression, and their virtues lie in their helplessness, their clinging to the past, and their defeat by an 'English'-dominated industrial society. How can such people be held responsible for the degradation that racialism imposes upon the blacks? They themselves represent victims within the white supremacist society itself; are they then not in the same boat as blacks?

Yet these are the people who, like English-speaking South African whites, conquered the blacks, who built a national pride out of their defeat by the British. These are the people whose votes gained political power and legislated, once and for all, the white man's will to overlordship.

It is an ironic illustration of the effect of South African politics upon literature to remark that while, in the 1920s, Plomer and van der Post were writing novels exposing the colour bar, they probably were not so much as aware of the existence of two remarkable fellow novelists of the time. These novelists were black. Thomas Mofolo's *Chaka*, written in Sesuto about 1910, was published in English in 1931, and is as extraordinary an achievement in terms of the writer's background, if not his age, as Plomer's *Turbott Wolfe*. It is, of course, a very different novel, in a way that was to be significant of the difference between white liberal or radical writings and the work of black writers themselves. It is written not *about* blacks, but as a black man. It is both a historical and political novel, based on fact and legend about the great nineteenth-century king Chaka, and its theme is dealt with in accordance with the author's own sense of the innate conflict in invoking Christian values to interpret an African power struggle. Mofolo, writing for original publication in a missionary journal, tried to approach the life of Chaka, the great despot, the Black Napoleon, as whites have called him, in the light of the Christian text: 'What shall it profit a man, if he shall gain the whole world, and lose his own soul?' But although Mofolo presents Chaka's brutal conquering excesses against his own people as sinful blood-lust, they also represent the neurotic paroxysm of a dying nation, turning to rend itself before colonial conquest. When the spears of fratricidal assassins are meeting in Chaka's body, Mofolo has him cry: 'It is your hope that by killing me ye will become chiefs when I am dead. But ye are deluded; it will not be so, for uMlungu [the white man] will come and it is he who will rule and ye will be his bondmen.'

The guns of white conquest are cocked over Mofolo's novel, but there are no white characters in it. In Sol Plaatje's *Mhudi*, also based on historical events, and set slightly later in the nineteenth century, uMlungu makes his entry for the first time in South African black literature. The Boers appear, trekking north, travelling with their families in hooded wagons and driving with their caravan their wealth of livestock into the hinterland in search of some unoccupied territory to colonise and to worship God in peace.

'But', asked Chief Moroka, 'could you not worship God on the South of the Orange River?'

'We could', replied Cillier, 'but oppression is not conducive to piety. We are after freedom. The English laws of the Cape are not fair to us.'

'We Barolong have always heard that, since David and Solomon, no king has ruled so justly as King George of England!'

'It may be so', replied the Boer leader, 'but there are always two points of view. The point of view of the ruler is not always the view point of the ruled.'

Quite. Despite its stylistic crudities, the novel skilfully explores the white man's double standard slyly posited here. Barolong and Boer find a temporary identity of interest in military alliance against the armies of another African tribe, Mzilikazi's Matabele; but once the battle is won, the white man expects to dictate the sharing of spoils, keeping the land for the Boers and handing over the captured cattle to the Barolong. 'What an absurd bargain,' says the Chief; 'will cattle run on clouds, and their grass grow on air?'

Similarly, although the white men all fight alongside the blacks, they wanted no personal relations with them. Juxtaposed with the power struggle between white and black there is in this book the sort of dream of its resolution in non-military, non-revolutionary, non-political terms that was to become the particular justificatory myth given expression by white liberal writers thirty years after Plaatje: a friendship between a young black and a young white. It is the literary wish-fulfilment of what South African society could be, would be, if only the facts of the power struggle conveniently could be ignored. The proposition cancels itself out. Ignored, the facts remain; they are not to be changed by turning to loving without changing the balance of power, to paraphrase Alan Paton's prophetic dictum in *Cry, The Beloved Country*, that by the time the whites have turned to loving, the blacks will have turned to hating. The apocryphal black–white brotherhood perhaps reached its symbolical apotheosis in Athol Fugard's tragedy as the *Blood Knot* between two men who are *actual* brothers, the skin of one reflecting the white side of their ancestry, the other the black. This friendship is a justificatory myth that embodies the yearning of many whites, and even some blacks, to escape the ugly implications of a society in which such apparently transcendental private relationships are in fact pretty meaningless, trapped in political determinism. Several of my own books explore these implications. In *Occasion for Loving* a young Englishwoman destroys a black man by indulging in a love affair with him and whose flouting of the power of segregation laws leaves him, once she has gone back to England, exactly where he was: carrying a pass and drinking himself to death in the black ghetto. The prototype friendship of Ra-Thaga and Viljoen, Barolong and Boer boys in Sol Plaatje's novel, survives until Viljoen sincerely offers Re-Thaga all that a white man can, in a white-orientated society: 'I will catch Mzilikazi alive, and tie him to the wagon wheel; then Potgieter will make me his captain, and you will be my right-hand man.' And Ra-Thaga sincerely rejects the hand-out: 'Oh no! . . . what would my children think of me if I were to be the right-hand man of a wifeless youth?'

South African literature seems to have developed by curious fits and starts; the explanation lies close to political developments in the country. In the 1930s and 1940s, of those writers whose work had been the most innovative in the 1920s, Plomer and van der Post were in exile, and Millin had turned her stridently detached attention mainly to the domestic dramas of Pauline Smith's poor whites now becoming industrialised in town. There were no more novels from Mofolo or Plaatje. Nor did any black writer emerge to follow their bold example of how black writers might, as Claude

Wauthier suggests in his *The Literature and Thought of Modern Africa*, reaffirm their origins, and use their present position. Why?

We have to look for an answer in the situation of black intellectuals at the time. With General Hertzog's 'final solution' to the 'native question', as exemplified in laws such as the Land Act of 1936, blacks were beginning to realise that Booker Washington faith in education as a means of gaining acceptance and a share in a common society was getting them nowhere in South Africa. The eloquence of a scholarly leader like Dr Jabavu had not succeeded in gaining a recognition of civil rights for blacks when the constitution of the South African Union had been drawn up more than twenty-five years before; the eloquence of a Benedict Vilakazi, outstanding Zulu poet of the 1930s and 1940s, did not succeed in rousing the white man to recognition of the black man's humanity, although he had the courage to tackle subjects such as the condition of black labour. A creative apathy took over among blacks, born of frustration; and not for the last time.

By way of comparison, for Afrikaner writers, this was a period of consolidation, through literature, of the importance of their possession of a mother tongue distinct from those imported from Europe. In a movement that finds its parallel only with the negritude movement among Caribbean and American negroes, and Africans outside South Africa, Afrikaners were engaged in affirming their political claim through a cultural identity. Afrikaans had been a patois; it became a language rich enough to be a literary language, hand over fist, so to speak, with their climb to political power. Fine Afrikaner poets, such as Langenhoven, made it so; others, such as van Wyck Louw and Uys Krige, internationalised it by bringing consciousness of the literary developments of the world outside into its orbit, in the field of poetry. The novelists continued to sing the saga of the rural Afrikaner, dealing with the black man as with the elements.

From the English-speaking population, little came but some poetry, sometimes fine, but often widely generalised in emotion, rather boring ontological thoughts on the Second World War. The war years had the effect, inhibitory to the development of an indigenous literature, of throwing the country back upon cultural links with Europe.

So far as it had become a literature of dissent, although it was soon to build up to its strongest impetus ever, South African literature began again, post-war, at a position somewhere behind that of William Plomer's *Turbott Wolfe*. It made a new beginning with Alan Paton's *Cry, The Beloved Country*, which suggested the need for a Christian solution to the political problem of racialism. It was a book of lyrical beauty and power that moved the conscience of the outside world over racialism, and, what is more, that of white South Africa, as no book had before. *Turbott Wolfe* was too radical for them, and no piece of writing was to move them again until the advent of Athol Fugard's plays, *Blood Knot* and *Boesman and Lena*, in the late 1960s and early 1970s.

The decade and a half through the 1950s to the mid-1960s produced a paradox between English-language literature and politics. The Afrikaner Nationalists, who were to formulate, codify and implement long-entrenched colour prejudice as apartheid, had come to power in 1948, and yet it was while this final processing of racialism was in progress that a wave of new South African writers, white and black, suddenly appeared to dig deep into the subsoil of South African society and give expression, in the dimensions of the creative imagination, to the kind of answers that 'every man, black, white or yellow' had given to Turbott Wolfe's 'question of colour'. Peter Abrahams, whose talent was given initial encouragement by white leftists (for so many years the only whites prepared to take seriously the possibility of a black writer being more than a sort of quaint freak, a literary albino) wrote the first proletarian novel, *Mine Boy*, the story of a tribal black man confronted with the twin experience of industrialisation and race discrimination in a city. My first novel, *The Lying Days*, published in 1953, was essentially about an experience many young white South Africans have shared. They are born twice: the second time when, through situations that differ with each individual, they emerge from the trappings of colour-consciousness that were as 'natural' to them as the walls of home and school. Dan Jacobson returned South African literature to the Karoo, in his brilliant first novel, *A Dance in the Sun*, making of the old colonial wilderness the stony ground of self-deception, doubt and questioning. The emphasis is on what happens to whites as oppressors. White Fletcher's attitude to black Joseph, whose wife has had a brat fathered on her by Fletcher's brother-in-law, is shown as the whole process of action and interaction between the personality of a man and the morality within which it exercises itself. The old woman in Alan Paton's *Too Late the Phalarope*, a later novel exploring the same moral theme, this time through a variation of Thomas Pringle's prophetic 'Brown Dinah' story, states a conclusion: 'We are not as other people any more.' Jack Cope, in a novel called *Albino*, made an ingenious attempt to sidestep the white writer's problems of politically decreed isolation within his white skin, by writing a novel about a young white boy brought up as a Zulu, in the words of one of the characters, 'a white with a black mind'.

But blacks were beginning again to write about themselves. Not in terms of the epic past but in direct terms of the present. The central experience of urban life on the dark side of the colour bar was bringing to paper 'the stench of real living people', as one of those writers, Lewis Nkosi, has said. The short stories of Ezekiel Mphahlele, Can Themba, Casey Motsisi, carried in Mphahlele's case by a sullen force, and in those of Themba and others jigged with a jaunty wit and self-lacerating humour, reflected survival characteristics developed by the nature of life in those human conglomerations, neither city nor suburb, now called black townships but once more accurately called 'locations', since they are sites chosen by whites to dump blacks outside the city limits, after work, just as they choose sites well out of the way for the city trash heap. Lewis Nkosi, in *Home and Exile*, a book of essays and literary criticism unique in South African literature, where literary criticism can scarcely be said to exist, wrote from the acrobatic position peculiar to African intellectuals in the 1950s, the audacious one of a young black who has a foot in the white liberal world and the other holding his place in the black proletariat of the 'township'. None of these writers, though undoubtedly their boldness was a reflection of confidence stemming from the existence of such movements, gave direct expression to the black liberatory movements that drew mass support at the time, the African National Congress and Pan-Africanist Congress. Subconsciously, their writings were aimed at white readers, to rouse white consciousness to black frustration. Even in the writings of the most talented black novelist since Peter Abrahams, Alex La Guma, who was a political activist, and in the poetry of Dennis Brutus, both later to be political prisoners on Robben Island, there was no overt commitment to a particular political line, nor did they use the vocabulary of political clichés. La Guma's moving novel *A Walk In the Night*, like his short stories set in prisons, backyards and cheap cafés, presents men and women who don't talk about apartheid; they bear its weals, so that its flesh-and-blood meaning becomes a shocking, sensuous impact. Few South Africans have been exposed to it, however; La Guma was a banned writer before it was ever published, abroad. As the black–white political tension rose, exploded at Sharpeville and culminated in mass imprisonments and the outlawing of black political movements, all these writers and more, with few exceptions, were forced into exile.

Work by white writers who tried to trace, through imaginative insights, in terms of political, social and spiritual options open to South African whites, the motivation of the young whites who turned to sabotage against the regime in the late 1960s, was banned. My novel *The Late Bourgeois World*, Mary Benson's *At The Still Point*, Jack Cope's *The Dawn Comes Twice*, C. J. Driver's *Elegy for a Revolutionary*, none of these has been read by South Africans themselves, who lived through the experience of that period. It all happened; it certainly exists within their memory; it does not officially exist in South African literature.

Again, by comparison, how was writing in Afrikaans developing in the 1960s? The changes were regarded as so fundamental that the era gave a generic term to the writers who emerged, the Sestigers (the Sixty-ers). In the words of one of them, André Brink, 'a conscious effort was made to broaden the hitherto parochial limits of Afrikaans fiction', to challenge certain cultural taboos in Afrikanerdom: the

Calvinist taboos on uncompromising religious exploration and the challenging of old, especially sexual, moralities. Against the background events of a country that seemed on the brink of a revolution, the Sestigers preoccupied themselves with just precisely these things, and with William Burroughs-inspired experiment in literary form. They challenged with sexual candour and religious questioning, taunting the church and the Afrikaans Academy of Letters; but the evidence that not one of them published anything that was banned shows how they turned away, astonishingly, from the deepest realities of the life going on around them. The Sestigers' outstanding prose writer, and indeed the most sweeping imaginative power in South African literature as a whole, Etienne le Roux, makes the lofty claim that his trilogy, *Towards a Dubious Salvation*, is a 'metaphysical' novel; but if a writer is part of the creative consciousness of the society in which he lives, is it not a form of betrayal, of creative as well as human integrity, to choose to turn away from the messy confrontation of man with man, and address oneself to God? In fact, reading this dazzling book, you sometimes have the feeling that Etienne le Roux *is God*, an infinitely detached Olympian observer, amusing himself by recording all those absurd and dirtily flamboyant little battles and copulations way, way down on earth.

Only in 1974, for the first time, has a book by an Afrikaans writer been banned. André Brink has written a novel that breaks the *political* taboos answering the challenge he himself published in a newspaper five years ago: 'If Afrikaans writing is to achieve any true significance within the context of the revolution of Africa (of which we form part) . . . it seems to me that it will come from those who are prepared to sling the "No!" of Antigone into the violent face of the System.' Not unpredictably, his novel suffers from the defiant exultation and relief of that cry, coming so belatedly from the Afrikaans novel, looting a newly seized freedom of expression on whose validity the seal of 'banned' was almost sure to be set. Perhaps it was inevitable that this novel should demand of its creator that it encompass all that is forbidden in the ninety-seven definitions of what the Censorship Act finds 'undesirable'; that it should roll up pell-mell all the forbidden themes and many of the cliché situations written about already by others. It follows that this novel cannot do André Brink justice, as a writer. Yet its exaggeration, its stylistic piling-up of words, images, events, like a series of blows – Take that! and that! and *that*! – remind one of the works of certain black South African writers, in which the truth is in the excesses and even absurdities because *this is the fantasy bred by our society*; it is the truth as evidence of the kind of nightmares that grow out of our kind of daylight.

That 'No!' of Antigone has come out loud and clear from Afrikaans literature once only before, and from a poet, Ingrid Jonker. Somehow she managed, without compromising her great gifts, to write a poem of the 1960s that sets the era's events in a perspective that takes in past and present and projects the future as no writer, black or white, has done after her. The poem refers to the pass-burning campaigns of the African National Congress and Pan-Africanist Congress, when women and children were killed in the course of police and military action.

The child is not dead
the child lifts his fists against his mother
who shouts Afrika! shouts the breath
of freedom and the veld
in the locations of the cordoned heart.
The child lifts his fists against his father
In the march of the generations who are shouting Afrika! shout the breath
of righteousness and blood
in the streets of his embattled pride.
The child is not dead
not at Langa nor at Nyanga
nor at Orlando nor at Sharpeville
nor at the police post in Philippi
where he lies with a bullet through his brain.
The child is the dark shadow of the soldiers
on guard with their rifles, saracens and batons
the child is present at all assemblies and law-giving
the child peers through the window of houses and into the hearts of mothers

this child who wanted only to play in the sun at Nyanga is everywhere
the child grown to a man treks on through all Africa
the child grown into a giant journeys over the whole world
Without a pass.

What is the position of South African literature in the mid-1970s, the era of Bantustan independence within the country while former guerrilla movements become constitutional governments in countries round about; the era of dialogue on black–white federalism; of streaky, if not exactly thoroughly mixed sport; and of the re-emergence of mass black action in the form of striking labour forces? The series of blood-lettings over the years, writers going into exile, emphasises the enormous influence of politics on literature not only in the obvious way, that so many writers *are* in imposed or self-imposed exile, but also in the state of South African society as reflected in their work if they continue to live here in South Africa, as opposed to the vision of the place held by writers now removed from the actual scene. A writer as immensely gifted as Dan Jacobson, after a series of novels rooted 'from memory' so to speak, in South Africa, has begun to write novels thematically remote from it. A liberation, of a kind . . .? Alex La Guma, in the gentle, beautifully written *In the Fog at the Season's End*, writes, like so many black exiles, as if life in South Africa froze with the trauma of Sharpeville. Since he is a good writer, he cannot create at the newspaper-story level, and cannot, from abroad, quite make the projection, at the deepest level, into a black political milieu that has changed so much since he left. Ezekiel Mphahlele's novel, *The Wanderers*, also suffers from this lack of connection. Only the poet Dennis Brutus seems to have drawn strength from the 'bitter bread of exile' and to have developed his gifts fully, if perhaps differently from the way he might have at home. In a collection of poems that places him perhaps higher in achievement than any of the younger generation, Arthur Nortje, exiled and dead before his book *Dead Roots* was published two years ago, writes the spiritual autobiography of exile on the most harrowing level. In the end, he who has had to make do with crumbs from the white man's table at home may find no stomach left for Europe's bounty:

> I drag my shrunken corpulence
> among the tables of rich libraries.
> Famous viands tasted like ash . . .

These are the terrors of exile, for a writer; and the decimation of a literature.

At home, significant South African drama in English has been created, single-handed, by Athol Fugard. The obvious major influence of Beckett on his work is a fascinating example of an esoteric mode, in which character is sacrificed to symbolic abstraction, and dialogue largely disembodied, returned to flesh and the individual involved rather than alienated. This is an interesting example of a writer's methodological response to his socio-political situation.

Of the new novelists, few and far between, who have emerged lately, a black one, Bessie Head, in exile but still on the continent of Africa, expresses an indiscriminate repugnance for *all* political aspirations in *all* races, and a white one at home, Sheila Fugard, takes into the arcane realm of Buddhist mysticism the old white liberal justificatory myth of the power of love to melt racialism. One of the two most interesting newcomers, J. M. Coetzee, with his two-part novel, *Dusklands*, links the behaviouristic conditioning of peoples by other peoples as a congenital flaw in human nature. His first narrative, that of a South African working in 1970 as a United States government official on a 'New Life Project' for the people of Vietnam, posits the choice offered by the anthropologist Franz Boas: 'if we wish to take over the direction of a society we must either guide it from within its cultural framework or else eradicate its culture and impose new structures'. It does not require much insight to understand where the reader's eyes are being turned: to that other society, in South Africa, where both these techniques of socio-political manipulation have been tried upon the indigenous population. And this could lead us obediently to a conclusion: if white South Africans are no better, they are merely just as bad as other people with the will to follow up military with psychological conquest. Like them, they run the risk of losing their own souls in the contest; the narrator retreats into madness in which he has 'high hopes of finding whose fault I am'.

The second narrative is a superbly written attempt of a dubious kind to which South African white writers are beginning to turn irresistibly, it seems, in unconscious search of a new justificatory myth: the explanation of the present in terms of the past; and therefore, does it not follow, a present as helplessly inexorable as the past? The narrator in this story set in 1760 goes hunting elephant and falls ill among hostile Hottentots. With a putrefying backside as the sum of his pain and humiliation, he enters the old Conradian heart of darkness. In order to survive, he must live as the people he despises as savages manage to live; he must admit, in himself, hideous instincts that he had attributed only to them. The final irony of some of his reflections would seem to make them those of a twentieth-century Coetzee, rather than an eighteenth-century one: 'To these people [the Hottentots] for whom life was nothing but a series of accidents, had I not been simply another accident? Was there nothing to be done to make them take me more seriously?' And again, 'I am an explorer. My essence is to open what is closed, to bring to light what is dark. If the Hottentots comprise an immense world of delight, it is an impenetrable world, impenetrable to men like me, who must either skirt it, which is to evade our mission, or clear it out of the way.' After his recovery and return to white settlement he goes back with a punitive expedition to the Hottentots who succoured and tortured him. He wipes them out in 'the desolate infinity of my power over them'. The fatalism, the detachment borrowed from history in this novel are best signified by the choice of epigraph for the second narrative, a quotation from Flaubert: 'What is important is the philosophy of history'.

Another newcomer, D. M. Zwelonke, apparently a member of Poqo, the underground wing of the Pan-Africanist Congress, has written a first novel in exile after a spell on Robben Island. His book takes its title from and is set on that prison island where once Makana, the prophet who wanted to drive the white man into the sea, was also imprisoned. Much of the writing is naive and sometimes even nonsensical, but where he deals with the dreams and nightmares that spring from spare diet, solitary confinement and the repetitious labour of endless stone-breaking, no polished 'imagining' of the situation by anyone, even a black writer, could

achieve his branding-iron impact. As for the book's vision of the
white man, here it is another new myth-making:

> We have seen the mole and a curse has befallen us. There is a
> time-old legend that he who sees the mole shall hear of a friend's
> relative's death. An evil omen was forecast: we have seen the colonial
> monster in his bathroom, naked, playing with his penis and anus.
> In consequence he was enraged. He caught us and dragged us to
> Makana Island, and there we were his prisoners. A curse has fallen
> on us. He is like the mole because he cannot see. He gropes in the
> blind alley of the tragedy of history.

All this is a long, long way from the world of black writer Lewis
Nkosi in the 1950s, the mixed parties where black and white argued
politics, arms around each other's necks, glass in hand ... And it
is the vision, too, that hovers in incantation over the resurrection of
black writing after the apathetic post-Sharpeville silence induced by
censorship and the relentless equation, in the minds of the Security
Police, between black articulateness and subversion. I believe these
new young black writers instinctively attempt poetry rather than
prose because poetry is the means of literary expression least accessible
to the rules of thumb employed by the Censorship Board. The deraci-
nation of their predecessors of the 1950s does not attract them; they
are street-corner poets whose work reflects an affirmation of black
identity aimed at raising black consciousness rather than rousing
white consciousness to the black man's plight. Blacks have seen white
culture, naked, for what it has proved to be, *for blacks*: long posited as
an absolute value, and eternally withheld from them. These writers
are interpreting the assertion of a particular kind of black separatism
which exists concurrently with, if discounted by, the official kind
accepted in dialogue between Bantustan leaders and white leadership
in and outside the South African government. Mongane Wally Serote
makes the black claim to the right to dictate terms:

> White people are white people
> They must learn to listen.

> Black people are black people
> They must learn to talk.

Irony is perhaps the best literary mode of expression, where passionate assertion will not pass the censors. James Matthews's book of poems *Cry Rage!* plumbs with passion not always matched by skill the hollowness of high-sounding apartheid terms such as 'separate development' and 'surplus people', but is banned. Another of these young poets, Don Mattera, has recently been picked off by being declared a banned person; one wonders how long the better-known Adam Small, who, like Mattera, has taken the decision of many people of mixed blood to see themselves now as blacks rather than half-whites, will go on being published if along with that abandoned half-white status he also abandons the idea of love, always acceptable to whites, as a weapon of a struggle. Judging from some of his statements lately, I do not think he will again be writing in terms such as these:

> You can stop me
> goin' to Groote Schuur
> in the same ambulance
> as you
> or tryin' to go Heaven
> from a Groote Kerk pew
> you can stop me doin'
> some silly thing like that
> but O
> there's somethin' you can
> never never do:
> true's God
> you can stop me doin'
> all silly things of that sort
> and to think of it
> if it comes to that
> you can even stop me hatin'
> but O

there's somethin' you can
never never do—
you can't
ever

ever
ever stop me
loving
even you!

In conclusion, to return to the situation in which all South African writers find themselves, whether black or white, writing in English, Afrikaans, Sesuto, Zulu, what-have-you – even if he successfully shoots the rapids of bannings and/or exile, any writer's attempt to present in South Africa a totality of human experience within his own country is subverted before he sets down a word. As a white man, his fortune may change; the one thing he cannot experience is blackness, with all that implies in South Africa. As a black man, the one thing he cannot experience is whiteness, with all that that implies. Each is largely outside the other's experience-potential. There is no social mobility *across* the colour line. The identification of class with colour means that breaching class barriers is breaking the law, and the indivisible class-colour barrier is much, much more effective, from the point of view of limiting the writer's intimate knowledge of his society, than any class barrier has ever been. The black writer in South Africa writes from the 'inside' about the experience of the black masses, because the colour bar keeps him steeped in its circumstances, confined in a black township and carrying a pass that regulates his movements from the day he is born to the status of 'piccanin' to the day he is buried in a segregated cemetery. The white writer, aseptically quarantined in his test-tube elite existence, is cut off by enforced privilege from the greater part of the society in which he lives: the life of the proletariat, the nineteen millions whose potential of experience he does not share, from the day he is born 'baas' to the day he is buried in his segregated cemetery.

The black writer would seem to have the advantage here; there are only four million whites. But this compartmentalisation of society works both ways. The black writer is extremely limited in his presentation of white characters, witness the frequency with which his are no more than cardboard or caricature. What he cannot know about the white man's life because of those large areas of the white experience he is excluded from by law, he supplies out of a fantasy distorted by resentment at the exclusion. The very force of the accusation he feels he must make against the white man sometimes loses the strength it should have. So it happens that you come across, in the work of a talented black writer, a white character so clumsily presented he seems to have no place in the work. A black South African, in exile in a nearby territory I visited recently, challenged my assertion that the presentation of white characters in work by black writers is *limited* by caricature: on the contrary, he countered, this is the way whites are, so far as blacks are concerned. I think he makes an interesting point. Caricature under these circumstances is perhaps not a deliberate distortion of the subject but a form of truth about those who see the subject that way. The idea relates to my own observation about André Brink's novel.

In the work of white writers, you often get the same gap in experience between black and white lives compensated for by the projection of emotions about blacks into the creation of a black typology. Guilt is the prevailing emotion there; often it produces cardboard and unconscious caricature just as resentment does.

The eminent authority on comparative literature, Professor Harry Levin, defines cultural identity as 'nothing more nor less than the mean between selfhood and otherness, between our respect for ourselves and our relationship with our fellow men and women'. The dilemma of a literature in a country like South Africa, where the law effectively prevents any real identification of the writer with his society as a whole, so that ultimately he can identify only with his colour, distorts this mean irreparably. And cultural identity is the ground on which the exploration of self in the imaginative writer makes a national literature.

1976

Letter from Soweto

I flew out of Johannesburg on a visit abroad two and a half months after the first black schoolchild was killed by a police bullet in Soweto. Since 16 June, when the issue of protest against the use of the Afrikaans language as a teaching medium in black schools, long ignored by the white authorities, finally received from them this brutal answer, concern had been the prevailing emotion in South Africa.

Concern is an overall bundle of like feelings in unlike people: horror, distress, anguish, anger – at its slackest manifestation, pity.

There was no white so condemnatory of black aspirations, so sure of a Communist plot as their sole source, that he or (more likely) she didn't feel 'sorry' children had died in the streets. Black children traditionally have been the object of white sentimentality; it is only after the girls grow breasts and the boys have to carry the passbook that chocolate suddenly turns black.

There was no black so militant, or so weary of waiting to seize the day, that he or she did not feel anguish of regret at the sacrifice of children to the cause. Not even a mighty rage at the loathed police could block that out.

I was away for the month of September. Henry Kissinger came to South Africa to discuss the Rhodesia settlement with Mr Vorster; six children were killed while demonstrating against his presence. A day or two after I arrived home in October, a girl of fifteen was shot by police at the Cape. The six were already merely a unit of the (disputed) official figures of the dead (now 358), some adult but in the main overwhelmingly the young, in unrest that has spread from blacks to those of mixed blood, and all over the country by means of arson, homemade bomb attacks, boycotts and strikes. The fifteen-year-old girl was added to the list of fatalities; no one, I found, was shocked afresh at the specific nature of this casualty: the killing of a child by a police bullet.

Like the passing of a season, there was something no longer in the air. People had become accustomed, along with so much else unthinkable, to the death of children in revolt.

I try to recognise and set out the reasons for this acclimation before daily life here, however bizarre, makes me part of it.

When striking children met the police that Wednesday morning in June in the dirt streets of Soweto and threw stones that promptly drew bullets in return, who would have believed that the terrible lesson of white power would not be learned? The lesson for these children wasn't free, any more than their schoolbooks are (white children get theirs for nothing); they paid with the short lives of some of their number. No one could conceive they would ever present themselves again, adolescent girls bobbing in gym frocks, youths in jeans, little barefoot boys with shirts hanging out as in a wild game of cops and robbers – to police who had shown they would shoot real bullets. But the children did. Again and again. They had taken an entirely different lesson: they had learned fearlessness.

Of course, white attitudes towards them began to change, even then. It was immediately assumed by the government and the majority of white people that since the issue of the Afrikaans language had been quickly conceded, and the children now demanded the abolition of the entire separate educational system for blacks, and then bluntly 'everything whites get', such intransigence must be the work of agitators. Among black people – among the outlawed liberation organisations inside and outside the country, and those perforce confined to balancing cultural liberation on a hair's breadth of legality within it – all began to claim credit for the first popular uprising since the early sixties. No one will know, for years perhaps, how to apportion the influence of the banned African National Congress and Pan-Africanist Congress – their leadership in prison and exile – in the development of schoolchildren's defiance into the classic manifestations of a general uprising.

Neither can one measure how much of the children's determined strategy was planned by older students of the black

university-based South African Students' Organisation. There
surely were – there are – agitators; if agitators are individuals
able and articulate enough to transform the sufferings and grievances of their people into tactics for their liberation. There surely
was – there is, has never ceased to be – the spirit of the banned
political movements in the conceptual political attitudes and
sense of self, passing unnamed and without attribution to their
children from the tens of thousands who once belonged to the
mass movements.

What neither the accusations of the white government nor the
claims of black adult leadership will ever explain is how those children learned, in a morning, to free themselves of the fear of death.

Revolutionaries of all times, who know this is the freedom
that brings with it the possibility of attaining all others,
have despaired of finding a way of teaching it to more than a
handful among their trained cadres. To ordinary people it is
a state beyond understanding. We knew how to feel outrage
or pity when we saw newspaper photographs of the first
corpses of children caught by the horrible surprise of a death
nobody believed, even in South Africa, would be meted out
by the police. Blacks still burn with an anger whose depth
has not yet been fathomed – it continues to show itself as it
did at the Soweto funeral of Dumisani Mbatha, sixteen, who
died in detention. Seven hundred mourners swelled to a crowd
of 10,000 youths that burned 100,000 rands worth of the
Johannesburg municipality's vehicles and buildings. Yet – not
without bewilderment, not without shame – black people have
accepted that the weakest among them are the strongest, and
thus by grim extension also accept the inconceivable: the death
of children and adolescents has become a part of the struggle.

We whites do not know how to deal with the fact of this death
when children, in full knowledge of what can happen to them,
continue to go out to meet it at the hands of the law for which
we are solely responsible, whether we support white supremacy or,
opposing, have failed to unseat it.

When you make men slaves you deprive them of half their virtue,
you set them in your own conduct an example of fraud, rapine and
cruelty, and compel them to live with you in a state of war . . .

Olaudah Equiano, eighteenth-century black writer

White people have turned away from concern to a matter-of-
fact preoccupation with self-protection. A Johannesburg parents'
committee has a meeting to discuss whether or not teachers at a
suburban school should be armed, as they might once have planned
a school fête. I bump into a friend who tells me, as if he were
mentioning arrangements for a cattle show, that he and fellow
farmers from a district on the outskirts of Johannesburg are gathering next day to set up an early warning system among themselves
– one of them uses a two-way radio for cattle control, the gadget
may come in handy.

Now it is not only the pistol-club matrons of Pretoria who regard
guns as necessary domestic appliances. At the house of a liberal
white couple an ancient rifle was produced the other evening, the
gentle wife in dismay and confusion at having got her husband to
buy it. Gunsmiths have long waiting lists for revolvers; 50 per cent
of small arms come illegally from Iron Curtain countries who call
for a total arms embargo against South Africa at the UN.

Certainly, in that house a gun was an astonishing sight. Pamphlets
appear with threats to whites and their children; although the black
movements repudiate such threats, this woman feels she cannot
allow her anti-apartheid convictions to license failure to protect
her children from physical harm. She needn't have felt so ashamed.
We are all afraid. How will the rest of us end up? Hers is the
conflict of whites who hate apartheid and have worked in 'constitutional' ways to get rid of it. The quotes are there because there's
not much law-abiding virtue in sticking to a constitution like the
South African one, in which only the rights of a white minority are
guaranteed. Gandhi had our country in mind when he wrote, 'The
convenience of the powers that be is the law in the final analysis.'

My friend Professor John Dugard, Dean of the Faculty of Law
at the Witwatersrand University, says that if whites do not show

solidarity with blacks against apartheid, their choice is to 'join
the white laager or emigrate'. Few, belonging to a country that
is neither in the Commonwealth nor the Common Market, have
the chance to emigrate. Of the laager – armed encampment – my
friend David Goldblatt, the photographer, says to me: 'How can we
live in the position where, because we are white, there's no place
for us but thrust among whites whose racism we have rejected with
disgust all our lives?'

There is not much sign that whites who want to commit themselves to solidarity with blacks will be received by the young
anonymous blacks who daily prove the hand that holds the stone
is the whip hand. They refuse to meet members of the Progressive
Reform Party, who, while assuming any new society will be
a capitalist one, go farther than any other white constitutional
group in genuine willingness to share power with blacks. They
will not even talk to white persons (there are still no white parties
that recognise the basic principle of Western democracy although
they would all call themselves upholders of the Western democratic system) who accept one man one vote and the rule by a black
majority government as the aim of any solidarity, and understand,
as John Dugard puts it, that 'the free enterprise system is not the
only system' to be discussed.

The black moderate Chief Gatsha Buthelezi, whose position
as a Bantustan leader fiercely attacking the government that
appointed him has made him exactly the figure – legal but
courageous – to whom whites have talked and through whom
they hope to reach blacks, lately is reported to have made a
remark about 'white ultra-liberals who behave as though they
are making friends with the crocodile so they will be the last to
be eaten'. He also said, 'Nobody will begrudge the Afrikaner his
heritage if it is no threat to the heritage and freedom of other
people.' It seems old white adversaries might be accepted but
white liberals will never be forgiven their inability to come to
power and free blacks.

Nevertheless, I don't think the whites he referred to would be
those with the outstanding fighting record of Helen Suzman, let

alone radical activists like Beyers Naude of the Christian Institute, and others, of the earlier generation of Bram Fischer, who have endured imprisonment and exile alongside blacks in the struggle.

If fear has taken over from concern among whites, it has rushed in to fill a vacuum. In nearly six months, nothing has been done to meet the desperate need of blacks that seems finally to have overcome every threat of punishment and repression: the need, once and for all and no less, to take their lives out of the hands of whites. The first week of the riots, Gatsha Buthelezi called for a national convention and the release of black leaders in prison to attend it. As the weeks go by in the smell of burning, the call for a national convention has been taken up by other Bantustan leaders, black urban spokesmen, the press, the white political opposition. After five months, the Prime Minister, Mr Vorster, answered: 'There will be no national convention so far as this government is concerned.' Most of the time he leaves comment to his Minister of Justice, Police and Prisons, Mr Jimmy Kruger. The only attempt to deal with a national crisis is punitive. It is Mr Kruger's affair. He continues to project an equation that is no more than a turn of phrase: 'South Africa will fight violence with violence.'

Three hundred and sixty people have died, of whom two were white. The police, who carry guns and still do not wear riot-protective clothing but army camouflage dress and floppy little-boy hats that could be penetrated by a slingshot, have not lost a single man.

Neither the Prime Minister nor his minister in charge of black lives, M. C. Botha (Bantu Administration, Development and Education), has yet talked to urban black leaders more representative than members of the collapsed Urban Bantu Councils. (They do not have normal municipal powers.) On their own doleful admittance, these are dubbed 'Useless Boys' Clubs' by the youths who run the black townships now.

Of the black leaders whom the vast majority of urban blacks would give a mandate to speak for them, Nelson Mandela and his lieutenants Walter Sisulu and Govan Mbeki, of the banned African

National Congress, are still imprisoned for life on Robben Island. Robert Sobukwe of the Pan-Africanist Congress is banished and silenced.

Black intellectuals who might stand in for these have been detained one by one, even while whites of unlikely political shades continue to affirm a fervent desire to talk to blacks, just talk to them – as if 300 years of oppression were a family misunderstanding that could be explained away, and as if everyone did not know, in the small dark room where he meets himself, exactly what is wrong with South African 'race relations'.

The government leaders refuse to meet the Black People's Convention, perhaps in the belief that by not recognising Black Consciousness organisations the power of blacks to disrupt their own despised conditions of life and (at the very least) the economy that sustains the white one will cease to exist. Fanonist theory of the black man as an image projected upon him by the white man takes a new twist; the white man goes to the door of his shop in central Johannesburg one September morning this year and fails to recognise the black man marching down the street shouting, in his own image, 'This is our country.'

The government won't speak to the Black Parents' Association, formed originally to finance the burial of Soweto children in June. In this ghastly bond, the association moved on under the leadership of Nelson Mandela's wife, Winnie Mandela, and Dr Manas Buthelezi, an important Black Consciousness leader about to be consecrated Lutheran Bishop of Johannesburg. It became a united front combining youthful black consciousness inspiration with the convictions of older people who followed the African National Congress and Pan-Africanist Congress.

Finally, the government does not consider speaking to the militant students themselves who are still effectively in leadership, sometimes preventing their parents from going to work (two successful strikes in Johannesburg). Daily and determinedly, they pour into the gutters the shebeen liquor they consider their elders have long allowed themselves to be unmanned by.

Meanwhile, since June 926 black schoolchildren have received punishments ranging from fines or suspended sentences to jail (five years for a seventeen-year-old boy) and caning (five cuts with a light cane for an eleven-year-old who gave the black power salute, shouted at the police and stoned a bus). They are some of the 4,200 people charged with offences arising out of the riots, including incitement, arson, public violence and sabotage. Many students are also among the 697 people, including Mrs Winnie Mandela, detained in jail for 'security reasons'; the other week one hanged himself by his shirt in the Johannesburg prison, an old fort two kilometres from the white suburban house where I write this.[1] Several students, not twenty years old, have just begun that reliable apprenticeship for African presidents, exile and education in Britain. When, in September, Mr Vorster met blacks with whom he will talk – his appointed Bantustan leaders – he would not discuss urban unrest or agree to a national conference of blacks and whites to decide what ought to be done about it.

There is a one-man commission of inquiry into the riots, sitting now. Mr Justice Cillie, the white judge who constitutes it, complains that few people actually present at these events have volunteered evidence. In fact, the schoolchildren and students themselves boycott it, and for the rest, South Africans' faith in the efficacy of commissions to lead to positive action has long gone into the waste-paper basket along with the recommendations the government steadily rejects. The Cillie Commission keeps extending the period in which it will sit, as the riots continue to be part of the present and not a matter of calm recollection. 27 January next year is the latest limit announced. Historical analogies are easily ominous. But a commission of inquiry was Tsar Nicholas II's way of dealing with the implications of the 'unrest' of Bloody Sunday, the beginning of the 1905 revolution.

---

1 The South African Institute of Race Relations in Johannesburg released on 8 November the following analysis gleaned from cases reported in the national press between 16 June and 31 October: 1,200 people have already stood trial. Three thousand are facing trials not yet completed. Of the 926 juveniles tried and convicted, 528 have been given corporal punishment, 397 have received suspended sentences or fines, and one has been jailed.

A chain-store owner whose business has been disrupted by strikes and the gutting of a store has burst out of the conventions of his annual report to shareholders to say, 'Decades of selfishness and smugness by South African whites is the principal reason for widespread unrest among blacks.'

Yet most changes suggested by whites do not approach a call for a national convention, with its implication of a new constitution and the end of white supremacy. Black certainty that nothing will bring equality without power is dismantled by whites into component injustices they can admit and could redress without touching the power structure. The Federated Chamber of Industries calls for job 'reservations' discriminating against blacks in industry to be ended, and has the support of the most powerful trade union group and the opposition parties. The National Development and Management Foundation goes further and calls for the ending of business and residential apartheid as well. Afrikaner big business, government supporters all, in their Afrikaanse Handelsinstituut ask for blacks to be given 'greater' rights in their own urban areas and training to increase their skills.

Although the Progressive Reform Party has demanded a national convention and the release of all people from detention, it was still necessary, before its 1976 congress agreed to change its education policy to enforced desegregation, for Helen Suzman to remind rank-and-file members that the separate-but-equal dictum for education had been 'thrown out by the United States twenty years ago'.

With unprecedentedly strong criticism of the government coming from its own newspapers and prominent Afrikaners as well as the opposition, it is baffling to read that at the same time 60 per cent of whites – an increase of 5 per cent over the majority gained by the government in the 1974 election – support Mr Vorster's National Party. The reliability of this particular poll is in some doubt; but perhaps the contradiction is not so unlikely after all. It is possible to see a dire necessity for change and fear it so greatly that one runs to give oneself to the father figure who will forbid one to act.

For months the white political opposition parties – Progressive Reform, United Party, and Democratic Party – have been trying to agree to some sort of realignment. If a liberal front comes about, it will trample the old sandcastle fort of the United Party, the conservative official parliamentary opposition, already eroded by the departure of most of its politically vigorous members to the Progressive Reform Party.

The numerical strength of such a front cannot be measured until it is known whether a major part of the United Party, which still polled 31.49 per cent in the 1974 elections, will enter it alongside the Progressive Reform Party, in the last few years grown from a pressure group to a real presence in parliament, with twelve seats and 6.25 per cent of the vote. (The crankish Democratic Party has a minute following.) Only when the extent of United Party commitment is revealed will it be possible to estimate roughly what percentage of the 40 per cent who voted against the government in the last election are liberals. There are rumours that some disaffected verligte ('enlightened') National Party MPs may defect to the front too.

The declared aim of the front is to protect the rights of whites while giving blacks, coloureds and Indians a direct say in government – which careful phrasing suggests its policy will be to the right of the present Progressive Reform Party. The spectral raison d'être of such a realignment is surely not the chance of ousting Vorster's government but of getting ready a white 'negotiating party' to treat with blacks on a shared-power basis when he finds he can no longer govern. The viewpoint of enlightened white politics now includes urgently the wide angle of acceptability to blacks, although they have no vote to be wooed. When Mr Vorster can no longer govern, it is not likely any other white government will be able to.

No one knows whether the Bantustan leaders are, in their different circumstances, preparing themselves for a particular role on that day. They meet at a Holiday Inn at Johannesburg's airport, exactly like Holiday Inns all over the world, down to its orgy-sized beds and cosy smell of French fried potatoes piped along with muzak, but deriving its peculiar status as neutral country outside apartheid from the time when it was the first hotel here to be declared 'international': not segregated – for foreign blacks, anyway.

From there the Bantustan leaders demand 'full human rights for blacks and not concessions'. With the exception of the Transkei and Bophuthatswana – the former having celebrated the homeland brand of independence on 26 October, the latter soon to do so – they reject ethnic partitions of South Africa. Which means they walk out on the many-mansions theory of apartheid, abandoning the white government which set them up inside; and they identify themselves as part of the liberation movement for an undivided South Africa. They present themselves to the black population in general as black leaders, not tribal leaders. Is this a bid for power? If Nelson Mandela were to come back from the prison island, would they step aside for him? Has the most imposing of them, Gatsha Buthelezi, a following cutting across his Zulu tribal lines?

Whites believe so. He attracts large audiences when he speaks in cosmopolitan black townships. Many blacks say no; and the African National Congress in exile continues to deride the Bantustan leaders as collaborators, making no exceptions. Other blacks imply that the best of the Bantustan men are keeping warm the seats of leaders in prison. Among politically articulate blacks, this year is their (Southern hemisphere) hot summer of brotherhood. Tsietsi Mashinini, the student leader who fled the police to exile in Britain, suggests that the tremendous force his movement shows itself to represent is loyal to Mandela. It does not seem to matter to blacks whether it is a Gatsha Buthelezi or anyone else who is the one to say to whites, as he has, 'The future is a Black future and we Blacks want our future now.'

From the Market Theatre, newly opened in what was the Covent Garden of Johannesburg, comes a strange echo – Cucurucu, Kokol, Polpoch and Rossignol, asylum clowns in Peter Weiss's *Marat/Sade*, singing: 'Give us our rights . . . and we don't care how – We want – our re-vo-lu-tion – NOW.' The author granted performances on condition everyone could see the work and has donated his royalties to a Soweto riot victims fund. His play has never been

performed before in a city atmosphere such as ours, it has never
been heard as we hear it.

During the 'quiet' years of successful police repression, before
the young emptied the Dutch courage of shebeens down the drain
and sent through people's veins the firewater of a new spirit, there
have been political trials in progress continually in South Africa.
Not only those of blacks who have left the country for military
training and re-entered illegally, but also those reflecting aspects
of the struggle against apartheid carried on by an intellectual elite.

While the riots have been taking place, two young white university lecturers in Cape Town have given the black power clench
and, avowing 'no regrets', have accepted long sentences under
the Terrorism and Internal Security Acts; their uncompromising
personal suffering serves as proof of solidarity with blacks that must
be granted even by those whites who abhor the white far left. In
Johannesburg I have been to hear the trial of four white university
students and a lecturer accused of trying 'to change South Africa'
by organising black workers, who have no recognised trade unions.
The five were charged under the Suppression of Communism Act,
and the state's principal evidence consisted of papers read at a
seminar.

The backs of these young men in blue jean outfits suggested a
pop group; but when they turned in the witness stand it was not
to greet fans but to smile at the wife of one of them, whose hands,
while she followed the proceedings, were working at a complicated
length of knitting – the danger of active dissent does make risk
of imprisonment part of the daily life of courageous people. Yet I
felt events had overtaken them. The segregated public gallery was
almost empty of white and black spectators. The struggle was a few
miles away in the streets of Soweto.

But it is another trial, which has gone on almost two years,
that seems to have the opposite relation to present events. Four
years ago, the nine black members of the South African Students'
Organisation accused under the Terrorism Act seemed to the
ordinary public, black and white, to represent a radical fringe
movement on the far side of the generation gap. The state's evidence

against them was literary and clumsily esoteric – it consisted of black plays in the idiom of New York black theatre of seven years ago, mimeographed Black Consciousness doggerel that couldn't compete with comic books, poetry readings that surely could appeal only to the educated young.

The paper flowers of literary rhetoric have come alive in the atmosphere of tragic exaltation and discipline that can't be explained.

In the city streets of Johannesburg black people go about their white-town working lives as they always did: the neat clerks, waiters in their baggy parody of mess dress, dashing messengers in bright helmets on motor scooters, shop-cleaners, smart girls who make tea in offices or shampoo the clients' hair in white hairdressing salons. Polished shoes, clean clothes; and most of the time, when the youngsters don't stop them from boarding township trains, people get to work every day.

How do they do it? Daily life in Soweto is in hellish disruption. One-third of the country's school-leavers may not be able to write the final exams of the school year that ends in December; not all schools in the Johannesburg area have reopened. Those that have function irregularly, either because militant pupils stop classes, or teachers suspected of sympathetic alignment with them are detained. Buses and trains don't run when stoning and burning start; commuters crush into the big old American cars that serve as taxis or walk to stations outside the area. No one knows when his neighbour's house may cave in, set alight because he is a policeman. If he himself owns a precious car, it too may burn, should he be suspected of being, or even be mistaken for, some less obvious form of collaborator.

While we white people picnic, Sundays are the most dreadful days of all in Soweto: funerals, the only category of public gathering not banned, have become huge mass meetings where the obsequies of the riot victim being buried are marked by new deaths and fresh wounds as the police attack mourners singing freedom songs and shaking black power salutes. A black intellectual whose commitment to liberation no one would question, although he risks the violent disapproval of blacks by still having contact with whites, tells me, 'When I go home tonight, I don't know which to be more afraid of – the police getting me when they shoot at anything that moves, or my own people getting me when I walk across the yard to the lavatory.'

White Johannesburg appears as it always was. Across the veld to the south-west Soweto *has* been severed from the city, to drift in its fury and misery. Refuse, carted away in municipal vehicles that are vulnerable symbols of white rule, is collected when it can be. The Johannesburg medical officer of health has warned of possible outbreaks of measles and diphtheria in Soweto, and the reappearance of poliomyelitis; the white doctors and nurses who staffed most clinics have had to be withdrawn. It is no longer safe for any white to enter there. Only the white police go in; stand guard, their chrome whiplash aerials giving away the presence of riot-squad cars and men in leaf-spattered jumpsuits at the crossroads where Soweto leads to Johannesburg. And the black workers come out every morning and go back every night, presenting faces that won't distress the white city.

What may the clean, ironed clothes and calm faces carry concealed, of disease and violence, to a city that has cut such things loose from itself?

Postscript: A Johannesburg newspaper asks if I will accept nomination for the 'Woman of the Year'. I decline. Someone else will have that honour, perhaps even a black woman from the small black professional elite. But this year the only candidates are surely Winnie Mandela, who came out of house arrest to stand between the police and the schoolchildren and be imprisoned, or any one of the black township women who have walked beside their marching children, carrying water to wash the tear gas from their eyes.

1976

What Being a South African Means to Me

Address at the University of Cape Town

What does it mean to be a South African? Who decides? What does it mean to me to be a South African? Do I qualify? Of course, only white people in South Africa ever feel the need to ask themselves or each other such questions. And this leads to the last one we shall ever have to find the answer to: Is there such a being as a white African? Who decides?

You will have had, or will have before these sessions are over, many criteria set up in answer to the first question. The geographical criterion will be generally taken for granted as inadequate; living here under Capricorn is not enough. The circumstantial one also is inadequate: living here under apartheid is not enough. The evidence is in a state of being that has passed, from some people of my grandfather's generation of locals who called Europe 'home' to some people of your generation who feel so detached from our ideologically dense environment that they are again no longer at home. There is an internal emigration that can be said to have lasted for four generations. A section of the white population has lived from conquest to decline without ever becoming South African-conscious.

But you don't want generalisations; you will want to garner your own, from various views. What does being a South African mean to me? First of all, what are my objective claims to be one?

I was born here, yes, and to me that is a fact of deeply emotional importance, because I not only believe along with the Jesuits and Freud that the early years of a child's life are carried within that child for always, he may live and discard many phases of experience, but that one, never. I also believe that the shock of confrontation with the physical world, the first landscape you open your eyes on, the first piece of earth you stagger to your feet on, the first faces that bend over you, although they pass beyond conscious recall, put a certain stamp on your perception and interpretation of the world. When I am in Europe or America, or anywhere away from Africa, my vision of home – in that half-waking state when time and distance don't exist – is burned veld round mine-dumps and coal-mine slag hills. Not a romantic vision. Not one that most Europeans would recognise as Africa. But Africa it is. Although I find it harsh and ugly, and Africa and her landscapes have come to mean many other things to me, it signifies to me a primary impact of being; all else that I have seen and know is built upon it. Many questions to which I shall die while still working out my answers began there.

I have found that my claim to regard myself as South African by virtue of the pre-memory perceptions of birth and infancy are sometimes contested – by fellow whites. I may have been born here more than fifty years ago, but that does not mean I have been here *long enough*. I am the daughter of immigrants, my mother from England, my father from Lithuania. They weren't the sort who called Europe 'home', but that doesn't help. In the opinion of some whites, it is necessary to be able to trace one's ancestry back to the Voortrekkers or the 1820 British Settlers in order to be accepted as South African.

Potato-famine Irish or pogrom-Jewish lineage is parvenu. As time goes by, and the tenure even of whites who can trace their family lines to van Riebeck is challenged by blacks, who for so long would not have been thought to have any say in the matter at all, the question of how many generations a white must have behind him in order to qualify as a South African seems quaintly irrelevant. I have an urbane Afrikaner intellectual friend, educated at Oxford and Leyden, who used to like to annoy me by clinching an argument with the observation, 'How European you are, Nadine!' Whereas he, of course – his covered-wagon pedigree and free-running child-hood on a farm among black children who now live not in South Africa at all but shunted off to Gazankulu or Bophutatswana – was a real South African. I wonder how he feels about being polarised, along with the parvenu, as white, simply white, to the proposition of black consciousness . . .

Having staked a territorial claim that goes further and further than a mere birth certificate, how does it seem to me my consciousness of being a South African took shape? Well, to go back to childhood: subconsciously, and *innocently* – by which I mean that the subconscious was storing impressions and experiences that were taken at face value. When you are a child, whatever is around you, in terms of human behaviour as well as physical environment, is the way the world is. Immutable. Adults present you with a manner of life; you know of no other. For this child there is a four-roomed house with a red *stoep*, a lawn in front and in the back yard a pepper tree, a room where a black servant lives. The father goes on a bicycle every day to open his shop. The child walks through the suburb of bungalows across the veld to school. Once a week she wakes to the sound of drumming and knows it is Sunday because the mine-boys are dancing at the compound. They are black, wear blankets and sometimes white ladies' church hats that have been thrown away; they pee by the roadside, they are always wandering between the mine and the town. A schoolfriend is the daughter of the mine secretary and invites the child to the Christmas party for staff children. The children are white, like her, like all the children at school. A pet dog is run over by a neighbour; the black servant goes to see a sick brother. *That is the way things are.*

There is another place where things are different: overseas; snow and robins and cowboys, a king and queen, read about in children's books. That place – the faraway – is a mystery; everything here is exactly what it is: the given facts are perfectly congruous, none stands out of category, the way an object would catch a bright child's eye in one of those puzzle pictures, meant to train the power of cognitive distinction, where a tool must be singled out among toys, or a fish on land. A long time goes by before the facts of daily life in that small Reef town begin to be sorted into heaps, in a tentative taxonomy. The dead pet will never reappear. The mine-boys are in fact men (there's evidence of that) although they don't know men don't wear ladies' hats, and although they aren't members of the Mine Recreation Club. The servant is a woman with a brother – another life – she's not only 'our Lettie' who embroiders pillowcases in the sun on the step of her room. The men and Lettie are black. They don't belong to clubs, they don't come on picnics, their children don't go to the Convent of Our Lady of Mercy, across the veld. The fact-sorting process speeds up; the little heaps mount, some merge. In the principle of selection, a norm is the set of facts governing the life of the child herself: if you are white, *you begin from the premise of being white*. Are *they* different because they are black? Or are they black because they are different?

To be born a South African is to be presented with *given* facts of race on the same level of reality as the *absolute* facts of birth and death. Perhaps that is what whites mean when they speak of the unfairness of black resentment against even 'innocent white women and children' (women being honorary children); and perhaps it is what blacks mean when they argue that every white is guilty, by birth, of oppression of blacks. I have spoken and written often, in my life, of the second or rebirth many South African whites go through. I mean by this simply what happens when the child begins to realise the fact that the black does not enter through the white's front door is not in the same category as the fact that the dead will never come back. From the childhood memories of black friends and from the writings of blacks I gather that, until very recently, and no doubt still, in vast areas of the country, young blacks have a converse emergence into a second consciousness – when they realise that it is not in any natural and immutable order of things to call the white children's father 'Baas' and 'Master'.

I date the development of my consciousness of being South African rather than having any other social identity from the birth into that second consciousness. The process is essentially the discovery of the lie. The great South African lie. In disagreement with popular beliefs, I myself don't equate this consciousness with guilt – that famous guilt white-anting the South African personality comes later, with the age of reason and the shame of consent . . . What comes of the immediate discovery of the lie is revelation: you cannot feel guilt for being conned. From the time I discovered that what was being concealed by my society was that blacks were people – not mine-boys, not our Lettie, but people, I had the opportunity to become what I think of as a South African. I had the responsibility to accept what I now knew. Which is to say that I believe that is where the identity is to be formed: working one's way through the central, definitive experience of black and white as people, with undifferentiated claims on life, whatever else – skin, language, culture – makes them differ from one another. Of course, I don't have to say that it is not as brusquely attainable and clear-cut as it sounds. When I reached the awkward age of reason, I sought ideological and political explanations and formulations for what whites were doing to blacks. To be a South African is to be one for whom none of these theories is abstract; long before you or I are old enough to read politics and economics we have demonstrated in ourselves capitalist exploitation of a peasantry and proletariat, lived this in our lives, going to a free school while our black siblings caddied for our fathers on the golf course or herded their cattle on the farms; long before we have heard of the race theories of a Gobineau or a Hitler, we have been part of a demonstration of the counter-Marxist, Western democratic theory that race discrimination and not class exploitation is the basis of oppression in our country.

For me, the black mine-workers were in the compound before the term migratory labour was stored in my mind. I heard in the mouth of a grown-up in that small town the words 'white kaffir' as an ordinary term of abuse between two quarrelling whites before complex analyses of the projection of fears, before the concept of the Other who epitomises one's own obstreperous idea came my way. Now I began to interpret. I began to understand that I was, as a white South African, in terms of social evolution, and to ask how – if – one might break out into another social role. Most important, contact with blacks as people and equals, sometimes very close and personal contact, shaped my consciousness through their ideas about whites, about me; rounded it out through their demands upon me and my dependencies upon them.

In this period of intense give-and-take between idea and flesh, between the theory and the daily reality not only of aspiring to something called justice but of aspiring to become human in the ways South African society was and is not, I was beguiled by the charm of a 'free society' within four walls, so to speak. But outside that room the iron colour bar remained on black backs, not mine. Like many others, I granted too much counterweight to the groups where there was no 'they' and 'we', only Us.

During this period – and it lasted more than a decade – I also had new relationships with whites that developed my awareness of what might be involved in being a South African. In particular there was my close friendship with a woman who already lived in a way that seemed to be evolved in particular response to the situation. She was an Afrikaner, but there were others like her, Jewish or of English descent. She was a white prepared to take full responsibility for the past that can't be changed and the future that must be. Through her I came to understand that we whites are not European and that in order to be *anything* we must change profoundly. It was in the 1950s, long before we had been frightened by the concept of black consciousness and before the concept of white consciousness had begun to be considered as anything but white supremacy. At the time it was still possible to work with blacks; she did just that: not *for* them. She considered proxy a crippling thing to those on whose behalf concessions were asked. She believed no one could assess black needs but blacks themselves: no one could decide for them how they could free themselves from white oppression: only they knew what it really was. She would argue political tactics passionately with blacks, but she did not expect to prevail by assumption of white-knows-best, if not out of despotism then out of an equally despotic compassion. I watched her in her daily life, as an organiser of a mixed trade union, then running a co-operative, willing and able to work under blacks in political activities on *their* terms, astonishingly free of any sense of self-sacrifice or nobility in the risks she ran, the naming and banning and periods of detention

– in simple, unshakeable acceptance that if she suffered it was as much to remake the meaning of being a white South African as to remake that of being black.

A lot of cant is talked in the context of whites like you and me suffering on full stomachs the psychic damage of over-privilege; but if we are to try to discover if there is any validity in a concept of white consciousness, we have to examine how privilege subconsciously hampers the will to change. And it still seems to me that people like my friend saw the real aspects of this and took their own hard way towards curing it.

Today men and women such as Beyers Naudé and some young people who have been student leaders show that same courage.

Jean Paul Sartre, as an old man in his middle seventies, says his only regret in life is that he was not more radical; I think it is likely that I, too, from that safe shore, may say the same. Certainly I am aware that I have not been nearly as brave as being a South African has turned out to require, and it so happens that active radicals and bravery have gone together, in South Africa.

How much can I blame on the tumbril of history, whose destination is unlikely to be that rendezvous where there is room for all? How much must I blame on the lingering sloth of privilege, convictions not matched by courage; the writer's fiercely exclusive sense of his existence through his work? It is hard to be honest about these things, even with oneself.

'Only connect' was a fragile bond. Part of my continuing consciousness of being a South African has been to accept, quite long ago, without sneering at the limited but undoubted value it had, that that bond between black and white has broken, defiled by 'dialogue', the zoo tea party at which noises remarkably like human exchanges are made. That bond has been rent like gossamer by brutish removals, medieval detentions, and finally, the shooting of children.

At no time in my life has my sense of being a South African been final and definitive, and it is not, now. Being a South African is a constant state of response to demands; continuing and changing demands. I often mark how different is the social state of being of American or English friends. They begin to seem to me a protected species; in one way, I could define my South Africanness by the extent to which they differ from me in their secure sense of what they are. Once mature, they may have to make adaptive changes to outward circumstances, they may have to face slumps and unemployment, changes in the standard of living, even the possibility of atomic annihilation together, but they will never have to change the concept of who and what they are in relation to their country.

This is exactly what is being demanded of whites in South Africa now: to change the concept of who and what they are in relation to South Africa now. After more than three hundred years, blacks are demanding it of whites; whites such as the students who have organised this series of discussions and inquiries are demanding it of themselves. In the political parties' understanding of the nature of the demand, there are varying degrees of sincerity and realism; what we have to keep foremost in our South African consciousness, there, is that although some wild things have come out of the mouth of Mr Andrew Young, and although the diplomatic notes of protest from the big powers as well as those of Mr Pik Botha fell thick upon Mr Andrew Young's head when he said South Africa's government was illegal, only legalistic, sophistic arguments can prove him wrong. Morally, our government is illegal. When our Nuremberg comes – and the trials go on in private, inside us, already – no one will be able to deny that the 'legality' of our government consists in its being legal in our country for a parliament representing only a white minority to make the laws . . .

I don't think the public platform is the place for me, but I am here because I take seriously the Student Representative Council's intention to examine the feasibility and validity of a white consciousness concept as a response to our present situation, psychological and practical. I am not prepared to dismiss white consciousness out of hand as merely the acceptance, black-dictated, of racialism in reverse. The rejection by young and not-so-young blacks of the white spectrum from liberal to radical is a traumatic experience, make no mistake about it, for whites. For myself, I can say that rationally I understand it and consider it necessary, but as individual experience I find it as wounding as anyone else does. It is not easy to take as a new starting point. Black thought insists that, beginning again from rejection, whites must work out a social and psychic route based on the idea that they will arrive so changed back at the point of departure that it will be possible, then, for there to be equality of acceptance. For blacks will emerge from their great pilgrimage into full selfhood; and the thread that leads out of the labyrinth of struggle will turn out to have been in the hands of both and to have brought them to a meeting place, not some hall where the petty apartheid signs have been hastily taken down.

Is this just a ghastly mirror-version of 'separate development'? I fervently hope not. I don't think so. Mongane Serote once wrote a little poem: 'White people are white people, they must learn to listen; black people are black people, they must learn to talk.' It has happened. But we must not expect blacks to tell us what *we* must do, or even what they want of us. It is frustrating that they will not, cannot.

If we declare an intention to identify fully with the struggle for a single, common South African consciousness, if there is such a thing as white consciousness as a way to human justice and honest self-realisation, whites will have to take their attitudes apart and assemble afresh their ideas of themselves. We shall have to accept the black premise that the entire standpoint of *being white* will have to shift, whether it is under the feet of those who loathe racialism and have opposed it all their lives, or those to whom race discrimi-nation is holy writ.

One of the most difficult things of all to face is that black thinkers talk at the moment as if they prefer, in principle, white racialists and conservatives, those who have decreed and pursued the persecution of blacks with pious cruelty and detached hubris, to those whites of the liberal-to-radical spectrum who have pursued the cause of black liberation, at worst, yes, out of self-interest disguised as paternalism, at best out of commitment to destroy self-interest as whites have known it, along with apartheid. There is no objective reason why the ugly sincerity of white racialists should be regarded as more 'sincere' than the sincerity of whites who want to ditch racialism. But the thing is those whites failed: failure in the ranks of those who have power is not forgiven by those without power. Yet this failure of whites has become one of the most important factors in black consciousness – in the form of the realisation that liberation cannot be gained on *one's behalf*, by others. Could white consciousness – once you have decided what it is and how to put it into practice – provide a means for whites to participate in the legal and economic and spiritual liberation of blacks? Will it find a way in which whites themselves may at the same time be liberated from the image of the Janus Oppressor, the two archetypal stereo-faces, grinning racialist or weeping liberal, of the same tyrant? Is this what consciousness is? You are making a Pascalian wager on it; and that's the only way to find out.

1977

Transkei

A Vision of Two Blood-Red Suns

Coming into the new 'black republic' of Transkei[2] from the north, I was out of it again almost at once and then in again. The road leads through an area and town 'excised' for whites. On the map these blobs and trickles of black and white, marking off the 87 per cent of the Republic of South Africa reserved by

---

2   Where I have used 'Transkei' – the term for the so-called 'independent homeland' – instead of 'the Transkei' – denoting the region – it does not imply any recognition on my part of this integral area of South Africa as a separate country.

4 million whites for themselves from the 13 per cent offered to
18 million blacks, are an ethnic Rorschach test whose logic is to
be understood only by initiates of the political ideology of apartheid; from the road, it's suddenly easy for anyone. Passing before
one's eyes, the perfect contours of vast lands ploughed and crops
reaped by machine, the barns full of bright farming equipment,
the pedigree stock, the privacy of trees and gardens drawn round
the fine farmstead of the white area change abruptly to the black
area's uneven strips cultivated by hand-plough, the bare hills
with their discs of mud huts and squares of spiky agave enclo-
sures for motley beasts herded by children. The only machinery
is the occasional wrecked car, dragged off the road and picked
clean.

A torchlight procession of hundreds of winter-blooming aloes –
red-flame, blue-flame, white-flame – passes a church upon a hill in
an infinity of empty hills. A range of shadows – the Drakensberg
Mountains that form Transkei's north-east border – fades with
the light that is leaving a feminine landscape of classical curves
broken here and there by ravines intimately furred with virgin
forest. Where this has been replaced by afforestation already there
is the inappropriate European dusk gathered by Northern pine. A
slope is a football field because racing youngsters are using it for
that purpose, and marks one of the 'rehabilitation' villages established to control landless people and soil erosion caused by random
grazing: several hundred rounds of mud and thatch instead of
hilltop crowns of two or three, the new tin flash of a windmill,
kilometres of wire fencing. Many women carrying across their
heads loads of wood twice their height, and one or two elderly
men in old business suits on horseback are making their way along
concourses undefined as the football field. Broad tracks made by
ox-drawn sleds lead only to sources of firewood and water. For
me, on the way to places with onomatopoeic names, *Tabankulu*,
Lusikisiki, there is the one fierce road. Stones and ruts; no signposts. As if to confuse an invader – but the invader is merely one
who doesn't know the signs of the terrain so firmly staked within
the lifetime range of the people who live here that they walk alone,

in the dark, old, female, as surely as and much more securely than
Western contemporaries find the way home from a suburban bus
stop.

Great space; and human intimacy. To think one has found it
even here is an illusion, so far as the sense of space is concerned.
This 1976 creation of a country (4.4 million hectares) larger than
Switzerland is so overcrowded in terms of agricultural potential
that it cannot survive unless enough industry can be established to
take half the people off the land.

But the human intimacy is no illusion. These people are innocent; innocent of alienation, our crime against ourselves. One
midday I was received in the empty round mud room that was
the home of a woman so poor there were not even any of the
usual home-made utensils to be seen. Her children had the peculiar, still sad air of malnutrition. She apologised with social grace
for not being able to offer food to her white guests, as if home
freezer supplies just happened to have run out – but no, I am
projecting my own kind of situation on one I couldn't conceive
of: she assumed, without loss of pride or self-respect, perfect
understanding of shared circumstances. Like the majority of families, hers had no adult male living at home – the men are away
working on the mines or canefields of South Africa – but three
youths had dropped in to visit. She was animated and charming in
her rags. The youngsters shared a cigarette rolled from a piece of
newspaper none of the company could read, but tranquil communication was strongly present as the smell of grass-thatch and
woodsmoke that comes from the skin and hair of these people as
you sit among them.

On a mountain-top with a view no multimillionaire could
secure to himself in Europe, I found three little girls alone in
possession of two huts, a tethered calf, a hen coop made of woven
branches and a field where mealies had been reaped. A figure out
of Grimm climbed into view with a load of wood and a bunch of
wild asparagus fern she had cut to make a broom. A child ran off
reverently to fetch a tin of water. The quizzically intelligent old
woman quenched her thirst. What did white people want to visit

a dirty homestead like hers for? A confident, welcoming joke. To submit at her invitation to the dim, wide, conical engulfment of her hut was to find the order of good housekeeping. Apart from the grindstone and pestle for maize and the huge clay pot for brewing maize beer that are the standard furnishings, there were gourd dippers and enamel store plates; the careful luxury of a bottle of paraffin hung among the hoe and scythe hooked under the eaves of the thatch. Around one curve the base of the wall extended to make a low clay bench like a window seat, and there were a couple of stacked carved stools: the men's side of the house. The grandmother and the children sank at once into a calm unit, close together, on the sleeping mats of the women's side. In place of the ticking of a clock, in these houses silence is the piping chip-chip of chicks whose tiny blur carries the light from the single source of the doorway as they pick grains of meal from the smooth mud-and-dung floor.

The old woman's son is in the mines; she provides and cares for the grandchildren out of her yearly R144 old age pension. What about the money her son earns? That pays taxes and supports his wife and their smallest children. A relative comes to plough the grandmother's steep field; she cultivates and harvests herself, just as she walks the mountains to fetch wood and water. The ideal love between women and children I see everywhere here — that is what it is made of: that great burden of toil. The sturdy little girls each find some surface of their grandmother's body to make tender contact with; this thin woman with the blue-black darkening of age in the wrinkles of capability is their bedrock. Grimmest facts of economic hardship are the ugly secret of such love.

The biggest contribution to the national income of Transkei is still the sale of men as migratory labourers. In the first elections that symbolised independence, 55 per cent of the people at the polls were women. After 300 years of white rule in South Africa the men of Transkei cannot earn a living at home. The land allotted them under the division of South Africa into white and black areas of occupation is not sufficient to support their families, and the cities

and industries they have given their labour to build over generations, the gold and coal mines they have manned, are hundreds
of kilometres from the poor portion they have been persuaded to
accept of South Africa, which could not have realised its rich potential without them.

Govan Mbeki is a man of the Transkei, educated, politically
capable, but not honoured by any chieftainship or cabinet appoint-
ment in the new black government. He is imprisoned for life on
Robben Island off Cape Town for political activities that asserted
the right of South African blacks to share non-racial government
over the whole of South Africa. I keep remembering how he has
written of the Transkei as a 'breeding camp' where the men come
home for three months a year to procreate, in these round huts, the
next generation of cheap labour for whites.

The white man had hardly set his spoor of boot and wheel upon
this part of Africa before visions of how to rid themselves of his
overlordship began to come to the indigenous people.

A hundred and twenty years ago a black Jeanne d'Arc saw and
heard the African ancestral dead. To Nongqause they foretold that
if her Xhosa people gave up witchcraft, killed their cattle and razed
their maize crops in sacrifice, on 18 February 1857 two blood-red
suns would rise and a hurricane would sweep the whites back into
the sea by which they had come. New fields of maize and new herds
of cattle would appear, and Xhosa warriors dead in frontier wars
would live again.

The Xhosa were fighting a battle that could not be won. Not
only was it the oxhide shield and assegai against the gun, but ultimately man's masterful technological attitude to his environment
– acquired in Europe's nineteenth-century industrial revolutions
– against the compact with his environment that is the ancient
pastoral society's solution to the problem and mystery of our place
in creation. The need of a miracle was the Xhosa reality: they did
as Nongqause's vision bid.

On 18 February 1857 the two blood-red suns did not rise, and
the whites were not swept into the sea. Sixty-eight thousand Xhosas

starved to death and those who survived did so by making their way to the Cape Colony to beg food and work from the white man.

In Transkei's capital, Umtata, among the rows of traders' stores and under the glass and steel mirrors of fine administrative blocks built with the South African government's money, there is a building unique in the history of all that was and is South Africa. The Cape Dutch-style colonial stateliness suggests perfectly what it was intended it should: a parliament just like the white man's. It was here that the vision of driving the white man into the sea underwent a transformation to become the constitutional vision of getting the vote and direct representation for blacks, along with whites, in the government of South Africa.

In the mid-nineteenth century the British of the Cape Colony controlled the Transkei through magistracies, and blacks had a qualified vote in the Cape legislature. The paring-down of the black franchise was successive until 1894, when the annexation of all chiefdoms of the Transkei to the Cape Colony was completed. Then Rhodes, the Empire-builder who wanted to see all Africa draped in the Union Jack, introduced an act that established a system of African representation *outside* a common society of black and white. A pyramid of councils, part elected, part white-government-nominated among chiefs, conveyed the Transkeians' needs to the white government; the black councillors had no powers of legislation and the government had no obligation to act on their advice.

The South Africa Act of 1909, which unified the country in the wake of the Boer War, took away from those blacks who still managed to qualify for the vote the right – never yet exercised – of electing a black to parliament. While that same act entrenched the African franchise in the Cape, the long-term process was clear. In the early thirties an unqualified franchise was given to all whites; by 1936 black voters in the Cape were removed from the common voters' roll. The Transkeian supreme council had moved into this elegant doll's house of power where, on a budget that ten years later did not yet amount to more than half the money spent by the South African government on printing and stationery, the council was allowed to deal only with local education, roads, agriculture, limitation of stock and tribal law.

The quaint 'natives' parliament' was called – both institution and building – the Bunga, derived from a Xhosa word meaning 'a discussion'. Apart from placating chiefs for their loss of authority to white magistrates, the Bunga incidentally gave educated Transkeians a chance (unique for South African blacks) to learn by frustration the workings of Western government administration.

The Bunga asked for direct representation for blacks in the South African government year after year; at the same time, it asked for greater administrative powers within the Transkei. These aims were never accepted by the Transkeians as mutually exclusive. In the 1950s apartheid made them so. The 'self-government' the new laws prepared for applied only to the eight 'Bantustans' – nascent black statelets – of which the Transkei was one. 'Self-development' was carried out by government-appointed and even government-created chiefs (the present Prime Minister was made a Paramount Chief) functioning as 'Tribal Authorities' whose decisions could be vetoed by the white government in Pretoria.

The Bunga as an institution dissolved itself in 1955. In 1976 the Bunga doll's house with its solemn panelling and gilded citations of democracy became Transkei's National Assembly, in return for the surrender of any claim for Transkeians ever to sit in the parliament of South Africa, or take any part in the central government of South Africa, where more than a third of the Transkei's people live and work.

Both private reception rooms at the Umtata Holiday Inn are called the Kaiser Matanzima Room. If this is caution, it isn't lack of imagination. Prime Minister Kaiser Matanzima gives no chances to rivals who might qualify to have their names honoured. One of the new administrative blocks is named after State President Chief Botha Sigcau, rewarded with that high office for his politically strategic importance as Paramount Chief of the rebellious Pondo people; but President Sigcau's portrait does not hang in

the Cabinet Chamber with Kaiser Matanzima's, and Matanzima
has not repealed the preventive detention act that, under South
African rule, kept the leaders of the opposition party in jail
during elections for the country's first independent government.
(The leader of the opposition was jailed again, by Matanzima,
while I was in Transkei.) George Matanzima, Minister of Justice,
now, but once struck off the lawyers' roster for professional
misconduct while practising in South Africa, seems content to
be the closest of siblings. The Brothers Matanzima have the same
Roman senator heads. Their family name means 'strong saliva';
the taste of power turns venomous when Kaiser Matanzima
attacks those who call him a stooge of the white South African
government, a man who has betrayed the black man's right to
share all South Africa. From time to time, venom flickers even at
the government that set him up.

Kaiser Matanzima's cousin, Nelson Mandela, and his other
compatriots Walter Sisulu and Govan Mbeki are serving life
sentences. The constitutional vision has receded further and
further. It is not difficult to see why Nongqause's vision of ridding
the blacks of white overlordship would be transformed, yet again,
into a third avatar. To some blacks, 13 per cent of the land seems
better than nothing; a beggarly black state within South Africa
could be regarded as a Trojan horse from which liberation could
overrun white domination.

Matanzima is the man, as well as the opportunist, of his time.
He carries within his personality the contradictions of the vision
transformed. He has opted for tribal nationalism, accepted and
approved apartheid; on occasion he lifts the black power fist and
declares solidarity with blacks in South Africa who reject apartheid and hold out for full rights in a unitary state. He pledged
he would not take independence until the South African government fulfilled Transkei's claims to additional land and guaranteed
such citizenship rights as there are for blacks in South Africa to
those Transkeians living and working there. He has got part of
the white-owned land he claimed – some of it as a gift of farms to
the Brothers Matanzima personally. But he has given up the right

to South African citizenship of the 1.3 million Xhosa-speaking people who do not live in Transkei. Thousands of them were not born in, nor have they ever seen Transkei. The language they speak is declared by the South African government as proof of Transkei nationality; in this way apartheid 'keeps South Africa white' by making 'foreign' sojourners of the majority of South Africa's urban black population. If they refuse to accept Bantustan citizenship, they become stateless. While I was in Transkei a vast settlement of squatters near Cape Town was bulldozed and 70 per cent of the inhabitants, Xhosa-speaking, were ordered to go 'home' to Matanzima, who had neither welcome, land nor work to offer them.

No foreign dignitary attended the Transkeian 'independence celebrations' in 1976: the countries of the world have not officially recognised the existence of this one.

The single gain Transkei made in the independence deal is the abolition of South Africa's lower standard of schooling for blacks. A scholarly Transkeian of the missionary college old boy network castigates UNESCO for refusing educational aid, now: couldn't I influence *anyone* – the Americans, West Germans – to give young Transkeians scholarships abroad? Even Amin's Ugandans get them! 'Everyone sneers at us for taking orders from Pretoria – why won't they help us train people to make our independence real? Orders . . . it's not true . . . Well, what can we do? D'you know that the library here in Umtata was opened to blacks only after the celebrations in '76! We're not stooges . . . we need teachers, librarians . . .'

His eyes move about his government office as if to catch out a filing cabinet listening and observing. Yet he gabbles indiscreet asides. His son has 'disappeared'; I know what that means? – yes, from South Africa where he was studying – fled abroad after detention during the riots in 1976. These young people want nothing to do with this independence . . . Out in the street he accompanies me courteously but I am merely a presence from which his preoccupation echoes. *Pretoria, Pretoria*, he murmurs – a ringing in his ears.

In the bar at an Umtata hotel a group of attractive black men wearing young executive clothes meets heartily every evening: a lawyer, an insurance man, 'reps' (travelling salesmen) from South African firms, and functionaries in the para-governmental Development Corporation, financed by South Africa. The Corporation is concerned with getting blacks into business as well as attracting white foreign industrialists by the inducement of tax remissions, no minimum wage and no trade unions. A game of cards is slapped down among the beer bottles, banter flies in a mixture of Xhosa and English, a tray of fried fish goes round in place of peanuts. The insurance man has just won his company's citation for the month's highest average of life insurance sales; the cosmetic 'rep' swaggers: 'A gold mine, I'm telling you, this country's a gold mine.'

To whom does one sell life insurance here?

To the grandmothers whose worth could not be compensated by any premium? To the men who tell me they don't know where to find the new R2.50 livestock tax payable on each head of cattle – their only capital?

In two years Umtata's population has risen from 25,000 to 31,400. Apart from imported skilled workers and administrators employed on the R20-million university, the hydroelectric scheme, the industrial and housing developments, the new affluent class is a bureaucracy and its hangers-on. R37.5 million invested in the country by South African and foreign industrialists, and R59.5 million from the South African-financed Development Corporation have provided only 12,500 jobs for Transkeians. Unless he works for the government or has the minimal education and maximum good luck to be able to take over a white store on finance borrowed from the Corporation, the Transkeian has little choice but to labour for low pay at home or hire himself out to the mines across the border.

The Umtata Town Hall clock has stopped and not even independence sets it measuring a new era. At noon by my watch old women in their tribal petticoats and turbans settled like huge black snails on their heads are watering the public gardens from cans; cheaper for the municipality than the outlay for a hose, I suppose.

Life down the road at the end of York Street remains the reality
of the capital for most people. Taxi drivers tout custom along the
bus queues; some vodka 'rep' has been zealous: all buses bear the
huge legend – SMIRNOFF, THE SPIRIT OF FREEDOM. In
the market a medicine man dressed like a respectable farmer sells
potions from bead-covered gourds which are his apothecary's jars,
and among business women sewing braided print skirts there is
one who sells teaspoons of snuff from a tin which she also uses
to mark out the circumference of the women's anklets she cuts
from the tubes of old tyres. And all along one side of the street are
the recruiting offices, with their neat and cheerful, fresh-painted
façades like white suburban houses, and their cajoling signs. The
older ones tell a picture-story: assegais and shields invoking manli-
ness, the homecoming of the beaming miner stepping off the train
into a company of admiring women and children. The latest recognises that tribal black men have entered the kind of contemporary
world offered them, abandoning hope of anything but money: no
human beings, no smiles – a miner's helmet, shown as a cornucopia
filled with notes.

In the yards of the offices are small buses and Land-Rovers that
pick up recruits from their villages. Men are waiting about with
their cardboard suitcases and blankets. Some look very young;
there is an atmosphere of detachment and silence in the stoicism of
an unavoidable destination, very different from the strutting confidence of government officials running up the broad steps of new
ministries, and the free-riding pleasure of the Rotary Club candidates on their nightly spree in a hotel bar their colour would have
excluded them from in South Africa.

'If I were to get a telex from Johannesburg asking me to send
a thousand men this week, I'd have no difficulty.' The white
recruiting officer for South Africa's biggest gold-mining company,
a group of coal mines, a construction company and a sugar-cane
growers' association, says that more men than ever are prepared to
go off for a nine-month stint as a contract labourer. Black miners'
wages have been raised considerably lately; but the wage gap
between white and black average monthly earnings on the mines

continues to grow – at present it is a staggering R700 in favour of whites. Blacks are housed in barracks and nutritiously fed, free, as units of labour, in the interests of efficiency that take no account of further, human needs.

In most old trading villages there are no whites now except those left behind under marble angels in the abandoned European cemeteries (the Xhosas mourn elaborately but plough and plant over their last season's dead). The trading stores, the butchery and the single hotel have all been taken over by blacks, and so have the recruiting concessions that used to be as much part of the white trader's turnover as the sale of sugar and blankets. In one of these villages I watched young black men in earrings, sniffing and hawking against the early morning cold, led into the magistrate's office by the local recruiting agent – a brisk black girl loud on plat-form shoes. The magistrate read to forlorn closed faces the terms of the agreement whereby they would go to the mines; the men touched a clerk's ballpoint in symbol of the illiterate's signature to the document. The girl wrote bus and rail passes for the journey. They were led out, launched on their career in a place where they are not permitted to stay longer than nine months at a stretch, and are forbidden to have wife, child or family come to live and make a home with them.

The Transkeians are people of twelve tribal clusters, each with its strong sense of identity and named terrain, although they all speak Xhosa dialects.

In the 1880s Pondoland was still an independent country governed by its own chiefs when a colonising party of Germans from South West Africa (Namibia) – then already annexed by Kaiser Wilhelm I – landed on its wild coast and obtained gran-diose concessions for mineral and commercial exploitation from an ancestor of the present President of the Republic of Transkei, Chief Botha Sigcau. In return, two sons of the tribe were taken to Germany to be educated. It would have been a good bargain for the Germans if the British had not ridden in to remind the Pondos, with a military escort, that Pondoland had *already* been given away

– to the British, by Sigcau's father. The Germans left; no one can tell me if the two young Pondos achieved their *Abitur*.

Pondoland was the last Transkeian territory to come under white rule and it seems it will be the last to accept the apartheid dispensation of independence. In the fifties at a meeting called to persuade Pondos to accept 'Tribal Authorities' as a form of self-government, a man literally turned his backside to Botha Sigcau, its protagonist-in-office, and was cheered: *Umasiziphathe uya Kusubenza sifile* – Bantu (tribal) authorities will operate over our dead bodies!

They did. A vast popular movement of resistance arose in Pondoland in 1960, concurrent with the general uprisings in South Africa that culminated in the police massacre of blacks at Sharpeville. Thousands of Pondos came down from their mountains on foot and horseback to demand, among other things, the removal of Paramount Chief Botha Sigcau. Tanks and guns from South Africa met them. Thirty Pondos died for their part in the revolt, 4,769 were held in preventive detention.

All this is not entirely in the past. Everywhere, burned-out huts, baked to rough pottery by fire, stand among occupied ones: oh yes, I am told, it happened last year, in 'the fighting'. Vendettas between chiefs and their people opened during the revolt continue, in forms dictated by the new status of the country. Every time the subject of the new livestock tax is mentioned there is, in the company of ordinary men smoking their pipes and women sorting grain from grit for the next meal, a flash of resistance taken for granted – 'No one will pay.' An interpreter extrapolates: 'They want to kill Sigcau.'

If it's true it would not be the first time he has had to flee for his life in this exalted landscape. Pondoland is at once peaceful and dramatic beyond reconciliation. On high terrible roads you move through the sky by way of mountains that set you down only when they reach the sea. Looking from mountains on to mountains: dark ploughed land cast like nets, there; velour of light on contours of rose, blond and bronze grasses. Where the grass has been burned, coal-blue shapes; where the first rains have fallen on these, stains of livid growth spread as the shadows of the clouds do. The lovely chimera's torso of the earth reclining; black, gold, brown, green

markings of its pelt; and down into the broad flow of a valley that
is scratched by reaped mealie fields where red cattle are stumbling,
the great paws of mountains stretch and flex. Rivers searching
through to the sea are too far below to be heard. They disappear for
kilometres behind mammoth slopes; suddenly, when it is almost
night, shine up from the dark clutches of the land.

The Pondos seem always to be seen in silhouette against the sky.
At a high snake-bend near the Umzintlava River, young men are
come upon, gathered on a rock. Behind them valleys fall sheer and
they live somewhere in what, to them, is the neighbourhood: this
or that mountain-top group of blind-backed huts whose doors –
and windows, if they have any – all face the same way, not at some
town-planner's dictate, but out of the older logic that a habitation
must turn its back to the direction from which bad weather blows.
Goats are shaking out their cries across space. There's a tiny store
balanced nearby but nobody is buying. The young men are not
going anywhere. They are merely out to be appreciated by each
other and anyone else who comes along. My inventory of what they
were wearing will be extraordinary but there is nothing outlandish
about it, here. Not only because this is as much local men's gear as
blue jeans and T-shirts are elsewhere in the world, but also because
Pondos have mastered an esoteric law of aesthetics, along with
dandies and Dadaists – style is a combination of incongruities.

They wear some of the endless varieties of headgear devised
among Transkeian men and women – a striped towel can be as
intricate and dashing as a piece of hand-beaded cloth or a beaded
diadem and locks. They wear long skirts not stitched but draped
skin-tight. Their midriffs are bare and suck in and out with sexually
self-confident male laughter. All carry knobkerries (home-carved
truncheons) and the pointed staffs that are a thinly disguised
substitute for the spear of warrior days, and still can and do kill, if
used in anger. One has glittering expanding watchstraps all up his
slim black arms; another wears dangling earrings. All wear golfer's
sleeveless cardigans with the air of starting a fashion. One has a
flowered tablecloth knotted nonchalantly round the wrist of the
hand he gestures with, and when the sun goes down he flounces the

cloth loose and it becomes a cloak arranged to fall in Grecian folds from his shoulders. It's taken his fancy to carry a child's plastic handbag. No matter. What is tribal dress? Something in a constant state of change since Africans began to wear anything. A plastic handbag is no more inauthentic than a turban introduced by Arab slavers. You just have to know how to make it your style.

These young men have the Vogue model's saunter. But names of mines they have worked in come quickly to their tongues: Stilfontein, Grootfontein, Durban Deep. On their mountain-top *piazza* it is difficult to imagine, crouched under a weeping rock-face, enclosed in dank dark with several kilometres of earth above them, their steel-helmeted heads.

The centres from which life is ordered for the people living in the round huts that seem to have come spinning to rest, like counters in a game, everywhere round the mountains, are not made out at first sight. But each airy community has its chief's Great Place. The weekly court is in session in one. Horses are tied in the traditional clearing under trees which was the original form of an African court where chief and tribal elders deliberated; there is a little schoolhouse-type building, broken panes patched with cardboard, an assembly squeezed close on benches and the floor, the well of the court demarcated by a barrier and witness stands of imposing carved wooden solidity certainly representing the justice of the early British magistracy.

The prosecutor is the only fat man I encounter in the Transkei, a black Orson Welles, skilled in sarcastic showmanship. Before the court are two striped blankets. The case is a charge of adultery, and these the husband's evidence that another man came to sleep with his wife and forgot his blankets when he left. The tribal elders of the jury pass remarks about the cuckold that need no translating. When the next case is called I find that the composed, handsome woman whose Maillol feet beside mine jingle columns of brass anklets, whose profile and long hair braided with clay and beads I have been aware of close to mine, is the plaintiff in a divorce. Her husband up in the dock is much older, with irritable veins raised in sunken temples. The jury take snuff and go in and out as their attention waxes or wanes. The young magistrate in sports jacket and shined shoes – a Tribal Authority appointee – who takes down his own court record in longhand, asks how many children the couple have. The woman says ten. The husband: 'I see eleven.' Her blanket hides that evidence. Now I understand the secret source of her confidence; a woman with a lover. She is unembarrassed and unrepentant. The husband wants her back to take care of the children, anyway. Her brother is there to tell the court that not only will she not return but the husband must pay her family a debt of bride-price still outstanding.

Now a witch doctor takes the stand. Barefoot, a dark raincoat; and all I can detect that is not entirely unremarkable in this face is deviousness. He claims he cured an epileptic child by a herbal inhalation and cuts in the skin, and was not paid the cow that was his fee. He has a shrewd, loyal, consciously modest wife who knows how to please the court but then contradicts a vital piece of evidence and loses her husband's case for him.

Lawyers are not allowed to plead in a chief's court and criminal cases are heard in the common law courts in trading towns. In this Great Place a one-eyed headman prods witnesses to attention with either malice or humour – he has a different expression on each side of his face, and it depends from which side I see him. The reason why the prosecutor is so well fed may be because people holding this position, I am told, can 'arrange' a verdict at a price. Yet for me something of the intangible truth about our lies has been arrived at in his cross-examination . . .

The sea into which the Xhosa's ancestral dead promised whites and their world would be swept is the southern boundary of Transkei. A long coastline has at every river-mouth a small resort created by the patronage of ordinary middle-class white South Africans who enjoy the luxury of nature not yet polluted by themselves.

The bungalow hotel at Umgazi River Mouth has been taken over by the Transkei Development Corporation, but it employs a white manager, and for the time being the habitué bird-watchers and fishermen still come. The dining-room walls are collages of glued paper fish recording catches. Oysters are 60c a dozen. You sleep in a thatched hut and don't need to lock the door for fear of any intruder, yet you have a private bathroom. The rush hour heard in the night is the splendid traffic of the Indian Ocean tide coming in. The pure, single sound at the bottom of the well of sleep at dawn is the ferryman's oarlocks as he rows to work from across the wide Umgazi; he will take hotel guests back and forth to the beach at their pleasure throughout the day. Like him, all the people who work as hotel servants come from the village on the hills on the other bank of the river. White resort and black village face each other. Sitting on the hotel terrace under coral-branch flowers of great erythrina trees people drink beer and follow without moving, like an idle tune they don't know their fingers are drumming, the rhythm of other lives, over there; the procession of bowed oxen under the whip of the boy taking the three-cornered sled to gather fuel from the beaches' sculpture galleries of driftwood; the women setting out and trailing back with on their heads the sacks of mussels, black as their wet legs, that change their gait. At night, dart games and after-dinner liqueurs in the bar; crowns of fire are suspended in the thick darkness – over there, the people are burning their steep pasture.

I went across with the hotel's night-watchman going home in the early morning. Kingfishers squabbled a cockfight in mid-air and the tide was so far out the huge Indian Ocean rollers were the sea's horizon, smoking like a waterfall. It was a long walk to his house in the village; over riverain fields, then through a forest of yellow-wood and milk-wood trees laced by butterflies, up a path it would have been easier to swing through, from branch to branch. Mussel shells littered the way like peanut husks cast by people nibbling while they walk. Friends of the watchman caught up with us; I was reminded that all my life, in Africa, has been lived among people who apologise when you trip and stumble.

The watchman's family was not put out by the early intrusion of a stranger. Always the same question: from *Egoli?* – 'place of gold', Johannesburg's African name, but to Transkeians it means the gold mines, anywhere over the border. The hut door is open before the black pigs belching by, the tattered dogs still stiff from the night's cold; it breathes quiet smoke. Inside, two women, both young and beautiful, are suckling babies – his wives. His mother, another one of those spare, authoritative old women who never give up the femininity of some adornment, sups tea from a saucer and the young mothers sip theirs slowly above the babies' heads. There is no food set out. No furniture in the hut except an iron bedstead and a small kitchen dresser, made of boxwood in crude imitation of one someone has seen in a white man's house. The wood fire that never quite dies in the shallow hearth round which everyone centres, smells sweet. A day has begun in poverty, without the alarm clock, radio, coffee and eggs, commuter's train that doesn't wait. It won't do to romanticise, but there is something here I have to formulate for myself: respect and wholeness. The watchman takes out a very small mandarin (he must have filched it from the hotel garden) and presents it to his elder child. The tiny fruit is brilliant and luxurious, in this house.

About 27,000 new jobs a year have to be found for Transkeians. Agriculturally, there are two irrigation schemes under way which could help to feed the people a little better, but there will be no surplus for export. Unless traces of nickel, copper and platinum, of which geologists so far have no great hopes, turn out to be extensive deposits, the region has none of the primary products the world needs. Coffee, tea, pyrethrum, nuts – beginning to be grown and processed under state schemes – and forestry with its corollary development of sawmills and furniture factories, provide an opening into modern productive activity that has some relation to what the country has and the people know. Most of the new factories in Butterworth, the nineteenth-century town designated the most important 'growth point' for the establishment of industry, have no relation at all. Factories owned by South African industrialists manufacture products such as those derived from coal, rubber and plastics imported duty free from South Africa under conditions of a new domestic colonialism. These plants have their cut-rate workers living literally outside their gates; row upon interchangeable row of identical brick cabins in barrack formation without any architectural reference points to community – add or subtract a row here or there, nothing would be noticed. I recognise the model at once: Soweto, the dreary paradigm of black segregated townships in South Africa. With all the world's experience of humanising low-cost housing at their planners' disposal, Transkeians are passing from their round thatched huts to this.

In the end, you have to look for people in their times of release – festivity or sorrow – in order to approach their identity with yourself. It comes while you stand back from the mystery of exotic mores: rooted, like your own, in myths without which the inevitable progression from birth to death would be a chain gang of mortality.

The people of the Transkei do not debar an outsider from places where their ceremonial rites still heavily underscore adaptation to those of church, court and industrialisation. In the dimness of huts, I had made out the Cross painted or the miner's badge nailed on the wall; but there were also circumcision retreats all over the countryside if one knew how to recognise the sign, a ragged yellow flag on a stick. I was allowed to enter one in Bomvanaland, although only mature men and pre-pubertal girls may visit the initiates who, for three months after being ritually circumcised, are isolated there; as a white woman whose sexuality is not codified under the same sanctions as blacks, I was to all intents unsexed, I suppose.

Two men rolled in blankets smoking at the roadside were doing their shift of the twenty-four-hour vigil kept over the retreat. The hills they led the way into on foot showed no human being or house; then there, in a groin of forest where I guessed there would be a hidden stream, there was also hidden a large, blind, woven grass hemisphere at the bottom of a clearing ringed by stakes fluttering scraps of coloured rag and plastic. There was something quietening about crossing that symbolic boundary. But from the lair of contorted trees their movements over months had hollowed out, three or four young men burst, sociably painting their faces with the gestures of women and actors. The cosmetic was *ngceke*, ground from a chalky white stone and mixed with water from the stream in the little gourd each wore dangling braceleted from his wrist. Each clutched a drab blanket around himself against the wind. There is nothing much to do all day for three months except keep repairing this make-up of white that covers the whole body from head to toe, as well as the face. The feminine gestures and the rough fooling-around and showing-off of any group of young males were confusing — an atmosphere of a harem and army camp, combined and yet out of place in this context for which I had no precedent or name.

Inside the grass shelter (not a hut or house; its feeling was unlike that of any habitation I have known) the frivolous mood fell away with the blankets discarded. These beings were naked except for the paint and a little sheath over the tip of the penis from which a long straw tassel hung stroking thighs as they moved. White lips made for oracles and the liquid dark of eyes, eyes so movingly, over-whelmingly alive in ghostliness and gloom suddenly asserted the yearning faculties of communication and comprehension — spirit and mind glowing against the presence dominated by bodies. If I was not a woman, among them, we were so fully human, there together.

Four of the eight young men had already been to the mines. They lay on the primitive shelf of branches that had been their communal bed for many weeks; there was a log to which they bent to light cigarettes; the fighting-sticks that recall old conflicts and the cursed-at dogs who have been companions through them all. No other possessions. Nothing in this straw cave but the shadows, in these beings' minds, of the world outside they will emerge into when their time is up and they wash off the white paint and burn, with the straw, the era before they were qualified to enter into the fullness of life, as men.

What is that going to mean, what will be open to them in the third avatar of Nongqause's vision?

1978

Relevance and Commitment

There is a question that bursts with the tenacity of a mole from below the surface of our assumptions: Do men and can men make a common culture if their material interests conflict?

Don't let us ignore the mole; though blind it knows instinctively where the daylight is.

The nature of art in South Africa today is primarily determined by the conflict of material interests in South African society. A philosophy of spiritual liberation requires, among other fundamentals, frank appraisal of the institutions and policies of the white communities that affect the arts in South Africa. We are all paradox. We have all the questions and few answers. Yet there is left to us no less embattled ledge from which to speak honestly and meaningfully about the arts. We must face the fact that the Appollonian brotherhood is no safer from fratricide than any other, where divided loyalties are demanded by immediate survival. We have to challenge ourselves, without cant.

For I take it we acknowledge that as racial problems, both material and spiritual, can hope to be solved only in circumstances of economic equality, so the creative potential of our country cannot be discussed without realisation and full acceptance that fulfilment of that potential can be aimed for only on the premise of the same circumstances.

Equal economic opportunity, along with civil and parliamentary rights for all 26 million[1] South Africans, is rightly and inev-

---

1 In 2010, 49,320,500. Unusual increase due not to birth rate but influx of refugees, principally from Zimbabwe.

itably the basis for any consideration of the future of the arts.
Man has no control over the measure in which talent is given
to this one and withheld from that; but man, through the state,
controls the circumstances in which the artist develops. Innate
creativity can be falsified, trivialised, deflected, conditioned,
stifled, deformed and even destroyed by the state, and the state
of society it decrees.

'Courage in his life and talent in his work' is the artist's text,
according to one of the greatest of them, Albert Camus. Every
artist, in any society, has to struggle through what the poet Pablo
Neruda calls the 'labyrinths' of his chosen medium of expression;
that is a condition of his being. As to his place in the outer world,
I doubt if any artist ever finds himself in the ideal condition of
Hegel's 'individual consciousness in wholly harmonious relationship to the external power of society'. But there can have been few
if any examples in human history of the degree, variety and intensity of conflicts that exist between the South African artist and
the external power of society. That external power is at its most
obvious in the censorship laws, running amok through literature
and lunging out at the other arts. But it is at the widest level of the
formation of our society itself, and not at any specific professional
level, that the external power of society enters the breast and brain
of the artist and determines the nature and state of art. It is from
the daily life of South Africa that there have come the conditions
of profound alienation which prevail among South African artists.
The sum of various states of alienation *is* the nature of art in South
Africa at present.

I am not invoking the concept of alienation in the Marxist sense,
as the consequence of man's relation to the means of production,
although that undoubtedly has its appositeness in the industrialisation of blacks under apartheid and therefore our society as a
whole. There are many ways in which man becomes divided from
others and distanced from himself. Alienation as such is a condition of rejecting and/or being rejected. The black artist lives in
a society that rejected his culture for hundreds of years. He has
turned his alienation in the face of those who rejected him and

made of his false consciousness the inevitable point of departure towards his true selfhood. The white artist belongs to the white culture that rejected black culture, and is now itself rejected by black culture. *He* is the non-European whose society nevertheless refused to acknowledge and take root with an indigenous culture. He is the non-black whom blacks see as set apart from indigenous culture. He does not know as yet whether this is a dead end or can be made a new beginning.

Any homogeneity in the nature of the work produced by these artists is brought about by what shackles them together rather than what they share. South African artists belong to the Dionysiac 'disintegrated consciousness' that Hegel defines by its antagonism to the external power of society – if by nothing else, they are united in the wish to be free of imposed social circumstances, although they would define these in accordance with a widely differing experience of circumstantial reality. From a disintegrated consciousness, all seek wholeness in themselves and a reconnection with the voltage of social dynamism. Opposition to an existing society implies a hunger to create and identify with another and better one. The abjuration of a set of values implies an intention to create and relate to another set. For the artist, these implications become part of the transformations of reality which are his work.

'Relevance' and 'commitment' are conceptualisations of this movement. They become the text claimed by artists who, individually, understand different things by them; they also become the demands made upon the artist by his people. Relevance and commitment pulse back and forth between the artist and society. In a time and place like this one, they have become, in the words of Lionel Trilling, 'the criteria of art and the qualities of personal life of men that may be enhanced or diminished by art'.

How close are these terms that question the existence of the painter, sculptor, writer, composer, photographer, architect, in South Africa today? In fact, they are juxtaposed as much as cognate. And in this, again, they are a signification of the tension between the artist and his society in which his creativity is generated. For relevance has to do with outside events; and commitment comes from within.

For the black artist at this stage in his development relevance is the supreme criterion. It is that by which his work will be judged *by his own people*, and *they* are the supreme authority since it is only through them that he can break his alienation. The Black Consciousness thinker, Bennie Khoapa, states that the black artist's only option is personal transformation; he must be ready to phase himself out of the role of being carrier to what the poet, Mafika Pascal Gwala, calls white official 'swimming pool and caravan culture'. The external reality to which relevance paces out the measure of his work is not a step away from him: another writer, Njabulo Ndebele, says 'blacks are operating' from within 'a crushing intellectual and educational environment'. Sartre's philosophical dictum sums up: 'The exploited experience exploitation *as their reality*' – the artist has only to do what every artist must in order to become one: face his own reality, and he will have interiorised the standard of relevance set up outside. Then, theoretically, he has solved the aesthetic and social problem, put himself in meaningful relationship to his society.

But relevance, in the context of the absolutes placed upon the black artist by the new society to which he is dedicated, has another demand. Struggle is the state of the black collective consciousness and art is its weapon. He accepts this as the imperative of his time. Weapons are inevitably expected to be used within an orthodoxy prescribed for the handling of such things. There is a kit of reliable emotive phrases for writers, a ready-made aesthetic for painters and sculptors, an unwritten index of subjects for playwrights and list of approved images for photographers. Agitprop binds the artist with the means by which it aims to free the minds of the people. It licenses a phony sub-art. Yet the black artist is aware that he is committed, not only as a voluntary act, but in the survival of his own being and personality, to black liberation. It is at this point that, as an artist, commitment takes over, from within, from relevance, and the black artist has to assert the right to search out his own demotic artistic vocabulary with which to breathe new life and courage into his people. His commitment is the point at which inner and outer worlds fuse; his purpose to master his art and his purpose to change the nature of art, create new norms and forms out of and for a people recreating themselves, become one aim.

For the black artist, the tendentiousness of the nature of art goes without question. He cannot choose the terms of his relevance or his commitment because in no other community but the predicated one which blacks have set up inside themselves are his values the norm. Anywhere else he is not in possession of selfhood. The white artist is not quite in the reverse position; that would be too neat for the complexity of the state of art, here. He can, if he wishes, find his work's referent in an aesthetic or ontological movement within the value-system traditional to whites. White South African culture will not repudiate him if he does. Even if he were to decide to be relevant to and find commitment only to himself, he could still find some kind of artistic validity so long as he were to be content to stay within the kind of freedom offered by that closed value-system. Yet the generally tendentious nature of art, overwhelmingly so in writing, if less consciously so in painting and the plastic arts, in South Africa, shows that few white artists take up these options. One could reverse the proposition and say they don't 'opt out' — if it were not for the fact that the rejection of whites-only values by no means implies a concomitant opting in: to black culture. The white artist, who sees or feels instinctively that exclusively white-based values are in an unrecognised state of alienation, knows that he will not be accepted, cannot be accepted by black culture seeking to define itself without the reference to those values that his very presence among blacks represents. Yet for a long time — a generation at least — the white artist has not seen his referent as confined within white values. For a long time he assumed the objective reality by which his relevance was to be measured was somewhere out there between and encompassing black and white. Now he finds that no such relevance exists; the black has withdrawn from a position where art, as he saw it, assumed the liberal role Nosipho Majeke defined as conciliator between oppressor and oppressed.

If the white artist is to break out of his double alienation, he too has to recognise a false consciousness within himself, he too has to discard a white-based value-system which it is fashionable to say 'no longer' corresponds to the real entities of South African life but which in fact never did. But unlike the black, he does not have a direct, natural, congenital attachment to these entities. We are not speaking of artistic modes and forms, here, but of the substance of living from which the artist draws his vision. Exploitation, which the blacks *experience as their reality*, is something the white artist repudiates, refuses to be the agent of. It is outside himself; he experiences it through a moral attitude or a rational empathy. The black creation of new selfhood is based on a reality he, as a white, cannot claim and that could not serve him if he did since it is not his order of experience. If he is to find his true consciousness, express in his work the realities of his place and time, if he is to reach the stage where commitment rises within him to a new set of values based on those realities, he has to admit openly the order of his experience as a white as differing completely from the order of black experience. He has to see the concomitant necessity to find a different way, from that open to the black artist, to reconnect his art through his life to the total reality of the disintegrating present, and to attempt, by rethinking his own attitudes and conceptions, the same position the black artist aims for: to be seen as relevant by and become committed to commonly understood, commonly created cultural entities corresponding to a common reality – an indigenous culture.

I suppose I shall be accused of using the schema of a Black Consciousness philosophy. It is an indication of the rethinking, remaking needed in South African cultural contexts that for years no one, not even blacks, ever questioned the exclusive use of white cultural analyses. In my view, this conference should not be afraid of having kick-me political labels pinned on its back; it should assert the urgent need and right to use whatever ideas, from

whatever source, that may reflect the facts of life here and penetrate the cataract of preconceptions grown over our vision. This is
consistent with an abandonment of the old positions of white and
black in culture and the scrapping of the assumption that white-
based culture is the mean, for white as well as black.

What I have outlined so far is a brief analysis of the imperatives laid upon South African artists by their society. Of course
it is all not so clear-cut as that. When we turn to the nature of
the work the artist produces, we become aware of the terrible
problems in which the artist is enmeshed while following those
imperatives, even if, as in the case of black artists, he feels sure
he knows his way. The nature of contemporary art here, in the
aspect of subject matter, is didactic, apocalyptic, self-pitying,
self-accusatory as much as indicting. Apartheid in all its manifestations, the petty jigger that niggles under the skin, the bullet
that reaches the heart, informs the ethos of what is produced even
by a non-objective painter or an architect seeking an aesthetic
for cheap housing to replace a demolished crossroads. As Pieyre
de Mandiargues says in one of his novels, 'When you have been
given a disaster which seems to exceed all measure, must it not
be recited, spoken?'

But when we posit a post-apartheid art – and we must, right *now*,
out of the necessity implied by the facts examined so far, and forth-
rightly expressed in the white artist Andrew Verster's question:
'Is there a South African art or is it still to happen?' – we switch
off the awful dynamism of disintegration and disaster. The black
artist is aware of a great force ready to charge *him*, the Yeatsian
drive to 'express a life that has never found expression', his part in
the recreation of his people in their own image. For him, the new
orientation may be already psychologically established; but it is by
no means fully formulated. The important cultural debate that was
taking place, in the early and mid-seventies in publications like the
yearly *Black Review* and the publications of the Black Community
Programmes, has been cut off by the banning of organisations and
individuals concerned. Black art has not really visualised itself
beyond protest. It has not even dealt with aspects of present-day

art that do a disservice to the very purpose relevance imposes upon them – for example, the commodity-maker of 'black image' sculpture and painting, the production of artefacts of protest that the white man hangs on his wall as he keeps a carved walking stick in his hall. These aspects may have grave effects on the future of art, carry over a distortion of the moment of identification between the artist and his subject that Proust defines as style. In the dragon's breath heat of the present, this neglect is more than understandable. But understanding does not shift aside problems that will confront the new black culture. Black thinkers are aware of them. Ezekiel Mphahlele and Lewis Nkosi began an inquiry twenty years ago, and their essays were banned. In this decade, it is a continuingly shameful and criminally stupid action on the part of the South African government to have reduced the black cultural debate to a clandestine affair showing itself here and there in white and/or literary journals.

Black artists are primarily concerned with a resuscitation of the pre-colonial culture as a basis, concreted over by the interruption of a purely white-based culture, for an indigenous modern African culture. They break through the concrete with the drums and folk epics that celebrate the past and effectively place the heroes of the present liberation struggle – Mandela, Sobukwe, Biko, Hector Petersen – in a parthenon of inspirational culture-heroes along with Plaatje and Mofolo, but to embody the objective reality of modern blacks they must synthesise with all this the aspirations of people who still want TV and jeans – what George Steiner calls 'the dream-life and vulgate' of contemporary, individual lives. It is comparatively easy to create a people's art – that is to say an aesthetic expression of fundamentally shared experience, during a period when the central experience of all, intellectuals, workers and peasants alike, is oppression: the pass laws are a grim cultural unifier. It is quite another matter when the impact of experience breaks up into differing categories of class-experience. The avowed black aim is a culture springing from and belonging to the people, not an elite. This new orientation involves turning away from Europe but at the same time setting up an essential relationship

between the past and the technological present recognised as
something distinct from the inherent threat of all-white culture,
something that cannot be denied and is with blacks in Africa for
ever. Post-apartheid, beyond liberation in the political sense, and
moving on within the total context of liberation in which black
culture sees its future – unless black artists can achieve a strong,
organic synthesis on these lines their art will be nostalgic, there will
be a hiatus between modern life and art, for them. They will be in
danger of passing into a new phase of alienation. The questions of
relevance and commitment will come up again. This may not seem
much of a concern in the fierce urgency of present dangers, but it
is one of the many that make the black artist's struggle towards
true consciousness a continuing one, and the future of art in South
Africa uncertain.

If the white artist is to move on to express a life that has
never found expression, this presupposes, on the one hand, that
white culture will remake itself, and on the other that black
culture will accept him as one who has struck down into liens
with an indigenous culture. That remaking could inform his
vision, it could replace the daemonic forces of disintegration
which both drove him into alienation and were his subject. But
unless this happens he will know less and less and see less and
less, with the deep comprehension and the inner eye necessary
to creation, of the objective realities he came to recognise when
he rejected the false consciousness constituted in traditional
white-based culture. In the post-apartheid era, the white's position will depend much more on external forces than will that of
the black artist. Having changed his life, the white artist may
perhaps stake his place in a real indigenous culture of the future
by claiming that place in the implicit nature of the artist as an
agent of change, always moving towards truth, true consciousness, because art itself is fixed on the attainment of that essence
of things. It is *in his nature* to want to transform the world, as
it is a *political decision* for those who are not artists to want to
transform the world. The revolutionary sense, in artistic terms,
is the sense of totality, the conception of a 'whole' world, where

theory and action meet in the imagination. Whether this 'whole' world is the place where black and white culture might become something other, wanted by both black and white, is a question we cannot answer; only pursue.

Although I am white and fully aware that my consciousness inevitably has the same tint as my face, when I have spoken of white attitudes and opinions I have not taken it upon myself to speak for whites, but have quoted attitudes and opinions expressed by whites themselves, or manifest (in my opinion) in their work. When I have spoken of black attitudes and opinions, I have not taken it upon myself to speak for blacks, but have quoted attitudes and opinions expressed by blacks themselves or (in my opinion) manifest in their work. It's difficult to end on the customary high note; the state of culture in South Africa does not encourage it. Yet when I go so far as to use 'we' to speak for our culture, the pronoun in itself expresses some kind of obstinate collective intention to assume that there is at least the possibility of a single, common, indigenous nature for art in South Africa. Any optimism is realistic only if we, black and white, can justify our presence by regarding ourselves as what Octavio Mannoni, in his study of the effects of colonialism, terms 'apprentices of freedom'. Only in that capacity may we perhaps look out for, coming over the Hex River Mountains or the Drakensberg, that 'guest from the future' that Nadezhda Mandelstam calls upon, the artist as prophet of the resolution of divided cultures.

1979

Pula!

Botswana

*P*ula. In the middle of southern Africa there is a country whose coat of arms bears, instead of some Latin tag boasting power and glory, the single word: *rain*.

On the map Botswana appears as a desert big as France. And sometimes, in Botswana, looking at the figures of men, the bole of thorn tree or palm, a single donkey, breaking the white light, it seems a vast sand-tray in which these are lead toys stuck upright. But they are rooted there. This Kalahari sand nourishes them – grasses, thorn bush, *mopane* forest, birds, beasts and 600,000 people. They live on it, in it and off it. In places it hardens into a crust of salt; it swallows, in the north-west, the waters of a great delta. But even the final desiccation of the south-west provides harsh sustenance for those – beasts and men – who know where to find it, and for those who know how to space their thirst, there is water if you dig for it.

A desert is a place without expectation. In Botswana there is always the possibility of rain. The hope of rain. Rain *is* hope: *pula* means fulfilment as well as rain. As a political catchword, the cry has a less muffled ring than the many variants of the word 'freedom'.

From the days of the late-nineteenth-century conquest of southern Africa by whites until 1966, Botswana was the British Protectorate of Bechuanaland and, except for parties of anthropologists for whom it was a trip back to the Stone Age culture of the Kalahari Bushmen, it meant the 'line of rail' connecting the Republic of South Africa with Rhodesia that ran up inside its border along the strip of fertile farmland settled by whites. The Line of Rail is still there, the two or three frontier towns – one street with hotel verandah and shops facing the railway station – but as a way of life it no longer sums up the country, only the colonial past. Botswana's railway was – and is – owned and operated by a neighbouring country, Rhodesia, and Botswana's capital was until recently a town just outside its borders, in South Africa. The brand new capital, Gaborone, is only just inside; the pull of economic gravity remains unavoidably towards the south, where are based the international mining companies whose discoveries of copper, nickel and diamonds beneath the sand will mean, ten years from now, the doubling of the per capita income, at present on the poverty line. Gaborone is set down on the Line of Rail but not of it, complete and ready-to-use: an Independence Expo in whose pavilions, after the celebrations, people stayed on. Flag-waving consular residences, a national museum, churches with contemporary bell-towers, the hotel/cinema/national-airline/shopping complex which even includes an American Embassy – one-stop urban civilisation. In the piazza of the shopping mall a few thorn trees have been left to assert the empty savannah outside, but the barbers, beggars and vendors of an African town are too overawed to set up business under them. Emancipated black girls drink beer among the men in a hotel bar, now, at midday. Out of the cheerful exchanges in the Tswana language there comes suddenly, in English, the authentic tone of Gaborone: 'I give it three years, and I buzz off.'

More than twenty years ago Seretse Khama, Chief-designate of the Bamangwato and Paramount Chief-designate of all the Botswanaian tribes, married a white girl while studying law in England and was exiled by the British colonial administration from his ancestral home in Serowe. It was one of the biggest political scandals in Africa, with all the private intrigues of an African dynasty, the Khama family, to complicate the issue. Sir Seretse Khama, knighted by the British, elected by democratic vote, is now first President of Botswana; the Bamangwato remain the biggest and most distinguished tribe; Serowe remains the seat of the Khamas as well as the capital of the wealthiest province and probably the last nineteenth-century African – as opposed to colonial – town south of the Equator.

In their Great Place where the Khamas lie when they die, they are not so much buried as set on final watch over the Bamangwato.

You reach the Great Place by a steep walk up behind the swept, stockaded *kgotla*, the open-air tribal court and meeting place beneath a big tree, and the silos where communal water or grain are stored. On a hill that gives out upon the whole town and beyond is a pink stone terrace of graves – the Grecian urns, marble scrolls and infant angels of 'funerary art'. The real monument is the one the earth has spouted and tumbled in an outcrop to one side, Thataganyana Rock. Little humpy *dassies* dart fussily in and out its petrified burst-bubble holes.

Thataganyana is a superb vantage place for the living as well as the dead; we leaned upon the warm wall of the terrace and looked down over the entire life of this town like no other town, a town ordered garland by garland, not in streets or blocks, loop after loop of green rubber plant hedging circular houses grouped round cattle stockades made of stony grey tree trunks. Far away, the square of a sports field marked in the same green, and then the fuzzy plain overlaid, by the eye, with thickness upon thickness of blond grass and grey bush until it laps a few hills, one flat-topped, that are exactly the single woolly hills drawn on ancient maps of Africa. A God's-eye view; you can also see into everyone's clay-walled, decorated back yard. A woman whirrs at her sewing machine. Gossiping men lean against walls. A baby staggers about in a G-string; an old man in a parson's black suit, with hat and stick, pays a visit. You can hear everyone's life as well: it is Saturday afternoon and those people who have decided to kill a goat, brew some maize beer and throw a party – a popular way of making money, since an entrance fee is charged – amplify African jazz above the hollow knock of wood being hewn. We stayed on while the moon came up and only the little bronze buck, symbol of the Bamangwato on top of the grave of Khama III, stood out clear. Just before the light went, a tiny girl ran from the houses and squatted to relieve herself in the security of the Great Place's shadow.

Down in Serowe in a gaunt cool house with the drinks and the guns ready on the verandah lives Sekgoma Khama, graduate of Dublin

University and cousin of the President. He is a princely young man, almond-eyed and handsome, with a strangely fateful laugh – when a gun went off among us while we were jolting in a truck over the veld after eland, the bullet searing the ear of his close friend, he broke the shock with that laugh, not in callous amusement but as a kind of baring-of-teeth at the hazards of life. The hunt itself was in the nature of a quest: as Tribal Authority (the democratic title for Chief; he is acting in that capacity in place of an elder brother studying the problems of developing countries, abroad) he has the right to bag himself a single head of the rare species a season. He set off early with us among a house-party of friends – a Jamaican, an African geologist (rarer even than the eland), a pretty Swedish girl who was helping to found a cottage textile industry in the town, and a whole entourage of gun-bearers. Half an hour out of Serowe the red hartebeest with their tarnished copper coats stood, not recognising death when one among them fell, but a small herd of eland were as elusive as any unicorn. Their broad light flanks always seeming to be presenting themselves one-dimensionally, just the way they look in ancient bushman paintings; they led us a dance from the grassland into the scrub forest, where they threaded away between screens of trees while even Sekgoma's crack shots fell short.

When his brother returns, Sekgoma Khama will take up again his full-time occupation of managing the Khama family's lands and cattle, and serving on the Land Boards that, as much as the switch to a money economy, will change the structure of Botswana society. He sees change not as abandonment but transposition of traditional institutions: cattle as wealth not capital – which was the basis of the economy – becomes 'a ranching operation'; the tribal monopoly of land loosens as allocation becomes a matter of applying to a government board instead of the local chiefs. He felt at home in Joyce's Dublin; lucky man, it has not made him feel any the less at home when he sits under the tree at the *kgotla*, settling some dispute among the 36,000 people of Serowe. He shows disquiet over only one thing: 'The mineral discoveries so far are all in our Central Province . . . it could be a delicate situation, politically . . .'

The Bamangwato, it seems, cannot escape being a favoured people; for them, the cry *Pula* does not go unanswered.

Like the ownership of cattle, hunting has always been the way of life of the people here, whereas in other parts of Africa in colonial times it quickly became only the privilege of whites. In a country without billboards (or even road signs) a pair of horns on a tree marks a turn-off or the way to a cattle post, and in every place of habitation bones and the skins of game pegged out to dry are homely as a front garden in the context of other lives.

In spite of this, Botswana is one of the few countries in Africa that still has great herds of game left, not only in reserves but living alongside men. The Kalahari, hostile to agriculture, is what has saved the animals, and they have learned to subsist sleek-coated through the dry months upon the heavy desert dew condensed on tough vegetation. There is conflict now between, on the one hand, the Government's reflection of the Western world's concern to preserve wild life in the Third World and, on the other, the curious unconscious alliance of interest between the Africans who've always shot for the pot and whites who have shot for trophies and fur coats. The fashionable vocabulary of environmental studies is invoked these days by people in the skin-and-bone trade. In Francistown on the Line of Rail, while walking through a 'game industry' past mounds of lopped-off elephant feet and vats of impala and zebra skins soaking, we were given an erudite lecture on the ecological viability of the whole highly profiable business – indigenous people continuing to live off indigenous animals, rather than the development of agricultural and industrial employment for the people and protection for the animals. The very balance of nature was being preserved, our cultured white informant said, by buying from Africans the skins of only plentiful species, and utilising every scrap of the product – and by this time we had left the sickish smell of the curing sheds and were in a workshop where beautiful and noble creatures like those we had pursued on the plain outside Serowe were emerging finally: as elephant-foot umbrella stands, ostrich-foot lamps and zebra-skin bar stools. In the taxidermy

department, some white safari hunter's lion was being tailored into
his skin, with little strips of cosmetic tape to hold it in place over
the stuffing. A ghastly ecological situation given dubious scientific
licence to continue colonial hubris in the beauty of wild animals
owned as kitsch.

There is only one road to the west and it leads three hundred miles
from Francistown to Maung, the last place on the map that signifies more than a store, a well and a mud village. Early on the way
the earth gives out, the Kalahari begins, then the road skirts the
rime of the Makgadikgadi salt pans and the heads of ilala palm
stand up like broken windmills. As if all their sundered parts
had flown together again, we encountered along the road impala,
gemsbok crowned with antennae-straight horns, kudu bulls with
elaborately turned ones, ostriches with legs like male performers in
ballet drag.

Maung reached has the unreality of any oasis; no relation
between the deep blue and green of the Thamalakane River
shining between towering wild fig trees and the monotonous
village of grey huts on endless grey sand not a hundred yards away.
Riley's Hotel (the old London Missionary Society mission station
converted by an Irish pioneer adventurer, now dead and legendary)
and Riley's Garage are the fount: the big pub behind mosquito
screening where white-collar Africans have taken up darts among
hefty white habitués, the grease pits where trucks and Land-Rovers
are relieved of the sand that clogs their innards. Lumbering four-
wheel-drive vehicles are to Maung what ships are to a port – their
image of power and freedom not only demarcates road from sand
by the impress of their tracks, it also dominates the imagination of
the black children: their toys are model trucks home-made of bent
wire on condensed milk-tin wheels.

Walking through the village we read a 'Wanted Man' notice
of a new kind. Reward was offered for Diphetho Monokrwa, 'last
seen following a herd of buffalo'. We came upon, at nine in the
morning, a party of women in Victorian dress embellished with
jewellery and eastern turbans, sitting like telephone-cover dolls in

the sand, making a leisurely meal of tea and porridge. Before the 1914–18 war Herero people fled from German genocide in South West Africa (Namibia); here they live still, their extraordinary women peacocking it among the Tswana hens. These are the women who played the Lysistrata act without ever having heard of her – they refused to bear children while the men submitted to German oppression. Only that sort of female spirit could sustain a vanity colossal as this, trailing wide skirts through the sand, boned up to the throat in the heat, ironing flounces with a flat-iron filled with burning coals, creating in poverty a splendour constantly remade out of bits of what has worn out. After the meal they passed round a cup of salt and a pocket mirror; each cleaned her teeth with a beringed finger, and took a critical look at today's face.

Maung is the last place you can buy a loaf of bread for many hundreds of miles. It is also the plenitude of the Okavango delta and you can skip the desolation and fly there in a few hours to canoe and fish and bird- and game-watch. The Okavango, misnamed a swamp, is really a vast system of clear bayous created by the Okavango River and seasonal flood-waters that come down from the highlands of Angola each May. At least one of the safari camps that are setting up business has its own airstrip. Just outside the Moremi Game Reserve, in a self-styled 'game kraal' built of reed and thatch to house a wealthy species of tourist, each suite has its pastel-coloured portable thunder-box and each guest his personal servant. For the hard-living Francis Macombers are being replaced by wildlife worshippers, and the white hunters, pushed as far south as Botswana, have gone about as far as they can go, and many are themselves turning for survival to leading photographic safaris and mugging up ornithology to please bird-watching clients. Derek 'Kudu' Kelsey is one of the adaptable ones, as ready now to aim the amateur photographer's camera so that he may bring back the trophy picture as once the white hunter was to put his client into the position where his gun couldn't miss. But while Mr Kelsey is a perfectionist, filing the wicked cat's-nail thorn off every knob of the magnificent *mukoba* trees of his 'kraal' lest a guest might suffer so much as a scratch at Africa's hands, he retains a dash of endearingly uncalculated zaniness from wilder, colonial times. In the morning he took us by canoe expertly along the water-paths made by hippos through papyrus that lead on for many days' journey up the Okavango; in the evening he appeared in dinner jacket and trousers worn above bare ankles and *veldskoen* shoes, and had arranged for 'dinner music' to be provided by the grandfathers, wives and babies of a nearby village, who sat round the fire clapping and singing their narrative chants. Later, there were dancing girls, in the form of the six- or seven-year-old daughters of the waiters, abandoning a sweet bashfulness to shake their little bodies frenziedly in grass skirts.

We bought that last bread in Maung.

Carrying our water and petrol as well as food we struck out west again, into the Kalahari. There are roads marked on the map, but a loose hank of tracks ravels the sand out of Maung and it doesn't much matter which spoor you choose, provided it fits the wheel-gauge of your vehicle, and you stick to it.

We arrived at Lake Ngami at night, put down sleeping bags on anonymous sand in an anonymous dark. Our headlights showed weirdly that the cabs of trucks had worn topiary tunnels in thick thorn trees. We didn't know which side the lake was, only that the few lights in the bush were the village of Sehithwa. One cannot always be sure if the lake will be there at all: when Livingstone saw it in 1849 it was seventy miles long, but there are years when it disappears altogether; it is one of the farthest points where the delta is quaffed by the desert.

This year it is there, about eight miles of it, in the morning. Like a long gleam seen between the slit of eyelids, at first. No trees on the banks; there are no banks. Sometimes for minutes, when nothing is flying, it looks empty of life. But again, from a certain angle, the skimming birds and the crenellations of the water are the same, so that the whole surface is made of grey wings. What appear to be verges of water and ooze are thousands of gliding duck, quiet and close; a white sandbank in the distance is really solid flamingo. The bush stands withdrawn, half a mile from the water.

Suddenly I see silent explosions of dust puff from it, and as I watch, herd after herd of cattle, black, russet, white and dappled, stippled and shaded variations of these colours, burst out of the bush and advance in slow motion, because of the heavy wet sucking at their hooves; across horizontals of grass, sky and water. Herdsmen on horseback with skinny dogs pushing rodent noses into every scent ride by now and then; among all these cattle, one of the men comes up and asks me for milk. Horses, knee-deep, shake their manes like vain girls bathing. Pelicans on the water turn the lake into a child's bathtub filled with plastic toys. The flamingoes will not stir until late afternoon, when the colour under their wings as they rise seems to leak into the water like blood from a cut finger. As the day moves on heat hazes interpose – between land and water, between one layer of birds or beasts and another – new glassy surfaces of a water that isn't really there. The peace, born of the passive uncertainties of this beautiful place, one year a lake, another a dried bed of reeds! Over the trembling horizon you can just make out two nubile hills – The Breasts of The Goat. In shallow years, they say, you can drive across through the lake and pass straight between those hills. It is the way to Ghanzi, where the great cattle drives going south pass; and on, deep in the desert, to the non-places where the Bushmen withdraw from the threat of other men.

No one had been able to agree where petrol or potable water would be available on the two hundred miles to the Tsodilo Hills. But then no one had told us, either, of the existence of Marcos's bar, suddenly come upon in the ash-pale desert of Sehithwa village, where we sat disbelievingly drinking iced whisky and arguing over the mathematical problem in a correspondence study course the young village barman was following.

Villages were more austere even than uninhabited stretches, scoured down to shadeless mud houses, a single store, in an emptiness cleared of thorn by the appetites of goats and the need for fuel. Austere but not desolate: the store was always full of people buying scoops of sugar and maize meal before wire-netted shelves offering blood tonics and gilt earrings, and racks where dusty dresses were chained together. There was no green thing to buy; only the chestnut-shiny fruit of the ilala palm, arranged in frugal pyramids on the sand. When I ate an orange from our supplies, I found myself tasting each suck and morsel down to the pith; the bright skin cast away was an extravagance of fragrance and colour.

The road as a total experience filled each mile and hour, whether you were the one swirling the wheel in split-second decisions and slamming to lower and lower gear, or were simply bent on keeping your balance in the passenger seat. In parts the sand was bottom-less, bedrock-less: pits covered with broken thorn and branches looked to be and were traps – the wheels of other vehicles had dug them. The company of the road was that of the marooned: great trucks beached, helpless, their passengers philosophically brewing tea and suckling infants in their shade. The code of the road, quite apart from its condition, made it impossible to say when you could hope to reach where, for you stopped to help, whether with water and cigarettes, or a tow-rope and whatever heaving manpower you could muster. There is a bush panache about the way the Batswana set out over this desert of theirs without a pump or spare wheel, calmly doubling up the human burdens of one truck upon another as they break down.

It becomes true that it is the journey and not the arrival that matters; we forgot we had a destination. Yet at the village of Sepopa we picked up a guide from the headman and were told there were only fifty miles more to go. An unidentified track turned off abruptly left, from nowhere to nowhere. For miles we found ourselves displaced, out of Africa, still lurching over sand, yes, but through a European beechwood, flaming with autumn – we were in a *mopane* forest. Behind it, the first sight of a hazy blue back; and then, as the forest thinned on to a pale plain, a whale-shaped hill came out of the bush, the Male hill of the Tsodilo.

The Tsodilo are called hills but whether a mountain is a moun-tain or a hill a hill is not a matter of height but presence. After hundreds of miles of the horizontals of sand, that mastodon of rock is the presence of a mountain; and the emotion one feels standing in the cold dark shadow it casts across the afternoon is the uneasy one engendered by the primeval authority of a mountain. Behind Male is Female Hill, the sheer and fall of soft chalky colours, stone flanks that are olive, rose, smoke-mauve, and behind her are a series of hidden amphitheatres, bays of heat and quiet. And as you climb in the last real luxury left, a boundless silence, years thick, you come with a strange contraction of perception upon paintings made upon the rock. It is as if, out of that silence, this place speaks. There are rhinoceros, zebra; on an umber battlement – quite clear of surrounding blocks of rock spangled with livid fish-scales of lichen – an eland and giraffe. In a cool cleft we lay on our backs (as the artist must have done, at work) to see a line of dancing men with innocent erect penises that have no erotic significance and persist as a permanent feature of Bushman anatomy, even today. Among the animals, schematic drawings and men, there were terracotta imprints of the hands of the artists, or perhaps of others, less talented, who wanted to assert their presence. They were the size of a child's hand; inevitably, I measured mine against them, clumsily touching across the past. Nobody knows exactly how old these Bushman paintings are, but the Bushmen have wandered this part of Africa for a thousand years and the surviving ones have long lost the art and have not been known to paint within living memory. The paintings were discovered to the world only in the 1950s; new ones are found by anyone who has a few days to spend looking. But very few people have seen even those that are known; by August, we were only the eighth group of travellers to come to Tsodilo that year.

There was a village of twenty-five or thirty people just beyond the reach of the afternoon shadow of the Male hill of Tsodilo. They were a little clan of Mbukushu, the home of whose creation-myth the Tsodilo Hills are. Nyambi (God) let people and animals down to earth from heaven on a rope to the Tsodilo, and so the world began.

We went over to visit with our guide, who had a letter for one of the villagers. Beyond Maung there are no post offices and a letter will be carried by whatever truck happens to be making for a point nearest its destination. No one in the village could read; the old woman for whom the letter was intended handed it back to our guide and settled on her haunches to listen while he read aloud to her. It was from her son, working on a gold mine near Johannesburg, more than a thousand miles away in the Republic of South Africa. Our guide had also, as a young man, been far away to the mines; one of the changes that Sir Seretse Khama's government is most determined on is the end of Botswana's necessity to export her men as contract labour, but the experience of going to the mines is one that has entered profoundly into remote lives and changed for ever ancient patterns of existence – that is the furthest reach, in consequence far beyond its military might, of the White South. The letter from the mines was read through again so that – one could see the vivid concentration of response wincing across the old woman's face – she would remember it precisely as if she could refer to the text.

Meanwhile, the women and children had gathered and I had doled out the remains of a packet of sweets I happened to have. Not enough to go round; but the asceticism bred of a begrudging environment has its own pleasures. These babies who never get sweetmeats exhibited the very opposite of lust for them. One sweet fed four, scrupulously divided from mouth to mouth. The wrapping paper was sucked. Fingers were licked so lingeringly that the pinkish-brown skin came through the dirt. A young Tannekwe Bushman girl and her small brother got their share – a shy yellow pair with oriental eyes and nostrils delicate as shells. They were probably the children of a family enslaved by the Mbukushu.

The black, round, pretty Mbukushu mothers had a queen among them, standing tall and a little apart, with a turned-down amusement on her sardonic mouth. She perversely wore an old striped towel half-concealing her kilt of handmade ostrich shell beads and hide thongs, and her long legs with their calf-bracelets of copper and hide, but her slender, male youth's shoulders and the flat breasts her body seemed almost to disdain, the assertion of her long neck and shaven head, resolved all aesthetic contradictions. The prow of Male hill rose behind her. Sometimes one comes across a creature, human or animal, who expresses that place in which it has its being, and no other. In the Kalahari, she of the Mbukushu was such a one.

When her ancestors migrated from the north in the early nineteenth century they gained among the Tswana tribes the reputation of great rainmakers. They practised human sacrifice to make rain; today rainmaking is being replaced by water conservation schemes, such as the Shashe River one in the south, and plans to water the desert from the Okavango, but the Mbukushu still speak for Botswana when their rainmaker asks of Nyambi, in the old formula: 'Do not make too much lightning; just give us quiet water so that we can have food.'

1979

The 1980s

The Prison-House of Colonialism

Ruth First's and Ann Scott's *Olive Schreiner*

W ho is qualified to write about whom? Subjects very often do not get the biographers their works and lives demand; they are transformed, after death, into what they were not. There must be a lot of fuming, beyond the grave.

Olive Schreiner has been one of the worst-served, from her spouse's version of her life, in accordance with what a husband would have liked his famous writer-wife to be, to the hagiographic selectivity of two or three other biographies which have appeared since her death in 1920. At last, the perfectly qualified candidates have presented themselves: two people who represent a combination of the dominant aspects of Schreiner's character; her feminism and her political sense; and each of whom corrects the preoccupational bias of the other.

Schreiner's feminism followed the tug of colonial ties with a European 'home', it was conceived in relation to the position of women in late nineteenth-century Europe; through her tract, *Woman and Labour*, she is a Founding Mother of women's liberation in Britain, and one of her two new biographers, Ann Scott, is a young English feminist. Schreiner's political awareness was specific, through her understanding of the relation of capitalist imperialism to racialism in South Africa; and Ruth First, her other biographer, is a South African radical activist,[1] thinker and fine writer who went into exile in Britain years ago but is now close to her – and Olive Schreiner's – real home again, teaching at the

---

1 Ruth First was assassinated by the apartheid regime in August 1982. An apparently ordinary parcel sent to her in Mozambique exploded – it contained a bomb – as she opened it, killing her. 2010: she is one of the revered heroes of the South African freedom struggle.

Eduardo Mondlane University in Mozambique.

First and Scott make a superb combination and one is curious about how they overcame the tremendous differences between their two ideological approaches. Take the statement: 'We have tried to create a psychologically believable woman of the late 19th Century largely on the basis of the psychoanalytic language of the 20th.' Was Ruth First able to follow this basic approach because of the new attitude to psychoanalysis that has been penetrating Marxist thinking through the work of Jacques Lacan and others since the failure of the 1968 student uprising in Paris? The book is a model of disinterested collaboration and scholarship, and the reconciliation it achieves between the viewpoints of the authors and their subject brings great rewards for the reader.

This biography establishes a level of inquiry no previous biographer was perhaps in a position to attempt. So far ahead of her own times, Schreiner was obscured in succeeding ones by the kind of critical assessment then prevailing. Now First and Scott can write:

> We see Olive Schreiner's life writing as a product of a specific social history. We are not only looking at what she experiences but at how she, and others, perceived that experience; at the concept with which her contemporaries understood their world, and, again, at the consciousness that was possible for her time – after Darwin, before Freud, and during the period when Marx's *Capital* was written.

Olive Schreiner was born in South Africa of missionary parents, and as a twenty-one-year-old governess in 1886 wrote *The Story of an African Farm*, a novel which brought her immediate world fame that has lasted ever since. In her work and life (she had the missionary sense of their oneness), it becomes clear from this study, she was hampered crucially by the necessity of fighting the ways of thought which imprisoned her and others, equipped only with the modes available within those concepts. Only once did she invent a form to carry her advanced perceptions: a literary one, for *The Story of an African Farm*. Her short novel about the conquest of Rhodesia, *Trooper Peter Halket*, shows as true an interpretation of historical realities, re-read during the week of Zimbabwe's independence celebrations, as Schreiner claimed it did when she wrote it, during Rhodes's conquest of Mashonaland: but it has the preachy, nasal singsong of a sermon. When she wanted to find a way to express her political vision, she took up the form of allegory typical of the hypocritical Victorian high-mindedness she had rejected along with religious beliefs.

About sex, she lied to herself continually – protesting to her men friends that she wanted 'love and friendship without any sex element' in letters whose very syntax paces out yearning sexual desire. She recognised the sexual demands of women in a period when they were trained to believe that their role was merely to 'endure' male sexual demands, but she used Victorian subterfuges (on a par with the 'vapours'), disguised as feminism to hide a sense of shame at the idea of her own sexual appetite. The spectacle of the rebel dashing herself against the cold panes of convention is that of a creature doubly trapped: by a specific social history, and by the consciousness possible to her in her time.

First and Scott suggest further that Schreiner's reputation as an imaginative writer has suffered by the 'persistent view that her social comment is obtrusive and damaging to her work'; the novel – *The Story of an African Farm* – on which that reputation rests has been acclaimed, sometimes by people who would not share even her liberal views, let alone the radical element in them, as having its genius in 'transcending politics', and by extension, Schreiner's political fervour. The present biographers will be interested to know that a reverse trend is now appearing in South African criticism; Schreiner is no longer praised for soaring above politics, but attacked for turning out to be nothing but the broken-winged albatross of white liberal thinking. C. I. Hofmeyer, a young white lecturer at an 'ethnic' university for South African Indians, said at a conference recently:

Although Schreiner was cognisant of the power of the speculator and capitalist to triumph because of their access to power, she none the less continued to harbour a tenuous optimism that justice,

equality and rightness of the liberal democracy would come to
triumph via the operation of the 'enlightened' liberal remnant of
the English community. Of course, it did not, and the bourgeois
democracy that Schreiner had hoped for soon developed into the
repressive colonial state. This development is significant in so far as
it shows the weaknesses in the thinking of Schreiner and her class.

If Schreiner was a 'genius', the lecturer continued, this was 'a critical category that obscures the extent to which she was rooted in
nineteenth-century assumptions'.

Whether or not one can swallow this (old) view of genius as
a class-determined concept rather than an innate, congenital
attribute – and whether Schreiner had it or not – the tension in
her relationship to these nineteenth-century assumptions, so brilliantly conveyed in this book, was the source of her achievements
and her failures.

Olive Schreiner, like other South African writers (William Plomer,
Roy Campbell, Laurens van der Post) up until after the Second
World War, when writers both black and white became political
exiles, looked to Europe and went to Europe. Some went permanently, after the initial success of work born specifically of their
South African consciousness. Some went ostensibly because they
had been reviled for exposing the 'traditional' South African way of
life for what it is (Plomer, *Turbott Wolfe*). But the motive generally
was a deep sense of deprivation, that living in South Africa they
were cut off from the world of ideas; and underlying this incontest-
able fact (particularly for Schreiner, in her time) was another reason
which some had a restless inkling was the *real* source of their alienation, although they could express it only negatively: that the act
of taking the Union Castle mailship to what was the only cultural
'home' they could conceive of, much as they all repudiated jingoism,
was itself part of the philistinism they wanted to put at an ocean's
distance from them. Even Sol Plaatje, one of the first black writers,
had this instinct, since he was using Western modes – journalism,
the diary, the novel – to express black consciousness.

They went because the culture in which their writings could

take root was not being created: a culture whose base would be the indigenous black cultures interpenetrating with imported European cultural forms, of which literature was one; and because the works they had written – or would have found it imperative to attempt, if they were to express the life around them – were solitary contradictions of the way in which that life was being conceptualised, politically, socially and morally.

Olive Schreiner felt stifled (the asthma she suffered from is a perfect metaphor) by the lack of any questioning exchange of ideas in the frontier society in which she lived. I suppose one must allow that she had a right to concern herself with a generic, universal predicament: that of the female sex. During her restless, self-searching years in England and Europe, and her association with Havelock Ellis, Eleanor Marx, Karl Pearson, women's suffrage and English socialism in the 1880s, she studied intensively theories on race and evolution, and participated in progressive political and social movements; but feminism was her strongest motivation. Yet the fact is that in South Africa, now as then, feminism is regarded by people whose thinking on race, class and colour Schreiner anticipated, as a question of no relevance to the actual problem of the country – which is to free the black majority from white minority rule.

Her biographers point out that, once living again in South Africa, she resigned from the Women's Enfranchisement League when its definition of the franchise qualification was changed so as to exclude black women. But in the South African context, where she always felt herself to belong, and to which she always returned, in the end to die there, the women issue withers in comparison with the issue of the voteless, powerless state of South African blacks, irrespective of sex. It was as bizarre then (when a few blacks in the Cape Colony had a heavily qualified vote) as now (when no black in the Republic of South Africa has a vote) to regard a campaign for women's rights – black or white – as relevant to the South African situation. Schreiner seems not to have seen that her wronged sense of self, as a woman, that her liberation, was a secondary matter within her historical situation. Ironically, here at least, she shared the most persistent characteristic of her fellow colonials (discounting the priorities of the real entities around her) while believing she was protesting against racism.

First and Scott give a fascinating account of the neuroticism of this amazing woman, in whose tortured, heightened sense of being all the inherent contradictions of her sex and time existed. One enters into their biography as into a good discussion with people better informed on the subject than oneself.

For myself, I am led to take up the question of Olive Schreiner's achievement exclusively as an imaginative writer, in relation to the conceptual determinants within which she lived, even while warring against them. First and Scott quote the argument – and I think they see her wronged by it – that after *African Farm* her creativity disappeared 'into the sands of liberal pamphleteering'. The observation was originally mine. Their book confirms, for me, that whatever else she may have achieved, Schreiner dissipated her creativity in writing tracts and pamphlets rather than fiction. This is *not* to discount her social and political mission; neither is it to attempt to nail her to the apartheid *Tendenzroman*. It is to assert that, by abandoning the search for a form of fiction adequate to contain the South African experience, after her abortive experiments with a 'distancing' allegory, she was unable in the end to put the best she had – the power of her creative imagination – to the service of her fierce and profound convictions, and her political and human insight. It is true that, as First and Scott claim, 'almost alone she perceived the race conflicts during South Africa's industrial revolution in terms of a worldwide struggle between capital and labour'. But she wrote *about* these insights instead of transforming them through the creation of living characters into an expression of the lives they shaped and distorted. This could have achieved the only real synthesis of life and work, of ideology and praxis, for Olive Schreiner, raising the consciousness of the oppressed from out of the colonial nightmare, and that of the oppressor from out of the colonial dream, and telling the world what she, uniquely, knew about the quality of human life deformed by those experiences.

1980

Letter from the 153rd State

We have to succeed in our bid to establish a non-racial society, in our bid to establish civil liberties . . . Once the reconciliation between the races is complete, once we have the opposing forces in harmony, then whatever the difference in the political sphere we will, at least, have that oneness which upholds a democratic society. I think it will also act as a consolidating factor for Mozambique, Zambia, Botswana, Angola, and even for the former High Commission territories, Lesotho and Swaziland. The progressive forces in South Africa will have a basis on which to demand that transformation take place as quickly as possible in their society.

. . . Let me say that our principles remain . . . as a party we stand by the socialist ideology deriving, to an extent, from Marxism and Leninism. We don't hide that. At the same time we are not governed by those principles alone. We also have our own tradition, and the principles that we have developed here under the influence of Christianity, while we were occupied by the West. In other words, while we adhere to definite socialist principles there is a streak of morality that runs through them, and this morality is a synthesis of our tradition and our Christian practice here . . . We have always lived as a collective society. Land belongs to all. True, each person has his own cattle and goats but there was always a distinction between what was communal and what the individual acquired as his own property. The rivers and the fruit trees have always been common to us all.

Robert Mugabe, Prime Minister, Zimbabwe

Just eighteen weeks after the creation of a new African state that not only its prime minister predicts will have a definitive influence on the future of all southern Africa, I had the chance to visit that state for myself. To go to Zimbabwe (or any other African country no longer ruled by a white minority) as a South African is different from going as a European or American; and to travel as a private person accustomed to observing from the underground point of view of the novelist is different from arriving with the journalist's conscious, skilled determination to find news. I was less informed than a good journalist would be; as someone both African and white, I think I understood what I saw for myself – as distinct from what I might be told or told about – rather more accurately than a visiting European or American could.

And yet it is difficult, in the sniffing-the-air alertness, the awkward solemnity of first setting foot on the tarmac of change, not to read in headline fashion what meets the eye. I always warn myself that there are two places from which I must not generalise any impressions: airports and bars. The white immigration officer at Salisbury airport turned the pages of my passport with a metal beak instead of a hand. At once I saw that brave adaptation as the machine gun beaten into the tool of peace. For me, the man had sacrificed his arm fighting a senseless war for Ian Smith's Unilateral Declaration of Independence, and his artificial hand, efficiently manipulated in the service of a black majority government, was acceptance that that war, like the flesh-and-blood hand, was lost and done with.

But what proof did I have that he hadn't had his arm severed in an ordinary road accident?

The bar at my second-rate hotel was full, of course, like the bars of grander hotels nearby, and during my stay it was never anything else. The faces were black, mostly young, the drink was beer, and the atmosphere no more thickly felted with voices and smoke than in comparable bars anywhere.

That scene was something I know how to read more certainly than the immigration officer's artificial hand. Where the colour bar has been grudgingly relaxed in white-ruled Africa, the practice has been to let blacks into public bars before opening to them libraries, sports and hobby clubs, and other facilities for amusement and activity created by whites for their own city leisure. This packing of the bars by young blacks doesn't signify to me that Zimbabweans, more than other city youngsters, are interested in no other pastime but drinking, but that bars were probably the first of the white man's pleasures opened to them when the Rhodesians were stalling power-sharing by giving placebos, and that the old colonial habits and leisure arrangements have not yet been replaced by new ones.

We all know how close the conviviality of the bottle is to the aggression of the bottle. One of the most stupid things whites ever did in Africa was to make the bar the first public place where they would mix with blacks socially, and drinking the first pleasure to be openly shared by black and white. Almost without exception, the scattered incidents of violence that are occurring in the new state, whether racial insults followed by blows between black and white, or political fights between blacks, happen in the vicinity of bars. The immediate answer for Zimbabwe lies, alas, only in hindsight: during their prosperous rule of ninety years in Rhodesia (I date this from the establishment of Cecil John Rhodes's Pioneer Column camp at Salisbury, September 1890) whites should have created more opportunities for white and black to get to know one another while sober. And whites should have opened to blacks places other than bars where the energies of men back from the war could be spent more constructively than dangerously.

The long-term answer will be taken up within the movement of the whole society itself, political and economic. At the moment the city of Salisbury[1] – the most beautiful colonial city in Africa – is a wide, sunlit stage set. The play for which British government, international mining and white settlers' agricultural and commercial headquarters were built – with their pillars, verandahs and palms they are more mansions than public premises, an imperialist architectural aesthetic expressing perfectly the concept of the colonies as a kind of greater country estate of the British Empire family – that play has closed.

Black urban couples with their children wander across the polo-field-sized streets window-shopping, old women in from the

---

1   Now Harare.

country carry long rolled mats balanced on their heads in a queer inversion of tightrope walking, young men hawk, discreetly as if offering dirty postcards, chess sets carved from local stone: all were here before, but now their presence has a different meaning. The props of the capital city are theirs, a city conceived by others; they seem not to have occupied it psychologically, yet. There are some constructions – not necessarily of white walls, handsome teak doors and brass fittings – they may never want to occupy, and others that their government, newly committing itself to socialism with a mixed economy, and land distribution and development to keep the rural population in agriculture, is determined to see they do not.

I spent most of my time in two of these colonial mansions. In both, the walls stood, but the internal human construction had been started anew. One was the House of Assembly. The official flunkey was a C. Aubrey Smith figure from the set of that play that has folded, wandered in to bear the golden turnip-topped mace before the Speaker of the House at those points in parliamentary procedure decreed by tradition. Here, the change of power from the minority of 230,000 whites to the majority of some 6.8 million blacks is set out clearly by change of colour as Lewis Carroll roses painted to order in the Duchess's garden. There is no official opposition to Prime Minister Robert Mugabe's government. It is dominated by his own ZANU-PF Party, which nevertheless includes Joshua Nkomo, leader of the rival Patriotic Front Party (he would have been prime minister if Rhodesia had become Zimbabwe as a result of early negotiation instead of ultimate civil war), and two white ministers. David Smith of the Rhodesian Front is Minister of Commerce. Whites have minority rights to a guaranteed number of seats in parliament for twenty years. The all-white Rhodesian Front's members sit together on one side of the House as if in a group photograph taken at some Old Boys' gathering. The good looks of the (segregated) clubman – pink faces, silver-touched hair – prevail. Acrimonious remarks from this side of the House – bitter saliva flies from both sides – come in British rather than colonial accents.

The black MPs are not only sharp-tongued, highly articulate men like Dr Herbert Ushewokunze. He is the Minister of Health whose irregular postponement, the day I was present, of a debate on ministerial estimates for which the Rhodesian Front had prepared its arguments led to sarcastic exchanges and a walkout by five RF members ('to the canteen', Dr Ushewokunze did not fail to suggest). Filling the backbenches ('back' in the parliamentary sense only) were men and women painstakingly self-educated beyond the miserable facilities provided by successive white governments in their pursuit of Cecil Rhodes's 'hinterland' paradise for whites. When a member from a rural constituency stood up to speak about Minister of Education Dzingai Mutumbuka's bill introducing free primary education for all children, the man on his feet in a lumpy Sunday suit was a schoolteacher whose own education, he explained, and that of his children, had meant hardship for his parents and, in turn, for himself. One by one, other men and women stood up eagerly, even passionately, putting forward in the supreme forum of parliamentary democracy the claims of the people in their districts for new schools and more teachers.

The language of parliament is English. Some did not always have the right words for the expression of their ideas; but the ideas corresponded with desperate sincerity to real entities in the lives of the people they represent. When these MPs thanked the minister for something all the decades of white rule in a rich country never provided, this was no Party back-slapping but the response to a realisation long withheld. During that week, when the British and American press was giving front-page scandal space to the alleged murder of a white farmer by a black cabinet minister, Edgar Tekere, and the 'defection' of General Walls from his curious position as commander of the ex-guerrilla forces he had once fought, I don't suppose there was more than a line for the truly enormous event of free education for Zimbabwean children.

The white MPs did not display much interest in the bill, for that matter. Well, there had always been government money for white children's schools. This hangover of racial divisions showed itself most depressingly in a debate on the employment bill of the

Minister of Labour, Mr Kumbirai Kangai. A clause the House grew
coldly tense over was that dealing with new legislation providing
for complaints by domestic servants against unfair dismissal. Voices
of the past seemed to be sounding hollowly through the mouth of
the present. As whites are (almost exclusively) the employers and
blacks are the servants, the debate, without anyone on either side
ever admitting it, was according to the familiar scenario. I could
have prompted the ensuing dialogue from my seat behind glass
(bulletproof? a precaution from the war?) in the visitors' gallery.

Some Rhodesian Fronters were very interested in this clause. With
ramrod decorum they approached it exclusively from the unexpressed
experience of the Master and the Madam with Boys and Girls. If the
servant's complaint of unfair dismissal was in fact itself dismissed,
would the exonerated employer be compensated for his time spent
at the hearing, and the working time lost by other servants in his
employ who might have wasted days giving evidence?

The black MPs, equally tight-buttocked, concealed their sympathies for the smarts and indignities of the back yard in an insistence
that the minister's raising of the status-less servant to a worker
with rights (and a minimum wage!) like any other worker not
be reduced by amendments. Surely there was no one, even of the
doctors, academics and other university-educated people among
the black men and women seated in that House, some member of
whose family had not cleared away 'the white man's scum!' (The
phrase is Ezekiel Mphahlele's – the black South African writer.)

The other mansion in which I spent my time was a real one, a
private house from the Rhodesian *Gone With The Wind* era.

'The Ranche House' stands on a ridge in what is now a Salisbury
suburb but must have held the sovereignty of its original owner's
eye over virgin grassland all the way to the hills of rock and the
msasa trees that turn as maples do, but in spring not autumn. The
garden with its formal perspective of wide shallow steps is still
there. The single-storey white house spreads even more widely than
climbing the steps had prepared me for – when it was built, for
those for whom it was built, there was all the space in the world,

for the taking. There was money to observe grace and style; on either side of the simple farmhouse gable a whim to place vents in the form of baroque ox-eye windows could be indulged. It is a very lovely façade. A pity architectural beauty often has its political implications . . .

I don't know the full story of the house's internal adaptation through Ian Smith's Unilateral Declaration of Independence in 1965 and the seven years of war that resulted; but its last occupation in the style and political philosophy for which it was built was surely that of Mr Justice Robert Tredgold, Chief Justice of the Central African Federation of Southern Rhodesia, Northern Rhodesia and Nyasaland. With the breakaway of Nyasaland as the new country of Malawi, this federation became a cartographical error almost as soon as it was drawn on the map, and by the time Northern Rhodesia became Zambia in 1964 seemed as distant and presumptuous a European piece of African map-making as the Berlin Conference of 1885 which shared Africa out among European powers. I gather that for some years The Ranche House has been used by various educational institutions; there are barrack classrooms, and a hall and canteen have been built where, by now, young black men and women talk French over their traditional African lunch of stew and *putu* (maize mash, like polenta and just as delicious) because they are doing an intensive course in that language as part of their training to staff Zimbabwe's new diplomatic missions abroad.

When I was there The Ranche House was also giving hospitality to a 'media workshop'. I was one of a collection of twenty or so unlikely characters who could only have been brought together by the search for an author like Mugabe. The blacks included conscientiously note-taking young men from the ruling party, public relations officers for ZANU-PF, journalists from the government information service, announcer/producers from the Zimbabwe (state) Broadcasting Corporation and TV, journalists from the principal newspapers, a research fellow with a film star's face from the literature department of the University of Zimbabwe. These tame titles in fact designated, among others, the two men sitting behind me who until a few months ago were regional commanders of the guerrilla forces, and a tall young man with the strong Semitic nose that Arab slavers seem to have left behind in their raids on Central Africa, who joined the liberation army straight from a rural school and spent part of the war in Egypt studying media at Cairo University.

Those black members of our workshop who had not been freedom fighters nearly all were veterans of periods of political detention in the white man's prisons; each curriculum vitae listed the career of being 'inside' if not 'outside' (infiltrating with the guerrilla forces), and military terms slipped into tea-break chatter – people would talk about waiting to be redeployed rather than about looking for a job. One of the ZANLA commanders wore a short-sleeved safari jacket of a vaguely military green for the first few days, and several copper bracelets looping over a watch of the military hardware kind on his elegant, iron-black arm; but he appeared in a perfectly hung 'redeployed' three-piece suit on the final day.

The white participants at the workshop consisted mainly of those Old Africa Hands, often in the para-journalistic occupations, who move from territory to territory, serving governments white and black, oiled with a professionalism that allows them to pass unharmed from hand to hand, from colonial to black capitalist to black socialist states, from democracies to dictatorships and vice versa. Here they were again: among a Press and Liaison Officer for Ministers of Government, an Editorial Training Officer for a newspaper group (still owned by a South African company), and an awesomely titled Senior Information Officer for All Media, was a jolly fellow who once managed a hotel I stayed at twenty-five years ago in Zambia. There was another – a Graham Greene rather than Pirandello character, this one, with a comedian's long jaw, a sharp regional humour from England, and close-to-the-nose bright eyes – whose previous job was that of head of President Kamuzu Banda's secret police in neighbouring conservative Malawi.

Yet with the exception of two irascible Germans vying in jealous whispers for the privilege of organising us all (the workshop was sponsored by the West German Friedrich Ebert Foundation, which seems close to the Social Democratic Party), there was no acrimony in this old mansion. Never, in six days of discussion, was a breath of the old hates exhaled in the House of Assembly. People addressed one another as 'comrade' and whether initially this was for some ideological carpetbaggers an insurance while for other participants an affirmation of political convictions, the title turned out to be an ordinary expression of comradely feeling that grew among all. Our discussions ranged with a charmed life over minefield subjects, from the point of view both of colour and party differences. ZANU-PF men in broadcasting and TV debated respectfully with people like Ronald Mpofu, a middle-aged individualist who complained that zealous ZANU-PF Party men among radio announcers slip into their disc-jockey patter what he called 'honeymoon slogans' plugging the Party. Stanley Mhondoro, the man who had gone to war straight from school, counselled: 'As a nation we must learn to distinguish Party matters from national issues.' When the subject of offensive terminology was raised by the young literary academic Musaemura Munya, opinions were not identifiable by colour; there was agreement that terms like *kraal*, whose literal meaning is a place where cattle are confined but which has been used throughout colonial English-speaking Africa to denote the homes of rural black people, should be dropped by the media, since men in independent Africa are not regarded as cattle.

The workshop's main business was with ways and means to open the minds of a long-neglected population not only to information but more importantly to education of a kind that provides the means to assess information intelligently. On this question, a few Old Africa Hands of a very different kind were raptly listened to. Alexander Katz, an American chartered accountant who many years ago quit the United States as a result of the McCarthy hearings and came to live in what was then Rhodesia, spoke about 'the colonialism of the professions'. In a colonial regime, 'the settlers know everything; the people nothing'. In the colonialism of the professions, which too easily survives the overthrow of colonialism, 'the professionals know everything; the ordinary public nothing'.

He proceeded to go through the annual report of the Zimbabwe Broadcasting and TV Corporation, pointing out how little this revealed of how public money had been spent during the Smith regime, and bluntly asking whether Zimbabweans were going to be intimidated by accountants' jargon into accepting a comparable state of ignorance about what were now their own public affairs. Ruth Weiss, an English journalist (once a child refugee, in South Africa, from Nazi Germany) having the status of foul-weather friend of Robert Mugabe himself, could speak some plain truths about interdependence and dependency among the states of southern Africa.

But the issue that contained all others was always there, and discussion faced with considerable if not complete honesty those sheer and slippery walls as it came up against them: will the ethics of the media be decided in the interests of the nation, or the truth?

Even as I write, I don't know whether to put the 'interests of the nation' in quotes, for that, too, is perhaps significant of a personal ethical bias . . . For a people just emerged from colonial rule as victors of a seven-year war in which they had to destroy their own homes as well as those of the people they were fighting, Lenin's dreadful 1920 dictum may seem the voice of reason and right: 'Why should freedom of speech be allowed? Why should a government which is doing what it believes to be right allow itself to be criticised?'

Time and again, the quasi-divine dispensation of 'doing what it believes to be right' was a syntactical presence in our discussion, if not an open statement; it will be hard for Zimbabwe not simply to compensate fiercely for what it *knows to be wrong*: the Smith government's absolute control of the media in exclusive promotion of views and information favourable to justification for white minority rule. But always among us was some black hand beckoning for the chairman's permission to raise the question – how inalienable is a government's *right to believe itself to be right*? What ethic silences criticism? The Minister of Information, Dr Nathan Shamuyarira, a former newspaper editor, abolished all the white Rhodesian government's restrictions on reporting and on the entry of foreign newsmen as soon as the Mugabe government took power. Some of the latter, he feels, have abused their welcome by sensational reporting, particularly of minor remarks as policy statements. When we all parted, it looked as if a Press Council may be set up as a result of The Ranche House workshop. The problem it will have to deal with is not, as the outside world might be quick to conclude, simply to preserve freedom of the press, but rather to create it within a continent where it scarcely exists, in a new country struggling with a past that, though both Western and white-dominated, alienated most people from any such tradition.

During the week I was in Zimbabwe the country became the 153rd member of the United Nations. Zimbabwe television still runs genteel British middle-class series (*The Pallisers* has followed *The Forsyte Saga*) and cute American children's programmes suited to the taste of the majority of people who can afford sets – whites to whom England is not home and the US is foreign, but who have no indigenous culture. On the night of the event we saw Robert Mugabe, a black man, the Prime Minister of the country we were viewing from, being smiled on beneath the flags of the international community of nations. His American hosts beamed with particular emotion in Washington. But he came home with nothing substantial. He said that President Jimmy Carter was 'well-disposed to giving Zimbabwe more aid, perhaps not in the near future, but in the long term'.

Indeed, not in this term; not until after the American presidential election; and then will money be forthcoming only if Ronald Reagan does not become President in Carter's place?

Seen from Salisbury, there was something shameful about those banquets, ringing speeches, fraternal handclasps far away. What does pomp signify, if not practical help to enable the new human entity to survive?

Mugabe came home with very little to a country which, though burgeoning with *potential* for world investors in minerals such as chrome and iron, agricultural products such as tobacco and sugar, even ethanol (fuel from maize), has now emerged from an economically devastating war and is enduring a drought that for two years has compounded the agricultural aspect of that devastation. Above all, Zimbabwe is facing the expectations of 30,000 freedom fighters who won the country's independence and are now waiting idle in camps,

waiting to live the normal life they fought for. At the Lancaster House
talks, the Patriotic Front Alliance agreed to compensate 'dispossessed' white farmers on the condition that Britain and the West
would provide the money to buy whatever land is needed to meet
the requirements of black Zimbabweans. The amount discussed was
between 560 and 800 million Rhodesian (then) dollars, and Lord
Carrington indicated that an African Development Bank would be
established with Britain supplying the initial capital and encouraging
wider Western support. The metamorphosis of freedom fighters into
citizens at peace is directly related to the question of land; it was
envisaged that most would cultivate the land under a project called
Operation Seed. But these promises from the West seem in danger
of becoming procrastination. Of the total of $250 million in interna-
tional aid available this year, so far the United States has given only
$22 million, and President Carter's statement in August to Robert
Mugabe seems to bring into doubt the $25–$30 million the US
promised for the fiscal year starting in October 1980, as well as the
$20–$25 million for housing guarantees now under discussion with
the US. Of the £750 million promised by Britain over three years,
only £7 million has been given.

Zimbabwe's people cannot wait for their country's potential to be
realised; Robert Mugabe cannot uphold through an indeterminate
transition period those civilised standards that the West now has
high hopes of from him in its turnabout from regarding him as a
terrorist. The West must put adequate aid into the country immediately, not merely because it was promised by Kissinger, or pledged by
the Lancaster House agreement, but because to ditch Mugabe now by
talk of helping him some tomorrow is to make it impossible for him
to attempt what those UN celebratory smiles and handshakes were
surely acknowledging – his 'bid to establish a non-racial society . . .
civil liberties . . . and a consolidating factor in all southern Africa'.[2]

1980

---

2   2010: now become a dictator, Mugabe has brought his country to suffering and disaster.

The South African Censor: No Change

Sharing the preoccupations of my fellow writers, I was the first to express the conviction, now become a general stand, that the release from ban of a few books by well-known white writers is not a major victory for the freedom to write, and that the action carries two sinister implications: first, those among us who are uncompromising opponents of censorship with wide access to the media can be bought off by special treatment accorded to our books; second, the measure of hard-won solidarity that exists between black and white writers can be divided by 'favouring' white writers with such special treatment, since no ban on any black writer's work has been challenged by the Directorate's own application to the Appeal Board.

I don't claim any prescience or distinction for early arrival at this conviction – *Burger's Daughter* (1979), my novel,[1] happened to be the first released as a consequence of the Directorate's new tactics. It was natural for me to examine the package very carefully when my book came back to me – apparently intact, after all the mauling it had been through. It was inevitable that I should come upon the neat devices timed to go off in the company of my colleagues. It was not surprising that they should recognise for themselves these booby-traps set for us all, since a week or two later André Brink received the same package containing his novel *A Dry White Season* (1979). And then, in time for April and the seating of the new Chairman of the Appeal Board, came Afrikaans literature's Easter egg, all got up for Etienne le Roux with the sugar roses of the old Appeal Board's repentance and the red ribbon defiant of Aksie Morale Standaarde, the NGK and Dr Koot Vorster – of course, *Magersfontein, O Magersfontein!*[2] was not released as the two other

---

1 Published and banned that year.
2 Etienne le Roux's novel.

books were, as a result of the Director's own appeal against his Committee's bannings, but its release on an ultimate appeal by the author's publishers transparently belongs to the same strategy in which the other two books were 'reinstated'.

I am one who has always believed and still believes we shall never be rid of censorship until we are rid of apartheid. Personally, I find it necessary to preface with this blunt statement any comment I have about the effects of censorship, the possible changes in its scope, degree, and methodology. Any consideration of how to conduct the struggle against it, how to act for the attainment of immediate ends, is a partial, pragmatic, existential response seen against a constant and over-riding factor. Today as always, the invisible banner is behind me, the decisive chalked text on the blackboard, against whose background I say what I have to say. *We shall not be rid of censorship until we are rid of apartheid.* Censorship is the arm of mind-control and as necessary to maintain a racist regime as that other arm of internal repression, the secret police. Over every apparent victory we may gain against the censorship powers hangs the question of whether that victory is in fact contained by apartheid, or can be claimed to erode it from within.

What exactly has changed since 1 April 1980?

What exactly does the 'born again' cultural evangelism staged with the positively last appearance of Judge Lammie Snyman and the previews of rippling intellectual musculature displayed by thirty-seven-year old Dr Kobus van Rooyen, mean?

The Censorship Act remains the same. It is still on the statute book. The practice of embargo will continue. The same anonymous committees will read and ban; a censorship committee having been defined in 1978 by the Appellate Division of the Supreme Court as 'An extra-judicial body, operating in an administrative capacity, whose members need have no legal training, before whom the appellant has no right of audience, who in their deliberations are not required to have regard to the rules of justice designed to achieve a fair trial, whose proceedings are not conducted in public and who are not required to afford any reasons for their decision'.

The enlarged panel of experts has some of the old names, among whom is at least one known Broederbonder, and the new ones are recruited from the same old white cadres. The powers of the Board are what they always were.

There is no change in the law or procedure, then. Nor is any promised, or even hinted at.

What we have is a new Chairman of the Appeal Board, in a position whose power we already know: although he does not make decisions alone, the Chairman of the Appeal Board is the ultimate authority and decision-maker in the whole process of censorship. We also know that the head of any institution – and censorship is an institution in our national life – interprets the doctrinal absolutes and directs the tactical course towards that institution's avowed objectives according to his own personal ideas of how these should be achieved. His flair – for which quality he will have been chosen, all other qualifications being equal – will influence procedure, make innovations in the way *the same things* are done, whether the institution is a bank accumulating capital or a Directorate of Publications controlling people's minds.

Therefore it can only be the philosophy and psychology of censorship that have changed. Why and how is something we shall have to delve into in the months to come, beyond a first snap understanding of what was plain behind the unbanning of a small group of books in quick succession – the hope to placate certain white writers, the suggestion of an attempt to divide the interests of black and white writers. These actions were surely already the product of Dr van Rooyen's thought, since he was running the Appeal Board for some time before he was appointed Chairman in April 1980. They were the first show of the quality of mind, the concept of culture, the concept of the relation of literature to society, to politics, to economics, to class as well as colour, the new Chairman has, and on which – as we see – the nature of what we are up against now will be dependent.

Since he took office he has made policy statements – signification from which it will be possible to trace the grid of his purpose. Taking as given the ordinary motives of personal ambition and good pay in his acceptance of the job of chief censor, we need to know how he sees his particular mission. We need to know what his sense of *self* and *other* is. For that is the vital factor in the praxis of censorship, the phenomenon of censorship as a form of social and cultural control. Philosophically speaking, on this sense of self and other is the authority of censorship conceived. A *we* controlling a *them*. Dr van Rooyen won't tell us what this private sense deciding his widely affective thoughts and actions is; but we have the right to find out. I'll ask you to look at the evidence of his statements presently; first I want to return to the evidence of his actions – or actions behind which his hand can be detected – the unbanning of certain highly controversial books.

André Brink has pointed out that the week that his novel, dealing with the death by police brutality and neglect of a black man in prison, was released from ban, Mtutuzeli Matshoba's story collection, *Call Me Not A Man*, was banned. The reason for banning supplied to Matshoba's publisher was objection to one of the stories only, 'A Glimpse of Slavery', dealing with the experiences of a black man hired out as prison labour to a white farmer.

Death in prison or detention; the abuse of farm labour. Both are subjects whose factual basis has been exposed and confirmed in the proceedings of court cases and, in one instance at least, a commission of inquiry. Two writers, each of whom can make with Dostoevsky a statement of the writer's ethic: 'Having taken an event, I tried only to clarify its possibility in our society'; the work of one is released, the other banned.

Now, in preparation for the new regime, from which we are being persuaded we may expect a new respect for literature, and are asked to accept this as a new justification for censorship, there has been much emphasis on literary quality in recent decisions by the Appeal Board. It seems that Dr Kobus van Rooyen wants to substitute the silver-handled paper-knife of good taste for the kerrie of narrow-mindedness and prudery, as the arbitrary weapon. But although it was decided by a censorship committee that there was 'not inconsiderable merit in much of the writing in this collection of short stories by the African writer Mtutuzeli Matshoba . . .

with regard both to the quality of the writing and to the author's insight in the human situations which he interprets', although the Committee members found the stories 'generally of a high quality', they banned the book because of a single story. They did this – again I let them speak for their anonymous selves – ostentatiously from the new 'literary' angle, claiming that this particular story was flatly written and the accumulation of its events improbable. But what was hatched beneath the peacock feathers was the ostrich with his familiar kick. They banned the book on one-seventh of its contents, to be precise. They returned, when dealing with a black writer, to the precept followed in the past, when a work was to be judged 'undesirable' or 'desirable' not in relation to the quality of the whole, but could be damned because of a single chapter, page or even paragraph.

The sole basis for the ban on Matshoba's book rested ultimately on a declared calculation made in the imperatives of political repression, not literary quality, although literary quality is invoked – the Committee stated that the appeal to the reader of the story 'lies not in the *literary creation* but rather in the *objectionable nature* of the events which are presented . . . even if all these situations . . . had occurred in this context in which they are set in the story, *the presentation of these scenes in a popular medium would be undesirable*'.

The italics are mine. The standard used by the censors here is that of political control over reading matter likely to reach the black masses. If this is not so, let us challenge the Directorate to act in accordance with Dr van Rooyen's statement that the banning of a book by the 'isolation method' would now be rejected, and therefore ask for the ban on Matshoba's book to be reviewed by the Appeal Board.

My novel, *Burger's Daughter*, was released by the Appeal Board although, among all the other sections under which it had been deemed offensive, there were numerous examples cited under D Section 47 (2) of the Censorship Act. One was the remark by English-speaking schoolgirls mouthing prejudices picked up from their parents: 'Bloody Boers, dumb Dutchmen, thick Afrikaners'.

Miriam Tlali's novel *Muriel at the Metropolitan* in the version found inoffensive and left on sale for several years, was banned in 1979 on the sole objection of three offences under the same section of the Act, the principal being the reference by the narrator-character to an Afrikaans-speaking woman as a 'lousy Boer'.

Well, these ugly racist epithets are not my personal ones, nor, I think, are they Miriam Tlali's; but they are heard around us every day, and there are certain characters whose habitual inability to express themselves without them is another fact about our society no honest writer can falsify. Yet Tlali's book, otherwise quite inoffensive from the censors' point of view, is ultimately banned while mine is ultimately released. Is it more insulting for a white South African to be abused by a black character in a book than by a white one? What is clear is that a censorship committee regards it as necessary to prevent black readers from reading their own prejudices, their own frustrations, given expression in the work of a black writer; outside the considerations assiduously to be taken into account by a new and enlightened censorship there is an additional one, operative for black writers only that nullifies most of the concessions so far as black writers are concerned – they may not say what white writers say because they are calculated to have a wider black readership, and to speak to blacks from the centre of the experience of being black, to articulate and therefore confirm, encourage what the black masses themselves feel and understand about their lives but most cannot express.

And with this trend taken by the Censorship Directorate in the period preparing us for the advent of a new Chairman, we come to the event itself, and the statements of policy made by Dr Kobus van Rooyen since 1 April.

He has not said much; and one of his statements has been to the effect that he intends to say even less: he has announced that he will take no part in public debates on censorship. *The Star* (5/4/1980) editorial pointed out, of public debates: 'these insights to the work-ings of a censor's mind were what helped speed the retirement of his predecessor. They will be missed.'

Indeed.

Dr Kobus van Rooyen would be unlikely to present the image

that emerged from the public appearances and statements of his predecessor. Nevertheless, Dr van Rooyen does not intend taking any risks. What interests us more is that he does not want openly to proselytise his philosophy of censorship any more than he intends to be open to the influence of counter views. This is an autocratic approach – let us not call it an arrogant one. From it we can understand that here is a man whose view of culture is elitist, someone in whose mind, whether consciously or not, is posited the idea of an official cultural norm. The fact that his version of that norm is likely to differ, here and there, in emphasis, does not mean that it is any less fundamentalist than that defined implicitly, along with the law, in the Censorship Act. The shift in emphasis is a realpolitik adjustment to catch up with the change in the relation of literature to life that has taken place in South Africa, and that a clever man cannot ignore. The concept – that there is a right for a single power group to decide what is culture, remains the grid on which, although – like the most functional of contemporary business premises – all manner of interior open-space arrangements may be made to suit the tenant, the total structure must be accepted. The myth of the South African culture sustains a man who is so convinced of his approach to his job that he is not prepared to discuss it let alone admit any necessity to defend it.

Roland Barthes points out that traditional myth explains a culture's origins out of nature's forces; modern myths justify and enforce a secular power by presenting it as a natural force. Sophisticated officials of this government may be openly sceptical of some of the more ritualistic aspects of our societal myth – the Immorality Act, the awful malediction of four-letter words, etc. – but sophistication must never be taken for enlightenment; acceptance of the concept of a culture based on an elite dispensation to the masses who cannot create anything valid for themselves, acceptance of the role of literature in life according to that culture, are still firmly based on a particular myth of power.

Only from within that myth could Judge Lammie Snyman have taken the cultural standpoint revealed when he said earlier this month that blacks are 'inarticulate people, who, I am sure, are not interested' in censorship (*The Star*, 8/4/1980). And what a lightning flash lit up a whole official mentality for us when, summing up his entire five years in which it was his responsibility to decide 'what was likely to corrupt or deprave an immature mind, or whether it was likely to horrify or disgust' the people of South Africa, he added: 'Of blacks, I have no knowledge at all.'

His 'average ordinary South African' – whose standards of morality and literary judgement he constantly invoked during his term of office – was not to be found among the majority of the South African population. For this reason, Dr Kobus van Rooyen has abandoned the creature. But not the idea that he has the right to create another of his own, whose imaginary or rather conditioned sensibilities and susceptibilities will be the deciding factor in what shall and shall not be read by all of us. What is regarded as Dr van Rooyen's most important statement is his announcement that his creature will be the 'probable reader'. Important it is, but not, I am afraid, for reasons assumed by some.

The assumption is that sexual explicitness as an integral part of sophisticated literature written in the idiom of educated people will now be passed. That complex works dealing with contentious or radical political characters and events above the level of simple rhetoric will also be passed. And there the effect of the change apparently ends, and so can only be regarded as beneficial; after all if you have not the educational background and trained intellect to follow these works, that is hardly the responsibility of the censors.

It is not? By putting on the top shelf, out of reach of those masses Lammie Snyman confessed he knew nothing about, imaginative, analytical presentation of the crucial questions that deal with their lives, is one not hampering the healthy cultural development censorship purports to be guarding?

We should like to be able to put that question to the new Chairman of the Appeal Board, who evidently does know a great deal about those masses. Does he see the justification of that hampering, in a mission to adjust the strategy of the myth of hostile forces he well understands?

Why may intellectual readers handle inflammables?

Is it because this readership is predominantly white, and radical initiative by whites has been contained by imprisonment, exile, bannings and the threat of right-wing terrorism while the moderate, let alone the revolutionary initiative for social change has passed overwhelmingly to blacks, and is not contained?

Why may white writers deal with inflammables?

Is it because the new censorship dispensation has understood something important to censorship as an arm of repression – while white writings are predominantly critical and protestant in mood, black writings are inspirational, and that is why the government fears them?

The definition of the 'probable reader' can be arrived at by the old pencil-in-the-hair and fingernail tests, believe me. The criterion for reading matter allowed him is not literary worth but his colour.

As a cultural and not merely a politically manipulable prototype, the 'probable reader' is a creature of class-and-colour hierarchy. He cannot be visualised, in our society, by those of us sufficiently free-minded to see that culture in South Africa is something still to be made, something that could not be brought along with mining machinery in the hold of a ship, nor has been attained by the genu-inely remarkable achievement of creating an indigenous language out of European ones. He cannot be visualised by anyone who understands culture not as an embellishment of leisure for the middle classes, but as the vital force generated by the skills, crafts, legends, songs, dances, languages, sub-literature as well as literature – the living expression of self-realisation – in the life of the people as a whole.

Behind the 'probable reader' is surely the unexpressed concept of the 'probable writer'. The new Chairman of the Appeal Board has assured *him* that 'satirical writing will be allowed to develop'. To most of us this is an elitist concession. Of course, nobody stops anyone from writing satire, whatever his colour. But in the rela-tion of literature to life at present, satire is unlikely to appeal to black writers. It requires a distancing from the subject which black writers, living their lives close within their material, are not likely to manage; it requires a licence for self-criticism that loyalty to the black struggle for a spiritual identity does not grant at present. So

effective weapon though satire may be, as a social probe in certain
historical circumstances or stages, it will not, so far as it is a concession by this government to freedom of expression, fall into the
hands of the 'wrong' probable writer . . .

Similarly, the new directive that the general public (probable
reader distinction again) 'does not have to accept literary works and
that a writer is a critic of his society and therefore often in conflict
with the accepted moral, religious and political values' will benefit
– if anyone, since we still have to prove ourselves unharmful and
inoffensive to whichever probable reader our work is allotted, in the
censors' consideration – will benefit writers of work in the critical
and analytical mode but lift no barriers for the inspirational. Yet
there is no ignoring the fact that the inspirational is a dynamic of
our literature at present. Franz Kafka's standard, that 'A book must
be an ice-axe to break the frozen sea inside us', is not the censors'.
Neither is there any sign of acceptance that in South Africa we
writers, white and black, are the only recorders of what the poet
Eugenio Montale calls 'unconfessed history'.

That has been made, and is being made every day, deep below
the reports of commissions and the SABC news; it is the decisive
common force carrying us all, bearing away the protective clothing
of 'probable readers' as paper carnival costumes melt in the rain.

In the final analysis, censorship's new deal is the pragmatic
manifestation of an old, time-honoured view of culture, already
dead, serving repression instead of the arts, and its belated recognition of literary standards is its chief strategy. This recognition
is shrewd enough to see what Lammie Snyman did not – that the
objective validity of literary standards as a concept (there are works
of genuine creation, there is trash) could be invoked for a purpose
in which, in fact, they have no place and no authority. The criteria
by which the quality of literature can be assessed have nothing
whatever to do with calculation of its possible effect on the reader,
probable or improbable. The literary experts who are instructed to
take this factor into account, and do so, are not exercising any valid
function as judges of literature.

And in affirmation of freedom of expression, which is the single uncompromised basis of opposition to censorship, the literary worth or otherwise of a work is not a factor – what is at stake each time a book falls into the censors' hands is the right of that book to be read. Literary worth has nothing to do with that principle.

We must not fudge this truth. The poor piece of work has as much right to be read – and duly judged as such – as the work of genius. Literary worth may be assessed only by critics and readers free to read the book; it is a disinterested, complex and difficult judgement that sometimes takes generations. There is a promise that future judgements by the censors will 'more readily reflect the opinions of literary experts appointed'. The invocation of literary standards by censors as a sign of enlightenment and relaxation of strictures on the freedom of the work; above all, the reception by the public of this respected and scholarly concept as one that could be enthroned among censors – both are invalid. Let us never forget – and let us not let the South African public remain in ignorance of what we know: censorship may have to do with literature; but literature has nothing whatever to do with censorship.

1981

Unconfessed History

Alan Paton's *Ah, But Your Land Is Beautiful*

Alan Paton's last novel, *Too Late The Phalarope*, was published almost thirty years ago. The events central to his new one are an oblique explanation for the gap: the political activism of the man prevented the writer from exercising what Harry Levin calls 'that special concentration of the ego' which enables a writer to 'discover the power within himself'. In honourable retirement from politics, Paton has freed the power within himself; and it is inevitable that it should find its expression in what Czeslaw Milosz

has called 'unconfessed history': the personal dimension of events
that can be perceived only through their recreation in imaginative
works.

The new novel, intended to be the first of a trilogy, begins roughly
in the period of South African history in which the previous novel
was set. *Ah, But Your Land is Beautiful* strides vigorously through the
years from the first Nationalist Afrikaner government to its ideological apogee, the accession in 1958 of Prime Minister Hendrik
Verwoerd, who, assuming the godhead of the chosen white *Volk*,
promised a creation of 'separate freedoms' for black and white that
would be achieved, not in six days, but by 1976. Some of the issues
occurring within the book's span (six years during the 1950s) were:
the Bantu Education Act, the Suppression of Communism Act, the
consolidation of the black 'homelands' (yes, 13 per cent of the land,
and the loss of South African citizenship for the black majority),
and the removal of 'coloured' voters of the Cape from the common
roll. The 1950s also witnessed the formation of the Liberal Party
(the only legal non-racial party, once the Communist Party was
banned); the establishment of the secret society *Broederbond*'s
control of government; the alliance of black, Indian, and coloured
mass movements and white leftist movements in the Congress of
the People, at which the Freedom Charter (similar to the United
Nations Charter, and now banned) was adopted; the beginning of
the boycott movement against racialism in South African sport,
and of the opposition of church to state on the question of 'mixed'
worship. It was the era of the great mass movements of black
(sprinkled with white) passive resistance to unjust laws. It saw the
beginning of white right-wing urban terrorism, many years before
the suppressed and outlawed black liberation movements turned
in tragic desperation to the sporadic urban terrorism that frightens
South Africans today.

In Paton's novels one hears voices. That is his method. It derives
perhaps – fascinatingly – from the secret level at which the supra-
rational of creative imagination and the supra-rational of religious
belief well up together in him. In *Phalarope* a voice bore witness to

the undoing of a young man by racist laws that made a criminal act out of a passing sexual infidelity. A loving relative watched what she was powerless to prevent; hers was the voice of compassion. In *Ah, But Your Land is Beautiful*, watcher has turned spy. Characters' actions are seen now by hostile, distorting eyes and recorded in the evil cadences of poison-pen letters. Paton's technique remains the same, but his viewpoint has changed from sorrowful compassion to irony. Compare the hushed shock with which Paton described Pieter van Vlaanderen's 'fall' (he has made love to a black girl) from the love of wife and family, honour and self-respect in *Phalarope*, with the prurient cackle of Proud White Christian Woman when she writes anonymously to Robert Mansfield, a leader of the Liberal Party: 'How are your black dolly girls? . . . Does your wife like to be poked by the same stick that has been poking the black dolly girls?'

The phalarope, rare bird of understanding that came too late between father and son in the earlier novel, is recognised between the generations in the proud acceptance by the wealthy Indian family, the Bodasinghs, of their daughter's involvement in the Defiance Campaign against unjust laws. And, much later in the narrative, the bird figures again in the rise of internal moral conflicts and their liberal resolution within formerly self-righteous racists, like Van Onselen, a civil servant and one of the 'voices', and his Aunt Trina, to whom his running commentary on central events and protagonists in the book is addressed. This type of happy-end conversion is sometimes difficult to believe and slightly embarrassing to read. Perhaps it is best taken as another symbol: that of Alan Paton the man's continued faith in the power of seeing the light, which is in tension with the writer's ironic doubt that its beam goes all the way to a change in power structure. Proud White Christian Woman's 'conversion', on the other hand, is brought about by brutal circumstance that, alas, seems closer to the actualities of change in South Africa: the threat of her own death. She is dying of cancer, as there are signs that white society is beginning to know it can die of apartheid.

*   *   *

Yet, with few exceptions, the writer wins out over the man. The most dangerous episode in the book, from the point of view of those who see Paton's assertions of faith as lapses into sentiment, is steely and silencing. An Afrikaner judge, in line for the highest legal honour in the land, disqualifies himself by ceremonially washing and kissing, in a black church, the feet of his old servant, to restore a breach of faith between the whites who administer a black ghetto and the blacks who live in it. The strangeness and awkward solemnity is somehow enhanced by devices of irony that also expose the incident's South African craziness. Comments within the book take the form of snippets of supposed newspaper reports wryly and slyly aping the attitudes and vocabularies of left and right. Criticism from the left is pre-empted:

> The episode is totally meaningless and irrelevant, and it shows once more how unrelated to our realities are the bourgeois values of goodwill and sporadic benevolence in our South African situation . . . an example of white condescension at its very worst . . . The wages that she earns probably amount to three or four per cent of the judge's salary. Such gross inequalities are not removed by any amount of washing or kissing.

Every word is true, and Paton knows it; but for him that truth lies alongside the other, his faith.

He probably will be accused, now, of Manichaeanism. The trouble with being a public, political figure as he has been is that the writer will always be judged in relation to that figure. But Paton ought, with this work, to be granted the writer's freedom and, indeed, obligation to show the Manichaean elements in the society that is his material. Since he is a fervently personal writer, his own convictions may dominate, but he fulfils a writer's vision by seeing everything that is *there*. He does not let himself shirk much. He is aware that if the 1950s were the high years of white liberalism, they saw more importantly the beginning of the revolutionary period for blacks. Chief Luthuli, talking to the fictional Robert Mansfield, Liberal Party leader, about the African National

Congress alliance with the Communist Party, says: 'When my house is burning down and we are all running to the fire, I don't say to the man next to me, Tell me first, where did you get your bucket, where did you draw your water?' From the mouth of another of the real personages who converse with fictional ones, Dr Monty Naicker, comes: 'This is going to be our life from now on. Some of us have to be destroyed now so that freedom can come to others later.'

Before I knew I was going to review this book, I read it and wrote to Alan Paton in response. What I said remains valid for me upon re-reading the book as critic rather than fellow writer, and I am going to take the liberty of paraphrasing myself below.

One cannot read this book without the total absorption that comes from recognition of its truth and admiration for the artistic truth into which that has been transposed. There are many characters, yet this is not so much a novel as a meditation on subjects and characters in a novel. Paton has made a meditation his own novelistic form. He seems more interested – and he succeeds in making the reader more interested – in his reflections on the characters and events than in these people and events themselves. When his characters speak – even the 'voices', the marvellous ventriloquist's acts of Proud White Christian Woman and Van Onselen – it is quite simply Alan Paton speaking. This was, I think, a fault in some of his earlier work. He did not always succeed in creating what Patrick White has called the 'cast of contradictory characters of which the writer is composed'. But this time, yes, Alan Paton is speaking, and such is his skill, so individual the music of his lyricism, the snap of his staccato, the beauty of his syntax, that what ought to be a failure becomes somehow the strength of the work. Style is a matter of finding the one way to say exactly what you have to say. What Paton wants to say here is so central to his own experience, at conscious and subconscious levels, that it is natural to hear it in his own voice.

Why a novel, then, and not just another volume of his autobiography (one was published recently)? Ah, but this is not *his* story; it is part of ours, the South Africans'. That demands an imaginative transposition. This one is achieved with shining intelligence and acerbity, a young man's book with the advantage of an old man's experience of the battle with life and words.

1982

Mysterious Incest

Patrick White's Flaws in the Grass: A Self-Portrait

What do you expect from an autobiography? Those who write them are as uncertain as those who publish them. They don't even use the term, any longer. Czeslaw Milosz subtitled his a search for self-definition; Sartre, endowed by nature with the physical possibility of never looking anyone in the eye, stressed that his autobiography was nothing but words. The Australian novelist Patrick White has written one of the two key autobiographies by contemporary writers (my other nomination is Milosz's) that fit the lock of the creative process. Yet he has insisted that his publishers misrepresent and undervalue his book by stating on the jacket that it is 'merely' a self-portrait in the form of sketches.

All these cautionary riders to the form: biography, well yes; *auto* – don't ask too much. Too much of what? There's another decision. A review I read in an English literary magazine sulked because Patrick White had not written enough about being a homosexual. I, personally, should have been disappointed if he had written more about being a homosexual than about becoming and being a writer. Is autobiography the story of a personality or the work that has made the subject an object of sufficient public interest to merit writing about him/herself? If the subject is an artist, and in particular a writer, for whom the act is performed in the medium of his own art, what one wants, expects, is a revelation of the mysterious incest between life and art.

In his own books, White finds something of the 'unknown man' thesis that writers expect to find when they visit the author, and that he is 'unable to produce'. That unknown man is the writer of this autobiography; neither White the novelist nor White the man, but of their dark union: *he* has produced the revelation. It is read by glares of Australian sun and flares of European war, in the first, main section, a broken narrative that carries perfectly the philosophical proposition of its title, *Flaws in the Glass*, and in the second section, 'Journeys', by a kind of reflection cast up in sea crossings that are also connections, of a non-narrative nature. The scrappy third section at first appears to be a filler the book could have done without. On reading cat-scratch anecdotes, wry incidents, and a brilliantly elliptical telephone conversation, one realises all these are the geneses of unwritten short stories – a condition that offers addenda to the existence of the unknown man.

Patrick White was born in England in 1912 of Australian parents and brought back to Australia about the time he was able to sit up. He had imported English nannies, and later fulfilled colonial parental ambitions by being sent 'home' – away – to Cheltenham, where he suffered traditional miseries endured by embryonic writers in English public schools – and then some, if we are to believe that anti-colonial jeers were as bad as racialism, at that time. (I myself wonder whether his own infant snobbery – suppressed dislike of being a colonial, shame of his own people's apparent crassness in comparison with the nasty genteel indifference of assured ancestry – doesn't make him exaggerate this paradoxical phenomenon of empire.) As a young adult, he came back to try living on the Australian land – the Monaro region that has continued working through its relationship with his consciousness, and is magnificently recreated fifty years later in *The Twyborn Affair*. Going to England for a university education, he stayed on after Cambridge to become a writer in a London bedsitter.

Of course. That is the pilgrimage of the colonial artist of the twenties and thirties – and before. In late-nineteenth-century South

Africa, Olive Schreiner felt 'stifled' (significant metaphor for the asthma sufferer she was, as White himself is) in drawing-room pockets of colonial culture, and went to England to breathe. In Australia, White could not 'come to terms with the inhabitants'; away from Australia, the 'consolation of the landscape' always drew him back: but – it was a 'landscape without figures'. Intermittent self-exile, in England, America, and during the war in Africa and the Middle East, represents the split in being that is the initial stage in life's painful pull towards art.

Australia was *mother*-land, *father*-land, in an extraordinary sense. White refers to his actual mother always as 'Ruth'; she is a character rather than the closest relative in the kinship of blood. He seems to feel he inhabited her, that is all, for a time – like any other lodging left behind. England – the mother country to colonial ones – proved as little of a mother surrogate to run to; her earth alien. When aged seventy he worries away at the puzzle of his relation to his father, father and fatherland become one in an analysis that opens out like a great wound beyond its familial references. 'Had I been able to talk to him, and if, at the risk of sounding priggish, there had been some vaguely intellectual ground on which we could have met, I would have loved my father.'

He would have loved *Australia*. If he had felt able to talk to Australians of his own upper crust, if there had been some ground . . . Australia would not have been for him an inescapable landscape without figures, a place of silence between the extermination of indigenous people and culture, and the burble of Sunday family lunch at the Sydney Club. This patrician-looking man (in Australia, he was the sole native I met whose Cambridge English had no comfy cadence of the miaow vowel) sought out the Lizzies, Flos and Matts who were family servants. He came to love them 'through their connection with everyday reality'. By contrast: '*I had never seen my father in the context of reality*' (my italics). This is no less than a definition of colonial culture. All its referents were in one or the other of the Old Countries. It was not connected with the real entities of the country it claimed. The Lizzies, the Flos and Matts claimed no culture; but they lived at one with everyday reality on

Australian earth. That was where the substance of a live culture would come from. The child's instinct led him faithfully.

Did the 'unreality' of colonial life create 'unreal' family relationships? The fact that I can generalise from Patrick White's experience to that around me in another colonial society gives the idea some credence. But writers 'make' themselves out of such impasses. White writes, 'I have stuck by my principles [the middle-class ones instilled by his parents] while knowing in my irrational depths what it was to be a murderer, or be murdered.' This knowing began by knowing what it is to be Lizzie, Flo and Matt. All writers have to find the way to knowledge that remains, for most other people, buried within themselves. Being pitched in to conflict between the unreality of colonial life (bourgeois safety) and the reality of native entities of land and/or people (revolutionary danger of untamed nature, masses and mores) is the beginning of the way for writers in colonial societies, whether or not colour is involved. White has 'come to terms' with Australians by recognizing the *in himself*, in the writer's irrational depths beyond class, race or sex, at the same time as he stands apart from them. He talks to fellow Australians of themselves through his creation of them in his work. Surprising that he still troubles, in this book, to answer accusations that he is hard on them; he is hard on himself, in them.

The problem of colonialism, social and political, was resolved for the life by the work – almost. There was another problem, fed from the same bloodstream. White knew from an early age that he was homosexual. This doubled his sense of exclusion, since he felt himself set apart, if differently, both in Australia and London. He knows now that a solitary existence is the normal condition for artists. But, leading that existence as a young writer in London, he blamed his seclusion 'wrongly on my homosexual temperament, forced, at that period anyway, to surround itself with secrecy, rather than on the instinctive need to protect my creature core from intrusion and abuse'.

Of homosexuality as a component in the development of a writer he makes the familiar claim that the homosexual temperament 'strengthens our hand as man, woman, artist', then, with the acerbity that is so much a part of his chameleon's-eye originality, swivelling to observe all from unfamiliar angles, he is unafraid to add: 'Homosexual society as such has never had much appeal for me. Those who discuss the homosexual condition with endless hysterical delight . . . have always struck me as colossal bores. So I avoid them, and no doubt I am branded as a closet queen. I see myself not so much a homosexual as a mind possessed by the spirit of man or woman according to actual situations or the characters I become in my writing.' White is a wizard at definitions. But this 'mind possessed' is a definition of any writer, of any sex; White would have had it even if he had married the girl his mother selected, and fathered six little Australians. We are all pansexual, at work. Again, he at one stage considered writing 'as a disguise'; in his case, for unapproved sexual desires – for other writers, for all writers, a disguise which is also a guise in which life becomes art?

Even if he had been born a generation later, it is doubtful if White would ever have had the temperament to be 'gay' rather than plain homosexual. The emotional isolation he felt was resolved for him when, during the Second World War, he met Manoly Lascaris. This 'unlikely relationship between an Orthodox Greek and lapsed Anglican egotist agnostic pantheist occultist existentialist would-be though failed Christian Australian has lasted forty years'. It is a relationship that describes its own parabola through White's work. And I am not referring only or principally to the character Angelos Vatzatis, composed of respect, love and irony in *The Twyborn Affair*. White chooses another symbol. He states with the single verbal gesture of deep emotion that Manoly Lascaris became 'the central mandala in my life's hitherto messy design'. That symbol, working inward, became central to one of his books, *The Solid Mandala*.

Any artist who knows what it means to sustain a long relationship with a human partner while the ego that is the genie of creation clamours through a lifetime will recognise a moving achievement in the service of the man and the genie. It is clear that Manoly has been able to temper the two worlds White could not live in – Australia and Europe. Manoly helped to resolve White's Australian/colonial/class alienation by solving the personal motherless/fatherless/homosexual alienation. This stranger and Greek was the one who was able to take Patrick White back to Australia, after the war, and make it possible for him to accept and inhabit it as home, an Australian among Australians, despite the Cambridge vowels and the lack of appreciation of his work (he alleges) until he became visible on the wide screen of the Nobel Prize. The genuine, essential link to Europe, through Manoly's culture and personality, has surely given White the freedom in which to re-create Australian consciousness in his unique grasp of the concrete, the relative and the transcendent. The responsibility of Europe for Australia is always there. There are no antipodes to which human nature can ship what is intrinsic to it.

Everyone is always immensely interested to know which of his works a writer thinks his best. White's list: *The Aunt's Story*, *The Solid Mandala*, and *The Twyborn Affair*. He is one of the few writers who care to, and are able to give the genesis of his novels without self-consciousness. What he cannot give, of course, is the magicking, half witches' brew, half elixir, that makes the old farmhouse he once lived in the eternal one of a novel, or twins two aspects of himself in his characters, the Brown brothers. Though the three novels of his choice – one an early work, one from his middle period, and the third his latest – are very different, *The Twyborn Affair* is the culminating expression of White's vision, a vision that has made of Australian boiled mutton and plum duff an Ensor carnival. The bobbing, oversize heads are recognisable everywhere. Like the spirit of carnival, he carries them through the streets, dancing beauties and vomiting drunks, in celebration of life; and in the knowledge that King Carnival is always to be killed.

The fishhook of White's social conscience (which seems to have kept up, if somewhat awkwardly, with his movement as a writer) winkled himself out of writers' seclusion to take to the public platform in support of the Gough Whitlam government and in hope of an Australia-with-a-human-face. Political finagling felled that government, and White sees himself once again as the 'skeleton at the Australian feast' of Mammon. What this great artist is grieving over, really – a grief encompassing disappointed hopes for Australian socialism – is the situation all contemporary artists complain of. The Futurists dreamed that by our time technology would have freed the imagination unlimitedly. What has happened is that technology has outstripped imagination in an unimaginable way; capturing human responses in the shallows, instilling a yearning for things instead of revelations. Looking up from the broken plastic and bottles afloat in Sydney harbour, the nearest White can get to optimism is the grim, cocky message: 'Don't despair . . . it is possible to recycle shit.'

1982

The Child Is the Man

Wole Soyinka's *Aké: The Years of Childhood*

It is not always possible to find the child again. Proust did, not only by reason of his genius but because the emotional force of the child–parent relationship was never exceeded by any other in his strange life. In this sense, he was never looking back; the child Marcel was with him. But other writers, even wonderful ones, are not as successful. Czeslaw Milosz finds his way back to the Issa Valley by what has never left him: the communion with nature that was the joy of childhood and – on the evidence of a recent interview – consoles the ageing exile, honoured far from home, who assures Americans that communion may be made just outside their violent cities. Yet the Issa Valley childhood is not reinhabited but consciously interpreted from the distance of the life that followed.

As autobiographer of childhood the African writer has an advantage as special as, if very different from, that of Proust. His sense of self is *au fond* his Africanness. Adult experience as poet, novelist, playwright, often exile, is mingled with other countries, languages, cultures from which his colour always distinguishes him. Childhood belongs to African experience and it is not over: it remains with him for ever in his blackness, an essential identity never superseded by any other. The history of enslavement, oppression and race prejudice secures this for him. The advantage extends to the reader. The old adage is paraphrased – one's pleasure in the autobiography lies in the fact that the child is not only father to the exceptional man, but still is the man. The Guinean writer Camara Laye's *Dark Child* (*L'enfant noir*), published in the early fifties, owes some of its status as a minor classic to this exoticism, which is more than territorial.

Wole Soyinka of Nigeria is an exceptional man indeed. Poet, playwright, novelist, he has done something Camus despaired of seeing any activist achieve – lived the drama of his time and been equal to the writing of it. During the Nigerian civil war he defied his Yoruba loyalties for a greater one, and campaigned against the sale of arms to either side. He tried to stop the war; he was tortured, imprisoned by General Gowon for two years under ghastly conditions, and survived to fulfil magnificently, with *The Man Died*, the need (in his own words) for 'a testimony of the political prisoner's isolation in solitude that would become a kind of chain letter hung permanently on the leaden conscience of the world'.

Soyinka, an elegant writer, has in his recent novels tended to be an overly self-conscious one. For the best of reasons – he is never complacent, always searching out the most striking and complete way to say what he has to say – he sometimes produces the bad result of making the reader aware of the writer's unresolved choices. Too many words, too many inversions, too many clamouring clauses which punctuation cannot handle intelligibly. This is the opening sentence of *Season of Anomy*: 'A quaint anomaly, had long governed and policed itself, was so singly-knit that it obtained a tax assessment for the whole populace and paid it before the departure of the pith-helmeted assessor, in cash, held all property in common, literally, to the last scrap of thread on the clothing of each citizen

– such an anachronism gave much patronising amusement to the cosmopolitan sentiment of a profit-hungry society.'

It is not surprising, then, that his approach to his years of child-hood should have more in common with *Tristram Shandy* than with Proust or Laye, although Laye's home was also in West Africa. For the first ninety pages or so, the tone is waggish. The 'worked-up' anecdotal dialogue of his parents and others reads like inventions based on what are really family sayings – whose origin is germane, a whole view of life rather than a response to a single happening. It is hard to believe that a boy under five thought of his mother as 'Wild Christian' although the fact that everyone referred to his father as 'HM' (headmaster) would have made it natural for him to see that as a name for intimate use, and not a title. It is hard to accept that a three-and-a-half-year-old's sassy ripostes were as well phrased as the supremely articulate adult now 'hears' them in memory. And as for rediscovering the time dimensions of childhood, the scrappy organisation of the first part of the book does not at all express the child's extended time spans and the size of events that swell with these, measured neither by seasons nor by dates.

Perhaps this section of the book is a collection of previously written fragments. There is, at least, one good story among the usual sort of reminiscence of punishments and pleasures that adults 'arrange' as the pattern of early years – the delightful tale of old man Paa Adatan, who, in return for the price of a meal from a market stall, undertook to defend any property against the arrival of 'dat nonsenseyeye Hitler one time'. His striking-force capacity ranged from drawing a magic line in the dust before a shop front ('If they try cross this line, guns go turn to broom for dem hand. Dem go begin dey sweeping dis very ground till I come back') to performing fearsome warrior dances. Like other wily misfits at different times and in different countries, he knew how to make of the world's villainy an excuse for his layabout existence: 'Na dis bastard Hitler. When war finish you go see. You go see me as I am, a man of myself.'

When the people in his village of Aké begin to be aware of the distant 1939–1945 war, the small boy Wole does seem to take over the interpretation of his own experience, maybe because by then he was just old enough to have sorted the hot and cold of sensuous impressions into some order available to memory. One forms the oblique picture of him for oneself, without the interference of the adult Soyinka's artifice. Wild Christian and HM are no longer ideograms of idiosyncrasy, but those most mysterious beings of our lives, parents. In the loving daily battle between the mother (who dispensed Christian charity and discipline as practically as the contents of her cooking pots) and father (scholarly agnostic towards both Christian and Nigerian gods) and their unpredictable child, he emerges as original innocence; not original sin, as his parents sometimes seemed to believe. Paying a family visit one Sunday at the palace of the Odemo, the titled head of HM's home village of Isara, the eight- or nine-year-old outraged the assembled African nobility by failing to prostrate himself before one of them. 'Coming directly from the Sunday service probably brought the response' to the child's head – 'If I don't prostrate myself to God, why should I prostrate to you? You are just a man like my father aren't you?'

Original innocence was still with the grown man when, knowing well, this time, he was defying the might of chauvinism and the world armaments industry, he took on his own 'side' as well as the Biafran 'side', identifying the only enemy as the war they were waging.

Parents are generally the scapegoats for all our adult inadequacies. Was there, then, something about Wole Soyinka's childhood, some security that produced the courage both physical and intellectual, and prepared him for the outlandish demands his era was to make of him? Yet his environment is revealed not as the natural paradise lesser writers edit, out of black yearning for a pre-conquest state of being or white yearning for a pre-industrial one, from the footage of reality. To begin with, his parents were middle-class, his mother a shopkeeper and debt-collector as well as a wild Christian, his father more interested in books than traditional status possessions; and the middle, in modern African societies, is the ground of the tug between the African way of life and the European way in which, as Chinua Achebe has definitively chronicled, things fall apart.

The tally of beatings, administered by every Aké adult in every kind of authority, is positively Victorian, although there's no suggestion that the British imported this style of punishment. In the 1940s in Nigeria even adolescent maidservants (black) were beaten by their mistresses (black) for wetting their sleeping mats; and, indeed, the high incidence of bed-wetters reported by the young Wole, who suffered creeping damp when sharing a communal sleeping mat, would in the West more likely be attributed to the beatings rather than 'cured' by them. Thirty-six strokes for an adolescent schoolboy who had 'made' a schoolgirl pregnant was regarded neither as cruel punishment nor as an injustice singling out one of the two it takes to make a baby.

Perhaps the trauma of all these beatings was dissolved in the witness that accompanied them? They did not take place in camera, between victim and castigator, alone with sin, but in the tumble of crowded households and even in a kind of dance through the streets. The purpose may have been public humiliation, but since every spectator had been or next time might be victim, there must have been a balm of fellow feeling flowing towards the wounds even as they were being inflicted. At any rate, the child never doubts that he is loved, which means that although he chafes against incidences of parental lack of understanding and a kind of sadistic, cock-fighting adult playfulness (setting him against his younger brother), he never seems to regard himself as unhappy, or rather seems never to have *expected* to be happier. Again, this may have something to do with the strong sense of community, not only with other children but with the particularly wide range of relationships the society provided – 'chiefs, king-makers, cult priests and priestesses, elders . . .'

Like a piece of *etú*, the rich locally woven cloth, social relations were a garment whose ceremonial weight was at the same time cosily enclosing. The child was never overawed by it; could snuggle up there just as the bedbugs (to the amused surprise of this middle-class white reader) had their own homely interstices in the Soyinka middle-class household with its servants and library. The different coordinates – which style of life goes with which class, which conventions with which kind of respect, which snobbishness with which pretension – are the source for non-Africans, who (of course) know only the styles of life that go with *their* social categories, of a fascination that takes hold with the hand of the child.

When the not-quite-heaven that was Wole's natal village of Aké extends, along with the parental relationship, to his father's natal territory at Isara, the fascination becomes complete. The grandfather, with a painful scarification ceremony, puts the boy in the care of the god Ogun just as Wild Christian has put him in the care of Christ. Again, the result is not a trauma but greater security for the child. And the writer finds his way to him with a felicity of evocation and expression on the 'axis of tastes and smells' along which the preparation of foods provides a family genealogy, a wonderfully sensuous *first* sense of self, other and belonging. The whiff of identical flavour in dishes prepared by different hands, different generations, is the child's own historiography and system of kinship. Just as the visitors and supplicants to HM's yard, despite the particular 'tang of smoke and indigo' they bring, remind one of Isaac Bashevis Singer's father's court in the Polish ghetto, so the patterns of living perceived through the tastebuds evoke Günter Grass's culinary interpretation of Europe's disasters and survivals. The pleasures of entering Wole Soyinka's childhood, for a stranger, consist not only in differences but in correspondences as well.

1982

Living in the Interregnum

Police files are our only claim to immortality.

Milan Kundera

I live at 6,000 feet in a society whirling, stamping, swaying with the force of revolutionary change. The vision is heady; the image of the demonic dance is accurate, not romantic: an image of actions springing from emotion, knocking deliberation aside. The city is Johannesburg, the country South Africa, and the time the last years of the colonial era in Africa.

It's inevitable that nineteenth-century colonialism should finally come to its end there, because there it reached its ultimate expression, open in the legalised land- and mineral-grabbing, open in the labour exploitation of indigenous peoples, open in the constitutionalised, institutionalised racism that was concealed by the British under the pious notion of uplift, the French and Portuguese under the sly notion of selective assimilation. An extraordinarily obdurate crossbreed of Dutch, German, English, French in the South African white settler population produced a bluntness that unveiled everyone's refined white racism: the flags of European civilisation dropped, and there it was, unashamedly, the ugliest creation of man, and they baptised the thing in the Dutch Reformed Church, called it *apartheid*, coining the ultimate term for every manifestation, over the ages, in many countries, of race prejudice. Every country could see its semblances there; and most peoples.

The sun that never set over one or other of the nineteenth-century colonial empires of the world is going down finally in South Africa. Since the black uprisings of the mid-seventies, coinciding with the independence of Mozambique and Angola, and later that of Zimbabwe, the past has begun rapidly to drop out of sight, even for those who would have liked to go on living in it. Historical coordinates don't fit life any longer; new ones, where they exist, have couplings not to the rulers, but to the ruled. It is not for nothing that I chose as an epigraph for my most lately written novel a quotation from Gramsci: 'The old is dying, and the new cannot be born; in this interregnum there arises a great diversity of morbid symptoms.'

In this interregnum, I and all my countrymen and women are living. I am going, quite frequently, to let events personally experienced as I was thinking towards or writing this paper interrupt theoretical flow, because this interaction – this essential disruption, this breaking in upon the existential coherence we call concept – is the very state of being I must attempt to convey. I have never before expressed so personal a point of view. Apart from the usual Joycean reasons of secrecy and cunning – to which I would add jealous hoarding of private experience for transmutation into fiction – there has been for me a peculiarly South African taboo.

In the official South African consciousness, the ego is white: it has always seen all South Africa as ordered around it. Even the ego that seeks to abdicate this alienation does so in an assumption of its own salvation that in itself expresses ego and alienation. And the Western world press, itself overwhelmingly white, constantly feeds this ego from its own. Visiting journalists, parliamentarians, congressmen and congresswomen come to South Africa to ask whites what is going to happen there. They meet blacks through whites; they rarely take the time and trouble, on their own initiative, to encounter more than the man who comes into the hotel bedroom to take away the empty beer bottles. With the exception of films made clandestinely by South African political activists, black and white, about resistance events, most foreign television documentaries, while condemning the whites out of their own mouths, are nevertheless preoccupied with what will happen to whites when the apartheid regime goes.

I have shunned the arrogance of interpreting my country through the private life that, as Theodor Adorno puts it, 'drags on only as an appendage of the social process' in a time and place of which I am a part. Now I am going to break the inhibition or destroy the privilege of privacy, whichever way you look at it. I have to offer myself as my most closely observed specimen from the interregnum; yet I remain a writer, not a public speaker: nothing I say here will be as true as my fiction.

There is another reason for confession. The particular segment of South African society to which I belong, by the colour of my skin, whether I like it or not, represents a crisis that has a particular connection with the Western world. I think that may become self-evident before I arrive at the point of explication; it is not the old admitted complicity in the slave trade or the price of raw materials.

I have used the term 'segment' in defining my place in South African society because within the white section of that society – less than one-fifth of the total population now,[1] predicted to drop to one-seventh by the year 2000 – there is a segment preoccupied, in the interregnum, neither by plans to run away from nor merely by ways to survive physically and economically in the black state that is coming. I cannot give you numbers for this segment, but in measure of some sort of faith in the possibility of structuring society humanly, in the possession of skills and intellect to devote to this end, there is something to offer the future. How to offer it is our preoccupation. Since skills, technical and intellectual, can be bought in markets other than those of the vanquished colonial power, although they are important as a commodity ready to hand, they do not constitute a claim on the future.

That claim rests on something else: how to offer *one's self*.

In the eyes of the black majority which will rule a new South Africa, whites of former South Africa will have to redefine themselves in a new collective life within new structures. From the all-white parliament to the all-white country club and the separate 'white' television channels, it is not a matter of blacks taking over white institutions, it is one of conceiving of institutions – from

---

1   Total population 1980, 20 million, of which 4.5 million are white. *Survey of Race Relations in South Africa 1981*, South African Institute of Race Relations, 1981.

nursery schools to government departments – that reflect a societal structure vastly different from that built to the specifications of white power and privilege. This vast difference will be evident even if capitalism survives, since South Africa's capitalism, like South Africa's whites-only democracy, has been unlike anyone else's. For example, free enterprise among us is for whites only, since black capitalists may trade only, and with many limitations on their 'free' enterprise, in black ghettos.

A more equitable distribution of wealth may be enforced by laws. The hierarchy of perception that white institutions and living habits implant throughout daily experience in every white, from childhood, can be changed only by whites themselves, from within. The weird ordering of the collective life, in South Africa, has slipped its special contact lens into the eyes of whites; we actually *see* blacks differently, which includes not seeing, not noticing their unnatural absence, since there are so many perfectly ordinary venues of daily life – the cinema, for instance – where blacks have never been allowed in, and so one has forgotten that they could be, might be, encountered there.

I am writing in my winter quarters, at an old deal table on a verandah in the sun; out of the corner of my eye I see a piece of junk mail, the brochure of a chain bookstore, assuring me of constantly expanding service and showing the staff of a newly opened branch – Ms So-and-So, Mr Such-and-Such, and (one black face) 'Gladys'. What a friendly, informal form of identification in an 'equal opportunity' enterprise! Gladys is seen by fellow workers, by the photographer who noted down names, and – it is assumed – readers, quite differently from the way the white workers are seen. I gaze at her as they do . . . She is simply 'Gladys', the convenient handle by which she is taken up by the white world, used and put down again, like the glass the king drinks from in Rilke's poem.[2] Her surname, her African name, belongs to Soweto, which her

---

2   Rainer Maria Rilke, 'Ein Frauenschicksal' (A Woman's Fate), in *Selected Poems of Rainer Maria Rilke*, translated by C. F. MacIntyre, University of California Press, Berkeley 1941.

smiling white companions are less likely ever to visit than New York or London.

The successfully fitted device in the eye of the beholder is something the average white South African is not conscious of, for apartheid is above all a habit; the unnatural seems natural – a far from banal illustration of Hannah Arendt's banality of evil. The segment of the white population to which I belong has become highly conscious of a dependency on distorted vision induced since childhood; and we are aware that with the inner eye 'we have seen too much ever to be innocent'.[3] But this kind of awareness, represented by white guilt in the 1950s, has been sent by us off into the sunset, since, as Czeslaw Milosz puts it, 'guilt saps modern man's belief in the value of his own perceptions and judgments', and we have need of ours. We have to believe in our ability to find new perceptions, and our ability to judge their truth. Along with weeping over what's done, we've given up rejoicing in what Günter Grass calls headbirths, those Athenian armchair deliveries of the future presented to blacks by whites.

Not all blacks even concede that whites can have any part in the new that cannot yet be born. An important black leader who does, Bishop Desmond Tutu, defines that participation:

This is what I consider to be the place of the white man in this – popularly called – liberation struggle. I am firmly non-racial and so welcome the participation of all, both black and white, in the struggle for the new South Africa which must come whatever the cost. But I want to state that at this stage the leadership of the struggle must be firmly in black hands. They must determine what will be the priorities and the strategy of the struggle. Whites unfortunately have the habit of taking over and usurping the leadership and taking the crucial decisions, largely, I suppose, because of the head start they had in education and experience of this kind. The point is that however much they want to identify with blacks it is an existential fact . . . that they have not really

3   Edmundo Desnoes, *Memories of Underdevelopment*, Penguin, Harmondsworth, 1973.

been victims of this baneful oppression and exploitation. It is a divide that can't be crossed and that must give blacks a primacy in determining the course and goal of the struggle. Whites must be willing to follow.[4]

Blacks must learn to talk; whites must learn to listen – wrote the black South African poet Mongane Wally Serote, in the seventies. This is the premise on which the white segment to which I belong lives its life at present. Does it sound like an abdication of the will? That is because you who live in a democracy are accustomed to exerting the right to make abstract statements of principle for which, at least, the structures of practical realisation exist; the symbolic action of the like-minded in signing a letter to a newspaper or in lobbying Congress is a reminder of constitutional rights to be invoked. For us, Tutu's premise enjoins a rousing of the will, a desperate shaking into life of the faculty of rebellion against unjust laws that has been outlawed by the dying power, and faculties of renewal that often are rebuffed by the power that is struggling to emerge. The rider Desmond Tutu didn't add to his statement is that although white support is expected to be active, it is also expected that whites' different position in the still-standing structures of the old society will require actions that, while complementary to those of blacks, must be different from the blacks'. Whites are expected to find their own forms of struggle, which can only sometimes coincide with those of blacks.

That there can be, at least, this coincident cooperation is reassuring; that, at least, should be a straightforward form of activism. But it is not; for in this time of morbid symptoms there are contradictions within the black liberation struggle itself, based not only, as would be expected, on the opposing ideological alignments of the world outside, but on the moral confusion of claims – on land, on peoples – from the pre-colonial past in relation to the unitary state the majority of blacks and the segment of whites are avowed to. So, for whites, it is not simply a matter of follow-the-leader

---

4   Bishop Desmond Tutu, *Frontline*, no. 5, vol. 12, April 1982.

behind blacks; it's taking on, as blacks do, choices to be made out of confusion, empirically, pragmatically, ideologically or idealistically about the practical moralities of the struggle. This is the condition, imposed by history, if you like, in those areas of action where black and white participation coincides.

I am at a public meeting at the Johannesburg City Hall one night, after working at this paper during the day. The meeting is held under the auspices of the Progressive Federal Party, the official opposition in the all-white South African parliament. The issue is a deal being made between the South African government and the kingdom of Swaziland whereby 3,000 square miles of South African territory and 850,000 South African citizens, part of the Zulu 'homeland' KwaZulu, would be given to Swaziland. The principal speakers are Chief Gatsha Buthelezi, leader of 5.5 million Zulus, Bishop Desmond Tutu, and Mr Ray Swart, a white liberal and a leader of the Progressive Federal Party. Chief Buthelezi has consistently refused to take so-called independence for KwaZulu, but – although declaring himself for the banned African National Congress – by accepting all stages of so-called self-government up to the final one has transgressed the non-negotiable principle of the African National Congress, a unitary South Africa.

Bishop Tutu upholds the principle of a unitary South Africa. The Progressive Federal Party's constitution provides for a federal structure in a new, non-racial South Africa, recognising as de facto entities the 'homelands' whose creation by the apartheid government the party nevertheless opposes. Also on the platform are members of the Black Sash, the white women's organisation that has taken a radical stand as a white ally of the black struggle; these women support a unitary South Africa. In the audience of about two thousand, a small number of whites is lost among exuberant, ululating, applauding Zulus. Order – and what's more, amicability – is kept by Buthelezi's marshals, equipped, beneath the garb of a private militia drawn from his tribal Inkatha movement, with Zulu muscle in place of guns.

What is Bishop Tutu doing here? He doesn't recognise the 'homelands'.

What are the Black Sash women doing here? They don't recognise the 'homelands'.

What is the Progressive Federal Party doing – a party firmly dedicated to constitutional action only – hosting a meeting where the banned black liberation salute and battle cry – '*Amandhla! Awethu!*': 'Power – to the people!' – is shaking the columns of municipal doric, and a black man's tribal army instead of the South African police is keeping the peace?

What am I doing here, applauding Gatsha Buthelezi and Ray Swart? I don't recognise the homelands nor do I support a federal South Africa.

I was there – *they* were there – because, removed from its areas of special interest (KwaZulu's 'national' concern with land and people belonging to the Zulus), the issue was yet another government device to buy support for a proposed 'constellation' of southern African states gathered protectively around the present South African regime, and to disposses black South Africans of their South African citizenship, thus reducing the ratio of black to white population.

Yet the glow of my stinging palms cooled; what a paradox I had accommodated in myself! Moved by a display of tribal loyalty when I believe in black unity, applauding a 'homelands' leader, above all, scandalised by the excision of part of a 'homeland' from South Africa when the 'homelands' policy is itself the destruction of the country as an entity. But these are the confusions blacks have to live with, and if I am making any claim to accompany them beyond apartheid, so must I.

The state of interregnum is a state of Hegel's disintegrated consciousness, of contradictions. It is from its internal friction that energy somehow must be struck, for us whites; energy to break the vacuum of which we are subconsciously aware, for however hated and shameful the collective life of apartheid and its structures has been to us, there is, now, the unadmitted fear of being without structures. The interregnum is not only between two social orders but between two identities, one known and discarded, the other unknown and undetermined.

Whatever the human cost of the liberation struggle, whatever 'Manichaean poisons'[5] must be absorbed as stimulants in the interregnum, the black knows he will be at home, at last, in the future. The white who has declared himself or herself for that future, who belongs to the white segment that was never at home in white supremacy, does not know whether he will find his home at last. It is assumed, not only by racists, that this depends entirely on the willingness of blacks to let him in; but we, if we live out our situation consciously, proceeding from the Pascalian wager that that home of the white African exists, know that this depends also on our finding our way there out of the perceptual clutter of curled photographs of master and servant relationships, the 78 rpms of history repeating the conditioning of the past.

A black man I may surely call my friend because we have survived a time when he did not find it possible to accept a white's friendship, and a time when I didn't think I could accept that he should decide when that time was past, said to me this year, 'Whites have to learn to struggle.' It was not an admonition but a sincere encouragement. Expressed in political terms, the course of our friendship, his words and his attitude, signify the phasing out or passing usefulness of the extreme wing of the Black Consciousness movement, with its separatism of the past ten years, and the return to the tenets of the most broadly based and prestigious of black movements, the banned African National Congress. These are non-racialism, belief that race oppression is part of the class struggle, and recognition that it is possible for whites to opt out of class and race privilege and identify with black liberation.

My friend was not, needless to say, referring to those whites, from Abram Fischer to Helen Joseph and Neil Aggett, who have risked and in some cases lost their lives in the political struggle with apartheid. It would be comfortable to assume that he was not referring, either, to the articulate outriders of the white segment, intellectuals, writers, lawyers, students, church and civil rights progressives, who keep the whips of protest cracking. But I know

<hr>

5   Czeslaw Milosz, 'The Accuser', in *Bells in Winter*, Ecco, New York, 1978.

he *was*, after all, addressing those of us belonging to the outriders on whose actions the newspapers report and the secret police keep watch, as we prance back and forth ever closer to the fine line between being concerned citizens and social revolutionaries. Perhaps the encouragement was meant for us as well as the base of the segment – those in the audience but not up on the platform, young people and their parents' generation, who must look for some effective way, in the living of their own personal lives, to join the struggle for liberation from racism.

For a long time, such whites have felt that we are doing all we can, short of violence – a terrible threshold none of us is willing to cross, though aware that all this may mean is that it will be left to blacks to do so. But now blacks are asking a question to which every white must have a personal answer, on an issue that cannot be dealt with by a show of hands at a meeting or a signature to a petition; an issue that comes home and enters every family. Blacks are now asking why whites who believe apartheid is something that must be abolished, not defended, continue to submit to army call-up.

We whites have assumed that army service was an example of Czeslaw Milosz's 'powerlessness of the individual involved in a mechanism that works independently of his will'. If you refuse military service your only options are to leave the country or go to prison. Conscientious objection is not recognised in South Africa at present; legislation may establish it in some form soon, but if this is to be, is working as an army clerk not functioning as part of the war machine?

These are reasons enough for all – except a handful of men who choose prison on religious rather than on political grounds – to go into the South African army despite their opposition to apartheid. These are not reasons enough for them to do so, on the condition on which blacks can accept whites' dedication to mutual liberation. Between black and white attitudes to struggle there stands the overheard remark of a young black woman: 'I break the law because I am alive.' We whites have still to thrust the spade under the roots of our lives; for most of us, including myself, struggle is still something that has a place. But for blacks it is everywhere or nowhere.

> What is poetry which does not save nations or peoples?
>
> Czeslaw Milosz

I have already delineated my presence in my home country on the scale of a minority within a minority. Now I shall reduce my claim to significance still further. A white; a dissident white; a white writer. I must presume that although the problems of a white writer are of no importance compared with the liberation of 23.5 million black people, the peculiar relation of the writer in South Africa as interpreter, both to South Africans and to the world, of a society in struggle, makes the narrow corridor I can lead down one in which doors fly open on the tremendous happening experienced by blacks.

For longer than the first half of this century the experience of blacks in South Africa was known to the world as it was interpreted by whites. The first widely read imaginative works exploring the central fact of South African life – racism – were written in the 1920s by whites, William Plomer and Sarah Gertrude Millin. What have been recognised now as the classics of early black literature, the works of Herbert and Rolfes Dhlomo, Thomas Mofolo and Sol Plaatje, were read by the literate section of the South African black population, were little known among South African whites, and unknown outside South Africa. These writers' moralistic works dealt with contemporary black life, but their fiction was mainly historical, a desperate attempt to secure, in art forms of an imposed culture, an identity and history discounted and torn up by that culture.

In the fifties, urban blacks – Es'kia Mphahlele, Lewis Nkosi, Can Themba, Bloke Modisane, following Peter Abrahams – began to write in English only, and about the urban industrialised experience in which black and white chafed against one another across colour barriers. The work of these black writers interested both black and white at that improvised level known as intellectual, in

South Africa: aware would be a more accurate term, designating awareness that the white middle-class establishment was not, as it claimed, the paradigm of South African life and white culture was not the definitive South African culture. Somewhere at the black writers' elbows, as they wrote, was the joggle of independence coming to one colonised country after another, north of South Africa. But they wrote ironically of their lives under oppression; as victims, not fighters. And even those black writers who were political activists, like the novelist Alex la Guma and the poet Dennis Brutus, made of their ideologically channelled bitterness not more than the Aristotelian catharsis, creating in the reader empathy with the oppressed rather than rousing rebellion against repression.

The fiction of white writers also produced the Aristotelian effect – and included in the price of hardback or paperback a catharsis of white guilt, for writer and reader. (It was at this stage, incidentally, that reviewers abroad added their dime's worth of morbid symptoms to our own by creating 'courageous' as a literary value for South African writers . . .) The subject of both black and white writers – which was the actual entities of South African life instead of those defined by separate entrances for white and black – was startingly new and important; whatever any writer, black or white, could dare to explore there was considered ground gained for advance in the scope of all writers. There had been no iconoclastic tradition; only a single novel, William Plomer's *Turbott Wolfe*, written thirty years before, whose understanding of *what our subject really was* was still a decade ahead of our time when he phrased the total apothegm: 'The native question – it's not a question, it's an answer.'

In the seventies black writers began to give that answer – for themselves. It had been vociferous in the consciousness of resistance politics, manifest in political action – black mass organisations, the African National Congress, the Pan-Africanist Congress, and others – in the sixties. But except at the oral folk-literature level of 'freedom' songs, it was an answer that had not come, yet, from the one source that had never been in conquered territory, not even when industrialisation conscripted where military conquest had already devastated: the territory of the subconscious, where a people's own particular way of making sense and dignity of life – the base of its culture – remains unget-at-able. Writers, and not politicians, are its spokespeople.

With the outlawing of black political organisations, the banning of freedom songs and platform speeches, there came from blacks a changed attitude towards culture, and towards literature as verbal, easily accessible culture. Many black writers had been in conflict – and challenged by political activists: are you going to fight or write? Now they were told, in the rhetoric of the time: there is no conflict if you make your pen our people's weapon.

The Aristotelian catharsis, relieving black self-pity and white guilt, was clearly not the mode in which black writers could give the answer black resistance required from them. The iconoclastic mode, though it had its function where race fetishists had set up their china idols in place of 'heathen' wooden ones, was too ironic and detached, other-directed. Black people had to be brought back to themselves. Black writers arrived, out of their own situation, at Brecht's discovery: their audience needed to be educated to be *astonished at the circumstances under which they functioned.*[6] They began to show blacks that their living conditions are their story.

South Africa does not lack its Chernyshevskys to point out that the highroad of history is not the sidewalks of fashionable white Johannesburg's suburban shopping malls any more than it was that of the Nevsky Prospekt.[7] In the bunks of migratory labourers, the 4 a.m. queues between one-room family and factory, the drunken dreams argued round braziers, is the history of blacks' defeat by conquest, the scale of the lack of value placed on them by whites, the degradation of their own acquiescence in that value; the salvation of revolt is there, too, a match dropped by the builders of every ghetto, waiting to be struck.

---

6   Walter Benjamin, 'What Is Epic Theater?' *Illuminations*, Schocken, New York, 1969.

7   Nikolai G. Chernyshevsky, *Polnoye sobraniye sochinenii*, vol. 3. Paraphrased from the quotation in the English translation by Tibor Szamuely, 'The Highroad of History Is Not the Sidewalk of the Nevsky Prospekt', *The Russian Tradition*, edited by Robert Conquest, McGraw-Hill, New York, 1975.

The reason for the difficulty, even boredom, many whites experience when reading stories or watching plays by blacks in which, as they say, 'nothing happens', is that the experience conveyed is not 'the development of actions' but 'the representation of conditions', a mode of artistic revelation and experience for those in whose life dramatic content is in its conditions.[8]

This mode of writing was the beginning of the black writer's function as a revolutionary; it was also the beginning of a conception of himself differing from that of the white writer's self-image. The black writer's consciousness of himself as a writer comes now from his participation in those living conditions; in the judgement of his people, that is what makes him a writer – the authority of the experience itself, not the way he perceives it and transforms it into words. Tenets of criticism are accordingly based on the critic's participation in those same living conditions, not on his ability to judge how well the writer has achieved 'the disposition of natural material to a formal end that shall enlighten the imagination' – this definition of art by Anthony Burgess would be regarded by many blacks as arising from premises based on white living conditions and the thought patterns these determine: an arabesque of smoke from an expensive cigar. If we have our Chernyshevskys we are short on Herzens. Literary standards and standards of human justice are hopelessly confused in the interregnum. Bad enough that in the case of white South African writers some critics at home and abroad are afraid to reject sensationalism and crass banality of execution so long as the subject of a work is 'courageous'. For black writers the syllogism of talent goes like this: all blacks are brothers; all brothers are equal; therefore you cannot be a better writer than I am. The black writer who questions the last proposition is betraying the first two.

As a fellow writer, I myself find it difficult to accept, even for the cause of black liberation to which I am committed as a white South African citizen, that a black writer of imaginative power, whose craftsmanship is equal to what he has to say, must not be

---

8   Walter Benjamin, 'What Is Epic Theater?'

regarded above someone who has emerged – admirably – from
political imprisonment with a scrap of paper on which there is
jotted an alliterative arrangement of protest slogans. For me, the
necessity for the black writer to find imaginative modes equal to
his existential reality goes without question. But I cannot accept
that he must deny, as proof of solidarity with his people's struggle,
the torturous inner qualities of prescience and perception that will
always differentiate him from others and which make of him – a
writer. I cannot accept, either, that he should have served on him, as
the black writer now has, an orthodoxy – a kit of emotive phrases,
an unwritten index of subjects, a typology.

The problem is that agitprop, not recognised under that or
any other name, has become the first contemporary art form that
many black South Africans feel they can call their own. It fits
their anger; and this is taken as proof that it is an organic growth
of black creation freeing itself, instead of the old shell that it is,
inhabited many times by the anger of others. I know that agitprop binds the artist with the means by which it aims to free the
minds of the people. I can see, now, how often it thwarts both
the black writer's common purpose to master his art and revolutionary purpose to change the nature of art, create new norms and
forms out of and for a people recreating themselves. But how can
my black fellow writer agree with me, even admit the conflict I
set up in him by these statements? There are those who secretly
believe, but few who would assert publicly, with Gabriel García
Márquez: 'The duty of a writer – the revolutionary duty, if you
like – is simply to write well.' The black writer in South Africa
feels he has to accept the criteria of his people because in no other
but the community of black deprivation is he in possession of selfhood. It is only through unreserved, exclusive identification with
blacks that he can break the alienation of being 'other' for nearly
350 years in the white-ordered society, and only through submitting to the beehive category of 'cultural worker', programmed,
that he can break the alienation of the artist/elitist in the black
mass of industrial workers and peasants.

And, finally, he can toss the conflict back into my lap with

Camus's words: 'Is it possible to be in history while still referring to values which go beyond it?'

The black writer is 'in history' and its values threaten to force out the transcendent ones of art. The white, as writer and South African, does not know his place 'in history' at this stage, in this time.

There are two absolutes in my life. One is that racism is evil – human damnation in the Old Testament sense – and no compromises, as well as sacrifices, should be too great in the fight against it. The other is that a writer is a being in whose sensibility is fused what Lukács calls the duality of inwardness and outside world, and he must never be asked to sunder this union. The coexistence of these absolutes often seems irreconcilable within one life, for me. In another country, another time, they would present no conflict because they would operate in unrelated parts of existence; in South Africa now they have to be coordinates for which the coupling must be found. The morality of life and the morality of art have broken out of their categories in social flux. If you cannot reconcile them, they cannot be kept from one another's throats, within you.

For me, Lukács's 'divinatory-intuitive grasping of the unattained and therefore inexpressible meaning of life' is what a writer, poorly evolved for the task as he is, is made for. As fish that swim under the weight of many dark fathoms look like any other fish but on careful examination are found to have no eyes, so writers, looking pretty much like other human beings, but moving deep under the surface of human lives, have at least some faculties of supra-observation and hyperperception not known to others. If a writer does not go down and use these – why, he's just a blind fish.

Exactly – says the new literary orthodoxy: he doesn't see what is happening in the visible world, among the people, on the level of their action, where battle is done with racism every day. On the contrary, say I, he brings back with him the thematic life-material that underlies and motivates their actions. 'Art lies at the heart of all events', Joseph Brodsky writes. It is from there, in the depths of being, that the most important intuition of revolutionary faith comes: the people know what to do, before the leaders. It was from that level that the yearning of black schoolchildren for a decent education was changed into a revolt in 1976; their strength came from the deep silt of repression and the abandoned wrecks of uprisings that sank there before they were born. It was from that level that an action of ordinary people for their own people made a few lines low down on a newspaper page, the other day: when some migrant contract workers from one of the 'homelands' were being laid off at a factory, workers with papers of permanent residence in the 'white' area asked to be dismissed in their place, since the possession of papers meant they could at least work elsewhere, whereas the migrant workers would be sent back to the 'homelands', jobless.

'Being an "author" has been unmasked as a role that, whether conformist or not, remains inescapably responsible to a given order.' Nowhere in the world is Susan Sontag's statement truer than in South Africa. The white writer has to make the decision whether to remain responsible to the dying white order – and even as dissident, if he goes no further than that position, he remains *negatively* within the white order – or to declare himself positively as answerable to the order struggling to be born. And to declare himself for the latter is only the beginning; as it is for whites in a less specialised position, only more so. He has to try to find a way to reconcile the irreconcilable within himself, establish his relation to the culture of a new kind of posited community, non-racial but somehow conceived with and led by blacks.

I have entered into this commitment with trust and a sense of discovering reality, coming alive in a new way – I believe the novels and stories I have written in the last seven or eight years reflect this – for a South Africa in which white middle-class values and mores contradict realities has long become the unreality, to me. Yet I admit that I am, indeed, determined to find my place 'in history' while still referring as a writer to the values that are beyond history. I shall never give them up.

Can the artist go through the torrent with his precious bit of talent tied up in a bundle on his head? I don't know yet. I can only report that the way to begin entering history out of a dying white regime is through setbacks, encouragements and rebuffs from others, and frequent disappointments in oneself. A necessary learning process . . .

I take a break from writing.

I am in a neighbouring black country at a conference on 'Culture and Resistance'. It is being held outside South Africa because exiled artists and those of us who still live and work in South Africa cannot meet at home. Some white artists have not come because, not without reason, they fear the consequences of being seen, by South African secret police spies, in the company of exiles who belong to political organisations banned in South Africa, notably the African National Congress; some are not invited because the organisers regard their work and political views as reactionary. I am dubbed the blacks' darling by some whites back home because I have been asked to give the keynote address at a session devoted to literature; but I wonder if those who think me favoured would care to take the flak I know will be coming at me from those corners of the hall where black separatists group. They are here not so much out of democratic right as out of black solidarity; para-doxically, since the conference is in itself a declaration that in the conviction of participants and organisers the liberation struggle and post-apartheid culture are non-racial. Yet there is that bond of living conditions that lassos all blacks within a loyalty containing, without constraining or resolving, bitter political differences.

Do I think white writers should write about blacks?

The artless question from the floor disguises both a personal attack on my work and an edict publicly served upon white writers by the same orthodoxy that prescribes for blacks. In the case of whites, it proscribes the creation of black characters – and by the same token, flipped head-to-tails, with which the worth of black writers is measured: the white writer does not share the *total* living conditions of blacks, therefore he must not write about them. There are some whites – not writers, I believe – in the hall who share this view. In the ensuing tense exchange I reply that there are whole

areas of human experience, in work situations – on farms, in factories, in the city, for example – where black and white have been
observing one another and interacting for nearly 350 years. I challenge my challenger to deny that there are things we know about
each other that are never spoken, but are there to be written – and
received with the amazement and consternation, on both sides, of
having been found out. Within those areas of experience, limited
but intensely revealing, there is every reason why white should
create black and black white characters. For myself, I have created
black characters in my fiction: whether I have done so successfully
or not is for the reader to decide. What's certain is that there is no
representation of our social reality without that strange area of our
lives in which we have knowledge of one another.

I do not acquit myself so honestly a little later, when persecution
of South African writers by banning is discussed. Someone links this
with the persecution of writers in the Soviet Union, and a young
man leaps to reply that the percentage of writers to population is
higher in the Soviet Union than in any other part of the world and
that Soviet writers work 'in a trench of peace and security'.

The aptness of the bizarre image, the hell for the haven he wishes
to illustrate, brings no smiles behind hands among us; beyond the
odd word-substitution is, indeed, a whole arsenal of tormented
contradictions that could explode the conference.

Someone says, out of silence, quietly and distinctly: *'Bullshit.'*

There is silence again. I don't take the microphone and tell the
young man: there is not a contrast to be drawn between the Soviet
Union's treatment of writers and that of South Africa, there is a
close analogy – South Africa bans and silences writers just as the
Soviet Union does, although we do not have resident censors in
South African publishing houses and dissident writers are not sent
to mental hospitals. I am silent. I am silent because, in the debates
of the interregnum, any criticism of the Communist system is
understood as a defence of the capitalist system which has brought
forth the pact of capitalism and racism that is apartheid, with its
treason trials to match Stalin's trials, its detentions of dissidents
to match Soviet detentions, its banishment and brutal uprooting

of communities and individual lives to match, if not surpass, the gulag. Repression in South Africa has been and is being lived through; repression elsewhere is an account in a newspaper, book or film. The choice, for blacks, cannot be distanced into any kind of objectivity: they believe in the existence of the lash they feel. Nothing could be less than better than what they have known as the 'peace and security' of capitalism.[9]

I was a coward and often shall be one again, in my actions and statements as a citizen of the interregnum; it is a place of shifting ground, forecast for me in the burning slag heaps of coal mines that children used to ride across with furiously pumping bicycle pedals and flying hearts, in the Transvaal town where I was born.

And now the time has come to say I believe the Western world stands on shifting ground with me, because in some strange pilgrimage through the choices of our age and their consequences the democratic left of the Western world has arrived by many planned routes and plodding detours at the same unforeseen destination. The ideal of social democracy seems to be an abandoned siding. There was consternation when, early this year, Susan Sontag had the great courage and honesty publicly to accuse herself and other American intellectuals of the left of having been afraid to condemn the repression committed by Communist regimes because this was seen as an endorsement of America's war on Vietnam and collusion with brutish rightist regimes in Latin America.

This moral equivocation on the part of the American left draws parallel with mine at the writer's congress, far away in Africa, that she has given me the courage, at second hand, to confess. Riding handlebar to handlebar across the coal slag, both equivocations reveal the same fear. What is its meaning? It is fear of the abyss, of the greater interregnum of human hopes and spirit where against Sartre's socialism as the 'horizon of the world' is silhouetted the chained outline of Poland's Solidarity, and all around, in the ditches of El Salvador, in the prisons of Argentina

---

9 *The Star*, Johannesburg, 4 August 1982.

and South Africa, in the rootless habitations of Beirut, are the victims of Western standards of humanity.

I lie and the American left lies not because the truth is that Western capitalism has turned out to be just and humane, after all, but because we feel we have nothing to offer, now, except the rejection of it. Communism, in practice since 1917, has turned out not to be just or humane either; has failed, even more cruelly than capitalism. Does this mean we have to tell the poor and dispossessed of the world there is nothing to be done but turn back from Communist bosses to capitalist bosses?

In South Africa's rich capitalist state stuffed with Western finance, 50,000 black children a year die from malnutrition and malnutrition-related diseases, while the West piously notes that Communist states cannot provide their people with meat and butter. In two decades in South Africa, three million black people have been ejected from the context of their lives, forcibly removed from homes and jobs and 'resettled' in arid, undeveloped areas by decree of a white government supported by Western capital. It is difficult to point out to black South Africans that the forms of Western capitalism are changing towards a broad social justice in the example of countries like Sweden, Denmark, Holland and Austria, with their mixed welfare economies, when all black South Africans know of Western capitalism is political and economic terror. And this terror is not some relic of the colonial past; it is being financed *now* by Western democracies – concurrently with Western capitalist democracy's own evolution towards social justice.

The fact is, black South Africans and whites like myself no longer believe in the ability of Western capitalism to bring about social justice where we live. We see no evidence of that possibility in our history or our living present. Whatever the Western democracies have done for themselves, they have failed and are failing, in their great power and influence, to do for us. This is the answer to those who ask, 'Why call for an alternative left? Why not an alternative capitalism?' Show us an alternative capitalism working from without for real justice in our country. What are the conditions

attached to the International Monetary Fund loan of approximately
$1 billion that would oblige the South African government to stop
population removals, to introduce a single standard of unsegre-
gated education for all, to reinstate millions of black South Africans
deprived of citizenship?[10]

If the disillusioned American left believes the injustices of
Communism cannot be reformed, must it be assumed that those of
capitalism's longer history, constantly monitored by the compassionate hand of liberalism, can be? The dictum I quoted earlier
carried, I know, its supreme irony: most leaders in the Communist
world have betrayed the basic intuition of democracy, that 'the
people know what to do' – which is perhaps why Susan Sontag
saw Communism as fascism with a human face. But I think we
can, contrary to her view, 'distinguish' among Communism and
socialist democracies just as among Western democracies, and I am
sure, beyond the heat of a platform statement, so does she. If the
US and Sweden are not Botha's South Africa, was Allende's Chile
East Germany, though both were in the socialist camp?

We of the left, everywhere, surely must 'distinguish' to the point
where we take up the real import of Sontag's essential challenge to
love truth enough, pick up the blood-dirtied, shamed cause of the
left, and attempt to recreate the left in accordance with what it was
meant to be, not what sixty-five years of power-perversion have
made of it. If, as she rightly says, once we did not understand the
nature of Communist tyranny, now we do, just as we have always
understood at first hand the nature of capitalist tyranny. This is
not a Manichaean equation – which is god and which the devil?
is not a question the evidence could easily decide, anyway – and
it does not license withdrawal and hopelessness. We have surely
learned by now something of where socialism goes wrong, which
of its precepts are deadly dangerous and lead, in practice, to fascist
control of labour and total suppression of individual freedom. Will

---

10 The US has a 20 per cent slice under the weighted voting system of the IMF and so
outvoted all loan opponents combined. The US consequently surely has a corresponding
responsibility for how the money South Africa receives is being spent. Is there any evidence that
this responsibility is being taken up?

the witchcraft of modern times not be exorcised, eventually, by this knowledge?

In the interregnum in which we coexist, the American left – disillusioned by the failure of Communism – needs to muster with the democratic left of the third world – living evidence of the failure of capitalism – the cosmic obstinacy to believe in and work towards the possibility of an alternative left, a democracy without the economic and military terror which exists, at present, in both left and right regimes. If we cannot, the possibility of real social democracy will die out, for our age, and who knows when, after what even bloodier age, it will be rediscovered.

There is no forgetting how we could live if only we could find the way. We must continue to be tormented by the ideal. This is where the responsibility of the American left – and liberals? – meets mine. Without the will to tramp towards that possibility, no relations of whites, of the West, with the West's formerly subject peoples can ever be free of the past, because the past, for them, was the jungle of Western capitalism, not the light the missionaries thought they brought with them.

1983

The Idea of Gardening

J. M. Coetzee's *The Life and Times of Michael K*

Allegory is generally regarded as a superior literary form. It is thought to clear the reader's lungs of the transient and fill them with a deep breath of transcendence. Man becomes Everyman (that bore).

From the writer's point of view, allegory is no more than one among other forms. But I believe there is a distinction between the writer's conscious choice of it, and its choice of him/her. In the first instance, loosened by time from ancient sources of myth, magic and morality, allegory is sometimes snatched from the air to bear aloft a pedestrian imagination or to distance the writer, for reasons of his own, from his subject. In the second instance, allegory is a *discovered* dimension, the emergence of a meaning not aimed for by the writer but present once the book is written.

J.M. Coetzee, a writer with an imagination that soars like a lark and sees from up there like an eagle, chose allegory for his first few novels. It seemed he did so out of a kind of opposing desire to hold himself clear of events and their daily, grubby, tragic consequences in which, like everyone else living in South Africa, he is up to the neck, and about which he had an inner compulsion to write. So here was allegory as a stately fastidiousness; or a state of shock. He seemed able to deal with the horror he saw written on the sun[1] only – if brilliantly – if this were to be projected into another time and plane. His *Waiting for the Barbarians* was the North Pole to which the agitprop of agonised black writers (and some white ones hitching a lift to the bookshop on the armoured car) was the South Pole; a world to be dealt with lies in between. It is the life and times of Michael K, and Coetzee has taken it up now.

Michael K (the initial probably stands for Kotze or Koekemoer and has no reference, nor need it have, to Kafka) is not Everyman. In fact he is marked out, from birth, by a harelip indelibly described as curled like a snail's foot. His mother is a servant in Cape Town, which means he is a so-called coloured, and he grows up fatherless in a home for handicapped children. His deformity distorts his speech and his actual and self-images. He shrinks from the difficulty of communication through words and the repugnance he sees holding him off, in people's eyes; thus he appears to be, and perhaps is, retarded – one of those unclassifiable beings that fascinated Dostoevsky, a 'simple man'. He is suitably employed as a gardener by the municipality of Cape Town. A civil war has been going on for an unspecified time – as such wars do, undeclared and unending – and in various parts of

---

1 'But wait till you can see HORROR,/my child, written on the sun.' Friston, the missionary, in South Africa, in William Plomer's *Turbott Wolfe*, The Hogarth Press, London, 1965.

the country – as such wars are waged in our time, Michael K's time – with roving destruction missing patches of stranded calm. Michael is no more aware of this war than of much else in society that ignores him (women, the possibility of friends), until his mother is dying of dropsy and neglect in an overcrowded hospital and begs to be taken 'home' to the farm in the near-desert country of the Karoo where she was born the child of labourers.

She and her purse of savings are taken on the road in a wheelbarrow shelter put together by her simple son. Turned back the first time because of lack of permits, set upon by thugs as desperately homeless as themselves, they do not get very far before the mother dies. A purpose for his apparently unnecessary continued existence coheres slowly in Michael K's mind: he will take his mother's ashes, presented to him as a brown paper parcel, to be buried at the 'home' she spoke of. He finds it, or what may be it, abandoned by the white owners; the coloured labourers no doubt long ago moved off the land under one of the schemes to herd blacks away from whites that were the beginnings of the war.

He lives there in the veld, sowing and tending a handful of pumpkin seeds, until frightened off by the arrival of an army deserter; is picked up and commandeered for a forced labour camp; returns to the farm, which is visited by guerrillas from whom he conceals himself only to be captured, starving, by the army. Interrogated as the guerrillas' suspected contact man, he is kept in the makeshift hospital of a 'rehabilitation' camp for captured rebels set up on a former race course in Cape Town. One night he disappears from his bed and is given up as lying dead somewhere beyond the walls.

But Michael K is alive. Fled – yet again – from the sinister care of a gang of beach nomads who dispense to him, out of pity, wine and sex (travesty of untasted joys), he is holed up among abandoned beach furniture in the apartment where his mother once worked.

I have escaped the camps; perhaps, if I lie low, I will escape the charity too.

The mistake I made, he thought, going back in time, was not to have had plenty of seeds, a different packet of seeds for each pocket . . .

Then my mistake was to plant all my seeds together in one patch. I should have planted them one at a time spread out over miles of veld in patches of soil no larger than my hand, and drawn a map and kept it with me at all times so that every night I could make a tour of the sites to water them.

This, then, is the simple story of a 'simple' man. And it begins unexceptionally, anybody's refugee plodding predictably away from hunger and homelessness without much hope that these will not be waiting again at the end of the journey. You can shake your head decently over yet another evocation of commonplace misery; the only particular reaction, this time, a slight sense of impatience – did it all have to be laid on so thick? Does the man have to be harelipped, etc., on top of everything else?

But Coetzee's mode, from the beginning, is soon seen to have arisen solely out of the needs of content, and is purely and perfectly achieved. As the reader is drawn into the novel there comes the extraordinarily rare occurrence of one's response to its events opening up along with that of the central character himself. This is the reverse of facile identification, a prehensile comprehension stirs to take hold where the grasp of familiarity doesn't reach. A fellow inmate of the labour camp says to Michael K, 'You've been asleep all your life. It's time to wake up.' For the reader, too.

It is here that allegorical symbols occur. The work speaks: a voice inside the reader. Michael K is a real human being experiencing an individual body, but for some of us he will be the whole black people of South Africa, whatever gradations of colour the South African Population Registration Act sorts them into; for some he will be the inmate of Auschwitz or Stalin's camps. Others will see the split lip and strangled speech as the distortion of personality that South African race laws have effected, one way or another, in all of us who live there, black and white. Similarly, white privilege may be seen to come to its end in one of Coetzee's implosive images, when the white guard's portable refrigerator is smashed and its contents spilled – 'a tub of margarine, a loop of sausage, loose peaches and onions . . . five bottles of beer'.

The abstraction of allegory and symbol will not give access to what is most important in this magnificent novel, however. Neither will seeing it as a vision of the future. If it is set ahead in time at all, then this is done as a way of looking, as if it had come to the surface, at what lies under the surface of the present. The harried homelessness of Michael K and his mother is the experience, in 1984, of hundreds of thousands of black people in South African squatter towns and 'resettlement' camps. A civil war is going on in 1984 on South Africa's borders, between black and white. Coetzee has won (or lost?) his inner struggle and now writes, from among the smell of weary flesh, a work of the closest and deepest engagement with the victimised people of Michael K's life and times.

Political statements are made implicitly through the situations and reactions of Michael K that have no obvious political meaning. The deserter who comes to the farm is the grandson of the white farmer from Michael's mother's girlhood: Visagie's descendant and that of his labourer are living a parallel life now that the old structure is destroyed, one a fugitive from duty within the army that hunts and kills, the other fugitive from its pursuit. In the presence of the two on the farm is contained the core of tenure – this is the land that was taken by conquest, and then by deeds of sale that denied blacks the right even to buy back what had been taken from them. Can't the fugitives accommodate each other? Neither knows how to do this outside the ghostly pattern of master–servant. So Michael instinctively runs; and when he returns to find the boy has gone, he does not even then move into the Visagie house.

When he articulates the reason, it comes not as from an author's mouthpiece, but as what lies developing inside Michael, unsaid, unable to be shaped by his misformed lip. 'Whatever I have returned for, it is not to live as the Visagies lived, sleep where they slept, sit on their stoep looking out over their land . . . It is not for the house that I have come . . . The worst mistake, he told himself, would be to try to found a new house, a rival line, on his small beginnings.' (His hidden pumpkins.) Here is the concrete expression, through the creative imagination, of political debate about the future of South Africa under black majority rule: whether or not it should take over what has been the white South African version of the capitalist system.

Yet the unique and controversial aspect of this work is that while it is implicitly and highly political, Coetzee's heroes are those who ignore history, not make it. That is clear not only in the person of Michael K, but in other characters, for example the white doctor and nurse in the 'rehabilitation' camp, who are 'living in suspension', although for the woman, washing sheets, time is as full with such tasks as it has ever been, and for the doctor it is a state of being 'alive but not alive', while for both 'history hesitated over what course it should take'. No one in this novel has any sense of taking part in determining that course; no one is shown to believe he knows what that course should be. The sense is of the ultimate malaise: of destruction. Not even the oppressor really believes in what he is doing, any more, let alone the revolutionary.

This is a challengingly questionable position for a writer to take up in South Africa, make no mistake about it. The presentation of the truth and meaning of what white has done to black stands out on every page, celebrating its writer's superb, unafraid creative energy as it does; yet it denies the energy of the will to resist evil. That *this* superb energy exists with indefatigable and undefeatable persistence among the black people of South Africa – Michael K's people – is made evident, yes, heroically, every grinding day. It is not present in the novel.

Except in the person of Michael K?

If so, then this can be only because Coetzee, while fiercely moved far beyond commonplace understanding of their plight, does not believe in the possibility of blacks establishing a new regime that will do much better. (If Michael K is shown to see himself 'like a parasite dozing in the gut', he can never develop the metaphor by becoming the internal underground rebel who destroys the body of the enemy society he inhabits.) Camps with high walls will always have their uses, reflects the camp doctor. Freedom is defined negatively: it is to be 'out of all the camps at the same time' according to Michael K, who in this context

seems occasionally to have conceptual musings that really belong
to the sophisticated intelligence of the doctor. While 'we have
all tumbled over the lip into the cauldron', the doctor, who takes
over the narrative in the first person towards the close of the
novel, finds Michael K 'a soul blessedly untouched by doctrine,
untouched by history', a creature no 'organ of state' would recruit
as one of its agents. This white liberal feels chosen by the victim
of his own society; wasted Michael K becomes the doctor's burden
and his only hope of salvation. He believes Michael K can lead
him out of history of those 'areas that lie between camps and
belong to no camp'. A revulsion against all political and revolutionary solutions rises with the insistence of the song of cicadas
to the climax of this novel.

I don't think the author would deny that it is his own revulsion.

And so J.M. Coetzee has written a marvellous work that leaves
nothing unsaid – and could not be better said – about what human
beings do to fellow human beings in South Africa; but he does
not recognise what the victims, seeing themselves as victims no
longer, have done, are doing, and believe they must do for themselves. Does this prevent his from being a great novel? My instinct
is to say a vehement 'No'. But the organicism that George Lukács
defines as the integral relation between private and social destiny
is distorted here more than is allowed for by the subjectivity that is
in every writer. The exclusion is a central one that may eat out the
heart of the work's unity of art and life.

For is there an idea of survival that can be realised entirely outside a
political doctrine? Is there a space that lies between camps? Again,
this book is unusual in positing its answer while writers custom-
arily say it is their business only to explore questions. The place is
the earth, not in the cosmic but the plain dirt sense. The idea is the
idea of gardening. And with it floods into the book, yet again, much
more than it seemed to be about: the presence of the threat not only
of mutual destruction of whites and blacks in South Africa, but of
killing, everywhere, by scorching, polluting, neglecting, charging

with radioactivity, the dirt beneath our feet. From this perspective the long history of terrible wars whose reason has been advanced as 'to augment human happiness' could, I suppose, be turned away from; only the death of the soil is the end of life. The single sure joy Michael K can experience is the taste of a pumpkin he has grown, hidden from the just and unjust of marauding history. Under the noise of the cicadas, with delicacy and sureness, Coetzee has been drawing upon the strength of the earth to keep his deceptively passive protagonist and the passionate vitality of this book alive.

All along, dying Michael K has been growing. It began when he fertilised the earth with the burden of his mother's ashes; that, hidden to him, was his real reason to be. The only time he is tempted to join history – to tag behind the guerrilla band when he sees them leaving the farm – he knows he will not go 'because enough men had gone off to war saying the time for gardening was when the war was over; whereas there must be men to stay behind and keep gardening alive, or at least the idea of gardening; because once that cord was broken, the earth would grow hard and forget her children. That was why.' Beyond all creeds and moralities, this work of art asserts, there is only one: to keep the earth alive, and only one salvation, the survival that comes from her. Michael K is a gardener 'because that is my nature': the nature of civilised man, versus the hunter, the nomad. Hope is a seed. That's all. That's everything. It's better to live on your knees, planting something . . .?

1984

Postscript: J. M. Coetzee took Australian citizenship in 2006.

New Notes from Underground

Breyten Breytenbach's *Mouroir*

Mouroir is the work of that rarity which Camus despaired of finding, an individual who has lived, as protagonist *and* victim, the central experience produced by his time and place and who possesses a creative ability equal to his experience. A poet and a painter, faced with injustice before which words and pigment seemed to fail, Breytenbach put away his pen and brush and became a revolutionary. Whether he was a good one or not is something for those of us safe behind our desks to argue over. He spent seven years in a South African maximum security prison, the ventricle-and-auricle of the struggle against oppression in South Africa. For a white man, to have gone through that is to have come as close as is possible to *the* experience in South Africa – that of black people.

Yet this is not a prisoner's book. It will be a crass injustice of underestimation and simplification if it is presented and received that way. In it the ordinary time focus of a man's perceptions has been extraordinarily rearranged by a definitive experience that, the writer understands, belongs as much to the time before it happened as to the time after. Prison irradiates this book with dreadful enlightenments; the dark and hidden places of the country from which the book arises are phosphorescent with it.

Breytenbach is polylingual; he wrote his book in English and Afrikaans under a French title. Although *mouroir* is the word for 'old people's home', it seems he has reinterpreted it as a dovetailing of *mourir* (to die) and *miroir* (a mirror). What Breytenbach knows, and shows by means of his recurring mirrors, eliding, reversing, breaking up events, emotions and perceptions, is that the death presence of prison is always there in a country where people oppress and are oppressed. A target on the stoep,[1] set up for the innocent amusement of Afrikaner youths enjoying themselves in a seaside cottage, is not only the black man their parents and mentors are preparing them to kill but also the youths themselves, to be killed in turn. 'Tuesday', an endless journey created under that title out of an actual journey and recalled throughout the book with the regularity of a calendar, is the day of release: the day on which Breytenbach himself came out of prison, and also the day of freedom, to which a name must be given if ever it is to come, to jailed and jailer, the day when, as Breytenbach expresses it *totally*, 'life must be tempted back to earth'. In another facet of the book is a passage that is a perfect metaphor for colonial culture:

With enormous trouble we transported grown trees, for instance, from the coast to the house – along the way the leaves and fruit dragged in the dust; it was the abduction of an exotic princess from a far-off empire; we then dug a deep hole and made the tree to stand upright in it. Occasionally it took several weeks, months even, before the transplanted tree shrivelled up entirely and had to be unearthed – that is, if it hadn't tilted over all by itself in the meantime . . . But it never took root. Trees or brushwood, anything that could capture the wind and give it sound, is even so always needed round a house. Because otherwise you lose all memory of yourself and are gobbled up by nothingness to become part of the night.

Breytenbach is a writer who carries his whole life with him, all the time. His work takes on the enormous task of assuming full responsibility for what he was and is; the self cannot be disowned, either by the young Afrikaner growing up as one of the chosen *Volk*, speaking the language of the master, or by the artist fled to Paris (two generations of Afrikaner intellectuals did flee, later than but like the Hemingways and Fitzgeralds, looking hopelessly for a way out of being what they were), or by the failed revolutionary. All these personae are present in every single moment of Breytenbach's

---

1 Terrace, verandah.

working consciousness – the consciousness of the writer, which is different from that which serves for shaving or for buying lettuce. This fusion is what makes it impossible for him to write a work that can conveniently be fitted into even the broad concept of 'story collection' or 'novel'.

This is not to say that Breytenbach has written a book of fragments, that there is no narrative in the work. Narrative is an old railway line on which service has been discontinued. But of course service does continue; other forms of transport perform the railway's function. Inner logic (concepts, dreams, and symbols) also narrates. It has a sequence of its own, and sequence of any kind is narrative. But this sequence – unlike that of time – is highly individual, different in each subconscious and consciousness, and very, very few writers have the ability to use it as the unique shape of their work. Breytenbach is one of these, the greatly gifted. This inner logic, for which there is no recognised literary form (certainly not the long-polluted stream of consciousness, nor surreal surrender of control) is his form. (Even he cannot label it: 'Mirrornotes of a Novel' – his subtitle – will hardly do.)

With the overthrowing of time values in Breytenbach's writing comes a concomitant freeing from attachment to individual characters. If you are not going to be told what happens to them next, you don't have any obligation to identify with Minnaar or Levedi Tjeling. As Breytenbach himself airily remarks (one of his mirrors is that of ironic self-regard), these two so-called characters 'disappear from the story since they were never of any importance for its development, except perhaps as wraiths to be addressed . . .' At first, for reasons of habit, one misses characters, word-skeletons to be dressed up in what happens to them 'next'. But soon an exhilarating liberty like that of a Buñuel film is granted: if someone walks into a room where the characters are being 'developed', why not drop them and go off with him into his life? Here is a work in which all choices (as to which way it might go) are present.

Is it, then, an alternative autobiography? (Breytenbach could have been, might be, all these people.) He writes of 'liquidating the "I"', but also of 'an "I", a departure'. He himself is the centrifuge from which all seeds are cast and sown again: the horror, the humour, the love, the knowing and unknowing, he has received from living in his world and era. Yet there is none of the self-obsession of a Henry Miller or a Céline. A world is not defined by self: he defines himself by a world – that world in which 'white is posture, a norm of civilisation'. South Africa has produced in this writer an exacerbated self-consciousness, exactly what Stalin's Russia created in Anna Akhmatova – what the English critic John Bayley has called 'the power . . . to generalise and speak for the human predicament in extremity.' Akhmatova wrote sublime lines about her husband's death, her son's imprisonment. She had been parted for years from the husband; her son had been brought up by his grandfather. The sorrow and anger of the poem were not for herself but for 'somebody else's wound', for others who were suffering tragedies like these. Breytenbach has (has earned) this power to extrapolate suffering beyond what he has suffered himself. And as for responsibility for suffering, a one-and-a-half-page parable/parody entitled 'Know Thyself' will leave a share of that lodged within every reader.

Writing in the English language, Breytenbach is a phenomenon of the Nabokovian rather than the Conradian order. (No space to take up what I believe is the fine difference here, except to say that Conrad is incomparably at ease in the language, whereas Nabokov's performance is *his* achievement.) A native speaker of a minor language – Afrikaans, derived mainly from Dutch – Breytenbach has a few failures in making new English words out of a collage of old ones. By contrast, his imagery is so exquisite, chilling, aphoristic, witty, that one is reminded how that ancient and most beautiful attribute of writing has fallen into desuetude in prose. Someone 'dons his trousers the way one would mount a horse' and has a 'thick black moustache tied like a secondary tie under the nose'; a rainy sky is 'heaven with its grey beard'. In an all-existent, rather than a non-existent, urban complex Breytenbach puts 'an artificial cherry orchard vibrating a wind'; of a prisoner sentenced to death (it's done by hanging in South Africa), he says, 'His life was to be reeled in with a cord.' Aural and visual are combined: murmuring voices behind the walls sound 'as if the whole prison were filled with fast-running water'. Visual and onomatopoeic: a 'flock-a-flap' of birds. Visual and visceral: the tide 'withdrawn a long way, like a huge thirst'. And again and again Breytenbach strikes a spark by turning a cliché into something new while retaining the original image: 'Life unfolds, gets folded, wrinkled.'

If Breytenbach's imagery is to be compared with anyone's it is that of Czeslaw Milosz, with whom he shares an intense response to nature and a way of interpreting politically determined events and their human consequences through the subtleties of the physical world. Once more a fusion of the creative imagination makes reality out of mere facts. For the rest, I do not think one need look for comparisons to evaluate Breytenbach's book. It is his own — perhaps the highest compliment any writer can earn.

Exactly what Breyterbach's politics are now is difficult to tell. The matter is not irrelevant; if it were, this beautiful and devastating book would be betrayed, since its chemistry is politics, that chemistry of man opposing man, of good struggling with evil, from which one sees — with a shudder — both mushroom clouds and works of art arise. Does Breytenbach, like Régis Debray (quoted by Walter Schwarz in the *Guardian* last March), regard himself as having been 'essentially emotional, not noted for his discernment, locked in mythical conceptions of the external world which he recreates as the effigy of his own obsessions'?

Breytenbach's political conviction is no mythical conception of the external world; he had a conviction of the indefensible concrete cruelty and shame of white oppression of blacks, and the necessity to ally oneself with the blacks' struggle to free themselves. His obsession was that to make this alliance it was necessary to jump the barbed fence between artist and revolutionary, what he calls 'the contradiction between dreams and action'. He fell — how hard and humiliatingly one gets some ideas. But when he laughs at or mourns the spectacle of himself, this does not mean he disavows the truth on which the obsession was based: that South Africa is rotting in its racism, as much under a new constitution (which makes blacks foreigners without rights in their own country, and with which Ronald Reagan's America chooses to be 'constructively engaged') as it was under the old name of apartheid.

He writes from the underground that is exile. It is impossible, for his countrymen and for all of us, to stop our ears against the excruciating penetration of what he has to say.

1984

The Essential Gesture

When I began to write at the age of nine or ten, I did so in what I have come to believe is the only real innocence – an act without responsibility. For one has only to watch very small children playing together to see how the urge to influence, exact submission, defend dominance, gives away the presence of natal human 'sin' whose punishment is the burden of responsibility. I was alone. My poem or story came out of myself I did not know how. It was directed at no one, was read by no one.

Responsibility is what awaits outside the Eden of creativity. I should never have dreamt that this most solitary and deeply marvellous of secrets – the urge *to make* with words – would become a vocation for which the world, and that lifetime lodger, conscionable self-awareness, would claim the right to call me and all my kind to account. The creative act is not pure. History evidences it. Ideology demands it. Society exacts it. The writer loses Eden, writes to be read, and comes to realise that he is answerable. The writer is *held responsible*: and the verbal phrase is ominously accurate, for the writer not only has laid upon him responsibility for various interpretations of the consequences of his work, he is 'held' before he begins by the claims of different concepts of morality – artistic, linguistic, ideological, national, political, religious – asserted upon him. He learns that his creative act was not pure even while being formed in his brain: already it carried congenital responsibility for what preceded cognition and volition: for what he represented in genetic, environmental, social and economic terms when he was born of his parents.

Roland Barthes wrote that language is a 'corpus of prescriptions and habits common to all writers of a period'.[1]

He also wrote that a writer's 'enterprise' – his work – is his 'essential gesture as a social being'.

Between these two statements I have found my subject, which is their tension and connection: the writer's responsibility. For language – language as the transformation of thought into written words in any language – is not only 'a' but *the* corpus common to all writers in our period. From the corpus of language, within that guild shared with fellow writers, the writer fashions his enterprise, which then becomes his 'essential gesture as a social being'. Created in the common lot of language, that essential gesture is individual; and with it the writer quits the commune of the corpus; but with it he enters the commonalty of society, the world of other beings who are not writers. He and his fellow writers are at once isolated from one another far and wide by the varying concepts, in different societies, of what the essential gesture of the writer as a social being is.

By comparison of what is expected of them, writers often have little or nothing in common. There is no responsibility arising out of the status of the writer as a social being that could call upon Saul Bellow, Kurt Vonnegut, Susan Sontag, Toni Morrison or John Berger to write on a subject that would result in their being silenced under a ban, banished to internal exile or detained in jail. But in the Soviet Union, South Africa, Iran, Vietnam, Taiwan, certain Latin American and other countries, this is the kind of demand that responsibility for the social significance of being a writer exacts: a double demand, the first from the oppressed to act as spokesperson for them, the second, from the state, to take punishment for that act. Conversely, it is not conceivable that a Molly Keane, or any other writer of the quaint Gothic-domestic cult presently discovered by discerning critics and readers in the United States as well as Britain, would be taken seriously in terms of the interpretations of the 'essential gesture as a social being'

---

1   From *Writing Degree Zero*, in *Barthes, Selected Writings*, edited and introduced by Susan Sontag, Fontana, London, 1983, p. 31.

called forth in countries such as the Soviet Union and South Africa, if he or she lived there.

Yet those critics and readers who live safe from the realm of midnight arrests and solitary confinement that is the dark condominium of East and West have their demands upon the writer from such places, too. For them, his essential gesture as a social being is to take risks they themselves do not know if they would.

This results in some strange and unpleasant distortions in the personality of some of these safe people. Any writer from a country of conflict will bear me out. When interviewed abroad, there is often disappointment that you are there, and not in jail in your own country. And since you are not – why are you not? Aha . . . does this mean you have not written the book you should have written? Can you imagine this kind of self-righteous inquisition being directed against a John Updike for not having made the trauma of America's Vietnam war the theme of his work?

There is another tack of suspicion. The London *Daily Telegraph* reviewer of my recent book of stories said I must be exaggerating: if my country really was a place where such things happened, how was it I could write about them? And then there is the wish-fulfilment distortion, arising out of the homebody's projection of his dreams upon the exotic writer: the journalist who makes a bogus hero out of the writer who knows that the pen, where he lives, is a weapon not mightier than the sword.

One thing is clear: ours is a period when few can claim the absolute value of a writer without reference to a context of responsibilities. Exile as a mode of genius no longer exists; in place of Joyce we have the fragments of works appearing in *Index on Censorship*. These are the rags of suppressed literatures, translated from a Babel of languages; the broken cries of real exiles, not those who have rejected their homeland but who have been forced out – of their language, their culture, their society. In place of Joyce we have two of the best contemporary writers in the world; Czeslaw Milosz and Milan Kundera; but both regard themselves as amputated sensibilities, not free of Poland and Czechoslovakia in the sense that Joyce was free of Ireland – whole: out in the world but still in possession of the language and culture of home. In place of Joyce we have, one might argue, at least Borges; but in his old age, and out of what he sees in his blindness as he did not when he could see, for years now he has spoken wistfully of a desire to trace the trails made by ordinary lives instead of the arcane pattern of abstract forces of which they are the finger-painting. Despite his rejection of ideologies (earning the world's inescapable and maybe accurate shove over to the ranks of the Right) even he senses on those lowered lids the responsibilities that feel out for writers so persistently in our time.

What right has society to impose responsibility upon writers and what right has the writer to resist? I want to examine not what is forbidden us by censorship – I know that story too well – but to what we are bidden. I want to consider what is expected of us by the dynamic of collective conscience and the will to liberty in various circumstances and places; whether we should respond, and if so, how we do.

'It is from the moment when I shall no longer be more than a writer that I shall cease to write.' One of the great of our period, Camus, could say that.[2] In theory at least, as a writer he accepted the basis of the most extreme and pressing demand of our time. The ivory tower was finally stormed; and it was not with a white flag that the writer came out, but with manifesto unfurled and arms crooked to link with the elbows of the people. And it was not just as their chronicler that the compact was made; the greater value, you will note, was placed on the persona outside of 'writer': to be 'no more than a writer' was to put an end to the justification for the very existence of the persona of 'writer'. Although the aphorism in its characteristically French neatness appears to wrap up all possible meanings of its statement, it does not. Camus's decision is a hidden as well as a revealed one. It is not just that he has weighed within himself his existential value as a writer against that of other functions as a man among men, and found independently in favour of the man; the scale has been set up by a demand outside himself, by

2   Albert Camus, *Carnets* 1942–51.

his world situation. He has, in fact, accepted its condition that the greater responsibility is to society and not to art.

Long before it was projected into that of a world war, and again after the war, Camus's *natal* situation was that of a writer in the conflict of Western world decolonisation – the moral question of race and power by which the twentieth century will be characterised along with its discovery of the satanic ultimate in power, the means of human self-annihilation. But the demand made upon him and the moral imperative it set up in himself are those of a writer anywhere where the people he lives among, or any sections of them marked out by race or colour or religion, are discriminated against and repressed. Whether or not he himself materially belongs to the oppressed makes his assumption of extraliterary responsibility less or more 'natural', but does not alter much the problem of the conflict between integrities.

Loyalty is an emotion, integrity a conviction adhered to out of moral values. Therefore I speak here not of loyalties but integrities, in my recognition of society's right to make demands on the writer as equal to that of the writer's commitment to his artistic vision; the source of conflict is what demands are made and how they should be met.

The closest to reconciliation that I know of comes in my own country, South Africa, among some black writers. It certainly cannot be said to have occurred in two of the most important African writers outside South Africa, Chinua Achebe and Wole Soyinka. They became 'more than writers' in answer to their country's – Nigeria's – crisis of civil war; but in no sense did the demand develop their creativity. On the contrary, both sacrificed for some years the energy of their creativity to the demands of activism, which included, for Soyinka, imprisonment. The same might be said of Ernesto Cardenal. But it is out of being 'more than a writer' that many black men and women in South Africa *begin* to write. All the obstacles and diffidences – lack of education, of a tradition of written literary expression, even of the chance to form the everyday habit of reading that germinates a writer's gift – are overcome by the imperative to give expression to a majority not silent, but whose deeds and whose proud and angry volubility against suffering have not been given the eloquence of the written word. For these writers, there is no opposition of inner and outer demands. At the same time as they are writing, they are political activists in the concrete sense, teaching, proselytising, organising. When they are detained without trial it may be for what they have written, but when they are tried and convicted of crimes of conscience it is for what they have done as 'more than a writer'. 'Africa, my beginning . . . Africa my end' – these lines of the epic poem written by Ingoapele Madingoane[3] epitomise this synthesis of creativity and social responsibility; what moves him, and the way it moves him, are perfectly at one with his society's demands. Without those demands he is not a poet.

The Marxist critic Ernst Fischer reaches anterior to my interpretation of this response with his proposition that 'an artist who belonged to a coherent society [here, read pre-conquest South Africa] and to a class that was not an impediment to progress [here, read not yet infected by white bourgeois aspirations] did not feel it any loss of artistic freedom if a certain range of subjects was prescribed to him' since such subjects were imposed 'usually by tendencies and traditions deeply rooted in the people'.[4] Of course, this may provide, in general, a sinister pretext for a government to invoke certain tendencies and traditions to suit its purpose of proscribing writers' themes, but applied to black writers in South Africa, history evidences the likely truth of the proposition. Their tendency and tradition for more than three hundred years has been to free themselves of white domination.

Art is on the side of the oppressed. Think before you shudder at the simplistic dictum and its heretical definition of the freedom of art. For if art is freedom of the spirit, how can it exist within the oppressors? And there is some evidence that it ceases to. What writer of

---

3 Ingoapele Madingoane, *Africa My Beginning*, Ravan Press, Johannesburg, 1979; Rex Collings, London, 1980.

4 Ernst Fischer, *The Necessity of Art: A Marxist Approach*, translated by Anna Bostock, Penguin, Harmondsworth, 1963, p. 47.

any literary worth defends fascism, totalitarianism, racism, in an age when these are still pandemic? Ezra Pound is dead. In Poland, where are the poets who sing the epic of the men who have broken Solidarity? In South Africa, where are the writers who produce brilliant defences of apartheid?

It remains difficult to dissect the tissue between those for whom writing is a revolutionary activity no different from and to be practised concurrently with running a political trade union or making a false passport for someone on the run, and those who interpret their society's demand to be 'more than a writer' as something that may yet be fulfilled through the nature of their writing itself. Whether this latter interpretation is possible depends on the society within which the writer functions. Even 'only' to write may be to be 'more than a writer' for one such as Milan Kundera, who goes on writing what he sees and knows from within his situation – his country under repression – until a ban on publishing his books strips him of his 'essential gesture' of being a writer at all. Like one of his own characters, he must clean windows or sell tickets in a cinema booth for a living. That, ironically, is what being 'more than a writer' would come down to for him, if he were to have opted to stay on in his country – something I don't think Camus quite visualised. There are South Africans who have found themselves in the same position – for example, the poet Don Mattera, who for seven years was banned from writing, publishing, and even from reading his work in public. But in a country of total repression of the majority, like South Africa, where literature is nevertheless only half-suppressed because the greater part of that black majority is kept semi-literate and cannot be affected by books, there is – just – the possibility for a writer to be 'only' a writer, in terms of activity, and yet 'more than a writer' in terms of fulfilling the demands of his society. An honourable category has been found for him. As 'cultural worker' in the race/class struggle he still may be seen to serve, even if he won't march towards the tear gas and bullets.

In this context, long before the term 'cultural worker' was taken over from the vocabulary of other revolutions, black writers had to accept the social responsibility white ones didn't have to – that of

being the only historians of events among their people; Dhlomo,
Plaatje, Mofolo created characters who brought to life and
preserved events either unrecorded by white historians or recorded
purely from the point of view of white conquest.[5] From this beginning there has been a logical intensification of the demands of
social responsibility, as over decades discrimination and repression
set into law and institution, and resistance became a liberation
struggle. This process culminated during the black uprising of
1976, calling forth poetry and prose in an impetus of events not
yet exhausted or fully explored by writers. The uprising began
as a revolt of youth and it brought to writers a new consciousness – bold, incantatory, messianically reckless. It also placed new
demands upon them in the essential gesture that bound them to
a people springing about on the balls of their feet before dawn-
streaks of freedom and the threat of death. Private emotions were
inevitably outlawed by political activists who had no time for
any; black writers were expected to prove their blackness *as a
revolutionary condition* by submitting to an unwritten orthodoxy of
interpretation and representation in their work. I stress unwritten
because there was no Writers' Union to be expelled from. But
there was a company of political leaders, intellectuals, and the new
category of the alert young, shaming others with their physical
and mental bravery, to ostracise a book of poems or prose if it were
found to be irrelevant to the formal creation of an image of people
anonymously, often spontaneously heroic.

Some of my friends among black writers have insisted that
this 'imposition' of orthodoxy is a white interpretation; that the
impulse came from within to discard the lantern of artistic truth
that reveals human worth through human ambiguity, and to see by
the flames of burning vehicles only the strong, thick lines that draw

5   See H.I.E. Dhlomo, 'Valley of a Thousand Hills', reprinted in his *Collected Works*, edited
by N. Visser and T. Couzens, Ravan Press, Johannesburg, 1985; Sol T. Plaatje, *Mhudi*, edited
by Stephen Gray, introduction by Tim Couzens, Heinemann, London; Three Continents Press,
Washington DC, 1978; *Native Life in South Africa*, Longman, London, 1987; and *The Boer War
Diary of Sol T. Plaatje*, edited by J. L. Comaroff, Macmillan, Johannesburg, 1973; Thomas Mofolo,
Chaka: An Historical Romance, new translation by Daniel P. Kunene, Heinemann, London, 1981.

heroes. To gain his freedom the writer must give up his freedom. Whether the impulse came from within, without, or both, for the black South African writer it became an imperative to attempt that salvation. It remains so; but in the 1980s many black writers of quality have come into conflict with the demand from without – responsibility as orthodoxy – and have begun to negotiate the right to their own, inner interpretation of the essential gesture by which they are part of the black struggle.[6] The black writer's revolutionary responsibility may be posited by him as the discovery, in his own words, of the revolutionary spirit that rescues for the present – and for the post-revolutionary future – that nobility in ordinary men and women to be found only among their doubts, culpabilities, shortcomings: their courage-in-spite-of.

To whom are South African writers answerable in their essential gesture if they are not in the historical and existential situation of blacks, and if (axiomatic for them in varying degrees) they are alienated from their 'own', the historical and existential situation of whites? Only a section of blacks places any demands upon white writers at all; that grouping within radical blacks which grants integrity to whites who declare themselves for the black freedom struggle. To be one of these writers is firstly to be presented with a political responsibility if not an actual orthodoxy: the white writer's task as 'cultural worker' is to raise the consciousness of white people, who, unlike himself, have not woken up. It is a responsibility at once minor, in comparison with that placed upon the black writer as composer of battle hymns, and yet forbidding if one compares the honour and welcome that await the black writer, from blacks, and the branding as traitor, or, at best, turned backside of indifference, that awaits the white, from the white establishment. With fortunate irony, however, it is a responsibility which the white writer already has taken on, for himself, if the other responsibility – to his creative integrity

---

6   Among the most recent examples: Njabulo Ndebele, *Fools*, Ravan Press, Johannesburg, 1983; Longman, London, 1986; Ahmed Essop, *The Emperor*, Ravan Press, Johannesburg, 1984; and Es'kia Mphahlele, *Afrika My Music*, Ravan Press, Johannesburg, 1984.

– keeps him scrupulous in writing about what he knows to be true whether whites like to hear it or not; for the majority of his readers are white. He brings some influence to bear on whites, though not on the white government; he may influence those individuals who are already coming-to bewilderedly out of the trip of power, and those who gain courage from reading the open expression of their own suppressed rebellion. I doubt whether the white writer, even if giving expression to the same themes as blacks, has much social use in inspiriting blacks, or is needed to. Sharing the life of the black ghettoes is the primary quali-fication the white writer lacks, so far as populist appreciation is concerned. But black writers do share with white the same kind of influence on those whites who read them; and so the categories that the state would keep apart get mixed through literature – an unforeseen 'essential gesture' of writers in their social responsibility in a divided country.

The white writer who has declared himself answerable to the oppressed people is not expected by them to be 'more than a writer', since his historical position is not seen as allowing him to be central to the black struggle. But a few writers have chal-lenged this definition by taking upon themselves exactly the same revolutionary responsibilities as black writers such as Alex La Guma, Dennis Brutus and Mongane Serote, who make no distinc-tion between the tasks of underground activity and writing a story or poem. Like Brutus, the white writers Breyten Breytenbach and Jeremy Cronin were tried and imprisoned for accepting the neces-sity they saw for being 'more than a writer'. Their interpretation of a writer's responsibility, in their country and situation, remains a challenge, particularly to those who disagree with their actions while sharing with them the politics of opposition to repression. There is no moral authority like that of sacrifice.

In South Africa the ivory tower is bulldozed anew with every black man's home destroyed to make way for a white man's. Yet there are positions between the bulldozed ivory tower and the maximum security prison. The one who sees his responsibility in being 'only a writer' has still to decide whether this means he can

fulfil his essential gesture to society only by ready-packaging his
creativity to the dimensions of a social realism *those who will free him
of his situation* have the authority to ask of him, or whether he may
be able to do so by work George Steiner defines as 'scrupulously
argued, not declaimed . . . informed, at each node and articulation
of proposal, with a just sense of the complex, contradictory nature
of historical evidence'.[7] The great mentor of Russian revolutionary
writers of the nineteenth century, Belinsky, advises: 'Do not worry
about the incarnation of ideas. If you are a poet, your works will
contain them without your knowledge – they will be both moral
and national if you follow your inspiration freely.'[8] Octavio Paz,
speaking from Mexico for the needs of the Third World, sees a fundamental function as social critic for the writer who is 'only a writer'.
It is a responsibility that goes back to source: the corpus of language
from which the writer arises. 'Social criticism begins with grammar
and the re-establishing of meanings.'[9] This was the responsibility
taken up in the post-Nazi era by Heinrich Böll and Günter Grass,
and is presently being fulfilled by South African writers, black and
white, in exposing the real meaning of the South African government's vocabulary of racist euphemisms – such terms as 'separate
development', 'resettlement', 'national states', and its grammar of
a racist legislature, with segregated chambers for whites, so-called
coloureds and Indians, and no representation whatever for the
majority of South Africans, those classified as black.

If the writer accepts the social realist demand, from without,
will he be distorting, paradoxically, the very ability he has to offer
the creation of a new society? If he accepts the other, self-imposed
responsibility, how far into the immediate needs of his society will
he reach? Will hungry people find revelation in the ideas his work
contains 'without his knowledge'? The one certainty, in South
Africa as a specific historical situation, is that there is no opting out

7 George Steiner, review of E. M. Cioran, *Drawn and Quartered*, *The New Yorker*, 16 April
1984, p. 156.

8 Vissarion Belinsky, 1810–48. The quote is from my notebook: unable to locate source.

9 Octavio Paz, 'Development and other mirages', from *The Other Mexico: Critique of the
Pyramid*, translated by Lysander Kemp, Grove Press, New York, 1972, p. 48.

of the two choices. Outside is a culture in sterile decay, its achievements culminating in the lines of tin toilets set up in the veld for people 'resettled' by force. Whether a writer is black or white, in South Africa the essential gesture by which he enters the brotherhood of man – which is the only definition of society that has any permanent validity – is a revolutionary gesture.

'Has God ever expressed his opinion?' – Flaubert, writing to George Sand. 'I believe that great art is scientific and impersonal ... I want to have neither hate, nor pity, nor anger. The impartiality of description would then become equal to the majesty of the law.'[10]

Nearly a century passed before the *nouveau roman* writers attempted this kind of majesty, taking over from another medium the mode of still life. The work aspired to be the object-in-itself, although made up of elements – words, images – that can never be lifted from the 'partiality' of countless connotations. The writers went as far as it is possible to go from any societal demand. They had tried so hard that their vision became fixed on Virginia Woolf's mark on the wall – and as an end, not a beginning. Yet the anti-movement seems to have been, after all, a negative variation on a kind of social responsibility some writers have assumed at least since the beginning of the modern movement: to transform the world by style. This was and is something that could not serve as the writer's essential gesture in countries such as South Africa and Nicaragua, but it has had its possibilities and sometimes proves its validity where complacency, indifference, accidie, and not conflict, threaten the human spirit. To transform the world by style was the iconoclastic essential gesture tried out by the Symbolists and Dadaists; but whatever social transformation (in shaping a new consciousness) they might have served in breaking old forms was horribly superseded by different means: Europe, the Far, Middle and Near East, Asia, Latin America and Africa overturned by wars; millions of human beings wandering without the basic structure of a roof.

---

10   *The Letters of Gustave Flaubert 1857–1880*, selected, edited and translated by Francis Steegmuller, Harvard University Press, Cambridge, MA and London, 1982.

The Symbolists' and Dadaists' successors, in what Susan Sontag terms 'the cultural revolution that refuses to be political' have among them their '. . . spiritual adventurers, social pariahs determined to disestablish themselves . . . not to be morally useful to the community' – the essential gesture withheld by Céline and Kerouac.[11] Responsibility reaches out into the manifesto, however, and claims the 'seers' of this revolution. Through a transformation by style – depersonalised laconicism of the word almost to the Word – Samuel Beckett takes on as his essential gesture a responsibility direct to human destiny, and not to any local cell of humanity. This is the assumption of a messenger of the gods rather than a cultural worker. It is a disestablishment from the temporal; yet some kind of final statement exacted by the temporal. Is Beckett the freest writer in the world, or is he the most responsible of all?

Kafka was also a seer, one who sought to transform consciousness by style, and who was making his essential gesture to human destiny rather than the European fragment of it to which he belonged. But he was unconscious of his desperate signal. He believed that the act of writing was one of detachment that moved writers 'with everything we possess, to the moon'.[12] He was unaware of the terrifyingly impersonal, apocalyptic, prophetic nature of his vision in that ante-room to his parents' bedroom in Prague. Beckett, on the contrary, has been signalled to and consciously responded. The summons came from his time. His place – not Warsaw, San Salvador, Soweto – has nothing specific to ask of him. And unlike Joyce, he can never be in exile wherever he chooses to live, because he has chosen to be answerable to the twentieth-century human condition which has its camp everywhere, or nowhere – whichever way you see Vladimir, Estragon, Pozzo and Lucky.

---

11 Susan Sontag, 'Approaching Artaud', in *Under the Sign of Saturn*, Farrar, Straus and Giroux, New York, 1980, p. 15: '. . . authors . . . recognised by their effort to disestablish themselves, by their will not to be morally useful to the community, by their inclination to present themselves not as social critics but as seers, spiritual adventurers, and social pariahs'.

12 Letter to Max Brod, quoted in Ronald Hayman, *K: A Biography of Kafka*, Weidenfeld & Nicolson, London, 1981, p. 237.

Writers who accept a professional responsibility in the transformation of society are always seeking ways of doing so that their
societies could not ever imagine, let alone demand: asking of themselves means that will plunge like a drill to release the great primal
spout of creativity, drench the censors, cleanse the statute books
of their pornography of racist and sexist laws, hose down religious
differences, extinguish napalm bombs and flame-throwers, wash
away pollution from land, sea and air, and bring out human beings
into the occasional summer fount of naked joy. Each has his own
dowsing twig, held over heart and brain. Michel Tournier sees
writers' responsibilities as to 'disrupt the establishment in exact
proportion to their creativity'. This is a bold global responsibility,
though more Orphic and terrestrial than Beckett's. It also could be
taken as an admittance that this is *all* writers can do; for creativity
comes from within, it cannot be produced by will or dictate if it is
not there, although it can be crushed by dictate. Tournier's – this
apparently fantastical and uncommitted writer's – own creativity
is nevertheless so close to the people that he respects as a marvel –
and makes it so for his readers – the daily history of their lives as
revealed in city trash dumps.[13] And he is so fundamentally engaged
by what alienates human beings that he imagines for everyone the
restoration of wholeness (the totality which revolutionary art seeks
to create for alienated man) in a form of Being that both sexes
experience as one – something closer to a classless society than to a
sexually hermaphroditic curiosity.

The *transformation of experience* remains the writer's basic essential
gesture; the lifting out of a limited category something that reveals
its full meaning and significance only when the writer's imagination has expanded it. This has never been more evident than in the
context of extreme experiences of sustained personal horror that
are central to the period of twentieth-century writers. The English
critic John Bayley has written of Anna Akhmatova:

---

13   Michel Tournier, *Gemini*, translated by Anne Carter, London: Collins; Garden City, NY:
Doubleday, 1981.

A violently laconic couplet at the end of the sections of *Requiem* records her husband dead, her son in prison . . . It is as good an instance as any of the power of great poetry to generalise and speak for the human predicament in extremity, for in fact she had probably never loved Gumilev, from whom she had lived apart for years, and her son had been brought up by his grandmother. But the sentiment [of the poem] was not for herself but for 'her people', with whom she was at that time so totally united in suffering.[14]

Writers in South Africa who are 'only writers' are sometimes reproached by those, black and white, who are in practical revolutionary terms 'more than writers', for writing of events as if they themselves had been at the heart of action, endurance and suffering. So far as black writers are concerned, even though the humiliations and deprivations of daily life under apartheid enjoin them, many of them were no more among the children under fire from the police in the seventies, or are among the students and miners shot, tear-gassed and beaten in the eighties, or are living as freedom fighters in the bush, than Akhmatova was a heartbroken wife or a mother separated from a son she had nurtured. Given these circumstances, their claim to generalise and speak for a human predicament in extremity comes from the lesser or greater extent of their *ability to do so*; and the development of that ability is their responsibility towards those with whom they are united by this extrapolation of suffering and resistance. White writers who are 'only writers' are open to related reproach for 'stealing the lives of blacks' as good material. Their claim to this 'material' is the same as the black writers' at an important existential remove nobody would discount. Their essential gesture can be fulfilled only in the integrity Chekhov demanded: 'to describe a situation so truthfully . . . that the reader can no longer evade it'.[15]

---

14   John Bayley, review of *Akhmatova: A Poetic Pilgrimage* by Amanda Haight, *Observer*, 31 October 1976, p. 29.

15   From Isaiah Berlin, *Russian Thinkers*, The Hogarth Press, London, 1978, p. 303.

The writer is eternally in search of entelechy in his relation to his society. Everywhere in the world, he needs to be left alone and at the same time to have a vital connection with others; needs artistic freedom and knows it cannot exist without its wider context; feels the two presences within – creative self-absorption and conscionable awareness – and must resolve whether these are locked in death-struggle, or are really foetuses in a twinship of fecundity. Will the world let him, and will he know how to be the ideal of the writer as a social being, Walter Benjamin's story-teller, the one 'who could let the wick of his life be consumed completely by the gentle flame of his story'?[16]

1985

Letter from Johannesburg

Dear—,
        What is it you need to know about us that you cannot read as plain reportage, I wonder?

Well, maybe there is an indication in the ambiguity of the pronoun 'us'. When I, as a white English-speaking South African, employ it in this context, of whom do I speak? Of whom do you Americans understand me to be speaking? For you ask about the 'position that non-Afrikaners find themselves in after the declaration of the State of Emergency in South Africa', and doubtless you would assume it is from that position that I respond because I am white, English-speaking, etc. But your question at once reveals that an old misconception is still current abroad: the Afrikaners are the baddies and the English-speakers the goodies among whites in our country; all Afrikaners support

---

16   'The Story-Teller', in *Illuminations*, pp. 108–9.

the State of Emergency[1] and the sadistic police and army actions that led up to it, and all English-speakers would implode apartheid tomorrow if it were possible to prevail against the Afrikaner army that mans the Afrikaner fortress. This surprises me because anyone who follows the reports of foreign press correspondents in South Africa must be aware that in November 1984 the then Prime Minister, Mr P. W. Botha, received an overwhelming 'yes' vote for his new constitution with its tricameral parliament for whites, Indians and so-called coloureds, and total exclusion of the black majority. The referendum held was open to whites only, Afrikaans and English-speaking; Mr Botha could not have received a mandate if the English-speakers had voted 'no'. 'Yes,' they said, voting along with Mr Botha's supporters in the National Party. 'Yes,' they said, 15½ million black people shall have no say in the central government of South Africa.

And 'yes' said the Reagan government, entering into constructive engagement with a policy destructive of justice and human dignity, while mumbling obeisance to abhorrence of apartheid like those lapsed believers who cross themselves when entering a church.

There is no such special position as 'one in which non-Afrikaners find themselves' now, nor has there been for a very long time. The categories do not fall so neatly into place. The actual division among whites falls between those – the majority – Afrikaner and English-speaking who support, whether directly or circuitously, the new constitution as a valid move towards 'accommodating black aspirations' (let us not invoke justice), and those – the minority – English-speaking and Afrikaner who oppose the constitution as irremediably unjust and unjustifiable. There are fewer Afrikaners than English-speakers in the latter category, but the support of English-speakers in the former represents a majority in their language group. When blacks speak about the 'Boere' these days, the term has become a generic rather than an ethnic one:

---

1 A 'State of Emergency' in South Africa was declared by government in 1960, lifted, redeclared, extended, through the years to 1986, on and off.

it is likely to refer to a mode of behaviour, an attitude of mind, a *position* in which the nomenclature encompasses all whites who voluntarily and knowingly collaborate in oppression of blacks. Not all Afrikaners are 'Boere', and many English-speakers with pedigrees dating back to the 1820 Settlers are . . .

States of mind and ways of life under crisis would be expected more or less to follow the lines of division, and I believe that states of mind do. Everywhere I go I sense a relaxation of the facial muscles among whites who had appeared to be tasting the ashes of the good life when Soweto was on fire in the week before the State of Emergency was declared. Approval of the state's action is not often explicit in my company because it is known that I belong to the minority-within-the-white-minority that opposes the constitution as a new order of oppression in contempt of justice, and sees the State of Emergency as an act of desperation: a demonstration of the failure of the government's atrocious 'new deal' only a few months after it was instituted. The general feeling among whites is that fear has been staved off – at least for a while. The police dogs are guarding the gates of paradise. Keep away from roads that pass where the blacks and the police/army are contained in their vortex of violence, and life can go on as usual. One can turn one's attention to matters that affect one directly and can be dealt with without bloodying one's hands: lobbying all over the world against disinvestment and sports boycotts – an area where sophisticated people understand one another in economic and leisure self-interests; for many, the only brotherhood that transcends nation and race. There is a physical and mental cordoning-off of 'areas of unrest'. The police and army take care of the first, and that extraordinary sense of whiteness, of having always been different, always favoured, always shielded from the vulnerabilities of poverty and powerlessness, takes care of the second. We whites in South Africa present an updated version of the tale of the Emperor's clothes; we are not aware of our nakedness – ethical, moral, and fatal – clothed as we are in our own skin. This morning on the radio the news of the withdrawal of more foreign diplomats from South Africa, and the continuing threat of the withdrawal by foreign banks, was followed by a burst of pop-music defiance by the state-owned South African Broadcasting Corporation, on behalf of Afrikaner and English-speaking whites. *Allies*, yelled a disco idol, *We're allies, with our backs against the w-a-ll* . . .

As for the less worldly among the white majority, they express openly their approval of government violence in the last few months, and there is a group that believes there has not been enough of it. 'The government should shoot the lot.' This remark was offered to my friend the photographer David Goldblatt in all crazy seriousness, not as a manner of speaking: there are whites in whose subconscious the power of the gun in a white man's hand is magical (like his skin?) and could wipe out an entire population nearly four times as large as that of the whites. This, in bizarre historical twinship, is the obverse of the belief of the mid-nineteenth-century Xhosa prophetess, Nongquase, who told her people that by following her instructions they could cause all those who wore trousers (the white men) to be swept away by a whirlwind . . .

It is not true that the South African government is bent on genocide, as some black demagogues have averred (the black man is too useful for that); but it is true that the unconscious will to genocide is there, in some whites. So is belief in the old biblical justification for apartheid that has been embarrassedly repudiated by even the Dutch Reformed Church. Over lunch on his father's Transvaal farm recently, I met a handsome young Afrikaner on leave from military service. Grace was said; when the young man lifted his bowed head he began an exposition of biblical justification that was all his own, I think: blacks are the descendants of Cain and a curse on humankind. I did not rise to the bait; but my eyes must have betrayed that I could scarcely believe my ears. When, among the women of the family, I was being shown their new acquisition, a pristine white dishwasher that had replaced the black maid, he took the opportunity to fire at me: 'Yes, it's a good white kaffir girl.'

During the weeks that led up to the State of Emergency, the Eastern Cape black townships had become ungovernable – even in the streets of Grahamstown, the English 1820 Settlers' Association show-piece answer to the Afrikaner Voortrekker Monument at Pretoria, soldiers and armoured vehicles had taken the place of festival visitors. Most whites in South Africa were in a state of anguish: over the outcome of the New Zealand government's determination to stop the All Blacks' rugby tour of South Africa. It was only when Soweto became a hell to which Johannesburg's black workers returned each night as best they could (buses would not venture farther than Soweto boundaries) that white faces in Johannesburg became strained.

But the state of mind of the minority-within-the-white-minority did not have to wait for any declaration to be aware of an emergency beyond the national rugby fields. People like Bishop Tutu, Reverend Beyers Naudé and Sheena Duncan of the Black Sash – a women's organisation that has done more than any other source to expose the appalling forced removals of black rural people – had been warning for months that an uprising was inevitable: built into the new constitution as its own consequence. The government was arresting trade union leaders and leaders of the non-racial United Democratic Front. Just as, abroad, one may mutter abhorrence of apartheid and go on funding it morally and materially, so the government continued (as it continues) to reiterate a litany of dedication to consultation and change while arresting almost every black leader with any claim to be consulted about change. On the minority side of the dividing line between white and white, a new organisation had grown in urgent response to the use of army recruits against the people of the black township of Sebokeng last October. Resistance to conscription was suddenly no longer some fringe defection on religious grounds by a handful of Seventh Day Adventists, but a wave of revulsion against 'defending one's country' by maiming, killing, and breaking into the humble homes of black people. In this horrifying domestic context, the End Conscription Campaign held a three-day gathering in Johannnesburg where a large crowd of young men and their families debated the moral issues of conscientious objection and defined their position not as pacifist but as a refusal to defend apartheid. I gave a reading there of poetry by South African writers black and white in whose work, like that of playwrights, lately, this has been the theme. The subject has to be handled gingerly, whether in poetry or platform prose; it is a treasonable offence, in South Africa, to incite anyone to refuse military service. The ECC is not yet a mass movement, and maybe will not be, but the government is sufficently alarmed by it to have detained several members.

For years, when one asked blacks why they allowed black police to raid and arrest them, they would answer: 'Our brothers have to do what whites tell them. We are all victims together.' Now, black youths are confronted with what surely always was clear would be the ultimate distortion of their lives by apartheid: brothers, co-opted as police informers and City Fathers by white power, becoming enemies.

Many of us who belong to the minority-within-the-white-minority already were accustomed, before the State of Emergency, to using the telephone for the kind of call not made outside thriller movies in your country. When the South African Defence Force raided the capital of one of our neighbouring countries, Botswana, earlier this year, we feared for the lives of friends living in exile there. For some days, we could piece together their fate only by exchanging guarded word-of-mouth news. For my fellow writer, Sipho Sepamla, the news was bad; he travelled across the border to Botswana to the funeral of a relative murdered in the raid, and we were nervous about his doing so, since the brutal raid – which resulted in indiscriminate killing, so that even children died – was purportedly against African National Congress revolution-aries, and the demonstration of any connection with even random victims could rub off as guilt by association. With the beginning of the State of Emergency there came mass arrests, and severe penal-ties for revealing without authority the identity of any detainee. The names we know are confined to those permitted by the police to be published. Who can say how many others there are? So our ominous kind of morning gossip has increased – and there remains the fear that the individual one calls may not answer because he or she has been taken.

Some of us have friends among those who are the accused in

the treason trials, mainly trade unionists and leaders of the United
Democratic Front, in session or about to commence. I telephone
my old friend, Cassim Saloojee, a social worker, and an office-bearer
in the United Democratic Front. He is at home on bail after many
weeks of detention before being formally charged with treason.
One discovers, these days, that genuine cheerfulness exists, and
it is a by-product of courage. He has only one complaint, which
is expressed in a way that catches me out: 'I've been spending
my time watching pornographic films.' And with my tactfully
unshockable laugh, I remember that active resistance to apartheid
is political pornography in South Africa. The state has seized video
cassettes of public meetings made by the United Democratic Front
as records of their activities. For the purposes of their defence, the
accused must study what may now be used as evidence against
them. 'Ninety hours of viewing . . .'

The case is *sub judice*, so I suppose I cannot give here my version
of whether the particular meetings I attended (the UDF is a non-
racial, non-violent and legally constituted movement) could
possibly be construed as violent and treasonous, but I hope that
among all that footage there is at least recorded the time when the
crowd in a Johannesburg hall heard that there was police harassment of some supporters in the foyer, and from the platform Cassim
Saloojee succeeded in preventing the crowd from streaming out to
seek a confrontation that doubtless would have resulted in police
violence.

While writing this letter I have had a call from a young white
student at the University of the Witwatersrand, down the road,
who himself is a veteran of detention, and whose brother is now in
detention for the second time. At last, after more than two weeks,
Colin Coleman's parents have managed to get permission to visit
Neil Coleman in prison – like well over a thousand others, he has
not been charged. The parents are founder members of the well-
established Detainees Parents' Committee, a title and status that
indicate the enduring state of mind, stoic but unintimidatedly
active on the part of all prisoners of conscience, black and white,
whether or not in the family, that prevails among white people like

these. Colin has called to ask me to take part in a panel discussion on South African culture to be held by the students' Academic Freedom Committee. Irrelevant while we are in a State of Emergency? Concurrently with engagement in the political struggle for the end of apartheid, there exists an awareness of the need for a new conception of culture, particularly among whites. Young people like these are aware that a *change of consciousness*, of the white sense of self, has to be achieved along with a change of regime, if, when blacks do sit down to consult with whites, there is to be anything to talk about. The arts in South Africa sometimes do bear relation to the real entities of South African life in the way that the euphemisms and evasions of white politics do not.

These are the *states of mind* of the majority of white South Africans, and of the minority within the white population. In the first, the preoccupations of the second are no more than newspaper stories you, too, read thousands of miles away: so long as the Casspir armoured monsters patrol the black townships and even mass funerals are banned, the majority feel safe, since there is no possibility that they may be imprisoned for a too-active sense of justice, or find any member of their families or their friends in detention, on trial, or in danger of losing a life in right-wing terrorist attacks. Nor is there any possibility that one of their lawyers might be gunned down, as was a member of a treason trial defence team outside her home a few nights ago.

The *conditions of life*, for whites, are a different matter. Even those few whites who have members of their families in prison themselves continue to wake up every morning as I do, to the song of weaver birds and mechanical-sounding whirr of crested barbets in a white suburb. Soweto is only eight miles from my house; if I did not have friends living there, I should not be aware of the battles of stones against guns and tear gas that are going on in its streets, for images on a TV screen come by satellite as easily from the other side of the world as from eight miles away, and may be comprehended as equally distanced from the viewer. How is it possible that the winter sun is shining, the randy doves are announcing spring, the domestic workers from the back yards are placing bets on the numbers game, Fah-Fee, with the Chinese runner, as usual every afternoon? In terms of *ways of life*, conditions of daily living are sinisterly much the same for all whites, those who manage to ignore the crisis in our country, and those for whom it is the determining state of mind. Some go to protest meetings, others play golf. All of us go home to quiet streets, outings to the theatre and cinema, good meals and secure shelter for the night, while in the black townships thousands of children no longer go to school, fathers and sons disappear into police vans or lie shot in the dark streets, social gatherings are around coffins and social intercourse is confined to mourning.

The night the State of Emergency was declared I was at a party held at an alternative education centre, the Open School, in the downtown area where banks and the glass palaces of mining companies run down into Indian stores and black bus queues. The school is directed by Colin and Dolphine Smuts (black, despite their Afrikaans surname) for black youths and children who study drama, painting, dance and music there – subjects not offered by government 'Bantu' education. The occasion was a celebration: the school, which had been in danger of closure for lack of funds, had received a Ford Foundation grant. Colin had not known until the evening began whether the new ban on gatherings might not be served on the celebration; Dolphine had gone ahead and prepared food. There were polite speeches, music, drumming, and the declamatory performance of poetry that has been part of resistance rhetoric since young people began to compose in prison in 1976, and which sets such gatherings apart from their counterparts in other countries. Soweto was sealed off by military roadblocks. Yet the black guests had come through somehow, thoroughly frisked in the 'elegantly casual' clothes we all, black and white, wear to honour this kind of occasion. I asked a couple I had not met before what it was like to be in Soweto now, looking at them in the inhibited, slightly awed way one tries not to reveal to people who have emerged alive from some unimaginable ordeal. The man took a bite from a leg of chicken and washed it down with his drink. 'In your street, one day it's all right. The next day, you can cross the street when a Casspir comes round the corner, and you'll die. It's like Beirut.'

Yes, if you want to know what it's like here, it's more like Beirut than he knew. I remember a film I once saw, where the camera moved from destruction and its hateful cacophony in the streets to a villa where people were lunching on a terrace, and there were birds and flowers. That's what it's like. I also remember something said by a character in a novel I wrote ten years ago. 'How long can we go on getting away scot free?'

1985

Huddleston: A Sign

Above this desk at which I write there are children's paintings, a poster showing Marcel Proust as a small boy with a large bow tie and a watch-chain, a carving from the Central African Republic that looks like a human sundial, and a photograph. These are my treasures, under whose signs I spend my working life.

The photograph was taken by my friend David Goldblatt at the beginning of his career, in 1952, at the Newclare squatter camp, Johannesburg. It is a night scene, lit only by a tin brazier. The light from lozenges of incandescent coal brings forward out of the dark a pair of gaunt, tightly clasped hands, the long fingers tautly interlaced, making a great double fist. They are the hands of a white man. Above them there is darkness again, until the furthermost reach of light leaps on the bright white band of a clerical collar, and, more softly, brings from oblivion the three-quarter face. There is a pointed ear standing alertly away from the head and lean jaw, and the tendon from behind the ear down the neck is prominent and tense. The ear is cocked intently and the eyes are concentrated.

The man is the young Father Trevor Huddleston. He is listening to and looking at someone you can't make out – a faint lick of light touching knuckles and thumb held towards the fire, a shirt collar framing the knot of a tie, and above that a shape almost one with the night, unrecognisable as a face. But the man, the black man, is there; he is there in the extraordinary, still, self-excluding attention of the young priest. Trevor Huddleston's immense *awareness* of black people, in a city and country and time when white people ignored their lives, categorised them as so many statistics, planned to move them about as so many plastic pins on a demographic map, is in the photograph. It is there as an emblem of the Defiance Campaign, in which Huddleston had currently engaged that attention of his, and which the whites in power crushed while their supporters turned their heads away. It is there as an omen of what was to come: Sharpeville, at the start of a new decade; the 1976 uprising; the school, rent and shop boycotts, the troops in the black townships, the detention of thousands without respect for childhood or old age, the strikes in factories and mines – and the deaths, the deaths, the unrolling death-scroll of constantly intensified state violence that, in the 1980s, inevitably brought forth counter-violence from its victims. Within the chiaroscuro of that photograph the black people of South Africa are wholly present in the attention of a white man who, from the beginning of his experience in our country, saw them not as statistics and movable counters in some ugly and insane plan to keep races apart and class domination in power, but as blood, heart, brain and spirit, as human beings dispossessed of their birthright and certain to regain it.

That is what is in the instant of a night in Newclare in 1952. I have no religious faith, but when I look at that photograph of a profoundly religious man, I see godliness in a way I can understand deeply, I see a man in whom prayer functions, in Simone Weil's definition,[1] as a special form of intelligent concentration.

---

1   '. . . prayer consists of attention . . . Not only does the love of God have attention for its substance; the love of our neighbour, which we know to be the same love, is made of this same substance . . . The capacity to give one's attention to a sufferer is a very rare and difficult thing; it is almost a miracle; it is a miracle . . . Warmth of heart . . . pity, are not enough.' Simone Weil, *Waiting on God*, Routledge, London, 1951, pp. 51, 58.

Everything that is in that photograph is what whites in South Africa have turned away from, towards deliberate fragmentation, callous and stupid denial, wild political distraction, mindless elevation of indifference; turned away to catastrophe.

Yet Trevor Huddleston's concentration remains. It asserts, always, that another way of thinking and living existed, and still exists. What is asserted there was passed on by Huddleston to many people and has never been forgotten or abandoned by them, but handed down to another generation. He belongs to the living history of the liberation movement in an ancestry all of us, black and white, who are involved in the movement now are inspired to claim. He is the only white man to have received the *Isitwalandwe* – the highest distinction in African society; that award was conferred upon him in a particular context at the Congress of the People in 1955, but I know of no one in any of the liberation organisations who, whatever their political ideology, does not revere him. Certainly, all whites in the struggle are under his sign.

Everyone in the contemporary world is familiar with the old pious condemnation of churchmen who 'meddle in politics'. In South Africa, it was invoked against the Reverend Michael Scott before Huddleston, and after Huddleston against Bishop Ambrose Reeves and others, as it is now against the Reverend Allan Boesak and (and how!) Archbishop Desmond Tutu. There is a more subtle and sophisticated form of attack – derogation. Its vocabulary, too, is worn smooth: 'sentimental liberalism', 'starry-eyed Utopianism'. 'Priests and pinkos' don't understand that politics is the 'art of the possible'. The inference is always that churchmen who accept political action as part of their responsibility for humankind are well meaning but unfitted for the task. In short, they lack the necessary specific intelligence.

Trevor Huddleston's place in South African history demonstrates exactly the reverse. In him, early on, it was clear that 'intelligence' in all its senses has combined to produce exactly what would have been *the* specific intelligence necessary to find a peaceful political end to racism in all its avatars, economic, social, religious. Intelligence means superior understanding and quickness of apprehension; inherent mental qualities. It also means what may be acquired: to have intelligence of something is to have news and knowledge of it. Then there is the dimension of Simone Weil's definition: the faculty of 'intelligent concentration' that is prayer. Trevor Huddleston summoned all three into synthesis. (How evident this is in his book, *Naught for your Comfort*.) His actions showed a superior understanding of the political future of South Africa far in advance not only of parliament but also of most liberal thinkers among people who had the vote – the white minority. Those actions were based on the first-hand knowledge, 'intelligence', gained working among the majority – the black South Africans whose lives were to be the decisive factor in South African politics. Through the focus of his Weilian faculty, he saw us all clearly, as few of us saw ourselves.

Some of the non-violent forms of resistance that have been seen to bring results, since, stem from his kind of specific intelligence. He saw before anyone else that a sports boycott would rudely waken the average 'non-political' white voter from the sleep of complacent tacit racism. His initiative has resulted in the most successful and long-lived anti-apartheid campaign ever sustained. His political action, supporting the ANC, encouraging the people of his parish in Sophiatown to resist one of the first population removals, was evidence of a prescient understanding and political forecast of what was to come: the vast and terrible shifting of whole populations, let alone townships, about the country, the isolation of people in ethnic backwaters dubbed 'states', the destruction of community life, and, finally, the stripping of black South Africans of their citizenship.

He was a good politician, that churchman. If our professional politicians had had his intelligence they would not have behind them today the failed Verwoerdian 'grand apartheid'; with them, the doomed Outhouses of Parliament for so-called coloureds and Indians only; and ahead an immediate future that, because of 'reforms' whose scenario is still projected in black and white, and whose script still keeps ultimate power in white hands only, promises only violence. Their tragic lack of intelligence – not being able to grasp the fact of the social forces of their own post-colonial era, not being open to the information that the majority was plainly giving them, not having any political morality other than that based on physical attributes of skin and hair – has brought this tragedy about.

I didn't know Trevor Huddleston well, personally. I met him in the early 1950s through our mutual friend Anthony Sampson, and, set beside my great admiration for the public figure, there is an endearing trivial memory. Some years later a party for Anthony Sampson was held in my house. While my husband Reinhold Cassirer and I were still preparing food and drink, the first guest arrived. It was Huddleston, and he and Anthony settled on the verandah. Our son, taking on hostly duties for the first time, kept offering a plate of stuffed eggs, and to his dismay the guest never refused, but kept absently reaching out and eating them. The small boy came rushing indignantly into the kitchen: 'Mum, the man in a skirt is finishing all the eggs!'

An uncharacteristic side-glance at that figure striding so ascetically through our lives in Johannesburg in the 1950s, less at home in white suburbia than in the Sophiatown of crowded yards, shebeens, vigorous street life, the blare of *pata-pata* music, and the roof-raising voices of the congregation singing in the people's lovely home on the hill, his Church of Christ the King. But wherever I encountered him, here or there, 'the man in a skirt' was an assurance that South Africa didn't have to be as it was, that the barriers set up between black and white must come down in situations other and greater than private affinities and friendships – those relationships which many of us in the 1950s enjoyed but which lacked the necessary political energy and dedication to bring freedom.

He left us, left South Africa physically. It was not of his own volition. But he hasn't gone, any more than Mandela, Sisulu, Mbeki, Kathrada and their fellow prisoners are not with us. He acted here, and has continued to act in exile, to achieve a different South Africa, which he knew was and knows is possible, and will be.

1988

The Gap Between the Writer and the Reader

When I am asked that interviewer's stock in trade, 'For whom do you write?' I reply irritably, 'For anyone who reads me.' The question is crass, giving away the press's assumption that a writer presumes 'audience potential'. It seems typical of one of the anti-art tenets of commercialism: give the public what they know. But writers – artists of all kinds – exist to break up the paving of habit and breach the railings that confine sensibility: free imaginative response to spring up like grass. We are convinced that we are able to release the vital commonality of the human psyche, our reach limited only by the measure of our talent. After all, isn't this what we ourselves have received at the touch of other writers?

If we are not manufacturing for Mills and Boon, if we are not writing political tracts disguised as works of the imagination, we do not have in mind a shadow company of heads out there, the chat-show groupies, or the Party supporters. But for some time now, I have felt a certain unease when I snap, 'Anyone who reads me'. The echo comes: 'Oh really? My, my!'

I begin to think there is a question to be asked, but it is not 'For whom do we write?' It is 'For whom can we write?' Is there not such a thing as writer potential, perhaps? The postulate reversed? And may I dismiss that one highhandedly?

These doubts – or more accurately suggestions – have come about in my particular case less from readings in literary theory over the years than as a result of experience out there in the world among, not ordinary people – to a writer no one is ordinary – among non-literary people. Which does not imply that they do not read, only that their reading does not take place within the culture most literature presupposes.

And here there must be a self-correction again. The suggestions are raised as much by the contradictions between literary theory

– which, of course, is concerned with the reader's perceptions as well as the writer's conscious and subconscious intentions – and the actual experience of the man or woman on the receiving end of all these deliberations: the generic reader.

For the generic reader surely must be the one I have in mind when I answer that I write for 'anyone who reads me'. More than twenty years ago, we were all entranced by or sceptical of (or both at once) the discoveries of structuralism and its analysis of our art and our relationship to the reader. The Freudian explanations that interested some of us seemed simplistic and speculative by comparison. The subconscious was ectoplasm in contrast with the precise methodology of a work such as, say, Roland Barthes's *S/Z*, which had been published in 1970 on the basis of work done in the sixties, and in which the whole emphasis of literature passed from writer to reader. Barthes's goal was 'to make the reader no longer a consumer but a producer of the text', of 'what can be read but not written'. The novel, the short story, the poem, were redefined as a 'galaxy of signifiers'.[1] As Richard Howard sums it up, Barthes's conviction of reading was that 'what is told is always the telling'.[2] And Harry Levin wrote,

> To survey his [the writer's] writings in their totality and chart the contours of their 'inner landscape' is the critical aim of current Structuralists and Phenomenologists. All of these approaches recognise, as a general principle, that every writer has his own distinctive configuration of ideas and sentiments, capacities and devices.[3]

Barthes's brilliance, with its element of divine playfulness, made and makes enthralling reading – for those of us who share at least sufficient of his cultural background to gain aesthetic pleasure

---

1   Roland Barthes, *S/Z*, translated by Richard Miller, preface by Richard Howard, Hill and Wang, 1974, p. 5.

2   Richard Howard, 'A Note on *S/Z*', preface to *S/Z* by Roland Barthes, p. xi.

3   Harry Levin, 'From Obsession to Imagination: The Psychology of the Writer', *Michigan Quarterly Review*, no. 3, vol. 12, summer 1974, p. 190.

and revelation from his cited 'signifiers'. It's a detective game, in which the satisfaction comes from correctly interpreting the clue – elementary, for Sherlock Holmes, but not for my dear Watson. Barthes, in the structural analysis of Balzac's novella *Sarrasine*, is the Sherlock Holmes who, deducing from his immensely rich cultural experience, instantly recognises the fingerprints of one cultural reference upon another. The reader is Watson, for whom, it may be, the 'signifier' signifies nothing but itself, if there is nothing in the range of his cultural experience for it to be referred to. It is a swatch of cloth that does not match any colour in his spectrum, a note that cannot be orchestrated in his ear. So that even if he is told that Balzac's clock of the Elysée Bourbon is actually chiming a metonymic reference to the Faubourg Saint-Honoré, and from the Faubourg Saint-Honoré to the Paris of the Bourbon restoration, and then to the restoration as a 'mythic place of sudden fortunes whose origins are suspect'[4] – there remains a blank where that reader is supposed to be reading 'what is not written'. The signifier works within a closed system: it presupposes a cultural context shared by writer and reader beyond mere literacy. Without that resource the reader cannot 'read' the text in Barthesian abundance.

'Words are symbols that assume a shared memory', says Borges.[5] Without that memory the Faubourg Saint-Honoré is just the name of a district, it has no elegant social or intellectual associations, either as an image conjured up from visits to Paris or as a symbol described in other books, visualised in paintings. The Bourbon restoration brings no association as a 'mythic place of sudden fortunes whose origins are suspect' because the reader doesn't know the place of the Bourbon restoration in French political and social history. The polymath interchange of the arts, letters, politics, history, philosophy, taken for granted by Barthes, is not the traffic of that reader's existence.

When one says one writes for 'anyone who reads me' one must be aware that 'anyone' excludes a vast number of readers who cannot

---

4 Roland Barthes, *S/Z*, p. 21.

5 Jorge Luis Borges, 'The Congress', *The Book of Sand*, translated by Norman Thomas di Giovanni, Penguin, 1979, p. 33.

'read' you or me because of concerns they do not share with us in grossly unequal societies. The Baudelairean correspondences of earlier literary theory cannot work for them, either, because 'correspondence' implies the recognition of one thing in terms of another, which can occur only within the same cultural resource system. This is the case even for those of us, like me, who believe that books are not made out of other books, but out of life.

Whether we like it or not, we can be 'read' only by readers who share terms of reference formed in us by our education – not merely academic but in the broadest sense of life experience: our political, economic, social and emotional concepts, and our values derived from these: our cultural background. It remains true even of those who have put great distances between themselves and the inducted values of childhood: who have changed countries, convictions, ways of life, languages. Citizenship of the world is merely another acculturation, with its set of givens which may derive from many cultures yet in combination becomes something that is not any of them.

'In our time, the destiny of man presents its meaning in political terms' – so said Thomas Mann, and I quoted this as an epigraph for one of my early novels. I saw the proposition then as the destiny of my characters: now I can see that it could be applied to the destiny of literature. For if politics interprets destiny, it must be accepted that the destiny of culture cannot be separated from politics. Posing to himself the big question, 'For whom do we write?' Italo Calvino wrote, 'Given the division of the world into a capitalist camp, an imperialist camp and a revolutionary camp, whom is the writer writing for?'[6]

While – if he has any sense – refusing to write for any camp, despite his personal political loyalties (and I think there are more of these than Calvino allows), the writer certainly writes from within one of them. And the reader reads from within one. If it is not the same as that of the writer, he is presumed at least to 'read' in the writer's signifiers some relevance to his own, different cultural background.

---

6   Italo Calvino, 'Whom Do We Write For?', *The Literature Machine*, translated by Patrick Creagh, Secker and Warburg, London, 1987, p. 86.

But frequently the reader does not find equivalents, in that culture, for the writer's referential range, because he has not 'read' that range. He cannot. The signifying image, word, flashes a message that cannot be received by a different set of preconceptions.

This happens even at apparently homogeneous cultural levels. In reviews of your fiction and the interviews to which you are subjected, this process can hatch in your text like a cuckoo's egg. What comes out is unrecognisable, but the reader, reviewer, journalist, insists that it is yours.

I experienced this when I came to the United States for the publication of a novel of mine entitled *Burger's Daughter*. The daughter and other characters in the story were centred around the personality of Lionel Burger, exemplifying the phenomenon – and problem – of ideology as faith in the family of an Afrikaner who, through becoming a Communist, devotes his life and his children's to the liberation of South Africa from apartheid.

In reviews, Burger was unfailingly referred to as a liberal: I myself was guilty of an unthinkable lack of deference to a famous talk-show personality when I contradicted his description of Burger as a noble white liberal.

'He's not a liberal, he's a Communist,' I interrupted.

But it was no good. None of these people 'read' me because in the ethos of mainstream American society a Communist could never, no matter in what country or social circumstances, be a good man. Yet it had to be acknowledged that Burger was a good man because he was a fighter against racism: therefore my signal must be that Burger was a liberal.

This is not a matter of misreading or misunderstanding. It is the substitution of one set of values for another, because the reader cannot conceive of these otherwise.

Yet not politics but class most calls into question the existence of the generic reader, the 'whoever reads me'. And by class I mean to signify economics, education and, above all, living conditions. The cultural setting from laws to latrines, from penthouse to poor-house, travelled by jet or on foot.

I grant that the difference between the material conditions of life signified in the text and those of the reader must be extreme, and manifest in the dogged daily experience of the reader, if the writer cannot be 'read' by him. And the powers of the imagination should never be underestimated. They sometimes can produce miracles of what, in the complexity of the work being read, is the most limited of referential links. As the seventeen-year-old daughter of a shopkeeper in a small mining town in Africa, I was able to 'read' *Remembrance of Things Past*. Why? Because, although the lineage Proust invented, so faithful to that of the French noblesse, genuine and parvenue, could not 'signify' much for me, the familial mores from which the book sets out, so to speak, and are there throughout – the way emotions are expressed in behaviour between mother and child, the place of friendship in social relations, the exaltation of sexuality as romantic love, the regulation of daily life by meals and visits, the importance of maladies – all this was within the context of middle-class experience, however far-flung.

And, by the way, where did I get the book from? Why, from the municipal library: and I could use the library because I was white – and so for me that also was part of the middle-class experience. No black could use that library: in the concomitance of class and colour a young black person of my age was thus doubly excluded from 'reading' Marcel Proust: by lack of any community of cultural background and by racist material conditions . . .

Hermeneutic differences between writer and reader are still extreme in our world, despite the advance in technological communications. There is a layer of common culture spread thin over the worlds, first, second and third, by satellite and cassette. The writer could count on the 'signifier' Dallas or Rambo to be received correctly and fully by any reader from Iceland to Zimbabwe, and almost any other points on the map culturally remote from one another. But the breadth of this potential readership paradoxically limits the writer: producing, it would seem, something close to the generic reader, it confines the writer to a sort of primer of culture, if he expects to be 'read'. It excludes signifiers that cannot be spelled out in that ABC. The writer's expectations of wider readership have diminished in inverse proportion to the expansion of technological communications.

And the effect of extreme difference in material conditions between writer and reader remain decisive. Such differences affect profoundly the imagery, the relativity of values, the referential interpretation of events between the cultural givens of most writers and, for example, the new class of literate peasants and industrial workers, emancipated by the surplus value of leisure earned by mechanisation and computerisation.

Writers, longing to be 'read' by anyone who reads them, from time to time attempt to overcome this in various ways. John Berger has experimented by going to live among peasants, trying to enter into their life-view as formed by their experience. He writes about their lives in a mode that signifies for us, who are not French peasants: we 'read' him with all the experience we share with him of literary exoticism, of life-as-literature providing the necessary layers of reference. He doesn't say whether the peasants read what he writes, but remarks that they are aware that he has access to something they don't have: 'another body of knowledge, a knowledge of the surrounding but distant world'.[7] A recent review of one of Bobbie Ann Mason's books sums up the general problem: '[She] writes the kind of fiction her own characters would never read.'[8]

In my own country, South Africa, there has been demonstrated recently a wider potential readership for writers in our population of 29 million, only 5 million of whom are white. Politically motivated, in the recognition that the encouragement of literature is part of liberation, trade unions and community groups among the black majority have set up libraries and cultural debate.

Now, I do not believe that one should be written down to. (Had I been confined in this way, I certainly never should have become a writer.) Once the love of literature ignites, it can consume many obstacles to understanding. The vocabulary grows in proportion

7   John Berger, 'An Explanation', *Pig Earth*, Pantheon, New York, 1979, p. 9.
8   Lorrie Moore, *New York Times Book Review*, 3 December 1989, review of *Love Life* by Bobbie Ann Mason, Harper and Row, New York, 1989.

to the skills of the writer in providing imaginative leaps. But these must land somewhere recognisable: and most writers share no assumptions with the kind of potential readership I have just described.

In Africa and many countries elsewhere, Updike's beautifully written genre stories of preoccupation with divorces and adulteries could touch off few referential responses in readers for whom sexual and family life are determined by circumstances of law and conflict that have very little in common with those of the professional class of suburban America. Their domestic problems are children in detention, lovers fleeing the country from security police, plastic shelters demolished by the authorities and patched together again by husband and wife. The novels of Gabriel García Marquéz, himself a socialist, presuppose an answering delight in the larger-than-life that can find little response in those whose own real experience outdoes all extremes. The marvellous fantasies of Italo Calvino require assumptions between writer and reader that are not merely a matter of sophistication.

Life is not like that for this potential readership. Books are not made of other books, for them. Furthermore, the imaginative projection of what life might be like is not like that. These texts cannot be 'read' even for the aspirations they suggest.

Surely this is true of most of us who are serious writers, in and from most countries where material conditions do not remotely correspond with those of the potential reader. It is most obvious in South Africa. White writers, living as part of an overprivileged minority, are worlds away from those of a migratory miner living in a single-sex hostel, a black schoolteacher grappling with pupils who risk their lives as revolutionaries, black journalists, doctors, clerks, harassed by the police and vigilantes around their homes. The gap sometimes seems too great to reach across for even the most talented and sensitive power of empathy and imaginative projection.

I am not saying, nor do I believe, that whites cannot write about blacks, or blacks about whites. Even black writers, who share with these readers disaffection and humiliation under racist laws, generally acquire middle-class or privileged, if unconventional, styles of living and working concomitant with middle-class signifiers, as they make their way as writers. Often it is only by a self-conscious effort of memory – using the signifiers of childhood, before they joined the elite of letters, or drawing on the collective memory of an oral tradition – that black writers can be sure they will be 'read' by their readers. Freedom of movement – weekend trips, stays in hotels, choice of occupation – which punctuates the lives of many fictional characters, signifies nothing to the migratory worker whose contract does not allow him to stay on in town if he changes jobs, and whose 'holiday' at the end of eighteen months down a mine is the return home to plough and sow.

The cosseted adolescent who rebels against the materialism of philistine parents signifies nothing to the child revolutionaries, an increasing phenomenon in Latin America as well as South Africa, often precociously intelligent, who have abandoned parents, never known home comforts, and taken on life-and-death decisions for themselves. Even among white-collar readers of this milieu, 'existential anguish' – Sartre's nausea or Freud's discontents – finds no answering association where there is a total preoccupation with the business of survival. *The Spoils of Poynton* cannot be read as the apotheosis of the cult of possession by someone who has never seen such objects to covet, someone whose needs would not correspond to any attraction they are presupposed to have – that given attraction taken as read, by the writer.

You might well object: who expects a poorly educated clerk or teacher to read Henry James? But, as I have tried to illustrate, many signifiers that are commonplace, assumed, in the cultural mode of the writer find no referents in that of the potential wider readership.

What can the writer count on if she/he obstinately persists that one can write for anyone who picks up one's book? Even the basic emotions, love, hate, fear, joy, sorrow, often find expression in a manner that has no correspondence between one code of culture and another.

The writer can count on the mythic, perhaps. On a personification of fears, for example, recognisable and surviving from the common past of the subconscious, when we were all in the cave together, when there were as yet no races, no classes, and our hairiness hid differences of colour. The prince who turns into a frog and the beetle Gregor Samsa wakes up to find himself transformed into are avatars of the fear of being changed into something monstrous, whether by the evil magic of a shaman or by psychological loss of self, that signify across all barriers, including that of time. They can be 'read' by anyone, everyone. But how few of us, the writers, can hope ever to create the crystal ball in which meaning can be read, pure and absolute: it is the vessel of genius, which alone, now and then, attains universality in art.

For the rest of us, there is no meta-culture. We ought to be modest in our claims. There is no generic reader, out there. The kiss of the millennium when art shall be universal understanding shows no sign of being about to release us from our limitations.

1989

Censorship — The Final Solution

The Case of Salman Rushdie

Riots, book-burning, the demand that a work shall be banned worldwide, publishers boycotted, the threatened toppling of a prime minister, five dead — has ever a book been the pretext for such a frenzy of righteous barbarism?

Reviled, sentenced to death by a religious authority, a price offered for his head, forced to flee his home and live under police guard — has ever a writer been persecuted as Salman Rushdie is? Victor Hugo, Flaubert, D.H. Lawrence and others may have suffered public opprobrium or exile. Milan Kundera, forbidden to write, had to earn a living cleaning windows. In Stalin's Soviet Union writers were banished to the Gulag. In South Africa, some writers have been forbidden to publish. Many books have been banned; some writers banned from any form of publishing their work. Even in the most repressive regimes, none – although they had offended public morals or political orthodoxy – was condemned to a double death: Rushdie's book to be expunged from world literature for ever, his life to be forfeited.

And this bloodthirsty baying comes from a pack of millions, not one fraction of one per *mille* of whom *have read the book*. That is clear from the simplistic reduction in which it is arraigned as being literally 'about' the Prophet Mohammed – and nothing else. Whereas anyone who actually has read, and been sufficiently literate fully to understand, this highly complex, brilliant novel knows that dominant among its luxuriant themes is that of displacement. Mohammed and the Muslim faith are the novelist's metaphors for, among other human dilemmas, spiritual displacement in the reversal of a process which brought imperialists to adjust themselves among the populations they conquered, and in our age brings people from those populations to reconcile the dichotomy between their own culture and the world of the West that has set them apart from that culture without granting acceptance in return.

The method being used by the Muslim leaders and communities against Salman Rushdie is (literally) a murderous refinement of the unchanging principle of censorship, which was and is and always will be to harness the word to the tyrant's chariot. The tyrant may be a dictator, a regime, moral or religious bigotry. For me, the Rushdie affair has revealed how any of these agents of censorship can advance, in collusion, its gains against freedom of expression. I am no stranger to censorship, living in South Africa. At various times,[1] three of my own books have been banned, and for several years, now, the press and media here have been grimly restricted under successive States of Emergency imposed to stifle opposition to apartheid. Yet it was an ugly revelation to find, in my country where the government outlaws freedom of expression, where all

---

[1] Three of Nadine Gordimer's novels were banned successively in South Africa: *A World of Strangers*, *The Late Bourgeois World* and *Burger's Daughter*.

who use the written word are fighting against the Publications Control Board and its ancillary laws, where individual Muslims have a proud and brave record in the liberation movements, that local Muslim extremists rose in fanatical response to a proposed visit by Salman Rushdie last November.

He had been invited to speak on censorship at a book week dedicated to that theme. The story is one that has become familiar: rabble-rousing meetings outside mosques, threats to burn book-shops, death threats not only to Rushdie but to those, including members of the Congress of South African Writers, involved in the invitation. And all this, of course, by people who had not read the book.[2] I know, because I had the single copy in the country, a proof sent to me by his American publisher. No matter; it was easy for the Muslim extremists to get the book banned, at once, *in absentia.* A word to the Publications Control Board (no doubt) from some member of the Muslim community with influence in the House of Delegates (the segregated 'house' of Indian collaborators in our apartheid tricameral parliament that excludes Africans), and it was done. We writers had the alternative of risking Salman Rushdie's life for our principles of freedom of expression or cancelling the visit. Now, with five dead in Pakistan, it can be seen that we made the only possible choice. But through religious thuggery the state has gained an ally in repression of the word, here.

I admit I have no religious sensibilities, of any faith, to be offended by a work of fiction. But I accept and respect that others have. Numerous books, plays, films have appeared in which Jesus Christ and the Virgin Mary, God himself, have been satirised, fictionally divested of divinity, and cast as imperfect mortals. The Christian faith remains unshaken. Surely Islam cannot be threatened by the fantasy of a single novel? Satan has taken a hand, all right, in the affair of *The Satanic Verses.* I can't believe that anyone's Divinity

---

2   I had gathered this information by questioning some reaction, from all those violently opposed to Rushdie's visit, to obvious points in the narrative any reader would recognise. Blank response. I was a member of a group of writers and journalists who met with the Muslim religious leader and his followers who declared to us that if Rushdie set foot on South African soil he would be killed.

could sanction what is being done to a writer. Religious fanaticism has discovered censorship's Final Solution for that enemy of darkness, the word. I write that with a shudder.

1989

The African Pot

My collection of African pots were bought at roadsides and village markets under trees. They were viewed at no *vernissage*, but among little pyramids of tomatoes, onions, bananas and mangoes. They have no provenance beyond my memory of where I found them. They are unsigned and I do not know if the artists are living or dead.

What is the relation of ownership to appreciation, I wonder? Since the great private collections of works of art must belong — because these people can afford to pay for them — to the rich, we jealously dismiss their appreciation as acquisitiveness. Because the shrewd and affluent middle class buy works of art as investment we decide pleasure doesn't come into it; they have price tags hanging on their walls. As democrats we assert the honest way to enjoy art is at the humble cost of a museum entry ticket. Art ought to belong to everybody, and this is the closest society can get to making it available to all, as a right, while preserving it for the benefit of all. (And, of course, some museums are free.) There's a moral convention that ownership must be punished by an inability to receive what the work of art has to offer.

But, looking at my pots, I realise that the special relationship I have with them doesn't come because I *own* them — ownership implies a market value or prestige, of which qualities they are innocent. It comes because I have the luxury of looking at them again and again, days without number, from the different perspectives of my daily life, in the objectivity of the different qualities of light that fall upon them, and in the subjectivity of my own moods. Leonardo da Vinci's *Virgin of the Rocks* is a painting I might choose as my favourite picture; but what chance do I have to drop in to the National Gallery in London more than once a year to renew my sense of the divine in her face?

Seen from the top of the stairs my pots strike me as a sort of keyboard – resonators of a musical instrument – where they are ranged on their low table. Or a choir. Their round apertures are open mouths, and the different circumferences of these, according to the size of the pot, suggest that they are actually mouthing, soundlessly, in close harmony: WAH wah WAHWAH wah-h . . . If I were to become sensitive enough to them, through long association, I might even be able to begin to hear it with my eyes and transpose the notation to my ears. Seen differently, at eye level, as you enter by the front door, the pots are pure volume; round, round-round, the elipses of their sides – but they have no sides, their spheres simply curve out of sight! – seeming to spin immobilely away from one another. They are ranged close but however clumsily I might shift them about they cannot be arranged faultily, so that they jostle: their roundness ensures that they touch only lightly, at their fullest diameter.

How can I write about one among my pots? In the anonymity of their creation – unattributed, traditional, functional in origin – they are, in a sense, all one pot.

Unlike other works of art, they do not attempt to recreate something in another medium: pigment on canvas creating a language of line and colour that stands for shape, space and light; marble standing for flesh. They are the earth they are made of. They are its colours – the colours of fields, swamps and river beds. Their common material is mediated only by fire, and on many of them fire has painted the only decoration, cloudy green-black shadings and inspired black brush-strokes sparse as those of Japanese masters. The fire is not the controlled one of a kiln, but the same open-air one where the cooking pots bubble. They are shaped not on a wheel but by hands; their surface texture has the faint striations of human skin. When you put your hand against my pots you are palm-to-palm with the unknown artist.

They are all as perfect, removed from their function, as they are *for* their function – which would be to hold water, maize, porridge or beer. They simply *are*. Their form can take on many concepts, material and abstract. Globe of the world/planet Earth; I twirl the large ones slowly. Hunger/repletion; I look down the inner maw or follow the promise of plenty in their calm rotundity. The big one I bought in Lesotho I held on my lap coming home by plane, thighs spread for its weight and arms round it for protection; a pot grand as a full womb. Then there is the little one that comes from Swaziland, blackened with the application of graphite from local outcrops, with its unique moulded ear-shapes in low relief. There is the one I found in Venda, with its incised curving bands, delicate as the veins on a leaf; and there's the very old one, its mouth not at the apex but obliquely tipped in balance, below, and its pale, grave-clay tints.

But I have put the Lesotho pot up on the desk before me and I know what I did not know until I began to think about my pots in the way one thinks anew of something one is going to write about. This pot is my favourite. Or rather, it favours me by answering some need. Perhaps it makes visible and concrete some proportion and wholeness I can't attain in my life. It's a large pot, yes, and the material of which it is made provides not only its shape but also its decoration. The base of sunset-rose clay is met at the widest part of the belly by dun bronze clay and is smeared over it in sweeping upwards strokes to form a calm garland of curves, like four suns rising above or sinking below a dim horizon. Its wide mouth is rimmed with the same sunset colour. The outline of the suns is not neat, and if I turn my pot I see gradations of colour, like the heart of flames, round its base. It stands firm if I rock it; and yet I know that integral to its beauty is its fragility, a thing of the earth meant to return to the earth. Enjoy it until it breaks.

To write about something is to remake it. I am now closer to my pot, to the maker of my pot, dead or alive, than I have ever been.

1989

The 1990s

A Writer's Vital Gift to a Free Society

The Satanic Verses

I 990. A new decade, freedoms rising – and while a writer comes out of prison to become president in one country, another writer is being hounded to death throughout the world.

As we move towards the end of the twentieth century we carry the abomination of the pillory of Salman Rushdie with us as the mark of Cain.

The 'anniversary' this week is not some celebration of the end of horrors that our century had overcome but the ghoulish reminder of a return of the repressed: the Nazi book-burnings of our time re-enacted only a year ago in an English city.

Salman Rushdie has not been seen for – how long? He has become one of the Disappeared, like those who vanished during a recent era in Argentina, and those who vanish under apartheid in South Africa. Repressive governments have the power to destroy lives in their own countries; when religions take over these methods, they have the power to terrorise, through their followers, anywhere in the world. The edict of the dead Ayatollah has jurisdiction everywhere, contemptuous of the laws of any country. Political refugees from repressive regimes can seek political asylum elsewhere; Salman Rushdie has nowhere to go. His oppression is unique. It is contemptible to read that some cultured people – including a few of his fellow writers – blame the victim for the savage and evil intolerance of his persecutors: he should have known that he would cause 'offence'. And this 'offence' is equated with the counter 'offence' of destroying the book and pronouncing death on the author – a punishment he should have expected.

As for the wrigglings of ecumenical 'understanding' of the Muslim position, it is incomprehensible that anyone in modern times who believes in God, under any name or avatar, could 'understand' the claim of divine authority to destroy a writer's creativity and end his life. No doubt the cry will go up: you are not a Muslim; you don't know our faith. But no erudite citations of text from the Koran or any other holy work can alter the fact that the basic tenet of all religions is the love of God manifest in the brotherhood of man. What did this writer commit against man? Does his novel anywhere suggest that people should harm one another? Does he, through his characters, advocate racism, fascism, hatred? There is no line in his pages that does anything of the kind. If those who are still baying after him had the ability, unblinkered by their prejudices, to read this book with the intelligence it deserves, they would receive its rewards.

The Italian writer, Primo Levi, who disappeared into Auschwitz for years because his Jewishness offended against the good Christian Nazis, has described 'a metamir . . . a metaphysical mirror that does not obey the law of optics but reproduces your image as it is seen by the person who stands before you'. A writer is a metamir. What Salman Rushdie sees, of his people Indian and British, their mores religious and secular, is something to be faced, not smashed. The crime against Rushdie is also a crime against the artist's vital gift to a free society, self-knowledge.

1990

Freedom Struggles out of the Chrysalis

I990. Euphoria: to be alive was – not exactly bliss, but certainly a high, as we saw and heard President de Klerk declare the African National Congress, the Pan-Africanist Congress and other liberation movements unbanned. The morning had begun with a more personal preoccupation for me and my three young comrades from the Congress of South African Writers. We'd set off early for the courts in Soweto, to attend a hearing of political charges against Mzwakhe Mbuli, our immensely popular musician and extraordinary poet-activist.

I took a small radio, so that we could hear de Klerk's speech in the long wait that invariably comes before a case is called before the magistrate. But as soon as the court opened it was merely remanded to a later date. So, somewhat downcast, we found ourselves able to get back to the city in time to watch on television the de Klerk speech at the opening of parliament.

We sat with mugs of tea in a backyard cottage occupied illegally in a white suburb by a black man. (The pressure of population and the mood of confidence among blacks is breaking down city segregation.) Of the four of us, I, the white, was the only one with the right to vote for the three-colour parliament we were looking at. Of the three black men, Mxolisi Godana, Raks Seakhoa and Menzi Nbaba, Raks had spent five years as a political prisoner on Robben Island, and Menzi had endured months in solitary detention in 1988.

De Klerk's address was skilfully divided for delivery alternately in English and Afrikaans. It was a cliffhanger. We waited a long time for him to come to any pronouncement on the banned organisations and Nelson Mandela. 'That'll be in English,' Menzi predicted wryly; and when it came, it was – perhaps to ensure there would be no mistranslation for the outside world, perhaps to protect the Afrikaner right wing at least from the affront of hearing the Afrikaans language soiled by the expression of such a statement.

What we had been conditioned to expect of de Klerk, by the media and our own speculations, was the announcement of Mandela's release. Put bluntly, Mandela is what the world wants from de Klerk in return for the lifting of sanctions. What Mandela and the Mass Democratic Movement want was somehow not in the barter. So it was with amazement, a singing in the ears, that we in that small room heard the leader of the South African government announce that the ANC, the PAC – even the South African Communist Party! – were henceforth unbanned.

We looked to one another, eager for confirmation – politicians are so clever, had we missed some catch? No. The plain words were coming out of the mouth of a South African white president. And I was hearing them in the company of three young blacks who were born after black liberation movements were banned at the beginning of the 1960s. They had never known what it was to have political loyalties and aspirations that do not break the law and lead to prison.

It was as if they were coming out of a chrysalis. Their movements, in the excitement, were the awkward ones of drying wings. Back-slapping and grasping hands wouldn't do. Everything seemed inadequate to express an event with so many consequences.

Maybe later in the day, after we'd parted, they joined celebrating crowds, but there among the tea mugs, the exhilaration snatched at personal possibilities. Mxolisi's mind flew to close friends in exile: 'They'll be able to come home! Bring their kids!' And we swapped the names of our writers who could soon be among us, as well as the politicians, away for a lifetime. And Mandela. For us, as for the great and revered man himself, it had never been what would have satisfied the world – his messianic deliverance from apartheid – but the freeing of the people, no less. Of course, what de Klerk had conceded in meeting some of the conditions of the Harare agreement was less . . . but still so much. Our minds flew through the stages by which, once the ANC was free to organise and the exiles return, with Mandela and Sisulu and the others together in leadership, the remaining conditions for negotiation would follow. Inevitably. Unstoppably. We locked the cottage door behind us and walked out into streets that surely couldn't, shouldn't look familiar?

I stopped by a liquor store to buy some celebratory libation, and a white man waiting for his beer asked the proprietor whether he knew if anything had happened there in Cape Town today? The white man behind the counter hadn't heard.

'The ANC and the PAC are unbanned,' I offered.

'Oh my God, all hell's going to break loose for us now!' – the customer loped out with averted eyes.

'Don't worry, don't worry!' the white proprietor yelled after him, not wanting a customer to leave with a bad memory of a moment in his shop. And he turned to me: 'I don't know about you, but the trouble is we've been told and told, since I was a kid, we just the only ones, we just everything here.'

The morning after: the chaff of euphoria has blown away. I still believe the unbanning of the liberation movement is the real beginning of the great release. But studying de Klerk's speech instead of listening to it, reading the comments of leaders at home and in exile, one sees what was left unsaid and undone. The President, dazzling us with the unbannings, said little or nothing about abolishing apartheid legislation. He did not speak of the Group Areas or the Population Registration Act; he did not touch upon the basis of apartheid that is under my feet as I write this – the land whose ownership remains forbidden to the blacks from whom it was taken by conquest, and by laws they had no part in making. The exiles my friends and I were so happy to welcome home, yesterday – some have already reminded us that they will not come back to live under apartheid laws of any kind, under apartheid justice. And I remind myself this morning that while de Klerk has said he is releasing Mandela unconditionally, he has not met all the conditions that Mandela himself set for his own release – in particular the repeal of apartheid laws.

The important move towards negotiated change that came about yesterday did so because of the growing power of the black people of South Africa to influence the economy and lifestyle of white South Africans, and the pressure of sanctions.

Mrs Thatcher is wrong when, in self-congratulation and hubris, she attributes change to her opposition to sanctions. Exactly the reverse is true. Without sanctions, there would have been no such speech in the House of Assembly yesterday. Within South Africa, we have to thank young people like the three with whom I heard the speech, who have never known freedom and have suffered imprisonment for a new South Africa; and in the outside world, we have to thank those who brought South Africa to some sense of reality through economic and political pressure, and who would serve our freedom best by continuing this policy until there are no gaps or silences in the momentous speeches to come.

1990

Sorting the Images from the Man

Nelson Mandela

I have just come home from the rally that welcomed Nelson Mandela back to Soweto. It was the occasion of a lifetime for everyone there; including the dot in the crowd that was myself, as one of the whites who have identified with the African National Congress through the years when it was a crime to do so. Overwhelmingly, the joyous gyrating mass that filled Soccer City Stadium, clung to retaining structures like swarming bees, even somehow hoisted one another up on old gold-mine headgear outside the fences, had been born and grown to adulthood – young whites as well as blacks – while Mandela spent twenty-seven years in prison. Yet all that time there was no black child in whose face, at the mention of his name, there was not instant recognition. And there were no whites – enemies of the cause of black freedom as well as its supporters – who did not know who this man was. His body was hidden behind walls; his presence was never obliterated by them.

When Bishop Desmond Tutu received the Nobel Peace Prize in the twentieth year of Mandela's imprisonment, he said he accepted it for Mandela, for all prisoners of conscience, and for all those ordinary black people whose employers do not know their workers' surnames. And on the day of Mandela's release, when Dr Nthato Motlana, himself a symbolic figure of resistance, was asked whether he didn't think Mandela should now come to live in Soweto 'among his people', Motlana said: 'He's not a Sowetan, he's a South African. Wherever he lives in our country he is among his own people.'

That may have sounded like a grandiose put-down but it is strangely true. Apart from the Afrikaner right wing, whose fringe of Nazi crazies give the swastika on their flag a new twist and wave 'Hang Mandela' posters at each other, whites have not merely accepted Mandela's return but turn to him now as the only one who can absolve and resolve: absolve the sin of apartheid and resolve the problems of reconciliation and integration. President de Klerk's boldness in freeing Mandela has as its ironic obverse a fervent submission to this idea. He counts on Mandela: without him, the legendary bird rising out of the bars, blue-winged and with a sprig of olive held ready for three decades in its beak, the transformation of South Africa into a place where de Klerk's white electorate can still live can't be realised. The blacks' personification of the hidden Mandela as the image of their ultimate liberation is superimposed by the whites' picture of him as their salvation, forming a single image.

So there were the faded photographs of a tall young man with smiling eyes and an old-fashioned part in his hair, umpteenth-generation reproductions that looked like ectoplasmic evidence, and there was the vision of the generic hero who (our Che Guevara if not messiah) could never be dead even if, as sometimes seemed only too likely, he were to die unseen. On the cover of *Time* his Identikit portrait appeared in final apotheosis in the guise of a beaming idol, something between Harry Belafonte and Howard Rollins.

And then there walked out of prison a man unrecognisable as any of these. The real man, with a face sculpted and drawn by the spirit within himself enduring through thirty years, by the marks of incredible self-discipline, of deep thought, suffering, and the unmistakable confidence of faith in the claims of human dignity. An awesome face.

Now he's here. He confronts us, the man among us. He spoke bluntly, in Soweto, to black and white, sparing us nothing. He cut through the adulation of the crowd to demand from blacks an end to violence between black people. He spelled out to whites their responsibility for the consequences of poverty, homelessness and unemployment caused by the laws they made and must abolish.

By contrast, few care to interpret in equally plain language the staggering responsibility that expectations lay upon Mandela. 'Reconciliation' in a 'new South Africa' by him ultimately means finding houses for hundreds of thousands of blacks whose needs dating back to World War II have never been met. It means finding the 4,000 skilled personnel the dwindling economy desperately needs, from among a population whose majority has received a hopelessly inadequate, segregated education. It means – turning up only one among monster problems the big buzzwords hide – transforming a police force and army which have been the brutal enemies of the people of South Africa for generations.

Big words: a kind of helplessness among whites – the government – has dumped on Mandela the problems of the moment as well as the long-term: violence, crowd control, black school attendance. The mantra is Mandela; the hum is everywhere, but does it really represent the guru? The man himself is not carried away. He reiterates firmly that 'no individual leader' can take on the enormous task of creating unity and remaking South Africa on his own, that any decision by which the bread of negotiation will be broken with the government will be made by the combined leadership of the ANC, of which he is 'a loyal and disciplined member'. The onus rests on whites; they must accept the policies of the ANC as a standpoint for negotiation as they accept Mandela. And he makes it absolutely clear that whether there will be feast or famine at that symbolic table depends on the whites' and blacks' understanding of what the big words really mean if they are to spell a united, non-racist, democratic and free South Africa. Mandela doesn't want to be worshipped. He wants the people of South Africa to remake themselves together. That's his greatness.

1990

Censorship and its Aftermath

It has been a long time since censorship could be symbolised by the blue pencil; even the word processor with its superhuman capacity for total erasure won't do.

We who read *Index on Censorship* and – in countries like my own, South Africa – the local pamphlets keeping track of what can't be printed, read or said, know that over vast tracts of the world censorship actually has been maintained by laws far beyond the control of any duly constituted Board of Censors. The vision of retired persons trying out on one another what passages may be sexually exciting or cause trembling at the prospect of subversion of the state are not the principal threat to the word. With television's banalisation of sex, half the mandate of the sedentary censor has gone the way of those dashes between first and last letters.

Political censorship has taken place of first importance since before the second half of our century. And it has been taken over, surely as never before, by the knuckle-duster imprisonment of writers and journalists, the banning of individual writers, the closure of newspapers, the prosecution of editors, the exclusion of television crews and journalists from the scene of events – all under laws that make conventional censorship appear namby-pamby. Repressive regimes from Hitler's, Stalin's, Franco's, to Verwoerd's and Botha's, taking in so many others on the way, East to West, from the Northern to the Southern Hemisphere, have maintained themselves with these laws that, at first appearing ancillary to censorship, ended by rendering it old hat, almost redundant.

Coming as I do from a country which has regarded itself as part of the Western world (a claim somewhat in dispute . . .), you will forgive me if I take as my paradigm what has prevailed there, with emphasis on the immediate past.

Censorship in the conventional sense we have had with us since the early 1960s, with some amendments to the law, over the years, that made it worse. The right of appeal to the courts of law was removed, and with it the Western principle of the accused being innocent until proved guilty. Ever since, the author of a banned work – book, play, film – has been declared guilty of offence *before* he/she has the right to appear before the mock-up court of the Publications Appeal Board with its jury of 'experts' appointed by the Minister of Home Affairs. The institution of Appeal Board hearings was one of the first of many moves by which the rule of law has been bypassed as the South African white minority has twisted and turned its avowed 'Western' values to maintain apartheid power.

In 1988, 824 publications, films and objects (this usually means calendars and posters) were banned. Few of these bans applied to what, even in the broadest sense, we writers would term literature. The fact is that latterly the banning of serious literature, even that dangerous stuff, political non-fiction, as distinct from tracts, which are consistently banned, has become rare. A factor has been the worldly sophistication of the man who was the Chairman of the Board until April 1990, Professor Cobus van Rooyen. He realised that in a country where the masses are neither book-literate nor have libraries which would help them to become so, serious literature, whether by black or white writers, at home or from abroad, and no matter how potentially 'inflammatory', reaches only a section of the population that already has contact with such influences. But the principal reason for apparent leniency is that a vast proportion of the masses *is* newspaper-literate, media-literate, and therefore the focus of state information and thought control must be the media.

For this purpose, the Publications Control Board has no authority, nor is it needed. In 1989, under the provisions of the second and third of our successive States of Emergency, four newspapers and journals were threatened with suspension, two were closed down, fifty-two journalists covering a protest march were arrested and held for some hours; there were twenty-four separate trials with 198 defendants involving journalists and a few other writers, and there were dockets opened against journalists from a spread of ten papers, both alternative press and mass circulation, for infringements under the State of Emergency and its related Acts.

The South African Broadcasting Corporation also had no need of the Publications Control Board, or even the State of Emergency, in order to censor: it admitted that there were about a thousand songs 'we just don't play', ranging from the soundtrack of *Cry Freedom* to George Michael's disc, 'I Want Your Sex'. I wonder whether the *Cry Freedom* track will ring out over the SABC, now that under the de Klerk regime of 'new enlightenment' the film has been released from ban; I don't know whether George Michael's plea will be heard . . .

In February this year, with President de Klerk's unbanning of the African National Congress, the Pan-Africanist Congress, the South African Communist Party and other political organisations prohibited since 1960 or earlier, the removal of a number of people from the list of those who may not be quoted, the lifting of gagging restrictions on other organisations and individuals, and the release of some political prisoners, a wall (on our side of the world, as well) was breached, and information and ideas dammed up for at least three decades began to flow in a way we had forgotten.

But as Gilbert Marcus of Witwatersrand University's Centre For Applied Legal Studies[1] notes, 'there remain over one hundred laws that restrict the free flow of information . . . the "new enlightenment" of February 1990 has left all of these laws untouched'. Journalists may be ordered out of an area or detained, organisations and the activities of individuals restricted. The Internal Security Act, with such powers, is still in force; the Police Act has severe controls on the reporting of police activity – my son, happening to have a camera on him when he dropped in to visit a friend in hospital last month, only just managed to talk his way out of arrest by attendant police when he paused to take a picture of a demonstration by hospital personnel on strike. There is the Prisons Act,

---

1   Gilbert Marcus, 'The New Enlightenment', Centre For Applied Legal Studies, University of the Witwatersrand, 1990.

which keeps what happens in prisons from public scrutiny, the Defence Act, which restricts reporting of any troop movements, and has on occasion made it possible for a military action never to be known about by the public, and the Protection of Information Act, which prevents the publication of information on virtually all official documents.

The Media Council, a conservative body, is now to review all legislative restraints on media reporting. ACAG, the Anti-Censorship Action Group,[2] is sceptical: 'It remains to be seen whether this is an exercise to gain the backing of media people for the *retention* of some of these laws.'

The government complains that we in radical opposition to censorship always move the goalposts when the law scores a piecemeal reform.

Of course we do; and that is why we have made the gains we have in our determination to win freedom of expression. Early this year the extraordinarily courageous editor of a newly-launched Afrikaans weekly, *Die Vrye Weekblad*, ran away with the grim game against suppression of information by exposing the existence and connection with the police of the incredibly named 'Civil Co-operation Bureau' – the death squad which, over more than a decade, has murdered opposition activists, including lawyers and an academic. Taken up by other newspapers and arousing public outrage, the exposé led to revelations of Defence Force involvement in the death squads with the possible knowledge of members of the government. A judicial commission of inquiry, the Harms Commission, was set up. That, we must grant 'the new enlightenment', is unlikely to have happened during the Botha regime. And the sticky network of revelations consequent upon a single editor's vigilance did not end there. Other papers took new courage in investigative reporting. Another commission, the Hiemstra Judicial Commission into 'alleged' irregularities in the Johannesburg City Council, revealed that the council has employed spies to infiltrate all manner of progressive gatherings

2 ACAG UPDATE, March 1990.

to report who said what. In addition there were files kept on many vocal local citizens, including myself.

Mr Louis Pienaar, Administrator-General of Namibia, was out of a job when Namibia became independent; in April he was appointed new Chairman of the Publications Appeal Board. The daily newspaper, *The Star,*[3] reported that he is 'widely regarded as an enlightened thinker in the field of the arts', but gave no examples of people who do the regarding. ACAG[4] recalls that he was certainly 'not noted for his support of the press' during his tenure in Namibia. *The Weekly Mail*[5] reminds us that he will find himself faced with a mass of appeals for the unbanning of African National Congress and other liberation organisations' media material; because of the ancillary laws I've cited, these have not been automatically released by the unbanning of the organisations themselves. We'll see how Mr Pienaar deals with this long-suppressed expression of the ideas of a vast majority of South Africans. While declaring[6] that he sees his most important task as promoting 'dialogue along with the changing circumstances in South Africa', he wants to 'make it clear . . . that violence and intimidation are not part of democracy, and where these appear in publications I will take very firm action'. Gilbert Marcus[7] comments: 'Democratic principles are predicated on freedom of expression as a priority. And for this reason there has to be respect for views which are contrary, strident and militant. The proper discharge of Pienaar's duties will also entail a recognition that people are generally moved to violence not by what they read or see, but because of the conditions under which they live.'

'Are we to believe that those who write literature have a greater right to free speech than those who write pulp?' John le Carré's statement,[8] vis-à-vis the Rushdie case, surprised some people and disgusted others – including myself.

3   *The Star*, 19 March 1990.
4   ACAG UPDATE, March 1990.
5   *The Weekly Mail*, 5–11 April 1990.
6   Ibid.
7   Gilbert Marcus, 'The New Enlightenment'.
8   John le Carré, *Guardian*, 15 January 1990.

Yes, yes, we *do* believe that. It is surely one of the tenets of the stand against censorship that the abuse of human sensibilities – which is what pornography and pornographic violence are, since their content is lifted completely out of the complex context of life to which sex and strife belong – cannot be confused with works in which that complex context is encompassed in the creative spirit of exploration and daring. The object of the one is selective exploitation; that of the other is the writer's huge and hazardous attempt to make sense of the whole of life.

We admit that it is difficult to protect society from the first while freeing the second. Yet the basic principle in doing so is to disavow the totally false equation. The task is to find a legal framework that will protect freedom of expression while dealing with the abuse of human sensibility, whether sexual, social or political.

This last – the political – is the great issue in South Africa. Albie Sachs, the African National Congress's constitutional adviser and a fine writer, visualises for the post-apartheid future 'an entrenched Bill of Rights in a constitution which declares certain fundamental rights and freedoms and establishes an independent judiciary to ensure they are maintained . . . Then, if parliament were to adopt any law, or if there were some executive act which abridged the freedom of speech in any unconstitutional way, a citizen could go to the courts and have that act struck down.' We should 'look at legislation in democratic countries throughout the world . . . study very carefully what they have done in relation to the limits of freedom of speech when it comes to racial defamation and incitement to racial hostility, and try to distil from that some kind of common minimum factor whereby the limits are set'. And he says what needs to be said for all of us, everywhere, who are concerned with the freedom of expression: '. . . the issues go well beyond speech. They touch souls.'[9]

To turn more specifically to writers of literature. There is not one of us writing in South Africa today who has not either begun or spent the major part of a working life under conventional

---

9   Albie Sachs, 'The Gentle Revenge at the End of Apartheid', *Index on Censorship*, April 1990.

censorship and the chain-mail laws which reinforce it. While most have chafed at and some fiercely fought censorship, we have got used to it. To paraphrase Graham Greene, every country becomes accustomed to its own restrictions as part of its own violence. We have defied censorship and/or found ways round it. At the same time, inevitably, it has brought about deeper reactive consequences in our writers. And what is true of us is surely true of any other country where the *very defiance* of oppression creates defining restrictions of its own. I was in Hungary at a Wheatland Conference last year, and the session devoted to our host Hungarian writers revealed in them what I can only call fear of freedom – fear, for a writer, meaning not knowing how you are going to write next. Although they were overjoyed, as citizens, at their new freedom, they were bewildered about its meaning at the internal level from which the transformation of the entities of living into the writer's vision takes place. With the head-clamps on the writer removed, there disquietingly is revealed – an aftermath of censorship I believe we've never considered – cramped and even distorted imagination.

For when I speak of the reactive consequences of censorship I am referring to the *other* pressure upon the writer that censorship calls into being. The counter-pressure of resistance also, ironically, screws down the head-clamp. Defiance of censorship and the regime it serves calls upon the writer to cut and weld his work into a weapon. It is necessary. But he may have to discard much of his particular insight in the process. It is impressed upon him that certain themes are relevant; certain modes are effective. Accustomed to the confines of allegory and allusion, our Eastern European colleagues now have to teach themselves the choice of numerous other modes to express life experience. Accustomed to the obsessive demands of choosing every situation and word for its trajectory against apartheid, South African writers will have to open themselves to a new vocabulary of life.

Many are ill-prepared, particularly the young writers. For everywhere where there has been censorship the counter-orthodoxy of resistance in literature has also come about. It has been an era when, in Brecht's words, 'to speak of trees is treason'. And to quote Albie Sachs again: 'Instead of criticism, we get solidarity criticism. Our artists are not pushed to improve the quality of their work, it is enough to be politically correct . . . It is as though our rulers stalk every page . . . everything is obsessed by the oppressors and the trauma they have imposed . . . What are we fighting for, if not the right to express our humanity in all its forms, including our sense of fun and capacity for love and tenderness and our appreciation of the beauty of the world?'[10]

We must not think that when tyrants fall and there is a new constitution in his/her country the writer regains all that has been lost. It is not a matter of not having anything left to write about. Only those who jumped on the anti-apartheid and anti-communist bandwagons, having nothing in their baggage but the right clichés, will lose their dubious inspiration and need to find some other way of selling themselves. The real writers, on the contrary, will have the less sensational, wonderfully daunting task of finding the way to deal with themes that have been set aside in second place while writing was in battle dress – the themes of 'humanity in all its forms', human consciousness in all its mystery, which demand not orthodoxy of any nature, but the talent and dedication and daring to explore and convey freely through the individual sensibility. Many writers, constricted by censorship on one side and the orthodoxy of the anti-mode on the other, have never developed the ability to deal with anything outside the events and emotions their historical situation prescribed.

And what of the writer under that most damning form of censorship, exile?

Does the possibility of a return home for Kundera, Milosz, mean that the moment they set foot there the years of imaginative growth on their home soil, lost to them, will be instantly restored? Who can give to South African writers in exile, Dennis Brutus, Mongane Wally Serote, Mandla Langa, a whole roster of others, the

10   Albie Sachs, 'Preparing Ourselves for Freedom', ANC In-house Seminar on Culture, 1990.

experience of the life and languages of their own people – a writer's bread and being – they have missed?

There is no form of censorship that does not affect a writer's sensibility, whether suffered for years or as an isolated event. Commenting on the indecency case against *Madame Bovary* after he won it in 1857, Flaubert[11] writes of this and of another aftermath of censorship: the establishment of spurious literary values. '. . . my book is going to sell unusually well for a writer's first. But I am infuriated when I think of the trial; it has deflected attention from the novel's artistic success, and I dislike to be associated with things alien to it. To such a point that all this row disquiets me profoundly . . . I long to return, and forever, to the silence and solitude I emerged from; to publish nothing; never to be talked of again.'

Which brings me to the ghastly reversed fulfilment of that particular traumatic response among many that censorship calls forth in its distortion of a writer's life. Salman Rushdie is not with us today, condemned to incarceration, silence and solitude, talked of endlessly under the cruellest and most depraved form of censorship this century has known, notwithstanding the Gulag. He is a writer of prodigious vitality and gifts, and nothing will stop him writing. But when he is free to live in the world again, nothing can give him back the time that evil religious fanatics took from him, and that the world allowed the perpetrators to take, nothing can restore to his novel, cleansed of the dirty fingerprints of those who manhandled it, raised from the ashes of those who burned it, the artistic attention that, *alone*, belongs to it.

While we rejoice at new freedom for writers in many countries long denied it, and work for freedom for writers in those countries where the many devices of censorship still prevail, some perpetrators carrying their gags and guns and book-burnings all over the world, we must also remember that writers are never freed of the past. Censorship is never over for those who have experienced it. It

---

11 *Letters of Gustave Flaubert* 1830–1857, selected, edited and translated by Francis Steegmuller, Belknap Press, Harvard, 1980, p. 224.

is a brand on the imagination that affects the individual who has suffered it, for ever. Where censorship appears to be swept away in the rubble of toppled regimes, let us make sure that it does not rise again to the demands of some future regime, for the generations of writers who will grow up, anywhere in the new world in the making. As Barbara Masakela,[12] Secretary for Culture in the African National Congress, has said bluntly, and surely for all of us: 'We are not prepared to see culture become a case of arrested development, frozen at the point of liberation. Nor will we be content with a culture vulnerable to becoming the fiefdom of some future oppressive ruling class.'

1990

Joseph Roth

Labyrinth of Empire and Exile

S trangely, while I have been writing about Joseph Roth, the wheel of karma – or historical consequence? – has brought Roth's territory back to a re-enactment of the situation central to his work. In Roth's novels – and supremely through the lives of the Von Trotta family in his masterpieces, *The Radetzky March* (1932) and its sequel *The Emperor's Tomb* (1934) – we see the deterioration of a society, an empire, in which disparate nationalities have been forced into political unity by an overriding authority and its symbol: the Austro-Hungarian Empire and the personality of Emperor Franz Josef. There the rise of socialism and fascism against royalism led to Sarajevo and the First World War. After World War II the groups that had won autonomy were forced together again, if in a slightly different conglomerate, by another all-powerful authority and its

---

12   Barbara Masakela, 'Possible Strategies for Culture in a Post-Apartheid South Africa', paper given at UNESCO Working Group on Apartheid, Dakar, Senegal, November 1989.

symbol: the Communist bloc and the personality of Joseph Stalin. Now restlessness and rebellion, this time against the socialism that has not proved to be liberation, brings once again the breakup of a hegemony. Passages in Roth's work, about the Slovenes, Croats and Serbs, could with scarcely a change describe what has happened in Yugoslavia in 1991.

Roth: he looks out from a book-jacket photograph. Just the face in a small frame; it is as if someone held up a death mask. The ovals of the eyes are black holes. The chin pressed up against the black shadow of a moustache hides stoically the secrets of the lips. A whole life, in bronze, seems there. And there's another image in that face: the huge sightless eyes with their thick upper and lower lids dominating the width of the face have the mysteriously ancient gaze of a foetus, condemned to suffer the world.

'Je travaille, mon roman sera bon, je crois, plus parfait que ma vie,' Roth wrote.[1] Prefaces to some translations of his books give the same few penny-life facts: born in 1894 in Galicia, served in the Austro-Hungarian army during the First World War, worked as a journalist in Vienna, Berlin and Prague, left for France in 1933, wrote fifteen novels and novellas mainly while taking part in the émigré opposition to the Nazis, died an alcoholic in Paris in 1939. I failed to find a full biography in English.[2] After having re-read all Roth's fiction available to me, I am glad that, instead, I know him in the only way writers themselves know to be valid for an understanding of their work: through the work itself. Let the schools of literary criticism, rapacious fingerlings, resort to the facts of the author's life before they can interpret the text.

Robert Musil, Roth's contemporary in Austria-Hungary,

---

1   In a letter to his translator, Blanche Gidon, quoted by Beatrice Musgrave in her introduction to *Weights And Measures*, Dent, London, 1983, p. 9. Roth lived in Paris for some years and two of his novels, *Le Triomphe de la beauté* and *Le Buste de L'Empereur*, were published first in French. *Le Triomphe de la beauté* probably was written in French; it appears not to have been published in German.

2   I have been told that the standard German biography, David Bronsen's *Joseph Roth: Eine Biographie*, Kiepenheuer and Witsch, Cologne, 1974, is now in the process of translation for Roth's English publisher, Chatto and Windus. Another biography by Nat Cohen of Toronto is planned for publication by the Overlook Press.

although the two great writers evidently never met, put into the mouth of his Ulrich 'One can't be angry with one's own time without damage to oneself';[3] to know that Roth's anger destroyed him one has only to read the great works it produced. The text gives us the man, not the other way around. The totality of Joseph Roth's work is no less than a *tragédie humaine* achieved in the techniques of modern fiction. No other contemporary writer, not excepting Thomas Mann, has come so close to achieving the wholeness – lying atop a slippery pole we never stop trying to climb – that Lukács cites as our impossible aim.

From the crude beginnings in his first novels, *The Spider's Web* (1923) and *Hotel Savoy* (1924), the only work in which Roth was satisfied to use the verbal equivalent of the expressionist caricaturing of Georg Grosz or Otto Dix, through *Flight Without End* (1927), *The Silent Prophet* (1929),[4] and all his other works with, perhaps, the exception of the novellas *Zipper and his Father* (1928) and *Fallmerayer the Stationmaster* (1933), his anti-heroes are almost all soldiers, ex-prisoners of war, deserters: former aristocrats, bourgeois, peasants and criminals all declassed in the immorality of survival of the 1914–1918 war. This applies not only to the brutal or underhand necessity that survival demands, but also to the sense that, in the terrible formulation of a last member of the Trotta dynasty, they had been 'found unfit for death'.

All the young are candidates for the solutions of Communism or fascism when there are no alternatives to despair or dissipation. Their fathers are unable to make even these choices, only to decay over the abyss of memory. All, young and old, are superfluous

---

3   Robert Musil, *The Man without Qualities*, vol. I, Secker and Warburg, London, 1961, p. 64, translated by Eithne Wilkins and Ernst Kaiser. Musil was born in 1880, and though long neglected as a writer outside German-speaking culture, was not forgotten as long as Roth. Musil became a figure in world literature in the fifties; Roth's work had to wait another twenty years before it was reissued in Germany, let alone in translation.

4   *The Silent Prophet* was edited from unpublished work, with the exception of fragments published in *24 Neue Deutsche Erzähler* and *Die Neue Rundschau* in 1929, and published after Roth's death, in 1966. The English translation by David Le Vay was published in the United States by the Overlook Press in 1980. The work appears to have been written, with interruptions, over several years. The central character, Kargan, is supposedly modelled on Trotsky.

men to an extent Lermontev could not have conceived. Women are attendant upon them in this circumstance. Roth, although he often shows Joyce's uncanny ability to write about women from under their skin, sees them according to their influence on men. 'We love the world they represent and the destiny they mark out for us.' While his women are rarely shown as overtly rejecting this male-determined solution to their existence, they are always unspokenly convinced of their entitlement to life, whether necessity determines it should be lived behind a bar, in a brothel bed, or as an old *grande dame* in poverty. No better than the men, they connive and plot; but even when he shows them at their slyest and most haughtily destructive, he grants them this spiritedness. If one reads the life (his) from the work, it is evident that Roth suffered in love and resented it; in most of his work desired women represent sexual frustration, out of reach.

The splendid wholeness of Roth's oeuvre is achieved in three ways. There's the standard one of cross-casting characters from one novel to the next. There's the far bolder risk-taking, in which he triumphs, of testing his creativity by placing different temperaments from different or (even more skilled) similar backgrounds in the same circumstances in different novels. There is the overall paradoxical unity of traditional opposition itself, monarchic/revolutionary, pitched together in the dissolution of all values, for which he finds the perfect physical metaphor: the frontier between Franz Josef's empire and the Tsar's empire, exemplified in Jadlowsky's tavern, which appears in both *The Radetzky March* and *Weights and Measures*. There, the rogue Kapturak, a Jew whose exploitation of others' plight stems from his own as a victim of Tsarist anti-Semitism, hides the Russian army deserters he's going to sell to labour agents in America and Australia. The only contacts between men are contraband; commerce of this kind is all that will be left of the two monarchic empires fighting each other to a mutual death, and the only structure that will still exist in the chaos to follow; the early twentieth-century class struggle will arise from that.

Roth's *petite phrase* in the single great work into which all this transforms is not a Strauss waltz but the elder Strauss's 'Radetzky

March', in honour of the Austrian field marshal who was victorious against Sardinia. Its tempo beats from the tavern through Vienna and all the villages and cities of Franz Josef's empire, to Berlin in those novels where the other imperial eagle has only one head. For Roth's is the frontier of history. It is not recreated from accounts of the past, as *War And Peace* was, but recounted contemporaneously by one who lived there, in every sense, himself. This is not an impudent literary value judgement; it is, again, the work that provides a reading of the author's life. Here was a writer obsessed with and possessed by his own time. From within it he could hear the drum rolls of the past resounding to the future.

Musil's evocation of that time is a marvellous discourse; Roth's involves a marvellous evanescence of the author in his creation of a vivid population of conflicting characters expressing that time. His method is to show a kind of picaresque struggle on the inescapable chain of the state. He rarely materialises as the author. There is his odd epilogue to *Zipper and his Father*, apparently some sort of acknowledgement that this, his most tender book (for while their situation makes both Musil and Roth ironic writers, Roth is tender where Musil is detachedly playful), is a form of the obeisance to the past that is autobiography. And there is his prologue to *The Silent Prophet*, his most politically realistic and least imaginatively realised book. In this prologue he comes as near as he ever will to an authorial credo with respect to his pervasive theme, the relation of the individual to the state. He says his characters are not 'intended to exemplify a political point of view – at most, it [a life story] demonstrates the old and eternal truth that the individual is always defeated in the end'.

The state or empire is the leg iron by which his characters are grappled. The political movement against the state, with the aim of freeing the people, in Roth forges a leg iron of its own by which the revolutionary is going to find himself hobbled.

Roth manages to convey complicated political concepts without their vocabulary of didacticism, rhetoric and jargon. In the bitter experiences of Franz in *Flight Without End*, disillusion with the revolutionary left conveys what must have been the one-time-revolutionary Roth's own experience more tellingly than any research into his life could, and points to the paradox that runs through his novels with such stirring dialectical effect on the reader. The old royalist, capitalist, hierarchic world of church and state, with kings assuming divine authority on earth, their armies a warrior sect elected to serve as the panoply of these gods, is what he shows ruthlessly as both obsolete and bloodthirsty. But the counter-brutality of the revolution, and the subsequent degeneration of its ideals into stultifying bureaucracy – surely the characterising tragedy of the twentieth century – leads him to turn about and show in his old targets, fathers, mothers, the loyalist, royalist land-owners and city fathers, enduring values in the very mores he has attacked. This hardly provides a synthesis for his dazzling fictional dialectic. One who came after him, Czeslaw Milosz, expresses the dilemma:

Ill at ease in the tyranny, ill at ease in the republic,
in the one I longed for freedom, in the other for the end of corruption.[5]

The ten years between 1928 and 1938 seem to mark the peak of Roth's mastery, although the dating of his novels in terms of when they were written[6] rather than when they were published is often uncertain, since in the upheavals of exile some were not published chronologically. *The Radetzky March* (1932), *Weights And Measures* (1937) and *The Emperor's Tomb* (1938) are both the culmination of the other novels and the core round which they are gathered to form a manifold and magnificent work. *Zipper and his Father* (1928) and *Fallmerayer the Stationmaster* (1933) are a kind of intriguing coda, a foray into yet another emotional range suggesting the kind of writer Roth might have become in another age, living another kind of life. Not that one would wish him any different.

Roth was a Jew in a time of growing persecution that drove him into exile, but as a writer he retained, as in relation to politics, his

---

5 Czeslaw Milosz, 'To Raja Rao', *Selected Poems*, Ecco Press, New York, 1980, p. 29.
6 The dates I give are generally the dates of first publications, in the original German.

right to present whatever he perceived. Jewish tavern keepers on the frontier fleece deserters. There is a wry look at Jewish anti-Semitism. In *Flight Without End* a university club has a numerus clausus for Jews carried out by Jews who have gained entry and in *Right and Left* – a novel Roth seems to have written with bared teeth, sparing no one – there is a wickedly funny portrait of the subtleties of Jewish snobbism and anti-Semitism in Frau Bernheim; she conceals that she is a Jew but, as soon as someone at dinner seems about to tell a joke, she 'fall[s] into a gloomy and confused silence – afraid lest Jews should be mentioned'. On the other hand, Old Man Zipper, like Manes Reisiger, the cabby in *The Emperor's Tomb*, is a man with qualities – kindness, dignity in adversity, humour, love of knowledge for its own sake – and, yes, endearing Jewish eccentricities and fantasies, portrayed with the fond ironic humour that was inherited, whether he was aware of it or not, by Isaac Bashevis Singer.

Fallmerayer, the country stationmaster, conceives a passion for a Polish countess who enters his humble life literally by accident (a collision on the railway line). It is an exquisite love story whose erotic tenderness would have had no place – simply would have withered – plunged in the atmosphere of Roth's prison camps or rapacious post-war Vienna and Berlin. It takes place in that era, but seems to belong to some intimate seclusion of the creative imagination from the cynicism and cold-hearted betrayals that characterise love between men and women in most of Roth's work. Helping to get the injured out of a train wreck, Fallmerayer comes upon a woman on a stretcher, in a silver-grey fur coat, in the rain. 'It seemed to the stationmaster that this woman . . . was lying in a great white island of peace in the midst of a deafening sea of sound and fury, that she even emanated silence.'

The central works, *The Radetzky March* and *The Emperor's Tomb*, are really one, each novel beautifully complete and yet outdoing this beauty as a superb whole. The jacket copy calls them a saga, since they encompass four generations of one branch of the Trotta family in *Radetzky* and two collateral branches in *The Emperor*. But this is no mini-series plodding through the generations. It is as if, in the years after writing *Radetzky*, Roth were discovering what he had opened up in that novel, and turned away from, with many dark entries leading to still other entries not ventured into. There were relationships whose transformations he had not come to the end of: he had still to turn them around to have them reveal themselves to him on other planes of their complexity. So it is that the situation between fathers and sons, realised for the reader with the ultimate understanding of genius in *Radetzky*, is revealed to have an unexplored aspect, the situation between son and mother in *Emperor*. And this is no simple mirror image; it is the writer going further and further into what is perhaps the most mysterious and fateful of all human relationships, whose influence runs beneath and often outlasts those between sexual partners. We are children and we are parents: there is no dissolution of these states except death.

No theme in Roth, however strong, runs as a single current. There are always others, running counter, washing over, swelling its power and their own. The father–son, mother–son relationship combines with the relationship of the collection of peoples in the empire to a political system laid as a grid across their lives; and this combination itself is connected to the phenomenon by which the need for worship (an external, divine order of things) makes an old man with a perpetual drip at the end of his nose, Franz Josef, the emperor-god; and finally all these currents come together in an analysis – shown through the life of capital city and village – of an era carrying the reasons for its own end, and taking half the world down with it.

> Though fate elected him [Trotta] to perform an outstanding deed,
> he himself saw to it that his memory became obscured to posterity.

How unfailingly Roth knew how to begin! That is the fourth sentence in *The Radetzky March*. His sense of the ridiculous lies always in the dark mesh of serious matters. Puny opposition (a lone person) to the grandiose (an empire): what could have led to the perversity of the statement? And while following the novel the reader will unravel from this thread not simply how this memory was obscured, but how it yet grew through successive generations and was transformed into a myth within the mythical powers of empire.

The outstanding deed is not recounted in retrospect. We are in the battle of Solferino and with Trotta, a Slovenian infantry lieutenant, when he steps out of his lowly rank to lay hands upon the Emperor Franz Josef and push him to the ground, taking in his own body the bullet that would have struck the Emperor. Trotta is promoted and honoured. A conventional story of heroism, suitable for an uplifting chapter in a schoolbook, which it becomes. But Captain Joseph Trotta, ennobled by the appended 'von Sipolje', the name of his native village, has some unwavering needle of truth pointing from within him. And it agitates wildly when in his son's first reader he comes upon a grossly exaggerated account of his deed as the Hero of Solferino. In an action that prefigures what will be fully realised by another Trotta, in time to come, he takes his outrage to the Emperor himself, the one who surely must share with him the validity of the truth.

> 'Look here, my dear Trotta,' said the Emperor, '. . . you know, neither of us shows up too badly in the story. Forget it.'
> 'Your Majesty,' replied the Captain, 'it's a lie.'

These are some of the most brilliant passages in the novel. Is honesty reduced to the ridiculous where 'the stability of the world, the power of the law, and the splendour of royalty are maintained by guile'? Trotta turns his back on his beloved army, and estranged by rank and title from his peasant father, vegetates and sourly makes of his son Franz a district commissioner instead of allowing him a military career.

The fourth generation of Trottas is the District Commissioner's son, Carl Joseph, who, with Roth's faultless instinct for timing, enters the narrative aged fifteen to the sound of the 'Radetzky March' being played by the local military band under his father's balcony. The DC has suffered a father withdrawn by disillusion;

he himself knows only to treat his own son, in turn, in the same formula of stunted exchanges, but for the reader, though not the boy, Roth conveys the sense of something withheld, longing for release within the DC.

Brooded over by the portrait of his grandfather, the Hero of Solferino, lonely Carl Joseph is home from the cadet cavalry school where he has been sent to compensate the DC for his own deprivation of military prestige. The boy is seduced by the voluptuous wife of the sergeant-major at the DC's gendarmerie post. When she dies in childbirth, Carl Joseph, concealing his immense distress from his father, has to pay a visit of condolence to the sergeant-major, and is given by him the packet of love letters he wrote to the man's wife. 'This is for you, Herr Baron . . . I hope you'll forgive me, it's the District Commissioner's orders. I took it to him at once after she died.'

There follows a wonderful scene written with the dramatic narrative restraint that Roth mastered for these later books. Devastated, Carl Joseph goes into the village café for a brandy; his father is there and looks up from a newspaper. 'That brandy she gave you is poor stuff . . . Tell that waitress that we always drink Hennessy.'

One has hardly breathed again after this scene when there is another tightening of poignantly ironic resolution. Father and son walk home together.

> Outside the door of the District Commissioner's office is Sergeant-Major Slama, helmeted, with rifle and fixed bayonet, his service ledger under his arm. 'Good day, my dear Slama,' says Herr von Trotta. 'Nothing to report, I suppose.'
>
> 'No, sir,' Slama repeats, 'nothing to report.'

Carl Joseph is haunted by the portrait of the Hero of Solferino, and though inept and undistinguished in his military career, dreams of saving the Emperor's life as his grandfather did. A failure, haunted as well by the death of Slama's wife (Roth leaves us to draw our own conclusion that the child she died giving birth to may have been Carl Joseph's) and his inadvertent responsibility for the death of his only friend in a duel, Carl Joseph fulfils this dream only when, incensed by the desecration, he tears from a brothel wall a cheap reproduction of the official portrait of the Emperor – that other image which haunts his life.

Roth reconceives this small scene at full scale when, at a bacchanalian ball that might have been staged by Fellini on a plan by Musil's Diotima for her 'Collateral Campaign' to celebrate Emperor Franz Josef's seventy-year reign, the news comes of the assassination of the Emperor's son at Sarajevo. Some Hungarians raucously celebrate: 'We all agree, my countrymen and I, that we ought to be glad the swine's done for.'

Trotta, drunk, takes 'heroic' exception – 'My grandfather saved the Emperor's life . . . I, his grandson, will not stand by and allow the dynasty of the Supreme War Lord to be insulted!' He is forced to leave ignominiously.

As the District Commissioner's son deteriorates through gambling and drink, Roth unfolds with marvellous subtlety what was withheld, and longing for release, in the father. The old District Commissioner's unrealised bond with his old valet, Jacques, is perfectly conveyed in one of the two superlative set pieces of the novel, when Jacques's dying is, first, merely a class annoyance because the servant fails to deliver the mail to the breakfast table, and then becomes a dissolution of class differences in the humanity of two old men who are all that is left, to one another, of a vanished social order: their life.

The second set piece both echoes this one and brings back a scene that has been present always, beneath the consequences that have richly overlaid it. The levelling of age and social dissolution respects no rank. The DC not only now is at one with his former servant; he also, at the other end of the ancient order, has come to have the same bond with his exalted Emperor. In an audience recalling that of the Hero of Solferino, he too has gone to ask for the Emperor's intercession. This time it is to ask that Carl Joseph not be discharged in disgrace from the army. The doddering Emperor says of Carl Joseph,

'That's the young fellow I saw at the last manoeuvres . . .' And since this confused him a little, he added, 'You know, he nearly saved my life. Or was that you?'

A stranger catching sight of them at this moment might have taken them for brothers . . . The one felt he had changed into a District Commissioner, the other, that he had changed into the Emperor.

The unity of Roth's masterwork is achieved in that highest faculty of the imagination Walter Benjamin[7] speaks of as 'an extensiveness . . . of the folded fan, which only in spreading draws breath and flourishes'.

Carl Joseph, firing on striking workers, hears them sing a song he has never heard before, the 'Internationale'. At the same time, he has a yearning to escape to the peasant origins of the Trotta family. Unable to retreat to the 'innocent' past, superfluous between the power of the doomed empire and the power of the revolution to come, he is given by Roth a solution that is both intensely ironic and at the same time a strangely moving assertion of the persistence of a kind of naked humanity, flagellated by all sides. Leading his men in 1914, he walks into enemy fire to find something for them to drink. 'Lieutenant Trotta died, not with sword in hand but with two buckets of water.'

Carl Joseph's cousin, of *The Emperor's Tomb*, has never met him although Roth knows how to give the reader a frisson by casually dropping the fact that they were both in the battle at which Carl Joseph was killed. But this Trotta links with the peasant branch of the family, through his taking up, first as a form of radical chic, another cousin, Joseph Branco, an itinerant chestnut roaster from Roth's familiar frontier town. Emotionally frozen between a mother who, like the DC, cannot express her love, and a young wife who turns lesbian after he leaves her alone on their wedding night while he sits with a dying servant (the vigil of the DC with Jacques

7   Walter Benjamin, 'One-Way Street', *Reflections: Essays, Aphorisms, Autobiographical Writings*, edited and with an introduction by Peter Demetz, translated by Edmund Jephcott, Schocken, New York, 1986, p. 83.

composed in a new key), Trotta forms his warmest relationship with Branco and Branco's friend, the Jewish cab driver. They go to war together, live together as escaped prisoners of war in Siberia, and in this phase of Roth's deepest reflection on the elements of his mega-novel, exemplify brilliantly his perception that consistency in human relations is not a virtue but an invention of lesser novelists. The ideal camaraderie of the three men cracks along unpredictable lines, just as the complexity of Trotta's love for and indifference to his wife, and her constant breaking out of what has seemed to be emotional resolutions to their life, are consonant with the jarring shifts of war and post-war that contain them.

As with all Roth's work, this phase is as wonderfully populous as any nineteenth-century novel, psychologically masterly, particularly in the person of Trotta's mother and the tangents of distress and illogical fulfilment in the relationship between him and her. But *The Emperor's Tomb* was one of Roth's last works, published only the year before he died, the year of the next war for which all that was unresolved in the previous one was preparing in his world, his time. Although he wrote at least two more novels after this one, he concludes this phase, and – for me – the summation of his work, with a scene in which Trotta is in a café. On that night 'my friends' excitement . . . seemed to me superfluous' – as it does to the reader, since it is not explained until, with Roth's power to shatter a scene with a blow of history:

> . . . the moment when the door of the café flew open and an oddly dressed young man appeared on the threshold. He was in fact wearing black leather gaiters . . . and a kind of military cap which reminded me at one and the same time of a bedpan and a caricature of our old Austrian caps.

The *Anschluss* has arrived. The café empties of everyone, including the Jewish proprietor. In an inspired fusion of form with content, there follows a dazedly disoriented piece of writing that expresses the splintering of all values, including emotional values, so that the trivial and accidental, the twitching involuntary, takes over. Trotta sits on in the deserted café, approached only by the watchdog. 'Franz, the bill!' he calls to the vanished waiter. 'Franz, the bill!' he says to the dog. The dog follows him in the dawn breaking over 'uncanny crosses' that have been scrawled on walls. He finds himself at the *Kapuzinergruft*, the Emperor's tomb, 'where my emperors lay buried in iron sarcophagi.'

> 'I want to visit the sarcophagus of my Emperor, Franz Joseph . . . Long live the Emperor!' The Capuchin brother in charge hushes him and turns him away. 'So where could I go now, I, a Trotta?'

I know enough of the facts of Joseph Roth's life to be aware that, for his own death, he collapsed in a café, a station of exile's calvary.

1991

Turning the Page

African Writers on the Threshold of the Twenty-first Century

In the beginning was the Word.

Over the centuries of human culture the word has taken on other meanings, secular as well as religious. To have the word has come to be synonymous with ultimate authority, with prestige, with awesome, sometimes dangerous persuasion, to have *Prime Time*, a TV talk show, to have the gift of the gab as well as that of speaking in tongues.

In the twenty-first century, the word flies through space, bounces from satellites, now nearer than it has ever been to the heaven from which it was believed to have come. But its most significant transformation occurred for us – the writers – long ago (*and* it was in Africa) when it was first scratched on a stone tablet or traced on papyrus, when it materialised from sound to spectacle, from being heard to being read as a series of signs, and then a script; and travelled through time from parchment to Gutenberg. For this is the genesis story of the writer. It is the story that *wrote* you or me into being.

It was, strangely, a double process, creating at the same time both the writer and the very purpose of the writer as a mutation in the agency of human culture. It was both ontogenesis as the origin and development *of* an individual being, and the adaptation, in the nature of that individual, specifically to the exploration of ontogenesis, the origin and development of *the* individual being. For we writers are evolved for that task. Like the prisoner incarcerated with the jaguar in Borges's story 'The God's Script' who was trying to read, in a ray of light that fell only once a day, the meaning of being from the markings on the animal's pelt, we spend our lives attempting to interpret through the word the readings we take in the societies of which we are part. It is in this sense, this inextricable, ineffable participation, that writing is always and at once an exploration of self and of the world; of individual and collective being.

Writers in Africa in the twentieth century interpreted the greatest events on our continent since the abolition of slavery, from Things Falling Apart in the colonialist regimes, crossing the River Between oppression and liberation, passing Up in Arms through the Fog at the Season's End, Down Second Avenue, singing the Song of Lawino on the Mission to Kala, overcoming Nervous Conditions and discarding the Money Order as the price of bondage, enduring the House of Hunger, challenging the World of Strangers created by racism, recognising we were shirking responsibility as Fools for Blaming ourselves on History. Confessing as An Albino Terrorist, telling as the Interpreters the Tough Tale of the struggle for Freedom.[1]

---

1   References here are to *Things Fall Apart* by Chinua Achebe, *The River Between* by Ngũgĩ wa Thiong'o, *Up in Arms* by Chenjerai Hove, *Fog at Season's End* by Alex L. Guma, *Down Second Avenue* by Es'kia Mphahlele, *Song of Lawino* by Okot P'Bitek, *Mission to Kala* by Mongo Beti, *Nervous Conditions* by Tsitsi Dangarembga, *The Money-Order* by Sembene Ousmane, *The House of Hunger* by Dambudzo Marechera, *A World of Strangers* by Nadine Gordimer, *Fools* by Njabulo Ndebele, *Blame Me on History* by Bloke Modisane, *The True Confessions of an Albino Terrorist* by Breyten Breytenbach, *The Interpreters* by Wole Soyinka and *A Tough Tale* by Mongane Wally Serote.

There is no prize offered for correctly identifying the writers of the books whose titles you should recognise strung together to tell the story in the account I have just given, nor will it be necessary to point out that these titles and writers are only a random few of those that have made manifest in our literature the embattled awakening of our continent.

We have known that our task was to bring to our people's consciousness and that of the world the true dimensions of racism and colonialism beyond those that can be reached by the media, the newspaper column and screen image, however valuable these may be. We writers have sought the fingerprint of flesh on history.

The odds against developing as a writer able to take on this huge responsibility have, for most of our writers, been great. But as Agostinho Neto said, and proved in his own life: 'If writing is one of the conditions of your being alive, you create that condition.'

Out of adversity, out of oppression, in spite of everything.

Before we look forward into the twenty-first century we have the right to assess what we have come through, and what it means to be here, this particular time and place that has been twentieth-century Africa. This has been an existential position with particular implications for literature; we have lived and worked through one of those fearful epochs Brecht has written of when 'to speak of trees is almost a crime'. Our brothers and sisters have challenged us with the Polish poet Czeslaw Milosz's cry: 'What is poetry which does not serve nations or people?' And we have taken up that challenge. Inevitably, the characteristic of African literature during the struggle against colonialism and, later, neo-colonialism and corruption in post-colonial societies, has been engagement – political engagement.

Now, unfortunately, many people see this concept of engagement as a limited category closed to the range of life reflected in literature; it is regarded as some sort of upmarket version of propaganda. Engagement is not understood for what it really has been, in the hands of honest and talented writers: the writer's exploration of the particular meaning that being has taken on in his or her time and place. For real 'engagement', for the writer, is not something set apart from the range of the creative imagination at the dictate of his brothers and sisters in the cause he or she shares with them; it comes from within the writer, his or her creative destiny as an agency of culture, living in history. 'Engagement' does not preclude the beauty of language, the complexity of human emotions; on the contrary, such literature must be able to use all these in order to be truly engaged with life, where the overwhelming factor in that life is political struggle.

While living and writing under these conditions in Africa, some of us have seen our books lie for years unread in our own countries, banned, and we have gone on writing. Many writers have been imprisoned: Wole Soyinka, Ngũgĩ wa Thiong'o, Jack Mapanje, Jeremy Cronin, Mongane Wally Serote, Breyten Breytenbach, Dennis Brutus, Jaki Seroke and a host of others. Many, such as Chinua Achebe and Nuruddin Farah, have endured the trauma of exile, from which some never recover as writers, and which some do not survive at all. I think, among too many, of Can Themba and Dambuze Marechera.

What has happened to writers in other parts of the world we cannot always dismiss as remote from being a threat to ourselves, either. In 1988, what the Greek novelist Nikos Kazantzakis called the 'fearsome rhythm of our time' quickened in an unprecedented frenzy, to which the writer was summoned to dance for his life. There arose a threat against writers that takes its appalling authority from something more widespread than the power of any single political regime. The edict of a world religion had sentenced a writer to death.

For three years now, wherever he is hidden, Salman Rushdie has existed under the pronouncement upon him of the fatwa. There is no asylum for him anywhere. Every time this writer sits down to write, he does not know if he will live through the day; he does not know whether the page will ever be filled. The murderous dictate invoking the power of international terrorism in the name of a great and respected religion is not something that happens to 'somebody else'. It is relevant to the themes that concern *us*, and will continue to do so, in African literature as part of worldwide post-colonial literature, for Rushdie's novel is an innovative exploration of one of the most intense experiences we share, the individual personality in transition between two cultures brought together in that post-colonial world. For the future freedom of the word, and for the human rights of all of us who write, the fatwa of death must be declared an offence against humanity and dealt with by those who alone have the power to do so – democratic governments every-where, and the United Nations. The precedent of the fatwa casts a shadow over the free development of literature on our continent as it does everywhere, even as we believe ourselves to be moving into the enlightenment of the twenty-first century.

What do we in Africa hope to achieve, as writers, in the new century? Because we are writers, can we expect to realise literally, through our work, that symbol of change, the turning to a fresh page?

What are the conditions under which we may expect to write – ideological, material, social?

It seems to me that these are the two basic questions for the future of African literature. I think it is generally agreed that consonance with the needs of the people is the imperative for the future in our view of African literature. This is surely the point of departure from the past; there, literature played the immeasurably valuable part of articulating the people's political struggle, but I do not believe it can be said to have enriched their lives with a literary culture. And I take it that our premise is that a literary culture is a people's right.

We shall all, as I have suggested, make the approach from our experience in the twentieth century; we shall all be hazarding predictions, since we do not know in what circumstances our ambi-tions for a developing literature will need to be carried out. We have our ideas and convictions of how literary development should be consonant with these needs of our people; we cannot know with what manner of political and social orders we shall have to seek that consonance.

I think we have to be completely open-eyed about the relations between our two basic questions. We have to recognise that the first – what we hope to achieve in terms of literary directions – is heavily dependent on the second: the conditions under which we shall be working as writers. A literary culture cannot be created by writers without readers. There are no readers without adequate education. It's as simple – and dire – as that. No matter how much we encourage writers who are able to fulfil, according to their talents, the various kinds and levels of writing that will take litera-ture out of the forbidding context of unattainable intellectualism, we shall never succeed until there is a wide readership competent beyond the school-primer and comic-book level. And where there are readers there must be libraries in which the new literature we hope to nurture, satisfying the need of identification with people's own daily lives, and the general literature that includes the great mind-opening works of the world, are available to them.

Will potential readers find prose, poetry and non-fiction in their mother tongues? If we are to create a twenty-first-century African literature, how is this to be done while publishing in African languages remains mainly confined to works prescribed for study, market-stall booklets and religious tracts? We have long accepted that Africa cannot, and so far as her people are concerned, has no desire to, create a 'pure' culture in linguistic terms; this is an anachronism when for purposes of material development the conti-nent eagerly seeks means of technological development from all over the world. We all know that there is no such workable system as a purely indigenous economy once everyone wants computers and movie cassettes. Neither, in a future of increasing interconti-nental contact, can there be a 'pure' indigenous culture. We see, a plain fact all over Africa, that the European languages that came with colonial conquest have been taken over into independence, *acquired* by Africans and made part of their own convenience and culture. (Whites, of course, have never had the good sense to do the same with African languages . . .)

But we cannot speak of taking up the challenge of a new century for African literature unless we address the necessity to devise the means by which literature in African languages becomes the major component of the continent's literature. Without this one cannot speak of an African literature. It must be the basis of the cultural crosscurrents that will both buffet and stimulate that literature.

What of publishing?

We write the books; to come alive they have to be available to be read. To be available, they have to be competently distributed, not only through libraries, but also commercially. Many of us have experienced trying to meet the needs of the culturally marginalised by launching small, non-profit publishing ventures in African literature. We find ourselves stopped short by the fact that the distribution network, certainly in the southern African countries (I don't imagine there is much difference in countries in the north), remains the old colonial one. Less than a handful of networks makes decisions, based on the lowest common denominator of literary value, on what books should be bought from publishers, and has the only means of distributing these widely to the public, since they own the chain bookstores that dominate the trade in the cities, and are the only existing bookstores in most small towns. In South Africa, for example, in the twentieth century, there have been and are virtually *no* bookstores in the vast areas where blacks have been confined under apartheid.

Another vital question: what will be the various African states' official attitude to culture, and to literature as an expression of that culture? We writers do not know, and have every reason to be uneasy. Certainly, in the twentieth century of political struggle, state money has gone into guns, not books; literature – indeed, culture – has been relegated to the dispensable category. As for literacy, so long as people can read state decrees and the graffiti that defies them, that has been regarded as sufficient proficiency. As writers, do we envisage, for example, a dispensation from a Ministry of Culture to fund publishing in African languages, and to provide libraries in rural communities and in the shanty towns that no doubt will be with us, still, for a long time? Would we have to fear that, in return for subvention, writers might be restricted by censorship of one kind or another? How can we ensure that our implicit role – supplying a critique of society for the greater understanding and enrichment of life there – will be respected?

Considering all these factors that stand between the writer's act of transforming literature in response to a new era, it seems that we writers have, however reluctantly, to take on contingent responsibilities that should not be ours. We shall have to concern ourselves with the quality and direction of education – will our schools turn out drones or thinkers? Shall we have access, through our writing, to young minds? How shall we press for a new policy and structure of publishing and distribution, so that writers may write in African languages and bring pleasure and fulfilment to thousands who are cut off from literature by lack of knowledge of European languages? How shall we make the function of writers, whose essential gesture, the hand held out to contribute to development, is in the books they offer, something recognised and given its value by the governing powers of the twenty-first century? We have to begin now to concern ourselves with the structures of society that contain culture, and within which it must assert its growth.

And there is yet one more problem to be faced by the naked power of the word, which is all we have, but which has proved itself unkillable by even the most horrible of conventional and unconventional weaponry. Looking back, many well-known factors inhibited the growth of a modern African culture, and African literature, in the century whose sands are running out through our fingers. One hardly need cite the contemptuous dismissal of all African culture by frontier and colonial domination; the cementing-over of African music, dance, myth, philosophy, religious beliefs and secular rituals: the very stuff on which literary imagination feeds. The creativity of Africa lay ignored beneath the treading feet of white people on their way to see the latest Hollywood gangster movie or to pick up from the corner store a comic with bubble text in American. And soon, soon, these were joined by black people in the same pursuit, having been convinced, since everything that was their own was said to be worthless, that this was the culture to acquire. The habit of chewing cultural pap is by now so deeply established among our people, and so temptingly cheaply purchased from abroad by our media – including the dominant cultural medium of our time, television – that literature in Africa not only has to express the lives of the people, but also has to assert the beauty and interest of this reality against the mega-subculture that, in my revised terminology in a vastly changing world, is the opium of the people.

Surely the powers of our writers' imaginations can be exerted to attract our people away from the soporific sitcom, surely the great adventures that writers explore in life can offer a child something as exciting in image and word as the cumbersome battle between Japanese turtles? We do not want cultural freedom to be hijacked by the rush of international subliterature into the space for growth hard-won by ourselves in the defeat of colonial cultures. That is perhaps the greatest hazard facing us as we turn the page of African literature and write the heading: twenty-first century.

Albert Camus wrote: 'One either serves the whole of man or one does not serve him at all. And if man needs bread and justice, he also needs pure beauty, which is the bread of his heart.' And so Camus called for 'Courage in one's life and talent in one's work.' We shall need courage in our lives to take part in transforming social structures so that African literature may grow.

Gabriel García Márquez wrote: 'The best way a writer can serve a revolution is to write as well as he can.' That goes for the peaceful revolution of culture, as well; without talent in our work, without ourselves writing as well as we can, we shall not serve African literature as we should.

I believe that the statements of Camus and Márquez and Neto (remember his words: 'If writing is one of the conditions of your being alive, you create that condition') might be the credo for all of us who write in Africa. They do not resolve the conflicts that will continue to come, but they state plainly an honest possibility of doing so, they turn the face of writers squarely to their existence, reason-to-be, as a writer, and the reason-to-be, as a responsible human being, acting like any other within a social and political context. Bread, justice and the bread of the heart, which is the beauty of literature: these are all our business in Africa's twenty-first century.

1992

Beyond Myth

Mandela's Mettle

On Friday, in Oslo, Nelson Mandela accepted the Nobel Peace Prize with South African President F.W. de Klerk for their efforts to end apartheid.

Nelson Mandela is one of the world-famous today. One of the few who, in contrast with those who have made our twentieth century infamous for fascism, racism and war, will mark it as an era that achieved advancement for humanity. So will his name live in history, the context in which he belongs to the world.

Of course, we South Africans are part of that context and share this perception of him. But he belongs to us, and – above all – we belong to him on another and different level of experience.

There are those of us who knew him in childhood in his home, the Transkei, and see, beneath the ageing face formed by extraordinary experiences of underground and imprisonment, the soft contours of a lively youth unaware of the qualities within him beyond a commonplace appetite for life. There are freedom fighters who sacrificed their lives and are not with us to match the image of the leader, in the struggle they shared, with the statesman who has brought it to its fulfilment. There are those who see, superimposed upon his public appearances, his image in newspapers and on television today, the memory of his face, figure and bearing as he spoke from the dock when he was given a life sentence for his actions against apartheid, and declared a commitment he has lived up to since, many times, through many dangers: 'I have cherished the ideal of a democratic and free society in which all persons live together in harmony and with equal opportunities. It is an ideal which I hope to live for and achieve. But if needs be, it is an ideal for which I am prepared to die.'

It is a temptation to be anecdotal about Mandela. To speak, each of us who has had even some brief point of contact with him, of the pleasure of being remembered as well as remembering. For this man with the Atlas-like weight of our future borne on his erect shoulders does have what appears to be some kind of mind-reading facility to pick up identities, some card-index mnemonic system (perhaps developed in the long contemplative years in prison) that enables him to recognise people he may not have seen for years, or whom he may have met fleetingly during recent weeks of hand-shaking encounters. But this is no trick of political showmanship. Seemingly insignificant, it is a sign of something profound: a remove from self-centredness; the capacity to live for others that is central to the character.

He moves about our country now and is a flesh-and-blood pres-ence to millions. For twenty-seven years he was imprisoned; in our midst – for Robben Island is in sight of Table Mountain, in Cape Town, and Pollsmore Prison is part of the city – and yet, in social terms, entombed. Silenced. Even his image removed; it was forbidden to reproduce his photograph in newspapers or other media. He could so easily have become legendary, his features recomposed as the icon of hopes that never would be realised and a freedom that always receded as each wave of resistance within our country was crushed and seemed defeated, and the outside world was indifferent.

But the people had a sense of his enduring what they knew: the harsh humiliations of prison were everyday experiences to black people under the apartheid pass laws and innumerable other civil restrictions that for generations created a vast non-criminal prison population in South Africa. When he and his colleagues were set to break stones and pull seaweed out of the Atlantic Ocean, ordinary people among the black population were being hired out by prison authorities as slave farm labour. His people kept him among them in the words of their songs and chants, in the examples of forms of resistance he had passed on to them, and in the demands for his release which were part of the liberation platform, maintained both by leadership in exile and the people themselves, at home. In such news of him that came out of prison, we came to know that his sense of himself was always part of all this, of living it with his people; he received them through prison walls, as they kept him with them. This double sense was intrinsic to the very stuff of resistance. The strong possibility that he would die in prison was never considered for acceptance. There never was the psychological defeat, for the liberation movement, of his becoming a mythical figure, a Che Guevara who might reappear some day only in mystical resurrection on a white horse, since once a personage becomes a myth he has disappeared for ever as a leader to take on the present in vulnerable flesh.

Of course, it remains difficult to write of a phenomenon like Mandela in terms other than hagiography. But he is not a god-like figure, despite his enormous popularity – and this popularity, in the era of successful negotiation between black and white, extends in all kinds of directions beyond the trust and reverence in which he is held by blacks and those whites who have been active in liberation from apartheid. I heard on the news while I was writing this that a poll of South African businessmen has revealed that 68 per cent wished to see Nelson Mandela as the future president of South Africa. Far from assuming a celestial status, Mandela's quality is, on the contrary, so fully and absolutely that of a man, the essence of a human being in all the term should mean, could mean, but seldom does. He belongs completely to a real life lived in a particular place and era, and in its relation to the world. He is at the epicentre of our time; ours in South Africa, and yours, wherever you are.

For there are two kinds of leaders. There is the man or woman who creates the self – his/her life – out of the drive of personal ambition, and there is the man or woman who creates a self out of response to people's needs. To the one, the drive comes narrowly from within; to the other, it is a charge of energy that comes of others' needs and the demands these make. Mandela's dynamism of leadership is that he has within him the selfless quality to receive and act upon this charge of energy. He has been a revolutionary leader of enormous courage, is a political negotiator of extraordinary skill and wisdom, a statesman in the cause of peaceful change. He has suffered and survived more than a third of his life in prison and emerged without uttering one word of revenge. He has received many personal family sorrows as a result of his imprisonment. He has borne all this, it is evident, not only because the cause of freedom in South Africa for his people has been the breath of his life, but because he is that rare being for whom the human family is his family. When he speaks of South Africa as the home of all South Africans, black and white, he means what he says. Just as he did when he stood in court and vowed that he was prepared to die for this ideal.

As Aimé Césaire says, at the rendezvous of victory there is room for all. Mandela's actions and words show he knows that without that proviso there is no victory, for anyone.

1993

Rising to the Ballot

What does an election mean in democratic Western countries? An election is a recurrent event of the social order, coming up like the obligation to fill out income tax returns. A day when, as a matter of routine in civic life, you go to make your mark in favour of the individual or political party whose policies for governing your life you believe will do this best. Unless one is oneself a politician, or actively campaigning for a political party, making that mark is not a major experience. I can project into this commonplace acceptance because, although I am a South African, I am white, and consequently I have had the right to vote since I was eighteen years old.

But because I am a South African, I also understand what I believe no one in the Western world can: what this week's election in the year 1994 in our country signifies for the great majority of South Africans, the blacks who, by law, have never before been allowed to cast a vote. And because I have been a protagonist, in my way, in the struggle against the racism that found its base in denying blacks the vote, the right to have a voice in the governments that proscribed every aspect of their lives, I also share what this election means to black people. That is why I shall speak of 'us' instead of 'them' when attributing that meaning.

To us, the election signifies not just a new beginning. It is a resurrection: this land rising from the tomb of the entire colonial past shared out in different centuries, decades and proportions among the Dutch, the French, the British and their admixture of other Europeans; this indigenous people rising from the tomb of segregated housing, squatter camps, slum schools, job restrictions, forced removals from one part of the country to another; from the burial of all human aspiration and dignity under the humiliation of discrimination by race and skin; this people rising, for the first time in history, with the right to elect a government: to govern themselves. A sacred moment is represented in the act of putting a mark on a ballot paper.

Yes, there are high emotions involved in this election beyond the obvious political ones of the contest for power as a democratic process. How to transform the emotion people feel into enablement, the ability to use that process, is another matter. The generations of subjection have produced their own psychoses. It is difficult to convince people whose lives have been totally controlled by white employers and the authorities that served the interests of those employers that anything one commits to paper – a signature, a thumbprint – is not open to the scrutiny of the white baas and his agents.

This is particularly true of farm workers. The blacks who work on white farms, although distinguished from slavery by being wage-earners, have belonged literally body and soul to the white farmer. They and their families live by his favour on his land – the land they work for him – and if dismissed lose their homes as well as their jobs. It is not easy to give them the democratic faith to believe that their vote will be secret, not even the baas will know against what party's name they made their mark. By the stroke of a pen in their own hand, they fear to lose whatever wretched security their lives have. Rural and urban people alike have been conditioned by something else, very different – one of the strategies of the liberation struggle that now, ironically, inhibits them from using the vote. One of the most successful campaigns against apartheid, adopted by both the African National Congress and the Pan-Africanist Congress, was that of refusing to carry the pass. The hated dossier that blacks had to exhibit, like a shackle, on demand, and for which they went to prison on failure to do so, was the document that restricted their freedom of domicile and their right to seek work in one area rather than another.

From this anti-pass campaign came a wariness of all official documents that has remained long beyond the abolition of the pass. Having been told, then, by the liberation movements to protest against apartheid by not complying with government bureaucracy's official records, many people retain a strong unconscious reluctance to apply for an identity document that each voter must produce at the polls.

Against this background, voter education has proved to be the essential first step in the curriculum of a new democracy. Very different from electioneering, voter education must teach people not for whom they should vote, but why they should exercise their rights through the vote, and how to do so. A number of organisations have been formed to provide this. Probably the most active, nationwide, is Matla Trust ('Matla' means strength in the Sotho language) on whose board I serve, and of whose activities I therefore can give account at first-hand, but which also are typical of the activities of such organisations in general, even if these do not share the same scope as Matla.

From its headquarters in Johannesburg, Matla serves a whole country of constituencies varied by many differences of language, levels of literacy, understanding of civic processes. With 60 per cent illiteracy among the people, the possibilities of voter education by the written word are limited. Using the daily press is the least effective of means. With a proliferation of languages – though many even illiterate black people speak three or four indigenous ones in addition to either English or Afrikaans, the official languages of the white regime — the task of reaching the population through oral programmes is a challenge. There is the great disparity between material possessions of urban and rural people. In the vast black townships around the cities, television sets are widely owned (some run on batteries, where electricity still has not been provided for black people), while in the rural areas a small transistor radio with restricted range is the only medium through which people can be reached in their homes. So that for the spoken word, and the spoken-word-plus-image, a separate approach is required.

Matla Trust has devised many strategies to reach responses to these problems. From the eleven branch offices around the country, field educators go out to villages, farms, factories, religious, youth and women's associations to explain to people in their own languages what the casting of the vote means to their future, and how to do it.

Matla's methods in this work have been so successful that the trust has run intensive courses to train field workers, as many as 500 at a time, from other voter-education programmes as well as its own. Brief informative dialogues, following the mode with which people are familiar in commercial advertising, are aired on radio stations. A fourteen-part TV mini-series featuring a popular black comedian was commissioned according to the ideas of the trust and has been shown on TV weekly at a peak hour in the run-up to the election. For the comic-book literate, a picture-story booklet in nine languages was distributed widely.

Perhaps the most original means of voter education has been the creation of six travelling theatre troupes of black actors who have both devised and acted a play, adapting it multilingually to areas and audiences throughout the country. I have seen the play evolve fascinatingly in response to the participation of audiences. With song and humour it presents a mock-up of a polling station, with the actors going through all the actual procedures — body-search for weapons, presentation of identity document, placing of hands under ultra-violet light and, after voting, into a special liquid, so that no one can vote twice — in the personae of various characters: the sceptical old crone, the swaggering youth carrying his deafening cassette player, the confidence trickster, the militant student, etc. People from the audience are invited to come up and make their mark on a board representing a ballot paper. The need for voter education has been startlingly clear when I have seen some cross out the names of parties they don't wish to vote for.

A jazzy song and dance about 'spoilt' papers deals with this sort of confusion. However, one must not conclude the confusion about the voting process means lack of understanding of political issues; many thousands of people are politically aware and informed of party policies, while simply never having had the chance to practise ordinary civic procedures. Which is what voter education is all about.

Matla Trust, like other voter educators, has been funded by overseas aid organisations and governments wishing to promote a democratic future in South Africa. If there is the great voter turn-out now expected on election day, donors can feel satisfied that their money was well used, for without these imaginative and effective programmes a vast number of South Africans would have missed the first opportunity to exercise the right to govern their own lives.

Matla, for itself, knows that the task is not over. Voter education is only the first step towards democracy; all its other processes, in community organisation, in accountability from those who govern to the people governed, will need to be learned during the five years of a government of national unity that begins after this week's election. Democracy is not an on-off affair; it has to be learned, day by day.

1994

Letter from South Africa

When I return to South Africa from abroad, now, I don't step down on to the earth of my old stamping ground, the Transvaal, where I was born, but on to new territory. It's named 'Gauteng' – 'Place of Gold'.

The airport itself is renamed. It used to be 'Jan Smuts Airport', now it is 'Johannesburg International Airport'.[1]

The former name – Transvaal – of my natal region derived, way back, from the geographical boundaries recognised by the Boer Republics: Transvaal – 'across the Vaal River' – was where the water divided the Boer Republic of Orange Free State from its counterpart on the other side, the Boer Republic of Transvaal. The former name of the airport commemorated General Jan Smuts, one of the heroes of the white regimes, who led South Africa into the war against Nazi racism but continued to head a racist government at home.

Now 'Gauteng' stoutly asserts not only that there will be no more white republics here, but that their latter-day apartheid counterpart, the slicing and chopping of the country into ethnic enclaves is over, for good. If 'Place of Gold' trails any historical trappings, these commemorate the labour of the black men who brought the underground metal to the surface, and made the country rich, as much as the Europeans who made the discoveries and supplied the technology. In abandoning the naming of an airport for some people's hero, I hope a principle is indicated whereby the naming of public utilities in honour of individuals will not be favoured – even if they are safely dead. The world is full of statues cast down on their broken noses, streets renamed for leaders celebrated and then deposed, requiring yet another street-name change, so that we may

---

1   2010: O. R. Tambo Airport, renamed for the great Oliver Tambo, a hero of the struggle against apartheid, up on the heights of Mandela.

lose our sense of direction, in more ways than one. Of course I make an exception, in the inconsistent manner of all human beings. My exception is Nelson Mandela.[2] He is no transient figure in human progress; one of the few mortals, like Mohandas Gandhi, whose name is invoked and will be, and whose image is revered and will be, even by his enemies.

I've become easily accustomed to the new Johannesburg, but when I've been away and I come home, fresh to it, my vision flashes back to the way it was, for fascinated comparison. I've lived here since 1949, and at most levels of that segregation reserved for whites. I've been a struggling young writer, divorced, with a child to support. I've ended up in a beautiful old tin-roofed house with room for my books. But wherever and however I lived, during the past regimes, it was where no black person could rent a room, a flat, or buy a house. When I went into the central city, it was one vast, white businessmen's club, with blacks coming in to run the errands, shine the doorknobs of the banks and insurance houses, sweep the streets, and keep out of any restaurant or coffee shop where clients could sit down. Of course they were more than welcome to spend their money in the businessmen's shops – so long as they cleared off, out of sight, to their segregated black townships, after hours.

In the eighties, things began to change. People in other countries tend to think that the elections in April last year achieved this from zero, overnight. It was not so. During this time, libraries, theatres and cinemas had been declared by law as open to everybody. Blacks could sit down to eat in a restaurant. Public transport was desegregated, and although a lot of legalistic pussy-footing to retain residential segregation remained, it was simply ignored by the growing confidence of black people moving into white high-density areas, and white landlords eager to fill vacancies where whites had retreated to the suburbs. Gradually, in the suburbs themselves, that old solvent of prejudices, class solidarity, discovered for whites that black neighbours – lawyers, doctors,

---

2   Oliver Tambo along with him; and the renaming of hospitals, many other institutions, and high roads for freedom fighters.

advertising executives, journalists, board members of white companies that were covering their backs for the future, followed the same
approved routine of driving their children to private schools in the
morning, and protected their property with the same intercoms
installed at electronic gates. Back in the city, the white government's lack of interest or success in providing transport to serve
black people in their daily to-and-fro between the white city and
the black ghettoes was replaced by a most disorderly but effective
form of transport, provided by thousands of minibuses owned by
black private enterprise.

These were the concessions made, and the changes helplessly
accepted, by the last days of apartheid, holed up in its bunker but
determined not to swallow the cyanide capsule.

The streets of Johannesburg's city centre are now totally transformed. A perpetual crowd scene has taken over what was a swept,
empty stage on which a few self-appointed leading actors performed
for one another. The pavements are a market where your progress
is a step-dance between pyramids of fruit and vegetables, racks of
second-hand jeans, spreads of dog-eared paperback lives from Marx
to Mandela, rickety tables set out with peanuts, sweets, sunglasses,
backyard concoctions labelled Chanel and Dior, hair straighteners,
Swatches and earrings. Traffic fumes are spiced by the smell of *boerewors*, a greasy farm sausage that is as much our national dish as thick
mealie-meal, the African polenta, for on every corner there are carts
frying circles of gut-encased meat over gas burners. You can have your
shoes re-soled while you stand in your socks; you can even have your
hair cut, right there. Like everyone else who has a car, I have had to
acquire new skills as a driver, after forty-seven years on the road: the
minibuses we call combis – a combination between a bus and a taxi –
stop on request signalled by a raised finger anywhere and everywhere.
You have to be ready with a foot on the brake and a quick swerve to
make it to the parallel lane, and usually that lane is full, anyway.

The city centre is dirty, yes. That private white club, that stage-set
for principal actors only, was not designed for non-members, the use
of the crowd, the entire population of this city. The dainty bins over-
flow with trash. And perhaps there is even an unconscious euphoria

among black people, in showing you can toss your cigarette pack and Coke can, even your old T-shirt, on to what whites kept so tidy, for themselves alone. It will take some time before people want to have clean streets because they have now claimed them.

I use the word 'unconscious' of this careless abandon in the streets because there is so little resentment of whites, in black South Africans. Not to be evidenced because, more importantly, simply not there, to be felt. I reflect on this as I write; but when I walk about Johannesburg these days I don't do so as a white among blacks, I'm not conscious of this at all, it's not there in the eyes, in the gait of people as they approach or pass me. And if we happen to bump one another, before I can apologise, the other will say 'Sorry, ma-Gogo', *I apologize, Grandmother* – in respect for my grey hair . . . I don't know of any other city in the world I've been in where you'd meet such courtesy on the street.

There are muggings, hijacks and house robberies to fear. And although it is easy for me to say these are the hazards of city life in many countries, certainly the developing post-colonial ones, it is a statistical fact that our city ranks very high on the crime scale. In one of the paradoxes of freedom, our country is no exception. For all the years of apartheid, we were isolated from the world, rightly shunned; now we are accepted with open arms and we ourselves are also open to the arrival from other countries of drug dealers and scam-men, and on a humbler but nevertheless damaging level, illegal immigrants from as far afield as Nigeria, Korea and China who compete with our own unemployed in the struggle to earn and eat.

The vast number of unemployed we inherited from the apartheid regime, like the millions in need of houses and schools, have created an industry of crime, with, as apprentices, homeless street children. It's a Dickensian situation apartheid bequeathed us and foreigners exacerbate, ironically, in our freedom. It's an inheritance not only from the years of apartheid, since 1948, but of the more than three and a half centuries of colonial racist rule under different names.

What has the Government of National Unity been able to do about this inheritance, this social malediction, no less, in a mere eighteen months of its existence in power?

I am surprised, somewhat incredulous, when people in the outside world call us to account in the quantitative terms *they* have decided. How many houses have we built? Too few, yes, too few, we are well aware. But how many do these South Africa watchers calculate, of the thousands required by several million shack and slum dwellers, could be built in a year?

This is not a game of Monopoly, where a house is a counter you put down on a chosen square.

Do they realise that land has to be legally acquired, in relation to where people have their work, that electricity and water reticulation have to be installed where they never existed, that – above all – banks have to be negotiated into providing low-cost housing loans for people who, because they were black and low-income earners, never before were eligible for bonds? These preparations are what has taken up the time. The fact that in the region where I live eighty thousand existing houses have been connected to electricity may mean little to you, who have been taking for granted electrical power ever since you were grown enough to reach a switch; but to people who live in those eighty thousand houses, touching a switch is indeed the beginning of a new life: let there be light.

We still lack schools and teachers better qualified than apartheid turned out. But in January, when the school year begins in the southern hemisphere, something happened that heartens me whenever I contemplate the vast problems we have to tackle. The schools were desegregated. Black children in their brand new uniforms registered along with white children and there were no police, army personnel or dogs necessary to protect black children, as there had to be, you will remember, when the American South opened its schools to all races. When I happen to pass a local, once all-white school at the end of the school day and see small children streaming out, the girls giggling together, the boys scuffling and shouting together, I know that statistics are only part of progress.

We have had a great number of strikes this year. The most important ones are those in the mines and related industries, because they are bound up with the colonial-established employment practice of migratory labour, that, in turn, is related to the recurrent violence which spills from the frustrations of hostel living conditions to adjacent black communities; violence begun by the fanatical determination of the individual who represents a danger to peace in South Africa, Mangosutho Buthelezi, to stir ethnic differences in reckless pursuit of his personal political ambitions. Other workers have been on strike – supermarket employees, transport drivers, even grave-diggers. These actions are deplored because they affect production (not the grave-diggers, of course . . .) and growth of the economy, but we have to remind ourselves, this is democracy in action . . . Under the old regime, police, dogs and guns were the only answer to workers' assertion of their rights.

Early this year I attended the inaugural sitting of the Constitutional Court. The case was brought by two men on death row, on the grounds that the death penalty violates South Africa's new constitution. It was a test case of tremendous significance to the constitution as the final arbiter of individual human rights. Among the judges, black and white, was Albie Sachs, the liberation activist whose arm was blown off and one eye blinded by a car bomb placed to kill him by the apartheid government's secret service; he, who might be thought to want to see assassins die, was eloquent for abolition of the death penalty. The court finally declared it a contravention of the constitution and it has been abolished. Eighty per cent of whites and 49 per cent of blacks, in a poll, had wanted it retained. Judge President Arthur Chaskelson said, 'This court cannot allow itself to be diverted from its duty to act as an independent arbiter of the constitution by making choices on the basis that they will find favour with the public.' We have, and need to have, this kind of protection of individual rights where we had so few. Those who kill will go to prison for life; the state will not become a murderer by killing them.

We have other kinds of murderers among us: political murderers who have never been brought to justice. In 1995 President Mandela signed into law a Truth and Reconciliation Commission. It is a country of reconciliation's preferred alternative to Germany's Nuremburg Trials. Those who come forward and confess what they did in the past may be granted indemnity. It's going to be a

process full of questions and difficulties, both for the perpetrators
of ugly and mortal deeds and for the families of those they killed
or maimed. But it is surely a rare and civilised way of dealing with
the past of a people who have to live with it, together. South Africa
is a human place to live in, today.

1995

Cannes Epilogue

*F*orrest Gump as the culmination of a hundred years of the art
of cinema: this appalling thought prompted me to accept an
invitation to serve on the jury of the 1995 Cannes Film Festival. I
belong to the first generation for whom film has been an art form,
along with literature, music, painting and sculpture, rather than
a technical discovery, the cinematograph, made in 1895 by two
French brothers, Auguste and Louis Lumière. The century has been
one of so much delight and revelation in the development of this
unique medium. How could we allow it to be marked by a laurel
wreath of confectioners' sugar placed upon the head of the only
hero an apparently weary civilisation, dwindled into sentimentality, could conceive of – a hero based on the premise that you have
to be brain-damaged to be fully human in this world?

So I went to Cannes hoping for a masterpiece: a film that goes for
all the possibilities in multimedia filmmaking; a film that extends
boundaries already attained by the great makers, from Chaplin
and Welles through Truffaut, Buñuel, Bergman and Bertolucci.
(Everyone may substitute her or his own list of those I revere but
have no space for.) Then there is, in the words of Satyajit Ray, 'the
presence of the essential thing in a very small detail which one
(screenwriter, director, cameraman, actor) must catch in order to
expose the larger things'.

I was intrigued to discover what the criteria of others on the jury
might be. My companions under the president, Jeanne Moreau,

were the French cinematographer Philippe Rousselot, the Italian director Gianni Amelio, the African director Gaston Kaboré, the Mexican critic Emilio García Riera, the Russian screenwriter Maria Zvereva, the French producer Michèle Ray-Gavras, the French actor/director Jean-Claude Brialy, and John Waters, about whom no American reader will ask, 'And who the hell is he?'

A mixed piece of casting – to some, even daring. The *Times* remarked that I might 'just be the one person in the world with whom Mr Waters has least in common'. Well, the *Times* was wrong. Though we may have differed now and then about the nature of masterpieces, we laughed together such a lot that we thought of having a photograph taken of ourselves, suitably enlaced, for the press.

The seclusion of the jury was not quite on the level of that which was prevailing concurrently for a certain trial jury on another continent. But it was a relief to have strict rules to adhere to when journalists pestered us for tips about which film was out in front in the laps of jury viewing. An icon of cinema glamour, immensely intelligent, truly literate in many cultural dimensions, Jeanne Moreau was a president from whose discipline we would not have dared to stray in blab. Her personality is an unlikely combination, at once imperious and lovable. She worked us hard, yet never once did she try to influence the opinion of any jury member. For myself, I learned from the exchange of preoccupations with others. A cinematographer reads the language of images while I receive the language of the script, an actor intuits where performance betrays or transcends a role, directors see structure, and producers see how much ingenuity and imagination are achieved in proportion to a little or a lot of money spent. To become aware of all these component aspects was to understand better what film sets out to do and how far it succeeds.

Film may re-create the past or create a future, but in its flickering beginnings it was the unique art form to capture, alive, the continuing present moment. Not surprising, then, that two themes were obsessive in a number of the films we saw. One was the new nihilism – youths on two continents living at the dead end of our century on emotionless sex and catatonic violence. The second was the self-destruction of Sarajevo.

Twelve days spent seeing films and discussing them. The lives, the countries, the world created out of the imagination I entered became the real world. To emerge from the Palais des Festivals on to the beachfront and into the glare of a concerted gaze – that was fantasy. Cannes is a city of voyeurs. What are they hoping for as they press to the glass of the flag-fluttering cars? Their faces sag in disappointment: alas, I am not Sharon Stone. And if I were? What solace could I offer for the fate of looking on?

By the way, there was the masterpiece I had hoped for, and we gave it the Palme d'Or. In it was the presence of the essential thing in small detail, caught in order to expose the larger things. Emir Kusturica's *Underground* is a splendid masquerade of life triumphant, in brass-band bravura, through half a century in the birthplace of the avatars of war which used to be Yugoslavia.

1995

Remembering Barney Simon

Theatre in South Africa without Barney Simon is unimaginable. With Athol Fugard – whose early plays he directed – back in the 1950s and 1960s, Simon broke the colonial mould of staging only those plays already applauded in the West End and on Broadway, discarded lack of confidence in our ability to judge theatre for ourselves, and opened the Brechtian road for South Africans to assert, as playwrights and actors, what Walter Benjamin called the 'ability to relate their lives'; the tragedy and vitality, the defiant humour of poverty in the underworld of black townships that was, in fact, the real South Africa. During those years, it was the alternative theatre that kept the head of culture above engulfing apartheid. Where books were banned, the stage got away with the wily genre of illusion. Barney Simon was one of the founders of the

Market Theatre, and from its beginnings in 1976 in the converted buildings of what had been our Johannesburg Covent Garden he put into its survival and growth as alternative theatre his very life. No one knows how many men and women who have become the makers of a unique black theatre and a unique non-racial theatre in South Africa, known over the world, come from his vision and patient energy as director/writer. His attitude was always not only to teach others what he knew, but – that was the brilliance of it – to draw from them what was deep in the streets and in themselves.

I remember, decades ago, Barney Simon came by and asked if I would like to come with him to meet two young men who were keen to devise a play. They were Percy Mtwa and Mbongeni Ngema, and they had the germ of an idea in two out-of-works chatting in a graveyard where the great African National Congress leader and Nobel Peace Prize winner Chief Albert Luthuli was buried. He got them to explore the idea, probing into the content; he told them to go home to Soweto and talk about it to street traders, crones, youths hanging around the bus stations, gangsters, taxi drivers, anyone – and come back with their gleanings a week later. From this material he nurtured their great talent as actors to shape with them *Woza Albert* (Come back, arise Albert), a marvellous work using music, mimicry, irony and stand-up comedy in a message of liberation. The play was the first of many successes for Mtwa and Ngema, a prototype of the new theatre, to be created by them and their contemporaries, that showed the world outside what the statute-book version of apartheid was really like in terms of black people's account of their own lives.

Simon was artistic director of the Market Theatre for virtually all his life, producing his own plays, international works and adaptations of others' stories – Can Themba's *The Suit* is one of them, running in London now – and in the last decade devoting enormous energy to the Laboratory, part of the Market's theatre complex, where aspirant playwrights could develop and stage their plays under his superbly creative guidance. What was Barney Simon like as a man? In contrast to his masterly professionalism in the theatre, he was often bamboozled by the mechanisms of daily life: a sort

of endearing Woody Allen character, defeated by burst pipes, car
breakdowns, and, in human relations, open to exploitation in his
kindness to anyone with a hard-luck story. He was a loving and
loved friend; the theatre was his family. Wherever theatre flourishes in this free South Africa his work helped bring about, his
spirit will be present: *Woza* Barney! Viva Barney!

1995

Our Century

A hundred years is the largest unit we can grasp, in terms of
human life. After a hundred years, quantification begins
again; it is not without significance that life is renewed in the
Sleeping Beauty's family castle after one hundred years. The turn of
a century is the prince's kiss of time. On the first morning of 2000,
the world will be awakened to a new calendar, perhaps a new life.

What has ours, our life in the twentieth century been?

Living in the twentieth century, we cannot look upon it from
the pretence of another perspective; nor should we try to if we are
to discover what only we, if secretly, suppressedly, know best: the
truth about ourselves, our time.

Has it been the worst of times?

Has it been the best of times?

Or should we combine the two extremes in Dickensian fashion,
and try 'It was the best of times, it was the worst of times'?

The brief conception of our century I propose now is inevitably
subjective; each of you will substitute or add your own, but there
are surely many we, shaped by the same period, share.

At once there arises from a flash brighter than a thousand suns
the mushroom cloud that hangs over our century. Exploded almost
exactly at the half-century, the atomic bombs that destroyed
Hiroshima and Nagasaki rise as unsurpassed evil done, even in this
century where more humans have been killed or allowed to die

of starvation and disease, by human decision, than ever before in history; and where the Nazi holocaust, fifty years on, has become household words of horror as 'ethnic cleansing' in the Balkans and Africa.

Unsurpassed evil laid at our door, certainly, because foremost of the 'firsts' our century can claim is that for the first time man invented a power of destruction which surpasses any natural catastrophe – earthquake, volcano eruption, flood. Thus the final conquest of nature, an aim pursued with the object of human benefit since the invention of agriculture in the Stone Age, has been achieved in our discovery of how to wipe ourselves out more quickly and efficiently than any force of nature. The demonic vow of our century seems to come from Virgil: 'If I cannot move Heaven, I will stir up Hell.'

The signing of a Nuclear Non-Proliferation Treaty is brokered among nations, and the threat of an atomic war, which for forty years depended on the press of a button in the Pentagon or the Kremlin, is complacently half-forgotten since one protagonist in a Cold War is *hors de combat*. But the French, in this last decade, have tried out their nuclear capacity as if these loathsome apocalyptic weapons were now old toys a safe world can play with reminiscently.

T.S. Eliot's prediction was that we would end with a whimper; ours is that we could go out with a bang. The mushroom cloud still hangs over us; will it be there as a bequest to the new century?

The strange relation between the forces of Good and Evil has been part of the mystery of human existence since we evolved as the only self-regarding creatures in the animal world. In our century, with its great leaps into what was formerly beyond human experience, the relation surely has become profoundly relevant and more inexplicable than ever. Einstein, exiled from his home country by the evil force of Nazism, split the atom, deciphering one of the greatest secrets of nature. What was intended to enrich humankind with an extension of knowledge of its cosmic existence, produced out of Good the malediction of our time: atomic capability, in whomsoever's hands it remains or passes to.

What is more puzzling and far more troubling is what appears to be a kind of symbiosis of Good and Evil. They pass from one into the other through some transparency we, bewilderedly, cannot fathom. We try to apply moral precepts to processes that function perhaps according to *quite other laws*, laws in which this human construct of ours, morality, does not exist at all. A sober contemplation for an age characterised by revolutionary scientific discovery.

If we turn away from the absolutes of opposing Good and Evil as we must see them while human values are to survive, we come to the lower level – of paradox. We have made spectacular advances in discoveries that have made life more bearable for some and more pleasurable for others. We have eliminated many epidemics and alleviated much pain with new drugs; we have raised the dead in a real sense, by taking vital organs from the dead and planting them to function again in the living. Air travel has revolutionised the possibility of physical presence. The bundle of telecommunications – computer, fax, email, mobile phone – has speeded up communication by the spoken and written word. We have lifted the burden of manual workers and housewives by machines programmed to do onerous tasks; with other devices we have brought music and moving images into every house. We have broken the sound barrier, explored space, entered the angels' realm, the sphere of the heavens. Most of us have enjoyed some of these embellishments of life.

The Italian Futurist painters in the early decades of our age depicted in their imagination this world which is now ours as a world of sleek cars whirling unhampered through streets, planes buzzing like happy bees gathering the nectar of a new age between skyscrapers and rainbows in a radiantly clear sky.

Their paintings look to us now like the work of a Grandma Moses of industrialisation; yet we shared this innocent ignorance of pollution, lacked with these artists the true vision of the future, which was that we would begin to choke on our technological progress, suffocate in our cities in our own foul breath of fumes and carcinogenic vapours. We have achieved much, but we have not always stayed at the controls of purpose.

It is also intriguing to observe in ourselves how technology has intervened in the intangible, telescoping our emotions. Those antipodean states, dread and anticipation, have been practically outdated. In our century, the ordeal of dread is banished by instant full communication from anywhere to anywhere. And as for anticipation, that becomes instant gratification. So, not for the first or last time, the advances of technology contradict theories of human satisfaction expounded by the savants of that other kind of advance in knowledge that has dramatically distinguished our century, psychoanalysis. Apart from its purely sexual application, Freud's deferred pleasure as a refinement of emotional experience does not compare, for us, with the immediate joy of hearing a lover's voice, or getting a friend's reply to a letter, at once, by email.

Even adventurism has been transformed by technology. The intrepid of the Euro-Russo-American world walk on the moon and dangle in space instead of 'discovering' jungles and rivers the indigenous inhabitants have known as home since their personal creation myths explained their presence there. The new adventurers *actually experience*, by weightlessness, *extinction while still alive*, become phantoms whose feet cannot touch earth. They are the successors to the angels we, alas, no longer believe in because we have probed outer space and found no heaven.

What has been the impact on the arts, in our century of unprecedented technological development?

Technology is the means by which one of the positive, progressive consequences of the revolutions of the century – bloody or peaceful, failed or surviving – the determination to break open the elitism of the arts, has been made practical. From the era of troupes of actors and art exhibitions travelling through the villages of Russia after the October Revolution, to this decade of the nineties when villages and even squatter camps in Africa, in India, in the Middle East, have transistor radios, and television sets are run on car batteries, culture in its most easily assimilable form – entertainment sugaring information – has been democratised. There has been a redistribution of intellectual privilege through technology.

Music has been brought to the masses by discs, and broadcasts which may be heard on the humblest of radios, whether it be pop or reggae or an opera performance many people would never have had the money or opportunity to attend. And by the same means a recognition and appreciation of the musical forms of the East and of Africa, from the ragas of Ravi Shankar to South Africa's *kwela* and *mbaqanga*, have spread internationally.

But it is television that has brought about the overwhelming cultural transformation.

Television has altered human perception. It has changed the means of knowing; of receiving the world. Of the five senses, sight now outstrips all others; watching is the most important form of comprehension. Although television speaks, it is its endless stream of images out of which the child, the youth, even the mature and old who have had considerable direct experience of life, construct reality. The visual other world of television is renewed in palimpsest, day after day, night after night, for millions the last vision before sleep and the first woken to in the morning. I know that every workshop of young painters in my country shows strikingly the imprinting of artists' creativity by television's imagery, iconography, television's *visual hierarchy of what is meaningful in our life*. Television has empowered the visual far beyond the capacity of the cinema, the art which democratised the enjoyment of leisure before the TV box entered homes. Through television, the service of technology to art developed in our century, we have produced a human mutation, a species that substitutes vicarious experience for the real thing.

'In our time the destiny of man presents its meaning in political terms.' These are the words of Thomas Mann, one of the greatest literary interpreters of the real thing, which he lived through in personal experience of the twentieth century's physical displacements and upheavals of perception.

But we are not only children of our time, we are also of our place. My own consciousness and subconscious, from which I write, come even in the most personal aspects of mind and spirit from destiny shaped by the historico-political matrix into which I was born. My personal sense of the defining events of our century is dominated

by two: the fall of Communism, and the end of colonialism. And
the two are linked subjectively, even contradictorily, for me, since I
was born a second-generation colonial in a capitalist-racist society
and as I grew up I looked to the Left as the solution to the oppression of the poor and powerless all around me, in my home country
and the world. When I was a toddler I was taken to wave a flag at
the Prince of Wales, the future Edward VIII, on his imperial visit
to the then British Dominion, South Africa. As I grew I was told
again and again of this momentous occasion, with a sense of values
to be inculcated: loyalty in homage to imperial power, white man's
power.

Nobody presented for the formation of my sense of values the
fact that Mohandas Gandhi had lived in, and developed his philosophy in and through the country where I was born and was to live
my life; the man who was to leave behind in that country principles
of liberation that were to be important to the struggle for freedom
by black people, my brothers and sisters unacknowledged by the
values of the whites who took me to make obeisance to an English
prince. The essence of the colonial ethos in which I was brought up
is contained in that flag I was given to wave.

It has become a truism to shake one's head in wonder at the end of
apartheid and the emergence of a free South Africa this century has
just seen.

A miracle; and coming to pass at the time when a new miracle is
yearningly needed to compensate for the miracle the first quarter
of the century promised for many – now a fallen star, the Red Star,
flickered out.

Human beings will always have the imperative to believe in the
possibility of a better world of their own making. In the words
of Jean Paul Sartre, socialism was seen as 'man in the process of
creating himself'. The depth of the sense of abandonment, now, not
only among those who were Communists but among all of us to
whom the broad Left, the ideals of socialism remain although these
have been betrayed and desecrated in many countries as well as in
the Gulags of the founding one – it is this sense of abandonment

that the collapse of the Soviet Union brings to our century, rather than the disillusion many in the West would triumphantly claim.

For whatever one's judgement of its consequences, the most momentous single date in the social organisation of our century was unquestionably the October Revolution of 1917, as a result of which one-third of humankind found itself living under regimes derived from it. The disintegration of the Soviet world before the end of the same century that saw its beginning: has it brought the triumph of democracy or only the return of the liberalism that failed, after the First World War, to prevent the poor and unemployed of Italy and Germany from turning to fascism as the solution of their circumstances, many of which exist again in many parts of our world today?

I can affirm that in my own country, South Africa, the Left's revelation of the class and economic basis of racial discrimination was one of the formative influences that, along with Pan-Africanism, joined the people's natural, national, inevitable will towards liberation. The other formative influence on the liberation struggle in South Africa is one of which I have already spoken, Mahatma Gandhi. He was one of the truly great individuals of our century whose lifetime within it we set against the monsters, from Hitler to Pol Pot, the century has produced. Gandhi was an original thinker on *the nature of power*, as distinct from power confined to the purely political concept as the tool for liberation, yet able to serve this tool as part of a high moral consciousness. His philosophy of *satyagraha*, 'the force which is born of truth and love', is perhaps the only genuine spiritual advance in an era of religious decline marked by crackpot distortions of faith, and, finally, by savage fundamentalism.

What Mohandas Gandhi began, out of a philosophy formulated in South Africa and applied tactically in India to bring about freedom from British imperial rule, Nelson Mandela has concluded. For Nelson Mandela's unmatched, unchallengeable prestige and honour in the world today is recognition not only of his achievement, with and for his people, in the defeat of the dire twentieth-century experiment in social engineering called apartheid. It is recognition that other ghastly forms of social engineering tried in our century were defeated where they had taken refuge, for apartheid with its blatant racist laws was an avatar of Nazism. And finally, it is homage paid to Mandela in recognition that what was at stake was something greater by far than the fate of a single country; it was final victory gained for humankind over the centuries-old bondage of colonisation.

The sum of our century may be looked at in a number of ways.

The wars that were fought, the military defeats that turned into economic victories, the ideologies that rose and fell, the technology that telescoped time and distance.

We could dip a finger in a dark viscous substance and write on the window of our time, OIL. Oil became more precious than gold; it has been the 'why' of many wars of our day; repressive regimes go unreproached by democratic countries who are dependent on those regimes for oil; men, women and children die, for oil, without knowing why.

In intimate human relations, we have won sexual freedom, and lost it – to Aids.

Freud changed emotional cognition and self-perception. Another kind of perception moved from Picasso's *Guernica* to a Campbell's soup can, to the Reichstag wrapped in plastic, illustrating our cycles: worship of force and destruction, worship of materialism, desire to cover up and forget these choices we have made.

Now that the deeds are done, the hundred years ready to seal what will be recorded of us, our last achievement could be in the spirit of taking up, in 'the ceaseless adventure of man',[1] control of our achievements, questioning honestly and reflecting upon the truth of what has been lived through, what has been done. There is no other base on which to found the twenty-first century with the chance to make it a better one.

1995

---

[1]   Jawaharlal Nehru, *The Discovery of India*, Meridian Books, London, 1951, p. 16.

The Status of the Writer in the World Today

Which World? Whose World?

A few months ago I was a participant in an international gathering in Paris to evaluate the status of the artist in the world.
There we were on an elegant stage before a large audience; among
us was a famous musician, a distinguished sculptor, several poets
and writers of repute, a renowned dancer-choreographer. We had
come together literally from the ends of the earth. At this stately
opening session we were flanked by the Director-General of our
host organisation, the representative of a cultural foundation
funded by one of North America's multibillionaire dynasties, and
France's Deputy Minister of Culture. The Director-General, the
representative of the multibillionaire foundation and the Deputy
Minister each rose and gave an address lasting half an hour; the
session, which also was to include some musical performance, was
scheduled to close after two hours.

An official tiptoed along the backs of our chairs and requested
us, the artists, to cut our addresses to three minutes. We humbly
took up our pens and began to score out what we had to say. When
the bureaucrats had finally regained their seats, we were summoned
one by one to speak in telegraphese. All did so except the last in
line. She was – I name her in homage! – Mallika Sarabhai, a dancer-
choreographer from India. She swept to the podium, a beauty in
sandals and sari, and announced: 'I have torn up my speech. The
bureaucrats were allowed to speak as long as they pleased; the
artists were told that three minutes was time enough for whatever
they might have to say. So – we have the answer to the status of the
artist in the world today.'

This experience set me thinking back to another that I have had,
on a deeper and more personal level.

In my Charles Eliot Norton lectures at Harvard, a year or two ago, which subsequently were published under the title *Writing and Being*, I devoted three of the six lectures to the writing and being each of Chinua Achebe, Amos Oz and Naguib Mahfouz. Edward Said, himself another writer whose work is important to me, reviewed the book extremely favourably in a leading English paper, while yet taking me to task for my indignant assertion that Mahfouz is not given his rightful place in contemporary world literature, is never mentioned in the company of such names as Umberto Eco, Günter Grass, etc., and certainly not widely read even by those whom one considers well-read; I know that a number of my friends read his work for the first time as a result of my published lecture.

Mahfouz neglected? – Said chided me.

Mahfouz not recognised for his greatness in world literature?

What world did I define him by, what world did my purview confine *me* to in my assessment? In the literature of Arabic culture, the world of the Arabic language, Mahfouz is fully established in the canon of greatness and, in the populist canon of fame, while controversial, is widely read.

Edward Said was right. What I was conceiving of as 'world literature' in my lecture, was in fact that of the Euro-North Americans into which only a few of us foreigners have been admitted. Naguib Mahfouz is recognised as a great writer in the world of Arabic literature, of whose canon I know little or nothing.

But wait a moment – Said, I saw, had hit intriguingly upon a paradox. *He* was placing the concept of another 'world literature' alongside the one *I* had posited with my eyes fixed on Euro-North America as the literary navel-of-the-world. In the all-encompassing sense of the term 'world', can any of our literatures be claimed definitively as 'world' literature? Which world? Whose world?

The lesson Edward Said gave me, along with the lesson provided by Mallika Sarabhai at the gathering in Paris, is a sequence, from the situation of artists in general, on the one hand, to the question of literary canons, on the other, that becomes the naturally relevant introduction to my subject, here among my brother and

sister African writers: our status, *specifically as writers*, in the worlds-
within-'the world' we occupy.

Status. What is status, to us?

First – it never can go without saying – the primary status must be
freedom of expression. That is the oxygen of our creativity. Without
it, many talents on our continent have struggled for breath; some
have choked; and some have been lost to us in that other climate,
the thin air of exile.

Suppression of freedom of expression by censorship and bannings
was in many of our countries a feature of colonial regimes – I
myself was such a victim of the apartheid government, with three
of my own works, and an anthology I collected of South African
writers' works, banned. Suppression of freedom of expression has
continued to be a feature of not a few of our independent regimes,
leading outrageously and tragically in one of them, Nigeria, to the
execution of one writer and the threat of death sentence placed
upon another. But thankfully, in many of our countries, including
mine, South Africa, and yours, Ghana, freedom of expression is
entrenched.

Freedom to write. We have that status; and we are fully aware
that it is one that we must be always alert to defend against all
political rationalisations and pleas to doctor our search for the truth
into something more palatable to those who make the compromises of power.

Quite apart from the supreme issue of human freedom, our claim
to freedom to write has a significance, a benefit to society that
only writers can give. Our books are *necessary*: for in the words of
the great nineteenth-century Russian writer, Nikolai Gogol,[1] they
show both the writer and his or her people *what they are*. 'The writer
is both the repository of his people's ethos, and his revelation to
them of themselves.' This revelation is what regimes fear, in their
writers. But if our status as writers is to be meaningful, that fear is
proof of our integrity . . . And our strength.

---

1   Quoted, in paraphrase, by Vladimir Nabokov, in *Nikolai Gogol* by Vladimir Nabokov,
New Directions, New York, 1961, p. 129.

Status, like charity, begins at home. The modern movement of African writers to define their status in this century was within our continent itself. With the impact of colonialism and its coefficient industrialisation, the keeper of the word – one who is marked for expression of the creative imagination with the 'ring of white chalk' round the eye by Chinua Achebe's old man of Abazon, in *Anthills of the Savannah* – with the impacts of colonialism the traditional status of the keeper of the word, the griot, was not, could not be adapted as a status for one whose poetry and stories were disseminated to the people-become-the-public at the remove of printed books, remote from any living presence of their creator in the flesh, their origin in the creative imagination. The keeper of the word became invisible; had no ready-defined place in society.

I am not going to reiterate, or rather regurgitate, the history, including the influence from the African diaspora in the United States and the Caribbean, that both preceded and coincided with the first congress of African writers and artists in 1956.[2] And it is significant, in terms of progress, to recall that it was not held in Africa at all, but in Paris.

I am looking at the modern movement from the distance made by events between then and now; from the epic unfurling of Africa's freedom from colonial rule in its many avatars, way back from Ghana's, the first, forty years ago, to South Africa's, the latest and final one.

In the broad sweep of hindsight one can see that Kwame Nkrumah's political postulation of Pan-Africanism had its cultural equivalent in the movement of negritude. Negritude, as a word, has long become an archaism, with its first syllable – although coming from the French language – suggestive of the American Deep South. But the *other* invented word, with which the young Wole Soyinka cheekily attacked the concept, has remained very much alive because over and over again, in the work of many African writers, Soyinka's iconoclasm has been proved mistaken. 'A

---

2 'Congress of Negro Writers and Artists', at the Sorbonne, Paris, under the auspices of *Présence Africaine*, 1956.

tiger doesn't have to proclaim his tigritude', he pronounced. But as each country on our continent has come into its own, in independence, the expression of Africanness, the assertion of African ways of life, from philosophy to food, has intensified: Africa measuring herself against her selfhood, not that of her erstwhile conquerors.

Africanness is fully established. So what status do we writers have, now, right here at home, in our individual countries?

Is it the kind of status we would wish – not in terms of fame and glory, invitations to dine with government ministers, but in terms of the role of literature in the illumination of our people, the opening up of lives to the power and beauty of the imagination, a revelation of themselves by the writer as the repository of a people's ethos? Alongside the establishment of African values – which in the case of our best writers included a lack of fear of questioning some, thus establishing that other essential component of literature's social validity – the criterion in almost all of our countries has been the extent to which the writer has identified with and articulated, through transformations of the creative imagination, the struggle for freedom. And this, then, indeed, was the role of the writer as repository of a people's ethos. Today the status, if to be measured on the scale of political commitment, is more complex.

Yes, economic neo-colonialism is a phase that threatens freedom, in a people's ethos. Yes, the greedy wrangles of the Euro-North American powers to manipulate African political change for the spoils of oil supplies and military influence are concerns in a people's ethos. Yes, the civil wars waged by their own leaders, bringing appalling suffering – these are all part of a people's ethos to be expressed, for now that our continent has rid itself of its self-appointed masters from Europe the sense of identity in having a common enemy has eroded and in many of our countries brotherhood has become that of Cain and Abel.

Between writers and the national state, the threat of death by fatwa or secular decree, from Mahfouz to Saro Wiwa and Soyinka, has become the status of the writer in some of our countries. Yet these and less grim political themes tend to be the *mise-en-scène* of contemporary writing on our continent rather than its centrality.

Africanism itself is an economic and cultural concept rather than an ideological one, now. For writers, the drama of individual and personal relations that was largely suppressed in themselves, and when indulged in was judged by their societies as trivial in comparison with the great shared traumas of the liberation struggle, now surfaces. When we in South Africa are asked, 'What will you write about now apartheid is gone', the answer is, 'Life has not stopped because apartheid is dead.' Life, as it did for you in Ghana after 1957 and for all the other countries of our continent after their liberation, begins again. There is so much to write about that was pushed aside by the committed creative mind, before; and there is so much to write about that never happened, couldn't exist, before. Freedom and its joys, and – to paraphrase Freud – freedom and its discontents, are the ethos of a people for its writers now.

So we have lost the status of what one might call national engagement that we had. Some few of us take on the responsibility to become writer-politicians – at random I think of poet Mongane Wally Serote, now in the Mandela government's Ministry of Culture and diplomats, like your own poet, Kofi Awoonor. But there are unlikely to be any future Senghors, poet-presidents. And I ask myself, and you: do we writers seek, need that nature of status, the writer as politician, statesperson? Is it not thrust upon us, as a patriotic duty outside the particular gifts we have to offer? Is not the ring of chalk round the eye the sign of our true calling? Whatever else we are called upon to do takes us away from the dedication we know our role as writers requires of us. As the cultural arm of liberation struggles, we met the demands of our time in that era. That was our national status. We have yet to be recognised with a status commensurate with respect for the primacy of the well-earned role of *writer-as-writer* in the post-colonial era.

How would we ourselves define such a status?

What do we expect, of our governments, our societies, and in return expect to give of ourselves to these? I have personally decisive convictions about this, constantly evolving as the country I belong to develops its cultural directions, and I am sure you have your convictions, ideas. And we need to exchange them, East–West,

North–South, across our continent; that, indeed, is my first conviction. We need to meet in the flesh, take one another's hands, hear
one another, at valuable encounters like this present opportunity
under the banner of the Pan African Writers' Association.

But you and I know that the best there is in us, as writers, is
in our books. The benefit and pleasure of personal contact is, in
any case, limited to a fortunate few. Much more importantly, we
need to read one another's work. We and the people of our countries need natural and easy access to the writings that express the
ethos of our neighbouring countries: what they believe, what they
feel, how they make their way through the hazards and joys of
living, contained by what varieties of socio-political and cultural
structures they are in the process of pursuing. Forty years after the
first country – yours – to attain independence, in the libraries and
bookshops of our countries you still will find, apart from works by
writers of each country itself, only a handful of books by the same
well-known names among African writers from other countries of
our continent. Every now and then, there may be a new one, a Ben
Okri who comes to us by way of recognition in Europe, along the
old North–South cultural conduit. Without the pioneering work of
Hans Zell, and the invaluable Heinemann African Writers Series,
the publication of journals from the old *Présence Africaine* to those
bravely launched, often to a short or uneven life, by writers' organisations or publishers in our various countries, the cross-pollination
of literature in Africa would scarcely exist where it should: among
ordinary readers rather than the African literati we represent, here.

The best part of two generations has gone by since the African
continent began its inexorable achievement of independence that
has now culminated: a priority in our claim for the status of writers
and writing in Africa surely is that there should be developed a
pan-African network of publishers and distributors who will cooperate – greatly to their own commercial advantage, by the way – to
make our writers' work as prominently and naturally available as
the Euro-North American potboilers which fill airport bookstalls.
This does not mean that we should export potboilers to one another!
It means that writing of quality which readers in your countries

and mine never see, unless they happen to have the resources to come across and mail-order from specialist book catalogues, would be beside our beds at night and in our hands as we travel on buses, trains and planes. There is a publishing industry on our continent, varying in different countries, as re-evidenced, after earlier studies, in Hans Zell's and Cecile Lomer's 1996 work, *Publishing and Book Development in Sub-Saharan Africa,*[3] and I understand there has been recently established the resource centre, the African Publishing Network, APNET. I would suggest that such a network doesn't yet exist, and welcome any such initiative to weave it.

You will say that the old obstacle of our Babel's Tower of languages rises before an African network of publishing. But the fact is that colonial conquest, with all its destruction and deprivation, ironically left our continent with a short list of *linqua francas* that have been appropriated to Africa's own ends in more ways than pragmatic communication for politics and trade. English, French and Portuguese – these three at least are the languages used by many African writers in their work – for good or ill in relation to national culture: that is another whole debate that will continue. These three languages have virtually become *adjunct African languages by rightful appropriation*; and the translation into them of African-language literature, which itself is and always must be the foundation and ultimate criterion of the continent's literature, is not an obstacle but an opportunity. Where are the translation centres at our colleges and universities, where young scholars could gain deep insights into their own languages while learning the skills of translation? Here is a field of cultural advancement, cultural employment in *collaboration with publishers*, waiting to be cultivated. We have an OAU uniting our continent, sometimes in contention as well as common purpose, on matters of mutual concern in international affairs, governance, policy and trade; we need an OAC, an Organisation of African Culture to do the same for Pan-African literature and the arts. Only then should we have a

---

3 *Publishing and Book Development in Sub-Saharan Africa: An Annotated Bibliography*, Hans Zell Publishers, Oxford, 1996.

'world literature': the world of our own, our challenge to the title each culturo-political and linguistic grouping on our planet has the hubris to claim for itself.

Professor Lebona Mosia,[4] an arts academic in South Africa, recently reflected on our Deputy President, Thabo Mbeki's concept of an African renaissance of roots, values and identity, remarking (I quote) that our people are emerging from an 'imaginary history . . . whose white folks believed that South Africa is part of Europe, America (the USA) and Australia. Blacks have always recognised that they are part of Africa.' The same 'imaginary history' of course applies to Pan-Africa, to the thinking of all ex-colonial powers.

Does Thabo Mbeki's renaissance sound like a renaissance of negritude?

I don't believe it is. Or could be. Circumstances in our countries have changed so fundamentally since that concept of the 1950s, when liberation was still to be won. The reality of African history has long begun to be recorded and established, from where it was cut off as anthropology and prehistory and substituted by the history of foreign conquest and settlers. One of the dictionary definitions of the wide meanings of renaissance is 'any revival in art and literature'; as we writers take to ourselves the right to vary or add to the meaning of words, I would interpret the meaning of renaissance in Mbeki's context not as reviving the past, whether pre-colonial or of the negritude era, but of using it only as a basis for cultural self-realisation and development in an Africa that *never existed before*, because it is an Africa that has *come through*: emerged from the experience of slavery, colonial oppression, the humiliating exploitation of paternalism, economic and spiritual degradation, suffering of every nature human evil could devise. A continent that has liberated itself; overcome.

Africans have established, beyond question, that our continent is not part of anyone's erstwhile empire. Secure in this confidence, and open-eyed at home as I hope we shall be to the necessity to

---

4   'Time To Be Truly Part of Africa', Lebona Mosia, Dean of the Arts Faculty, Technikon Northern Gauteng, Soshanguve, *The Star*, Johannesburg, 26 September 1997.

apply ourselves to developing Africa's literary variety to and fro across our own Pan-African frontiers, it's time to cross new frontiers on our cultural horizon, to turn the literary compass to measure whether we still should be pointing in the same direction towards the outside world.

Which world? Whose world? The North–South axis was the one on which we were regarded so long only as on the receiving end, and which, latterly, we have somewhat culturally reversed: African writers have won prestigious literary prizes in England and France, and even Nobel prizes; African music has become popular abroad, the international fashion industry presently has a vogue for somewhat bizarre adaptations of African traditional dress – well, Africa dressed itself up in Europe's three-piece suits, collar and tie; now Europe wraps itself in a pagne, a dashiki, a bou-bou . . .

Of course we do, and should, retain our freedom of access to, appropriation of, European and North American literary culture. I believe we have passed the stage, in the majority of our countries, of finding Shakespeare and Dostoevsky, Voltaire and Melville, irrelevant. I believe that, as writers and readers, all literature of whatever origin *belongs* to us. There *is* an acceptable 'world literature' in this sense; one great library to which it would be a folly of self-deprivation to throw away our membership cards.

What *has* happened is that the works of our own writers, imparting the ethos of our peoples, have firmly and rightfully displaced those of Europeans as the definitive cultural texts in our schools and universities.

But if you place the compass on a map you will see not alone that South–South and not North–South is our closer orientation, but that if you cut out the shape of South America and that of Africa you can fit the east coast of South America and the west coast of Africa together, pieces of a jigsaw puzzle making a whole – the lost continent Gondwana, sundered by cosmic cataclysms and seas.

This romantic geographical connection is merely symbolic of the actual, potential relationships that lay dormant and ignored during the colonial period when our continent of Africa was set by European powers strictly on the North–South axis. Climate and terrain are primary experiences for human beings; many South American and African countries share the same kind of basic natural environment, which determines not only the types of food they grow and eat, but the myths they created, and the nature of city life they have evolved. Both continents were conquered by European powers, their culture overrun and denigrated. Both have won their freedom from foreign powers through suffering, and suffered subsequently under brutal dictators in internecine wars among their own people. Both bear a burden of their people's poverty and confront neo-colonialism exacted in return for their need of economic aid. Finally, there is the strange reciprocal bond: with those communities in South America descended from slaves brought from Africa.

All this in common, and yet we know so little of South American writers' work and life. Aside from some few big names, such as Borges of Argentina, Machado de Assis of Brazil, Mario Vargas Llosa of Peru, and now Gabriel García Márquez of Colombia, we do not know the work of the majority of South American writers, with whom, in many ways, we have more *existential* ties than with writers in Europe and North America.

Industrialists and entrepreneurs are opening up their South–South routes of trade, matching the exchange of raw materials, processing and expertise which countries in South America and Africa can supply for one another. They are giving more than a side-glance away from the fixed gaze of North–South development. Earlier this year Mongane Wally Serote and I visited Argentina, Brazil and Uruguay, and there met writers from other South American countries, as well. All were eager to grow closer to their recognition that our literatures are reciprocal in the ethos of our many shared existential situations, from the colonised past to the development problems of the present, both material and cultural. If the industrialists and entrepreneurs are paying attention to the material reciprocity, why are we, as writers, not looking South–South in a new freedom to choose which world, whose world, beyond our own with which we could create a wider one for ourselves?

In our first concern, which is to develop an African 'world

literature' as our status, we should keep well in mind the words of the great Mexican poet, Octavio Paz.[5] With the exceptions of the pre-Hispanic civilisations of America, he writes, all civilisations – including China and Japan – have been the result of intersections and clashes with foreign cultures. And the Congolais writer, Henri Lopez,[6] in his novel, *Le Lys et le Flamboyant*, is speaking not only of the mixed blood of tribe, race and colour of many of our people in Africa, but of the interchange of ideas, of solutions to a common existence, when he writes, 'Every civilisation is born of a forgotten mixture, every race is a variety of mixtures that is ignored.' The nurture of our writers, our literature, is a priority which should not create for us a closed-shop African 'world literature', a cultural exclusivity in place of the exclusion, even post-colonial, that has kept us in an ante-room of self-styled 'world literatures'. Let our chosen status in the world be that of writers who seek exchanges of the creative imagination, ways of thinking and writing, of fulfilling the role of repository of the people's ethos, by opening it out, bringing to it a vital mixture of individuals and peoples recreating themselves.

Finally, at home in Africa, in the countries of our continent, let Rosa Luxemburg's definition be at the tip of our ballpoint pens and on the screens of our word processors as we write: 'Freedom means freedom to those who think differently.' Let the writer's status be recognised as both praise-singer and social critic. Let us say with Amu Djoleto:[7]

> What you expect me to sing, I will not,
> What you do not expect me to croak, I will.

1997

---

5   Octavio Paz, *In Light of India*, translated from the Spanish by Eliot Weinberger, Harcourt Brace, 1997.

6   Henri Lopez, *Le Lys et le Flamboyant*, Éditions du Seuil, Paris, 1997. My translation from the French.

7   Amu Djoleto, 'A Passing Thought', *Messages: Poems from Ghana*, edited by Kofi Awoonor and Adali-Mortty, Heinemann, London, 1971.

The Poor Are Always with Us

The Eradication of Poverty

These are the poles of perception between which we meet today. These are the oppositions of the phenomenon of want.

The first is ancient, an implied acceptance of a destined lot, everyone conditioned by class (each in his place); by religion (the meek shall inherit the earth) to be content to have no place and inherit nothing.

The second proposition refuses to accept poverty as part of human destiny. The United Nations General Assembly's designation of the International Decade for the Eradication of Poverty is a *mission* statement in the true sense. It is surely the boldest expression of faith in human endeavour ever made. It comes from the most representative body in the world. It posits perhaps the greatest human advancement ever embarked upon, an adventure greater than any attempted in the progress of humankind since we could define ourselves as such. And most important, it produces convincing proof that the goal is attainable.

Beginning last year, the United Nations Development Programme has launched an exhaustive, worldwide initiative to debunk poverty as destiny; with its partners, the United Nations system, organisations of civil society, academic institutions, the private sectors and international donor community, research has been produced which identifies the extent and nature of poverty in its many forms – and destiny.

I do not propose to cite the statistics of the world of want. They are all here, devastating, in the invaluable publications of the United Nations Development Programme – the staggering material facts of race, racial prejudice, political and social administration, geography, gender, ethnicity, agricultural practice, technological practice, industrial production, health services – everything, from the drying up of a stream to the closing down of an arms factory – that produces the phenomena of poverty as lived by the world's 1.3 billion poor.

When you read this evidence of physical, mental and spiritual deprivation, you can reach only one conclusion: poverty is a trap. Brought about by many factors other than the obvious ones you may always have had in mind, poverty is the nadir of disempowerment.

It is a disempowerment that has existed and does exist in democracies as well as dictatorships, links them, in a way we are reluctant to have to admit. The ballot box of free and fair elections has failed to empower the poor in most of the democratic countries. The dictatorship of the people failed to do so in most countries of the Soviet empire. And since the fall of Communism, the West's claim of freeing those countries to the establishment of a market economy and prosperity means nothing to the old people who now beg in the streets of Moscow, as the homeless do in the streets of cities of the only great power left in the world, this United States of America. In Brazil, in Argentina, in Africa, in India – where in this world except for the small welfare states of the North, are there not people in the nadir of poverty? No need to enter into ideological differences, no need to make any value judgements, here: each country has produced – or failed to end – the shameful human end product, poverty.

What is a decade, in terms of centuries of acceptance that *the poor are always with us*?

Our answer surely is that the world now has the knowledge, the scientific and technological ability to do away with most of the causes of poverty, and to turn around the consequences of causes it cannot prevent. There are identified practical means: what is needed is the money and commitment of governments, regional, national and bodies of world governance, to cooperate and carry out these means. And what is needed to bring *this* about is a roused awareness and admittance among the peoples of the world that whether there is proved to be life on Mars, and whether you may conduct your affairs electronically without leaving your armchair, the new century is not going to be a new century *at all* in terms of the progress of humanity if we take along with us acceptance of the shameful shackles of the past, over a billion men, women and children in poverty, and we offer only charity, that palliative to satisfy the conscience and keep the same old system of haves and have-nots quietly contained.

In view of this need for roused awareness I think it is important for us to consider, how do different people conceive poverty? How do they think about it? Historically, where did it begin?

In prehistory early humans lived by what we would call now a subsistence economy: you hunted, you gathered, and when these resources of your group ran out in one place, you moved on; only nature discriminated, making one area more salubrious than another, but there was space enough to make of this an advantage rather than a deprivation. It was with the arrival of surplus value that the phenomenon of rich and poor began; with the cultivation of the valleys of the Euphrates and the Nile, when food was grown and could be stored instead of foraged and hunted, able to satisfy only short-term needs. As soon as there was more than sufficient unto the day, those who grew more than they could eat became the haves, while those whose harvest provided no surplus became the have-nots.

Basically, nothing has changed since then. Except that it is no longer possible for society to move on from one disadvantaged environment to a more salubrious one – the colonial era of the European powers was perhaps the last such movement to take place successfully, the final enactment of an obsolete solution to social problems. On an individual scale, immigrants in contemporary days generally find themselves received by locals with resentment as competitors in the labour market of the country of their aspirations, and quickly sink to a place among the poor of that country. Nothing much has changed, over the centuries, except that we have evolved what might be called a philosophy of acceptance of poverty.

Firstly, there is the question of different class perceptions of what poverty is, and how these are arrived at. There is the upper-class perception. There is the middle-class perception. And there is that of the poor themselves.

For the rich, any contingency that they themselves might sink into poverty is so remote that it need not enter their minds. They are also in the position of being *bountiful* so that, curiously, while they may be genuinely concerned about the existence of the poor, poverty is also a source of self-esteem. Do not be shocked by this remark; without the philanthropy of wealth, the manner in which the world has dealt with, alleviated, poverty up till now could not have been maintained at all. But this overspill of wealth is too sporadic, too personally dependent on what aspects of poverty, piecemeal, donors happen to favour, to be a solution.

I read recently that if the wealth of the ten richest individuals in the world were to be made available, the problem of the world's 1.3 billion living in poverty could be solved. Well, one cannot expect these individuals to give up their wordly goods *in toto* for the world, any more than any of us, I suspect, are prepared to sacrifice our – we consider – reasonable privileges entirely for those who have none. What is asked is for those who possess and control great wealth to look at the economic structures in their countries which have made that wealth possible and yet have created conditions that make philanthropy necessary – regimes that have failed to establish the means, in adequate pay for work, in education and training, in environment, by which people may provide for themselves in self-respect and dignity. That is the thinking that will face the facts of redistribution of the world's wealth.

The wealthy and powerful who control the consortiums and international companies, and the government agencies who plan with them, need to take responsible heed of the emphasis placed by the United Nations Development Programme on 'putting people at the centre of development', on the concept of development enterprises as not only or even primarily advancing the credit balance of a country and providing X number of jobs, but as the instigation of a series of social consequences that will affect the implicated community in many ways. What may put pay in the pockets of the income-poor this year may be offset, over their lifetime, by destroying their environment. Development becomes a dangerous form of social engineering it if discounts the long-term effects on social cohesion. Profit and loss, in the book-keeping of the eradication of poverty, will be a calculation of how many people's daily lives can be entered, in the long term, on the credit column.

For the broad middle class, which includes the skilled working class in many countries, the possibility of descending to poverty is subliminally present. Their concept of poverty is tinged by fear, as well as by concern for those who suffer it: there but for the grace of God go I. A change of government, inflation, a form of affirmative action whether on principle of colour, race or simply replacement of older employees with the young – these contingencies threaten middle-class safety with its home ownership, its insurance policies and pension funds. All the things that poverty strips one of; all the safety nets the poor do not have . . . Poverty is regarded as a blow of fate that just might come. Alternatively, whose fault is it? Perhaps, since the middle class is by and large industrious and ambitious – and has the possibility of advancement in terms of money and status, having a base to start from which the poor have not – the middle class often feels that it is lack of will, initiative and commitment to work as they themselves do, that keeps the poor in that condition.

The basic perception of poverty is the man begging in the street; the conclusion: surely there's *something else* he could do? Unemployment is suspect as lack of ability; and well it may be in many developing countries where lack of skills makes people literally unemployable, unable to be active in sectors where employment would be available. But what has to be realised is how that lack comes about in the general disempowerment of poverty itself. To abolish the spectre of the man begging in the street, the woman huddled on her park bench home, the children staring from a refugee camp, is first to make the effort to understand what factors create this disempowerment.

How do victims themselves perceive their poverty?

They live it; know it best, beyond all outside conceptions. What, apart from the survival needs of food and shelter, do *they* feel they are most deprived of? Researchers moving among them have learned much that is often ignored, such as the perception of women that, as those who with their children suffer most, attention to their advancement through skills and education should take more than a marginal 'special interest' place in transformation of the lives of the disadvantaged in general. Consultation with how communities in poverty see themselves in relation to the ordinary fullness of life other communities take for granted is now recognised by research as integral to harnessing the negatives of social resentment and passivity into vital partnership for change. It is the fortunate world outside dollar-a-day subsistence that needs to begin to see the impoverished as our necessary partners in world survival, to be listened to in respect of the components of what a decent life is. It is the privileged world that needs to come to the realisation that a 'decent life' cannot be truly lived by any of us while one-quarter of the developing world's population exists in poverty.

If economic poverty began when some had surplus production and some did not, and nothing much has changed in principle, the second cause of poverty as a phenomenon of human history is war, and nothing much has changed there, either. Wars, social conflict, whether at international, national or inter-ethnic level, still produce hunger and homelessness, the prime characteristics of poverty, and now, it seems, on a rolling action scale. The eradication of poverty implies a hand-in-hand relation with agencies of the non-violent resolution of conflict. The peace-keeping, peace-promoting work of United Nations and other formations, fraught with difficulty, danger and frustration, and controversial as it is, must be seen as a vital component of the decade's aim.

The violence of nature – flood, drought and earthquake – is another factor that has caused poverty since ancient times, and that is something which is not within human capability to prevent, as wars are. But the violence perpetrated *by* humankind *on* nature is increasingly one of the causes of poverty. The destruction of indigenous forests, the pollution of oceans, the leaching out of the land by indiscriminate use of chemicals; these take away from communities their livelihood. The leakage of nuclear waste makes water unpotable and the very air unbreathable. The problem of poverty cannot be solved while the earth and its oceans that feed us are abused by ruthless government planning and blinkered human greed.

What are the moral perceptions of poverty?

These are governed by those looking on, looking in, so to speak, from the outside. 'Poor but honest': consider the dictum. Why do the rich never make the qualification, 'Rich but honest'? No one has commented on moral attitudes in this context better than the German poet and playwright, Bertolt Brecht. Here is his poem:

> Food is the first thing. Morals follow on.
> So first make sure that those who now are starving
> Get proper helpings when we do the carving.

Is for people to be honest when they are starving our measure of virtue, or is it a measure of our hypocrisy? Common crime, up to a certain level – economic white-collar crime is the prerogative of the wealthy – is a product of poverty and cannot be countered by punitive methods alone. Some of the funds that citizens, living in urban fear of muggings and robberies, want to see used, as the saying goes, to 'stamp out crime' with more police and bigger prisons, would have better effect diverted to the aim of stamping out poverty. No one will be safe while punishment and pious moral dicta are handed out in place of food. The campaign against poverty is the best campaign against crime.

Finally, the definition of poverty does not end with material needs; the aim of its eradication will not be completed or perhaps even attainable without the world's attention to the deprivation of the mind: intellectual poverty. As food is the basic need of the starved body, literacy is the basic need of the starved mind. According to the United Nations Development Programme's 'Human Development Report', in the past fifty years adult illiteracy in the world has been reduced to almost half. If it can be virtually ended by early next century, it will be a great force in the six-point global action plan provided by the Report, and not only because the ability to read and write is crucial to participation in development, the open sesame to the world of work, mental skills and self-administration that is economic freedom. To be illiterate or semi-literate is to be deprived of the illumination and pleasure of reading, of one's rightful share in and exploration of the world of ideas; it is to spend one's life imprisoned between the walls of one-dimensional experience.

Illiteracy cruelly stunts the human spirit both as a cause and result of the disempowerment we now dedicate a decade to bring to an end. We are here to celebrate and discuss the means we know we have at our disposal; and I want to close with what I believe can be our text, for the day and the decade. It comes from William Blake. I quote:

> Many conversed on these things as they labour'd at the furrow
> Saying: 'It is better to prevent misery than to release from misery:
> It is better to prevent error than to forgive the criminal.
> Labour well the Minute Particulars, attend to the Little ones,
> And those who are in misery cannot remain so long
> If we do but our duty: labour well the teeming Earth.'

1997

From a Correspondence with Kenzaburo Oe

Dear Kenzaburo,
Your letter brings the pleasure of realisation that we are simply taking up from where we were interrupted by the end of our encounter in the Tokyo hotel six years ago. There was so much to exchange; it has existed, in the parentheses of separate lives, ready to continue any time. The ambiguity, the connections that criss-cross against chronology between that short meeting and what was going to happen – an invisible prescience which would

influence our individual thinking and writing – *that* turns out to have presaged the links of our *then* and *now*. You came to our meeting unknowingly in the foreshadow of the terrible earthquake that was to devastate a Japanese city later that year, and that I was to use, in a novel as yet not conceived, as a metaphor for apocalyptic catastrophe wreaked by nature, alongside that of contemporary devastation by humans upon themselves in Eastern Europe and Africa.

And so now I should not have been surprised that you, writing to me, are preoccupied by the question of violence entering deeply into your awareness, just as it has made its way into mine. This is a 'recognition' between two writers; but it goes further. It is the recognition of writers' inescapable need to read the signs society gives out cryptically and to try to make sense of what these really mean.

I must tell you that when I began to write *The House Gun* it came to me as the personal tragedy of a mother and father whose son, in a crime of passion, murders their human values along with the man he kills. The parallel theme, placing their lives in the context of their country, the new South Africa, was that they – white people who in the past regime of racial discrimination had always had black people dependent upon *them* – would find themselves dependent upon a distinguished black lawyer to defend their son. That was going to be the double thesis of my novel. But as I wrote (and isn't it always the way with us, our exploration of our story lures us further and further into the complexity of specific human existences?) I found that the context of mother, father and son was not existentially determined only geographically and politically; there was the question of the very air they breathed. Violence in the air; didn't the private act of *crime passionel* take place within unconscious sinister sanction – the public, social banalisation of violence?

You make the true and terrible observation 'all the children of the world, in their perception and consciousness of their era, are the mirrors upon which the massive universal violence is reflected'. You are rightly most concerned about the situation of children, and I'll come to that, but first I must comment on the extraordinary, blinkered attitude to violence which I have just recently been subjected to rather than encountered, in Europe and the United States.

Whenever I was interviewed, journalists would propose the question of violence in South Africa as an isolated phenomenon, as if street muggings, burglaries, campus 'date rapes', brawls resulting in serious injuries between so-called sports matches were not part of everyday life in their countries.

Let me admit at once that South African cities have at present a high place on the daunting list of those with the worst crime rate in the world. Some South American cities have been prominent on that list so long that this has come to be regarded complacently by the rest of the world as a national characteristic, a kind of folk custom rather than a tragedy. Conversely, South Africa's violent crime is seen as a *phenomenon of freedom* – interpreted among racists everywhere (and there are still plenty) as evidence that blacks should have been kept under white hegemony for ever.

The reasons for the rise of crime in South Africa, however, are not those of black people's abuse of freedom. They are our heritage from apartheid. What the world does not know, or chose not to know, was that during the apartheid regime from 1948, state violence was quotidian and rampant. To be victims of state violence was the way of life for black men, women and children. Violence is nothing new to us; it was simply confined to daily perpetration against blacks. They were shut away outside the cities in their black townships at night, or permanently banished to ethnically defined territory euphemistically known as 'homelands', from which only male contract workers were allowed to come to the cities. This was how urban law and order was kept. Violence, and the desperate devaluation of life it called forth, was out of sight. Now that the people of our country are free in their own country to seek work and homes wherever they please, they flock to the cities. But the cities were not built for them; there is no housing for such vast numbers, and their presence on the labour market has swelled the ranks of the unemployed enormously. Their home is the streets; hunger turns them, as it would most of us who deplore crime on full stomachs, to crime, and degradation degenerates into violence. These are the historical facts that make the reasons for violence in South Africa exceptional. Economic development has the chance to change this deal with violence, here, although it is not a total solution, to a significant extent.

As for the matter of guns as domestic possessions along with the house cat – while I was in the USA two schoolboys aged eleven and thirteen shot and killed several classmates and their teacher, and while I was in Paris a schoolboy shot and killed his classmate. Why did these children have access to guns? Where did they get them? The American children took the guns from the house of their grandfather; the French child from that of his father. The guns were simply there, in these family homes, commonplace objects, evidently not kept under lock and key, if they had any legitimate place at all in household equipment. I've just read American statistics revealing that a gun in the house is forty-three times more likely to kill a member of the household than an intruder. And now you tell me that a Japanese boy killed a companion and hung up the victim's head in public; a boy fatally stabbed his teacher; an old man was beaten to death by two girls; and a father was killed by his son and the son's friend.

This brings us to what is the ultimate responsibility of adults in your country, in mine, in the whole world: why could children cold-bloodedly kill? What has made them horrifically indifferent to the pain and death of others, so that they themselves are prepared to inflict these? What has happened to their 'tender years'?

Setting aside the particular experience of South Africa, I think the woman who challenged you, citing environmental causes – an environment created entirely by the power and will of adults – was correct. If you look back at your own childhood experience, Kenzaburo, and I look back at mine, surely we shall see how our morality, our humanity was distorted by the agenda of adults, something we had to struggle with and shed by our own efforts as we grew: a confirmation of your conviction that there is the 'power of recovery inherent in children themselves', yes. You were brainwashed – no less – into believing the immortal worth of the

Emperor was such that you must be prepared to kill yourself at his command. I was brainwashed – no less – into believing that my white skin gave me superiority and absolute authority over anyone of another colour.

Children are not subjected to this sort of evil conditioning today. Then what is it, in countries dedicated to peace and democracy, reformed in aversion to the authoritarian cruelties of the past, that makes violence acceptable to children? I know it's easy to lay responsibility on the most obvious – the visual media, television and electronic games, now also part of home furnishings. But the fact is that these household presences have become the third parent. They raise the child according to a set of values of equal influence to that of the biological parents. The power of the image has become greater than the word; you can tell a child that a bullet in the head kills, a knife in the heart kills. The child *sees* the 'dead' actor appear, swaggering in another role, next day. This *devaluation* of pain, with its consequent blunting of inhibitions against committing violence, has become, with the acts of glamorous gangsters, mortal-ray-breathing heroes of outer space, the daily, hourly formation of youthful attitudes. It is hauntingly clear to me that these children who kill do not have – it's like an atrophied faculty – the capacity to relate to pain and destruction experienced by others. I think this is what has happened to the 'inner psyche of these juvenile delinquents' you speak of.

What can we do, all of us adults, to take up the responsibility to children, 'restore their normal selves', how rouse 'the power of self-respect inherent in them originally'?

If we place a large share of the blame for their condition upon the media, are we then advocating censorship? The idea is repugnant and frightening to me, who spent decades fighting censorship of information, literature, the arts, in my country. I have in mind something so difficult to bring about that it may seem naive to mention it. Is it not possible that writers, actors, directors and producers of these programmes that make violence acceptably banal could reconsider their values? It is said in what is euphemistically known as the 'entertainment industry' – it has also become a brainwashing industry – that the industry simply gives the public what they want. But the public are long conditioned to want what the industry dictates. And why is that public so passive under this self-appointed authority? Is it because the visual media are the true representation of much accepted adult behaviour? The violence in the air has become the exhalation of being?

You know – more telling, even, than any statement in your letter – years ago you made a remarkable implicit claim for the ability of children to restore the power of self-respect inherent in them. The children in your story (in English translation entitled 'Prize Stock') are the ones in a remote Japanese village who, by their actions and attitudes, teach the adults that the black American airman who has fallen into their hands during the war is a human being, capable of emotional response and suffering. Taking your premise that the power of self-respect is inherent in children, this means that it also must *exist*, dormant, in the substance of adult men and women. How can we release this power of restoration in our present era and circumstances?

Kenzaburo, you did not know how much you were speaking for the end of our millennium when you used these words for an early story: 'Who will teach us to outgrow our madness?'

Sincerely,
Nadine

1998

Octavio Paz: Poet-Archer

I first met Octavio Paz in the seventies, as a guest in his home in Mexico City. A long lunch, accompanying which was the benison of his rich mind. He was a man with a very large head, could have been a model for an Easter Island monolith, and his high white expanse of forehead held back, in a line straight across its cranial limit, the drama of tight-curled black hair. As you listened to him, that forehead seemed a headlight from which beamed illumination.

Every subject he touched upon was bright and new.

We had sporadic contact after that, and in the last year of his life a correspondence when he and I were trying to arrange for him to visit South Africa under the auspices of the Congress of South African Writers. He was keenly interested in our country, our engagement in transition from oppression to freedom, in particular freedom of the word, and it was only poor health that brought his plans to naught.

As a great contemporary poet, Octavio Paz defined himself more precisely as a *Spanish* American poet. For language was, to him, not only the instrument of his poetry, the harp of his lyricism – he saw it as the fundamental operative in the fate of human society; a sure barometer of the condition of ideological, political and social situations, and of individual responsibility for these. In one of his classic prose works, 'The Other Mexico: Critique of the Pyramid', he wrote: 'When a society decays, it is language that is first to become gangrenous. As a result, social criticism begins with grammar and the re-establishing of meaning.'

Of the question of corruption, he wrote:

Although moralists are scandalised by the fortunes amassed by the revolutionaries [in Mexico], they have failed to observe that this material flowering has a verbal parallel: oratory has become the favourite literary genre of the prosperous . . . and alongside oratory, with its plastic flowers, there is the barbarous syntax in many of our newspapers, the foolishness of the language on loudspeakers and the radio, and the loathsome vulgarities of advertising – all that asphyxiating rhetoric.

And, as so often with the writings of Octavio Paz, he might have been speaking of and for much of the rest of the world.

Like Pablo Neruda and Federico Garcia Lorca, Octavio Paz was one of those superb poets whose brilliance makes nonsense of the notion of lesser minds that taking on the turmoil and conflict in one's society and its extension in the world, carrying contentious political and social substance up into the sacrosanct ivory tower, corrupts and destroys true creativity.

Octavio Paz risked activism in many ways during Mexico's recurrent crises. I think of his resignation as his country's ambassador to India in 1968, when the Mexican government fired upon and killed student protesters in Tlatelolco Plaza.

But the most enduring aspect of his activism – his intellectual activism, if one may make such distinctions in the personality of such a *total* man – the treasure he bequeaths us along with his poetry, is the ranging ontology of his essays. There, stemming from his philosophy of language, the significance of literature, history, politics and concepts of time interplay in perfect lucidity of discourse on our being. One of my favourite examples of such symbiosis is this one:

> Every time the Europeans and their North American descendants have encountered other cultures and civilisations, they have called them *backward*. This is not the first time a race or a civilisation has imposed its forms on others, but it is certainly the first time one has set up as a universal ideal, not a changeless principle, but change itself. The Muslim or Christian based the alien's inferiority on a difference of faith: for the Greeks or Toltecs, he was inferior because he was a barbarian, a Chichemecan. Since the eighteenth century, Africans or Asiatics have been inferior because they were not modern. The Western world has identified itself with change and time, and there is no modernity other than that of the West . . . the new Heathen Dogs can be counted in the millions . . . they are called 'underdeveloped peoples'.
>
> 'Underdeveloped' – this adjective belongs to the anemic and castrated language of the United Nations. The word has no precise meaning in the fields of anthropology and history. It is not a scientific but a bureaucratic term . . . Its vagueness masks two pseudo-ideas: the first takes for granted that only one civilisation exists, or that different civilisations may be reduced to a single model – modern Western civilisation; the second affirms that changes of societies and cultures . . . are linear and progressive and that they can be measured.

Yet Octavio Paz was not a pessimist.

The beauty of imagery in his poetry, the elegant joy with which he handles the language whose power he reveres, and which triumphantly survives even translation – these are an affirmative love of life. I quote from one of his poems:

> To see, to touch each day's lovely forms
> The light throbs, all arrows and wings.
> The wine-stain on the tablecloth smells of blood.
> As the coral thrusts branches in the water
> I stretch my sense to this living hour;
> the moment fulfills itself in a yellow harmony.
> Midday, ear of wheat heavy with minutes, eternity's brimming cup.

This sensibility coexisted in Octavio Paz along with rebellious anger against a succession of corrupt and/or incompetent governments. I quote from another poem:

> We have dug up Rage
> . . . The lovers' park is a dungheap
> The library is a nest of killer rats
> The university is a muck full of frogs
> The Altar is Chanfalla's swindle
> The brains are stained with ink
> The doctors dispute in a den of thieves
> The businessmen
> Fast hands slow thoughts
> officiate in the graveyard.

Out of every experience, remote as it might seem to be from inspiration for poetry or imaginative prose, he brought sensuous and intellectual creativity. Out of his formal stint in India came, later, in 1995, a remarkable collection of essays moving, from personal celebration of his days there, through an exploration of India's art, literature, music and religions, to a comparison of Islamic, Hindu and Western civilisations in the course of world history.

He writes: 'India did not enter me through my mind but through my senses.'

And yet he quotes an anonymous Indian poet who says:

> Admire the art of the archer
> he never touches the body and breaks the heart

The collection of essays in this late work is entitled *In Light of India*. In light of everything Octavio Paz wrote, all of us who read him receive his light.

And his was the art of the poet-archer, that goes straight to the heart and mind, where the centre of being is one.

1999

When Art Meets Politics

I take it that we are excluding propaganda from our consideration of where and why art meets politics. Propaganda, in word and image, has its necessary justification in conditioning people to go to war, buy things, vote for political parties, but has nothing to do with originality, since it comes from the certainty of orthodoxies; is never a quest, an individual exploration.

Of course, the arts are many, and their expression of social issues springs to mind from Picasso's *Guernica* via Goya as the apotheosis of wars, to – in film – Costa-Gavras's and Semprun's *Z* of the Greek colonels as the apotheosis of junta oppression, Schlöndorff's *Tin Drum* as that of the social deformations, the dwarfing of humanity during Nazism, to Kusturica's *Underground* and Neil Jordan's *The Crying Game* as that of conflict which continues above ground, even today, and Spike Lee's *Do The Right Thing* vision of racism in America.

As a writer, however, I naturally concentrate on our subject in relation to the art I myself practise and know best in the work of my fellow writers, dead and alive – literature.

First a look back at works in which most obviously art meets politics, on different levels and in differing ways. One should begin with the Bible, of course, both Old Testament and New; the lyrical source-books of politics secular – the politics of tribal succession – and politics religious – the power struggles for the soul, between human beings and God. Then I pass over the centuries, the ancient Greeks and Dante, to *Uncle Tom's Cabin* and *Cry, The Beloved Country*. These last two show how a sentimental story can be an effective form of expression of a social issue, since, a century apart, Harriet Beecher Stowe's Uncle Tom and Alan Paton's Reverend Kumalo brought the issues of slavery and racism into the consciousness of millions of readers who might not have admitted these if presented any other way.

Ralph Ellison and James Baldwin despised sentiment as inadequate to express the realities of race prejudice, revealing the black persona as the one of whom *Nobody Knows My Name*, the 'Invisible Man' rejected by whites.

Joseph Roth used the picaresque mode to epitomise patriotic hubris and the end of the Austro-Hungarian Empire with the von Trotta generations in *The Radetzky March*.

Malraux gave expression to the mood of *Days of Hope* in the doomed early resistance to fascism in the Spanish Civil War, while Hemingway proposed the sexual stimulus of war as a social phenomenon – the earth moved by orgasm rather than by bombs.

Thomas Mann used the snowy isolation of the very place we find ourselves in today – Davos – to signify the complacency of a Europe skiing towards disaster, from which to pitch his anti-hero, Hans Castorp, into the 'universal feast of Death' which Mann saw as the 1914 war.

Milan Kundera took his art from a Communist regime that turned the writer into window-washer, away to the labyrinth of exile, returning always upon itself in the sense that *Life Is Elsewhere*, and Ariel Dorfman, also from exile, writing *Death and the Maiden*, revealed the social situation of a woman in the reconciliation of an emerging democracy, confronted with her former torturer as house-guest. I myself sought understanding for self and others through writing of the predetermination of a father's political faith on the life of the next generation, in my novel *Burger's Daughter*, and lately, with *The House Gun* explored the social significance of a *crime passionnel* in the world climate of urban violence we live in now. Jorge Semprun is one who has interiorised the social and ideological conflicts of our time as autobiography in the valediction *Adieu, vive clarté*.

Why have these writers, and many others, taken on themselves the meeting of art with socio-politics?

We are fatally linked to the political and social consequences of whatever our society, our country, that country's politics, may be, and further, to the flux and reflux of the globalisation we are beginning to live through. That is why original expression is inexorably linked to politics. It is, as Kafka wrote, 'a leap out of murderers' row, it is a seeing of what is really taking place'.[1]

The next question is what is the effect of the writer's original expression of social issues on the individual consciousness of society? I am told that one of the criteria for the Nobel Prize in Literature, apart from the quality of the means of expression, is that the works of the writer should be of 'benefit to mankind'. The way in which art's original expression of social and political issues is of benefit to mankind lies surely in the engagement of the artist with these issues at his or her deepest level of independent, searching understanding, the ability of the creative imagination to mine for the unexpressed in human motivation, the unadmitted, the necessary insights that the facts can never reveal.

Now this is not to deny that writers themselves have been and are hotly divided on whether or not art should be involved with an imperative of political and social issues. Proust judged that such issues as 'whether the Dreyfus affair or the war' simply 'furnished excuses to the writers for not deciphering . . . that book within them'.[2] The Marxist critic, Ernst Fischer, cuttingly pronounced,

---

1   Franz Kafka, *Kafka's Diaries*, 1922.
2   Marcel Proust, *In Search of Lost Time*.

'The feature common to all significant artists and writers in the capitalist world is their inability to come to terms with the social reality that surrounds them.'[3] Picasso – never at a loss for words: 'What do you think an artist is? An imbecile who has nothing but eyes if he is a painter, or ears if he is a musician, or a lyre at every level of his heart if he is a poet . . . Quite the contrary, he is at the same time a political being, constantly aware of what goes on in the world, whether it be harrowing, bitter or sweet, and he cannot help being shaped by it . . . painting is not interior decoration. It is an instrument of war for attack and defense against the enemy.'[4] While Flaubert complains: 'I have always tried to live in an ivory tower, but a tide of shit is beating at its walls, threatening to undermine it . . . it's not a question of politics but of the mental state of France.'[5]

George Steiner, speaking of writing under totalitarian rule, calls for the writer to stop writing 'a few miles down the road from the death camp . . . when the words in the city are full of savagery and lies, nothing speaks louder than the unwritten poem'.[6] But hear Neruda: 'Can poetry serve our fellow men? Can it find a place in man's struggles? . . . I felt a pressing need to write a central poem that would bring together the historical events, the geographical situations, the life . . . of our peoples.'[7] And Rilke, looking at a Cézanne painting, exclaims: 'Suddenly one has the right eyes',[8] and Kundera sees writers and artists as vital witnesses of the twentieth century as an age marked by tyranny, saying: 'People regard those days as an era of political trials, persecutions, forbidden books and legalised murder. But we who remember must bear witness; it was not only an epoch of terror, but also an epoch of lyricism, ruled hand in hand by the hangman and the poet.'[9]

Finally, for us – writers and artists bringing original expression

3   Ernst Fischer, *The Necessity of Art*.

4   Pablo Picasso, *Lettres Françaises*.

5   Gustave Flaubert, letter to Turgenev, 13 November 1872, *The Letters of Gustave Flaubert 1857–1880*, translated and edited by Francis Steegmuller.

6   George Steiner, *Language and Silence*.

7   Pablo Neruda (my notebooks do not give the source – probably his autobiography).

8   Rainer Maria Rilke, *Letters on Cézanne*, translated by Joel Agee.

9   Milan Kundera, *Life Is Elsewhere*.

to politics and social issues at the end of this century where neither socialism nor capitalism has achieved justice and human fulfilment for all – Czeslaw Milosz has the rubric:

> Ill at ease in the tyranny, ill at ease in the republic
> In the one I longed for freedom, in the other for the end of corruption.[10]

1999

A Letter to Future Generations

Dear citizens of the twenty-first century,
     There is no escaping the past, and so one must take an honest look at your inheritance from the twentieth century. There are many aspects; I choose that of the new, never-before concepts that arose during my life as a child of the time. One that is of great significance to your lives as you take over is the concept of globalisation.

The feasibility of globalisation has been made possible by the huge technological advances of the twentieth century, particularly in means of communication, from the satellite up among the stars to the computer on every office table. Information may be exchanged across the world in *real time*; distance means nothing so long as jet aircraft have the fuel to overcome it. Globalisation has all the means of efficiency to regulate itself as it is conceived so far: primarily as a one-world of investment, a super-tool of international finance.

Has it a human face?

The real necessity for globalisation – which you will have to tackle – is nothing less than the question of whether the gap between rich and poor countries can be narrowed by it. What role can globalisation play in eradicating world poverty? For poverty

---

10   Czeslaw Milosz, 'To Raja Raó', *Selected Poems*, Ecco, New York, 1980.

puts an inhuman, outcast mask on more than three billion of our world's population.

If globalisation is to have a human face in your century its premise is that development is about people in interaction on the planet we have occupied, so far, without sharing.

This will not be achieved, however, through worldwide shopping by internet. In the twentieth century consumption has grown unprecedentedly, reaching around $24 trillion in 1998, but the spending and devouring spree, far from widely benefiting the poor, in some aspects undermined the truly human prospects for globalisation: sustainable development for all.

Runaway consumption by the developed world has eroded renewable resources such as fossil fuels, forests and fishing grounds, polluted local and global environments, and pandered to promotion of needs for conspicuous display in place of the legitimate needs of life.

While those of us who have been the generations of big consumers need to consume less, for more than one billion of the world's poorest people increased consumption is a matter of life and death and a basic right – the right to freedom from want. And this is not want of food and clean water alone; there are other forms of want – illiteracy, lack of technological skills: the basic qualifications for benefiting from the concept of globalisation. Illiteracy is the basis of global cultural deprivation, and it exists among great numbers of the world's population. From it comes isolation from many of the forms of culture that are essential to the human right to develop individual potential for a full life. There can be no global culture while there are inhabitants deprived of the ability to read, to have access to the powers of the imagination released through the written word, through literature; deprived of the intellectual and spiritual bounty of libraries.

Then there is the matter of translation of the world's munificent store of literary enlightenment. With all the ease of technological reproduction of the written word now attained there remains the fact that the human process of translating creative literature from one language to another – which certainly, so far, cannot be achieved by any electronic brain – is not recognised as a highly important means of bringing about the ideal of global *understanding*; which surely must be the underlying *philosophy* of globalisation?

In the new millennium there will be the need to remedy this by establishing schools of translation in universities (they are rare in the twentieth century); by the action of publishers to cooperate in joint enterprise across language boundaries; for government ministries of arts and culture to provide subsidies for this work; and for the ministries of foreign affairs to wake up and realise that this is an initiative of diplomacy effective beyond the conventional cultural limits of providing cultural exchange mainly in the form of scholarships abroad.

Consumption is necessary for human development when, as cultural consumption does, it enlarges the capabilities of and improves people's lives without adversely affecting the lives of others. And a brake on material consumption need not, as some fear, bring about closed industries and shops if the power of becoming consumers is extended among the population of the globe.

Whose responsibility will it be to bring these things about?

That of many, international and national.

It is the responsibility of the European Community, which flouts the principles of globalisation through its blatant protectionism. It is the responsibility of national governments to bring about just consumerism. Theirs is a legal one: the framing of laws in each country for justice in the access to and share of its resources. And it is the responsibility of international law, an aspect of globalisation long contested in respect of fishing rights, for example, and towards the end of the twentieth century, at last, in the essential process of establishing an international criminal court. For globalisation, we must admit, posits the most difficult secular morality possible: a moral authority above all those individual ones of the global concept's component countries.

Non-governmental and civic organisations have the responsibility both in building human capability and in ensuring that a development philosophy prevails that projects are not imposed upon people according to others' ideas of their needs, but are planned and brought into being only with the beneficiaries themselves, according to their knowledge of their community and environment. Let the remnants of the age of social engineering be deeply buried in the twentieth century, not with a backward glance, but a shudder.

Now if we are realistic we have to see that on the doorstep of the new century there is delivered a new threat to globalisation with a human face. Thirty-five per cent of our world is in recession as the old century ends. Many countries are in strife. This means more millions of refugees, driven homeless and starving to swell the count of the globe's three billion poor, calculated before the tragedies of Kosovo and Angola, to name only two. In Russia the winter of 1988–9 froze over impoverished people in their disillusion with international openness in trade and investment; these elements of globalisation as it has been evidenced so far have not shown them a human face.

But we know what you absolutely must not do is allow the shadow of a world economic recession that fell upon the last decade of the twentieth century, reaching from Asia over West, North and South, to become an excuse to postpone the inescapable responsibility of the developed world, in the new millennium, to pursue the eradication, rather than the traditional band-aid amelioration, of poverty which exists alongside the globalisation of economic power.

Send not to ask for whom the bell tolls – when it sounds in one stock exchange its note reverberates throughout the world, shaking the Haves as well as casting down even further the Have-nots.

Global free markets mean nothing in the end, if there is no one able to come to buy. The hazard of decline through the very interdependence created by globalisation of world economies: this negative impact upon the progressive and positive in the concept is what surely must cause even the most complacent acceptors of the time-disgraced division of the world's resources between rich and poor, to realise that the billions of fellow men and women in abject poverty are in coexistence with *them*, not safely quarantined in isolation. The financier George Soros has come to the reflection: 'There are collective interests that don't find expression in market values'.[1]

---

1   George Soros, 'The International Crisis: An Interview', *New York Review*, interview with Jeff Madrick, January 1999.

And perhaps those five permanent members of the Security Council – Britain, China, France, Russia, the USA – who among others enrich their national economies by selling arms for the globe's conflicts and wars, will hear when Amartya Sen, 1998 Nobel Laureate in Economics, says of production of arms, 'Human benefits that flow by redirecting these forces can be remarkably large',[2] and when Kofi Annan says, 'No development without peace; no peace without development'.[3]

No globalisation without a human face.

The twenty-first century will achieve a new and radiant definition of progress if you can work to put that face upon your world.

1999

Five Years into Freedom

My New South African Identity

When I was young, in South Africa during the Second World War, I was far removed from the bombs, the nights in underground shelters, the rationed food, in Europe. I read reflections by those living through this experience, and these were not what I had in my mind as the way life must be, there; I had constructed their lives out of a projection of my own priorities in what makes life, my own fears of what would be most threatened in imagined circumstances.

Our war – South Africa's liberation struggle – is over. On 2 June, we shall cast our votes in our second post-apartheid elections. We have been led to that day by one of the great men of this century. He now displays the ultimate wisdom in closing his

---

2   Amartya Sen, 'Economics Laureate Condemns Arms Sales', *The Star*, Johannesburg, 5 January 1999.

3   Kofi Annan, Secretary-General of United Nations, speech at launch of UNDP 'Eradication of Poverty' programme, UN, 1997.

era at his peak of accomplishments, the final one being the assurance that his successor is the one equal to the era about to begin. We have lived five years of freedom. Whatever the frustrations as well as triumphs we've tackled, it is an achievement placed toweringly beside the years of apartheid racism and before them the years of colonial racism – five years against three centuries. Yet I see that this period is often the object of the same kind of subjective projection I imposed on the reality of wartime Europe fifty years ago.

Again and again, when I am interviewed or find myself in encounters with other people abroad, the burning question is, 'What is happening to whites?'

And again and again, my genuinely surprised response is: 'What about blacks? Don't you believe there are challenges to be met in their new lives?'

There are two obvious assumptions to be made of this approach to South Africa by Europeans and North Americans. The majority of them being white, they identify only with whites, whether consciously or subconsciously. Because I am white, they assume I do the same. It's the Old Boys/Old Girls Club producing its dog-eared membership card. The projection is of the priorities of their lives, along with the old colonial conditioning that these belong with whiteness and are incontrovertibly, always, for ever, threatened by the Otherness – blackness.

Five years into freedom. What kind of fossil should I be, unearthed from the cave of bones that was apartheid, if my essential sense of self were to be as a white?

There are some who still have this sense – suffer it, I would say, and unnecessarily, so it becomes a form of self-flagellation. I don't posit this in any assertion of smug superiority; I should just wish to prod them into freedom from confinement. And there is also the other – unadmitted – side of feeling superior as white: being ashamed of being white. An over-compensation for the past, useless for living fully in the present.

If you put the question to me, I hear it as, 'What about us?' – South Africans going as best we can about the business of living together. Being white as a state determining my existence is simply not operative. I was privileged through racism, I rejected and actively opposed racism, I played my small part in the liberation struggle and I know that as a result I am a South African and nobody else, living in a country we are in the difficult, thrilling process of creating. That we must create; for despite its natural resources, its sophisticated infrastructure, its advanced technology, what we want never existed for us before: a truly human society.

Grand words. How does it feel to live day to day under their imperative? Five years into freedom: for me, the great change comes from others, from the change in atmosphere in the cities, the streets. It is nothing new for me to 'mix' with people of all colours; my closest friendships and working relationships have been in this context for many years. But the old life existed counter to everything that defined and characterised the country. It was – even if triumphantly always in opposition – surrounded by the laws, the state, secular and religious traditions that represented everything it was not. Although we said 'our country', this was in reference to that which people were suffering, striving, surviving to bring about – there was no identity with the official entity called South Africa. We had no country.

I am aware now, every day, in so many ways, big and small, happy and troubling, that I can speak of 'our country'. If the air of taking possession can be palpable, I feel it when I walk out of my gate. I hear it in the volume of traffic. I know it when I pick my way between vendors of everything from mobile phones and fake French perfume to tomatoes and toilet rolls on the pavements. I see it out of the corner of my eye when I stand in a queue at my local post office and eavesdrop on the black postmaster giving instruction to the young Afrikaans employee at the counter. I hear it in the accents of our many languages, listeners speaking English on radio phone-in programmes. It is that indefinable quality called confidence; even the member of the vast number of unemployed who guides me theatrically into a parking bay has it – yes, a contradiction of his actual circumstances.

Well, I live in Johannesburg. A city in transition is full of such contradictions.

Recently my bag was snatched from the car when the friend driving stopped at a traffic light; I had forgotten to lock the passenger-seat door – our routine precaution, like the free distribution of condoms against Aids. I was indignant. House keys, credit card, ATM card – the fact that they were filched by someone living on the streets who had no middle-class status to own such things did not assuage me. But on the same streets in the press of people flowing and dodging round one another, the great mass who had been shut out of the city in ghettos and 'ethnic home-lands', if someone jostles me, I hear, 'Sorry, maGogo' ('I apologise, Grandmother'). Ordinary good manners, you will say. No. He apologises. He accepts me as a common relative in the human family; after he and his forebears have been decreed outcast from it for generations, both subtly and brutally, colonialist patronage to apartheid rejection. The benison of human feeling at once shines out against, and is threatened by, violent crime. The second question fired by individuals from abroad is one with a target that can't be missed. Back to the first proposition of the contradiction: the snatched bag. 'What about crime?' I shall not duck. The impersonal statistics are there, never mind my credit card. The city I live in is among those with the highest crime rates in the world. That my French granddaughter, a student in Nice, has had her little old car stolen is an incident of urban crime all over the world, but it doesn't add up to the indicting total in one city, one country, the way the loss of my bag will in the calculation of those passing judgement on the progress of a country with a five-year commitment to democracy as against the several hundred years' experience of its evolution in the West.

The curious view from abroad is that only whites are threatened by, and concerned about, street crime, hijackings and housebreaking and the violence these involve. Again and again, there are descriptions of suburban razor wire and Rottweilers as the prevailing flora and fauna of the white suburbs. The facts are that homes, humble as well as substantial and even complete with swimming pool, in what are still the black townships of greater Johannesburg, are also armed with wire and dogs. Black professional and businessmen and women who now take a place among the affluent owners of fine cars (regarded primly as suspect conspicuous consumers by observers who do not have the same moral judgement of whites driving the same models) are also victims of hijacking. We face the problems together.

But if you move about in my city, you don't need a criminologist to identify the reason for crime's prevalence. And it is not a bleeding-heart apologist response when the blunt answer is: unemployment.

I have taught myself to drive, all over again, fifty or so years after I was first licensed, because there has to be a new, nippy know-how and understanding of an unwritten code among drivers to weave among the buffalo herd of the road, the minibuses. We call them 'combis' because they are combination buses and taxis and conduct themselves as a hybrid, which is confusing to the uninitiated driver of a car. They hoot continuously, to attract the attention of potential passengers; they stop anywhere at the signal of a raised finger from the kerbside, the way a hailed taxi responds; they have regular routes they follow like a bus but no obligation to restrict themselves to any designated bus stops. They are always packed to suffocation limit: they have solved the transport question, which a succession of white regimes dealt with as the decision that blacks use their legs. To me, the combis are symbols of the immeasurable influx of people to the city since freedom was confirmed at the ballot box in 1994, the trek of many thousands who come to find work, and for whom there will be little or no possibility of finding it. When the humiliation of begging fails, desperation offers one way to survive – crime.

This phenomenon of crime is not, as some observers take smug satisfaction in regarding it, the phenomenon of freedom.

Things were not better in the old days of the apartheid regime: they were kept out of sight. The unemployed and underemployed who come to the city hungry in every way for a better life now were corralled in that extraordinary experiment in social engineering,

poverty-ridden 'ethnic homelands'. The social disease, unemployment, was quarantined; migratory labour from the rural areas, and
from one province to another, was permitted to enter the city only
in numbers determined healthy by the needs of industry. And these
workers were legally forbidden to take their families with them. I
have to remind myself of this when I see among us that sad devel-
oping-world category of childhood, street children; now they are
there before our eyes instead of underfed and undereducated in the
'homelands' of apartheid.

It is not a politically correct convenience to blame the past,
apartheid, for unemployment. The plain fact is that dammed-up
unemployment has burst upon us from the inhuman confines of
the past; it is not something inherent in freedom, a kind of punishment for our people's audacity in defeating whites-only rule. As
a result of the policies of the past, black people come to the city
doubly disadvantaged. First, industrial development, hampered
through sanctions that were necessary to end apartheid, has only
limited employment to provide in a period when, despite every
effort towards expansion, such development is affected by quaking
conditions in world finance. Second, the majority of the unemployed do not have the education or skills to take on such jobs as
are available. Many are illiterate or semi-literate, the products of
the contemptible level of education apartheid decreed for blacks.
Few have any of the basic skills demanded by an increasingly technological labour market.

I cannot shrug and dismiss them as a lost generation. I am one
who will press for innovative large-scale government projects that
will institute skills training and employment at the same time.
When the adults are providers, the children will not be on the
streets. And I am encouraged by the government's chivying of
business to give training in financial processes, and the condition
laid down to foreign investors that there must be a training component in their most welcome decisions to profit from investment
opportunities here.

There is enthusiasm among Haves in the city to see a solution to
the unemployment of Have-nots in what they call, broadly, small

business, and there are formations that commendably provide modest finance for this. Yet when I pass, near a supermarket, a young man mending shoes in a booth he has been supplied with, I can't help thinking this is something of a dead end for him: couldn't he be learning to be an electrician or plumber, even if he cannot become one of the millennium's computer-literate? His 'small business' venture doesn't seem to have the vigour of self-initiated brisk trading by those pavement vendors whom I note, month by month, acquiring the acumen of what will arrest the gaze of customers beyond a mere pile of bananas – the latest sports-club logo on a cap, the look-alike Nikes. South African blacks are new to shopkeeping, having been barred from owning shops in the city. They don't have the capital to do so, yet, but you can see they're learning fast – the hard way.

In awareness of sharing as a post-apartheid ethos, at what levels is this evident? At the top economic level, which used to be exclusively that occupied by whites, like begins to live beside like. It was a pejorative – aimed at white privilege in general – to refer to 'Houghton', but now our President Mandela lives in that residential area, more modestly than he would if he made the conventional choice of the official residence occupied by the white regimes' presidents in Pretoria. Sandton – the most luxurious of garden suburbs – can't really be regarded as the generic symbol of white capitalist living any longer, because black dignitaries in professions, business, communications and the arts now also favour the landscaped town house complexes complete with security service. They are a minority among blacks, of course. At the broadest, basic level of the new social pyramid there are changes that are not less contrasting, in their way, with the living conditions of the past. Late last year, I was in the city's old black township of Alexandra, in the brand-new three-room house, built with government subsidy and a low-interest bank loan, into which the Mashabela family of five had just moved after seventeen years in a one-room shack housing fourteen people. This kind of levelling of material conditions is my primary criterion of justice in my country, the city I live in.

I know it could not possibly be brought about in five years, or ever can be completely achieved, on the evidence of the chasms between the life of rich and poor in developed capitalist countries that have declared themselves dedicated to it for several hundred years, and the failure of socialist countries (of socialism – so far in human history, but not for ever, in my belief) to avoid making freedom a prisoner of its own dictates. South Africa – like its combis – has had to choose pragmatically to be a hybrid: a mixed economy, with every bias it can afford towards making the legal equality, now achieved, meaningful in economic, material form for the impoverished majority.

It follows that community of purpose is particularly decisive for us, coming as we do, rawly, from our divided, racist past. My own natural preoccupations, within my life as I see it as a responsible citizen, have always been in the arts, what are called (rather embarrassingly for my taste) cultural formations, in which race or colour or even language differences were an irrelevance in common enthusiasms, the realm of the imagination that couldn't be annexed, even by apartheid. But now, as it should be, in pursuit of South Africa as an African country rather than an Africanised outpost of the West, the initiatives and much of the innovation in culture are taken up by blacks – a form of unofficial, organic affirmative action that creates a balance that was missing while partnerships between black and white were always weighted by the fact that whites, by law, in the ordinary pursuits of daily life, had access to opportunities blacks did not have. I feel at home – in the real sense of the concept – as never before, even in working with my long-time close friend Mongane Wally Serote, poet, former freedom fighter, now a member of parliament with a high position in the Department of Arts and Culture, and with Walter Chakela, director of the Windybrow Centre for the Arts, in a total context that didn't exist for them and for me before.

Perhaps that may be regarded as a rather special area of race relations, far from 'Sorry, maGogo' in the street. In between, I reflect on my feelings when, moving about the city and suburbs, I pass a school at the hour when classes end. It was a whites-only school I knew well. I see the kids coming out, the small boys scuffling with one another, the little girls tangling hands and giggling together. They are all shades of colour – South African black, South African Indian, South African *mélange*, South African white. They are growing up with a common initiating experience, into life. They will never be subject to the unspeakable horrors that the Truth and Reconciliation Commission has exposed to us, and that have been so vital for us to face, what we did or what we allowed to happen. These children are not being kept apart to learn to hate, to fear the unknown, the untouched in one another.

One of the generation that was the victim of the horrors of apartheid, Tokyo Sexwale, lately Premier of Gauteng, of which Johannesburg is the capital, and now a black-empowerment crusader married to a white woman, said something this month that could be our rubric to live by: 'If blacks get hurt, I get hurt. If whites get hurt, that's my wife, and if you harm coloured people, you're looking for my children. Your unity embodies who I am.'

1999

Hemingway's Expatriates

A Way of Looking at the World

There is surely no writer in the English-speaking world, born in the generations after Ernest Hemingway, who does not share this centennial celebration through having been influenced in some way by his work. I am of the first generation after his. On another continent, I grew up against a similar small-town background. The Middle West, USA, and a gold-mining town in South Africa shared something beyond their backwoods limitations: mine shallowly occupied by whites as opposed to indigenous Africans, his shallowly occupied by whites as opposed to indigenous American Indians, although in his environment the Indians were perhaps a ghostly rather than a material presence, and in mine the Africans were very much alive, a majority left out in colonialism's double book-keeping of who counted.

Both twentieth-century environments were at 'the ragged edge of a newly formed and still forming cultural universe';[1] from there, he and I went different ways, I to enter through moving deeper into the reality of my own country, he through seeking reality in the moveable feast of the world outside.

But in the craft with which I provisioned myself as a writer there were certain skills I learned from him and am grateful for, along with the invaluable workshop handed on by Chekhov, D. H. Lawrence and Eudora Welty. I am speaking of the writing of short stories specifically, and I am not referring, as every writer knows, to the amateur's process of imitation. What a beginning writer learns from a master (of either sex) is the range of the imagination working upon life – what literature can go after, what is missed by those who do not have what Chinua Achebe has noted as the invisible ring around the eye that marks the writer.

From Ernest Hemingway's stories I learned to listen, within myself, when writing, for what went *unsaid* by my characters; what can be, must be, conveyed in other ways, and not alone by body-language but also in the breathing spaces of syntax: the necessity to create silences which the reader can interpret from these signs. Hermeneutics doesn't belong in the locked cupboards of academic circles: it's part of the illumination and pleasure of the reader, and Hemingway knew superbly how to bring it about. There is also, I believe, a misperception about his dialogue – it is not realistic but aphoristic, and there Beckett and Pinter are ones who came after and are a presence at the centennial.

Something else I learned to consider – judiciously – for myself, from Hemingway, was the use of repetition: we need to coin another term to honour him, conveying repetition transformed in his hand as a special term for emphasis; used well, repetition becomes the Beethoven note, a knell laden with resonant meaning. Of course,

1   Walter Berthoff, 'Fitzgerald and Hemingway in the 20s', *American Trajectories 1790–1970*, Penn State Press, 1990.

like most of us fallible writers, even Hemingway, who used it with perfect timing, overdid it sometimes, parodying one of his own strengths.

Then there is the power of the deliberate non sequitur. 'And we went up into the town to the Plaza and those were the last people who were shot in the village.' This is a quote from a novel, *For Whom The Bell Tolls*, but I would say it was learned from the *way of telling* Hemingway taught himself with the stories (I avoid the word 'technique' because writing is organic, it cannot be learned as a technique.)

A short story succeeds, if it does, as a series or play of echoes. Its marvellously rigorous discipline does not allow for explanation, whether authorial or disguised through a protagonist. Beginning with the conjunction, the echoes in this non-sequitur sentence of Hemingway's text sound back and forth through everything that has happened in the novel: the blessed banal continuity – and the horror of it – that life goes on with violence as something that can be measured in acceptance – they were the sum of it, the 'last people' to be shot – along with the daily round, up at the Plaza. The devastating reflection of how people are, what circumstances make of them, what they consent to become: all this is there. Tight-lipped? On the contrary, an oracle sounding back and forth.

In the novels, Hemingway indulged luxuriantly in the soliloquy, particularly in *For Whom The Bell Tolls*, recycled from the authorial interventions of nineteenth-century novelists. To overhear what is going on in the head of Robert Jordan as a subtext to what we are experiencing with him, through him – and he is a character who buttonholes you like the Ancient Mariner and you don't want to break free – is no contrivance. But the many pages of Pilar recounting, with dialogue formal between quotes, etc., the flailing of the fascists in a village, is a contrived set-piece from which a young aspiring writer such as I was would do best not to learn. *Hemingway* does it dazzlingly; but it is *Hemingway*, not Pilar, speaking. And he knows it; he gets round it by having Robert Jordan reflect: 'If that woman could only write . . . He would try to write it and if he had luck and could remember it perhaps he could get it down as she told it.' Hemingway tried, and didn't, because Pilar couldn't possibly have remembered and reconstructed the experience in the imaginatively ordered way he allowed himself to present it.

That Hemingway, indeed, didn't let Pilar tell it in her own idiom – the one he created for her throughout the rest of the novel – is an aside pertinent to a general question. At one time in the volatile attention of socio-literary criticism there was much discussion about Ernest Hemingway's decisions in writing direct speech as translation from another language. We are not talking of the task of an interpreter sitting up in a box at a conference. We are talking of the liberties a writer may or may not take in *inventing* – no less – a language that is neither the original nor an English equivalent, since this last is impossible. The intention is to convey the mode of expression, the musical beat, the harmony and dissonance, the *states of mind* that are the integument of the language's ancient formation.

The first consideration must be how well does the writer know the original language? And my premise must be that Hemingway the linguist knew Spanish very well. It was the tongue of one of his two love affairs with the world outside his own – the other love affair I shall come to later.

So the use of idiomatic expressions, which he often manages the best way, by giving them in the original, in contexts from which their meaning soon becomes clear, cannot be faulted. But for the flow of the speaker, all must be Hemingway's own invention, based on his ear for the original, but surely influenced selectively by what he finds most attractive, subtle, coarse, not only in the language but his outsider's version of the mind and spirit behind it.

A piece of theatre. When he sets himself to convey this in English, he must make casting decisions, subconsciously and *subjectively*: whether it is a peasant, a fascist or a bull-fighter, speaking Spanish. What one could learn from him, here, was caution: to be less sure than he of the possibility of bringing off this doubly creative act: to accept its very real limitations. Much as I have admired what to me is his masterpiece in the genre of the novel, I am always aware that

the virtuoso performance I am responding to so strongly is that of
Ernest Hemingway in the hired peasant outfit of Pilar or Anselmo.
If the liberty he has taken can have been part of his influence on
literature in English, there are doubts about its legitimacy that
have not yet been solved . . .

'He made the English language new. He changed the rhythms of
the way both his own and the next few generations would write
and speak . . . a certain way of looking at the world.'[2]

This is Joan Didion's claim, in a recent outstanding essay on
Hemingway. I agree that he was one of those, in the English-
speaking and writing world, who opened new spaces for the way it
was possible to write – as for speaking, I should think that would
apply only to his fellow Americans.

It was James Joyce who made the English language new, with
contributions coming from Ernest Hemingway and, some would
say, Virginia Woolf.

As for changing the way of looking at the world – I think we in
the English-speaking and -writing countries need to ask ourselves
what was happening in *this way* in other cultures, other uses of
language and literature. Another anglophone writer and critic,
V.S. Pritchett, no less, wrote of Hemingway: 'He has defined for us
the personality of our own time.'[3]

Whose time? Where?

The way Hemingway may have defined 'the personality of our
time', 'changed the way of looking at the world' cannot be claimed
as that of *the world*: the world of the Japanese, the Russians, the
people of India, the people of Islam . . . you name the global list.
Let's keep a sense of proportion in our cultural and linguistic places
in the world, whichever these may be. Ernest Hemingway himself
surely would have recognised the perspectives opened up by the
newly ground lenses of Marcel Proust, Thomas Mann, Robert
Musil, Yukio Mishima, and a handspan of poets from Apollinaire

---

2   Joan Didion, 'Last Words', *The New Yorker*, 9 November 1988.
3   Berthoff, *American Trajectories*.

to Rainer Maria Rilke. His expatriate personality would imply a certain roving itinerary of reading.

What do I mean by an expatriate personality?

It becomes necessary to explore this in the tension between living and writing from which Ernest Hemingway's work, like that of all of us, comes. And to do this I must go back to the similarity of early backgrounds between the Middle West of the USA, and the gold-mining town on the veld in South Africa. In both, Europe was the Mecca of culture for whites; in order to live the painter's life, *the writer's life*, the far-flung devotee yearned to go and *become*, there; kiss the Black Rock, receive the white ring around the eye. Hemingway wrote his Nick stories, his early truth in beauty wonderfully achieved, and received some recognition. But it was Europe that beckoned, Europe that counted; I don't believe of him, as I don't believe of us in South Africa, that it was so much the desire to broaden our experience as it was the idea to be recognised as a writer where to *be* a writer, an artist, was the highest calling, far above any of the commercial or professional activities recognised in what were, not long before, frontier towns. In the Nick stories, life vibrates; but for the writer – to borrow from Milan Kundera in a very different context – life was elsewhere.

Hemingway pursued it, and never really came home again, did he?

The difference between him and the other most illustrious expatriates, Joyce, Mann, Brecht, and later followers such as Kundera, Achebe, Soyinka, Solzhenitsyn, is that they became expatriate through political persecution or revulsion against the particular regimes in their countries, and Hemingway had no motivation of either. What he *did* have, or rather developed, was the beginnings of a broader human consciousness beyond nationalistic operatives, good or bad: and he made his choice of one of the causes of justice that was threatened in the cultural Mecca of Europe.

Why and how?

I am not concerned with what Ernest Hemingway did or did not do, in his own body, his own person, out of his own courage, in the Spanish Civil War. What I follow with fascination in his work, in this geographical area of its scope as in others, is the fictional expatriate persona he so profoundly created there. Warner Berthoff says of Hemingway in his later writing life 'he began making books out of activities and places he had elected for the sake of the pleasure he anticipated from them – Africa and the Caribbean, fishing and big game hunting' and remarks that in these books there is a 'palpable loss of control'.[4] This is one aspect of the exposition of the persona – in decline, so to speak. But in the periods when there was full-throttle control, enormous writing skill, the expatriate protagonist Hemingway creates has become one for different reasons.

I have cited a concern for human justice, to which Robert Jordan in *For Whom The Bell Tolls* (a cult book for my generation, published when I was nineteen) takes up a cause at great risk of hardship and loss of his life. And yet Jordan, it becomes clear as one reads, is fighting this war for personal emotional reasons rather than a dedication to justice as the ethical base of humanity itself. Jordan fights in this war because of his exogamous love affair with the Spanish people; because *Spanish people* believe in the Republic as something worth dying for. There is an apologist tone when he comes – it always seems embarrassedly – to define ideological motivations. I quote: 'He was under Communist discipline for the *duration of the war* [my italics], they were the only party whose programme and discipline he could respect. What were his politics then? He had none, now, he told himself.'

And he doesn't reveal what these were, *before*.

Whenever he confronts revolutionary concepts, he does so in literary terms, thinks of them merely as clichés, not statements that, however banal-sounding, stand for convictions held. A kind of conservative individualism (there is another kind!) collides in self-satisfaction with the claims of the wider concern for humanity, however flawed that credo might be. I quote Jordan: 'When you were drunk or when you committed either fornication or adultery you recognised your own personal fallibility of that mutable substitute for the apostles' creed, the party line.'

---

4   Berthoff, *American Trajectories*.

The expatriate fights for a cause – in this case the Left – while retaining the unexamined values, the buried fears of ideological choices within him – he has *no politics*, he tells himself: neither the Communist one he serves under nor the Democratic one, accepted like church on Sunday, that he has turned his back on, at home.

'I would rather have been born here.'

Away; away from all the Midwests, urban or rural, of the world, which stand for what there is to be faced at home.

'I would rather have been born here.'

Thus Robert Jordan, in Spain, formulates perfectly the credo of the self-elected expatriate. It is also the credo of those others, men and women, who are created within that second love affair of Ernest Hemingway – both of which being the only kind I think it my business to be interested in – the love affair with Africa.

Ernest Hemingway was in love with Africa. And as with others in such a state of emotion, in love with a woman or a man, he constructed for himself according to his own needs and desires something that had little relation to the reality of its object. I hope I won't offend with heresy when I say that Hemingway never had both feet down on Africa. Never really was in Africa. For a country is its people; Africa is its people. Never really was there, if we are to read the novels and stories for which he chose Africa as one of those panoramic three-dimensional postcards where at first light the animals seem to leap out of the thorn bush. I am interested in how this illuminates the expatriate persona, in *fiction as a way of looking at the world* – something beyond an individual writer's life and personal satisfactions.

The stunning, ruthlessly ironic story 'The Short Happy Life of Francis Macomber' does not take place in Africa but in marital hell; the expatriate persona, male and female, carries this hell with him or her wherever they go, the venue only brings it out like sweat. That's what 'Africa' is there for.

I would not go so far as to quote from a Hemingway text, as some have done, that it is a place to 'work the fat off', a gym for the soul, for in that process there could be implied some sort of commitment to what those onlookers, the people, the Africans – nameless most of the time under the generic of nigger or native – are engaged in striving for: their liberation from the status of onlookers to the world of foreign power which determines their lives; some sort of commitment to the people's freedom like Robert Jordan's commitment to the Spanish people against fascism.

But the expatriates in the Africa narratives are not aware of the rising sense of counter-identity in the impassive face of the gun-bearer as he hands over the white hunter's weapon, the subservience veneering the certainty that it will not be long before the power of the gun will be in black hands.

'The Snows of Kilimanjaro', one of the greatest short stories ever written, paradoxically has nothing to do with Africa; it is about death. It is the creative apogee of the painful, fearful exploration of the meaning of death that is the reverse side of Hemingway's two love affairs, the preoccupation with death – one of his major themes – that has been so often projected, in his fiction, upon the Other: the agony of the bull, the matador gored in the belly, the big fish struggling on the hook, the wounded Spanish partisan shot in mercy, the peasant Anselmo left behind at his own request, to die, the splendid lion – like the bull, man's innocent adversary – with half its head blasted away. The expatriate experiences death through these projections: now, at last, *it comes to him* – and it is a chosen death because it is an expatriate death, it happens *elsewhere*. 'I would rather have been born here.' I would rather die here.

I find it distasteful, to say the least, that one could think of approaching the unfinished novel *Truth at First Light*, as some seem eager to do, with the motive of 'finding out', deciding whether or not the experience of the particular expatriate hero in this novel that Ernest Hemingway so much wanted to write is intimately Hemingway's own. It does not matter a damn in the achievements of Hemingway as one of those who has *written our century*, whether or not he slept with a Wakamba girl. It is an insult to his lifelong integrity to his art to regard his work in this shabby, prurient way.

Again, what matters to literature is to find whether, in the persona of the expatriate character, sleeping with the girl was just another service, part of the package deal the white client buys, another kill along with so many heads of this beast, so many skins of that, or whether it is the beginning of something new to him, some late-come realisation that all the gun-bearers and room boys, campfire cooks, and all those women and children viewed as a frieze among their huts, are, like this single girl, part of himself, of the human family, in which there are none who can opt out by expatriatism and leave behind the black men and women and children of home – America – while taking into his arms just one of those whose ancestors were shipped on the Middle Passage.

Toni Morrison has written with ominous measuredness: 'My interest in Ernest Hemingway becomes heightened when I consider how much apart his work is from African-Americans.'[5]

Mine becomes heightened when I consider how far it is from Africans, and when I consider the revelation of the expatriate persona that can come only in the long reach of fiction. How there, the intuitions of imaginative power overcome self-protective inhibitions and justifications; how that persona assumes in a symbolic embrace of acceptance what he has evaded in his own country, his own society – that portion of the world primary to his being. The white hunter-writer did not have to go to Africa to recognise the existence of blacks as integral to his own existence, they were there where he came from, back in America. He did not have to wait to *become aware* – and only as a possibly bothersome interruption, by a straggling Mau-Mau raid, of the pleasant round of hunting and drinking and reading Simenon – of the revolt of blacks against racist domination gloved as patronage. The revolt was rising back in his natal United States of America. Hemingway's titles were always brilliant, and in this case, what belonged to one novel is strangely apposite to the situation in another. *To Have And Have Not*: this perfectly expresses the embrace of the black girl by the expatriate persona.

'The author is not personally accountable for the acts of his fictive creatures, although he is responsible for *them*.'[6] (My italics.) Toni

---

5   Toni Morrison, 'The Kindness of Sharks', *Playing in the Dark – Whiteness and the Literary Imagination*, Vintage, New York, 1992.

6   Ibid.

Morrison again: I take it she means the author has *chosen* to create
these creatures rather than others, or his life experience has *chosen*
him to make those choices. In each writer, the achievement is how
far his/her imaginative discoveries of the mysteries of our existence
has gone. This is how I see Hemingway's creation of the expatriate persona in all its complexity, as part not only of the essential
literature of but also a model produced by the twentieth century,
the violent and bloody assembly line of our time during which we
have invented so much, learned so much without learning how to
live together and find that place in ourselves which would make
this possible. On Ernest Hemingway's centennial too much will
be speculated about him, too much spoken about him, too much
written about him, including my own part in this. When we go
home, let us leave his life alone, it belongs to him, as he lived it.
Let us read his books.

1999

The 2000s

Personal Proust

There are two ways in which great literature impacts upon society. The one is cultural, in narrow definition of culture as practice of the arts: the writer breaks the traditional seals of the Word, takes off into exploration of new modes of expression, challenges and changes what fiction is. After Proust, after Joyce, yes, the novel could never be the same.

The other impact of great literature is its power of changing the consciousness of the reader – even if that lay reader were to have no awareness of how it has been done, the literary techniques and devices the writer has taken up, reinvented or invented. As a fiction writer I have been alertly privy to and no doubt learned from the literary innovations of Marcel Proust. But a writer finds her/his own voice or is not a writer. What has remained with me for a lifetime is the influence of Proust's emotional and aesthetic perceptions. So what I want to talk about is this other impact. The Proust who influences the persona. The Proust after reading whom the reader can never be the same.

This is a grave matter; wonderful. Perhaps dangerous. For there are those among us whose epiphany comes not from the faiths of religion, philosophy or politics, but the illumination of the subterranean passages of life by the imaginative writer.

I was at quite an advanced age – late teens – for one who had lived in books since early childhood, when long after Tolstoy, Dostoevsky, Balzac, Flaubert, I came upon that mistitled *Remembrance of Things Past* in the Modern Library edition of the Scott Moncrieff translation. I had survived a lonely mother-love-dominated childhood and so my first response was one of recognition; here was a writer who understood that childhood better than I did myself: an identification. But later as I read and returned to that book its effect was something different, exegetical, prophetic to the series of presents, existential stages I was coming to, passing through.

Holed up in an armchair in the tin-roofed house of a mining town in the South African veld, far, far in every way from the Méséglise Way, Swann's Way, Combray, Balbec and the Boulevard Haussmann, I discovered that the intense response I had to natural beauty, to flowers, trees, and the sea visited once a year, was not something high-mindedly removed from the drives of existence I was struggling with, but part of a sensuality which informs, belongs with awakening sexuality, the conflation of emotional and aesthetic formation. Every time, any time, one turns back to The Novel one finds the delight of something relevant to a past perception that one had missed before . . . For example, in my recent re-reading of *À la Recherche du Temps Perdu* (my third in French) I have seen how pollen recurs, the natural product become a metaphor – the wind-distributed fecundity part of the very air we breathe – first coming from the regard of the girl the narrator follows with his eyes on the drive with Madame de Villeparisis in *A L' Ombre des Jeunes Filles en Fleurs*. And then there's the bumblebee that enters the courtyard with pollen that signifies the attraction cast in the air between noble Baron de Charlus and the lowly waistcoat-maker, Jupien. Proust himself pollinates ineffable connections between needs and emotions aroused by various means, in us.

In the context of projected existence, I came to Proust from D. H. Lawrence and Blake; sexuality was fulfilment guaranteed to the bold, anyone who would flout interdictions and free desire: 'Abstinence sows sand all over/The ruddy limbs and flaming hair,/ But Desire Gratified/Plants fruits of life and beauty there.'[1] And this gratification between men and women was the image of Fred Astaire and Ginger Rogers dancing on simulated clouds – like Italo Calvino, I had formed my notion of future emotional life as innocently, lyingly portrayed by movies of the time. The processes of loving, as exemplified in the desperate pilgrimage of Swann – what a Way that is, ecstatic, frustrating, impossible to turn away

---

[1]   William Blake, *The Notebook of William Blake*.

from, viewing the pursued beloved from the terrible angles of suspicion, losing the will to continue, grabbed by the will to go on; always, moving along with him, one has moments when one wants to shake him: stop! And sees he cannot, will not. Maybe that's the principle of love . . . And in the end, that devastating conclusion: this woman, for whom he has spoiled years of his life, was really not his type at all.

Proust reformed, informed my youthful understanding of the expectations of sexual love, showed me its immense complexity, its ultimate dependency on the impossibility of knowing the loved one – the very defeat of possession – and the concomitant process of self-knowledge, often dismaying.

The cloud-mating of Fred and Ginger dispersed for ever. In the life of the emotions I was embarked upon my expectations were tutored by the greatest exploration ever made of the divine mystery of the sexual life in its ambient world of sensuality. No time to discuss the continuation of the theme with Albertine; only to observe that not only does it not matter a damn if an Albertine was really an Albert transformed by the alchemy of imagination rather than a sex-change operation – himself a homosexual, no one has written better than Marcel Proust of heterosexual relations. Perhaps literary genius can be defined yet once again: as a creativity that is all things, knows everything, in every human.

After early readings of The Book I read, of course, *Les Plaisirs et Les Jours, Jean Santeuil, Contre Sainte-Beuve*, but to these I have not returned. Like all of us, I have more or less the gamut of Proust scholarship in English and French. But all have been surpassed, for me, by the publication this year of Roger Shattuck's *Proust's Way*, an amazing feat of originality where one would have thought that all the gold-bearing ore had long been brought to the surface. My present reading of The Book has become a new one, filled with new understanding, possibilities, and new joys, through the variety of lenses provided by Roger Shattuck's radiant vision.

Marcel Proust is a writer with whom one moves along, for life; reading and re-reading without ever exhausting the sources he reveals only when one is ready for, or made ready for them. At the grand and poignant final social-gathering-of-all-social-gatherings narrator/Marcel finds past friends and acquaintances unrecognisably changed by age, while still having the sense of himself as he had been back in his mother's eyes. He replies to a young woman's invitation to dine: 'With pleasure, if you don't mind dining alone with a young man' and only when he hears people giggle, adds hastily 'or rather an old one'. Later he realises that the span of time represented by the aspect of the gathering not only had been lived through but was his life, presented to him.

As I grow old I find myself ready for the revelation, Time Regained, of this Proustian source when, among old friends with whom I was always the youngest of the circle, I realise we are, now, all alike, disguised in the garb of ageing. I, like everyone else, have to be introduced – to myself. Proust makes it another epiphany.

2000

Africa's Plague, and Everyone's

Sixty-nine per cent of the world's victims of HIV and Aids are in sub-Saharan Africa. This figure is not easy to take in. Aids seems to have come upon everyone while we were looking the other way: it happened to some sex or colour other than our own; it was endemic to some other country.

In South Africa it was quite some time before the realisation that the disease was not the unfortunate problem of our poorer neighbouring countries, but was our own. Now, out of South Africa's 43 million people, about 4 million have been infected by HIV and a further 1,700 are infected daily. Recently, in a Johannesburg home caring for orphaned or abandoned babies born with Aids, there was a service in memory of forty who had died there not long before. While South Africa is the most highly developed country on the African continent, we are faced with this kind of future for the generations to come.

But every community, every affected country, has to decide how to approach what is no longer a problem but a catastrophe. There is prevention, and there is cure. The ideal is to seek both at once, but this is beyond the capacity of most countries where the disease is rampant. Cure, and prevention by inoculation, are not within the capacity of lay people; these are in the hands of medical science, which implies money to be provided to advance research. Immediate prevention is in the hands and initiative of each population itself. I believe we cannot emphasise bluntly enough that the cure and vaccine development depend on money. And until recently, the country that has the money, the United States, perhaps inevitably has concentrated on a vaccine for a subtype of Aids prevalent in the Northern Hemisphere. It was only at the World Economic Forum's meeting this year that President Clinton announced that large-scale aid for vaccine development would be forthcoming from the United States. Only now has the International Aids Vaccine Initiative announced a third international development project, based on those subtypes of the virus most prevalent in the direly affected regions of Southern and East Africa, the subtypes C and A. It is encouraging that the project is being pursued in wide collaboration among researchers of the United States, South Africa, Kenya and Oxford University, and that the philosophy of the initiative is that of 'social venture capital', meaning that in return for financing, it has secured rights to ensure that a successful vaccine, when it is achieved, will be distributed in developing countries 'at a reasonable price'. The formation of an International Partnership Against HIV/Aids in Africa is to be welcomed as extremely important in the same context.

The question of money – price – is vital in terms of the palliatives available to arrest the disease and alleviate symptoms. It is another piercing example of the gulf between the world's rich and the world's poor that the suffering from Aids may be alleviated, and even the lives prolonged, of those victims who can afford expensive treatment. The same principle applies to prevention. Everywhere in Africa moral and humanitarian decisions are a common dilemma, with money the deciding factor.

At the level of international – global – responsibility, the total sum needed annually for Aids prevention in Africa is in the order of $2.3 billion. Africa currently receives only $165 million a year in official assistance from the world community.

Other questions that rest with the world community become relevant: debt relief for developing countries, for example. The Director-General of the World Health Organization said last year that debt relief should be reviewed in light of the resources that governments with large debts need to confront HIV. The role of governments in financing is another example. Where does the defence budget not far exceed the public health budget to combat Aids? Nevertheless, what HIV and Aids mean to the capability to govern, ultimately, was revealed in South Africa by the Minister of Public Service and Administration in February. The public service is the largest employer in the country and the fundamental government structure. In 1999, one in eight South Africans was HIV-positive. It is estimated that 270,000 out of 1.1 million public servants could be infected by 2004. This looming crisis in governance exists almost everywhere on the African continent. If, in developing countries, defence budgets continue to leave HIV budgets relegated to a footnote, all we shall have left to defend in the end is a graveyard.

Aids is not only a health catastrophe, a challenge to medical science. It is socially enmeshed in the conditions of life that obtain while it spreads, just as the medieval plague was in its time. Although Aids is no respecter of class or caste, slum conditions, ignorance and superstition (it is a white man's disease; it is a black man's disease) make the poor its greatest source of victims. In working to prevent the spread of the virus, we must accept the idea that promiscuity is difficult to condemn when sex is the cheapest or only available satisfaction for people society leaves to live on the street. On another socio-economic level, casual sex thrives among young people who are materially privileged yet whom society has failed to endow with the real values of human sexuality, the knowledge that fulfilment involves contact with the other's personality, that the sexual act is not some mere bodily function like evacuation – which is what some campaigners seem to reduce it to. There are subtleties, important ones, connected with any campaign against HIV and Aids, if it is to succeed in changing attitudes towards sexual mores. For there will be a cure discovered, there will be a vaccine – and after that? How shall we restore the quality of human relations that have been debased, shamed, reduced to the source of a fatal disease? The free condom dispenser is not the panacea. Neither, alone, is sex education restricted to anatomical diagrams and dire warnings in schools. The entire meaningfulness of personal sexual relations will need to be restored. That is what social health means, along with inoculation and survival. Self-interest cannot be discounted. So, to the developed world, a pragmatic word from the stricken African continent: call not to ask for whom the stock exchange bell tolls and the figures on the computer sound the alarm – the toll is for Europe, for the United States, even for those countries where HIV and Aids victims are few. For if the markets and vast potential markets for the developed world's goods fail – if decimated populations mean there is no one left economically active with money to spend – that bell tolls for thee, globally.

HIV/Aids is everyone's disaster. It has, finally, something to do with our whole manner of existence. It confronts us with questions that must be answered historically: what have we done with the world, politically? What are we doing with the world? What do we mean by development? Some Ugandans who had been in the audience of an Aids information play were asked what message it had brought them. One said, 'Don't go out with bar girls.' Another said, 'Stick to one partner.' Then an older woman said: 'Aids has come to haunt a world that thought it was incomplete. Some wanted children, some wanted money, some wanted property, and all we ended up with is Aids.'

Maybe she spoke for Africa.

2000

What News on the Rialto?

The re-publication of a book by Natalia Ginzburg has brought back to me not only a work I found uniquely beautiful in its tranquil honesty when I read it in translation from the Italian in the sixties; it has opened an overgrown way, that I thought to be a cul-de-sac, in my own life.

Natalia Ginzburg's *Family Sayings* – are what? Fictionalised family history? What was actually said; and what has been invented by Natalia that went on out of her hearing, in her Italian family from the thirties through the fifties: added exchanges between its members, imaginatively created by familiarity and the emotions, love, resentment, understanding, of which she was part?

But she writes: 'The places, events, people in this book are all real. I have invented nothing. Every time that I found myself inventing something in accordance with my old habits as a novelist, I have felt impelled at once to destroy everything thus invented.' Not for her the usual disclaimer, all characters are fictitious, no living personages, etc. 'The names are all real . . . Possibly some may not be pleased to find themselves described in a book under their own names. To such I have nothing to say.' And yet, again, from this translator of Proust (*À la Recherche du Temps Perdu*, no less),[1] the other, self-admonition: 'I must not be beguiled into autobiography as such.' Her blindfold trail into the past is not signposted by an uneven paving stone or the bite into a madeleine, but by over-hearing, echoing in her present, the intimate lingua franca of vanished family life.

---

[1]   *In Search of Lost Time*: now accepted as a more accurate translation of Proust's title formerly in English as *Remembrance of Things Past*.

The past is crowded out by the present during the day. Early in the morning I lie in bed eavesdropping on the birds and the rubrics heard in childhood surface from that past.

Natalia's family sayings are concerned with family relationships increasingly affected by conflicting views on, and eventually actions of, fascists and anti-fascists – her family belonged to the latter. When I overhear in recollection my own family's sayings, this is in the ambience of a different but related context: racism, first of the colonial kind, then that of its apogee, apartheid. But although Natalia Ginzburg married a foreigner, a Russian Jewish revolutionary, her own half-Jewish family was Italian, deeply rooted in their native country. There was no Old Country, not far behind them.

Now that family sayings come back to me from the house in a South African gold-mining town where I was born and grew up, I begin to see that, involved as I was in the clamour of racism and anti-racism, I did not hear that other voice whose significance I've never pursued. It's a given: you don't know your parents, ever, no matter how venerably stable your social background may be. But it is immigrant parents you particularly don't know, if they have taken you, as I was, completely and unquestioningly into their assimilated life of the country of *your* birth, not theirs. My mother and maternal grandparents (the only ones I was ever to know) came to South Africa from England; my father from Latvia. There were revolutions and wars in Europe, nobody went back. Like Natalia, I don't intend to be beguiled into autobiography. I can only confirm to myself that we lived entirely in the present, in the mining town and in the city where my grandparents lived. For me, the lives of parents and grandparents began with mine. My time, my place. Only now I'm led to decode from family sayings what these meant as clues to the life, the drowned Atlantis of the past where they had lived without me, back beyond me. The family sayings have become my small glossary of where they came from, not as marked on a map of the world but in attitudes and perceptions formed to deal with life – elsewhere; or to counter the immigrant's alienation in the country he had adopted without assurance it had adopted him.

My grandfather Mark Myers was in love with his old wife Phoebe, one could see that, but sceptical of her intelligence as a shopper. He was a connoisseur of fruit, as perfectionist as any wine buff. When she arrived back at their Johannesburg flat from the greengrocer she would have to unpack her string bag before his eyes. He would pick up and sniff the melon; then run a finger over a peach's down, alert for bruises. Perhaps it was the avocado that caught her out, too hard, overripe, he would shake it gently to hear if there was an answer from the pip detached from the flesh. Then derisory judgement, softened by use of a love-name from the old life: 'Bob, they saw you coming.'

The reproachful quip didn't exist in South African idiom. Mark Myers was a cockney, streetwise from Covent Garden. None of us knew what his work was before he came 'out to Africa' to prospect unsuccessfully for diamonds in Kimberley. But the saying became ours; if anyone in the family was conned, the affectionate jeer was to hand, from London. Bob, they saw you coming.

If my grandfather's past was still extant, privately, for him, in the copies of the *News of the World*, the yellow press London paper he subscribed to by mailship, my father's past was sunk five fathoms. The inevitable shtetl in the region of Riga had disappeared or been renamed on the side of new frontiers, its remaining inhabitants killed in pogroms or later in war. He had left school when perhaps eleven years old, apprenticed as a watchmaker, and after emigrating to South Africa at thirteen for some years plied his trade along the gold mines and rose to become the owner of a jewellery store where he prospered enough to employ someone else to repair watches. That much we knew. And that was all: clearly his origins were humble in comparison with the middle-class ones of my mother, whose father made his modest living by the sophisticated means of playing the stock exchange – a respectable gambler. My mother was the product of a good school for girls, and played the piano. She did not reassure her husband in any way about his origins; when they quarrelled she had the last word with her family saying: he came from people who 'slept on the stove'. He never spoke of his Old Country and I, no doubt influenced by my mother's dismissal of his lowly foreign past, never asked him about it.

My father's sense of inferiority conversely had a sense of superiority: he had married 'above himself' as my mother made sure he realised. He might not have known the phrase, but he was aware of its significance. He had not sent back to the Old Country as some other immigrants did, before it disappeared, for a wife of his own kind from among those, cold and poor, who slept on the stove.

But of course the principal and enduring source of his superior inferiority was that my mother was a native English speaker with genuine English-speaking parents. It was due to the advantage of living with her, listening to her, and having at least his own good fortune to have a parrot's ear, that he spoke that language almost entirely without the accent of Eastern European Jews that provides material for stand-up comics. Yiddish must have been his mother tongue – there was no one to speak it with, of any generation, in our family; a dead language for him. When some German speaker, result of a new immigration, this time from Nazi pogroms, was a customer in his shop, it was revealed my father could speak a little German learned in his short spell of schooling. During the Second World War, when there was news from the Russian front, it appeared that he also knew some Russian; he could pronounce all the unpronounceable names of cities and generals. He had picked up enough Afrikaans to deal with customers, Afrikaner whites, in the town – had to. Even more evident of the exigencies of immigrant survival, he had taught himself something invented by colonial mining companies in order for the white bosses to be able to communicate with the black indentured men who came from all over Southern, Central and East Africa to work in the mines – a curt pidgin of verbs and nouns believed to be more or less understandable to all, a mixture of Zulu, Afrikaans and English, dubbed Fanagalo. *Be like – do – like this*; more or less the accepted, certainly intended meaning. It consisted mainly of commands. He must have acquired it – had to – in the early days of his immigration when he went from mine to mine mending workers' watches.

All this was mimicry, wasn't it – surely the first essential for survival as an immigrant in any country, any time?

He knew English. He was fluent enough for all the purposes

of our daily communication. He had refined his pronunciation through his choice of an 'English' wife. He had 'English' daughters who read beside him, in the evenings, *Doctor Dolittle* and *Little Women*, books he had never heard of from a culture that his wife assured him did not belong to him.

Yet – I hear it again. When he came home from his shop at the end of the day and my mother's friends were gathered over their gin and vermouth, he would greet everyone with 'What news on the Rialto?'

Where did that quotation come from, to him? He did not read anything except a newspaper; he certainly had never read *The Merchant of Venice*. What painstaking early struggle with a phrase-book, what lessons in English he must have scrimped and saved to afford, does that family saying represent? *His* news was that he was part of the taken-for-granted cultural background of the company, by a tag if nothing else.

My grandfather's cockney sayings affirmed his past; my father's, his need to hold a place in his present. When people complained about a misfortune, the shortcomings of the city council or the problems of making a living, he had another saying, this one more expressive in his adoptive Afrikaans than its equivalent might be in English: 'So gaan dit in die wêreld' – that's the way of the world. He was ready with 'Môre is nog 'n dag' – tomorrow's another day – if someone despaired in a troubling circumstance or lost the first round of a golf tournament. These sayings heard over and over, I didn't recognise as the immigrant's tactics, seeking acceptance. The stranger my father was, calling out. He was reinventing something: himself.

How much of self-esteem comes from defining someone as lower than oneself on the ladder of human values?

Where, on whom, from his precarious foothold, can an immigrant look down? An element of racism is identifying that person even while at the same time being identified by others as beneath them. By chance and history my father had come to a country where self-esteem via racism was indulged by those who were in absolute political power and social control, far from insecure. (The turn of history on them was to come much later, with the end of white rule . . .) That white community of South Africa – to which he could 'belong' at least by the pallor of his skin – despised the black people whose country they had colonised and ruled by force. So even an immigrant from a people who slept on the stove was provided with someone, some humankind, to regard as beneath him. My father conformed to the racist social judgements of white townspeople, our family friends, his shopkeeper colleagues, using a saying of this extended family of whites as they did. The strongest condemnation of a white man's crude behaviour, drunk or sober, was to call him 'a white kaffir'.

This was not a saying ever pronounced by my mother; in fact there would be in her face yet another confirmation of all that she found crude in my father; that he, of all people, should think it insulting for a white man to be called black.

There were subtleties in racism among the sayings familiar to me in our town. Here, even my mother, who was not racist when it came to black and white, would make use of them. Among Jews, there was the other expression of disgust, 'he's a real Peruvian'. 'He' would be a Jew whose loud behaviour, flamboyance and vulgarity offended. The 'real Peruvian' did not come from Peru and the insulting implication surely devolved upon Peruvians as much as it did on the man so scorned. Why such behaviour should be asso-ciated with Peru, where no one in the community had ever been, and there was no one from that country among our white popu-lation of English, Scots, Irish, Welsh, Dutch, Jewish, German, Greek origin, I can explain only by suggesting that to the speaker Peru was the end of the earth, beyond civilisation, the last place God made; remote as Africa might seem to Peruvians. Perhaps the outlandish epithet also served to distance local Jews from conduct that might give a toehold of credence to anti-Semitism, which rumbled among Afrikaners – themselves discriminated against by the English-speaking whites.

Fifty or more years later, I decode these family sayings as the echoes of lost home – Grandpa Myers's – in an immigrant culture, or the innocently crafty attempt – my father's – of survival in escape from that culture. These days, I walk past elegant shopping malls in the suburbs of Johannesburg through sidewalk markets where, capered about before me, dangled at me, are masks and jewellery, carvings and sculpture, cowrie-and-seed rattles. I'm importuned by strangers' mimicry of South African sales-talk English. The vendors have come from all over Africa, they speak among themselves the mother tongues of their Old Countries, Mali, Nigeria, Congo, Zimbabwe, Zambia, Kenya, Senegal, Ethiopia, anywhere and everywhere there is war, natural disaster of flood and drought, and poverty by comparison with which we are a rich country, despite our own share of the poor and workless.

Their cajolings, reproduction of phrases understood by them only in sense of intention, are their family sayings. They're the latest arrivals of the endless no-nation of immigrants, forming and reforming the world, a globalisation that long, long predates any present concept. That's the news on the Rialto; nothing new. Just survival.

2001

The Dwelling Place of Words

People always want to know when and where you write. As if there's a secret methodology to be followed. It has never seemed to me to matter to the *work* – which is the writer's 'essential gesture' (I quote Roland Barthes), the hand held out for society to grasp – whether the creator writes at noon or midnight, in a cork-lined room as Proust did or a shed as Amos Oz did in his early kibbutz days. Perhaps the questioner is more than curious; yearning for a jealously kept prescription on how to *be* a writer. There is none. Writing is the one 'profession' for which there is no professional training; 'creative' writing courses can only teach the aspirant to look at his/her writing critically; not *how to* create. The only school for a writer is the library – reading, reading. A journey through realms of how far, wide and deep writing can venture in the endless perspectives of human life. Learning from other writers' perceptions that you have to find your way to yours, at the urge of the most powerful sense of yourself – creativity. Apart from that, you're on your own.

Ours is the most solitary of occupations; the only comparison I can think of is keeper of a lighthouse. But the analogy mustn't go too far, we do not cast the beam of light that will save the individual, or the world from coming to grief on its rocks.

Another standard enquiry put to fiction writers: what is your message? Milan Kundera has provided the response. The message is: 'A novel searches and poses questions . . . The wisdom of the novel comes from having a question for everything. It does not prescribe or proscribe answers.' We have the right and obligation of honesty to imply moral judgements we know people have, as exemplified in our fictional characters because – I paraphrase Goethe – wherever the writer thrusts a hand deep into society, the world, there will come up in it something of the truth. The writer her/himself stands before what has been dredged to light just as the reader will; what either makes of it will be individual moral judgement: her or his, writer's or reader's self-message.

That is the low-wattage beam I would claim for my own writings cast from my lighthouse, and those of the great writers who have illuminated my life. For me, writing has been and is an exploration of life, the safari that will go on into that amazing wilderness until I die. That is why my novels and stories are what I call open-ended; I've taken up an invention of human beings at some point in their lives, and set them down again living at some other point. My novel written in the 1980s, *July's People*, ends with a central character, a woman, wading through a shallow river, running from a situation. To what? I am often asked. The answer is I don't know. The only clues I have, and pass on there for the reader in the text of the novel that has gone before, are the social and historical context, the conflicting threats and pressures, personal and aleatory, of a time and place that would make up her options – what she could or might attempt next. The sole conclusion – in terms of reading a signpost – was one that I myself could come to, after I had re-read the novel (for a writer becomes reader when the publisher's proofs arrive), was that crossing through the water was some kind of baptism into a new situation, new life, however uncertain, hazardous, even unimaginable in the light of *how she had lived thus far*.

One can't even say that an individual death is the end of a story. What about the consequences the absence is going to have for others?

What about the aftermath of a political and societal conflict apparently resolved, in a novel whose final page leaves the men and women, the country, the cities, the children born to these, at that point? Again, the reader has the narrative and text that has gone before, to waken his/her own awareness, own questioning of self and society.

If the writer does not provide answers, is this a valid absolution from the ordinary human responsibility of engagement with society other than as the 'essential gesture', extended through literature?

Does the writer serve the *raison d'être* that every human being must decide for the self, by asserting the *exploration of the word* as the end and not the means of the writer's being? 'Words became my dwelling place.' The great Mexican poet and writer, Octavio Paz, wrote this; but in his superb life's work, on his intellectual journey, he invaded that place; he also wrote 'I learned that politics is not only action but participation, it is not a matter of changing men but accompanying them, being one of them.' The reason-to-be was a bringing together of the dwelling place of the artist and the clamorous world that surrounded it.

The great Günter Grass told me: 'My professional life, my writing, all the things that interest me, have taught me that I cannot freely choose my subjects. For the most part my subjects were assigned to me by German history, by the war that was criminally started and conducted, and by the never-ending consequences of that era. Thus my books are fatally linked to these subjects, and I am not the only one who has had this experience.'

He certainly is not the only one.

In Europe, the USA, Latin America, China, Japan, Africa – where in the world could this not be so? There are none of us who can 'choose our subjects' free of the contexts that contain our lives, shape our thought, influence every aspect of our existence. (Even the fantasy of space fiction is an alternative to the known, the writer's imaginative *reaction* to it.) Could Philip Roth erase the tattoo of the Nazi camps from under the skin of his characters? Can Israeli writers, Palestinian writers, now 'choose' not to feel the tragic conflict between their people burning the dwelling place of words? Could Kenzaburo Oe create characters not bearing in themselves the gene of consciousness implanted by Hiroshima and Nagasaki; could Czeslaw Milosz, living through revolution and exile, not have to ask himself in his poem 'Dedication', 'What is poetry which does not save/Nations or people?' Could Chinua Achebe's characters not have in their bloodstream the stain of a civil war in Nigeria? In Africa, the experiences of colonialism, its apogee, apartheid, post-colonialism and new-nation conflicts, have been a powerful collective consciousness in African writers, black and white. And in the increasing *interconsciousness*, the realisation that what happens somewhere in the world is just one manifestation of what is happening subliminally or going to happen in one way or another, affect in one way or another, *everywhere* – the epic of emigration, immigration, the world-wandering of new refugees and exiles, political and economic, for example – is a fatal linkage, not 'fatal' in the deathly sense, but in that of inescapable awareness in the writer. I have just written a novel, *The Pickup*, within this awareness, taking up at one point and leaving at another point in their lives, characters in our millennial phase of this eternal exodus and arrival.

However, when a country has come through long conflict and its resolution, its writers are assumed to have lost their 'subject'. We in South Africa are challenged – top of the list in journalists' interviews – 'So what are you going to write about now that apartheid has gone?'

Apartheid was a plan of social engineering and its laws; novels, stories, poetry and plays were an exploration of how people thought and lived, their ultimate humanity out of reach of extinction. Life did not end with apartheid. 'The new situation must bring new

subjects' – Czech writer Ivan Klíma wrote this, in exile, and out
of the breakup of his country. In South Africa there is not breakup and its violent consequences, but a difficult and extraordinary
bringing-together of what was divided. The new subjects, some
wonderful, some dismaying, have scarcely had time to choose us.

'What do we know / But that we face / One another in this
place' – William Butler Yeats. That is surely the subject that in the
dwelling place of words, everywhere, chooses the writer.

2001

The Entitlement Approach

'Governance': 'the action or manner of governing', 'the state of
being governed'. In the past this dictionary definition was
taken as referring specifically to national governments and their
people. But in our age of globalisation, of global resources and
certainly global problems, the concept of governance in relation to
tackling world poverty starts at a much higher level, the Everest of
international finance. Governance in individual countries is influenced by and in many instances prescribed by these. So we have to
begin by facing the opposing conceptions most widely held about
the devolution from the heights, down to earth.

Recipient countries of loan funds through the IMF and World
Bank resent conditions imposed by the agencies of the financial
Everest as to the ways in which the money is to be used. They
even assert that development – the object – is hampered by such
conditions.

The agencies cite stringent necessity for conditions in order to
counter their experience of corruption as a government conduit
through which the funds disappear without any development
reaching a country's population.

So governance begins above a country's own laws and administration. Whether debt owed to the Everest should be written off, in

view of crippling interest payments required even from countries which *do* use the money for sustainable development, is another question – should Everest be a usurer, or should it be the real agent of redistribution of wealth?

There are encouraging signs of a change in conception on the part of donors and recipients. Mamphele Ramphele, speaking as Managing Director of the Human Development Unit of the World Bank, says that the approach now needed is for 'countries to take ownership' of development rather than 'receive prescribed programmes of action . . . to leverage their own destiny and build capacity for themselves'.[1] Senegalese President Abdoulaye Wade says of Africans who have been 'financing debt by loans and aid for years', 'Those instruments don't take us far . . . we must first understand how we got into debt in the first place.'[2] This facing of reality by both donor and debtor gives credence to the claim by ten African leaders conferring with the IMF and World Bank this year, of a 'major step forward to define a new approach to fight poverty in Africa'.

What principal areas of national life depend on good national governance if poverty is to be tackled on the ground, within each country? Foremost, surely: unemployment, post-colonial land redistribution, use and exploitation of natural resources, health care with emphasis on the Aids epidemic, education; and not least, corruption. There is a determining condition if these are to be addressed: press and media freedom. There is no good governance without a population free to participate in open debate on government policy and practice, to effect for themselves progress in the condition of their lives.

'Entitlement relations'[3] – Amartya Sen's phrase defines for me what global governance through international finance and national

1   Mamphele Ramphele, 'World Bank Will Reward Good Governance', *Sunday Independent*, South Africa, 11 March 2001.

2   President Abdoulaye Wade, 'African Leaders, IMF and World Bank forge new strategy on poverty', *The Star*, Johannesburg, 21 February 2001.

3   Amartya Sen, *Poverty and Famines: An Essay on Entitlement and Deprivation*, Clarendon Press, Oxford, 1981.

governance on the ground need to have with a population on the premise that they are to tackle poverty the only effective way – together. And here UNDP, with partnership stressed as its mode of operation in the twenty-first century, provides a model in its proven dedication to be, itself, a partner in enterprises of and for good governance. Experience in project innovation has taught the lesson that success is dependent on making sure governance of a country has the minimum means, and the will, to cooperate – the *capacity*. This implies that capacity training is, in itself, a project in the partnership of governance with poverty elimination. A project cannot succeed where the capacity to implement it – whether through lack of trained personnel, communication facilities – is not at least in a parallel state of development. To reach the end, there must be the minimal means. Then the energy and determination of the population can, and does, take off for success.

The developing world, the peoples of that world, have entitlement; entitlement to the redistribution of the world's wealth rather than the euphemistic 'aid', entitlement to just, incorruptible governance. The right to recognition of, and action within, the interdependence of governance and the millennial, global problem, poverty.

2001

The Ballad of the Fifth Avenue Hotel

The Fifth Avenue Hotel. Easter 1954. Dim purple lighting on toy bunny rabbits perched over our heads all around a ledge beneath the restaurant ceiling. I am thirty years old, I have published two books of stories and a first novel; I am in the USA for the first time and I'm seated at table with a famous American writer – a Southerner, like myself, although my South is Africa – whose work I greatly admire. She is Carson McCullers. We have been brought together, in my neophyte's privileged anticipation, by the kindness of her sister, Margaret Smith, and Cyrilly Abels, editors of *Mademoiselle*, then a literary-innovative women's magazine that, along with *The New Yorker*, had published some of my stories. There before me is that life-questioning image, the wonderful face of a wise child who was born devastatingly knowing too much – the face of the being who wrote *The Ballad of the Sad Café*.

What *I* didn't know was that Carson had just come out of long weeks of detoxification, shut away somewhere. What I also didn't know was what that experience could do to the victim; how dazed was the return to the world. What followed was surely a scene written by her friend Tennessee Williams. Carson kept saying to Margaret, 'Sister, I think we need a a new beau.' It wasn't ironic or in lunch-table jest; it was a grave and determined conclusion. With me was my new husband (of one month). All through the meal Carson leaned a hand with a delicate fork, taking morsels from his plate. The questions I had ready to ask the writer who had meant much to me fled my mind. I managed somehow to tell her of my admiration for her work; don't remember that brought any response.

Bunny rabbits sister we need a new beau.

So America was a purple-lit fantasy with a foreboding message. If this was what fame could mean for a writer, I didn't think I wanted it ever to come to me. My husband (my new beau) was more compassionately moved, less judgemental; less frightened, although he himself had just taken on that risky mate, a writer.

Meeting those emissaries of American culture, the writers, has been mostly good and reassuring since that sad ballad of the Fifth Avenue Hotel. Soon there was Eudora Welty, American Chekhov, whose stories had early influenced me: Eudora in Jackson, Mississippi, as wonderful in person as she is as a writer. An American original of a special kind.

I haven't always encountered American writers in their home country. John Updike and I met happily in Australia, where at the Adelaide Festival we looked like a comedy duo, he so gangling tall, I so small. Kurt Vonnegut literally embodied a wry American brand of humour at a writers' get-together in Sweden. I met James

Baldwin in France and we talked as if we'd known each other always; perhaps we had, in our experience of racism, he in his country, I in mine – what this means for the transformations of the writer's imagination.

Some encounters have resulted in precious friendship. At a literary conference there was a woman with a damn-you-all beautiful face and swirling black hair, sitting on a step outside the venue: I recognised Susan Sontag. We fled the deliberations and explored the foreign city; the first of many exhilarating times together. Elisabeth Hardwick lent me Robert Lowell's den-apartment with library, in New York; gave me the freedom of her rich mind as well as the place where she still lives.

Of course I'd met America through their writings – all of them – along with the America of Melville, Hawthorne, Faulkner, Fitzgerald, Miller, Hemingway *et al*. (he more definitively American abroad than at home); had been confronted with the country in this deepest way, before coming face to face.

2001

Chinua Achebe and *Things Fall Apart*

Things fall apart.

Chinua Achebe's title, quoted from a poem by William Butler Yeats, seems a challenging declaration: what chaos will the reader be confronted with when taking up the opening pages of this book, first published in 1958?

But the title is a presentiment: Achebe is going to create *what was complete* before the situation in the title is to come about. Only then can the revelation of disintegration be fully understood. Achebe did not begin this first novel, and does not begin his later ones, with description of the setting of the story. In what country his characters live, what kind of life in what sort of landscape, city, village – he plunges us immediately among the people themselves in their full activity, and their physical surroundings of a region of Nigeria, West Africa, emerge as part of their identity as the reader follows. Okonkwo, the central character, is introduced in the first paragraph as a young man who has brought honour to his village by his fame as a wrestler, never thrown by opponents in any of the bouts of the traditional sport popular in the region. 'The drums beat and the flutes sound and the spectators held their breath . . . Amazile was the great wrestler who for seven years was unbeaten . . . he was called the Cat because his back would never touch the earth. It was this man that Okonkwo threw in a fight which the old men agreed was one of the fiercest since the founder of their town engaged a spirit of the wild for seven days and seven nights.'

Achebe has the master story-teller's knowledge that the present – what is happening to his characters now – can be totally meaningful only if (the way it is in our own lives) the past that has formed these people is shown as still within them, directing their lives. Okonkwo's story is taken up in an actual period not long before Nigeria's independence from British rule. 'That was . . . twenty years ago or more, and during this time Okonkwo's fame had grown like a bush fire in the harmattan.' Okonkwo's father was a failure by the standards of this Nigerian village of the Ibo clan with which we have quickly been made familiar through lively anecdotal exchange. Idle, owing thousands of cowries (the local currency), he had never qualified to take the series of traditional titles which recognise honour and success in Umuofia, and which are marked not by the medals that are presented to dignitaries in the European world, but by special anklets worn by those honoured. Even after his father has been dead for ten years, the driving motive in Okonkwo's life is to be everything his father was not. Okonkwo has triumphed in tribal battles, he's a wealthy farmer with three wives, and has taken two titles while still young. But this distinction and success bring about an obligation that Achebe introduces as natural, unexceptional in a close-knit society, yet whose consequences he is going to lead us to discover along with him, without advance warning – such is his power to engage the reader rather than tell a story.

Now an introduction must not reveal too much of what is in the book itself, only arouse anticipation; so I shan't recount the dramatic warring dispute between Umuofia and a neighbouring village, Mbaino, which results in Okonkwo being given the responsibility of taking into his household Ikemefuna, an Mbaino boy, given as reparation. The child at first is terrified, cannot understand what is happening to him, but he is a lively boy, becomes popular in Okonkwo's household and a special friend of Okonkwo's son Nwoye. Okonkwo, who regards the show of any emotion as weakness (the weakness of his father), is inwardly fond of the boy and so treats him familiarly like everybody else – 'with a heavy hand'. Ikemefuna calls him Father and sometimes has the honour of being allowed to carry Okonkwo's stool and goatskin bag to village ancestral feasts.

Ikemefuna takes part with the whole family in the planting of the yam. The yam is introduced here as 'the king of crops', the beautiful, bustling detail of its cultivation both the cycle of seasons and, as life-sustaining food, the cycle of human existence; from this first novel can be traced further the yam's compelling emergence, in Achebe's later work, as a philosophical and political symbol: life and death in the opposition of the yam and the knife.

The Feast of the New Yam is a two-day village celebration with feasting, palm wine and the customary great wrestling match between Okonkwo's village and its neighbours. It's a joyful interlude in which Achebe generously, for the reader's pleasure, uses his gifts of creating a whole community of men, women and children as people we instantly get to know intimately, recognising their individual ways of expressing themselves. The comedy of sharp exchanges and laughter sounds against the drums beating out the wrestling dance; you can almost smell the scents of the cooking. There are delightful conversations to be overheard between the women, half pidgin English, half to be followed as translated by Achebe from the rich imagery of the Ibo language. The undercurrent of the order of life for the Umuofians is revealed in what appears to be ordinary talk, gossip and conventional polite enquiry. Ezinma, Okonkwo's favourite daughter, comes to our attention. A woman who knows the girl's mother and has seen a number of her children die early, asks about Ezinma. The mother says: 'She has been well for some time now. Perhaps she has come to stay.' 'I think she will stay,' says the other woman. 'They usually stay if they do not die before the age of six.'

Now Ikemefuna has lived in Okonkwo's household for three years and Okonkwo is pleased that his influence on Nwoye is excellent. He encourages the two boys to sit with him, manly, in his *obi* – his quarters. He tells them stories of tribal wars and his own bold exploits. Nwoye prefers the folk stories and legends his mother used to tell him, and which enrich this novel with a cast of wily characters – including cosmic Earth and Sky – that make Disney's pale by contrast. The time of harmony, peace and plenty continues with the arrival of the great sky-darkening horde of locusts – here, not the curse of the biblical locusts but a delicacy everyone turns out to catch and eat.

Achebe's exploration of life – which is what all literature, all art is – through the wonderful powers of his imagination, reveals in all his writings the particular vulnerability of human beings when they are most happy. It is then that some almost forgotten conflict in the past suddenly raises the knife against the yam. Okonkwo is in his *obi* with Ikemefuna and Nwoye, crunching locusts and drinking palm wine, when the village elder, Ezeudu, arrives and asks to see Okonkwo outside. There he says something incomprehensible to Okonkwo, presenting Ikemefuna as an outcast who cannot continue to be accepted by the Umuofians. The Oracle of the Hills and Caves has declared he must be killed. The old man says, 'That boy calls you father. Do not bear a hand in his death . . . They will take him outside Umuofia as is the custom, and kill him there. But I want you to have nothing to do with it. He calls you father.'

How Okonkwo is fatefully involved in this inescapable murder is told mainly through the thoughts of the boy who, believing he is being returned to his home village, is being escorted by the

Umuofians to his death. As he is struck by the matchet of one of the men he runs towards Okonkwo, calls out ' "My father, they have killed me!" Dazed with fear, Okonkwo drew his matchet and cut him down. He was afraid of being thought weak.'

For a time Okonkwo can neither eat nor sleep. He drinks wine 'from morning till night, and his eyes were red and fierce like the eyes of a rat when it was caught by the tail and dashed against the floor'. For the sacrifice of Ikemefuna, his son Nwoye will never forgive him, with fateful consequences to unfold in his own life and that of his father.

But Okonkwo recovers: 'he is not a man of thought but of action; it is the season to tap his palm trees for wine, and the family of a suitor for his daughter, sixteen-year-old Akueke, is about to arrive'. The negotiations between the two families over cowrie bride-price and the amount of palm wine the bridegroom's family is expected to provide are enchantingly comic and slyly character-revealing, without malice – a feature of Achebe's humour, particularly in his early work, before the ugly and terrible times of civil war and post-independence corruption within which he was writing sharpened humour into teeth-clenched satire.

It is in the chatter at the marriage negotiations that the white man enters for the first time in Umuofia and the novel. There is discussion about different customs among different villages. Someone remarks

'But what is good in one place is bad in another place . . .'
    'The world is large,' said Okonkwo, 'I have even heard that in some tribes a man's children belong to his wife and her family.'
    'That cannot be,' said Machi. 'You might as well say that the woman lies on top of the man when they are making the children.'
    'It is like the story of white men who, they say, are white like this piece of chalk,' said Obierika '. . . And these white men, they say, have no toes.'
    'Have you ever seen them?' asked Machi.
    'Have you?' asked Obierika.

'One of them passes here frequently' [says Machi.] 'His name is Amadi.' Those who knew Amadi laughed. He was a leper, and the polite name for leprosy was 'the white skin'.

The people of Umuofia are great talkers. They become lively companions of the reader, who is overhearing their memories, rivalries, opinions, teasing, original views, all expressed with humour and intimate imagery that come from their way of life, its continuum of history, legend, security of place. The joking reference to the fact that no one has seen a white man is merely a snatch of the exchanges that criss-cross from subject to subject. The white man is butt of a laughable anecdote; he is not there yet, with his Bible and his gun. But Achebe has sounded the single beat of a distant drum, just as subconsciously in our own everyday talk there may occur an unnoticed reference to something that is looming, one day to change our lives.

Okonkwo is just beginning to be able to reconcile himself to – thrust aside – his part in the death of Ikemefuna when his favourite daughter, Ezinma, of whom he thinks so proudly that he has paid her the highest compliment in wishing that she were a boy, falls ill. *Iba* – malaria – does not respond to the treatment Okonkwo and her mother Ekwefi, one of his wives, give her. With this event, Ekwefi emerges from the wings where so far the village women have remained while men take the centre stage in the story. She is to be the first of a series of women characters, each growing in the author's intuition of women and recognition of their qualities, their pilgrimage towards the self-realisation that is equality with men in life's decisions and activities, which was to culminate in the character of Beatrice in his 1987 novel *Anthills of the Savannah*. Bearing and rearing children is the purpose and dignity allotted to women in Umuofia society. Achebe, the most honest of writers, simply allows us our own judgement of the facts: the fate of local women. Ekwefi has borne ten children and all but Ezinma died in infancy; it is his other wives who have given Okonkwo sons. Ekwefi's suffering speaks for itself in her natural, dramatic, poetic lament:

Her deepening despair found expression in the names she gave her
children. One of them was a pathetic cry, Onwumbiko – 'Death,
I implore you'. But Death took no notice; Onwumbiko died. The
next child was a girl, Ozoemena – 'May it not happen again'. She
died, and two others after her. Ekwefi then became defiant and
called her next child Onwuma – 'Death may please himself'. And
he did.

So Ezinma at ten years old is the single survivor, best beloved
of both parents. It is generally accepted in the village that she is
an *ogbanje*. The concept is rather like that of *karma*: one who dies
in one life returns to live again. But here the rebirth represents a
curse.

> Some of them [the children] did become tired of their evil rounds
> of birth and death, or took pity on their mothers and stayed.
> Ekwefi believed deep inside her that Ezinma had come to stay . . . a
> medicine man had dug up Ezinma's *iya-uwa*. The *iya-uwa* was the
> bond with the world of *ogbanje*, and the discovery meant that the
> bond had been broken.

But Ezinma's latest grave illness suggests that the *iya-uwa* might
not have been the genuine one. In desperation the parents summon
the medicine man, Okagbue, to find out from the child where it
is believed she herself has buried her real *iya-uwa*. Ezinma leads
Okagbue, her parents and a following crowd on a wild-goose chase
(perhaps mischievously!) beyond the village and then back again
to an orange tree beside her father's *obi*. The medicine man digs a
pit there so deep that he can no longer be seen by the tense crowd.
Finally, he throws out a rag on his hoe; some women run away in
fear. Ceremoniously he unties the rag and the fetish, a smooth,
shiny pebble, falls out. ' "Is this yours?" he asked Ezinma. "Yes,"
she replied. All the women shouted with joy because Ekwefi's
trials were at last ended.' But Achebe, weaving his diviner's creative texture of life back and forth, suddenly announces that all this
happened a year before the point at which his narrative has arrived

now, and Ezinma is once more shivering with *iba*. This time, Okonkwo cures the attack with an inhalation brewed from grasses, roots and barks of medicinal trees. Natural science, rationality, has won over superstition.

The presence of the supernatural, however, in its particular forms is among and embodied in the Umuofians' daily life just as the supernatural, in their particular forms of belief, is embodied in Christianity, Judaism, Islam, Hinduism, Buddhism and other beliefs.

One of the forms the supernatural takes in Umuofia is the ancestors in the guise of – inhabiting, it is believed – a masquerade of men which among other purposes, administers justice in disputes. The law: not in the judge's wig and gown, but the fearsome appearance of the *egwugwu*, ancestral spirits emerging from a sacred hut to sound of drums and flutes. The masquerade faced 'away from the crowd, who saw only its backs with the many coloured patterns and drawings' of their masquerade costumes. We can see some of these costumes today in many of the museums of the world, and they are recalled to us from books on African art, for they are recognised as a spectacular and profound art form. Symbolic, like all religious art, they represent, as one of the crowd gathered says, 'what is beyond our knowledge'.

The case to be heard by the representatives of the ancestors this time is a commonplace enough one: a wife and children have been abducted from her husband by her family. He demands that they shall return the bride-price he paid for her.

A member of her family, Odukwe, declares what the man has said is true; but what is also true is that 'My in-law, Uzowulu, is a beast . . . no single day passed in the sky without his beating the woman . . . when she was pregnant, he beat her until she miscarried.'

Uzowulu shouts: 'It is a lie. She miscarried after she had gone to sleep with her lover.'

To roars of laughter from the crowd, Odukwe, no mincer of words, continues: the wife may be allowed to return to her husband 'on the understanding that if he ever beats her again we shall cut off his genitals for him.'

And one elder in the crowd says to another, 'I don't know why such a trifle should come before the *egwugwu*.' Here is Achebe delighting in puncturing solemnity with a sly aside.

The interaction between the lively, happy daily life of the village, centred by Achebe on Okonkwo's family, and the ever-present darkness of supernatural beliefs beneath it continues at this pre-colonial stage in the community's history. The reader is listening in to a cosy, wonderful evening of story-telling exchange between Ezinma and her mother when the graphic legend of the Tortoise, who names himself 'All of You', who engages with the birds, named 'People of The Sky', is shattered by the arrival of Chielo, priestess of the god Agbala. She claims Ezinma as 'her daughter' and declares that Agbala demands that the child come to him 'in his house in the hills and the caves'. Okonkwo protests; the priestess screams, 'Beware Okonkwo! Beware of exchanging words with Agbala. Does a man speak when a god is speaking?'

There follows an exciting night-long ordeal of tension and dread as the priestess, with Ezinma on her back, takes the trail, terrified Ekwefi following. The priestess and Ezinma disappear into a narrow cave mouth. Ekwefi vows that if she hears Ezinma cry out she will 'rush into the cave to defend her against all the gods in the world. She would die with her.' Okonkwo has decided to follow: he suddenly appears and they wait together until dawn. Achebe understands so well the curious process by which memory distracts, sustainingly, from the most fearful events. Beside Okonkwo, Ekwefi finds herself thinking of their youth. Another dawn: she was going to fetch water. His house was on the way to the stream. She knocked at his door. 'Even in those days he was a man of few words. He just carried her to his bed and in the darkness began to feel around her waist for the loose end of her cloth.'

Achebe leaves us in suspense, on that intimate pause. The story is taken up surprisingly next day: Okonkwo's friend Obierika is celebrating a joyous occasion, the wedding of his daughter: life goes on; whatever fears and disasters threaten individuals, the yam and the knife eternally contend. For Okonkwo, tragedy has been averted: we learn, as the preparations for the feast begin, that Ezinma is sleeping safely in her bed – the priestess brought her back and laid her there, unharmed. On the turning wheel of human life, the festive scene of the wedding is followed by another ceremony in the cycle, the funeral of a man who had the distinction of having taken three anklet titles out of the four created by the clan. Okonkwo is among the men who, to drumming and dancing, fire a last salute to the dead dignitary. Then comes 'a cry of agony and shouts of horror. It was as if a spell had been cast.' And it is as if a spell has been cast on Okonkwo: his gun has exploded and killed the dead man's sixteen-year-old son. Achebe does not, and doesn't have to remind us of the echo here of the other crime Okonkwo was led into by circumstance – the final death-blow he gave Ikemefuna – we hear it.

'The only course open to Okonkwo was to flee from the clan. It was a crime against the earth goddess to kill a clansman . . . the crime was of two kinds, male and female. Okonkwo had committed the female, because it had been inadvertent. He could return to the clan after seven years.'

Seven years.

Okonkwo has become an exile; of a kind. For he takes his wives and children to the village of Mbanta, from where his mother came and where she was returned for burial. He is well received by his mother's kinspeople, given land, helped to build an *obi* and huts for his family, supplied with seed-yams. '. . . but it was like beginning life anew . . . like learning to become left-handed . . . his life had been ruled by a great passion – to become one of the lords' in his clan in Umuofia. 'That had been his life-spring. And he had all but achieved it. Then everything had been broken.' To Okonkwo, personally, has come to pass this prophecy of Achebe's title *Things Fall Apart*.

The second section of the novel is taken up in the second year of Okonkwo's exile. The white man makes his real, ominous entry this time. A visit of an old friend from Umuofia brings news of the destruction of their neighbouring village, Abame.

During the last planting season a white man had appeared in their clan.

'An albino' suggested Okonkwo.

'He was not an albino. He was quite different. He was riding an iron horse. The first people who saw him ran away; but he stood beckoning to them . . . The elders consulted their Oracle and it told them that the strange man would break their clan and spread destruction among them . . . And so they killed the white man and tied his iron horse to their sacred tree because it looked as if it would run away to call the man's friends. It was said that other white men were on their way.'

They were indeed; they came to the market day and killed everyone there. Okonkwo's friend Obierika says

'We have heard stories about white men who made the powerful guns and the strong drinks and took slaves away across the seas, but no-one thought the stories were true.'

'There is no story that is not true' said someone else. 'The world has no end, and what is good among one people is an abomination with others.'

Two years pass once again. The white man, in the person of missionaries, has come to both Umuofia and Mbanta. Okonkwo's son has appeared in Umuofia as a convert. Obierika comes to Mbanta to tell Okonkwo that when he asked Nwoye ' "How is your father?" Nwoye said, "I don't know. He is not my father." ' But Okonkwo does not want to speak of the son who has rejected his origin for God the Father.

Achebe, having dropped this bombshell, reels the story back to create the scene of the arrival of the missionaries, which has already taken place. The event is bitingly hilarious. When they had all gathered the white man began to speak to them. He spoke through an interpreter who was an Ibo man. Many people laughed at the way the white man appeared 'evidently' to be using words strangely. According to the interpretation, instead of saying 'myself' he always said 'my buttocks'. But he was a man of commanding presence and the clansmen listened attentively.

> He said he was one of them . . . The white man was also their brother because they were all sons of God. And he told them about this new God, the creator of all the world and all the men and women. He told them they worshipped false gods, gods of wood and stone . . . the true God lived on high and that all men when they died went before him for judgement.
>
> 'We have been sent by this great God to ask you to leave your wicked ways and false gods and turn to Him so that you may be saved when you die.'
>
> 'Your buttocks understand our language,' said someone light-heartedly and the crowd laughed.

When the white missionary speaks of the Son of God,

> Okonkwo, who only stayed [at the gathering] in the hope that it might come to chasing the men out of the village or whipping them, now said: 'You told us with your own mouth that there was only one god. Now you talk about his son. He must have a wife, then.'
>
> The crowd agreed. . . . 'Your buttocks said he had a son,' said the joker. 'So he must have a wife and all of them must have buttocks.'

But Nwoye, that day, had been impressed and moved. 'It was the poetry of the new religion, something felt in the marrow. The hymn about brothers who sat in darkness and fear seemed to answer a vague and persistent question . . . the question of Ikemefuna who was killed. He felt a relief within as the hymn poured into his parched soul.'

The missionaries ask for land to build a church and the elders give them land – in the Evil Forest, where were buried people who died of evil diseases, and which was the dumping ground for the potent fetishes of great medicine men when they died. 'They boast about victory over death. Let us give them a real battlefield in which to show their victory.'

The missionaries begin to build their church; 'The inhabitants of Mbanta expected them all to be dead within four days.' None of them died. 'And then it was known that the white man's fetish had unbelievable power. It was said that he wore glasses on his eyes so that he could see and talk to evil spirits.' Nevertheless, the missionaries begin to make converts.

Nwoye kept his attraction to the new faith secret, for fear of his father. But someone sees Nwoye among the Christians and reports this. When the boy comes home Okonkwo is overcome with fury and grips him by the neck.

'Where have you been.' [Nwoye struggles to free himself.] 'Answer me!' roared Okonkwo, 'Before I kill you!' [He seizes a stick and gives the boy savage blows.]

'Leave that boy at once' said a voice in the outer compound. It was Okonkwo's uncle, Uchendu. 'Are you mad?'

Okonkwo did not answer. But he left hold of Nwoye, who walked away and never returned.

The conflict between the white man's religion and the religion of the Ibo people of Umuofia and Mbanta is personified for Okonkwo in Nwoye, a Christian convert now at a missionary school in Umuofia from which Okonkwo is exiled. '. . . his son's crime stood out in stark enormity. To abandon the gods of one's father and go about with a lot of effeminate men clucking like old hens was the very depth of abomination. Suppose when he died all his male children decided to follow Nwoye's steps and abandon their ancestors?' But his distress is soon to go beyond the defection of his son. Animosity and hostile acts between the Christian missionaries and converts and the people of Mbanta was threatening to disrupt the entire way of life. And '. . . stories were gaining ground that the white man had not only brought a religion but also a government. It was said that they had built a place of judgment in Umuofia to protect the followers of their religion. It was even said that they had hanged one man who killed a missionary.' In these observations and rumours of the Ibos Achebe brings alive to the reader how what goes under the Western label 'colonialism' – the guise of conquest by means other than war itself – was seen, realised, experienced by the people themselves: how they visualised the church and the courthouse in their own words, their own ideas of social order. Okonkwo becomes active among the elders in their response to church and court. The decision finally is made to ostracise the Christian converts: the unity that had existed in each village through countless generations is fractured.

At this time Okonkwo's seven years of exile are about to end. After the cassava harvest he announces his farewell.

'I am calling a feast because I have the wherewithal. I cannot live on the bank of a river and wash my hands with spittle. My mother's people have been good to me and I must show my gratitude.' And so three goats were slaughtered and a number of fowls . . . It was like a wedding feast. There was foo-foo and yam pottage, egusi soup and bitter-leaf soup and pots and pots of palm wine.

An elder makes a speech. 'A man who calls his kinsmen to a feast does not do so to save them from starving. They all have food in their own homes . . . We come together because it is good for kinsmen to do so. You may ask why I am saying all this. I say it because I fear for the younger generation, for you young people because you do not understand how strong is the bond of kinship. You do not know what it is to speak with one voice. And what is the result? An abominable religion has settled among you. A man can now leave his father and his brothers. He can curse the gods of his father and his ancestors, like a hunter's dog that suddenly goes mad and turns on his master. I fear for you; I fear for the clan.'

Okonkwo has returned from exile.

. . . seven years was a long time to be away from one's clan. A man's place was not always there, waiting for him. As soon as he left, someone else rose and filled it. The clan was like a lizard: if it lost its tail it soon grew another . . . He knew that he had lost the chance to lead his warlike clan against the new religion, which he was told, had gained ground. He had lost the years in which he might have taken the highest titles in the clan. But some of these losses were not irreparable. He would return with a flourish, and regain the seven wasted years . . . the first thing he would do would be to rebuild his compound on a more magnificent scale.

If Nwoye is a traitor whose existence is no longer recognised by his father, that father would show his wealth by initiating his five other sons in the *ozo* society. 'Only the really great men in the clan were able to do this. Okonkwo saw clearly the high esteem in which he would be held, and he saw himself taking the highest title in the land.' Among his sons and daughters Ezinma is still his favourite child and he continues to wish she were a boy; as a compensation for what her strong character could have achieved as his son he envisages that her beauty and personality will attract a son-in-law who would be a 'man of authority within the clan'.

Returning to his clan and village, Okonkwo seems to have left behind, along with the years of exile, the Mbata elder's fearful warning. Okonkwo's vision of re-establishment is that within the traditional society which has in reality changed irreparably – the tail the lizard has grown is not the same as that of the old body grown whole again. There are many men and women in Umuofia who realise that 'The white man had indeed brought a lunatic religion, but he had also built a trading store and for the first time palm oil and kernel became things of great price, and much money flowed in Umuofia.' They have entered the world of production not only for their own consumption, but for sale and profit. '. . . And even in the matter of religion there was a growing feeling that there might be something in it after all, something vaguely akin to method in the overwhelming madness.'

The current white missionary, Mr Brown, was not over-zealous in his task of conversion to Christianity, he was a peacemaker 'who came to be respected even by the clan, because he trod softly on its faith. He made friends with some of the great men of the clan and on one of his frequent visits to the neighbouring villages he had been presented with a carved elephant tusk, which was a sign of dignity and rank.' And the numbers of converts to the church was steadily growing. One of the great men had given a son 'to be taught the white man's knowledge in Mr Brown's school'. Learning to read and write was an achievement, even if not on the same great level as the anklet of the clan's titles. '. . . it was not long before the people began to say that the white man's medicine was quick in working.'

Mr Brown's school produced results. A few months in it were enough to make a literate court messenger or even a court clerk. Some Umuofians became teachers or pastors as new schools and churches were built by the British. The establishment of colonial occupation provided such opportunities. But – 'From the very beginning religion and education went hand in hand.' If you wanted the one it had to be in the grasp of the other. Achebe's integrity as a writer in search of truth, and his honesty as a man, recognise that progress was real – in the forms of knowledge as it exists essential to the modern world in which Africa was so soon inevitably to become part; for gain or painful loss in terms of its own forms of knowledge and wisdom.

Achebe has the playwright's gift of making a conversation between people of opposing faiths and ideas an exciting to-and-fro. In Chapter 21 the missionary, Mr Brown, and the elder, Akunna, have a brilliant exchange on their different religious beliefs. Neither succeeds in converting the other, of course, but they learn more about their different beliefs; so do we, and about the apparently common human need to have a divine explanation and guidance for existence on earth.

Akunna says,

'You say there is one supreme God who made heaven and earth. We also believe in Him and call Him Chukwu. He made all the world and the other gods.'

'There are no other gods' said Mr Brown. 'Chukwu is the only God and all others are false. You carve a piece of wood . . . and you call it a god. But it is still a piece of wood.'

'The tree from which it came was made by Chukwu, as indeed

all minor gods were. But He made them for His messengers so that
we could approach Him through them. It is like you. You are the
head of your church.'

[Mr Brown:] 'No. The head of my church is God himself.'

[Akunna:] 'I know, but there must be a head in this world among
men.'

[Brown:] 'The head of my church in that sense is in England.'

'That is exactly what I am saying. The head of your church is in
your country. He has sent you here as his messenger . . .'

And now politics enters the verbal contest.

'Or let me take another example, the District Commissioner . . .
Your Queen [Queen Victoria] sends her messenger, the District
Commissioner. He finds he cannot do the work alone and so he
appoints *kotma* [assistants] to help him. It is the same with God
or Chukwu. He appoints the smaller gods to help him because his
work is too great for one person.'

[Mr Brown:] 'You should not think of Him as a person. It is
because you do that you imagine he must need helpers. And the
worst thing about it is that you give all the worship to the false
gods you have created.'

'That is not so . . . when his servants fail to help us we go to the
last source of hope. We appear to pay greater attentions to the little
gods but that is not so. We worry them because we are afraid to
worry their Master.'

. . . 'You said one interesting thing' said Mr Brown. 'You are
afraid of Chukwu. In my religion Chukwu is a loving Father and
need not be feared by those who do His will.'

'But we must fear him when we are not doing his will,' said
Akunna. 'And who is to tell his will? It is too great to be known.'

Okonkwo's homecoming has turned out 'not as memorable as he
had wished . . . Umuofia did not appear to have taken any special
notice of the warrior's return. The clan had undergone such
profound change during his exile that it was barely recognisable.

The new religion and government and the trading stores were very much in the people's eyes and minds . . .' Now he, too, 'mourned for the clan, which he saw breaking up and falling apart'.

The sense of presentiment which Achebe creates as we read takes the form of a new upheaval in the person of Mr Brown's successor. Reverend Smith 'saw things as black and white. And black was evil. He saw the world as a battlefield in which the children of light were locked in mortal conflict with the sons of darkness.'

There was a saying in Umuofia that 'as a man danced so the drums were beaten for him. Mr Smith danced a furious step and so the drums went mad. The over-zealous converts . . . now flourished in full favour.' This culminates in the disastrous clash between church and clan that has been gathering since Mr Brown left. One of the most heinous crimes against the clan was the sacrilege of unmasking an *egwugwu* – remember the masquerade of the embodied spirits of the ancestors? Now, during the masquerade ceremonies a Christian convert, Enoch, dares to do just this. An ancestral spirit has been desecrated by the act and the whole of Umuofia is thrown into violent confusion. Reverend Smith and the members of his flock decide to protect their fellow Christian, the violator, hiding him from the wrath of the band of *egwugwu* and the people. Smith stands before the mob and refuses to give up Enoch; there is terrible tension as it seems Smith is going to be killed. But the head of the ancestors, Ajofia, makes a dramatic intervention.

'The body of the white man, I salute you,' he said, using the language in which immortals spoke to men . . .' Tell the white man that we will not do him any harm,' he said to the interpreter, 'Tell him to go back to his house and leave us alone . . . But this shrine must be destroyed . . .'

. . . He turned to his comrades, 'Fathers of Umuofia, I salute you' and they replied with one guttural voice.

He turned again to the missionary. 'You can stay with us if you like our ways. You can worship your own god. It is good that a man should worship the gods and spirits of his fathers.'

The church is burned down.

For a few days the people's anger is pacified, although all go about armed with a matchet or gun in case of attack by Christian zealots. Then the District Commissioner sends for the leaders of Umuofia to come to his headquarters for what he calls a 'palaver'. Okonkwo is one of the six, warning the others to be fully armed. ' "An Umuofia man does not refuse a call" he said. [However:] "He may refuse to do what he is asked . . ." '

The District Commissioner wants to hear the elders' account of what happened at the masquerade. His manner, and the atmosphere, is calmly official, conveyed in the terse, cool style Achebe uses here. The leader of the six is about to speak, when the District Commissioner says, 'Wait a minute, I want to bring in my men so that they too can hear your grievances and take warning.' Like Okonkwo and his companions the reader is unprepared: 'It happened so quickly that the six men did not see it coming. There was only a brief scuffle, too brief even to allow the drawing of sheathed matchet. The six men were handcuffed and led into the guardroom.'

The District Commissioner:

'We shall not do you any harm if you agree to co-operate with us. We have brought a peaceful administration to you and your people so that you may be happy. If any man ill-treats you we shall come to your rescue. But we will not allow you to ill-treat others. We have a court of law where we judge cases and administer justice just as it is done in my own country under a great queen. I have brought you here because you joined together to molest others, to burn people's houses and their places of worship . . . I have decided that you will pay a fine of two hundred cowries.'

Imprisoned, after three days of hunger and bullying by the warders the six begin to talk about accepting the fine in exchange for their release.

'We should have killed the white man if you had listened to me' Okonkwo snarled.

'We could have been in Umuru now waiting to be hanged' [someone says to him.]

'Who wants to kill the white man?' asked a messenger who had just rushed in. 'You are not satisfied with your crime, but you must kill the white man on top of it.' He carried a strong stick and he hit each man a few blows on the head and back. Okonkwo was choked with hate.

The villagers collect two hundred and fifty cowries, just to be sure to appease the white man, unaware that the messengers will pocket the extra fifty – one of Achebe's ironic asides on the beginnings of corruption. Okonkwo goes home to his *obi* where Ezinma has come with food prepared for him; but he cannot eat; Ezinma and friends who have gathered see where the warder's whip has cut into his flesh.

During the night the gong of the village crier announces a meeting to be held next day. 'Everyone knew that Umuofia was at last going to speak its mind about the things that were happening.'

We find sleepless Okonkwo in a strange state of mind: '. . . he had brought down his war dress, which he had not touched since his return from exile. He had shaken out his smoked raffia skirt and examined his tall feather headgear. The bitterness in his heart was now mixed with a kind of childlike excitement.'

He lies on his bamboo bed and thinks about the treatment he received at the white man's court. 'If Umuofia decided on war, all would be well. But if they chose to be cowards he would go out and avenge himself.'

When Okonkwo and his fellow elder Obierika arrive at the meeting-place there are already so many people that – one of Achebe's uniquely original images – 'if one threw up a grain of sand it would not find its way to earth again'. Okonkwo distrusts the man Eginwanne who is due to address the crowd. Obierika asks.

'Are you afraid he would convince us not to fight?'

'Afraid? I do not care what he does to *you*. I despise him and those who listen to him. I shall fight alone if I choose.'

'But how do you know he will speak against war?'

'Because I know he is a coward.'

But before the man can begin to speak, Okika, 'a great man and a great orator', leaps to his feet and salutes his clansmen.

'Whenever you see a toad jumping in broad day-light, then you know that something is after its life ... When I saw you all pouring into this meeting from all quarters of the clan so early in the morning, I knew something was after our life ... This is a great gathering. No clan can boast of greater numbers of greater valour. But are we all here? I ask you: Are all the sons of Umuofia with us here? ... They are not. They have broken the clan and gone their several ways ... our brothers have deserted us and joined a stranger to soil our fatherland. If we fight the stranger we shall hit our brothers. Our fathers never dreamt of such a thing, they never killed their brothers. But a white man never came to them. So we must do what our fathers would never have done. Eneke the bird was asked why he was always on the wing and he replied: "Men have learnt to shoot without missing their mark and I have learnt to fly without perching on a twig." We must root out this evil. And if our brothers take the side of evil we must root them out too. And we must do it *now*.'

The tragic climax of this incomparable creation of a society in a time and place of inescapable, irrevocable upheaval and change closes the circle where it began: with the man whose life embodies it – Okonkwo. But it is not for me, it is for Chinua Achebe himself to tell you, for you to read for yourself the stunningly unexpected last pages of this story, the unforeseen consequences, decided by Okonkwo himself, of violent means he has resorted to under the pressures of that time and place, old Africa and the impact of colonial rule, with his own stormy personality fully revealed by the novelist. And there is a surprise postscript to the dramatic end of his story. Suddenly an about-turn in the viewpoint from which it has been told. Now the tragic events are as seen by the eyes and realised in the words of the District Commissioner, not the individuals of Umuofia with whom we've become so familiar. And I shan't reveal the final twist in the last sentence, with its challenge to the reader to laugh, and grimace with disgust, at the same time, at a white colonial mentality.

Things Fall Apart is a work that delights and shocks, rousing many questions. Does Chinua Achebe glorify the past? In this work of the imagination transforming history as poetry – lyrical imagery – common speech, anecdote, suffering, celebration, humour, the *extraordinariness* a great writer discovers in ordinary life – he makes no such sweeping judgements. He does not deny the inevitability of change; only looks into its ruthless processes with a steady and deeply human gaze.

In Chinua Achebe's second novel, Nwoye, Okonkwo's son converted to Christianity, appears, *No Longer At Ease* (the book's title) carrying continuity to the epic of dealing with change begun with *Things Fall Apart*. And later, with the brilliant satire, *A Man Of The People*, Achebe takes up the story when change has been established, four years after Nigeria's independence; his unmatched personal and intellectual nerve exposing, in the words of the narrator, Odili Samalu, 'with deepening dismay the use to which our hard-won freedom was being put by corrupt, mediocre politicians'. A dismay that comes to its conclusion in one of the most devastating final sentences of a book ever written: the words of Odili, 'I say, you died a good death if your life had inspired someone to come forward and shoot your murderer in the chest – without asking to be paid.'

2002

Joseph Conrad and *Almayer's Folly*

What does one expect to find, returning to a writer's first novel after years of reading his others have overlaid it? Outdistanced it?

The most widely read of Joseph Conrad's novels is *Heart Of Darkness*, whose very title has passed idiomatically into a metaphor for the evil of humankind in oppression of one another. As colonialism in its peculiarly historical form – conquest military, religious, commercial – began to near its end from the middle of the twentieth century, Conrad's narrator's recollection of what he found in a trading station up the Congo River in the late nineteenth century came to epitomise, for many readers and literary critics, *the* document of the colonialist phenomenon. For some it is the finest proof of Conrad's genius, laying bare with passion and irony that the heart of darkness is within the white exploiters of other peoples and not in the jungle Congolese whose hands were amputated by Belgian King Leopold's philanthropic company if they did not produce the required quota of wild rubber. For others, including the great African writer, Chinua Achebe, the novel is literary colonialism, representing Africans as savages with whom contact brings degradation for whites. Conrad's view of his novels set in the world outside Europe: 'The critic . . . seems to think that in these distant lands all joy is a yell and a war dance, all pathos is a howl and a ghastly grin of filed teeth, and that the solution of all problems is found in the barrel of a revolver or on the point of an assegai. And yet it is not so . . . There is a bond between us and that humanity so far away.'[1]

Conrad's other major novels are *Nostromo* (1904), *The Secret Agent* (1907) and *Under Western Eyes* (1911), read not alone for the transporting skill of Conrad's story-telling and evocation of land- and

---

1   Author's note to *Almayer's Folly*.

water-scapes, but for the astonishing relevance his themes have to our recent past and our present international preoccupations. The secret agent is not only to be found in Conrad's London just before the Russian Revolution; the way the agent operates matches for us the known but unseen presence of other secret agents of contemporary causes. Under Western eyes there is today the aftermath of Soviet Communism whose desperately dramatic beginnings and complex individual human psychology between the forces of faith and betrayal are his theme in St Petersburg. Nostromo, Italian immigrant shadily employed by the vast European-owned silver mine company which controls every aspect of life of the indigenous population of a South American country, is put to use between it and the abortive revolutions in which one set of indigenous corrupt politicians is toppled and replaced by another; a theme of the three-cornered act between capitalism, the poverty of underdevelopment and local corruption, seen every day on our millennial television.

So much prescience, so much genius of understanding the concept of progress and its perilous gains, the moral market of human action and feeling that we now posit as globalisation.

Are the themes that Conrad was to spend his life exploring for what ultimate meaning a single writer can hope to reach, already present in his first use of the imagination on what has been observed and/or experienced? His three great themes were the sea and its contributing rivers, colonialism and revolution. In some of his works all three are combined. A sailor from the age of seventeen, Conrad knew well the coast and rivers of the Malay Archipelago, and his first novel, *Almayer's Folly,* is created there as Sambir, on the Pantai River. Colonialism and the sea are indissolubly linked, here, as the superbly, cosmically indifferent sea is the means by which the trader-colonialist venture, Nietzsche's 'world as the will to power' comes about.[2] Revolutionary action as such is not the subject, but in the rivalry of the indigenous rajas co-opted on this

---

2 'The world is a will to power – and nothing else besides.' Nietzsche, *Will To Power*, translated by Walter Kaufmann, Random House, New York, 1967, p. 550. Quoted by Edward W. Said, 'Conrad And Nietzsche', in his collection *Reflections on Exile and Other Essays*, Harvard University Press, Cambridge, 2000, p. 75.

side or that of the Dutch, English and Arabs seeking control of the region, it is – for the post-colonial reader – foreshadowed.

Almayer's Folly is also a story of racism (which Conrad was to plumb further with *Heart of Darkness*, *Nostromo* and other works) in the ultimate, intimate expression of colonialism affecting individual relationships – an 'also' that grows with a complex narrative of other concerns with such insidious skill that its explicit dominance climaxes as a shock. There! says Conrad.

Captain Lingard, known on the coast as 'King of the Sea', runs supply ships for 'The Master', trader Hudig, whose warehouses are filled with 'gin cases and bales of Manchester goods', a demand for which has been created among the local Malays. Lingard is legendary for having 'discovered' (colonialists were always 'discovering' features known to indigenous peoples from ancient times) a river; a profitable trading highway whose location he keeps to himself. He takes a fancy to the young English-speaking Dutchman, Kaspar Almayer, who is a clerk in Hudig's warehouse. Almayer begins his association with Lingard clerking for him on sailings up and down the Archipelago. Lingard has an adopted daughter, a Malay girl taken from a boat in one of his forays against pirates; he demands that Almayer should marry her. 'And don't you kick because you're white. None of that with me! Nobody will see the colour of your wife's skin. The dollars are too thick for that . . . And mind you, they will be thicker yet before I die. There will be millions, Kaspar! And all for her – and for you, if you do as you're told.'

The beckoning dollars are too thick for qualms. Almayer marries the girl, is provided with a modest house and set up to run Lingard's trading post at Sambir.

It is a loveless match with a woman with whom colour and cultural differences are never overcome. Her relationship with Almayer is that of harridan, avaricious and aloof, knowing herself despised. But she gives him a daughter, Nina. Almayer's desire for wealth (he has built a pretentious house, symbol of wealth not yet attained, known on the Archipelago as 'Almayer's Folly', in which he doesn't live) becomes one with the passion of his love for this girl-child. On the first page of the novel, ageing Almayer's thoughts are

. . . busy with gold; gold he had failed to secure yet . . . He absorbed himself in his dream of wealth and power away from this coast . . . forgetting the bitterness of toil and strife in the vision of a great and splendid reward. They would live in Europe, he and his daughter. They would be rich and respected. Nobody would think of her mixed blood in the presence of her great beauty and his immense wealth.

Nina was sent away to Singapore to be educated as an English lady and has returned as a young woman, having been rejected by the woman in whose care she was because her beauty distracted the attention of suitors intended for the daughters of the house. In Sambir she lives strangely impassively, alienated from her mother despite her share of Malay blood, isolated in her father's adoration. The realisation of his dream of her future depends on his conviction that there is a mountain of gold deposits, Gunong Mas, to which he has planned a secret exploratory expedition with Dain, a raja's son from Bali. Lakamba, the local raja in Sambir, is also involved, for a share of the gold, while Lingard, who discovered it, left for Europe to raise capital for the venture and has not been heard of in years. Unknown to Almayer, Dain and Nina are attracted to each other.

All these intense personal preoccupations are going on within historico-political changes in the Archipelago. Almayer's trade has been taken over by the Arabs, his warehouse is empty, bankrupt. The Dutch, the British, the Arabs and the raja, the up-river Dyak tribes – all are embroiled in territorial and trade rivalries, which inevitably have extended to include smuggled gunpowder. Dain, on behalf of his father, the independent raja of Bali, in conflict with the Dutch, has first come to Sambir to buy it; Almayer has been persuaded to obtain the gunpowder, with the collusion of Lakamba, on Almayer's condition that Dain would help him in his enterprise at Gunong Mas. Almayer's friend, sea-captain Ford, would buy the gunpowder in Singapore and smuggle it from his ship to a brig by which Dain would bring it to his father. But a Dutch ship spies the brig, and when Dain runs it ashore inside the reefs, the Dutch follow in their boats, killing Dain's crew and losing two of their own men in the ensuing struggle. It is believed in Sambir that Dain is among the dead.

Nina's reaction to the news is mysterious to the reader; Conrad is master of the tension of withholding reasons for reactions. Stunned or impassive, it seems, she calmly brings her desolated father a glass of gin. 'Now it is all over, Nina.' The gold of Gunong Mas will never be his to take her away to 'a civilisation . . . a new life . . . your high fortune . . . your happiness'.

But Dain is alive; Nina in her great love, and her mother in her avarice (she has received a bride-price in dollars from him and sees her particular ambitions for her daughter to be realised as the wife of a future raja) revive him when he drags himself to the Almayer compound at night. They help him haul a body of one of the drowned men on to the river bank and the mother defaces it unrecognisably and forces Dain's ring and anklet upon a finger and leg. Dain is hidden in a nearby settlement. There a hawker of cakes, Taminah, who is in love with him although he has barely ever acknowledged her existence who discovers he is not the dead man and his life is in danger. She knows the white men – the Dutch – will be seeking him; she could tell them all. 'Did they wish to kill him? . . . no, she would say nothing . . . she would go to him and sell him his life for a smile, a gesture even . . . be his slave in far-off countries' away from her jealous hatred of Nina.

A party of Dutch officers arrives at Almayer's compound. They believe he knows where Dain is.

> 'And he killed white men!' [Nina says.]
>
>   'Yes, two white men lost their lives through that scoundrel's freak.'
>
>   '. . . Then when you get this scoundrel will you go? . . . Then I would get him for you if I had to seek him in a burning fire . . . I hate the sight of your white faces . . . I hoped to live here without seeing any other white face but this.'

She touches her father's cheek. The Dutch are led by drunk, embittered Almayer to the corpse that has been brought into the courtyard. 'This is Dain.'

With the connivance of Babalatchi, go-between of Lakamba, Nina and her mother, plans are made for Dain's escape. And here this first novel, like a rising gale bringing a tempest, elevates Conrad's powers as a writer to forecast – in my opinion to outreach – what he will achieve in works that were to come. For there is an almost prudish discretion, an averting of the eyes from any description of sexual love in Conrad's otherwise flouting of conventions in nineteenth-century literature. The love of father for daughter, mother for son, sister for brother, is generally his most explicit depiction of human emotion. But this work is the exception. At the reunion of Nina and Dain in his hideout, the wild answers of the body to the tensions and danger – the *unreasonableness*, in terms of the other kind of love, Almayer's vision of his daughter's fulfilment – are truly erotic. Their power clashes with the gigantic despair of Almayer become Lear; all pleading and violent reproach having failed to get her to stay with him, Almayer casts his desperate sorrow like a curse: 'I shall never forgive you, Nina; and tomorrow I shall forget you.'

Her love of Dain is a betrayal of her father's love; betrayal is increasingly to be a theme of Conrad's deeply delved situations between political imperatives and personal lives, as well as in the relationships between men and women. (It is fascinating to foresee, here, its apogee to come in *Under Western Eyes*.)

Where lesser writers are content to have reached in relative fulfilment, one finality, Conrad, even in this first novel, is not, although the vision of old Almayer on his knees obliterating the footprints of his daughter in the sand where she has walked away with her chosen love to a boat is one that leaves its imprint on the mind long after the book is closed. Almayer burns the past; burns down the fine house known as Almayer's Folly and dies, an opium smoker in the sole company of an old Chinaman. Shortly before his death he has said, to himself rather than to the rare visit of Captain Ford: 'I cannot forget.'

The curse was pronounced upon himself, as well as on his daughter. It is compounded, symbolic in his abandoned loneliness, by the situation itself as the alienation of the coloniser. So, for

Conrad, there is no finality in the way human lives *might have gone*, and he will spend the rest of his writing life in restlessly brilliant quest of their possibilities, the *realised* becoming the *unrealised*, to be followed in another and another working of the imagination on elusive reality. The constructions he evolved to do this began with his first novel, where he was then and thereafter to break the linear narrative. Almayer's story is not told sequentially, it moves as our human consciousness does, where what happened in the past seamlessly interrupts the present, and what is to come occurs presciently between these. He makes demands on the reader to follow him in the cut-and-paste interplay of that consciousness: an invigorating pleasure only great writers can offer. A nineteenth-century writer who died early in the twentieth, Conrad's work hurdled over modernism and practised post-modern freedom that was to enter literary theory long after his death.

Conrad's writing is lifelong questioning: even the title of this book poses one. What was 'Almayer's Folly'? The pretentious house never lived in, his obsession with gold, his obsessive love for his daughter, whose cogenitors, the Malay woman's race, he despised? All three? As if to answer some of these questions, Conrad did something else highly original, if doubtful in its success as an example of his work. A year after the publication of *Almayer's Folly* in 1895, he produced – what shall I call it – a prologue-novel to it, *An Outcast Of The Islands*, in which Almayer and his then small daughter are also central characters. But I don't advise reading Conrad in the way he obviously did not choose to be read; don't start with *An Outcast Of The Islands*; open the first pages of Conrad's magnificent literary creation by taking up *Almayer's Folly*.

2002

A Coincidence of Wills?

There comes a time in a reading life when you realise – there, on your bookshelves, are books you may never re-read. Books that once changed your sense of being. That opened your eyes, your understanding of human emotions, the context of your consciousness in the world.

Proposing the literature of the imagination as truth out of the reach of histories, I've often said 'If you want to know about Napoleon's famous retreat from Moscow, you have to read *War and Peace*, not a history book.'

Now facing me is the scuffed, monumental one-volume *War and Peace*. When did I last read it, and when shall I read it again – ever?

So now I have. And I understand that just as you discover new meaning in situations that recur in your life as changing social and political mores contain you, so every time you re-read a great work you discover something you missed because you and an earlier period were not ready for it: a hidden message for the particular present.

Count Lev Nikolayevich Tolstoy was born in 1828 and the novel was published in 1864. The time-span it covers is that of the Napoleonic wars in Russia from 1805 to 1812. It therefore chronicles events that happened before he was born. He was not writing about his own time, and I'm not reading about my own time. What the author and I have in common is that we are illuminating, each his own time, with intimations for the present that were there in the past. For him about 52 years distant; for me in 2003, 191 years.

The grandeur of the story moves from society salons around Tsar Alexander I, with the intrigues of love, its concomitant bargaining power in money and noble names, to the battlefields where none of these counts in snow, pain, hunger and death. The themes run concurrently, with fictional characters mixed with historical ones, invented gossip with actual military despatches. Tolstoy was a post-modernist nearly two centuries ago; his fiction brilliantly appropriated anything it demanded: life itself is incongruity.

Among the characters who emerge from the salons, Pierre Bezukhov is the most extraordinarily alive for me. He is rich, a count if only by a nobleman's liaison with a mistress; educated abroad, he is of no particular career. He himself makes a misalliance, falling in love and marrying the *femme fatale*, Helen. The choice of the name a touch of Tolstoy's wry humour. She is unfaithful, and there begins what was latent in Pierre's character, the examined life as a search for existential meaning. He tries Freemasonry (in the 1960s he would have been barefoot chanting Hare Krishna in the street), he tries good works among slave-peasants, his disillusion with materialism foresees the discontents of the well-endowed swallowing Ecstasy in our millennium of great riches and greater poverty. For Pierre the war against Napoleon's invasion of Russia was his saviour. First Napoleon's prisoner of war, then ragged and hungry in the ruins of Moscow, he finds among his fellow wretches that the will to live is itself the joy in life.

But it is not the bold and subtle understanding of personal conflicts that makes this 139-year-old novel contemporary. It is its amazing prescience of the nature of endless violence, the confusion and hopelessness of its persistent use to solve human problems between peoples and nations, multiplying them down the centuries.

Tolstoy calls into question the cause of catastrophic events being attributed to a single symbolic individual. A Napoleon, Hitler – now, for us, a Bin Laden, a Saddam Hussein. 'To the question as to what is the real causation of historical events . . . the course of this world depends on the coincidence of the wills of all those who are concerned in the issues . . .' The world, in 1812, was what its peoples made it, not Napoleon or Alexander I, as ours is what we have made and are making of it. The hollowness of victories achieved by violence is there when Napoleon retreats from Moscow, and the Russian peasants come in from the country to loot from their own people; it is there when we see the same desperate moral breakdown in the Congo, Côte d'Ivoire, Kosovo, Burundi, every month somewhere new. On the day 80,000 men, Russians, Frenchmen, were killed at Borodino, 'Napoleon neither fired a shot nor killed a man'. This is not the old fact that the leaders sit safe while they send Everyman out to kill or be killed. Tolstoy implies, beyond time and changing circumstances, the days of empires become our day of globalisation, that as individuals we bear responsibility for our world, which creates symbolic messianic politicians and leaders, taking us into chaos and foretelling our own corruption.

Re-reading Tolstoy's book is to realise that we live, not as a brave new millennium so much as an epilogue to what is revealed in that book of the senseless, persistent suffering and demoralisation of violence as the inhuman condition.

2003

Witness – Past or Present?

Like all witnesses to human acts that come second-hand, the reactions of visitors to museums dedicated to horrors perpetrated in the past, differ.

The United States Holocaust Museum in Washington opened in 1993. The Apartheid Museum in Johannesburg, 2001. The Jewish Museum in Berlin, 2001. While no one questions the need for such institutions to confront us with a past still within living memory of many, there are criticisms that come between awed acceptance and total dismissal of the achievement.

I think we have first to consider the way in which the definition 'holocaust' has come to be dispersed in meaning quite far from the dictionary one: the intent of genocide. We now report any massacre between factions, nations, as a holocaust, though the violent intention is to gain power over others, not wipe them off the face of the earth. This brings into question whether the old narrow definition was correct, and a case is demonstrable in the differences between the three museums. The Washington museum illustrates a holocaust, the intention to kill all Jews in Germany and the countries it occupied. The Berlin museum and the Johannesburg museum share with it a related but different, double purpose: the Jewish museum chronicles the political and cultural history of Jews in Germany before the Nazi extermination came into practice, as well as the experience of that period; the apartheid museum creates the African pre-colonial background, the period of early white settlement, the effect of exploitation, industrialisation, loss of land tenure on Africans, as well as their political subjection, and focuses on the black population's struggle to attain ultimate freedom. Perhaps the present-day meaning of 'holocaust' extends to any attempt by any means to kill the right of a people to live without discrimination and oppression?

The three museums are all subject to criticism in both their shared and specific aspects. We visitors are onlookers at a distance of time and space. The process called perspective.

A recurrent criticism of the Holocaust Museum is that a museum of the Nazi holocaust should be one encompassing and dedicated to the experience of all who suffered it, six million Jews, five million anti-Nazi activists, homosexuals, Gypsies and others. The counter-argument is that the Nazis' avowed holocaust was the culmination of a unique 2,000-year-old history of persecution of Jews. The lingering smell of the shoes of gas-oven victims, relics in the museum, perhaps brings ominous understanding, *unspecified*, of what genocide means.

For eighteen months after the opening, the Jewish Museum in Berlin was empty. I visited when the exhibits were in place, but there was something new to me – the impact of architecture as a blow-in-the-chest statement. Daniel Libeskind's building is an affront in itself: the affront of harassment, enclosure, the persecution of walls, material and ideological. Some opinions are that it should have been left empty, in that statement. The exhibits attempt to recreate the life, culture and beliefs of German Jews since medieval times, even earlier. Critical debate has been rough:

the museum creates 'a Disney world aesthetic',[1] it is 'a gigantic misunderstanding . . . a failure . . . simplifying the facts'. Yet it is demonstrably honest about the uncomfortable facts of the assimilation attempts of German Jews in the nineteenth and early twentieth centuries, as well as their remarkable contributions to German cultural life – which drained away under Nazi persecution, mainly to the benefit of the United States. There is displayed the German-Jewish Christmas tree, and the silver basin and ewer provided by a prominent family who desperately tried to hedge prescience of a coming fate by having some of their sons baptised Christian while the others remained Jewish. The holocaust documents and photographs are somehow more personal than the evidence in the Washington museum. There is criticism that this testimony of the dead needs to be completed by accounts of the lives of German Jews in the diaspora; apparently the extension is planned.

A casino deal was the origin of the Apartheid Museum in Johannesburg. Bidders for a gambling licence were awarded it on condition they include in their amusement complex a 'social responsibility' project. The fact that the museum shares a site with a giant roller-coaster offends people like me, who find this demeaning of the dignity of the South African freedom struggle – but the fact is we, our African National Congress majority government and the political movements to which we belong, talked about but never achieved an apartheid museum for ourselves. Once your back is turned on the roller-coaster-casino complex, the museum building, work of South African architects, has much of the impact of the Libeskind one, indeed recalls it, bringing two forms of stark racism appropriately together, the Nazi and the apartheid.

At the entry you buy a plastic card: if you are white, it states you are black, if you are black, it labels you white. You enter through separate adjoining spaces; so black experiences the privilege of being white, and white experiences the discrimination of being black. The journey within the museum has this striking underlying theme, with the documents, the vocabulary of discrimination, its

1 Jorg Lau, *Die Zeit*, 2000 (no precise date given).

crudity and cruelty. But emphasis, finally, is on resistance – the freedom movements and their heroes. There is much criticism of who and what is left out. Some see the museum as concentrating on the role of the African National Congress in liberation, although there was an alliance of the ANC with the South African Indian Congress and the South African Communist Party. White liberals say they have been ignored; the Pan-African Congress finds its role in liberation underplayed; there are faces and names, deeds, missing or passed over in a TV clip.

What is the object of such museums? It's accepted that by confrontation with the gross inhumanity of the past in the Washington Holocaust Museum, the Berlin Jewish Museum, the Johannesburg Apartheid Museum, what we witness we shall never be any party to. It shall never happen again.

But while facing the past, it *is* happening again in parts of our globalised world; has been happening: from ethnic cleansing in Bosnia, tribal genocide in Rwanda, to the devastation of lives in conflict between the Christian faithful and the Muslim faithful in Côte d'Ivoire, the destruction of Palestinian lives by Israel and the taking of Israeli lives by Palestinian suicide bombers. A visitor to the Washington Holocaust Museum remarked to writer Philip Gourevitch in 1995, 'We know the atrocities that happen in the world right now. And what are we doing? We're sitting in a museum.'[2]

We're still there, eight years later.

2003

---

2   Philip Gourevitch, 'What They Saw at the Holocaust Museum', *New York Times Magazine*, 2 December 1995.

Fear Eats the Soul

Can there be the phenomenon of a world state of mind?
Some such surely has existed for the past many weeks,
except, perhaps, in those enclaves, isolated by nature – if impenetrable forest, impassable ice haven't been finally invaded by information technology. There used to be people who were come upon in their remote fastnesses, after wars, unaware that war had happened. We have a conscious world as never before; awareness of an impending war between the dominant power among nations and an opposing power of amorphous capacity (who knows for sure who will join forces in religious solidarity) has been an all-pervading change of global climate which we all have breathed in. On an ostensible issue of weapons of mass destruction many reactions come forth: anger, belligerence, disbelief, holy outrage from the Faithful of Democracy and the Faithful of Islam. Among enemies, fearing poison gas and unseen infection by disease (for won't the gas blow back upon, won't the disease infect those who distribute it) there's a miasma of that climate no special clothing, no masks and plastic-hung shelters can protect against. Fear. It's unacknowledged; shared by friend and foe if nothing else is.

One looks for some sort of wisdom in how others have contemplated fear. There's the gung-ho of Franklin D. Roosevelt's inaugural address back in 1933. Was it Hitler's rise to power, so distantly European, he had in mind when he pronounced 'Let me assert my firm belief that the only thing we have to fear is fear itself.' Sounds hollow now, after new forms of human extermination we've discovered for ourselves since then.

Can fear be a force for the good?

Remember the old adage 'Best safety lies in fear'. But that, it will be morally countered, condones cowardice; shrinking from the duty to defend at risk the values your society holds. Thucydides was the first philosopher I educated myself with as an adolescent; it's natural that I go back to him now and find in an old notebook another take on the phenomenon of fear. 'That war is an evil is something that we all know, and it would be pointless to go on cataloguing all the disadvantages involved in it. No one is forced into war by ignorance, nor, *if he thinks he will gain from it, is kept out by fear.*' (My italics.) The mass protests against the United States war on Iraq are made on the conviction that the gain, by war, of control of the world's second greatest oil fields is not 'kept out' by fear that thousands of the people categorised as 'enemy led' will be killed and body bags of the righteous young victors will never require fuel oil again.

'Fear has many eyes and can see underground' observes Cervantes. Didn't the fear of what is happening – the roar is in our ears – begin within us when 11 September 2001 buried the invincible? If time is on a plane of existence great writers sometimes penetrate, doesn't T. S. Eliot wander ahead over Ground Zero when he writes, way back in 1922, 'And I will show you something different from either/Your shadow at morning striding behind you/or your shadow at evening rising to meet you; I will show you fear in a handful of dust.'

I am one of those who live far from the terrible threat of strike and retaliation across oceans and skies. But I am not in that now non-existent enclave of isolation, out-of-this-world. And like many who are distant from the continents of battle, I have nevertheless a personal stake in this war: someone closest to me lives with his young family in the vulnerable heart of New York. He tells me that the children's school has notified parents that the school basement has been equipped as a shelter, with water supplies and an adapted ventilation system that will keep out noxious elements. Some people, he says, have packed up and left the city, the obvious target of violence, direct or insidious. Is this ceding ground to those who threaten? Or is it a sensible option for people who have the means to absent themselves from their wage-earning posts and have some place to go: somewhere safe. Safe: who can tell what and where is beyond striking distance of the unconventional weapons we are told come from laboratories, not armouries?

I ask: What are you going to do?

So he reminds me: What did you and your kind do during the crises of apartheid, when there was danger of being arrested by the political police, or having some right-wing fanatic put a bomb to blow you up in your car?

Go carry on with your life.

Dangers are relative, over time and distance; fear is relative, whether it menaces a multitude or a single life, but it always demands the same answers: a yes, or a no. Capitulate within oneself, or refuse to submit to attrition, fear that eats the soul.

2003

Living with a Writer

There seems to be some confusion, here: I *am* the writer. So I can only conclude that I shall be relating what it is like to be living with myself. Not that there isn't a situation cited: everyone is faced with the basic problem of the self. A secret intimacy which, it is said, influences all others. First Know Thyself. Perhaps the most difficult relationship of all?

I've had to live with myself through a long life as a writer and as a woman. It wouldn't have been much different existentially had that life been between the writer and a man. Whatever the gender, we writers have to make, no matter how, clear distinction between what life-space is reserved for the writer and what must be that of the – what shall I term it? – socio-biological life. Sounds grandiose, that term, but I can't settle for 'emotional life' because there are strong emotions involved in the product of the writing life.

The apportionment of time and attention means self-discipline of a very strict kind. A journalist has a deadline to meet. The poet, novelist is her/his own boss. The publisher may specify, in a contract, when the manuscript shall be delivered, but this is on the writer's estimate, as task-master, of when it shall be fulfilled by the workings of an imagination which keeps no clock or calendar. If the advance payment runs out before the work is achieved, that's the nature of the gap between creativity and commerce.

It goes without saying that no writer waits for what people who are not writers call inspiration. Not that it doesn't come; but usually not in the hours set down for the writing table, the type-writer, word processor (or whatever the tool may be). Those hours are for the transformation of something already occurred, themes that take hold, beneath some other activity or situation. Waking up in the middle of the night. Ceasing to hear what the babble in a bar or a meeting is about. A displacement to a level of another irresistible, intense concentration elsewhere. I think I began to write, relating narratives, conversations, impressions silently to myself as a child sitting in the back of my parents' car on drives long or short. Now I often have this same sort of experience on long-distance flights; between a *here* and a *there*, the demands of exchange with other people, I'm living with myself: the self of the individual imagination. (The collective imagination is what you and I enter through literature, theatre, films.)

I believe writers, artists in general, have something of the monster in their personality. If selfishness is monstrous. Like most writers – I'll guarantee – I've had to accept in myself that I would have to without compunction put the demands of my writing gener-ally before human obligations – except, perhaps, while falling in love. On the principle that every businessman or woman executive is protected from random visitors and telephone calls by a guard of receptionist and secretary, I long ago made it clear to everyone, even those closest and dearest to me, that during my working hours no one must walk in on me, expect to reach me. Since the house where I live with others is also my workplace, I've made as an exception only an interruption to tell me the house is on fire. When my children were too young for boarding school my writing hours were those when they were absent at day school, and during the holidays the monster-writer decreed that they keep out of sight and sound during those same hours. But I got what I no doubt deserved one day when my small son transgressed, playing outside near my window, and I heard him reply to a friend's question 'What's your mother's job?' – 'She's a typist.' His response to living with a writer.

I've found myself to be a secretive person to live with. I don't know if this is general, for writers. I have been unable to share with anyone the exigencies, the euphoria at having arrived at what I wanted in my work or the frustration at finding it lacking. I cannot understand how the great Thomas Mann could bring himself to read the day's stint of writing aloud to his assembled family each evening. I've always been convinced no one could reach what I really was saying in a piece of writing until I had satisfied myself *finally* that it was the best I could possibly do with it.

My man, Reinhold Cassirer, with whom I lived for forty-eight years, sharing everything else in our lives, never saw a story or novel of mine in the making, although he was always the first to read it when it was done. He completely respected and protected this, my privacy.

A novel might take as long as three or more years. He should have been the one to respond to what it must have been like, living with a writer.[1]

2003

Edward Said

If the great contemporary intellectuals can be counted on one hand, Edward Said is the index finger pointing to some of the most profound existential questions of our time, and going back, invaluably, to search out their beginnings. What we humans have made of ourselves in the collective that is the world.

The obituaries have focused on the aspect of Said's life most newsworthy today: the tragedy of the Israeli-Palestinian conflict.

---

1 Reinhold Cassirer died in 2001.

The great conviction, dedication, activist faith of Said's life was, indeed, the Palestinian cause. He served it with courage and a nobility that excluded fundamentalism of any kind.

To say that there was more to his achievement than that is not to demean its urgency and the irreplaceable loss of its best spokesperson. He stood for real justice and peace for both Palestinians and Israelis.

But Said's unique brilliance was that he was the most eclectic intellectual of our time. He fused extraordinary literary talent – the writer, master of the beauty of language – with a philosophical, political, cultural, psychological quest of human motivation, bringing power-politics and the third eye of creative intuition into a synthesis of revelation. Proof that *we* cannot be understood in our motivations – the world cannot be understood – one without the other.

He was an academic of celebrated originality of mind; students did not fall asleep in Professor Said's seminars. He was by avocation a pianist of performance level, sometimes playing under the baton of his friend, Daniel Barenboim.

Reading his works, one is dismayed to be confronted with the limits of one's own supposedly wide reading: he had read everything in a number of languages and would pass on the benefit with lucidity and grace. Above all, along with enormous erudition, Edward Said had an *intelligence of feeling*. It glowed through his works and his physical presence.

In his greatest book, *Orientalism*, and its equally matchless successor-cum-sequel, *Culture and Imperialism*, he analyses the concept of Otherness, definitive in Orientalism. Orientalism is the projection, on people other than oneself, of one's idea of what they are.

Said in this marvellous work reveals Orientalism's origins and development from ancient times, in the textual representations conceptualised from the fragmentary experience of wandering explorers, the romantic and religious mysticism (the Orient an artefact, belonging to the past), the writings of poets and novelists, from Gérard de Nerval to Flaubert, Jane Austen to Conrad, the philologists and anthropologists who made a scientific subject out of it.

'The Orient' first referred to Islam and later encompassed Africa. India, Asia. Anywhere there were faiths, colours and cultures not Western and white. Said writes:

> Modern Orientalism derives from secularising elements in 18th century European culture . . . the expansion of the Orient further east geographically and further back temporally . . .
>
> Reference points were no longer Christianity and Judaism . . . the capacity for dealing historically (and not reductively, as a topic of ecclesiastical politics) with non-European and non-Judeo-Christian cultures was strengthened as history itself was conceived of more radically than before; to understand Europe properly meant also understanding the objective relations between Europe and its own previously unreachable temporal and cultural frontiers.

The result was 'the Orient henceforth would be *spoken for*'.

The precept on which colonialism is justified, out of Orientalism, was established. The Orient-Other is in the same position to this day, striving to speak and be heard for itself in the global structures that are attempting to re-form a world of Haves and Have-nots. For still, Said writes: 'The white middle-class westerner believes it is his human prerogative not only to manage the world but also to own it, just because by definition "it" is not quite as human as "we" are. There is no purer example than this of dehumanised thought.'

New millennium Orientalism is surely United States President George Bush's government's crusade to decide 'for them' what the Iraqi people are and what their constitution and future should be.

In his 2003 preface to the twenty-fifth anniversary edition of *Orientalism*, Said writes of the present 'threatened by nationalist and religious orthodoxies disseminated by the mass media as they focus ahistorically and sensationally on the distant electronic wars that give viewers the sense of surgical precision but in fact obscure the terrible suffering produced by "clean" warfare.'

Said reveals the full concept of Orientalism in its ultimate avatar, evolved through its justification of colonialism, imperialism, to western hegemony in the new world order: a sum of inhumanly divisive, disruptive forces.

His life was subject to many of them. He was born in Jerusalem sixty-seven years ago, uprooted when a child from his natal country, as a Palestinian, and was acculturated to the West through education in England and the US. Yet in his person he posits unchallenge-ably, with the magnificent achievement of his own life-conduct and scholarship, the thesis self-evident in his enthrallingly moving memoir, *Out of Place*.

The title proposes that to be so, in a sense, may be a way to better understanding between individuals and nations, an open state of being attained against the monolithic cages of nationalism, religion and closed cultures.

He *used* these multiple identities, made them into the crea-tion of a complete personality, a man of genius with an invaluable perspective to offer the world. In him, contradictions become a way of grasping something of the elusive truth that is somewhere in human coexistence.

I hope that without presumption, as his friend, and disciple in all I learned from him up to his last days, I may see as Edward's credo the words of Dimitry, on trial in Dostoevsky's *The Brothers Karamazov*. We are accountable to life 'because we are all responsible for all'.

2003

With Them You Never Know

Albert Memmi

It is hardly usual to begin an introduction with a caveat of the limitations of the work it prefaces. In the case of Albert Memmi's *The Colonizer and The Colonized*, I believe this is necessary in order to establish the classic work's continuing validity. That validity is in its invaluable presentation and brilliant analysis of the condition of colonised people, the results of practical *enactment* of man's inexhaustible capability of inhumanity to man; in this classic aspect of power, the work is timeless. What Equiano[1] wrote of this power in 1789, what Memmi wrote of it in the late 1950s, is as true in our new millennium. Slavery was not abolished, it evolved into colonisation. Retrospect has not altered, by perspective, the meaning of what was done to subject peoples in their own land.

That said, Memmi's study was first published in 1957, before Ghana became the first colonially occupied country in Africa to become independent. The book therefore pre-dates by what ideological forms, specifically in terms of participation of Leftist colonisers with the colonised, freedom from colonisation has been achieved in many countries, over the forty-six years since then. Memmi's predictions about the role of the Left have been proved a fallacy.

He begins his book with 'A Portrait of the Colonizer', but in view of my homage to the nature of the work's achievement, despite its shortcomings, I'll reverse the order of chapters and begin with Chapter Two, 'Portrait of the Colonised'. I take permission for this chronological impertinence from the very first sentence of the chapter: 'Just as the bourgeoisie proposed an image of the proletariat, the existence of the colonizer requires that an image of the colonized be suggested.' That image is where colonisation begins; its premise, its ikon.

The subtitle of the chapter has the rider 'The *Mythological* Portrait of the Colonized' (my italics) – Memmi's wry comment on the 'dialectic exalting the colonizer and humbling the colonized'. In colonialist mythology the colonised is a litany of faults and inadequacies. He's unbelievably lazy – at the same time this authorises his low wages. Skilled work is done by the coloniser's compatriots, imported; and if Memmi's typecast of their physique and demeanour is a caricature, it's sketched with the quick flash of humour. Irony makes its point in that light: 'The colonized . . . is asked only for his muscles; he is so poorly evaluated that three or four can be

1 Olaudah Equiano, *Equiano's Travels: The Interesting Narrative of the Life of Olaudah Equiano or Gustavus Vassa the African.*

taken on for the price of one European.' Memmi turns the reader
to the conclusion left out of the coloniser's evaluation: '. . . one
can wonder, if their [the coloniseds'] output is mediocre, whether
malnutrition, low wages, a closed future, a ridiculous conception
of a role in society, does not make the colonized uninterested in
his work'. The coloniser having established that the colonised is a
'hopeless weakling', from this, Memmi shows, comes the concept
of a 'protectorate': it is in the colonised's own interest that he be
excluded from management functions, and that those heavy responsibilities be reserved for the coloniser. 'Whenever the coloniser adds
. . . that the colonised is a wicked, backward person, he thus justifies his police and his legitimate severity . . . The humanity of the
colonised, rejected by the coloniser, becomes opaque . . . Useless . . .
to try to forecast the coloniseds' actions: ("They are unpredictable!"
"With them you never know!").' Memmi chips in to these too-often
overheard remarks: 'The colonized must indeed be very strange, if
he remains so mysterious after years of living with the coloniser.'

'The colonised means little to the coloniser . . . The colonised is
not this, is not that.' This mythological portrait Memmi draws is
of a stunning negation. For the coloniser, the colonised is nobody.

It is not only the rough-and-ready man who saw the conquered
and colonised as the ultimate other. An intellectual began his work
in Africa on the same premise. In 1928 a psychiatrist from Europe
practising in a mental hospital for South African black men 'made
a startling discovery . . . the manifestations of insanity . . . are
identical in both natives and Europeans . . . This discovery made
me inquisitive to know if the working fundamental principles of
the mind in its normal state were not also the same.'[2] But maybe
Cecil Rhodes the empire-builder had the last word in assessment of
the human worth of the colonised: 'I prefer land to niggers.'[3]

---

2   Wulf Sachs, *Black Hamlet – The Mind of an African Negro Revealed by Psychoanalysis*,
Geoffrey Bles, London, 1937; Johns Hopkins University Press, Baltimore, 1996; Witwatersrand
University Press (with a new introduction by Saul Dubow and Jacqueline Rose), Johannesburg,
1996.

3   Cecil Rhodes, attributed by Olive Schreiner, *Trooper Peter Halket of Mashonaland*, T. Fisher
Unwin, London, 1897.

'We should not, however, delude ourselves . . . by thinking that if only the colonizers would have been more generous, more charitable, less selfish, less greedy for wealth, then everything would have been very much better than it is now – for in that case they would not have been colonizers.'[4]

'Does The Colonial Exist?' The title of the first part of Memmi's analysis of the coloniser brings a semantic question to be got out of the way. Memmi's use – or perhaps his translator's use, in this English edition of the book – of the terms 'colonial' and colonizer' as interchangeable. But a *colonialist* is one who advocates the policy of colonisation; further, he may be one delegated, within the Colonial Service, to administer that policy, a colonial functionary in the European power's governance of territory taken by conquest of the original inhabitants. He is not a citizen of that territory, *his* country remains one across the world. A *coloniser* is a settler in the conquered territory, coming from another country but taking up residence and citizenship (usually granted after a period specified by the colonialist power). He occupies and owns, either under a settler dispensation to extend the 'mother' country's domains, or purchased from it, land taken by that colonialist power from the indigenous people. The coloniser regards himself as a permanent inhabitant. The difference is important. Memmi does have a subcategory to his concept of the colonial/coloniser. This one, identified as the 'European living in a colony having no privileges' – a class distinction within the ruling class that places him barely above the colonised – certainly didn't exist in the colonial countries I have known. The mere fact of skin colour guaranteed kith-and-kin privileges decreed by the colonial power. The category may have been singular to Tunisia.

It is with the coloniser's indubitable existence that Memmi's study recedes honourably to the shelves of the classic past. He sees the coloniser as one taking 'simply a voyage towards an easier life'.

---

4 O. Mannoni, *Prospero and Caliban: The Psychology of Colonization*, translated by Pamela Powesland, Praeger, New York, 1964.

There follows a fascinating account of the components of that easy life of the time – servants, climate, automatic qualification for superior status over the multitude. What Edward W. Said has defined as 'How you supply the forces of world-wide accumulation and rule with a self-confirming ideological motor.'[5] The coloniser, Memmi continues 'has not yet become aware of the historic role which will be his. He is lacking one step in his new status . . . the origin and significance of this profit . . . This is not long in coming. For how could he fail to see the misery of the colonised and the relation of that misery to his own comfort?' The colonised kept underfoot are 'no longer a simple component of geographical or historical decor. They assume a place in his life . . . He cannot even resolve to avoid them.' He must constantly live in relation to them, for it is this very alliance which enables him to lead the life which he decided to 'look for in the colonies; it is this relationship which creates privilege'. Memmi posits that the coloniser soon 'knows, in his own eyes as well as those of his victim, that he is a usurper . . . He must adjust to being both regarded as such, and to this situation.'

What is missing in this analysis is what any coloniser knows – yes, I speak as a coloniser's offspring – that the coloniser justified his/her situation by asserting that the colonisers brought enlightenment, technical as well as religious, to the indigenous people living in the heart of darkness. (It is almost obligatory to make a bow to Conrad, here.) On the coloniser's scale there was a trade-off balance, a straight deal that could ignore morality. Memmi in turn seems to ignore this forced deal in its psychological impact on both sides. (He deals with it only in his 1965 preface.)

Studying the coloniser, Memmi gives much attention to the grades of privilege he says are accorded in the colonial situation, and it is here that it is most evident his perspective was coming from the Maghrib, culturally arabised territories, while only propositionally extended to the rest of the African continent and colonised countries everywhere. This leads to conclusions that do not necessarily hold good for colonisation generally. He draws interesting

---

5   Edward W. Said, *Culture and Imperialism*, Knopf, New York, 1993.

distinctions between the societal positions arrived at by colonisers coming from various countries to Tunisia and Algeria, for example, Italians, Maltese, Corsicans, Spaniards and Jews (who even if they are from Morocco evidently are from that non-place, the diaspora). These are candidates for assimilation at various levels. The different levels of their acceptance by the already settled coloniser population – what the colonised thought of the continuous invasion did not count – didn't apply in any of the African countries I know. In these, if you were white you were welcomed by the colonial government and colonisers to shore up the white population, though as the colonial powers had been officially Christian since the Crusades, you were more welcome if you were of that faith. In South Africa right up to the end of the apartheid regime in 1994, whites only were accepted as immigrants. Once legally established, their situation in 'black' Africa was that of the indiscriminate privilege of being white. Even Jews did not, as Memmi avers in general, find themselves 'rejected by the colonized' and sharing 'in part the physical conditions of the colonised, having a communion of interests with him'. In South Africa, which was to become the most prosperous and highly industrialised of countries on the African continent, some Jewish colonisers[6] became founders of the gold and diamond industry, and their only share of the condition of the colonised was to employ them in their thousands to work underground as migrant labourers. Christian colonisers made the laws that ensured this labour supply, enforcing through taxes a cash economy in place of traditional land-based agricultural sufficiency.

Many of Memmi's conclusions, prognostications one might call them, have not been borne out by events. He considers the options of the coloniser, once he is aware 'under the growing habit of privilege and illegitimacy' that 'he is also under the gaze of the usurped'. There is 'his inevitable self-censure'. With the chapter

---

6   Generations later, among South African whites who joined the South African black liberation struggle, Jews were prominent, including Dennis Goldberg, sentenced to life imprisonment, Albie Sachs (post-apartheid Constitutional Court judge for fifteen years in free South Africa) who lost a leg and the sight of one eye when a bomb was hidden in his car, and Ruth First who was killed by a parcel bomb. Both these acts the work of the apartheid forces.

'The Colonizer Who Refuses' it is assumed that he is in this crisis of conscience for the sins of the fathers and his own. And now one must pause to set aside another of the confusions of terminology in the work. Memmi has visualised the *coloniser* as one in this condition who 'immediately thinks of going home' but 'being compelled to wait until the end of his contract, he is liable to get used to the poverty [of the colonised]'. That man cited is a *functionary* of the colonial government, there is an official limit to his confrontation with guilt, he will leave it behind when his span of duty ends. The *coloniser* cannot be seen as one with him; the coloniser has no contract that will elapse. He has no determined span of the life he has been living; he is committed to it. Many continued to live as before, counting on the mother country to hold off change, keep the colonised at bay indefinitely.

Another coloniser 'no longer agrees to become what his fellow citizens have become'. He is the genuine 'Colonizer Who Refuses'. He remains – but vows not to accept the role of protagonist of colonisation. He will reject that disgraced position.

But how? Here Memmi's analysis leaps – as it does impressively when he's using his philosopher's vision to relate a specific to an eternal human situation. 'It is not easy to escape mentally from a concrete situation, to refuse its ideology while continuing to live with its actual relationships. From now on, he lives his life under the sign of a contradiction which looms at every step, depriving him of all coherence and all tranquillity . . . What he is actually renouncing is part of himself . . . How can he go about freeing himself of the halo of prestige which crowns him?' If the coloniser persists in refusal 'he will learn that he is launching into an undeclared conflict with his own people'. Granted; but he will also discover others among colonisers who are ready to oppose, to one or another degree of courage, the regime that is defined in its very name – colonialism – as a give-away of injustice.[7]

History has proved that there were more options open to the

7 A colony: in Roman usage 'a settlement of Roman citizens in a hostile or newly conquered country', *Oxford English Dictionary*. Colonialism: 'a policy whereby a nation maintains or extends control of foreign dependencies', *American Heritage Dictionary of the English Language*.

refusenik than Memmi would allow. There was the 'humanitarian romanticism' Memmi himself recognises, and says is 'looked upon in the colonies as a serious illness . . . the worst of all dangers . . . no less than going over to the side of the enemy'. It is extraordinary that Memmi does not acknowledge that what was regarded as the worst of all dangers was not the reformist liberalism 'humanitarian romanticism' implies – in a black man's definition 'the role of the liberal as the conciliator between oppressor and oppressed'[8] – but the theory and tactics of Communism reaching the colonised.

Going beyond liberalism, the coloniser's refusal has 'closed the doors of colonialism to him and isolated him in the middle of the colonial desert'. No – *he* has isolated *himself* from the doomed false values of the colonial desert, voluntarily. But Memmi continues to follow the rebel's downfall as he sees it: 'Why not knock at the door of the colonized whom he defends and who would surely open their arms in gratitude?' Memmi is dismissive of that knock at the door. 'To refuse colonization is one thing; to adopt the colonized and be adopted by them seems to be another; and the two are far from being connected . . . To succeed in this second conversion, our man would have to be a moral hero.' Memmi, still (out of habituation?) using the old condescending colonial vocabulary: 'adopt', 'adopted', evidently believes such men couldn't exist. The hero 'discovers that if the colonized have justice on their side, if he can go so far as to give them his approval and even his assistance, his solidarity stops there . . . He vaguely foresees the day of their liberation and the reconquest of their rights, but does not seriously plan to share their existence, even if they are freed.' Memmi gives no example of a like situation he has observed. On what evidence – before the historical event – was his assumption based?

Again, I make no apology for the fact that as Memmi's perspective peers into the subject from the Maghrib, mine comes from the Southern and Central African continent, with consonant limitations but also the experience implied. To suggest that the coloniser's rebellion could serve no purpose in liberation of the colonised is to

---

8   Nosipho Majeke, *The Role of the Missionaries in Conquest*, publisher unknown.

deny the possibility – outlawed, evidently, by what Memmi sees as the racially congenital deficiencies of all the colonisers – of a range of actions taken by rebels among them, from Stewart Gore-Brown accompanying UNIP's Kenneth Kaunda to negotiate return of a territory, named for the arch-imperialist Rhodes, back from the British for rebirth as Zambia, to Ronnie Kasrils, white South African, becoming Head of Military Intelligence and Joe Slovo, white South African, as chief strategist, in South Africa's liberation army, Umkhonto we Sizwe, during the guerrilla war against apartheid. Men and women Leftist colonisers in South Africa were imprisoned, as Nelson Mandela and thousands of his fellow black South Africans were, tortured as Steve Biko was, for activities with the liberation movements. Two of them, white South Africans Bram Fischer and Dennis Goldberg, were given life sentences.

This brings us to Memmi's other summary dismissal of the Left in liberation from colonial regimes. For the Leftists of his generation, he states, 'the word "nationalism" still evokes a reaction of suspicion, if not hostility'. For doctrinal reasons, yes, and in some experiences of his time, the 1950s, the Left felt 'ill at ease before nationalism'. But political accommodation did not end there. In liberation movements that followed, from Ghana and Guinea-Bissau to Mozambique, Angola and beyond, the precepts and methods of the Left were adapted boldly in nationalism's service. It was, if you like, ironical that an ideology from the white world should prove an effective tool of participation in overcoming the colonial powers of that world. (Of course it was the only solution, according to Marxist theory.) That Leftist ideology in Stalinist form overran nationalism, in some countries, with disastrous results for the freed colonised, is something one wonders how Memmi regards. Has he seen this as an extension of his thesis of the inadequacies of the colonised Left to take the true path of the Left and influence effectively the future of the colonised? And what does he think of the role of the Left today, in its renaissance after the collapse of the mother country, the Soviet Union, as now a force along with the Green and Feminist, Gay and Lesbian, multiple non-governmental groups, together against globalisation which leaves the former colonised still as the poorest in the world?

One of the tributary sources of Memmi's failure of vision vis-à-vis the contribution of Leftist colonisers to the development of liberation movements is that he does not allow that the progeny of colonisers could *earn* a civic and national status other than that of coloniser, eternal outsider. Demonstrably, it is not valid to make the claim on natal grounds; that's not enough. But he doesn't allow that foreign plants might mutate and strike roots. As we have witnessed, history subsequent to his writing of this book has proved him in part right, in part wrong.

He is right, in that during the period of liberation movements arising and the post-colonial era that ensued, a majority of colonisers in many countries did not recognise the right of the colonised to liberation movements, nor were prepared to live under the independence of colonial rule these won. They made of themselves an anachronism, fossilised in the past. Many left; but deracinated from Europe, fled to wherever white rule might last a few more years – for example, from Angola, Mozambique and the Rhodesias to South Africa.

Memmi was wrong, in that there *was* a minority of colonisers mainly of the Left spectrum, who identified themselves with the position that colonialism was unjust, racist and anti-human, and were prepared, first to act against it along with the great mass force of the colonised, and then to live under that force's majority government. That is the logic of freedom; these colonisers saw that colonialism had misshapen them, too, its privileges were distortions, and the loss of these in post-colonial society would be and is normality they had never had a chance to experience. This logic reinforces, does not attempt to deny or diminish in any way, with white hubris, the fact that the colonised have *freed themselves* – no other could have done that in their name, out of the principles of any ideology. Theirs was 'a kind of historical necessity by which colonial pressure created anti-colonial resistance'.[9]

In examining the anachronism 'The Coloniser Who Accepts', Memmi makes *en passant* an extraordinary statement. 'Compared to colonial

_____

9   Said, *Culture and Imperialism.*

racism, that of European doctrinaires seems transparent, barren of ideas and, at first sight, almost without passion.' This written by a Jew in the 1950s, after the Nazi doctrine had sent millions of Jews, Gypsies and others to their death on its fanatically pursued racist theory. The colonial racist doctrine, extremely interestingly examined by Memmi, is summed up by him: the coloniser and the colonised, a definitive category formed by the colonial mind to justify that doctrine, 'is what it is because they are what they are, and neither one nor the other will ever change'. How was this racial stasis to be maintained?

Memmi refutes religious conversion as one of the means to keep the colonised subservient, the coloniser's authority standing in for the Divine Will on earth. 'Contrary to general belief, the colonialist [coloniser] never seriously promoted the religious conversion of the colonised.' He certainly did. Indeed, missionaries preceded colonisers in most territories, conquest advanced, gun in one hand and Bible in the other. 'When colonialism proved to be a deadly, damaging scheme, the church washed its hands of it.' The 'deadliness' was that 'conversion of the colonized to the colonizer's religion would have been a step towards assimilation'. The facts disprove this. While the church resigned many to freedom available to them only in heaven, reinforcing the colonialist creed of no such availability on earth, it produced others inspired by the rebel Jesus's example, rebels themselves against the colonial system, unreconciled to it. The church establishment itself was highly ambiguous in its functions of representing Divine Justice, blessing slaves to save their souls before they were shipped.

If any such was needed, Memmi does establish eloquently that racism was not 'an accidental detail, but . . . a consubstantial part of colonialism . . . the highest expression of that colonial system'. He takes leave of 'The Colonizer Who Accepts' with a sardonic salute: 'Custodian of the values of civilization and history, he accomplishes a mission; he has the immense merit of bringing light to the colonized's ignominious darkness. The fact that this role brings him privileges and respect is only justice; colonization is legitimate . . . with all its consequences . . . Colonization is eternal and he can look to his future without worries of any kind.'

If this coloniser who accepts to stay on in the country after liberation, living as he always did, tolerated by the independent government of the former colonised and privately retaining his old privileges – greasing a palm or two so that he may carry on farming the vast lands that were taken from the colonised – he may find he does have worry of a final kind. The land is seized back from him by those whose it was before colonisation stole it.

'Colonisation is eternal.'

Perhaps in his devastating appraisal of colonialist arrogance Memmi spoke more prophetically than he knew.

Could one expect him in the 1950s to have looked all the way ahead to neocolonialism? Maybe it is unfair; one should be satisfied to have his deep and dread probing into the condition of people living under a unique combination of racism and greed: the colonial will to claim right to take as booty other people's lives, other people's lands, that was fundamental colonialism. But he might have foreseen that if colonies freed themselves of colonial governance, colonialism would not give up so easily. Mannoni did in 1947: 'We must not, of course, underestimate the importance of economic relations, which is paramount; indeed it is very likely that economic conditions will determine the whole future of colonial peoples.' In his 1965 preface Memmi affirms that for him 'the economic aspect of colonization is fundamental' but in his book he does not deal with those aspects of the economics of colonialism that were prescient when he wrote it. He remarks only that the self-appointed colonial mother complained that the colony was costing more to maintain than it was worth. What the original liens of colonialism established in trade mean in worth in post-colonial times, is plenty. There are former colonies whose natural resources, from cocoa to gold, are still bought low and sold high. One of globalisation's immense tasks is to serve as the means of tackling this final form of colonialism. And it cannot be done *for* the developing countries that once were colonies (supposing there would be the will to do so . . .) but *with* them, in full recognition of their essential place in policy decisions.

The sickness of the world, technologically boastful, humanly inadequate, cannot be healed by traditional masters of the world alone. Events are proving that they themselves are not immune to anything, from terrorist attacks to HIV/Aids. Fanon saw this from the past, went further: 'The Third World . . . faces Europe like a colossal mass whose aim should be to try to resolve the problems to which Europe has not been able to find the answers.'[10] The only update necessary is the amendment: to which Europe, the USA and other rich countries have not been able to find the answers.

2003

William Plomer and *Turbott Wolfe*

'I think Turbott Wolfe may have been a man of genius.'
     The first sentence boldly stakes out William Plomer's power as a writer. He has taken you, the reader, by the scruff of the neck, for your attention. And it is up to him never to let it flag. For this is an extraordinary claim for a novelist to follow in the creation of his central character: produce the goods. How a genius? An artist? A writer? A thinker? There's the caveat 'may have been', with the canny calculation that the verdict is going to be for the reader to find out, decide for him/herself. Plomer's great gift in involving the reader controversially in his story is there, right away.

     Plomer chose for his first novel the Conradian device of having the writer be narrator at second hand. Turbott Wolfe is introduced as a kind of Marlow, telling his tale not as an old salt – Marlow in *Heart of Darkness* – but a sick man with little time ahead of him and much to tell.

     It turns out that Turbott Wolfe is only a leisure-time writer, an amateur artist; if he may be a genius, it is not as that sort of visionary. His vision is that which dares to venture through the

10   Frantz Fanon, *The Wretched of the Earth*, Grove Press, New York, 1967.

blinding density of moral, political and social acceptances of the colonial era to a reality that could be obscured but not banished.

He is telling his story late, in a reverse exile, back in the banal, rose-patterned chintz comforts of England, from where he left as a young man 'sent out to Africa' in the 1920s for his health and to make his colonial fortune. He was set to run a trading store in Lembuland, 'a region neither too civilized nor too remote', and in preparation spent his parental annuity on stocking up with books, paint, pens, ink, paper, and – unlikely provision but significant of his idea of the life he expected to lead – a piano. The baggage of a genteel 'civilized' European life transported to Ovuzane, in remote South Africa. He began there organising his time between 'trade and folk-lore [research on the spot] and painting and writing and music'. What an anachronism this was is soon evident as three realities invade its superficiality: the vast, undomesticated splendour of the landscape, the pettiness, crudity, sanctimoniousness of the local white population of colonial officials, farmers and missionaries, and the unselfconscious dignity and physical beauty of the blacks whom he served in his store.

Wolfe (or his creator, Plomer) is sharp-tongued but if some of his descriptions of the white locals are pitiless caricature, that stands for the total caricature of human relations that is the set-up of colonialism. His earliest experience of Ovuzane society is when he comes upon 'Schönstein's Better Shows', a travelling funfair where his few darting observations, like film clips that will develop coherence later, reveal the nature of the place and people in which and among whom he finds himself. To the roar of the hurdy-gurdy 'a gross European in one of the swing-boats' kisses a coloured girl and she flings away from him, to jeering laughter; the fair owner has a wife 'barefaced by day and barebacked by night'. In a mob, 'English, Dutch, Portuguese, nondescript were the whites; Bantu, Lembu, Christianized and aboriginal, Mohammedan negroes were the blacks; and the coloureds were all colours and all races fused. It came upon me suddenly in that harsh polyglot gaiety that I was living in Africa; that there is a question of colour.'

Then there are encounters with white neighbours given wickedly Dickensian names – Bloodfield, Flesher, mischievously label their coarse nature – who are jealous of what they see as his cultural snobbishness in having a 'studio', and disgusted when it is discovered that he has black people sit as models for his paintings, makes music there with them on their traditional instruments and his piano. 'Surely you don't have these blooming niggers in here?'

It is at once exceptional that a young man of Wolfe's conventional background should have so quickly shed any illusions he must have had about his presence. Plomer makes it not only believable, but inescapable for him: 'There would be conflict between myself and the white; there would be conflict between myself and the black.'

Wolfe describes these whites with an undisguised loathing and pokes gentle but demeaning fun at the old missionaries, such as Bishop Klodquist, who came to save souls among the Africans with 'a Bible and a bottle of *vin ordinaire* . . . no pyjamas, and not a word of Lembu'.

Wolfe blurts angrily, 'Give me a good old criminal lunatic any day, rather than ask me to breathe the same air as Flesher and Bloodfield.'

And just when you, the reader, find Turbott Wolfe to be proving himself as bigoted as the people he despises, Plomer catches you out in too hasty a conclusion. Judgement is not as simple as that. There's the self-searching of Wolfe's *own* conclusion, 'And seeing continually incessant lines of natives trooping in and out of the store I turned my feelings, in escape from the unclean idea of Flesher and Bloodfield, far too much into sympathy with the aboriginal.'

So he tends, at first, to idolise the blacks in apposition to loathing the whites. With a lens of overcompensation for the local Europeans' dehumanising image of Africans, 'My eye was training itself to admire to excess the over-developed marvellous animal grace of each Lembu individual. I was becoming ecstatic . . . over the patriarchal grace of each old man . . . over the aged women . . . warm-handed tender daughters.' But again there are no easy resolutions in the pace of this restlessly, relentlessly questioning novel. At the same time, Wolfe becomes aware 'I was losing my balance . . . I suspected danger. I found myself all at once overwhelmed with a suffocating sensation of universal black darkness. Blackness. I was being sacrificed, a white lamb, to black Africa.'

The image resurrects, from the subconscious of the young white man, colonialism's self-justification in the concept of Christianity in battle with paganism. But as Mongane Wally Serote, the South African novelist and poet, has written, 'You cannot fight yourself and be in an army of the people. The spirit must tear itself from the ghosts, it must sense and know its destiny. It must take care and charge of itself.'[11]

It is not as a white lamb but a man in love that Turbott Wolfe gains, through pain, his equilibrium of human vision. Since he has no woman, the local name the Africans have given him is 'Chastity Wolfe'. Now a particular young woman is among the black people who buy from his store. 'I was very strongly attracted . . . by a native girl . . . She took away the breath of Chastity Wolfe.' The description of the girl is exaltation: 'An aboriginal, perfectly clean' in contrast to the grubby spirit of the Bloodfields and Fleshers, 'perfectly beautiful . . . She was an ambassadress of all that beauty . . . outside history, outside time, outside science.' And the paean to the girl is interrupted by a tirade against missionary Christianity. 'She was . . . of a type you will find nowhere now: it has been killed by the missions, the poor whites and the towns. There was a chance . . . to build up a new Christianity . . . But it is too late now. The missionaries brought them [the Africans] the sacrament, but I could give you more than one instance where they brought them syphilis too. They took away everything from the natives . . . and what on earth did they give them instead? . . . Christianity is dead. It is a lost cause.' The girl 'was a living image of what has been killed . . . by our obscene civilization that conquers everything'. And yet: 'As soon as I had fallen in love with Nhliziyombi *I was afraid of falling in love with her.*' This was surely the last pull of the shackles of race consciousness dragging at the freedom of vision struggling to be attained along with his growing political awareness.

The emergence of the new, post-colonial man was not to be born through fulfilled sexual love, although love in its total sense, free of glib religious or political edicts, is the only human approach

11   Mongane Wally Serote, *Scatter the Ashes and Go*, Ravan Press, Johannesburg, 2002, p. 55.

in which iconoclastic Wolfe believes. He loses Nhliziyombi after unresolved, half-enchanted, half-agonised passion marvellously conveyed. He emerges to face both the angry opprobrium of Bloodfield, Flesher and company for having descended to falling in love with a black (while they have black mistresses bearing their children – but in the back yard, not the white man's house) and the moment of truth flung down before him by a white woman. Mabel van der Horst has the response to the question of colour that Wolfe found himself confronted with at Schönstein's Better Shows: 'there is no native question. It isn't a question. It's an answer.'

To give the answer expression, Wolfe, Mabel, a newly arrived missionary of a different kind, Friston – who is secretly a Communist – Zachary Msombi, a half-Western-educated young black man, and his cousin Caleb, Wolfe's assistant in the store, found an association, grandiloquently named 'Young Africa, an Important New Movement for the Regeneration of Our Country'.

HORROR was written on the sun.

A moment – of insight as genius? – flashing the image in a poem Plomer chooses to attribute to Friston, not Wolfe; it is what colonialism has scrawled on the face of Ovuzane, of Africa.

'Young Africa' becomes confused and dazzled; Friston drugs himself into delirium over jealousy as Mabel makes love with Zachary in an adjoining room. Did she want to found a revolutionary movement only in order to justify her choice of a black husband? Friston recovers sufficient sobriety – or gains enough change of heart and head – to officiate at the wedding before disappearing to be arrested as a Communist in some other colonially occupied territory. As for Wolfe – hounded by the colonial commissioner, reviled by the Bloodfield cohort who demand his deportation, he pre-empts this by taking his own decision to leave. He puts the trading store up for sale and I shan't pre-empt the author's final, devastating laconic thrust by revealing who snaps at the opportunity to own it. Turbott Wolfe sums himself up: 'I am an egoist,' he tells the black man Caleb, 'I have just enough money to go and live quietly in England . . . In England I shall be pointed at as an eccentric, because I try and use my brains . . . You will marry and settle down in your own country, among your own people . . . You will find happiness and I shall find emptiness.'

Tantalising for anyone living in the post-colonial world, it is for the reader to decide: was Turbott Wolfe a failure as a man of his time? Perhaps he was in Africa too soon? The day of the answer had not yet come.

William Plomer was nineteen years old when he began to write *Turbott Wolfe*. He was – yes – working in a trading store in Zululand, South Africa, in the 1920s. Only once is he identified as the author to whom Turbott Wolfe is telling his story. As Wolfe lies '. . . I know I am dying) in this cold and mothy bed' he addresses by name 'My good William Plomer'. A bit of an obvious ploy on the part of William Plomer to warn the reader not to assume (in fact the reader knows . . .) that Turbott Wolfe is William Plomer's creation of an alternate self. As all characters a fiction writer creates are alternate selves: the people we might have been by the mysterious accident of birth.

William Plomer was born of English parents in South Africa in 1903 but always insisted that he could not claim himself as South African 'since nobody, if a cat happened to have kittens in an oven, regards them as biscuits'. His childhood and education were divided back and forth between England, his ancestral home, and South Africa, where his father held various posts in colonial administration and did some farming. Nor very successfully; the trading store turned out to be the sole support of the Zululand farming venture.

Turbott Wolfe, written in pencil in school exercise books of the kind sold in a trading store, was sent to Leonard and Virginia Woolf at their Hogarth Press in London. Knowing nothing of publishers and the unlikelihood of them wanting to take on outlandish works by unknown writers, young Plomer couldn't have been more fortunate in his stab at finding a publisher. The Woolfs recognised the extraordinary originality of the novel, both in subject and style, in reference to what Edward Said, speaking of various literatures, terms 'historical modes of being'.[12] In this instance, the world-historical mode of colonial being, for both the coloniser and the colonised. It is an inexplicable lapse on the part of literary scholars and critics that *Turbott Wolfe* is not recognised as a pyrotechnic presence in the canon of renegade colonialist literature along with Conrad. While the work is only intermittently satire – and does not spare the narrator anti-hero, Turbott Wolfe himself, often attacked out of his own mouth, so to speak – it reveals William Plomer as that rarity, a writer brilliant enough to present deep, passionate seriousness with trenchant wit.

Turbott Wolfe was a success in England when published in 1926; disturbing, critically acclaimed. In New York a critic wrote, 'Look elsewhere for your bedtime story.' In South Africa the book drew down upon Plomer's head such outrage that the twenty-two-year-old author could not have continued to find any kind of social acceptance there, and in the context of *Double Lives* (title of his later autobiography) – his life already a consciousness evolved between one continent, one culture, and another – he went to try yet another culture, Japan. He learned the language, worked as a literature teacher, formed some of the most important relationships of his adulthood and stayed for several years. From that period came his second novel, *Sado*.

But like Turbott Wolfe, he spent the rest of his life in England, where he wrote more fiction, autobiography and biography, and became one of the best poets of his generation, along with Auden, MacNiece, Spender, much quoted for his vivid humour and subtle critique of humbug of any kind.

William Plomer returned to South Africa once, briefly, in 1956, after thirty years away. We met at last the writer of the only novel of poetic vision to come out of our country since Olive Schreiner's *Story of An African Farm*. A tall man, quietly and handsomely dressed, exquisitely courteous, receiving with a slight smile the gushing

---

12   Edward W. Said, 'Challenging Orthodoxy and Authority', *Culture and Imperialism*, Knopf, New York, 1993, p. 319.

accusation: Mr Plomer, why have you written so few novels, why haven't you gone on writing about Africa? But he had given the answer elsewhere, when he wrote 'Literature has its battery hens; I was a wilder fowl.'

He died in 1973 and did not live to see the end of that epitome of the age of colonialism, apartheid, overcome in the victory of the South African black liberation movements. The native question as the answer. But he had heard and understood the answer, half a century before.

2003

Atlantis

If there was one thing I knew about Cuba, it was as a country emerged from the staggering burden of a colonial past and a dictatorship – Batista's, as we emerged from apartheid's white minority one – but Cuba now, uniquely, subjected for more than forty years to a USA blockade. If Castro's regime, as long as Soviet Communist power existed, was a launching pad against the USA, militarily and ideologically, neither threat has any existence today. I am a signatory to the international protest demanding that the USA lift the blockade; and I'm aware that in the USA there is a considerable body of opinion that wants it abolished.

I am a member of the African National Congress in South Africa, but not of the South African Communist Party, one of its alliance partners. I didn't go to Cuba prepared to celebrate uncritically what the Fidel Castro regime has achieved, nor rejoice in Western glee over its failures to provide important freedoms.

Cubans are poor, yes. Even the writers, academics and cultural administrators I spent time with are poor by the modest standards of people working in the arts in Europe, the USA and even my own country. In the crowds at the opening of the Havana International Jazz Festival, pelvis-to-buttock, breath-to-breath in standing room only, there was a calm equilibrium that could be sensed. A Cuban companion joked, 'We aren't jealous of the ones who found seats. We don't own property. There's no keeping up with the Joneses, you see. We don't have any Joneses.'

Storming the bourgeoisie is the convention of revolution; taking over its ruin there is a reality. Creating a new and more just life may take longer than the forty-four years since the beginning of the Castro regime. This reality of taking over the grandiloquent ruins of colonio-capitalism in economic circumstances brought about by factors in the present is nakedly in your face as you drive along the sweep of the ancient fortressed harbour towards old Havana. Here are the empty hulks of a long façade of vast mansions that must have been merchants' headquarters or sumptuous residences – but no, *not* empty. Where even three walls stand at one of the jagged, roofless levels people are bravely living. Glimpse of a table, bed.

Terrible living conditions, comparable to those in parts of Johannesburg where illegal immigrants from neighbouring countries in conflict, squat. In a shopping alley that runs off a grand square of exquisite seventeenth- to nineteenth-century buildings, I was among dignified people, wearing the T-shirts and jeans of our international uniform, buying pizzas from hole-in-the-wall vendors. The minimum wage in Cuba is twelve dollars a month. How does one subsist? Education and medical care are good and free, and here are shed-depots where everyone exchanges their ration tickets for basic foods at low prices payable in pesos. A wartime measure – but then the USA blockade is a wartime action against a country where no one is at war with anyone.

I was driven more than 350 kilometres from Havana to a resort of the Caribbean Paradise style dating from Batista's time, available in dollars only. It was uncrowded, since tourists – unfortunately for the island's economy – due to the USA's ban on its citizens' travel to Cuba, were confined to a Canadian party and several French people. USA 'exemptions' allowed 176,000 Americans to visit in 2001, and 25,000 came clandestinely; but I encountered very few anywhere.

Everywhere royal palms are watchtowers over the Cuban

landscape. The roads were walled with sugar cane interrupted by villages. I had the displaced feeling I was in the old Deep South of the USA; these rows of cabins, with someone sitting out in a rocking chair. But this wasn't the Deep South, it was rural Cuba 2003. The poor in their rocking chairs had big cigars in their mouths. Almost the only cars and buses were on the single highway; there are few private cars in Cuba, these mainly vintage Oldsmobiles, de Sotos and Chryslers. The weekend family outing was measuredly taking place by horse and cart.

In Havana I had asked a writer why there were no independent newspapers in Cuba, no freedom of expression, stressing the difference there is between a press seeking to bring down a regime and a newspaper advocating reforms within it. Money, rather than fear of state retribution, he said. The only funds available to any reformist group for paper and printing would come from the Cubans in Florida whose sole intention is to topple Castro, and the importance of whose vote in USA elections keeps the blockade in force. But I knew that dissident Cuban journalists land in prison . . .

I see Cuba as a place of symbols. An Atlantis risen to confront us. The fall of the Soviet Empire drowned the island in our time as a relic of twentieth-century power-politics. To visit it is to come upon a piece of our not distant past, significantly surfaced.

Here is all that is left of Marxist-Leninist orthodoxy of our twentieth century, in the form it took as the utopian dream for a just world.

Here is the flotsam of vulgar capitalist materialism: the forties and fifties cars with their airflow flourish, fishtail embellishments, somehow kept running!

Two features from our past: the once great solution to an unjust world, Marxist-Leninism, become another kind of honourable folk-wisdom to follow, rather than the unquestionable solution to that world; and the trivial values of that world: they seemed shockingly reduced to the same level against the realities of our twenty-first-century survival. One of Cuba's intellectuals asks 'Cuba: socialist museum or social laboratory?' Could it be the latter? A social democracy of the Left already showing a tendency to follow the inspiration of José Marti: could Fidel Castro (or his successor) make use of the ideas of his original mentor for human justice, facing inevitable millennium facts, testing globalisation's universality, without betraying an evolved revolution?

The end of the USA's strangulation blockade will not solve magically the problems of a country with few natural resources. But the beginning of *any transformation* of Cuba's nobly borne hardship and poverty is the lifting of the outrageous edict. The blockade is a shameful and meaningless act of an overweening power, senseless in terms of world politics since the Soviet Union doesn't exist.

2003

Thirst

Turn a globe and it seems our world is awash with endless water. A paradox, that delegates to the World Water Forum taking place in Kyoto come with a crisis agenda that the future of our planet is a growing thirst which threatens all living matter. While 70 per cent of our earth's surface is covered by water, 97.5 per cent is salt water. Good only for whales, fish, crustaceans, and so on. Of the 2.5 per cent of fresh water on which life subsists, almost three-quarters is frozen in ice caps. Not unexpected that water resources can be a source of conflict between communities and territories. But necessity demands that water be shared for everyone's survival. Perforce it becomes a catalyst for international cooperation: water is also an agent for peace.

We are prodigal in our use of the precious liquor of life. In the twentieth century its use grew at twice the rate of the world population growth. Changing climate patterns, pollution, reckless deforestation, draining of wetlands – all contributed to the colossal binge. While extravagance was and is in progress for some countries and people, more than a billion lack access to a steady supply of clean water. Over 2.2 million, mostly in the developing countries, die each year from diseases carried by the impure water that is all they have to drink. Six thousand children die *every day* – yes, I stop, appalled, as I write this – of the same cause.

The benefice of water affects many less obvious aspect of poverty. While campaigns proceed to provide life-prolonging drugs to sufferers in Africa's plague of HIV/Aids, the success of treatment regimes requires the physical resistance booster of decent living conditions – and these begin with clean water. The edict 'Water is life' takes on many nuances.

The provision of a water supply to communities is only half a solution to its lack. Absence of effective sanitation means that the supply becomes polluted by seepage of faecal matter. The thirst is quenched but disease is imbibed with it. So access to effective sanitation *along* with fresh water supply is now recognised as the essential two-fold provision to meet human needs.

There are high-sounding terms which link the water supply factor indivisibly to others in the broad concept of providing a liveable environment now, and ensuring it for the future. 'Sustainable development', 'biological diversity', 'resource management', 'streamline existing'. Not least emphasised is 'good governance' to be implemented by both territorial and international policies. At the launch of the African-European Union Strategic Partnership on Water Affairs and Sanitation last year, the Presidents of South Africa and Nigeria, Thabo Mbeki and Olusegan Obasango, and Presidents of the European Council and European Union, Andus Fogh Pasmussen and Romano Prodi, issued a statement 'underlining that water resource management needs to be addressed at all levels' and that 'a balance between water needs and those of the environment can contribute to the goal of halting the loss of environment resources by 2015'. They stressed the dependency of this goal on the new strategic long-term partnership between governments . . . the relevant stakeholders . . . civil society and the private sector.' In fact everybody who ever turned on a tap or filled a glass. Human interdependence; it even specifies that water resource development should be 'gender sensitive'.

If this last looks like a nervous nod granting feminists the equal experience of thirst, it is in fact serious recognition of the (literally) heavy responsibility of women in the distribution systems of water in vast areas of the world. Theirs is the biblical category of drawers of water. And too often, in many countries, they carry it in vessels on their heads for many miles. Their generations-long role in what one might call human reticulation has been greatest on the African continent; in South Africa, coincident with the World Water Forum in Japan, there will be the presentation of 'Women In Water Awards' by the Department of Water and Forestry, to 'highlight and promote the participation of women in water resources management' both as the old bearers of its weight and their new role in overseeing, educating their communities in the fair-sharing and conservation of fresh water supplies.

The 'World Water Report', outcome of the Forum, will gather its conclusions from delegates' projects dedicated to conserve the world's water and to ensure that it does not favour the private swimming pools of the rich countries while the taps of the poor run dry. A leading proposition before the Forum is the United Nations Development Programme 'Community Water Initiative', with a budget of 500,000 dollars for this year alone, rising to a target of 50 million over five years. It will support 'innovative, community-level approaches to water supply, sanitation and watershed management to an increasing number of developing countries as one part of the UNDP's drive to halve, by 2015, the number of the world's people who are without access to potable water'.

There are so many threats to our continued existence; one hardly need name them. Some affect specific countries, regions defined by power groups. They are resolved or bring disaster to this or that part of the world. And if we can keep our patch of the planet clear of them, well, we turn away and hope to flourish through the next generation's day. But one threat applies to us all. If we do not recognise our global life-dependency on water, we shall thirst, on a parched planet.

2003

Questions Journalists Don't Ask

A nybody who has any kind of public persona – pop star, sports hero, politician, artist, writer – knows the predictable questions a journalist will ask in an interview, according to whatever defining area of professional achievement the interviewee belongs. (We could reply in our sleep.) Such is fame or notoriety – pop stars and politicians the best copy. Writers – none of whose achievements have been or are famous on that scale, except perhaps *Romeo and Juliet*, *Gone With The Wind* and Harry Potter – are obliged, by their publishers, to be interviewed. I am one of them. (The authors of the Bible are a collective, agents of a Creativity said to be in heaven, therefore inaccessible.)

As years have gone by in a long writing life, I have musingly assembled in memory a short list of the questions journalists don't ask. These sometimes would seem to me much more interesting – better copy? – than the ones they do. So I've decided to interview myself, and see what I can winkle out that they don't think to. This implies I must also answer myself no matter how reluctant that self may be? Yes. Not I'll be the judge, I'll be the jury, but I'll be the journalist, I'll be victim. Some sample questions from me to me:

N.Q.   What is the most important lack in your life?

N.A.   I've lived that life in Africa without learning an African language. Even in my closest friendships, literary and political activities with black fellow South Africans, they speak only English with me. If they're conversing together in one of their mother tongues (and all speak at least three or four of each other's) I don't understand more than a few words that have passed into our common South African use of English. So I'm deaf to an essential part of the South African culture to which I'm committed and belong.

N.Q.   What's the most blatant lie you've ever told?

N.A.   Really can't distinguish. Living through apartheid under
        Secret Police surveillance made those of us who opposed
        the regime actively, accomplished liars. You lied that
        you didn't know the whereabouts of someone the police
        were looking to arrest, you lied about your encounters and
        movements; had to, in order to protect others and yourself.

N.Q.   You've achieved something as a writer, OK; but you have a
        daughter and a son, how do you rate as a mother?

N.A.   Ask them. If you don't want to hear any other self-protective
        lies.

N.Q.   What was the best compliment you've ever been paid?

N.A.   When I was, years and years ago, on a camping trip on a
        farm, I was bitten by ticks that had brushed off the long
        grass I'd been walking through. When I complained of
        this, the old and very unattractive farmer said 'If I was a
        tick, I'd also like to bite you.'

N.Q.   What is the most demeaning thing said about you as a
        writer?

N.A.   My eight-year-old son, when asked by a schoolfriend what
        his mother's job was, said 'She's a typist.' True, I was in my
        study typing some fiction or other at the time; I overheard,
        through my window, his judgement in the garden.

N.Q.   You were awarded the Nobel Prize in Literature at the
        hands of the King of Sweden. Do you look back on that as
        the best moment in your life?

N.A.   Best moment? Reinhold Cassirer and I had just married,
        and were at a party in London. He had gone to find a friend
        in an adjoining room. I found myself standing beside a
        woman I didn't know, both of us amiably drinks in hand.
        He appeared in the doorway. She turned aside to me and
        exclaimed excitedly, 'Who's that divine man?' I said: 'My
        husband.'

N.Q.   How do you react to a bad review of one of your books?

N.A.   Ignore it if it's by some hack, easily recognised by his/her
        poor understanding of what the book's about. Pretend (to

myself) to ignore it if it's written by one whose judgement and critical ability I respect; and then take that judgement into account when, as my own sternest critic, I judge what I achieved or didn't in that book.

N.Q. How gratified are you to have your writing praised?

N.A. Same answer as the one above: not at all, if I don't respect the judgement of the one who praises, gratified when I believe the piece of work justifies such recognition coming from someone whose honesty, intellect and level of literary judgement I respect.

N.Q. While writing, do you take drugs, smoke marijuana or drink alcohol to beef up your creative imagination?

N.A. Only a double Scotch; hours after my writing day is over. (Wow! That quiz would be a tough one for many of my fellow writers, starting off with De Quincey.)

N.Q. Do you think a writer should also know how to cook?

N.A. Yes. The ivory tower has no kitchen. Work done there needs the earth of the ordinary tasks, distractions of everybody's existence, although we writers complain like hell about this.

N.Q. As a liberated woman, would you nevertheless prefer to have been born a man?

N.A. Both sexes experience the joys of love-making. If she chooses, a woman has the additional extraordinary experience of growing a life inside herself, and presenting the world to it. It's painful – all right. But the wider experience in life a writer has, the better the ability to identify with lives other than the writer's own, and create varieties of character, states of being, other than his/her own. I sometimes think, for example, I've missed out on extending emotional experience by never having been sexually attracted to a woman. Anyway, a writer *as such* is a special kind of androgynous creature, all sexes and all ages when creating fictional characters, all the people he or she has known, observed or interacted with. So while I'm a woman, as a writer I'm a composite intelligence.

N.Q.   Why did you instruct your publisher to withdraw a novel of yours from the shortlist of the English 'Orange Prize' for women writers?

N.A.   I don't think the sex of a writer is any criterion for literature. We are heterogeneous in our imagination, I believe. Writers black, female, gay, lesbian do the cause of recognition of their talents disservice in measuring their achievements particularly, exclusively, against themselves. Oh – you'll note that, as far as I know, there is no category of prizes for males only, or whites, or for heterosexuals only.

N.Q.   You're seventy-nine years old – when are you going to write your autobiography?

N.A.   Autobiography? Never. I am much too jealous of my privacy. Secretive, if you like. It's all one has, in the end. Whereas anyone's biographer has to make do with what's somehow accessible, by hook or by crook.

N.Q.   Do you think people will still be reading books – printed on paper, bound – in the future?

N.A.   No. I think a hundred years or less from now, the image of words projected on screens of limitless kinds and flowing directly as sound into ears – even beyond what technological means exist at present – will have made the book like a stone tablet dug up by archaeologists. I'm shudderingly relieved to know I won't be around to be so deprived.

Well: I can now draw my own conclusions about the character of the individual I was interviewing . . . It would be interesting to hear from other interviewee victims, what questions they – thankfully? – are never asked.

2003

'To You I Can'

Gustave Flaubert's *November*

N ovember. 'When the trees have shed their leaves, when the sky still keeps in twilight the russet tint that gilds the faded grass, it is sweet to see extinguishing itself all that not long ago still burned in you.'

Autumn. And it is with a man's recall of that season of life that there begins the most beautiful, unsparing, shaming and unashamed, emotionally and morally pitiless evocation of its antithesis, the season of fires ignited. Flaubert's novella is an unsurpassed testament of adolescence.

Gustave Flaubert was barely twenty years old when he completed it in 1842. He was the one burning. 'The puberty of the heart precedes that of the body.' As a schoolboy aged fifteen he fell worshipfully in love with somebody's wife. On his first travels beyond Rouen, where he was born, and still a virgin at eighteen despite tortuous sexual desires, he was made love to by the daughter of the proprietor of the hotel where he lodged in Marseille. He did not forget either conquest the women made of him, soul or body; they were transposed into one, the woman Marie, in this book.

This I learn from reading the many biographies of the author. Flaubert, more than any other fiction writer I can cite, including Marcel Proust, has been subjected to the process of taking the writer's creation as a kind of documentary basis for what is more interesting to explore: his/her life. It's not what you write, it's who you are. This guesswork on the processes of the imagination is surely a denigration, if scholarly unconscious, of literature: the act of creation itself. Fiction cannot be 'explained' by autobiography; it remains, like the composition of music, a profound mystery while a source of human understanding only the arts can offer.

I give the hotel-keeper's daughter simply as an example of the still fashionable literary methodology – not outdated along with the psychological novel but somehow reinforced by post-modern theory that anything pertinent to the author, even childhood snaps reproduced in the text, belongs in his/her fiction. I don't care, and frankly, I think Flaubert's reader won't care whether or not the transporting experience of this book is really that of the author's young life. All that counts is that it is a work of genius written by a twenty-year-old. Genius: as always on that extremely rare level of mind and spirit, the exploration of human motivation, action and feeling remains relevant, becomes again and again astonishingly contemporary in generations long after that within which it was conceived.

The years on which the narrator looks back from his November were the reign of King Louis Philippe, 1830–1848, years of post-Napoleonic disillusion, when revolutionary change as an agent to bring about justice, end privilege and corruption, create values to replace those shabbily glittering, seemed impossible. There was nothing to believe in, secular or religious, that was not a sham in relation to deep needs. Nothing to aspire to beyond materialism; and if resigned to this, no youth had the chance of access without sponsorship in high places. There are many countries in our twenty-first century where young people today experience the same frustration, malaise, updating the nineteenth-century escape to absinthe and opium by whatever alcoholic concoction at hand, and shooting up heroin.

Flaubert's reluctant law student, from a provincial bourgeois family with unrealised Voltairean ideas, has no name as narrator, drawing one without intermediary breath-to-breath into his life. He dispenses with his study assignments summarily in favour of poetry, unlikely ambitions in the arts, and fantasies: 'I would go as far as I could into my thought, revolve it in all its aspects, penetrate to its farthest depths . . . I built myself palaces and dwelt in them as an emperor, plundered the mines of all their diamonds and strewed them in bucketsful over the road I was to traverse.'

The awakening of the imagination comes through the evocative power of words, and so does the sexual awakening. 'Woman, *mistress* especially . . . bowled me over . . . the magic of the name alone' threw the adolescent 'into long ecstasies'. This is the genesis of an erotic narrative, an achievement that has nothing to do with pornography and everything to do with acknowledgement of the sexual drive in symbiosis with the spirit and intellect.

The 'mystery of woman' obsesses him in the streets with small details enchantingly described, from which he creates for himself the whole woman, tries to attach to each passing foot 'a body, a body to an idea, all these movements to their purposes, and I asked myself where all these steps were going'. Out of unsatisfied desires comes the revenge of rejection of what's denied. He's taken pleasure in watching prostitutes and seeing rich beauties in their carriages. This turns to savage disgust for them all, and extends to both levels of society they represent. The rebel without a cause, an empty heart, wants to lose himself in crowds. 'What is this restless pain, that one is proud of . . . and that one hides like a love?' (We'd diagnose depression, today.) His desperate plunges into commune with nature are no consolation; forces as erotic as sexual fantasies are what he enjoys there, only reinforcing his sexual frustration.

'Nothing but a great love could have extricated me.'

Unable to act, suffocated by youthful arrogance and fantasy – the young man not only has not realised the love, sexual and ideal, he places at the centre of being; he still looks for the sign that will beckon him to it. Seeking distraction, he responds to a sign that would seem to have no relation to this depth of need; he accepts the invitation in the eyes of a prostitute. If he has no name of his own he cares to give the reader, she has called herself Marie. Relieved of his virginity with a voluptuousness beyond the conceptions of his fantasies, he goes home with self-repulsion and returns with renewed desire. What would be described too inadequately as an affair, begins. She is older than him, in every way, years and breadth of experiences; a beauty in whom we recognise some of the characteristics of the unapproachable women he has idealised. The complexity of what we glibly term sexual satisfaction is conveyed subtly, marvellously, as something that truly can be *read*. Hyperbole has to be revaluated, in this prose. The professionally uncalled-for passion that has come about between her and this young initiate bonds the paradox of the situation into a communion of melancholy and sensuality. Love?

He has not known love. She has been used by many men but not known love; both despair of ever knowing it yet while doubting its existence within the morals and mores of their time, continue tortuously to seek it. From her, the woman who belongs to every man, he hears 'the first words of love I had heard in my life'. With her body lying upon him, in exquisitely described awareness of her physicality he is led to receive her in her whole being, not a means, a substitute for the unattainable. 'Contemplating this woman so sad in pleasure . . . I divined a thousand terrible passions that must have riven her . . . to judge from the traces left, and then I thought I would enjoy hearing her tell her life, since what I sought in human existence was its vibrant pulsating side.' He begs her for her story. Marie is aware that a prostitute's life outside the bed is not a story clients want to be reminded of. But as often throughout this book the flow of intimacy, irony, contemplation and self-scrutiny is suddenly stoppered: there's a curt statement that switches your mind to a new possibility of revelation.

'To you I can.'

And in her four words there's unspoken nuance on the strange nature of their closeness. Why 'to him'?

She begins a soliloquy that could be lifted out of the book as a novella in itself. Flaubert complained in his early writings that language is inadequate to depths of feeling. This is overwhelmingly disproved by himself in Marie's telling of her story. One might doubt whether a woman of her brutally humble background could have such a command of words to embody feelings. What can't be questioned, only received with amazement, is how a male writer could enter identity with a woman out of his class and kind, so utterly. This is the writer's clairvoyance, that all writers share to a certain extent, which this time is beyond what inevitably comes to mind in comparison – James Joyce's creation of inner musings of Molly Bloom. The twenty-year-old Flaubert achieved close to the great Hungarian writer-critic Georg Lukács's definition of the fiction writer's unachievable ultimate aim: wholeness; how to express *all*. Flaubert's narrator says he is 'like a bee gathering everything to nourish me and give me life'. Flaubert, creating him and the woman Marie, attains this – for *his work*. The brief novel, with its hurtingly fresh evocation of passion for nature and sexual love as two fused expressions of the same primal source, its implicit social critique, linking individuals to their time, is shocking, yes – not in the sense of offensive but of awakening as you read, areas of thought evaded, hidden. I leave it to you, the reader, to reach The End – at what point the author puts aside his account of his narrator's life, turns away to begin the novels of his celebrated maturity, including *Madame Bovary*.

Gustave Flaubert's famously cryptic remark of that period: 'Madame Bovary, c'est moi.' Madame Bovary is myself. In this early novel, all the manifestations of life revealed are somewhere buried in all of us. We were or are young. *C'est nous*. It's us.

2004

Leo Tolstoy and *The Death of Ivan Ilyich*

Tolstoy plunges the reader directly into his stories; no ponderous scene-setting used by other nineteenth-century writers. *War and Peace* begins with the broadside announcement by a St Petersburg socialite, Napoleon has taken Genoa and Lucca – the era of the Napoleonic wars is instantly stage-set. The opening of *Anna Karenina* is a calm bombshell: 'Everything had gone wrong in the Oblonsky household.' *The Death of Ivan Ilyich* thrusts the reader into the office of the court among lawyers to hear 'Gentlemen! Ivan Ilyich has died.'

The story begins at its end. But this is not just a familiar novelistic device, followed by a rewind of a life. The intention is to shock – and in an unconventional way. It succeeds. These are Ilyich's lawyer colleagues and friends; and their unspoken reaction to the sad news is, 'What about that, he's dead; but I'm not.' His intimate colleague Pyotr Ivanovich is anxious to be done with the obligatory visit to pay respects to the corpse lying in the deceased's home and get away to his game of cards. To make up for this irreverence he crosses himself repeatedly until the formula seems excessive as he gazes at the dead man's face; he sees there a 'reproach or a reminder to the living' but it has 'no relevance' to him. So tolls an ominous note that resounds throughout the story: no one wants to face the mystery of death as inevitable in his or her own person. The note resonates with a prevailing materialism that makes a brassy travesty of life's final event. Praskovya Fyodorovna, Ivan's wife, weeps while she enquires 'most thoroughly' about the price of the burial plot and whether she could not somehow extract more compensation money for her husband's demise from the government in which he had a prestigious position as a member of the Chamber of Justice. Only the peasant servant Gerasim, handing Pyotr Ivanovich his fur coat, remarks innocently, 'It'll be the same for all of us.'

What did Ivan Ilyich die of? – the gentlemen asked.

Will it be the same for all? Tolstoy has a devastating diagnosis which will be revealed through his unflinching genius in this short novel which encompasses such great themes.

Ivan Ilyich was the son of a civil servant who 'made the sort of career . . . that gets people to a position in which . . . though it proves clear they are unfit to do any real job, nonetheless, due to their . . . rank, they . . . are given fabricated, fictitious posts and non-fictitious thousands . . .' of roubles. Ivan consequently 'assimilated . . . their ways, their outlooks on life, and established friendly relations with them'. His acquired characteristics Tolstoy lists as sensuality, vanity and – somewhat misplaced, it would seem, in the same category as something reprehensible? – liberalism. But that may be explained when the reader comes to understand that the story is being told in the context of the writer's convictions when he wrote it in 1886.

After law school, Ivan is provided by his father with a post as an officer in a provincial government for which he is kitted out

materially from the most luxurious shops. He is urbane, suitably obsequious to the Governor, popular with the men and has
amorous liaisons in accordance with what is manly and fashionable. I'm tempted to quote directly from Tolstoy time and again,
since his castigation in the form of wry wit makes his observations
so succinct in comparison with any lame attempt at paraphrase.
'Everything took place with clean hands, in clean shirts, with French
words . . . in the very highest society.' Five years later, Ilyich's
career takes off with the new judicial initiatives put in place as a
result of the freeing of the serfs in 1861. He becomes examining
magistrate in a different province. The higher post brings within
him a sense of the power of the ruling class. He doesn't directly
abuse this power; more subtly, its seduction lies in trying to 'emol-
liate its manifestations': the classic ethos of liberalism exposed by
Tolstoy, as when Ilyich dismisses 'from his mind all *circumstances*'
(my italics) relating to a case; but Tolstoy's infallible skill implants
in the reader's subconscious what will be recalled when exposition comes later, as one realises that Tolstoy is accusing society of
creating criminals out of unjust social conditions. The implication
follows that in accordance with the general hypocrisy of his way of
life Ilyich was not dispensing justice.

Outward form is what he follows in everything.

'Indeed, why on earth shouldn't I get married?' He marries an
attractive, intelligent girl of the right class. Not a great love. But
suitable. Marriage in that milieu is, like death, a matter of accoutrements. 'Conjugal caresses' are simply an adjunct to the right
furnishings and objects d'art to keep up with the Tsarist high society
Joneses. But with pregnancy and the advent of crying babies, the
suitable wife becomes fractious and there are vulgar scenes between
the couple. The pleasant decorum of bourgeois life seems to be
unfairly disrupted by primal reality. To escape it – though Ilyich
does not or will not see this as a retreat from reality – he devotes
himself obsessively to his work. There, too, there is no satisfaction,
only an insufficient salary and, after seventeen years at middle-level
posts, the evidence that he has been passed over for advancement to
a presiding judgeship. The angry single purpose of his life, now, is

to 'get a post with a salary of five thousand roubles'. Again, as his father managed for him when he was a youth, he finds such a post through knowing the right people. Pride and pocket rejoice: 'Ivan Ilyich was completely happy.' This is expressed the only way he knows how. He sets about furnishing the finest house he's ever had with the luxuries which will surely please his wife and cushion the hell he has found in marriage. Supervising the interior decorating himself, he falls while adjusting the drape of a curtain and hurts his side, but, in the general euphoria, ignores the mishap as trivial.

Where does moral downfall begin in our lives? What is trivial in the distortion of human values? Tolstoy, the self-accusatory moralist who was excommunicated by the Russian Orthodox Church for rejection of what he declared distortion of Christ's original teachings, has the genius of dramatising, through his individual characters in apparently trivial actions, how we become what we are. Ivan Ilyich's slow death begins soon in the splendid new house, and in his struggle to fulfil the duties of the five-thousand-plus-fringe-benefits post, while suffering an illness which doctors quarrel over attempting to diagnose. It is a new source of shrill reproaches from his wife: illness is his fault, as everything that affects her adversely always is. The only individual who waits upon the suffering man and does not resent his infirmity as deliberately spoiling a pleasant personal life is that servant Gerasim whom we overheard saying of death in the opening pages of the story, 'It'll be the same for all of us.' Yes – the creative mastery of Tolstoy, in which every detail has significance, nothing occurs just to be forgotten, brings this man back into the story. He empties the bedpan without revulsion and it is he who quite naturally takes the burden of Ilyich's legs up on his strong shoulders to ease pain. Of course, Tolstoy is glorifying the human values he saw in the peasants who had been – and despite the abolition of serfdom still were – despised by the privileged class who betrayed these values flamboyantly, destructive of humanity both in themselves and towards others. Isn't the peasant behaving as the powerless vassal subservient to a master? Yet the passages in which Ilyich and Gerasim are alone together are so moving that they seem, and perhaps intentionally are, an underlying theme in the overall disillusion of this book; it is possible that people could become truly human in their relations to one another, despite the contrary evidence of history, of race, economic and social class, the material accoutrements of division that have been allowed by Ivan Ilyich to determine his life. Whether it is so or not, he believes his terminal illness was caused by his forgotten mishap when he fell trying to adjust the drape of a curtain – a symbol of privilege gained and stolen by injustice: the private ownership of vast lands, the indiscriminate exile to Siberia of the desperately poor turned to petty crime, and the blessing of the church over all this.

The story is usually regarded as an amazing narrative of the experience of dying, a search for the meaning of death. It is all that, and more: it's a great questioning of what is and what ought to be, in a human life.

What did Ivan Ilyich die of?

He was fatally sickened by his times.

2005

Susan Sontag

Going back to my shelf of Susan Sontag books it's as if, although I've known them so well, it has taken her death to make me realise the extraordinary range of her achievement. Seven volumes of essays, six novels, two film scripts, several plays, all the outstanding insight, great searching intelligence and imaginative power.

Of her fiction she said: 'To tell a story is to say: this is the important story. It is to reduce the spread and simultaneity of everything to something linear, a path.' To her non-fiction writing and her personal philosophy one had best apply her own words rather than attempt a lame summing up. She said: 'To be a moral human being is to be obliged to pay certain kinds of attention.'

Hers was the unsparing attention of a brilliant mind interpreting in the many modes she commanded, our times, our world. It was a scrutiny, an empathy unmatched. Sontag was one of a handful of universal intellectuals who represent and create contemporary thought at the highest essential level. Sontag matters; through her writings she will continue to matter in our era of conflict and bewildering ambiguity of values from which she did not flinch but took on responsibilities with her talents as an artist and her qualities as a human being.

Sontag was never satisfied with what she had achieved if changing circumstances meant that she must return with a further perspective to the implications of the accomplished work. Her 1973 book, *On Photography*, is a classic on the claims of photography as an art and, in history, the most influential interchange between reality and the image. She was not content to leave it at that. Her experiences in Vietnam, and more recently in Sarajevo, where she produced a play to keep alive the defiant survival of the spirit under bombardment, returned her to the extremes of the significance of turning the camera on human experience. In 2003, her most recent work daringly and controversially returned her to the role of photography and its ultimate viewers in *Regarding the Pain of Others*.

An accusation? To herself and the rest of us? 'Non-stop imagery (television, streaming videos, movies) is our surround, but when it comes to remembering, the photograph has the deeper bite . . . Images of the sufferings endured are so widely disseminated now that it is easy to forget how recently such images became what is expected from photographers.' This short book, written as if with one deep breath taken, questions whether in any claim to be moral human beings we are paying 'certain kinds of moral attention' to our reception of horrifying images.

Sontag never turned her strong, beautiful face from any aspect of human life. Her gaze did not spare herself. In 1978, after cancer, she wrote *Illness As Metaphor*. Her subject was not physical illness itself but stigma and socio-religious metaphors representing the condition as punishment for misdemeanour of some kind. In 1989, with consciousness that Aids as an epidemic with primary sexual associations had become a new metaphor, she needed the alertness of profound thought to add to the earlier book. Beginning *Aids and its Metaphors*, she says: 'Metaphor, Aristotle wrote, consists in giving the things a name that belongs to something else . . . Of course, all thinking is interpretation. But that does not mean it isn't something correct to be against interpretation.' To use the metaphor 'plague' for Aids is to stigmatise its sufferers with the image of the untouchable, as for victims of the medieval bubonic plague. She makes me aware that I myself am guilty of this . . . Isn't it the special quality of a marvellously original mind to shake up one's thinking? To personify illness as a curse is, in a sense, primitive, when the reality is nurturing the spirit of people to resist disease physically while under treatment, and for medical science to find the cure. That is her thesis. She was to meet her own death by illness, with fighting courage.

I had the immense good luck to be Sontag's friend. In her exhilarating presence you came alive with new zest. Along with formidable intellectual drive, her familiarity with many cultures, the arts and politics, she was a warm and loving person, quick with a witty riposte to stupidity but sensitive to the feeling of others. She certainly would challenge me now: and what about my novels? She often felt she had been drawn away, by her own convictions of how life should be taken on, from her vocation of the imagination: fiction. She wrote, 'Many things in my world have not been named . . . even if they have been named, have never been described.'

The last day I talked to her, on the telephone to her bed in hospital, she told me two things most important to her. If she recovered once again from cancer she had beaten twice before, she wanted to come back to South Africa, the people and the landscapes with which she had immediately bonded in 2004. That her time with us was to be her last of many ventures to understand and interpret the world so meaningfully is something for us to be glad of.

The second important thing was that she must survive to continue a new work begun. I am sure it was the novel she wanted to write – the novel that was still to come from her. I hope that her adored son, David Reiff, himself a fine writer, will find what she had already written and we shall hold, published, the proof of a marvel of creative force that was Sontag, until the end. We shall not see her like again. But her unique writings exist, as her being.

2005

Home Truths from the Past

Machiavelli or Erasmus?

Signposts to the human condition lie toppled down all over the past, from the stele marking Roman military bases to the rubble of what were once homes, relic of the latest conflict in – you name which country comes to mind.

It's a given cliché that we have only the past to learn from. At least, the opposition of great thinkers who took boldly contending different directions may have relevance to our human condition in the brave new millennium. For example, Machiavelli or Erasmus, who has most to say to us in the twenty-first century? Each was committed to the situation between the ruler and the ruled; the empowered (to use contemporary jargon) and the disempowerable (to invent my own), which term carries a present condition of powerlessness further.

Machiavelli and Erasmus – are they really dead? In speaking of the perceptions of their own shared era, they could be speaking of ours. The century we've only just left behind and the one we've only recently begun. No reminder needed of the bloodstains of the twentieth which are appearing afresh on the twenty-first, from Iraq to the Sudan. And every week, new bloodshed elsewhere. The world is as beautiful and as ugly as it was nearly six centuries ago, albeit transformed in many ways by scientific achievements.

I turn first to Machiavelli because he seems to have had no less than prescience of our time when he was analysing human aspirations in the fifteenth and early sixteenth centuries in Italy. His title *The Prince* is simply another nomenclature for the presidents and prime ministers, the dictators, fanatical religious leaders, the families ennobled by ownership of corporations – our cast on the globalised stage. Machiavelli's premise that 'the end which every man keeps before him is glory and riches' is as evident today as it was in his day. His most famous work *The Prince* is a manual for politicians that proves to have six centuries of shelf-life. His 'principalities' stand for the national states of this, our era spanning the twentieth century and its heritage in the twenty-first. He advocates the absolute necessity of war to defend principalities and provides the methodology to gain support of the people who lose their lives in war. The prince, he says, must himself have a warrior image. He must uphold that if the principality is not fully armed it will be despised by other principalities. Machiavelli certainly would have been Bush's ally in the invasion of Iraq. He would have appreciated the phrase 'axis of evil'. What would he have thought of nuclear capability? Welcomed it as the ultimate in arms, refused to sign the non-proliferation treaty? With grim subtlety accepted nuclear power as the end of power, in its power of annihilation?

As for the pandemic wars largely fought by mercenaries, going on around us fired by religious differences and fuelled by the resources of oil fields rival principalities want to secure for themselves – he gives timely warning: the prince who relies on mercenaries to shore up his power must know 'they are ambitious and unfaithful, valiant before friends, cowards before enemies'.

The Machiavellian rules for a prince's conduct if he is to keep himself in power domestically as well as at war are practised in some of our principalities at present. It is recognised, as he says 'that how one lives is so far distant from how one ought to live'. Yes, but let's be practical. For a prince to hold his own it is 'necessary for him to know how to do wrong . . . for if everything is considered carefully, it will be found that something which looks like virtue, if followed, would be his ruin; whilst something else, which looks like vice, yet followed brings him security and prosperity'.

Machiavelli's concept of liberalism is not as we understand liberalism politically in terms of freedom of expression and tolerance.

His liberalism refers to material possessions, land grants and money buying loyalty to the prince; and surely this concept is followed today while liberal bribes are the recognised process of arms deals brokered by government ministers?

As for statecraft, tackling whether it is better to be loved than feared by the people, he advises 'every prince ought to be considered clement and not cruel', but because it is difficult to unite ferocity and love in one prince: 'it is much safer to be feared than loved when one of either must be dispensed with'.

He was wrong about the either/or: think of the adoring crowds worshipping Hitler at the same time that he was murdering Jews, Gypsies and homosexuals. Saddam Hussein had his share of adulation. We have new principalities that have hard-won their freedom from colonialist princes in the twentieth century; some now have their Idi Amins both loved and feared at once.

Should we accept for the new princes Machiavelli's dictum that it is impossible for them to avoid imputation of cruelty, owing to the new states, wherever in our world, being full of dangers threatening their power? This posits that if the world's tolerance of oppression is immoral, it is also realistic. That's Machiavelli. What of the prince's fear of the people who have experienced his salutary cruelty? There's a precept for that eventuality: 'Men ought to be well treated or crushed, because they can revenge themselves for lighter injuries, of more serious ones they cannot; therefore the injury done to a man ought to be of such a kind that one does not stand in fear of revenge.'

Seize the people's incipient revolt by the jugular, with all the powers of decimation in forced population removals, indefinite detention and torture, whose practice the new millennium's princes have inherited from the twentieth century when they themselves suffered these methods.

Machiavelli still shocks, six centuries later. But when he is at his most machiavellian his unsparing vision of humankind pokes a forefinger into one's own probable moral ambiguity. It's not easy to feel innocent of this in relation to public life and the princes one votes for, as one reads: 'It is unnecessary for a prince to have all the good qualities . . . but it is *very necessary to appear to have them* . . . to appear to have them is useful.'

God's principality – in Machiavelli's dealings with his time – is approached much as the secular principalities are. He details the historical machinations of the popes and those who made use of the power of religious authority in worldly struggles for power and wealth. He comments almost jealously, as a statesman in and out of favour of princes, that 'religious leaders alone have states and do not defend them . . . subjects and do not rule them . . . such principalities are secure and happy . . . being exalted and maintained by God'.

So God is not invoked in Machiavelli's morality. Only when this may be – Machiavelli's prime criterion – useful. As when writing of Pope Leo he manages to link the Pope's power to the secular might of armaments: 'Pope Leo found the pontificate most powerful and it is to be hoped that if others made it great in arms, he will make it still greater . . . by his goodness and other virtues.' A papal post-blessing on the arms trade. We certainly do not have that, but we still have with us protagonists of war who claim God's or Allah's blessing for their sides in conflict. God is useful.

In the mind and spirit, the values and actions of Erasmus, God is paramount.

While taking the great risk of criticising and castigating as a departure from that faith the outward pomp of church practices, Erasmus's concept of the relation of the ruler to the ruled is measured by the founding religious principle of the power of ultimate morality coming from on high. That authority is Christianity, of course, through God's endowment of Christ to the world. Erasmus's enterprise was the regeneration of Christendom. Neither Erasmus nor his direct opponent in the view of human conduct, Machiavelli, considers the power of other faiths over the human condition. Here, neither the man of transcendent religious values nor the cynical pragmatist offers much relevance to the world we are attempting to create now, where the validity of many different faiths, held by Christians, Jews, Muslims, Hindus and others, has to be recognised as an absolute human right, honoured and respected equally if there is to be survival of anything like what we call civilisation. As I write of civilisation, this morning, comes the news of attacks on the underground transport system that takes the people of London to work every day. So far, about forty reported dead and over seven hundred injured. There is immediate debate of whether the source of this savage show of destructive power is religious fervour against Britain's involvement with the United States' war in Iraq and its aftermath, or whether it is directed at the G8 summit as a ghastly alternative form of protest to that of concerts demonstrating with music and song the failure of the rich countries to 'make poverty history'. Either/or; there is a connection in the state of our present human condition.

'How one lives is so far distant from how one ought to live.'

If Machiavelli confronts us with some home truths about how we live in our own times, Erasmus offers the possibility of how we ought to live. It is natural to be drawn to him on the *positive* side of the relevance of these thinkers to our times. Machiavelli determined it was the foremost duty of princes to make war. Erasmus determined it was the foremost duty of princes to avoid war. We know there is no question of which is the only future for humankind in our era, since we have means of destruction unknown to past ages.

Erasmus was so brilliant that it is difficult to single out one quality, one advocation from another in his grasp of the moral complexity of human affairs. That he was virtually the inventor of the concept of arbitration is perhaps, for us, his most relevant. Whether domestically in a trade union dispute with the bosses or the conflicts in the Middle East, Africa, Europe, the solution we look to, strive for now in desperate pursuit of peace and justice is arbitration. His presence surely sits with sessions at the UN, with the commissions on human rights. We share with him in our time his restless preoccupation with the welfare of society, measure this against the professed ideals of those responsible for it.

Erasmus's lifelong great enterprise in the regeneration of Christendom was not, is not, fundamentalism in the sense we know and fear it today. His early support for the young Luther ended significantly in his rejection of Luther on grounds of the need for a humanistic intellectual culture as well as, and within, return to the basic faith of Christ's life and teaching. How relevant to our age when we experience that vital movements for change we support can become in turn oppressive.

His belief in a humanistic culture included educational methods we're still trying to advance today – he would applaud computer competency for the young, but as a writer who saw literature as a basic component of humanist culture would deplore the decline of reading. In an age of specialisation such as ours, his intellectual sweep is challenging. He was not content to be the subject of academic debate; his dazzling use of satire (*In Praise of Folly*) as a non-violent cauterising of hypocrisy made him a best-seller centuries before ours. The great scholar and philologist didn't refrain, either, from controversial opinions on such apparently diverse matters as the correct pronunciation of Greek, 'abstinence from meat', and sharp observation on Christian marriage.

About the latter, he of the glorious open mind might just have been biased, as a homosexual. But that's an aside.

Machiavelli and Erasmus, contentious beings – aren't they both men of our time?

2005

Witness: The Inward Testimony

HORROR was written on the sun.

William Plomer, *Turbott Wolfe*

The prophetic words of the poet William Plomer.
The horror of Hiroshima and Nagasaki were part of the unspeakable horrors of a past war. The world has come to coexist in, witness the horrors of Twin Towers New York, Madrid bombings, London Underground train explosions, the dead in Afghanistan, Rwanda, Darfur, Sri Lanka . . . the list does not close.

What place, task, meaning will literature have in witness to disasters without precedence in the manner in which these destroy deliberately and pitilessly; the entire world become the front line of any and every conflict?

Place. Task. Meaning.

To apportion these for us, the world's writers, I believe we have first to define what *witness* is.

No simple term.

I go to the *Oxford English Dictionary* and find that definitions fill more than a small-print column. *Witness*: attestation of a fact, event, or statement, testimony, evidence; one who is or was present and is able to testify from personal observation.

Television crews, photographers, are pre-eminent witnesses in these senses of the word, when it comes to catastrophe, staggeringly visual. No need for words to describe it; no possibility words *could*.

First-hand newsprint, elaborately descriptive journalism becomes essentially a pallid after-image. Television made 'personal observation', 'attestation of a fact, event' a qualification of witness not only for those thousands who stood mind-blown aghast on the scenes of disaster but everyone worldwide who saw them all happening on television.

The place and task of attesting the fact, event, or statement testimony, evidence – the qualification of one who is or was present and is able to testify – this is that of the media. Analysis of the disaster follows in political, sociological terms, by various ideological, national, special or populist schemas, some claiming that elusive reductive state, objectivity. And to the contexts – political, sociological – in this case, according to the dictionary there must be added analysis in religious terms. For number eight in the list of definitions cites: 'One who testifies for Christ or the Christian faith, especially by death, a martyr.' The *Oxford English Dictionary*, conditioned by Western Christian culture, naturally makes the curious semantic decision to confine this definition of the term *witness* to one faith only. But the perpetrators of terrorist acts often testify as witness, in this sense, to another faith – a faith which the arrogance of the dictionary does not recognise: to the faith of Islam, by death and martyrdom.

Such attacks may be against an individual; one was threatened against Salman Rushdie. One almost took the life of the great writer in whose name we have the honour of gathering today – Naguib Mahfouz.

Harold Pinter in his Nobel Prize speech 2005 spoke these words:

> A writer's life is a highly vulnerable almost naked activity . . . The writer makes his choice and is stuck with it. But it is true to say that you are open to all the winds . . . You are out on your own, on a limb. You find no shelter, no protection – unless you lie – in which case of course you have constructed your own protection and, it could be argued, become a politician.

Naguib Mahfouz never constructed his own protection, took the risk of the writer's naked activity, refusing the lie, even when writing of politicians, in the times he lived and wrote through.

Place; task; meaning.

Meaning is what cannot be reached by the immediacy, the methodologies of expert analysis. If witness literature is to find its place, take on a task in relation to the enormity of what is happening in acts of mass destruction and their aftermath, it is in the tensions of sensibility, the intense awareness, the antennae of receptivity to the lives among which writers experience their own as a source of their art. Poetry and fiction are processes of what the *Oxford English Dictionary* defines the state of witness as 'applied to the inward testimony' – the individual lives of men, women and children who have to reconcile within themselves the shattered certainties which are as much a casualty as the bodies under rubble in New York, Madrid and the dead in Afghanistan.

Kafka says the writer sees among ruins 'different (and more) things than others' . . . it is a leap out of murderers' row; it is a seeing of what is really taking place.'¹

This is the nature of witness that writers can, surely must give, have been giving since ancient times, in the awesome responsibility of their endowment with the seventh sense of the imagination. The 'realisation' of what has happened comes from what would seem to deny reality – the transformation of events, motives, emotions, reactions, from the immediacy into the enduring significance that is meaning.

If we accept that 'contemporary' spans the century in which all of us here were born, as well as the one scarcely and starkly begun, there are many examples of this fourth dimension of experience that is the writer's space and place attained.

'Thou shalt not kill': the moral dilemma that patriotism and religions demand be suppressed in the individual sent to war comes inescapably from the First World War pilot in W. B. Yeats's poem: 'Those that I fight I do not hate, Those that I guard I do not love.'² A leap from murderers' row that only the poet can make.

The Radetzky March and *The Emperor's Tomb* – Joseph Roth's peripatetic dual epic of frontiers as the Scylla and Charybdis of the twentieth-century breakup of the old world in disintegration of the Austro-Hungarian Empire – is not only inward testimony of the ever-lengthening host of ever-wandering refugees into the new century, the Greek chorus of the dispossessed that drowns the muzak of consumerism. It is the inward testimony of what goes on working its way as a chaos of ideological, ethnic, religious and political consequences – Bosnia, Kosovo, Macedonia – that come to us though the vision of Roth.

The statistics of the Holocaust are a ledger of evil, the figures still visible on people's arms; but Primo Levi's *If This Is A Man* makes extant a *state of existence* that becomes part of consciousness for all time. Part unavoidably of the tangled tragic justifications made behind the violence perpetrated in the Israeli–Palestinian conflict.

1   Franz Kafka, *Diaries*, 1921.
2   W. B. Yeats, *Collected Poems*.

The level of unflinching imaginative tenacity with which the South African poet Mongane Wally Serote witnessed the apocalyptic events of apartheid amid which he was suffering and living goes into territory beyond the concepts of justice. He writes: 'I want to look at what happened;/That done,/As silent as the roots of plants pierce the soil/I look at what happened . . . /when knives creep in and out of people/As day and night into time.'[3]

In an earlier age, Conrad's inward testimony finds that the heart of darkness is not Mistah Kurtz's bedecked river station besieged by Congolese, but back in the offices in King Leopold's Belgium where knitting women sit while the savage trade in natural rubber is efficiently organised, with a quota for extraction by blacks that must be met, or punished at the price of their severed hands.[4]

These are some examples of what Czeslaw Milosz calls the writer's 'fusing of individual and historical elements'[5] and that Georg Lukács defines as the occurrence of 'a creative memory which transfixes the object and transforms it . . . the duality of inwardness and the outside world.'[6]

No writer sums up the lifetime experience of the creative memory which 'transfixes the object and transforms it', the long journey of the writer, the impossibility of escaping, as Mahfouz reveals exquisitely in Dream 5 of his late work *The Dreams*.

I am walking aimlessly without anywhere particular to go when suddenly I encounter a surprising event that had never before entered my mind – every step I take turns the street upside-down into a circus. The walls and buildings and cars and passers-by all disappear, and in their place a big top arises with its tiered seats and long, hanging ropes, filled with trapezes and animal cages, with actors and acrobats and musclemen and even a clown. At first I am so happy that I could soar with joy. But as I move from street to street where the miracle is repeated over and over, my pleasure

---

3   Mongane Wally Serote, *Yakhal' Inkomo*.
4   Joseph Conrad, *Heart of Darkness*.
5   Czeslaw Milosz, *Native Realm, Selected Poems*.
6   Georg Lukács, *The Theory of the Novel*.

subsides and my irritation grows until I tire from the walking and
the looking around, and I long in my soul to go back to my home.
But just as I delight once again to see the familiar face of the world,
and trust that soon my relief will arrive, I open the door – and find
the clown there to greet me, giggling.

There's no respite for the great writer to evade searching the
meanings behind the circus that is the world, the 'nauseating age
of slogans' a father speaks of in the days of the Sadat regime, the
era of Mahfouz's *The Day The Leader Was Killed*, and which applies
as aptly to our own. An era when 'Between the slogans and the
truth is an abyss' literature must struggle out of, bearing inward
testimony.

I have spoken of the existential condition of the writer of witness
literature in the way in which I would define that literature. The
question raises a hand: how much has the writer been involved in
his or her own flesh-and-blood person, at risk in the radical events,
social upheavals for good or bad ends – the threats to the very bases
of life and dignity? How much must the writer in the air or on earth
be at risk, become activist-as-victim? No choice of being just an
observer. In other terrible events – the wars, social upheavals – like
anyone else the writer may be a victim, no choice. But the writer,
like anyone else, may have chosen to be a protagonist. As witness
in her or his own person, victim or protagonist, is that writer not
unquestionably the one from whom the definitive witness literature must come?

Albert Camus believed so.

Camus believed that his comrades in the French Resistance who
had experienced so much that was physically, mentally both devastating and strengthening, appallingly revealing, would produce
writers who would bring all this to literature and into the consciousness of the French as no other form of witness could. He waited in
vain for the writer to emerge. The extremity of human experience
does not make a writer. An Oe surviving atomic blast and fallout, a
Dostoevsky reprieved at the last moment before a firing squad; the

predilection has to be there, as a singer is endowed with a certain kind of vocal cords, a boxer is endowed with aggression. Primo Levi could be speaking of these fellow writers as well as of himself, as an inmate of Auschwitz, when he realises that theirs are stories each to be told 'of a time and condition that cannot be understood except in the manner in which . . . we understand events of legends . . .'[7]

The duality of inwardness and the outside world: that is the one essential existential condition of the writer as witness. Marcel Proust would be regarded by most as one among great writers least confronted by public events. But I accept, from Proust, a signpost for writers in our context: 'the march of thought in the solitary travail of artistic creation proceeds downwards, into the depths, in the only direction that is not closed to us, along which we are free to advance – towards the goal of truth'.[8] Writers cannot and do not indulge the hubris of believing they can plant the flag of truth on that ineluctable territory. But what is sure is that we can exclude or discard *nothing* in our solitary travail towards meaning, downward into the acts of terrorism. We have to seek this meaning in those who commit such acts just as we do in its victims. We have to acknowledge them. Graham Greene's priest in *The Comedians* gives a religious edict from his interpretation of the Christian faith: 'The Church condemns violence, but it condemns indifference more harshly.' And another of his characters, Dr Magiot, avows, 'I would rather have blood on my hands than water like Pilate.' There are many, bearing witness in one dictionary definition and another who remind the world that the United States of America, victim of ghastly violence, has had on its hands the water of indifference to the cosmic gap between its prosperity and the conditions of other populations – a recent survey showed the richest 10 per cent of 25 million (plus) Americans had a combined income greater than the combined income of the 43 per cent poorest of the world population.

Georg Büchner's character in the play *Danton's Death* makes

---

7   Primo Levi, *If This Is a Man.*
8   Marcel Proust, *Within a Budding Grove* (from *Remembrance of Things Past*).

a chilling declaration: 'Terror is an outgrowth of virtue . . . the revolutionary government is the despotism of freedom against the tyranny of kings.'

Where does the despotism of terrorism begin to grow in our contemporary world; why? And where will it end? How? This is the mined territory of meaning, in the crisis of the present, from which the writer's responsibility cannot be absolved. 'Servitude, falsehood and terror . . . Three afflictions are the cause of silence between men, obscure them from one another and prevent them from rediscovering themselves.'⁹ That is what Camus found in that territory. It is a specification within Milan Kundera's credo: 'for a novelist, a given historical situation is an anthropological laboratory in which he explores the basic question: What is existence?'And Kundera goes on to quote Heidegger: 'The essence of man has the form of a question.'¹⁰

Whether this question is unanswerable, just as final truth is unattainable, literature has been and remains a means of people rediscovering themselves. Which may be part of the answer to terrorism and the violent response it evokes. Literature has never been more necessary, vital, than now, when information technology, the new faith, has failed to bring this rediscovery about.

Is there inevitably a loss of artistic liberty for the writer in inward testimony as witness?

A testy outburst not from a writer, but a painter, Picasso, replies, vis-à-vis their creativity, for artists in every medium. 'What do you think an artist is? An imbecile who has nothing but eyes if he is a painter or ears if he is a musician, or a lyre at every level of his heart if he is a poet . . . quite the contrary, he is at the same time a political being, constantly aware of what goes on in the world, whether it be harrowing, bitter or sweet, and he cannot help being shaped by it.'¹¹ Neither can the art. And there emerges *Guernica*.

Witness literature is not anathema to, incompatible with experiment in form and style, the marvellous adventures of the word. On

9   Albert Camus, *The Rebel*.
10 Milan Kundera, postscript to *Life is Elsewhere*.
11 Pablo Picasso, from my notebooks, unknown source.

the contrary, when writers, as André Pieyre de Mandiagues asks, 'have been given a disaster which seems to exceed all measures, must it not be recited, spoken?'

There is no style and form ready-made for witness literature. If it is to be a poem, it has to be found among all the combinations of poetics, tried or never tried, to be equal to the unique expression that will contain the event *before and beyond the event*; its past and future. As Yeats did with his pilot at war. If witness is to be a story or novel, that final demand – the expression of the event before and beyond the event – is the same. Among all the ways of plumbing meaning, existing and to be, this has to be discovered. Julio Cortàzar, Carlos Fuentes, Gabriel García Márquez, Kenzaburo Oe, Octavio Paz, José Saramago, Günter Grass, Naguib Mahfouz, . . . these are writers who discovered it unsurpassably for their own people, own countries, and by the boundlessness of great writing, for the rest of us who see the same responsibility of discovery to be pursued in our own countries.

I have had my own experience as that of a writer given evidence of a disaster which seemed to exceed all measure. In South Africa racism in its brutally destructive guises, from killing in conquest to the methodology of colonialism, certified as divine will by religious doctrine, took the lives of thousands of Africans and stunted the lives of millions more; *systematically*. I grew up in the Union that came out of wars for possession between the British and descendants of the Dutch, the Boers. The Africans had already been dispossessed by both. I was the child of the white minority, blinkered in privilege as a conditioning education. But because I was a writer – for it's an early state of being, before a word has been written, not an attribute of being published – I became witness to the unspoken in my society. Very young, I entered a dialogue with myself about what was around me; and this took the form of trying for the meaning in what I saw by transforming this into stories based on what were everyday incidents of ordinary life for everyone around me: the sacking of the back-yard room of a black servant by police while the white master and mistress of the house looked on unconcerned; later, in my adolescence during the Second World

War, when I was a voluntary aide at a gold mine casualty station, being told by the white intern who was suturing a black miner's gaping head wound without anaesthetic, 'They don't feel like we do.'

As time and published books confirmed that I was a writer and witness literature, if it is a particular genre of my circumstance of time and place, was mine, I had to find how to keep my integrity to the Word, the sacred charge of the writer. I realised, as I believe many writers do, that instead of restricting, inhibiting, coarsely despoiling aesthetic liberty, the existential condition of witness was enlarging, inspiring aesthetic liberty, breaching the previous limitations of my sense of form and use of language through necessity: to create form and sense anew.

Aesthetic liberty is an essential of witness literature if it is to fulfil its justification as meaning. And the form and use of language that will be the expression for one piece of work will not serve for another. I wrote a novel in the 1970s; it was, in terms of witness literature, an exploration of inward testimony to revolutionary political dedication against apartheid, invoked as a faith like any religious faith, with edicts not to be questioned by any believer, and the consequences of this, the existential implications handed down from father to daughter, mother to son. Witness called on aesthetic liberty to find the form and language, in order for the narrative to be fulfilled in meaning. Modes of lyricism and irony that had served best for some of my other fiction would not serve where a daughter's inner survival of personality depended on fully recovering her father's life of willing martyrdom, his loving relationship with her and its calculating contradictions in the demands his highest relationship, political faith, made upon her; his actions, motives, other personal attachments, which the condition of revolutionary clandestinity perforce made a mystery. A novel where, indeed, actual documents must be encompassed to be deciphered in terms of inward testimony. Through aesthetic liberty I had, so to speak, to question this story in many inner voices, to tell it in whatever I might hope to reach of its own testimony submerged beneath public ideology, discourse and action.

This is the search for Zaabalawi.

In his short story of that name the genius of Naguib Mahfouz sends a man to seek the saintly sheikh, Zaabalawi; everywhere to find always he has just missed the one who has the answer to the questions of being, personal, political, social, religious – the inward testimony. Zaabalawi knows the human mystery is revealed not alone in high places – he frequents Cairo bars, and the man is told he will be found at a particular haunt. Wearily waiting there for hours, the man falls asleep. When he wakes he finds his head is wet; others in the bar tell him Zaabalawi came while he was sleeping and sprinkled water on him to refresh him. Having had this sign of Zaabalawi's existence, the man will go on searching for him all his life – 'Yes, I have to find Zaabalawi.' Yes, we writers have to find the inward testimony our calling, literature, demands of us.

A writer who did is Naguib Mahfouz.

In *Khufu's Wisdom*, an early novel in which Mahfouz's brilliant creativity was already evident, Pharaoh Khufu leaves the palaces of worldly power and takes to the pyramid he had built as his tomb; there, he has decided to write 'a great book guiding the souls and protecting the people's bodies with knowledge'.

Naguib Mahfouz has drunk the cup and gone, leaving us behind in the shabby grim presence of worldly power, but he's left *his* wisdom, his writings, his inward testimony, the wisdom of great literature.

2006

Desmond Tutu As I Know Him

I am an atheist. But if anyone could have launched me into the leap of a religious faith – any denomination – it would have been Archbishop Desmond Tutu. Being so respectful of others' rights, even those of unbelief, he has never tried, on the occasions in my life when I have turned to him for personal but secular counsel. I am a Jew; for me, to be born Jew as to be born black are existential states not religiously determinate, and neither a matter for pride or shame, whatever the world tries to make of this. We are simply of the great human tribe.

If Desmond hasn't caused by his matchless example as a man of faith to lead me to find my own humble way to one, he certainly has influenced my life. Truly vitally, in the complex and often confusing, dismaying choice of reactions and attitudes called upon for response in the second half of the twentieth century and the new millennium in our country, South Africa.

First impressions: he is not a man of whom that of one's first meeting is going to have to be revised as one gets to know him. He has no façade. The open interest, the fellow warmth that radiate from him then are what he *is*. As he has risen to the Himalayas of public life, become world famous, this hasn't been blunted in any way. I'd call his lack of self-consciousness one of his inherent gifts; the others have been developed by the exercise of character, the spiritual and intellectual muscle-building he has subjected and continues to subject himself to in service of the human congregation. He's taken on no less than that.

His playfulness I recognised early as deeply serious. When he danced down the aisle after giving his sermon during our worst of times, it was not to be dutifully seen as symbiosis of conventional Christian forms of worship and traditional African forms. It was the assertion of sacred joy in life, the unquenchable force that no apartheid oppression could get at within people.

His playfulness was serious, for all of us; his sense of humour was directed often against himself.

He won't mind if I have my particular memory of the splendid occasion when my husband Reinhold Cassirer and I were fortunate to be invited to the ordination of Desmond Tutu as Bishop of Johannesburg. We sat in St Mary's Cathedral following the ceremonial process, the display of robed dignitaries, our spirits uplifted by the choir and awaiting in anticipation the speech of the newly mitred bishop. Such ceremonies *are* transformational; the individual enters with one public identity and emerges with another, whether the endowing authority is a religious one, such as this occasion, or a secular one, the induction of a president. Bishop Desmond Tutu smiled, but not down, on us all as if we'd just arrived at the door of his house in Orlando. After the formal acknowledgement to those who had received him into high office, he told us, 'In our hotel this morning Leah said, I've woken up in bed with a bishop!'

Anti-apartheid activities brought me into contact with Bishop Tutu in the years that were to come. The recognition he gave to the smallest effort as much as the largest initiative against the dehumanising apartheid regime made me aware of hasty judgemental dismissals I held against the effectiveness not only of some others, but of my own efforts. His own boldness was never punitive; the power he always has had is to make it impossible for any group, any formation, any persons not to recognise their responsibility for what they do to demean and brutalise others.

What is a man of the world? What do we mean by that designation? Usually it implies sophistication, a certain easy ambiguity in matters of money, friendships and sexual love. Desmond Tutu is not morally ambiguous in any of those designations. But he has shown me there is another definition to be entered in the human dictionary. He is a man of the world in a different way.

We had a parental bond in that our sons, his Trevor and our Hugo, were schoolmates at Waterford-Kamhlaba School in Swaziland. As it turned out, there came another bond in our personal concern about a mutual friend, one both respected and highly expected — by those of us looking ahead, then, to who would take leadership positions after the end of apartheid — as a young man qualified by courage, intelligence and integrity in the liberation movement. The secret love affair of the man was suddenly no secret. It was news, printed in and heard on the media. When I came to Desmond with my concern that what was to me a private matter, as the law provides, between consenting adults, was being regarded as a betrayal of political morality and integrity, I was very uncertain of what Desmond's attitude would be.

I found in him analysis and understanding of human sexuality. Not a judgement of its urges as sin. An acceptance that the unfortunate occurrence of submitting to such an urge while this causes pain and betrayal in the context of marriage, responsibility for which cannot be denied, must be borne; in the nature of humankind the happening is not decisive in the complete character of the individual. Desmond Tutu didn't give in to disappointment in the behaviour of the individual, I think, because in his fearless dedication to truth he allows himself no illusions. He did not condemn; he said he wished the man had come to him. I do not know what he would have done for him; I only know the capacity Desmond Tutu has to make one deal with oneself.

Came the 1980s and a crisis in the milieu of the Congress of South African Writers, of which I was among the founders. The Congress had for some hard years proved itself in actions to defend freedom of expression, not alone against the banning of books but in support of those of us who were detained, arrested on treason charges, their typewriters seized, their employment as teachers, journalists, forbidden. With our extremely limited funds, we hired legal representatives for them, alerted the world to the enforced stifling of their talent and had examples of their banned writings published abroad. But the political attitude towards the efficacy of what might be called fringe movements against apartheid, movements in the arts, was changing. The black consciousness movement was in the forefront of the growing decision that any cooperation with whites, whatever their anti-apartheid record short of underground revolutionary activity, ran counter to the apparent evidence that such concessions were part of the failure of liberalism to deliver the goods – freedom could be grasped only by black solidarity in all aspects of public life. Our Congress was headed by a black president, our editorial board and trustees were black and white Africans who were close as colleagues and comrades who trusted one another in common cause. But the pressure on the black writers was strong; they withdrew from the Congress and the choice was to carry on as a white organisation or close down. There was anger among some white members; they wanted to continue as such. For myself, I saw that the move on the part of our president and other black colleagues was necessary at this urgent final phase in the freedom impetus, psychologically and tactically. But I felt abandoned, confused; if I could have no part *as a writer* in the freedom movement in which I was active in other ways, as a citizen, my usefulness seemed truncated.

I went to Desmond. He is such a good listener. You don't sense him having snap reactions, making judgements, while you come to him in the full tide of your problems. He wants all the details, even those you think don't matter; he knows better. He is the man of wholeness. I wish I could recall his exact flow of words. He told me that my position was not useless. It was the right one; on the one hand I recognised the need for those blacks who saw withdrawal from white cooperation as necessary to go it alone, to attain freedom; on the other hand I had taken my right to refuse to belong to a segregated organisation. That was my usefulness to the freedom movement. With this counsel I was enabled without any resentment to continue the personal relations my black writer comrades never ceased to maintain with me.

Desmond Tutu's supreme achievement so far has been the Truth and Reconciliation Commission. That scarcely requires stating. I recall what I wrote near the beginning of the chance to pay tribute: 'His boldness was never punitive; the power he has always had is to make it impossible for any persons not to recognise their responsibility for what they do to demean and brutalise others.' Was this not the principle of the Commission? Its faith? It did not offer dispensation for confession but reconciliation with the victim by total public admittance of responsibility for terrible acts committed. A much more difficult attempt at resolution of crimes against humanity than a Nuremberg. The truth is harsh, shocking, terribly wonderful: Desmond has never accepted the evasion that truth is relative, for himself. At the Commission I understood that he extended that ultimate condition to our people and our country as the vital necessity for living together in survival of the past. The acceptance of that, he has taught, has to come from within.

When placing the TRC as his greatest achievement I added the proviso 'so far'. Desmond Tutu continues to be a bold and zestful force in our society, our country, completely unfazed if the convictions his human conscience and care demand, mean that his interventions may be unwelcome to the government. He gives his full support in the many initiatives it takes to create fulfilment of the needs of a free people still feeling the wounds of the past. But the other honest test of loyalty to a regime surely is to have the guts (Desmond often favours colloquial language!) to speak out when its actions are deficient. A vital example is his outspokenness on the devastation of HIV/Aids among our people and its consequences for the country's development. He has not been afraid to come forth and say that the level of official response, turning away from leadership of the tremendous effort needed to combat the threat, is low and seems deliberately blinkered. Whatever else happens in our country that may require to be faced by us without compromising the truth, Desmond Tutu certainly will be there to turn us towards problems we have to solve if we care for one another and our country. I know it's been a blessing for me – from whatever chance or good source that directs human destinies – to have lived along his seventy-five years in the same time and the same country as this splendid life-enhancing personality.

Tutu.

2006

Lust and Death

Philip Roth's *Everyman*

Nor dread nor hope attend/A dying animal . . ./Man has created death.

Philip Roth quotes not these lines from Yeats but those of Keats as epigraph to his latest novel: 'Here where men sit and hear each other groan;/Where palsy shakes a few, sad, last grey hairs, / Where youth grows pale, and spectre-thin, and dies;/Where but to think is to be full of sorrow.'

For three of the world's best novelists, Fuentes, García Márquez and Roth, the violent upsurge of sexual desire in the face of old age is the opposition of man to his own creation, death.

The final kick of the prostate, my old physician friend called it. But it cannot be summed up, so wryly and glibly, when it is the theme of contemporary fiction by these writers from the two Americas. García Márquez's *Memories of My Melancholy Whores*, Fuentes's *Inez*, Roth's *Human Stain* and *The Dying Animal* and now *Everyman* have in common in their wonderful transformations the phenomenon – presented as similar to that of adolescence – of late sexual desire. The last demanding exuberance in the slowly denuded body, when 'to think is to be full of sorrow': the doubt that comes about the unquestioned superiority of the rewards of the intellect. David Kepesh in *The Dying Animal* claims the phenomenon as the undeniable assertion of 'erotic birthright', and this holds good for Philip Roth's unnamed – perhaps because he is, Roth forces us to admit – Everyman.

His story begins when he is dead. But we recognise him immediately: he's in a cultural profession (if a doubtful one), advertising, with an avocation as an amateur painter; he's been married several times; he has adult progeny with whom he is in various states of lack of relationship. He's the man Roth has long chosen to take on our human burdens, as a writer has always to select particular beings from among us for attention. The Cultural Journalist in the grave has been a resident in a retirement village for several years before his death. The relatives, an ex-wife, etc., are at the graveside. It has been the decision of his most-loved child, Nancy, to bury him in a half-abandoned Jewish cemetery although she knows he was an atheist: he loved his parents and he will be close to them in their graves.

Roth takes the writer's free acknowledgement of many literary modes while unceasingly experimenting with his own. From the graveside nod to Dickens, the man unseen there is tracked back to life and even before his individual conception. Here, the chronology of living isn't that of a calendar but of cross-references; soon we're at an earlier graveside. After a re-creation of the Cultural

Journalist's childhood as he waits for one of the medical 'interventions' that maintain his geriatric body, he turns back the pages of
self to the day of his father's funeral. It is in the same cemetery, the
old Jewish one founded by immigrants. That day, as he watches, his
father's jewellery store is vividly present. It opened in 1933 with
an immigrant's audacity as the only capital: 'Diamonds – Jewelry
– Watches'. In order to 'avoid alienating or frightening away the
port city's tens of thousands of churchgoing Christians with his
Jewish name, he extended credit freely . . . he never went broke
with credit, and the goodwill generated by his flexibility was more
than worth it'. A good man, as his son recognises.

Perhaps it's possible to be good only in a life with a number
of limitations? So much is intriguing, left for the reader to ask
himself or herself in Roth's writings. The reason to risk opening
a store in the bad times of the Depression 'was simple': he 'had to
have something to leave my two boys'. This, in Roth's context, is
not sentimental; it's an unstated principle of survival with connotations waking the reader to the unending presence of the immigrant,
generation after generation, country to country, Jew, Irishman,
Muslim, no roots but shallow ones scratched into someone else's
natal soil.

If descriptive amplitude went out with the nineteenth century,
Philip Roth, who strides the whole time and territory of the word,
has resuscitated it – in description revved with the power of narrative itself. This father's graveside is – for the canny reader, not
the son – a post-premonitory experience, intended to lead back
to the graveside at which Roth chose to begin the son's life, a tug
at the lien between the son and his antecedents ignored by him.
He has never before witnessed the Jewish Orthodox ritual whereby
the mourners and not the cemetery professionals literally bury
the coffin. What he sees is not a symbolic sprinkling of a handful
of dust, but the relatives and friends heaving shovels of earth to
thud on the coffin, filling the hole to obliteration. As he becomes
'immersed in the burial's brutal directness' what comes to him is
not reverence but horror. 'All at once he saw his father's mouth as
if there were no coffin, as if the dirt they were throwing into the

grave was being deposited straight down on him, filling up his mouth, blinding his eyes, clogging his nostrils and closing off his ears . . . He could taste the dirt coating the inside of his mouth well after they had left the cemetery and returned to New York.' The taste of death.

'Professor of Desire'. One may so name Philip Roth, writer, without disrespect and in admiration, with an epithet that was the title of one of his earlier novels. Roth has proved by the mastery and integrity of his writing the difference between the erotic and the pornographic, in our sleazy era of the latter. The premise of his work is that nothing the body offers is denied so long as it does not cause pain. With rather marvellous presumption he seems unknowingly to have written the Kama Sutra of the twentieth and twenty-first centuries. He asserts the joy of loving sexual intercourse, the splendid ingenuity of the body. His men are not disciples of de Sade, though it may be difficult to accept (in *The Dying Animal*) the man licking a woman's menstrual blood off her legs as not exploitation of the privacy of a bodily function, quite different from the evocation of 'the simplicity of physical splendor' which is manifest in sexual desire, and beautifully celebrated for all of us in his latest novel.

If Portnoy has never been outgrown, only grown old, he is, in his present avatar, an everyman whose creator makes the term 'insight' something to be tossed away as inadequate. What Roth knows of the opposition/apposition of the body and the intellect is devastatingly profound and cannot be escaped, just as Thomas Mann's graffiti on the wall of the twentieth century cannot be washed off: 'In our time the destiny of man presents its meaning in political terms.' Roth has dealt with this other great theme in human existential drives – politics – as searchingly as he has sexuality. Roth's people, whether politically activist or not, live in our world – and the bared-teeth decorum of academe is its gowned microcosm – terrorised by fear of the Other abroad and state authoritarianism at the throat at home. His superbly matchless work, *The Plot Against America*, has the power of political fantasy moving out of literature into the urgent possibilities of present-day reality. With that novel he conveyed the Then in the Now. Hero-worship of Charles Lindbergh makes it feasible that he becomes President of the United States, despite his admiring embrace of Hitler; Bush never embraced Nazis, but the enthusiasm he elicits, through instilling fear in Americans who voted him into power and whose sons have come back in body bags along with the gruesome images of Iraqi dead, is no fantasy. And Lindbergh's anti-Semitism foreshadows the fundamentalisms that beset us in 2006.

One comes away from the strong political overtones in *Everyman* with the open truth that subservience, sexual connotations aside, is a betrayal of human responsibility. The strength of resistance derives from even further back within us than the drive towards freedom. Terminal Everyman's memory of a sensuous experience, relived, invokes the glory of having been alive even while 'eluding death seemed to have become the central business of life and bodily decay his entire story'.

> Was the best of old age . . . the longing for the best of boyhood, for the tubular sprout that was then his body and that rode the waves from way out where they began to build, rode them with his arms pointed like an arrowhead and the skinny rest of him following behind like the arrow's shaft, rode them all the way in to where his rib cage scraped against the tiny sharp pebbles and jagged clamshells . . . and he hustled to his feet . . . and went lurching through the low surf . . . into the advancing, green Atlantic, rolling unstoppably toward him like the obstinate fact of the future.

Another ecstasy. Not to be denied by mortality. Philip Roth is a magnificent victor in attempting to disprove Georg Lukács's dictum of the impossible aim of the writer to encompass all of life.

2006

Faith, Reason and War

Although I was involved in the struggle against apartheid as an active supporter of the banned African National Congress, I should like to concentrate on another aspect of war: that of the war against writers. War against the word. My own personal experience as a writer and the continuing war, much graver, deadly, as it threatens the very lives of journalists and writers in current conflicts. Recently, journalists have been taken hostage in wars in a number of countries, particularly that of international involvement in Iraq. Before this, a journalist was killed in one of these countries after an unspeakable ordeal as hostage.

In his Nobel Prize acceptance speech last year, laureate Harold Pinter said 'a writer's life is a highly vulnerable, almost naked activity. We don't have to weep about that. But it is true to say that you are open to all the winds, some of them icy indeed.' There is, of course, a long history from ancient times of action against writings judged as religious heresy. The Catholic proscribed list continues to exist. But in modern times the banning of books generally has been on grounds of sexual explicitness, while heresy has been invoked as a transgression against political correctness. *Madame Bovary* and *Lady Chatterley's Lover* come to mind immediately on the first count – sex – and may I be forgiven for recalling a personal experience as a footnote among the fate of many books banned on the second ground, political heresy. On this ground the South African apartheid regime banned three of my novels in succession.

Works banned on political counts, preventing their distribution and sale, and more drastically those outlawed by public burning, apparent acts of reason, are in fact actions perpetrated by faith of another kind – not religious but ideological. An ideology passionately held becomes a faith by which its adherents live and act. Hitler's purity of race, Stalin's pursuit of elimination of a class – only two examples of the means of eliminating freedom of expression in the name of political ideologies, exalted to a faith. Each self-appointed as salvation against the existence of the *other* in humankind. Faith and reason: one had become accustomed to acceptance that these apparent opposites were in fact one, a symbiosis in the bannings of literature decreed by oppressive political regimes. You have only to read the country-by-country reports by PEN's Writers in Prison Committee.

Then came an action against a writer inconceivable in modern times: our time. An edict of death was pronounced on a writer. Salman Rushdie. The grounds were religious heresy in a novel. 'I never thought of myself as a writer about religion until religion came after me', Salman Rushdie says. 'Religion was part of my subject, of course . . . nevertheless . . . I had to confront what was confronting me and to decide what I wanted to stand up for in the face of what so vociferously, repressively and violently stood against me. At that time it was difficult to persuade people that the attack on *The Satanic Verses* was part of a broader global assault on writers, artists, and fundamental freedoms.'[1] The faith that authorised this assault was a religious one: Islam. Nothing on the scale of a death fatwa has been invoked in respect of other writers who have been declared offenders on charges of religious or political heresy, sexual explicitness, though banned or imprisoned. Actions outrageous enough. The death sentence pronounced upon Rushdie was indelible writing on our wall by the hand of fundamentalisms that in our contemporary world threaten and operate not only against freedom of expression, but in many other areas of contemporary life.

How is one to approach, not specific conflict-by-conflict, depredation-by-depredation, the causes deeper and beyond these acts of fundamentalism in its hydra-head manifestations? And what guidance can one contemplate towards a possible solution? Amartya Sen offers a convincing analysis, with the consequence of a guidance for us to consider, in what he cites as

---

1   Salman Rushdie, *Guardian*, 19 November 2005.

the miniaturization of people . . . the world is frequently taken to be a fixed federation of 'civilisations' or 'cultures', ignoring the relevance of other ways in which people see themselves, involving class, gender, profession, language, science, morals, and politics. This reductionism of high theory can make a major contribution, if inadvertently, to the violence of low politics . . . people are, in effect, put into little boxes . . . ignoring the many different ways – economic, political, cultural, civic and social – in which people relate with one another within regional boundaries and *across* them . . . the main hope of harmony in our troubled world lies in the plurality of our identities, which cut across each other and work against sharp divisions around one single hardened line of vehement division that allegedly cannot be resisted. Our shared humanity gets savagely challenged when our differences are narrowed into one devised system of powerful categorisation.[2]

Isn't this one of the answers to the fundamentalists of faith and reason? As amply evidenced in his other writings, Amartya Sen is the last economist who could ever be accused of bypassing the fundament of the gap between rich and poor. This, his other aspect of human order, is a revelation of some of the methodology that maintains the great divide.

2006

Naguib Mahfouz's *Three Novels of Ancient Egypt*

'What matters in the historical novel is not the telling of great historical events, but the poet's awakening of people who figure in those events. What matters is that we should re-experience

---

2   Amartya Sen, *Identity and Violence – The Illusion of Destiny*, W.W. Norton & Co., New York, 2006.

the social and human motives which led men to think, feel and act just as they did in historical realities.'[1]

Naguib Mahfouz adds another dimension to what matters. Reading back through his work written over seventy-six years and coming to this trilogy of earliest published novels brings the relevance of re-experience of Pharaonic times to our own. The historical novel is not a mummy brought to light; in Mahfouz's hands it is alive in ourselves, our twentieth and twenty-first centuries, the complex motivations with which we tackle the undreamt-of transformation of means and accompanying aleatory forces let loose upon us. Although these three fictions were written before the Second World War, before the atom bomb, there is a prescience – in the characters, not authorial statement – of what was to come. A prescience that the writer was going to explore in relation to the historical periods he himself would live through, in the forty novels which followed.

Milan Kundera has spoken for Mahfouz and all fiction writers, saying the novelist doesn't give answers, he asks questions. The very title of the first work in Mahfouz's trilogy, *Khufu's Wisdom*: it looks like a statement but it isn't, it's a question probed absorbingly, rousingly, in the book. The fourth dynasty Pharaoh, ageing Khufu, is in the first pages reclining on a gilded couch as he gazes into the distance at the thousands of labourers and slaves preparing the desert plateau for the pyramid he is building for his tomb, 'eternal abode'. Hubris surely never matched. His glance sometimes turns to his other provision for immortality: his sons. And in those two images Mahfouz has already conceived the theme of his novel, the power of pride against the values perhaps to be defined as wisdom. King of all Egypt, north and south, Khufu extols the virtue of power. Of the enemies whom he has conquered, declares: '. . . what cut out their tongues, what chopped off their hands, but power . . . What made my word the law of the land . . . made it a sacred duty to obey me? Was it not power.'

---

1   Georg Lukács, *The Historical Novel*, translated by Hannah and Stanley Mitchell, Merlin Press, London, 1965.

His architect of the pyramid, Mirabu: 'and divinity, my lord'. The gods are always claimed for one's side. If the Egyptians both thanked and blamed them for everything, in our new millennium warring powers each justify themselves with the claim, God is on their side.

Mahfouz even in his early work never created a two-dimensional symbol, however mighty, always has taken on the hidden convolutions in the human personality. For Khufu, contemplating the toilers at his pyramid site, there's 'an inner whispering . . . Was it right for so many souls to be expended for the sake of his personal exaltation?' He brushes away this self-accusation and accepts a princely son's arrangement for an entertainment he's told includes a surprise to please him.

There is that intermediary between divine and earthly powers, the sorcerer – representative of the other, anti-divinity, the devil? The surprise is Djedi, sorcerer 'who knows the secrets of life and death'. After watching a feat of hypnotism, Khufu asks whether the man/woman has the kind of authority over the Unseen as over the mind of created humans: 'Can you tell me if one of my seed is destined to sit on the throne of Egypt's kings . . .' What's unspoken is that this is not an audience-participation TV show but a reference to the greatest political question of the times, succession to the reign of the Pharaoh.

The sorcerer pronounces: 'Sire, after you, no one from your seed shall sit upon the throne of Egypt.'

Pharaoh Khufu is sophisticatedly sceptical. 'Simply tell me: do you know whom the gods have reserved to succeed them on the throne of Egypt.'

He is told this is an infant newly born that morning, son of the High Priest of the Temple of Ra. Crown Prince Khafra, heir of the Pharaoh's seed, is aghast. But there's a glimpse of Khufu's wisdom, if rationalism is wisdom: 'If Fate really was as people say . . . the nobility of man would be debased . . . No, Fate is a false belief to which the strong are not fashioned to submit.' Khufu calls upon his entourage to accompany him so that he himself 'may look upon the tiny offspring of the Fates'.

Swiftly takes off a narrative of epic and intimacy where Mahfouz makes of a youthful writer's tendency to melodrama, a genuine drama. The High Priest Monra has told his wife that their infant son is divinely chosen to rule as successor to the God Ra. The wife's attendant, Sarga, overheard and she flees to warn Pharaoh Khufu of the threat. Monra fears this means his divinely appointed son will therefore be killed. He hides mother and newborn with the attendant Zaya on a wagon loaded with wheat, for escape. On the way to the home of the High Priest Khufu's entourage encounters Sarga in flight from pursuit by Monra's men; so Khufu learns the facts of the sorcerer's malediction and in reward orders her to be escorted to her father's home.

When Khufu arrives to look upon the threat to his lineage he subjects the High Priest to a cross-examination worthy of a formidable lawyer in court.

> 'You are advanced in both knowledge and wisdom . . . tell me: why do the gods enthrone pharaohs over Egypt?'
> 'They select them from among their [the pharaohs'] sons, endowing them with the divine spirit to make the nation prosper.'
> 'Thus can you tell me what Pharaoh must do regarding his throne?'

'He must carry out his obligations . . . claim his proper rights.'
Monra knows what he's been led to admit. There follows a scene of horror raising the moral doubt, intellectual powerlessness that makes such over-the-top scenes undeniably credible in Mahfouz's early work. Obey the god Ra or the secular power Khufu? There comes to Monra 'a fiendish idea of which a priest ought to be totally innocent'. He takes Khufu to a room where another of his wife's handmaidens has given birth to a boy, implying this is his son in the care of a nurse. With the twists of desperate human cunning Mahfouz knows so instinctively, the situation is raised another decibel.

Monra is expected to eliminate his issue. 'Sire, I have no weapon with which to kill.' Khafra, Pharaoh's seed, shoves his dagger into

Monra's hand. In revulsion against himself the High Priest thrusts it into his own heart. Khafra with a cold will (to remind oneself of, much later) has no hesitation in ensuring the succession. He beheads the infant and the woman.

There is another encounter, on the journey back to Pharaoh's palace, another terrified woman, apparently pursued by a Bedouin band. Once more compassionate, he orders that the poor creature with her baby be taken to safety – she says she was on her way to join her husband, a worker on the pyramid construction. Mahfouz, like a master detective-fiction writer, lets us in on something vitally portentous his central character, Khufu, does not know; and that would change the entire narrative if he did. The woman is Zaya. She has saved the baby from Bedouin attack on the wheat wagon.

Mahfouz's marvellous evocation, with the mid-twentieth-century setting of his Cairo trilogy[2], of the depth of the relationship between rich and aristocratic family men and courtesans, pimps, concurrent with lineal negotiations with marriage brokers, exemplifies an ignored class interdependency. His socialist convictions that were to oppose, in all his work, the posit that class values, which regard the lives of the 'common people' as less representative of the grand complex mystery the writer deciphers in human existence, begins in this other, early trilogy. The encounter with Zaya moves his story from those who believe themselves to be the representatives of the gods, to the crowd-scene protagonists in life. The servant Zaya's desolation when she learns her husband has died under the brutal conditions of pyramid labour, and the pragmatic courage of her subsequent life devotedly caring for baby Djedef, whom she must present as her own son, opens a whole society both coexistent with and completely remote from the awareness of the Pharaoh, whose desire for immortality has brought it about. The families of his pyramid workers have made in the wretched quarter granted them outside the mammoth worksite Pharaoh gazed on, 'a burgeoning low-priced bazaar'. There Djedef grows to manhood.

2   Naguib Mahfouz, *Palace Walk, Palace of Desire, Sugar Street*, translated by Peter Theroux, Doubleday, New York, 1990.

Zaya, one of Mahfouz's many varieties of female beauty, has caught the eye of the inspector of the pyramid, Bisharu, and does not fail to see survival for herself and the child in getting him to marry her. Mahfouz's conception of beauty includes intelligence; he may be claimed to be a feminist, particularly when, in later novels, he is depicting a Muslim society where women's place is male-decreed: a bold position in twentieth-century Egypt, though nothing as dangerous as his criticism, through the lives of his characters, of aspects of Islamic religious orthodoxy that brought him accusations of blasphemy and a near-fatal attack by a fanatic.

Djedef chooses a military career; his 'mother' proudly sees him as a future officer of the Pharaoh's charioteers. While his putative father asks himself whether he should continue to claim this progeniture or proclaim the truth? But that once again would be a different novel and the one whose heights Mahfouz is mounting will not have the pyramid inspector determine a route.

Pharaoh Khufu has been out of the action and the reader's sight; it almost seems the author has abandoned the subject of Khufu's wisdom. But attention about-turns momentously. As Djedef rises from rank to rank in his military training, Pharaoh has the news from his architect: the pyramid is completed, 'for eternity it will be the temple within whose expanse beat the hearts of millions of your worshippers'.

Fulfilment of Khufu's hubris? Always the unforeseen, from Mahfouz. Khufu has gone through a change. He does not rejoice, and when Mirabu asks, 'What so clearly occupies your mind, my lord?', comes the reply, 'Has history ever known a king whose mind was carefree . . . is it right for a person to exult over the construction of his grave?'

As for the hubris of immortality: 'Do not forget the fact that immortality is itself a death for our dear, ephemeral lives . . . What have I done for the sake of Egypt . . . what the people have done for me is double what I have done for them.'

He has decided to write 'a great book', 'guiding their souls and protecting their bodies' with knowledge. The place where he will write it is the burial chamber in his pyramid. If the wisdom claimed for the Pharaoh in the book's title has appeared to be intended to be ironic, it now proves to have been the counter-line of tension only a writer of subtle strength may hold between himself and the reader.

There are more changes of identity, outward ones.

The first notes in Mahfouz's recurrent theme of that other power, sexual love, life-enhancing or destructive, is heard in army commander Djedef's passion for a peasant girl who really is a princess.

Crown Prince Khafra's professed love for his father is really an impatience to inherit the throne.

Mahfouz puts Khufu's wisdom to what surely is the final test of any such concept: attempted parricide. The horror is foiled only by another: Djedef killing Khufu's own seed, Crown Prince Khafra. What irony in tragedy conveyed by vivid scenes of paradox: it is the sorcerer's pronouncement that is fulfilled, not the hubris of an eternal abode. Djedef of divine prophecy is declared future Pharaoh with the seemingly unattainable princess as consort, after a moving declaration by a father who has seen his own life saved – only by the death of his son. He calls for papyrus: 'that I may conclude my book of wisdom with the gravest lesson that I have learned in my life . . .' Then he throws the pen away. With it goes the vanity of human attempt at immortality; Khufu's wisdom attained.

The second novel of the trilogy opens in Hollywood if not Bollywood flamboyance with the festival of the flooding of the Nile. The story has as scaffold a politico-religious power conflict within which is an exotic exploration of that other power, the sexual drive.

This is an erotic novel. A difficult feat for a writer; nothing to do with pornography, closer to the representation of exalted states of being captured in poetry. The yearly flooding of the Nile is the source of Egypt's fertility, fecundity, source of life, as is sexual attraction between male and female.

There are two distractions during the public celebration before the Pharaoh; omens. A voice in the throng yells 'Long live His Excellency Khunumhotep'; the young Pharaoh is startled and intrigued by a woman's golden sandal dropped into his lap by a falcon. The shout is no innocent drunken burst of enthusiasm for the Prime Minister. It is a cry of treason. The sandal isn't just some bauble that has caught the bird of prey's eye, it belongs to Rhadopis.

The Pharaoh, 'handsome . . . headstrong . . . enjoys extravagance and luxury and is rash and impetuous as a raging storm', intends to take from the great establishment of the priesthood, representative of the gods who divinely appoint pharaohs, the lands and temples whose profits will enable him to 'construct palaces'.

His courtiers are troubled: 'It's truly regrettable that the king should begin his reign in confrontation.'

'Let us pray the gods will grant men wisdom . . . and forethought.'

His subjects in the crowd are excitedly speculating about him. 'How handsome he is!'

His ancestors of the sixth dynasty, 'in their day how they filled the eyes and hearts of their people . . .'

'I wonder what legacy he will bequeath?'

A beautiful boat is coming down the Nile from the island of Biga. 'It is like the sun rising over the Eastern horizon.'

Aboard is 'Rhadopis the enchantress and seductress . . . She lives over there in her white palace where her lovers and admirers compete for her affections.'

No wonder Mahfouz later wrote successful film scripts; already he knew the art, the flourish, of the cut. If the technique was to serve him for films, the close-ups of the courtesan and her sumptuous ambience as she wields erotic power through the relations not only of men with her, but of men with men, their dealings in financial and political power, forecast the woman Zubayda (in the Cairo trilogy), whose influence on the life of Cairo during the thirties and forties of British occupation in forms it took during peace and war, even after Egyptain independence in 1922, is so vividly created.

Rhadopis of Nubia is the original femme fatale. The ravishing template. Not even descriptions of Cleopatra can compare. The people gossip: enthralled, appalled, 'Do you know that her lovers are the cream of the kingdom'; spiteful, 'she's nothing but a dancer

... brought up in the pit of depravity ... she's given herself over to wantonness and seduction'; infatuated, 'her wondrous beauty is not the only wealth the gods have endowed her with ... Thoth [god of wisdom] has not been mean with wisdom and knowledge'; sardonic, 'To love her is an obligation upon the notables of the upper class, as though it were a patriotic duty.'

Mahfouz is the least didactic of writers. He's always had nimble mastery of art's firm injunction: don't tell, show. Overhearing the talk one's curiosity is exhilaratingly aroused as if one were there among the crowd, even while unnoticingly being informed of issues that are going to carry the narrative.

Prime Minister Khunumhotep favours, against the Pharaoh's intent, the case of the priests' campaign to claim their lands and temples as inalienable right. The bold challenge of calling out his minister's name on a grand public occasion has hurt and angered the Pharaoh; his Chamberlain Sofkhatep and courtier Tahu are concerned. There's juxtaposed another kind of eavesdrop, on an exchange between these two which goes deeper than its immediate significance, dispute over the priests' possessions.

Tahu urges Pharaoh, 'Force, my lord ... Do not procrastinate ... strike hard.'

Sofkhatep, 'My lord ... the priesthood is dispersed through the kingdom as blood through the body ... Their authority over the people is blessed by divine sanction ... a forceful strike might bring undesirable consequences.'

Here is a palace revolution in place of one of succession – Khufu's seed – and it carries the ancient and ever-present (in *our* present) opposition of force versus wisdom, religious causes versus secular humanism. Pharaoh chillingly responds, 'Do not trouble yourselves. I have already shot my arrow.' He has had brought to him the man who cried out, told him his act was despicable, awed him with the magnanimity of not ordering him punished, declaring it 'simple-minded to think that such a cry would detract me from the course I have set upon ... I have decided irrevocably ... that from today onward nothing would be left to the temples save the land and offerings they need.'

Something that does distract the young Pharaoh from problems of his reign is the fall from the blue – the gold sandal. Sofkhatep remarks that the people believe the falcon courts beautiful women, whisks them away. Pharaoh is amazed: the token dropped in his lap is as if the bird 'knows my love for beautiful women'. The gold sandal is Rhadopis's, recognised by Tahu. He seems perturbed when Pharaoh asks who she is; a hint dropped of a certain circumstance that will give him an identity rather different from official one of courtier. He informs that she is the woman on whose door distinguished men knock. 'In her reception hall, my lord, thinkers, artists and politicians gather . . . the philosopher Hof has remarked . . . the most dangerous thing a man can do in his life is set eyes upon the face of Rhadopis.'

Pharaoh is intrigued and will set his upon that face. Of course he cannot join the men, however highborn, who knock on the Biga Island palace door. It seems odd and amusing that there is no rivalry for her bed and favours shown. Is Mahfouz slyly exposing another side of that noble quality, brotherhood – decadence? They share her. There is music and witty exchange, she may dance or sing for them if the mood takes her and there's informed political debate in this salon-cum-brothel before she indicates which distinguished guest she will allow to her bed at the end of the entertainment.

If kingly rank had not proscribed Pharaoh from joining the brotherhood he might have gained political insight to the issues facing his kingdom. Aside from the demands of the priests, there is a rebellion of the Maasaya tribe, and from the aristocratic company comes the familiar justification of colonialism which is to be exposed with such subtlety and conviction in Mahfouz's future fiction.

One of Rhadopis's admirers questions 'Why the tribe should revolt' when 'Those lands under Egyptian rule enjoy peace and prosperity. We do not oppose the creeds of others.'

The more politically astute supporter of the imperial-colonial system: 'The truth is that the Maasaya question has nothing to do with politics or religion . . . they are threatened with starvation . . . and at the same time they possess treasure [natural resources] of gold and silver . . . and when the Egyptians undertake to put it to good use, they attack them.'

There's argument, for and against, over the priests' demands and Pharaoh's intransigence.

'The theocrats own a third of all the land in Egypt . . .'

'Surely there are causes more deserving of money than temples?'

The ironic dynamism of the story is that it is to be how the 'cause' of young Pharaoh's desire to build palaces and acquire a woman whose extravagance matches his – political power and erotic power clasped together – contests the place of 'most deserving'.

Yes, it's Milan Kundera's maxim, the novelist asking questions, not supplying answers, that makes this novel as challengingly entertaining as the conversation in Rhadopis's salon. House of fame, house of shame? As she becomes Pharaoh's mistress and obsession, is she the cause of his downfall, his people turning against him, their worshipped representative of the gods, because of his squandering of the nation's wealth on a courtesan? Or is Pharaoh a figure of the fatality of inherent human weakness? Is it not in our stars – fall from the sky of a gold sandal – but in ourselves, the Pharaoh himself, to fulfil personal desires? And further: isn't it the terrible danger in power itself that it may be used for ultimate distorted purpose? Dictators, tyrants. Mahfouz sets one's mind off beyond the instance of his story.

Rhadopis herself. Beginning with the introduction as prototype Barbie doll as well as femme fatale, the young Mahfouz achieves an evocation of the inner contradictions of the kind of life she lives that no other writer whose work I know has matched. Zola's Nana must retire before her. On the evening at the end of the Nile festival, Rhadopis's admirer-clients knock on her door as usual. The class-based denial of the existence of any critical intelligence in menial women, including prostitutes, is always an injustice refuted convincingly by Mahfouz's women, whether serving in that category or another. After dancing suggestively at the men's request, 'sarcasm overcame' her dalliance. To Hof, eminent philosopher among them: 'You have seen nothing of the things I have seen.' Pointing to the drunken throng, '. . . the cream of Egypt prostrating themselves at my feet . . . it is as if I am among wolves.' All this regarded amid laughter, as her titillating audacity. No one among these distinguished men seems to feel shame at this degradation of a woman; no one sees it as a consequence of the poverty she was born into, and from which it was perhaps her only escape. This night she uses the only weapon they respect, capriciously withholds herself. 'Tonight I shall belong to no man.'

A theatrical 'storm of defiance' is brewing in her as she lies sleepless. It may read like the cliché passing repentance of one who lives by the sale of her body. But the salutary mood is followed next night by her order that her door should be kept closed to everyone.

That is the night Pharaoh comes to her. No door may be closed to him. He is described as sensually as Mahfouz does his women characters. The encounter is one of erotic beauty and meaning without necessity of scenes of sexual gyration. It is also the beginning of Pharaoh's neglect of the affairs of state for the power of a 'love affair that was costing Egypt a fortune'. The price: Prime Minister Khunumhotep has had to carry out Pharaoh's decree to sequester temple estates. Pharaoh's choice is for tragedy, if we accept that the fall of the mighty is tragedy's definition, as against the clumsy disasters of ordinary, fallible people. Rhadopis, in conflict between passion for a man who is also a king and the other, epiphany of concern for the Egyptian people of whom she is one, uses her acute mind – after all, let's remind ourselves she was perforce wily in her former precarious life – to devise a means by which Pharaoh may falsely claim that there is a revolt of the Maasaya tribes in the region of the priests' lands and summon his army there to overcome the real rebellion, that of the priests. The intricate subterfuge involves the ruthless exploitation of an innocent boy – also in love with her – by Rhadopis's resorting to her old powers of seduction to use him as messenger.

Tragedy is by definition inexorable as defeated Pharaoh speaks after the priesthood has exposed his actions to his people and the mob is about to storm the walls of his palace. 'Madness will remain as long as there are people alive . . . I have made for myself a name that no Pharaoh before me ever was called: The Frivolous King.'

An arrow from the mob pierces his breast. 'Rhadopis,' he orders his men, 'Take me to her . . . I want to expire on Biga.'

We hardly have been aware of the existence of Pharaoh's unloved wife, the queen; how impressively she emerges now with a quiet command, 'Carry out my lord's decision.'

Mahfouz's nascent brilliance as, above all political, moral, philosophical purpose, a *story-teller*, is in the emotional pace of events by which *this* story meets its moving, questioning end, with the irony that Rhadopis's last demand on a man is to have the adoring boy messenger find a phial of poison with which she will join Pharaoh in death, final consummation of sexual passion. For the last, unrequited lover, asked how he obtained the phial, Mahfouz plumbs the boy's horror in the answer: 'I brought it to her myself.'

What was the young writer, Mahfouz, saying about love?

The Nile is the flowing harbinger of Egypt's destiny in the scope of Mahfouz's re-imagined pharaonic history, starting with *Khufu's Wisdom*, fourth dynasty, continuing with *Rhadophis of Nubia*, sixth dynasty, and concluding with *Thebes At War*, seventeenth to eighteenth dynasty.

A ship from the south arrives up the Nile, at Thebes. On board not a courtesan or a princess but the Chamberlain of Apophis, Pharaoh by conquest of both the north and south kingdoms. Again, through the indirection of an individual's thoughts, anticipation is roused as one reads the musing of this envoy: 'I wonder, tomorrow will the trumpet sound . . . will the peace of these tranquil houses be shattered . . . Ah, how I wish these people knew what a warning this ship brings them and their master.' He is the emissary of an ancient colonialism. Thebes is virtually a colony of Apophis's reign. The Southerners are, within the traditional (unchanging) justification of colonisation, different. The classic example for that and all time: darker than self-appointed superior beings – in this era the Hyksos of the north, from Memphis. Compared with these, a member of the Chamberlain's mission remarks, the Southerners are 'Like mud next to the glorious rays of the sun'. And the Chamberlain adds '. . . despite their colour and their nakedness . . . they claim they are descended from the loin of the gods and that their county is the well-spring of the true pharoahs'. I wonder what Naguib Mahfouz, looking back to 1938 when his prescient young self wrote his novel, thinks of how we now know, not through any godly dispensation, but by palaeontological discovery, that black Africa – which the Southerners and the Nubians represent in the story – is the home of the origin of all humankind.

After this foreboding opening, there comes to us as ludicrous the purpose of the mission. It is to demand that the hippopotami in the lake at Thebes be killed, since Pharoah Apophis has a malady his doctors have diagnosed as due to the roaring of the animals penned there! It's a power pretext, demeaning that of the region: the lake and its hippos are sacred to the Theban people and their god Amun. There is a second demand from Pharoah Apophis. He has dreamt that the god Seth, sacred to his people, is not honoured in the south's temples. A temple devoted to Seth must be built at Thebes. Third decree: the governor of Thebes, deposed Pharoah Seqenenra, appointed on the divide-and-rule principle of making a people's leader an appointee of the usurping power, must cease the presumption of wearing the White Crown of Egypt (symbol of Southern sovereignty in Egypt's double crown). 'He has no right . . . there is only one kind who has the right' – conqueror Apophis.

Seqenenra calls his Crown Prince Kamose and councillors to discuss these demands. His Chamberlain Hur: 'It is the spirit of a master dictating to his slave . . . it is simply the ancient conflict between Thebes and Memphis in a new shape. The latter strives to enslave the former, while the former struggles to hold on to its independence by all means.'

Of the three novels, this one has the clearest intention to be related to the present in which it was written – British domination of Egypt which was to continue through the 1939–1945 war until the deposing of King Farouk by Nasser in the 1950s. It also does not shirk the resort to reverse racism which inevitably is used to strengthen anti-colonial resolves. One of Seqenenra's military commanders: 'Let us fight till we have liberated the North and driven the last of the white with their long dirty beards from the

Land of the Nile.' The 'white' are Asiatic foreigners, the Hyksos, also referred to as 'Herdsmen' presumably because of their wealth in cattle, who dominated from Northern Egypt for two hundred years.

Crown Prince Kamose is for war, as are some among the councillors. But the final decision will go to Queen Tetisheri, Seqenenra's wife, the literary ancestress of Mahfouz's created line of revered wise matriarchs, alongside his recognition given to the embattled dignity and intelligence of courtesans. Physically, she's described with characteristics we would know as racist caricature, but that he proposes were a valid standard of African beauty, 'the projection of the upper teeth that the people of the South found so attractive'. A questioning of the validity of any people's claim to an immutable aesthetic standard of human form . . . Scholar of the Books of the Dead and books of Khufu's teaching, Tetisheri's was the opinion to which 'recourse was had in times of difficulty': 'the sublime goal' to which Thebans 'must dedicate themselves was the liberation of the Nile Valley'. Thebes will go to war.

Crown Prince Kamose is downcast when told by his father that he may not serve in battle, he is to remain in Seqenenra's place of authority tasked with supplying the army with 'men and provisions'. In one of the thrilling addresses at once oratorical and movingly personal, Seqenenra prophesies 'If Seqenenra falls . . . Kamose will succeed his father, and if Kamose falls, little Ahmose [grandson] will follow him. And if this army of ours is wiped out Egypt is full of men . . . if the whole South falls into the hands of the Herdsmen, then there is Nubia . . . I warn you against no enemy but one – despair.'

It is flat understatement to acknowledge that Seqenenra dies. He falls in a legendary hand-to-hand battle with javelins, the double crown of Egypt he is defiantly wearing topples, 'blood spurted like a spring . . . another blow scattering his brains', other blows 'tipped the body to pieces' – all as if this happens thousands of years later, before one's eyes. It is not an indulgence in gore, it's part of Mahfouz's daring to go too far in what goes too far for censorship by literary good taste, the hideous human desecration of war. The war is lost; Kamose as heir to defeat must survive by exile with the family. They take refuge in Nubia, where there are supporters from among their own Theban people.

From the horrifyingly magnificent set-piece of battle, Mahfouz turns – as Tolstoy did in *War and Peace* – to the personal, far from the clamour, which signifies it in individual lives. Kamose leads the family not conventionally to the broken body but 'to bid farewell to my father's room'. To 'face its emptiness'. With such nuance, delicacy within juggernaut destruction, does the skill of Mahfouz peretrate the depth of responses in human existence.

And the emptiness of that room will become of even greater significance. Kamose has Seqenenra's throne taken from the palace to the Temple of Amun, where the body of Seqenenra lies. Prostrate before the throne, he speaks: 'Apophis shall never sit upon you.'

Ten years have passed. The story is taken up again along the Nile. A convoy of ships is pointing north, now, from Nubia to the border with Egypt, closed since the end of the war. The sailors are Nubian, the two commanders Egyptian. Beauty and rightfulness go together in early Mahfouz's iconography. The leading commander has 'one of those faces to which nature leads its own majesty and beauty in equal proportion'. Here is Isfinis, a merchant bringing for sale the precious jewels, ivory, gold and exotic creatures that are the natural resources of Nubia. The convoy lands first at Biga, that island from which Rhadopis's siren call once sounded, where now the merchant bribes the local governor with an ivory sceptre in exchange for intercession to be received by the Pharaoh Apophis.

Isfinis is not a merchant and Isfinis is not his name. His purpose is not business but justice; we overhear him saying to his 'agent', courtier Latu, 'If we succeed in restoring the ties with Nubia . . . we shall have won half the battle . . . the Herdsman is very arrogant . . . but he is lazy . . . his only path to gold is through someone like Isfinis who volunteers to bring it to him.' So this merchant must be disguised Kamose, Seqenenra's heir, come for retribution?

Mahfouz is the writer-magician, pulling surprise out of the expected. No, Isfinis is Ahmose, Seqenenra's grandson, last heard of going as a child into exile with the defeated family.

A royal vessel sails near the merchant convoy and a princess with her slave girls is amazed at the sight on the merchant's deck of an item of cargo never seen before. It is a pygmy. Her Pharaonic Highness sends a sailor to say she will board the merchant ship to look at the 'creature' – if it is not dangerous.

Isfinis presents the pygmy with a show of obsequiousness: 'Greet your mistress, Zola!' A wryly mischievous scene of the cruel sense of absolute superiority in race, hierarchy of physique, follows.

The princess asks, 'Is he animal or human?'

Isfinis: 'Human, Your Highness.'

'Why should he not be considered an animal?'

'He has his own language and his own religion.'

To her the pygmy is like anything else the merchant might offer, something to own or reject; '. . . but he is ugly; it would give me no pleasure to acquire him'. From some other examples of the merchant's wares she picks a necklace; it's simply assumed he will have to come to the palace to be paid.

The satirical social scene explodes as Latu cries angrily, 'She is a devil, daughter of a devil!'

In this tale of doubling-up identities Isfinis/Ahmose realises that this woman he's attracted to is the daughter of the 'humiliator of his people, and his grandfather's killer'.

On land, the merchant takes lodgings at an inn among fishermen. In the bar (as later, the Cairo trilogy) inhibitions dissolving in drink mean people reveal in banter the state of the country. It's serious social criticism and delightful entertainment, at once.

'You're certainly a rich man, noble sir . . . but you're Egyptian, from the look of you.'

Isfinis/Ahmose: 'Is there any contradiction between being Egyptian and being rich?'

'Certainly, unless you're in the rulers' good graces'; this bar 'is the refuge of those who have no hope . . . The rule in Egypt is that the rich steal from the poor but the poor are not allowed to steal from the rich.'

Mahfouz has the rare gift of rousing a subconscious alertness in the reader: a kind of writerly transmission so that one moves on for oneself, as if before he does, to how things will develop and why. Nothing is an aside. A man bursts into the inn's rowdiness to tell how someone the locals know, Ebana, has been arrested on the pretext that she attacked a Herdsman officer who was soliciting her. When Isfinis hears the woman will be flogged because she's unable to pay a fine, he insists on going to the court to do so. The apparently irrelevant good deed that a man principled against injustice may casually settle with cash. But perhaps one has been prompted. Who is this woman?

And indeed her presence is invoked in context of Isfinis's mission when, at another of the progressively hierarchal meetings that must precede granting of audience with Pharoah Apophis, the judge from the woman's trial happens to be present, and he remarks superciliously of the merchant, 'It seems he is ever ready with himself and his wealth, for he donated 50 pieces of gold to save a peasant woman charged with insulting Commander Rukh.'

And Princess Amenridis – she's there too, sarcasm her form of baiting flirtation, 'Isn't it natural that a peasant should roll up his sleeves to defend a peasant woman?' Echoing tones of Rhadopis; but the courtesan was arming herself against her vulnerability as a despised woman, while Amenridis is amusing herself by taunting a man beneath her class, albeit attractive. Mahfouz hasn't cloned from a previous creation, he's making a statement that the caprice of the privileged is not the need of the dispossessed.

Merchant Isfinis, ready to produce a bribe of the Governor's choice, reveals the splendour of objects he wants to offer before Pharoah Apophis. The Princess enjoys making a sensation by saying, of the merchant, to the judge, 'I am in his debt.' She relates how she was drawn to the merchant's convoy by the weird sight of the pygmy and picked out from his other wares the necklace with its emerald heart she is now wearing.

The Governor joins the mood of repartee and innuendo: 'Why choose a green heart . . . pure white hearts, wicked black hearts but what might be the meaning of a green heart?'

The Princess: 'Direct your question to the one who sold the heart.'

Isfinis: 'The green heart is the symbol of fertility and tenderness.'

The Beatrice and Benedict volley will develop into the taming of the shrew, this arrogant beauty who privately wishes 'she might come across such a man as this merchant in the body of her own kind . . . instead she had found it in the body of a brown-skinned Egyptian who traded in Pygmies'.

The – blessed or cursed – complication of sexual attraction along with the imperative will to political power causes Isfinis 'out of beguilement and tactics to keep in with those who can take him to Pharoah', to decide he can't ask payment for the green heart.

A sharp-minded reader is required to follow the shifts in identity of protagonists in this marvellous chronicle; and he/she will be rewarded by zest of entering the stunning agility of the author's mind. Ebana was, indeed, no simple incident illustrating Isfinis/Ahmose's compassion. She is the widow of Pepi, the courtier killed with Seqenenra ten years ago, since when she has concealed herself among the poor fisher community of enemy territory, Memphis. Pepi had named their son Ahmose, after the grandson of Seqenenra, born the same day. It is more than coincidence; this *other* Ahmose is also twinned in bravery and dedication with Ahmose-disguised-as-Isfinis, to win back for Thebes the double crown of Egypt.

The dynastic Ahmose hears through Ebana that the fishermen's quarter is full of former owners of estates and farms, dispossessed by Apophis. He tells them – and lets on to the reader for the first time – the true purpose of his 'trade mission' is to link Egypt to Nubia by getting permission to transport these men ostensibly as workers to produce the treasures of Nubian resources for Memphis's acquisitive taste. 'We shall carry gold to Egypt and return with grain and men . . . and one day we shall come back with men only . . .'

Eros, too, is relentless; while Ahmose is engaged in planning this great campaign an 'invading image' causes him to shudder. 'God, I think of her . . . And I shouldn't think of her at all.' Amenridis, daughter of the enemy, the Pharoah Apophis.

The day of his reception by the Pharoah brings another emotional experience Ahmose cannot let disempower him: the garden of the palace usurped by Apophis was his grandfather Pharoah Seqenenra's where in childhood he would play with Nefertari – now his wife, whom Mahfouz knows, in his skill at conveying the unstated merely by an image, he does not have to remark that Ahmose is betraying.

In the palace Apophis falls to the trap of demeaning himself by discarding his crown and putting on his head the vanity of a fake, bejewelled double crown the merchant presents him with along with the gift of three pygmies. They are to amuse him; or to remind of something apposite to His Majesty, in guise of quaint information. 'They are people, my lord, whose tribes believe that the world contains no other people but themselves.'

The scene of greedy pleasure and enacted sycophancy is blown apart by the charging in of Apophis's military commander Rukh, the man who brought Ebana to court accused of insulting him. He is drunk, raging, and demands a duel with the Nubian trader who paid gold to save her from flogging.

Ahmose is strung between choices: flee like a coward, or be killed and his mission for his people lost. He's aware of Princess Amenridis regarding him with interest. Is it this, we're left to decide, which makes him accept Rukh's challenge? As proof of manhood? For the public the duel is between class, race: the royal warrior and the peasant foreigner. Commander Rukh loses humiliatingly, incapacitated by a wounded hand. Whatever Ahmose's reckless reason in taking on the duel, his present mission is fulfilled; the deal, treasures to Pharoah Apophis in exchange for the grain and workers, is granted. He may cross the border for trade whenever he wishes.

Aboard his homeward ship in what should be triumph, Ahmose is asking himself in that other mortal conflict, between sexual love and political commitment, 'Is it possible for love and hate to have the same object?' Amenridis is part of the illicit power of oppression. 'However it be with me, I shall not set eyes upon her again . . .'

He does, almost at once. Rukh pursues him with warships, to duel again, and, 'This time I shall kill you with my own hands.'

Amenridis has followed on her ship and endowed with every authority of rank stops Rukh's men from murdering Ahmose when he has once again wounded Rukh. Ahmose asks what made her take upon herself 'the inconvenience' of saving his life.

She answers in character: 'To make you my debtor.'

But this is more than sharply aphoristic. If he is somehow to pay he must return to his creditor; her way of asking when she will see again the man she knows as Isfinis. And his declaration of love is made, he will return, 'My lady, by this life of mine which belongs to you'.

His father Kamose refuses to allow him to return in the person of Merchant Isfinis. He will go in his own person, Ahmose, only when 'the day of struggle dawns'.

Out of the silence of parting comes a letter. In the envelope is the chain of the green heart necklace. Amenridis writes she is saddened to inform him that a pygmy she has taken into her quarters as a pet has disappeared. 'Is it possible for you to send me a new pygmy, one who knows how to be true?'

Mahfouz discards apparent sentimentality for startling evidence of deep feeling, just as he is able to dismantle melodrama with the harshness of genuine human confrontation. Desolate Ahmose: 'She would, indeed, always see him as the inconstant pygmy.'

The moral ambiguity of a love is overwhelmed by the moral ambiguities darkening the shed blood of even a just war. The day of struggle comes bearing all this and Kamose with Ahmose eventually leads the Theban army to victory, the kingdom is restored to Thebes.

Mahfouz, like Thomas Mann, is master of irony, with its tugging undertow of loss. Apophis and his people, his daughter, have left Memphis in defeat. It is a beautiful evening of peace. Ahmose and his wife Nefertari are on the palace balcony, overlooking the Nile. His fingers are playing with a golden chain.

She notices: 'How lovely. But it's broken.'

'Yes, it has lost its heart.'

'What a pity!' In her innocent naivety, she assumes the chain is for her.

But he says, 'I have put aside for you something more precious and beautiful than that . . . Nefertari, I want you to call me Isfinis, for it's a name I love and I love those who love it.'

'Are you still writing?'

People whose retirement from working life has a date, set as the date of birth and the date of death yet to come, ask this question of a writer. But there's no trade union decision bound upon writers; they leave practising the art of the word only when their ability to transform with it something of the mystery of human life, leaves them.

Yes, in old age Naguib Mahfouz is still writing. Still finding new literary modes to express the changing consciousness of succeeding eras with which his genius created this trilogy and his entire oeuvre, novels and stories. In the rising babble of our millennium, radio, television, mobile phone, his mode for the written word is distillation. In a current work, *The Dreams*,[1] short prose evocations drawing on the fragmentary power of the subconscious, he is the narrator walking aimlessly where suddenly 'every step I take turns the street upside-down into a circus'. At first he 'could soar with joy', but when the spectacle is repeated over and over from street to street, 'I long in my soul to go back to my home . . . and 'trust that soon my relief will arrive'. He opens his door and finds – 'the clown there to greet me, giggling'. No escape from the world and the writer's innate compulsion to dredge from its confusion, meaning.

2007

Experiencing Two Absolutes

'The moment when I am no longer more than a writer, I shall cease to write.'

The little strip of planet Earth where two peoples of common ancient origin, Israelis and Palestinians, contest to live – but not together.

---

1   Naguib Mahfouz, *The Dreams*, Dream 5, The American University in Cairo Press, Cairo and New York, 2005.

I went there not at the invitation of the Israeli government. I was invited by Israeli writers to an international festival of writers. I accepted because the quotation above, by Albert Camus, is my credo. I believe that the writer within integrity to his/her creativity has a responsibility as a human being for recognition of oppression perpetrated against people, whoever they are, in the society in which the writer has his/her being. Just as the opera singer has particular qualities of the vocal cords, the writer has an insight bringing the responsibility to bear particular witness to the writer's time and place. I want to testify that writers, rejecting political correctness and using the gifts of insight witness, may dredge up some of the truth, beyond the surface of information, about their society and country.

'Witness: The Inward Testimony' was the subject of the address I gave. It had, of course, particular reference and relevance to the place, Israel, and the Israeli writers among those present. In the depths of profound confusion, while peace talks as the foundation of justice for both peoples flounder and revive, I found there are two absolutes: for Israelis, the right of Israel to exist, denied by Hamas and jihad Palestinians; and the return of the occupied territories to Palestine.

Among Israeli writers, including the vociferous Amos Oz, renowned internationally for his brilliant novels and bold, critical publication of possible solutions for two-state justice, every Israeli writer I met was against the occupied territories and the harsh measures used against the Palestinian inhabitants. I was informed by people at conference sessions that the majority of Israelis are against their government's policies of occupation. A minority spoke to me in defence of the occupied territories as acquisitions of the 1967 changes to partition lines in divine accord with biblical prophecy.

I had made arrangements before leaving South Africa to visit East Jerusalem, the Palestinian sector. A car from the Palestinian Authority picked me up at a curiously named no-man's-land, the American Colony Hotel. I was received by Professor Sari Nusseibe, a fellow writer whose work I know. I talked with a gathering of students, many of them aspirant writers, answering their questions about the pressures of political conflict on the freedom of expression.

But literature did not turn out to be the portent of this occasion for me. I was taken to the faculty which houses a unique documentation, for which 'museum' is not the right word. The smiling director was himself a prisoner of Israel for seventeen years of Palestinian-Israeli conflict. Not only had he assembled the minute scraps of testimony scribbled on shreds of paper or cloth that were smuggled out of prison, and photographs of men under merciless interrogation; he has a library of written accounts by ex-prisoners whom he seeks out to set down living memories of pain and humiliation under interrogation. No doubt there are the same kind of memories of suffering among Israeli prisoners interrogated by Palestinians.

The inhumanity of humans towards humans knows no boundaries.

Al Quds University is close to what is referred to as the Jerusalem suburb, Abu Dib, through which the wall that divides Palestine from Israel has part of its monumental path. The wall defies any conventional image. I stood beside one of its gigantic convolutions across streets and houses. It is as high as a wall from floor to ceiling in a one-storey house. I was with a doctor at the entrance to his home. The wall slices toweringly across his and a neighbour's garden and their street. His clinic is a few blocks away, on the other side of the wall. He has to drive (I was with him) several kilometres to the nearest gate and checkpoint to cross and reach his clinic back near the very point he set out from. He told of critically ill patients on the east side of the wall whose life-saving treatment was available only at a specialised hospital on the west side, on occasion someone dying while guards delayed perusal of medical documents that authorised the crossing. In Israel, I was told by friends that nevertheless there are times when the 'unconscious' patient and the attending 'doctor' are let through. They are suicide bombers coming to explode murder among the Israeli men, women and children in public places.

Meanwhile, I watched children coming through the gate from their school on one side of the wall to reach their homes on the other side. The everyday disruption of Palestinian lives is inconceivable, even as you experience some small part of it.

Through my friendship with the late Edward Said, outstandingly brilliant intellect of our time, dedicated proponent of Palestine complete with just borders, and his wife Miriam Said, I was enabled to be received in what is known as the heart and mind of the occupied West Bank, Ramallah. Despite my participation in the International Festival of Writers, boycotted by Palestine, I was warmly welcomed by Dr Mustafa Barghouti, the secretary of Al Mubadara, 'the Palestine national initiative for the realisation of Palestinian national rights and creation of a just, durable peace' – a group whose members were assembled. They drove me about Ramallah, informing me of what I was seeing again as the results of occupation. Around a table for lunch at Al Mubadara, I learned first-hand about the political standpoint, tactics and work of the Palestine Initiative. They reject the Hamas denial of the right of Israel to exist, while pursuing a non-violent but inexorable struggle against the present and ongoing occupation of Palestine.

Dr Barghouti is a member of the Palestine parliament who achieved second place behind Mahmoud Abbas in the 2005 elections, focusing major attention on the demand to end further construction of Israel's wall and the dismantling of its existence. He talked about customary rhetoric among political leaders, encouraging colleagues to speak. I heard how the Palestine Initiative, while ineluctably dedicated to a Palestinian state on acceptable, just frontiers, is also concerned with internal Palestinian divisions. 'Just' being under endless disagreement, where both Israel and Palestine each believe they have an ancient right to the entire territory, even while bitterly recognising, *force majeure* of the contemporary world, that would only be achieved by unspeakable bloodshed in a horrific war.

I left for the Other Side with a huge poster: '40 years under occupation', reproducing coloured maps, green for Palestine splattered with red spots indicating Israeli 'colonies', incredible rearrangements, swaps of bitterly disputed territory, from 1948 to present – with a final blank map for the future, bearing only a question mark. There are some extraordinary responses to the blank map of the future. Returning from occupied territory to the conference in Jerusalem, the car in which I was transported plunged into a deep, long tunnel off the highway. My Palestinian escort told me this was one of those envisaged by Israel to connect, along 1967 lines, the far-flung pieces of Palestine that Israel recognises, without using the highways that lead through Israeli territory.

The question mark remains.

It hangs over peace negotiations – that vital base for the answer an outsider who believes in justice surely must support: two fully independent states on agreed, realistic frontiers. Israeli and Palestinian poets and fiction writers bear their particular responsibility of inward witness, not for the television and newsprint immediacy of the day, but in lasting works that bring up from beneath the news something of the contradictions of the human condition, enduring, living in hope, a time and place.

2008

The Lion in Literature

I am black: hasn't a black man eyes? Hasn't a black man hands, organs, dimensions, senses, affections, passions, fed with the same food, hurt with the same weapons, subject to the same diseases, healed by the same means, warmed and cooled by the same winter and summer as a white is: if you prick us, do we not bleed? If you tickle us, do we not laugh? If you poison us, do we not die? And if you wrong us, shall we not revenge? If we are like you in the rest, we will resemble you in that. If a black wrongs a white, what is his humility, his revenge? If a white wrongs a black, what should his sufferance be by white example, why revenge? The villainy you teach me I will execute, and it shall go hard but I will better the instruction.'

You will have no difficulty in recalling a different version of this monologue.[1] In fact, the two will be playing along in your mind, as in mine, as the same text in two voices; and it is the volume they

---

1   See Shylock's speech in *The Merchant of Venice*, Act III, Scene i.

create together that will be what I shall be venturing to put before you.

Colonialism was not only the conquest of land and the dispossession of peoples; it was also, as Edward Said has established with his term Orientalism, a *representation* of peoples through literature written by others. In his work *Culture And Imperialism*, he writes, 'I study Orientalism as a dynamic exchange between different individual authors and the large political concerns shaped by the three great empires – British, French, American – in whose intellectual and imaginative territory the writing was produced.' Jane Austen and the British Empire, Flaubert and the Middle East, Conrad and Kipling in Africa – even Thomas Mann and the Death in Venice that Mann assumes to be an infection from the tainted Other, the Orient – these are some examples of the literary concept of the Other, in the culture of domination. 'Texts are protean things,' Said says, 'they are tied to circumstance and to politics large and small . . .'

Imperialism was the big one. In his book entitled *Orientalism* he focuses mainly on the phenomenon of Orientalism as applicable to the Middle East and Far East, but we can recognise it as just as valid for Africa and even the way Africans were seen in the African diaspora, that ironic form of reverse colonisation by Africans in the home countries of the old colonial masters. Africa, Africans *were*, existed, as literary exoticism – half attraction, half contempt for the Other – that formed an ethos which inspired, accompanied and supplied self-righteous justification, even for slavery, in a worldwide conquest by dominant powers. To turn Rabbie Burns's famous dictum on its head: for Africa it was not a matter of 'Would the Lord the giftie gie us, to see ourselves as others see us' but would whatever gods may be give us the gift to see ourselves *as we know ourselves to be*, and to make the world recognise this reality.

It has been a long haul, and I am not going to roll-call all the great names in Africa and her diaspora who have achieved it. 'Being you, you cut your poetry out of wood.' That is Gwendolyn Brooks's metaphor for the process. Thinking of his appropriate metaphor for the beginning of the African story, Chinua Achebe recounts a proverb: 'Until the lions produce their own historian, the story of the hunt will glorify only the hunter.'

Africa was slow, perhaps, for many reasons, to produce her own historians in the strict sense of history as a separate literary discipline – the pace has accelerated, and in the case of South Africa is really only beginning, not only with the rewriting of school history books, but in dramatic resuscitations in drama and dance, as well as novels, of the past that was buried under colonial versions. But in fiction as prose and poetry, haven't Africa's pride of lions produced their own historians? Haven't they established incontrovertibly literature as what Edward Said calls 'a form of political memory': the past and present as created by Africans themselves, their characters and lives, their view of self and their regard on the world, fully emerged from the regard of the world upon *them*? Africa is no longer the world's invention, but herself, confident of this whether on the African continent or in its diaspora.

How strong is that confidence? How deep does it go? Is it by now, the twenty-first century, become so firm a foundation that we, of Africa, are ready to take up a reconnection with the literary culture of the outside world on a new basis, on our terms? The African Literature Association was created and has met through the crisis years of African cultural identity to defend and nurture the creativity on which that identity depended. I ask myself, is it not time to lift the horizon of that splendid identity and accept that literature, the illumination of the human imagination, has no frontier guards, no immigration laws, thank whatever gods may be. All literature belongs to all of us, everywhere. Once free of censorship, it is pure intellectual freedom, any limitations to be overcome by translation. And this conference is dealing with the highly important practicalities of relations between translators, publishers and critics. Why do we not glory in this freedom, take advantage of it? A positive globalisation among some dubious ones.

This call is redundant, yes, even absurd, in our gathering here – all in this company of literati have read, all their lives, world literature. But I raise the question before you out of serious concern in a wider context. I must speak now about the situation in South

Africa, which is the one I know intimately, but I more than suspect, from my reading of critical and literary journals in other countries, that something like prevails in the United States.

Young black readers and, most important, aspirant writers confine themselves to reading African and African-American writers. The lion's African story, it goes without question, is the one that must take first place; therein emerges the ethos of the people and the land. But to find writings from Western Europe, Eastern Europe, the Arab countries, India, the Far East, etc. 'irrelevant' is to re-enter – voluntarily, this time! – a cultural isolation formerly imposed by the arrogance of imperialism. The same principle applies to any African writing that is not more or less narrowly contemporary; except for some student painstakingly assembling a thesis at a university, I have found no young reader/writer in Southern Africa who has heard of, let alone read, in the canon of African literature, Olaudah Equiano;[2] even Plaatje[3] is just a name to them, if respected at a distance.

Internationally, the range of reading might – it is just beginning to – include one or two of the Latin American writers, principally because our country's government has begun to break the North–South axis and promote trade, investment and exchange of technological skills South–South with Latin American countries; trade followed the Bible and gun in colonial times, now cultural exchange follows the opening up of trade. (Although, in the case of music, between Latin America and Southern Africa, the happy exchange preceded trade as a move in globalisation.)

I should like to give account of a recent gathering in Johannesburg where the self-limitation of literary experience was explicitly evidenced in all its manifestations and even delusions. On Writers' Day there was a celebration held at Windybrow Cultural Centre, appropriately an old mansion, once the grand home of a colonial mining magnate, now the fine shabby complex of two theatres, music, drama and film workshops, in an area that has 'gone black'

---

2   Olaudah Equiano, *Equiano's Travels: The Interesting Narrative of the Life of Olaudah Equiano or Gustavus Vassa the African*.

3   Sol T. Plaatje, *Native Life in South Africa*.

since the end of apartheid and racial segregation. There were readings of poetry and prose by young rap and other poets, and by a few old hands such as once-banned Don Mattera and myself, but the main dynamism was the discussions started in the audience. That audience was overwhelmingly young, about 150 black men and women, and, as usual, there was a vivid articulacy of complaints from them.

Some of these were of a politico-social nature about which we all share concern in the new dispensation of South Africa from which we expect so much. Libraries are still almost exclusively in the areas where whites and the new black affluent class live. The paucity of libraries, the total absence of school libraries – except for a dusty shelf of Teach Yourself Accounting, How-To-Do-It books – is unchanged in what are and will long remain the areas where the greatest concentration of black citizens live. This was one of the valid answers given from the floor to why there is a poor reading culture in our country, stemming from the basic reason, high illiteracy and semi-literacy, and culminating in the lack of access to books. But challenges came from those of us on the platform who mingled with the audience. The plaintiffs were all fully literate and claimed to be reader/writers: What – on the premise that you cannot be a writer unless you are a reader, that is our only true schooling – did they read?

The responses were alarmingly uniform: they read African literature from the African continent, mainly from South Africa. We were celebrating Chinua Achebe's seventieth birthday as a focus of Writers' Day 2000, but few had read more of his work than *Things Fall Apart*, which had been a set work in high schools. Only one mentioned Wole Soyinka, one other, Toni Morrison, another Fanon; Mahfouz was an unfamiliar name to them. The assertion was: *we* want to read about *ourselves, our lives*. Don Mattera countered with the discovery of oneself to be found in Dostoevsky. The riposte was: too far away and long ago. The director of Windybrow, Walter Chakela, a poet and playwright who runs workshops that have discovered and nurtured new talent among the young and unknown, and whose own plays bring to life and light African heroes both of the distant past and the recent one of apartheid, stunned the vociferous with the quiet announcement that he had begun to think as a poet, to range mentally in the imagination, from having to learn Wordsworth at school. He spoke of the identification with the intimacies of human feeling which are to be found in contact with great creative minds in all kinds of eras, countries. Finally, the audience was in rejection and derision of the fact – a litany – that Shakespeare was 'stuffed down' their necks at school; and what did Shakespeare know about *them?*

And so now you, who have been patient, know why I quoted my version of a Shakespearean discourse.

Shakespeare – why Shakespeare? Because in Shylock's speech any of these children of apartheid with their history of racism in their veins will find, here in the experience of another race, their people, themselves: *hasn't a black man eyes? Hasn't a black man hands? If you prick us, do we not bleed? If you tickle us, do we not laugh? If you poison us, do we not die?* And if, as many young people struggle within themselves against the acid desire for revenge upon those who oppressed their parents and destroyed their childhood, they come to read these lines: 'The villainy you teach me I will execute, and it shall go hard but I will better the instruction' – will they not find something of their secret selves?

In the end it is a self-deprivation to approach literature, as Caryl Phillips says of history, through the prism of your own pigmentation.

That's what whites did, first.

Rightful pride in African literature should not create a literary ghetto. Surely there have been enough ghettoes. It's the end of Orientalism; for in African literature, Indian literature, Arabic literature, the Euro-American, Western world now begins to find something of *itself*. So surely the time has come for African literature to connect, beyond exclusive discourse at scholarly level about itself, its achievements, its problems, with the world of literature, the expansion of literary consciousness to which it belongs. Surely young people from among whom are our hopes for new African writers, should be urged to read widely, to set aside the dominant criterion of 'relevance' that belongs to the era when it was an essential element of consciousness-raising tactics of politics against racism. The struggle against racism is not over, as we well know, around the world, but if literature is to be the political memory of the present and future in which young people will live out their lives, should it not reflect, and reflect upon, between literatures, what Achebe calls 'preliminary conversations . . . participations in a monumental ritual by millions and millions to appease a long and troublesome history of dispossession and bitterness, and to answer "present" at the rebirth of the world?'

The lion's telling of his story has another, cogent, urgent, reason for identification with the literatures of that world.

In the beginning was the Word. The Word was with God, signified God's Word, the Word that was Creation. Its secular transformation came to us when it was first scratched on a stone tablet or traced on papyrus, and when it travelled from parchment to Gutenberg. That was the genesis of the writer, of literature.

In literature now we are indivisibly in a situation that did not exist when the lion's telling began. It did not exist when Langston Hughes, Léopold Sédar Senghor, Es'kia Mphahlele, Ngũgĩ wa Thiong'o, Agostinho Neto, Kofi Awoonor began to write. But all literatures are conjoined today under threat of the image against the Word. We are certainly aware of that rival, self-appointed, but with plenty of independent popular corroboration. From the first third of the twentieth century the image has been challenging the power of the written world as a stimulation of the imagination, the opening up of human receptivity. The bedtime story of middle-class childhood has been replaced by the hours in front of the TV screen; in shack settlements all over the poor countries of the globe there is the battery-run television where no single book is to be found. We already have at least one generation grown that looks instead of reads. Yes, TV images are accompanied by the spoken Word, but it is the picture that decides how secondary the Word's role shall be. The story-telling of the TV medium is the Big Picture; even in documentaries the spoken word is an accessory consisting generally of the most banal and limited vocabulary. Anyone who has run workshops for aspirant writers will know, as I do, how the mini-series vocabulary is often all that aspirants can command to express what are often original ideas. I am still waiting for some proof that, as has been claimed, TV has encouraged reading.

'A picture is worth a thousand words.' Whoever it was – a public relations savant, no doubt – who came up with the adage, the rejoinder is: 'For how long?'

The image disappears from the screen; to recall it you have to have an apparatus, a cell, a battery, access to an electric power connection. The written word is simply there, in your pocket. The book in your hand can be read on the bus, in bed, in a queue, on a mountain-top, beside a stream, in a traffic jam. The American writer William Gass argues our case for us:

> We shall not understand what a book *is*, and why a book has the value many persons have, and is even less replaceable than a person, if we forget how important to it is its body, the building that has been built to hold its lines of language safely together through many adventures and a long time. Words on a screen have visual qualities, to be sure, and these darkly limn their shape, but they have no materiality, they are only shadows, and when the light shifts they'll be gone. Off the screen, they do not exist as words. They do not exist to be reseen, reread, they only wait to be remade, relit . . . I cannot argue in their margins . . .

And the lions of our African literature are confronted suddenly, just as other literatures, with another, the latest factor in the threat to debase the written word, this time presented by information technology as, indeed, an *advancement* in the dissemination of literature. Although it seems something of a gimmick, so far, with one thirty-page novel (Stephen King's) written 'for' and 'published' on the internet, and one can hardly imagine Soyinka's *The Interpreters* let alone *War and Peace* republished in this way, there is every likelihood that at a certain broad level there is going to be a public deprived for a lifetime – because it is going to be told by international websites what it needs, what cultural fulfilment *is*; deprived of the pleasures and intellectual fulfilment I have described and quoted. People are going to 'read', not books, but texts passing on a screen, soon to be available like telephone messages to appear on the matchbox screens of mobile phones.

So the mobile phone, Kindle, and other devices become the paperbacks of the future – rivalling, anyway, the printed volume's portability? And the beguilement (or shall we say the corruption) of the writer to 'publish' in this ephemeral way cannot be discounted. Apparently the money is good; better and quicker than royalties. The seduction of the image, away from the printed word, has extended, in one instance already, to the very *process of writing* becoming an image. An American actor-turned-writer has fitted a tiny special camera to his computer and written his science fiction novel watched by a webcam. The linkage of his study at home to the internet by this means will bring him $2 million as a deal with a software company promoter. The reader as voyeur.

Vast advances in IT communications are an information revolution that has great possibilities for social development if well used, which means made economically available to the millions in the world, the underdeveloped and developing world whose lives will otherwise be bulldozed by the financial oligarchy of globalisation. But in literature, technology cannot ever replace with the image the illumination that comes from the written word, self-contained, self-powered, in print on paper, infinitely accessible for rumination on and return to, between hard or soft covers.

First it was the book of the movie.

Now it is the book of the website.

This is the lion's problem just as it is that of the rest of the world's literature.

2006

SOURCE ACKNOWLEDGEMENTS

Pieces in this collection first appeared in the following publications: A South African Childhood; Cannes Epilogue (*The New Yorker*); Hassan in America (*The Forum*); Egypt Revisited (*National English Review*); Chief Luthuli; New Notes from the Underground (*Atlantic Monthly*); Apartheid; The Congo; Party of One (*Holiday*); A Bolter and the Invincible Summer; Taking into Account; Pula! (*London Magazine*); Censored, Banned, Gagged (*Encounter*); Great Problems in the Street; Madagascar (*The Essential Gesture* by Nadine Gordimer, ed. Stephen Clingman); Notes of an Expropriator; The Prison-House of Colonialism (*Times Literary Supplement*); One Man Living Through It (*Magazine of the World Press*); Why Did Bram Fischer Choose Jail?; Letter from Johannesburg; The Short Story in South Africa (*Kenyon Review*); Merci Dieu, It Changes (*Atlantic Travel African Development*); Pack Up, Black Man; Unchaining Poets; Censorship – The Final Solution; Five Years into Freedom: My New South African Identity; Africa's Plague, and Everyone's; Lust and Death (*New York Times*); The New Black Poets (*Dalhousie Review*); A Writer's Freedom; The South African Censor: No Change; Censorship and its Aftermath (*Index on Censorship*); English-Language Literature and Politics in South Africa (*Journal of Southern African Studies*); Letter from Soweto; Letter from the 153rd State; Mysterious Incest; The Child Is the Man; Living in the Interregnum; The Idea of Gardening; The Gap Between the Writer and the Reader; Joseph Roth (*New York Review of Books*); What Being a South African Means to Me (*South African Outlook*); Transkei: A Vision of Two Blood-Red Suns (*GEO*); Unconfessed History (*New Republic*); The Essential Gesture (*The Age Monthly Review*); Huddleston: A Sign (*Trevor Huddleston: Essays on His Life and Work*, ed. Deborah Duncan Honor);

The African Pot (*Die Zeit*); A Writer's Vital Gift to a Free Society; Atlantis (*Guardian*); Freedom Struggles out of the Chrysalis; Remembering Barney Simon (*Independent*); Sorting the Images from the Man (*Newsweek*); Turning the Page (*Transition*); Beyond Myth; Rising to the Ballot; The Dwelling Place of Words (*Washington Post*); Personal Proust (*Salmagundi*); What News on the Rialto? (*Los Angeles Times*); Edward Said (*Sunday Independent* (Johannesburg)); Susan Sontag (*Sunday Times* (South Africa)); Desmond Tutu As I Know Him (*Tutu As I Know Him*, eds Lavinia Crawford-Browne and Piet Meiring); Experiencing Two Absolutes (*The Star* (South Africa)). The following pieces were first published as introductions to editions of the works discussed: Chinua Achebe and *Things Fall Apart*; Joseph Conrad and *Almayer's Folly*; With Them You Never Know; William Plomer and *Turbott Wolfe*; 'To You I Can'; Leo Tolstoy and *The Death of Ivan Ilyich*; Naguib Mahfouz's *Three Novels of Ancient Egypt*. The following pieces were first delivered as addresses or lectures: Relevance and Commitment; Letter from South Africa; Our Century; The Status of the Writer in the World Today; The Poor Are Always with Us; Octavio Paz: Poet-Archer; When Art Meets Politics; A Letter to Future Generations; Hemingway's Expatriates; The Entitlement Approach; Living with A Writer; Home Truths from the Past; Witness: The Inward Testimony; Faith, Reason and War; The Lion in Literature.